HOLMAN
New
Testament
Commentary

HOLMAN
New
Testament
Commentary

Romans

GENERAL EDITOR

Max Anders

AUTHORS

Kenneth Boa and William Kruidenier

HOLMAN
REFERENCE

Nashville, Tennessee

Holman New Testament Commentary
© 2000 Broadman & Holman Publishers
Nashville, Tennessee

ISBN 0–8054–0206–3

Romans / Ken Boa
     p.   cm. — (Holman New Testament commentary)
Includes bibliographical references.
ISBN 0–8054–0206–3 (alk. paper)
   1. Bible. N.T. Romans—Commentaries.   2. Bible. N.T. Romans—Commentaries. I. Title.   II. Title: Romans.   III. Series
226.6'07—dc21   98–39365
                                                CIP

5 6 05 04
D

In honor of all who, like the apostle Paul, have given their lives to take the gospel, the power of God unto salvation, to the ends of the earth.

William M. Kruidenier

I dedicate this book to my beloved wife Karen, our daughter Heather, and our son-in-law, Matthew.

Kenneth Boa

May 2000

Contents

Contents

Editorial Preface

Today's church hungers for Bible teaching, and Bible teachers hunger for resources to guide them in teaching God's Word. The Holman New Testament Commentary provides the church with the food to feed the spiritually hungry in an easily digestible format. The result: new spiritual vitality that the church can readily use.

Bible teaching should result in new interest in the Scriptures, expanded Bible knowledge, discovery of specific scriptural principles, relevant applications, and exciting living. The unique format of the Holman New Testament Commentary includes sections to achieve these results for every New Testament book.

Opening quotations from some of the church's best writers lead to an introductory illustration and discussion that draw individuals and study groups into the Word of God. "In a Nutshell" summarizes the content and teaching of the chapter. Verse-by-verse commentary answers the church's questions rather than raising issues scholars usually admit they cannot adequately solve. Bible principles and specific contemporary applications encourage students to move from Bible to contemporary times. A specific modern illustration then ties application vividly to present life. A brief prayer aids the student to commit his or her daily life to the principles and applications found in the Bible chapter being studied. For those still hungry for more, "Deeper Discoveries" take the student into a more personal, deeper study of the words, phrases, and themes of God's Word. Finally, a teaching outline provides transitional statements and conclusions along with an outline to assist the teacher in group Bible studies.

It is the editors' prayer that this new resource for local church Bible teaching will enrich the ministry of group, as well as individual, Bible study, and that it will lead God's people to truly be people of the Book, living out what God calls us to be.

Holman Old Testament Commentary Contributors

Vol. 1, Genesis
ISBN 0-8054-9461-8
Kenneth O. Gangel and
Stephen J. Bramer

Vol. 2, Exodus, Leviticus, Numbers
ISBN 0-8054-9462-6
Glen Martin

Vol. 3, Deuteronomy
ISBN 0-8054-9463-4
Doug McIntosh

Vol. 4, Joshua
ISBN 0-8054-9464-2
Kenneth O. Gangel

Vol. 5, Judges, Ruth
ISBN 0-8054-9465-0
W. Gary Phillips

Vol. 6, 1 & 2 Samuel
ISBN 0-8054-9466-9
Stephen Andrews

Vol. 7, 1 & 2 Kings
ISBN 0-8054-9467-7
Gary Inrig

Vol. 8, 1 & 2 Chronicles
ISBN 0-8054-9468-5
Winfried Corduan

Vol. 9, Ezra, Nehemiah, Esther
ISBN 0-8054-9469-3
Knute Larson and Kathy Dahlen

Vol. 10, Job
ISBN 0-8054-9470-7
Steven J. Lawson

Vol. 11, Psalms 1–75
ISBN 0-8054-9471-5
Steven J. Lawson

Vol. 12, Psalms 76–150
ISBN 0-8054-9481-2
Steven J. Lawson

Vol. 13, Proverbs
ISBN 0-8054-9472-3
Max Anders

Vol. 14, Ecclesiastes, Song of Songs
ISBN 0-8054-9482-0
David George Moore and Daniel L. Akin

Vol. 15, Isaiah
ISBN 0-8054-9473-1
Trent C. Butler

Vol. 16, Jeremiah, Lamentations
ISBN 0-8054-9474-X
Fred M. Wood and Ross McLaren

Vol. 17, Ezekiel
ISBN 0-8054-9475-8
Mark F. Rooker

Vol. 18, Daniel
ISBN 0-8054-9476-6
Kenneth O. Gangel

**Vol. 19, Hosea, Joel, Amos,
Obadiah, Jonah, Micah**
ISBN 0-8054-9477-4
Trent C. Butler

Vol. 20, Nahum, Habakkuk, Zephaniah, Haggai, Zechariah, Malachi
ISBN 0-8054-9478-2
Stephen R. Miller

Holman New Testament Commentary Contributors

Vol. 1, Matthew
ISBN 0-8054-0201-2
Stuart K. Weber

Vol. 2, Mark
ISBN 0-8054-0202-0
Rodney L. Cooper

Vol. 3, Luke
ISBN 0-8054-0203-9
Trent C. Butler

Vol. 4, John
ISBN 0-8054-0204-7
Kenneth O. Gangel

Vol. 5, Acts
ISBN 0-8054-0205-5
Kenneth O. Gangel

Vol. 6, Romans
ISBN 0-8054-0206-3
Kenneth Boa and William Kruidenier

Vol. 7, 1 & 2 Corinthians
ISBN 0-8054-0207-1
Richard L. Pratt Jr.

Vol. 8, Galatians, Ephesians, Philippians, Colossians
ISBN 0-8054-0208-X
Max Anders

Vol. 9, 1 & 2 Thessalonians, 1 & 2 Timothy, Titus, Philemon
ISBN 0-8054-0209-8
Knute Larson

Vol. 10, Hebrews, James
ISBN 0-8054-0211-X
Thomas D. Lea

Vol. 11, 1 & 2 Peter, 1, 2, 3 John, Jude
ISBN 0-8054-0210-1
David Walls & Max Anders

Vol. 12, Revelation
ISBN 0-8054-0212-8
Kendell H. Easley

Holman New Testament Commentary

Twelve volumes designed for Bible study and teaching to enrich the local church and God's people.

Series Editor	Max Anders
Managing Editors	Trent C. Butler & Steve Bond
Project Editor	Lloyd W. Mullens
Marketing Manager	Greg Webster
Product Manager	David Shepherd
Page Composition	TF Designs, Mt. Juliet, TN

Introduction to

Romans

It could not be more appropriate for the Protestant Reformation to have been kindled by a spark from Paul's Epistle to the Romans. This letter that has brought spiritual salvation and freedom to so many, awakened faith in the heart of a Roman Catholic monk named Martin Luther. Perhaps no one before or since has agonized so deeply and despaired so thoroughly over the condition of his soul. The depth of Luther's travail could only have been relieved by the writings of one who had sounded similar depths and lived to tell about it.

Accomplice to murder, persecutor, ridiculer—the pre-apostle Saul had his own reasons for torment and agony after coming face-to-face with his Lord on the Damascus Road. How could he, "the worst of sinners" (1 Tim. 1:16), be saved? Paul discovered, and later wrote down in Romans, how he was saved, how Martin Luther could be saved, and how anyone who has agonized over his standing with God is saved: by the power of the gospel of Jesus Christ.

When the first rays of the gospel began to dawn in Martin Luther's heart, he knew he had the answer. To be righteous, he discovered, one must live by faith—*sola fide*—by faith alone. Luther's discovery of the gospel transformed a moribund monk into a channel of power that infused life into a near-dead church. Nearly a half-millennium later, the Epistle of Paul to the Romans continues to awaken hearts and empower hands to spread the life-giving gospel of Christ. Is it any wonder that Luther said of this letter, "[Romans] is worthy not only that every Christian should know it word for word, by heart, but occupy himself with it every day, as the daily bread of the soul. It can never be read or pondered too much, and the more it is dealt with the more precious it becomes, and the better it tastes."

As you prepare to teach the Epistle to the Romans, may its words quicken afresh in your own heart the power of the gospel. May you become to those you teach, as Paul was to Martin Luther, a living example of a life transformed by the gospel of grace.

AUTHORSHIP

It is impossible to understand the purpose and theme of the Epistle to the Romans without understanding the author. A book that for nearly two thousand years has been the benchmark of Christian truth could only have surfaced in the life of one whose life was continually, and even ultimately, sacrificed for that truth. Words that set readers free can only flow through the heart and pen of one set free himself. Scottish scholar F. F. Bruce has so aptly called the apostle, "Paul: apostle of the heart set free" (see Bibliography). No man was more free than the apostle Paul. He lived to please no one except the Lord who confronted, confounded, and converted him (Gal. 1:10). His letter to the Romans becomes, as we shall see, a means for continuing to please his Master and carry out the commission he was given.

Details of the background and conversion of Paul to faith in Christ are well-known among Bible students and need not be repeated here (see Acts 9:1–19; 22:3–16; 26:4–18; 2 Cor. 11:22; Phil. 3:5–6). Suffice it to say that his theological training in the Old Testament and zeal for Judaism prepared him eminently for the task to which God had called him—a task which had its roots in the prophecies of Isaiah. It was no small task to which Paul was called, and it is in the larger context of his life's mission that the letter to the Romans fits.

In Pisidian Antioch, on his first missionary journey, Paul (accompanied by Barnabas) proclaimed the gospel in a Jewish synagogue. A week later, Paul's message had stirred up so much excitement in the city that the Jews spoke "abusively" against what he was saying (Acts 13:45). Paul declared that the Jews' rejection was only a confirmation of the direction God had called him: to take the gospel to the Gentiles. Quoting Isaiah 49:6 in Acts 13:47—"I have made you a light for the Gentiles, that you may bring salvation to the ends of the earth"—Paul reveals publicly the mission to which God had called him. The Gentiles in Antioch rejoiced at this, and many believed. But the Jews—how might you expect them to react toward one of their own who takes a messianic prophecy and applies it to himself? Paul and Barnabas were "expelled . . . from their region" (Acts 13:50), leaving a band of rejoicing Gentile disciples in their wake.

Paul had studied the Old Testament. He knew that the prophecies of Isaiah indicated that spiritual light would come to the Gentiles. It was to be in the last days that Jerusalem would be raised above the hills and the nations (Gentiles) would stream to it (Isa. 2:2; Zech. 8:23). The nations would turn to the root of Jesse, the Messiah, as the Lord drew his people out of those nations unto himself (Isa. 11:10–11). The Servant of God (Messiah) would be raised up to establish justice among the nations and the coastlands. He would be "a covenant for the people . . . a light for the Gentiles" (Isa. 42:6; 49:8). As a result, from the ends of the earth, from the islands and coastlands, would come forth praises to God (Isa. 42:10; see also Deut. 32:43; 2 Sam. 22:50; Pss. 18:49; 117:1).

None of this was problematic to the Jews; it was their most profound prophet who declared these things. It was *how* God chose to fulfill Isaiah's prophecies that the Jews could not reconcile. First, a poor carpenter and his wife enter the temple in Jerusalem with their forty-day old son, and an aging prophet named Simeon declares that the infant is the Messiah: "My eyes have seen . . . a light for revelation to the Gentiles and for glory to your people Israel" (Luke 2:30–32, quoting Isa. 42:6). Next, jump ahead thirty-five years. The carpenter's son, Jesus, was crucified for blasphemy, yet was resurrected and confronted the zealous Saul of Tarsus on the road to Damascus. Through a Jew named Ananias, the confused Jewish scholar learns from Jesus that he is the "chosen instrument to carry my name before the Gentiles and their kings" (Acts 9:15).

Who could fault Paul for taking ten years to sort things out? One day he is persecuting the followers of Jesus, the next decade he is committed to representing Jesus to the entire world (the world minus the Jews = the Gentiles).

Ten years later, when Paul's head had stopped spinning, he began describing his experience as he went on missionary journeys throughout the Mediterranean world. God began saving Gentiles along with Jews (Acts 10:45), the Jewish leaders began recognizing what God was doing (Acts 11:18), Jews and Gentiles began being addressed as one (Acts 13:16,26), and Jews and Gentiles began believing the gospel and forming the new, corporate body that Paul called the *ekklesia*—the assembly—or the church. It is hard for us today to imagine the trauma this new salvific paradigm produced, but it did (read Acts 15:1–35; Gal. 2:11–21). A significant part of Paul's apostolic ministry was spent mediating—blending the two groups into one body.

Paul's ministry to the Gentiles came to be accepted by the Jewish leaders of the church (Gal. 2:2–9), and his commission from God was documented extensively by Luke in Acts (Paul's speeches before Jewish leaders and pagan kings and the record of the Jerusalem Council, Acts 15:1–35) and in his own epistles (Rom. 9–11; 15:7–22; Gal. 1:16; 2:2–9; 3:8,14; Eph. 2:11–3:21; Col. 1:27; 1 Tim. 2:7; 2 Tim. 4:17). Nowhere is the heart of the apostle seen more than in his words to the church at Ephesus. He speaks of the inclusion of the Gentiles into the *ekklesia* as a "mystery" (Eph. 3:3–4,6,9), something revealed to him by God for delivery to the nations. It was revealed in the Old Testament, but not clearly; it was a mystery as to how God would accomplish through Israel the salvation of the world.

And now to Paul, more than to any other living human being, has the solution to the mystery been revealed. Though the beauty, humility, and passion of his Ephesian words come chronologically a few years after Romans was written, the heart of the man was the same.

Though the great apostle was in constant danger of being harmed by the very peoples whom he was commissioned to serve (Acts 21:11; 26:17; 1 Cor.

1:23; 2 Cor. 11:26), he never digressed from his path. It is impossible to fully appreciate anything written by the apostle Paul without understanding the radical transformation of his own life. There was both a means and an end to his ministry. The end of his ministry was "the ends of the earth" (Acts 1:8). Until the last Gentile on earth heard the gospel of the grace of God, Paul could know no rest. The means to his ministry was the mystery that God had revealed to him, the unifying of Jew and Gentile alike into a corporate body of believers, filled with and therefore empowered by the Holy Spirit.

Jesus Christ had walked on the earth for three years in a ministry first "to the lost sheep of Israel" (Matt. 10:6; 15:21–28) which broadened to the Gentiles as Israel failed to respond to him (Matt. 21:43; Luke 10:1–12). Perhaps the Twelve in Luke 9:1 represent the twelve tribes of Israel, and the seventy/seventy-two in Luke 10:1 represent the table of nations in Genesis 10. For the rest of history, Christ would walk on the earth again through his body, the church, made up of Jews and Gentiles "from every tribe and language and people and nation" (Rev. 5:9). And Paul was the steward of that mystery.

The church's mission was to disciple the nations (Matt. 28:18–20). Paul's mission was to explain the mystery of the body of Christ, the inclusion of the Gentiles into the blessings of the Jewish covenants, so that Jews and Gentiles alike would see themselves as the body of Christ on earth, continuing Jesus' work of seeking and saving what was lost (Luke 19:10). In order for him to be an effective steward of his own apostolic ministry, he had to communicate God's plan to the church. The most extensive example of that communication is the letter to the church at Rome.

Paul's letter to the Romans, when taken within the context of his missionary travels, reveals two things about Paul that are worthy of emulation. First, he was obedient. Paul received his commission from the Lord and turned his face toward "the ends of the earth." An overview of his missionary journeys shows that each time he traveled he made it further west. There is even some speculation that he made it as far west as Spain, which was his stated goal (Rom. 15:24,28).

Second, he was flexible. Though he was commissioned to take the gospel to the Gentiles, he still preached to the Jews as well. Being the "apostle to the Gentiles" (Rom. 11:13; Gal. 2:8) did not mean that Paul would not preach to Jews. Rather, it meant that his field was beyond Israel, both geographically and spiritually. God had revealed to him the mystery of the Gentiles' inclusion in the promises of God, and it was his job to explain that good news both to them and to the Jews. As much as the "apostle to the Gentiles," he was the "apostle of the mystery." The mystery had to be preached to the Gentiles so they might be saved, and to the Jews so they would understand God's new economy and know they had not been set aside by God.

Paul never lost sight of his goal and pursued it relentlessly (Acts 28:31), but he allowed God to set the timetable and direct his path. As to Paul being the actual author of the letter bearing his name and received by the church in Rome (Rom. 1:1), there is little need for discussion. The commentaries are filled with relevant information substantiating his authorship. Everett Harrison summarizes the situation as well as any: "From the postapostolic church to the present, with almost no exception, the Epistle has been credited to Paul. If the claim of the apostle to have written the Galatian and Corinthian letter is accepted there is no reasonable basis for denying that he wrote Romans, since it echoes much of what is in the earlier writings, yet not slavishly" (Harrison, pp. 3–4).

SETTING OF ROMANS

It is agreed upon by most that the letter to the church in Rome was written during Paul's third missionary journey, probably in Corinth, in late A.D. 56 or early 57. The following outline of events surrounding the writing of the letter puts us in the apostle's shoes and frame of mind:

First Missionary Journey, Acts 13–14 (A.D. 48–49)
1. Paul and Barnabas are sent out from church in Antioch.
2. They plant churches in the region of Galatia (modern Turkey).
3. Paul writes the letter to the Galatians.

Jerusalem Council, Acts 15:1–35 (A.D. 49–50)
1. Issue of inclusion of Gentiles is settled in Jerusalem.
2. Paul and Barnabas "taught and preached the word of the Lord" in Antioch (Acts 15:35). This was a critical point in the ministry of Paul vis-à-vis his calling to take the gospel to the Gentiles. The leaders of the church in Jerusalem confirm that God indeed is working through Paul to reach the Gentiles, and with fresh confirmation he continues to teach the church accordingly.

Second Missionary Journey, Acts 15:36–18:22 (A.D. 50–52)
1. Paul (with Silas) journeyed from Antioch through Galatia, into Macedonia, through Achaia and Greece and returned by ship via Ephesus to Caesarea and Jerusalem, returning to the church at Antioch.
2. On this trip, Paul spent one and one-half years in Corinth (Acts 18:11) and wrote the two letters to the church at Thessalonica. This period in Corinth saturates Paul, a believer with a strict, orthodox Jewish heritage, with the defiled practices of pagan culture. Nearby Athens was a seat of intellectual arrogance, and Corinth a seat of immoral arrogance. Paul got a full dose of the downward spiral of

depravity, so forcefully addressed later in Romans 1, on this trip and his three-month stay in Corinth later (see below).

3. This was his deepest foray into the Gentile nations. He experienced imprisonment for the sake of the gospel and encountered both opposition and belief from Jews and Gentiles. Another turning point for Paul was in Corinth when he "shook out his robes in protest" against the Jews and declared, "From now on I will go to the Gentiles" (Acts 18:6). The Lord confirmed his ministry in a vision in the night (Acts 18:9).

Third Missionary Journey, Acts 18:23–21:16 (A.D. 53–57)

1. Paul left Antioch and traveled through lower Galatia to Ephesus, where he stayed approximately three years (see his reference on his return voyage in Acts 20:31) and wrote 1 Corinthians perhaps in A.D. 55 (1 Cor. 16:5–8). Second Corinthians was probably written later that same year from somewhere in Macedonia (2 Cor. 2:13; 7:5). From Ephesus he journeyed to Macedonia and Greece, where he remained (most likely in Corinth) for three months, probably around the end of A.D. 56 and the beginning of 57 (Acts 20:1–3). From there he returned back through Macedonia, stopping to visit the Ephesian elders briefly (Acts 20) in an attempt to reach Jerusalem by Pentecost (Acts 20:16).

2. It was during his three months in Corinth that Paul probably wrote Romans. Near the end of his second missionary journey he had expressed a desire to go to Rome (Acts 19:21), and perhaps wanted to journey there from Corinth. Two things stood in the way: he wanted to deliver the money contributed by the Macedonian churches to the church in Jerusalem, and a plot against him by the Jews was discovered while he was in Corinth. Whether the letter to the Romans was in lieu of a personal visit at that time, we do not know (see below on "Purpose of Romans"). But the money for the Jerusalem church appeared to be in hand (Rom. 15:26), so Paul wrote his letter to the Roman church (A.D. 57), apparently sent it to Rome by Phoebe from nearby Cenchrea (Rom. 16:1–2), and escaped the Jewish plot by returning overland through Macedonia to Philippi where he sailed for Jerusalem (Acts 20:6).

3. It is obvious that Paul wanted to get to Rome (Rom. 1:8–17), but the way had not been opened. Therefore, at the end of his third missionary journey, in A.D. 57, Paul had extended his westward reach into the Gentile nations with the gospel only as far as Greece. He would eventually get to Rome, but not in a way he anticipated.

PURPOSE OF ROMANS

As the apostle to the Gentiles, Paul succeeded in taking the gospel throughout the northern regions of the Mediterranean world. At the end of his third missionary journey (around A.D. 57–58), his sights were focused on "the regions beyond" the Mediterranean (2 Cor. 10:16)—Spain at a minimum (Rom. 15:24,28) and no doubt further north into (present day) Europe after that.

The message of salvation under the old covenant was to have had a centripetal effect, drawing the nations to God in Jerusalem. Israel was to have been a "kingdom of priests" (Exod. 19:6) whose purity of life and love for God would be a beacon and a banner to the nations. God would dwell in his temple in Jerusalem and the nations would be drawn there to worship. Foreshadowings of this effect were seen at the height of the theocratic monarchy (theocracy) in Israel. When the queen of Sheba "heard about the fame of Solomon and his relation to the name of the LORD" (1 Kgs. 10:1), she came to Jerusalem to see for herself if the reports were true. In short, "she was overwhelmed" (1 Kgs. 10:5) and offered praise to God for what he had done in Israel through Solomon (1 Kgs. 10:9). That is how it was supposed to work in the Old Testament.

Though Peter declared that the church also was a "holy priesthood" (1 Pet. 2:5), this was not in a theocratic sense. Rather, the message of salvation was to travel in a manner opposite to that under the old covenant. Instead of drawing the nations to Jerusalem, God began sending apostolic ambassadors from Jerusalem to the nations (Acts 1:8). The so-called "Great Commission" is the most well-known statement of the peripatetic ministry of evangelism that the church was to undertake (Matt. 28:18–20; see also Mark 16:15; Luke 24:46–47).

This centrifugal effect would require "gospel outposts," or way stations, as the evangelistic movement extended further and further away from Jerusalem. Jesus' statement in Acts 1:8 is a perfect picture of the progress of the waves of expansion. The evangelistic pebble went into the pond in Jerusalem, with ripples washing first over Judea, then Samaria, and finally landing on the last shores at earth's end.

Syrian Antioch was the first of these mission stations, and it served adequately as a base for three Mediterranean mission journeys. But as Paul prepared to fulfill his mandate to take the gospel to the Gentiles, he looked for the next city that could serve as a launching pad to the regions beyond. Rome was not only the largest and most important city in the world at that time, but it also was on the western edge of the gospel's advance. Rome would serve as the perfect place for Paul to use as the base for his next series of missionary journeys. He seems to imply this in his letter to the Romans, saying he wanted to pass through Rome on his way to Spain (Rom. 15:28).

The church at Rome was likely large, and consisted both of Jews and Gentiles. Yet it had grown in importance without the benefit of direct apostolic guidance and teaching. Traditions to the contrary notwithstanding, there is no biblical or reliable traditional evidence to support Peter, or any other apostle, being the founder of the church in Rome. It was probably started by Jews who returned there after being converted and baptized under Peter's preaching in Jerusalem at the Feast of Pentecost (Acts 2:10). In addition, it is possible that converts from other churches started by Paul (in Macedonia, Asia, or Greece) migrated to Rome and helped to strengthen and establish the church in Rome.

Though the church at Rome was large and in a resource-rich city, there was a significant contrast between Paul, who wanted to go there, and the believers in that church. Paul was the "senior" apostle in the body of Christ. He had been a believer more than two decades when he wrote Romans (converted in A.D. 35, Romans written in A.D. 57). The first decade he had spent "in school" in and around Antioch, Tarsus, Arabia, Damascus, and Jerusalem. It took a while for the church to warm up to this former persecutor, and for him to receive and understand the stewardship God was giving him.

The second decade-plus, however, consisted of intense ministry. The record of his experiences during this period are phenomenal: walking and sailing all over the Mediterranean world, being beaten, shipwrecked, jailed, run out of towns, ridiculed—all the while carrying on a ministry of leadership development and written correspondence to the churches. Paul knew the problems, the people, the heresies, the objections—and he knew the truth.

He also knew that in order for the church at Rome to serve as the base for his future apostolic ministry, it needed to be convinced of the purpose and power of the gospel—the very gospel that he was preparing to take to Spain and beyond. They would need to understand its power to save both Jew and Gentile because all stood equally condemned before God. They would need to be clear on how one receives salvation. They would need to know what salvation looks like in the life of the believer (sanctification), and they would need to understand why it was imperative that Paul take the gospel beyond Rome to the Gentile nations, and how his mission related to the promises of God given to the Jews (Rom. 9–11).

Without this corpus of understanding, strife could easily develop between the Gentile and Jewish portions of the Roman church (as it possibly already had; see Rom. 14). Finally, the church would need to understand how the gospel has power to bring greatly diverse peoples together into one body that loves and serves and supports one another while furthering the Great Commission (chaps. 12–16).

Paul's experiences in Jerusalem (Acts 15) and Antioch (Gal. 2) had prepared him well for the possible challenges of building up and encouraging a Jewish-Gentile church in the world's most powerful city. Paul understood more than the Roman believers did that they were to play a key role in his apostolic mission. In order for them to participate in the promulgation of the gospel, they had to be convinced of—and experience personally—the power of the gospel to save and sanctify and equip for service. Paul sets forth in Romans everything he wanted the church at Rome to know that would equip them for the role they were to play in his ministry.

The length and size of Paul's letter have caused some to argue that Romans is simply his theological *magnum opus* which just happened to be sent to the church at Rome. While it undoubtedly had widespread distribution and value to other churches, it was still written specifically to the believers at Rome for the purposes outlined above. The maturity and depth of the letter is occasioned no doubt by the maturity of Paul's thinking and ministry in A.D. 57, the end of his third missionary journey. He was full of insights and spiritual wisdom about what it takes to bring both "halves" of humanity— Jew and Gentile—together for God's purposes in one body.

Additionally, the size and importance of Rome, and the church established there, required an "impressive" presentation. It must be thorough, convincing, and irrefutable. Paul's polemic tone betrays his desire to convince. Finally, the apparent lack of direct apostolic presence in the church, and the size of the task ahead of Paul, required him to write a letter that was exhaustive in scope, enthusiastic in tone, and equipping in result.

Therefore, Paul's letter to the Romans reflects the warp and woof of his personal and apostolic agenda: to declare the riches of the grace of God to the uttermost parts of the earth. Being practical as well as idealistic, Paul knew that another stepping stone—first Jerusalem, then Antioch—would be needed for the extension of the gospel, and Rome was the obvious choice. The purpose of his letter to the Romans is to teach them, equip them, and unite them in the faith. A church that would serve as his connecting point to the "outside world" must be a mature church; one that would support him prayerfully as well as materially—and be as strong when he returned as when he left.

Paul was not using the church at Rome for a personal agenda. He simply recognized the sovereign and unfolding plan of God for him to go to Spain and beyond and the placement of the church of Rome right in his path. His apostolic ministry would find much fruit as he built up the Roman church, first by letter and then in person (Rom. 1:11–13), as he carried out the command of Christ "to carry my name before the Gentiles and their kings and before the people of Israel" (Acts 9:15). Reading Romans in light of Paul's motivation and ministry gives his message the context it needs.

It is easy in Romans to get sidetracked into any one of Paul's subpurposes in the book. To lead a church into doctrinal and practical maturity means covering lots of doctrinal ground, which he does. The righteousness of God, the reality of sin, the depravity of man, the means of salvation, law versus grace, flesh versus Spirit, the sovereignty of God, the place of Israel in God's redemptive plan, Christian liberty, and life and love in the body of Christ—all are covered and serve as subpurposes of the apostle. Interestingly, Paul writes almost nothing about church life—leadership, ordinances, structure—or Christology or the return of Christ. Perhaps the church was grounded in these areas.

Suffice it to say that Paul's purpose was not to write a systematic theology that he happened to send to the church at Rome. Paul was preparing a large and potentially influential body of believers to be colaborers with him in a world-class task, for which he authored a world-class epistle.

RECIPIENTS OF ROMANS

Assuming that the Jewish converts at Pentecost in Jerusalem (Acts 2:10) formed the core of the church upon returning to Rome, God-fearing Gentiles in Rome would have begun making up perhaps the majority of the church. Jews were undoubtedly a small minority of the population of Rome. Demographically speaking, there is no particular reason to assume that the church would not gradually represent a cross-section of the population. Assuming it was founded soon after Pentecost in the year of Christ's death and resurrection, it would have existed for twenty to twenty-five years before receiving Paul's letter (depending on whether one holds an A.D. 30 or an A.D. 33 date for the crucifixion).

Acts 18:2–3 offers a historical reference to the Roman emperor Claudius's expulsion of all Jews from Rome which probably occurred around A.D. 49–50 (with the likely exception of Jews who were Roman citizens). Since Claudius's reign ended in A.D. 54, much of the Roman Jewish population would not have been in Rome for several years prior to the receipt of Paul's letter in A.D. 57. It is likely that many would have resettled permanently between A.D. 50 and 54 and not returned to Rome, allowing for a possible reduction in the number of Jewish believers in the church at Rome.

Paul's letter itself gives ample evidence of both Jewish and Gentile populations in the church. It is impossible to state with certainty which group would have been in the majority, nor is it necessary to know. Keeping Paul's focus in mind relieves the pressure on undeterminable details: Paul's mission was to unite and strengthen the church for the purpose of launching an outreach to the regions beyond. There were Jews in the church; there were Gentiles in the church; but from the perspective of the grace given to Paul "there is neither Jew nor Greek for [they were] all one in Christ Jesus" (Gal. 3:28).

Parts of Romans that reflect a Gentile presence include 1:13; 11:13; 11:28–31; 15:15–16, while 2:17–3:8; 3:21–4:1; 7:1–14; and 14:1–15:12 clearly reflect concerns related to Jewish believers. The famous passages in chapters 9–11 that deal with the interplay between Gentile believers and the nation of Israel were obviously of critical importance to all. They reflect the heart of the apostle's stewardship, showing how all people everywhere (the Gentiles) were being offered the opportunity to participate in the covenant blessings given to Israel. The danger was pride on the part of the Gentiles and anger on the part of the Jews.

Paul's mission as an apostle was to help the church in all locations work through the transition from salvation under the old covenant to salvation under the new covenant; from the primacy of physical Israel to the primacy of the church; and from being Mediterranean-minded to being missions-minded. The quickest way for any church to rise above "who's who" is to focus on a larger mission that all can participate in. Paul's goals for the church at Rome are a model in this regard.

STYLE OF ROMANS

The New Testament contains clear literary forms. There is history (Acts), biography (the Gospels), letters (the Epistles), and apocalyptic (Revelation). Epistles were letters, sent to specific people for specific purposes. Paul even identifies Romans as a letter (Rom. 16:22). But Romans is a different type of letter. It is not personal like Philemon, nor is it primarily problem-oriented like the two Corinthian letters. Rather, it seems to be purpose-oriented; it seems to be a letter written by the apostle to achieve his purpose directly, meeting the church's needs as a subset of that purpose.

Rather than answering questions either sent to him by members of the church or reported by others as he did in 1 Corinthians (1:10; 5:5; 6:1; 7:1; 8:1; 11:17; 12:1; 15:1; 16:1), Paul asks and answers questions and issues in Romans according to his own agenda. The discussion of the weak and strong brother (Rom. 14:1–15:13) may be evidence of some internal conflict in the church at Rome, but for the most part Paul takes them through a survey of truth in an order not unlike that of Ephesians: doctrinal first, then practical. In the most basic sense Paul seems to be saying in Romans, "The gospel . . . is the power of God for the salvation of everyone . . . therefore . . . offer your bodies as living sacrifices, holy and pleasing to God" (1:16; 12:1). Because of the gospel that has touched us, he says, Jew and Gentile alike (1:16), let us offer ourselves to God for his service, which is to extend this gospel for his glory to the whole world.

That paradigm dictates the style of Paul's letter. Chapters 1–11 lay out the most logical and systematic presentation of God's righteousness effecting salvation for humankind that has ever been penned. Chapters 12–15 are the "therefore"—the practical outworking of such a great salvation. Chapter 16 is a personal postscript from the apostle that brings this exemplary epistle down from polemic heights to peoples' hearts—people whom Paul knew and cared deeply about. The same man who wrote 1 Corinthians 13 also wrote the letter to the Romans. Different style, same heart, unified purpose.

The greatest danger in analyzing the style of Romans is to forget that it was, first and foremost, a letter to a specific church for a specific purpose. To suggest otherwise is to suggest a loss of focus on the apostle's part. To discover the reasons for Paul's style, we have to get inside his heart and understand his purpose. When that is clear, his epistolary style for this letter becomes easy to reconcile with that of his other letters.

THEME OF ROMANS

Paul hangs the key to the theme of this letter right by the front door: "I am not ashamed of the gospel, because it is the power of God for the salvation of everyone who believes: first for the Jew, then for the Gentile" (1:16). In the very next verse, that which is often identified as the theme of Romans is found: the righteousness of God. But rather than the righteousness of God being the theme of Romans, the righteousness of God is shown to be a component of the gospel, as he himself states: "For *in the gospel* a righteousness from God is revealed" (1:17; emphasis added). The key to quickly identifying the theme of Romans is to remember the purpose of the apostle—to be the "sent one" to the Gentiles, to deliver the good news that God had invited them to enter a relationship with him on the basis of the death and resurrection of Christ.

For Paul, theology was a means to an end, not the end itself. The end was the gospel being taken to the regions beyond. Paul would spare no one's feelings in making sure the gospel was the true gospel (Gal. 2:11–21). But once the theology was settled, his mission was to extend the gospel. Therefore, the righteousness of God is a critical part of the gospel message, but not the gospel itself. When Paul wrote a letter to the church at Rome, his theme was that which he knew every church should be about—manifesting and multiplying the impact of the gospel. In Romans, it is more pronounced at the beginning of the letter due to his specific plans for the church at Rome to serve as an outreach base for his ministry to Spain and beyond.

Paul was not confused about his mission or the "theme" of the church, and therefore was clear about the theme of his letter to the Roman believers. We will read Romans with new appreciation when we see his theme as the gospel that is the power of God. The outline for this commentary reflects the manner in which Paul's theme is evident throughout his letter.

COMMENTARY OF ROMANS

As the Editorial Preface to this book indicates, the Holman New Testament Commentary is for those who teach the Word of God. But because teachers of the Bible need several kinds of resources for their preparation, further distinction is needed. Probably no other book of the New Testament has been "commented" on more than Romans, as evidenced by the large number of commentaries in print at any given time—not to mention the volumes that have passed out of active circulation. There is no syllable of the Greek text of Romans which has gone unscrutinized, no verb unconjugated, no noun undeclined, no pericope unexegeted, no chapter unoutlined. Therefore, this commentary will not repeat those exercises. It will be based on exegesis and the best resources available, but the pages will not be taken up repeating what is available so readily in other sources.

Rather, the approach of this commentary on Romans will be to discover the heart of the author, the apostle Paul, and reveal it so the teacher may reveal it to others. The assumption is that what Paul wanted to communicate to the Roman church, and did so eloquently and profoundly, the modern church needs to hear as well. Rather than a "what?" commentary on Romans, this will be a volume that explores "why?" The driving question in each chapter will be, Why and how does Paul support his theme—the power of the gospel—in this chapter? What can the modern church learn from the apostle Paul about the most profound doctrinal and practical deposit of truth revealed from heaven since Mt. Sinai—*the revelation that God is spiritually uniting all believers everywhere into a unified body which can reveal the power of God and the gospel to a hurting and needy world?*

It is assumed that the primary use of this commentary will be by those teaching laymen and laywomen, not scholars, in the church. In other words, the same kinds of people who populated the Roman church! Paul viewed the Roman Christians as his potential partners in the gospel, those who would help him take the gospel to Spain and beyond. If he were writing this letter to your church, would he be expecting any less? Therefore, the goal of the commentary is to help you, the teacher, represent the apostle Paul to those you teach; in representing Paul, you can expect those you teach to capture and keep a passion for reaching the world with that most valuable of possessions—the gospel of Jesus Christ. The reflections on Romans offered in this volume are offered to that end.

The Bibliography at the end of this volume will list some of history's ablest commentators on the Epistle to the Romans, and you are encouraged to avail yourself of their wisdom. But in the following pages, our prayer is that you will have a fresh and intense confrontation with the power of the gospel as revealed through Romans; that the nations of the world that Paul longed to reach will become the objects of your own spiritual longing; and that the horizons of the earth that filled his eyes will fill your own as you contemplate the fields that are yet white unto harvest, and that you will consider the one thing, the only thing, that can bring the fruit into the storehouse—the power of the gospel!

Romans 1:1–17

Paul and the Romans: Potential Partners in the Gospel

I. **INTRODUCTION**
What Was Driving Columbus?

II. **COMMENTARY**
A verse-by-verse explanation of the chapter.

III. **CONCLUSION**
Prepared for "Come What May"
An overview of the principles and applications from the chapter.

IV. **LIFE APPLICATION**
Belief Determines Identity
Melding the chapter to life.

V. **PRAYER**
Tying the chapter to life with God.

VI. **DEEPER DISCOVERIES**
Historical, geographical, and grammatical enrichment of the commentary.

VII. **TEACHING OUTLINE**
Suggested step-by-step group study of the chapter.

VIII. **ISSUES FOR DISCUSSION**
Zeroing the chapter in on daily life.

> ## Quote
>
> "*O*ur calling is not primarily to be holy men and women, but to be proclaimers of the gospel of God. . . . Paul was not conscious of himself. He was recklessly abandoned, totally surrendered, and separated by God for one purpose—to proclaim the gospel of God."
>
> Oswald Chambers

Romans 1:1–17

 IN A NUTSHELL

*P*aul, known only by reputation to the large Christian community in Rome, introduces himself and his message to the church. Wanting to enter into a long-term partnership with the Roman church, he boldly sets forth his credentials and his message: called by God to preach the gospel of God.

Paul and the Romans: Potential Partners in the Gospel

I. INTRODUCTION

What Was Driving Columbus?

*C*hristopher Columbus labored for seven years to convince European monarchs to finance his seaborne explorations. Finally winning the support of Queen Isabella of Castille and King Ferdinand of Aragon, he set sail on August 3, 1492. Thinking he was on the way to India, he "discovered" the new world on October 12, 1492. In his *Libro de las Profecias* (*Book of Prophecies*), Columbus recorded a remarkable set of perspectives on his voyage. He was not sailing or exploring for himself; he was sailing by the will of God.

"I prayed to the most merciful Lord about my heart's great desire, and He gave me the spirit and the intelligence for the task: seafaring, astronomy, geometry, arithmetic, skill in drafting spherical maps and placing correctly the cities, rivers, mountains and ports. I also studied cosmology, history, chronology and philosophy," Columbus wrote. "It was the Lord who put into my mind (I could feel His hand upon me) the fact that it would be possible to sail from here to the Indies. All who heard of my project rejected it with laughter, ridiculing me. There is no question that the inspiration was from the Holy spirit, because he comforted me with . . . the Holy Scriptures . . . encouraging me continually to press forward, and without ceasing for a moment they [the Scriptures] now encourage me to make haste," he professed.

His continuing remarks give evidence of an unshakable confidence in the purposefulness of his "calling": "All things must come to pass that [have] been written by the prophets. . . . I am a most unworthy sinner, but I have cried out to the Lord for grace and mercy. . . . I have found the sweetest consolations since I made it my whole purpose to enjoy His marvelous presence. . . . No one should fear to undertake any task in the name of our Savior. . . . The working out of all things has been assigned to each person by our Lord. . . . The fact that the gospel must still be preached to so many lands in such a short time, this is what convinces me."

If one did not know the source of these statements, it would be easy to think they came from a same-generation protégé of the apostle Paul. Christopher Columbus lived many years after Paul, but he had a remarkably similar outlook on life: God is the ruler of all things; we are his servants; he communicates his will to us; we are responsible to fulfill it; the Scriptures are our guide; the Holy Spirit is our strength; courage is our banner; and the gospel is our message.

While no one should claim that Christopher Columbus was a perfect Christian, or that he had apostolic credentials, one thing can be said: his identity as a faithful servant of God is clear. Unfortunately, history books have removed much of his Christian identity, but the writings from his own hand make it clear. Nothing mattered more than to fulfill God's will for his life. And Romans 1 reveals the same thing about the apostle Paul. There was no mistaking Paul's identity by those who knew him, nor for those of us who read his writings. He was without question a charter member of the company of the committed.

Remember—the Romans had never met Paul personally. Undoubtedly, many or all of the Roman Christians had heard of him. But Paul's letter was a prelude to a future visit—a letter of introduction, if you will—and he wanted to make sure that the church in Rome could separate fact from fiction regarding his identity. Therefore, he clears away any confusion in the first chapter: "There are three things I am committed to," Paul said in essence: "My calling from God (my ministry is not my idea), my concern for you (I believe God wants us to be partners in the gospel), and my understanding of the gospel (it is the only thing that can save the world)."

To the degree that Paul is an example for all believers (1 Cor. 4:16), our identity should be like his—and like that of William and Catherine Booth, founders of the Salvation Army. The Booths' daughter, Evangeline, characterized her parents this way: "Very early I saw my parents working for their people, bearing their burdens. Day and night. They did not have to say a word to me about Christianity. I saw it in action" (Hughes, *Stories*, p. 59). There should never be a question about the identity of those called by God, concerned about people, and committed to the power of the gospel.

II. COMMENTARY

Paul and the Romans: Potential Partners in the Gospel

MAIN IDEA: *Paul is identified by commitment to his calling, commitment to people, and commitment to the gospel.*

A Paul: Called by God (1:1–6)

SUPPORTING IDEA: *Truth is validated by its source.*

Tony Campolo tells the story of a friend who discovered his true calling in life. He had been a college English teacher, but suddenly quit his position—to become a mailman. After hearing the man's reasons for resigning from teaching to become a mailman, Campolo tried to encourage him with the old Protestant work ethic: "Charlie, if you're going to be a mailman, then be the best mailman in the world!" To which his friend replied, "I'm a lousy mailman, Tony. I'm the last one to get back to the post office every day, and besides, I can't sleep at night." When he asked for an explanation, here is what Campolo heard: "There are so many lonely people on my route who never had anyone visit them until I became their mailman. Have you ever tried to sleep after drinking fifteen cups of coffee in one day?" (Hughes, *Stories,* pp. 337–339). Tony Campolo reached an important conclusion about his friend Charlie: "He was alive with the excitement that comes to a person doing something meaningful with his life."

There is nothing so debilitating as life without purpose. Conversely, there is nothing so energizing as life filled with purpose. A life purpose will bring focus and drive to anyone, be they Christian or non-Christian. And it does not even have to be a particularly spiritual purpose. But if a mundane purpose can empower an ordinary person, think what a divine purpose could do in the life of one who is linked to the eternal purposes of God! Outside of the Lord Jesus Christ himself, the apostle Paul is perhaps the best example we have of a life transformed and empowered by living out a divinely-ordained life purpose.

1:1. The apostle **Paul** began his letter with an expanded introduction. Because his future mission to Spain and beyond involved the church at Rome, and because the believers there had never met Paul, he made extra efforts to validate himself in their sight. He wanted them to know, as he wanted the Galatians to know several years prior (Gal. 1:1, 10–12), that what they were about to read in his letter was not his own invention. His letter to them was part of a divine mission, and what he wrote, he wrote for God.

The common form of a letter introduction in Paul's day was "X to Y, greetings . . ." Paul followed this pattern with only slight variation in most of his letters, but here the "to" comes in verse 7. Paul takes six verses to identify himself and establish his credentials and mission. In fact, it can be said that Romans 1:7–16:27 is simply an explication of Romans 1:1–6. In these initial six verses Paul summarizes who he is and what he does: a servant of Christ who calls people from the nations of the world to come to faith in Christ.

"Easy for Paul to say," we think to ourselves. "He was an apostle. He had been knocked flat on the ground after being accosted by Christ on the Damascus Road, being blinded in the process. He was smart; he was goal-oriented; he was committed; he was single without a family; he was . . ." and on and on. Our reasonings somehow make us think that apostles are supposed to live simply-defined lives (with the obvious implication being that it is okay if we do not!). Granted, all those things are true of Paul, but it is not those things to which we attribute the simplicity of his self-definition and identity. In fact, when Paul was saved by Christ, he was the same thing that the Romans are now to Paul, and that you and those you teach are now as well: potential partners in the gospel.

Remember, Paul was the enemy of Christ when he was saved, meaning he was only a potential partner in the gospel. He became a partner, a colaborer with Christ, through obedience—the same "obedience that comes from faith" (v. 5) to which he is calling the Romans and all who would read his letter, including us.

Paul was single-minded (Jas. 1:7–8) and uncluttered (Heb. 12:1–2)—characteristics which are to be found in every believer. Therefore, the potential exists for our identity to be the same as Paul's: servants of Christ committed to calling the nations of the earth to faith in Christ. If that is not our true identity now, perhaps we will be closer to it as we study Paul's great epistle to the Romans. The church has, after all, inherited the Great Commission which Christ entrusted to the original disciples (Matt. 28:18–20) and is presently under obligation (see Rom. 1:14) to fulfill it.

For all the theology and logic and reason and profundity that is rightfully attributed to the apostle Paul—and which the church commendably imitates—it must be remembered that it all served one purpose in his life: to fulfill the mission he had been given to take the gospel to the nations of the world. If there is a lesson for the church in Romans, it is that theology serves missions. If it did in the life of the greatest apostle, and the One who sent him on his mission, surely it must in our lives as well.

Three things characterized Paul: he was a **servant**, he was **called to be an apostle**, and he was **set apart for the gospel**. Perhaps the most radical evidence of the transforming power of the grace of God in Paul's life was what happened to his will. The transformation was subtle and therefore easy to miss—so subtle that many in the leadership of the contemporary church may have missed it. Paul was not changed from an active to a passive person; if anything, he was perhaps more active and goal-oriented after his conversion than before. The difference is that he submitted his activity to one whom he now knew personally and loved. He willingly subjected himself to the plans and purposes of a lord who was his master. He lived only to do the will of God (cf. the same perspective in the life of Christ as highlighted in John's Gospel: 4:34; 5:30; 6:38; 8:26; 9:4; 10:37–38; 12:49–50; 14:31; 15:10; 17:4).

Servant here is the familiar *doulos*, the word in the vernacular for "slave." Its background is in the Old Testament provision for a servant voluntarily choosing to remain with a master after a required period of servitude was completed (Exod. 21:5–6; Deut. 15:12–17; see Ps. 40:6–8 and the NIV's rendering of "pierced" in v. 6 as a possible reference to King David's self-positioning of himself as God's bondservant). The owner pierced the ear of his voluntary servant with an awl; such a mark identified him forever as belonging to the master.

The words of a hypothetical servant to his master in Deuteronomy 15:16—"I do not want to leave you because I love you and your family and am well off with you" (author's translation)—have stunning ramifications for the one today who would call himself a servant of God. Paul surely understood the implications, but do we? Can every believer, but especially those who teach and lead as did Paul (Jas. 3:1), say with integrity that we do not want to leave? That we love God and the family of God? That we are better off with him—regardless of the trials and problems that attend us—than we would be anywhere else in the world? For how many is Christian "service" a vocation rather than a voluntary profession of loyal love?

Note also how Paul used a term (**servant**) that would have shocked the Gentiles in the church at Rome while appealing to his Jewish brethren. Rome was filled with slaves; some have estimated that the majority of the population was in forced servitude of one sort or the other. To be a slave in the Gentile mind was to be at the bottom of the social order. Servanthood was something to escape; freedom was a goal to attain. How arresting it must have been to the Gentile believers to learn that Paul had "given up" his freedom and willingly submitted himself to **Christ Jesus**, the Jewish Messiah.

Paul delivers a book-in-a-word on freedom when he calls himself a *doulos* of Christ. As Francis Schaeffer beautifully puts it, "Paul had [a slave's] iron band around his neck, not because it had to be there but because he held it there by the fingers of his own will" (Schaeffer, *Finished Work of Christ*, p. 14).

To the Jewish believers, however, being a servant of God called to mind a roll call of those used by God in the Jewish nation. Abraham (Gen. 26:24), Moses (Num. 12:7–8), David (2 Sam. 7:5, 8), Isaiah (Isa. 20:3), and the prophets (Amos 3:7) were all called the servants of the Lord in the Old Testament. His Jewish readers would have noted immediately the formulary "servant of the Lord" being replaced by "servant of Jesus Christ" in Paul's salutation. The seamless transition from *Yahweh* in the Old Testament to Jesus Christ in the New Testament would not have been lost on the careful Jewish reader.

But Paul's use of the Old Testament label "servant" was not for class purposes. Paul had no interest in being a member of anyone's Hall of Fame. But Hall of Faith? That was a different story, and one he was willing to tell. As he would tell the Ephesians, writing from a jail cell after finally making it to Rome, he became a servant in response to God's grace (Eph. 3:7). But even that grace, and the faith to receive it, was God's gift (Eph. 2:8–9). If anyone deserves credit it is God, for "inviting" him to become a servant.

In addition to being a **servant**, Paul is **called to be an apostle**. Paul got to be an apostle the same way the Twelve did: Jesus called him. Remember the purity and simplicity of Jesus' calling of the disciples? "Come, follow me," he said to Peter and Andrew, who followed him at once (Matt. 4:18–20). Then he called James and John, who likewise followed (Matt. 4:21–22). Then, a few years later, he called Paul (Acts 9:1–19; 22:6–16; 26:12–18). An apostle is a "sent one" without necessary reference to the identity of the sender.

Before his conversion, Paul was sent by the Jewish leaders in Jerusalem to capture and incarcerate believers in Damascus (Acts 22:5). As such, he was a "sent one," an apostle. After his conversion, he was sent by Christ to do the same thing that Christ was sent to do: release the captives and set the prisoners free (Luke 4:18–29; Gal. 1:1). By whom one is sent determines the kind of ministry one will have.

Who has sent you? Hopefully, the words of Jesus to the first twelve that he sent out have been your commission as well: "As the Father has sent me, I am sending you" (John 20:21). Two thousand years removed from the personal sending ministry of Jesus, it can become hard to sort out "who is sending whom" in today's ecclesiastical world. But two questions bear asking in this regard (and are especially tied to the issue of servanthood previously mentioned by Paul).

First, as best you are able to prayerfully and humbly determine, are you where you are in ministry as a teacher as a result of the "sending" ministry of Jesus Christ? This is not asking if you are an apostle, a "sent one." That office was apparently reserved for those who had seen and could testify to the reality of the risen Christ (Acts 1:22; Eph. 4:11). Rather, it is the principle of going and doing according to the will of Christ.

Second, is anything standing in the way of your going where you feel you are sent? Your own will perhaps; a human institution; a lack of resources; an ecclesiastical permission structure? And what about those whom you are teaching? How would they answer the same two questions? Tasks which flow from authority structures result in someone going somewhere and doing something. The church is an authority structure, we have a task to do, and therefore can assume that we are going to be sent by our Master to accomplish his mission. It is healthy to pause and take stock of where we are and what we are doing, and make sure that we are where we have been sent by Christ.

Finally, Paul's third designation is as one who was **set apart for the gospel of God**. While we will explore issues concerning the gospel more in "Deeper Discoveries," it is important here to note that Paul only views himself as set apart for one thing: the gospel. Part of this stems from his commission to preach the gospel as the apostle to the Gentiles—a formal commissioning which he alone received from the Lord. But part of it also stems from the centrality of the gospel in Paul's life and thinking, a focus that the entire church of Jesus Christ is to embrace and maintain (Matt. 28:18–20).

Did Paul have a soul mate in the person of the weeping prophet Jeremiah? God told Jeremiah that he had been set apart in his mother's womb to be a prophet to the nations (Jer. 1:5). Paul likewise knew that God had set him apart from birth so that he might preach Christ among the Gentiles (Gal. 1:15). In ways that parallel the ministry of Jeremiah, Paul showed a no-holds-barred approach to fulfilling that for which he was set apart.

Other clues exist to the depth of the apostle's spiritual understanding of his "set apartness." The Greek word for "set apart," *aphorizo*, has the same root (p-r-s) as the Hebrew word on which "Pharisee" is based. While the meaning of "Pharisee" is murky, the practice of Pharisees was crystal clear. They had set themselves apart, dedicated to the practice of the Law of Moses. Paul had been "in regard to the law, a Pharisee" (Phil. 3:5), yet now he finds himself set apart as a "gospelizer," a spreader of the good news about Jesus Christ.

Because Paul mentions the gospel ten different times in this letter, we will encounter many facets of it in our study. Unfortunately, the contemporary church has so compartmentalized the gospel that it has lost touch with its full-orbed meaning. Many churches preach an evangelistic message every Sunday to an audience that is 98 percent Christian, boring the believers and turning them off to "the gospel." Other churches never mention the gospel in their meetings since the gospel is (allegedly) for the unsaved, not for believers. As a result, believers know little of the gospel's ongoing relevance for their lives.

Yet Paul says in Romans 1:15 that he is "eager to preach the gospel also to you who are in Rome," referring to the believers. We will discover from Paul the gospel's relevance for the church. F. F. Bruce provides a clue when he defines the gospel as "the joyful proclamation of the death and resurrection of [God's] Son, and of the consequent amnesty and liberation which men and women may enjoy through faith in him" (Bruce, p. 68). It is the first half of Bruce's definition with which we are most familiar since it echoes Paul's own words in 1 Corinthians 15:3–5. In the second half resound the words of Jesus himself in Luke 4:18–19, a quote from Isaiah 61:1–2. Indeed, the good news has its roots in the Old Testament, its fruit in the New. Paul had a broad and biblical (meaning Old Testament, for him) view of the gospel, and it was this gospel for which he had been set apart.

1:2–4. Which gospel is Paul going to expand on to the Romans? He tells them clearly to make sure that they are receiving not another gospel or a new gospel or a different gospel, but the *gospel* gospel, the one **promised beforehand through [God's] prophets in the Holy Scriptures.** The gospel is serious business for Paul. It is the heart of the message about the kingdom of God and its impact, and he wanted to make sure that the Romans had confidence in what they were about to hear. Paul was preparing to tell them more about the gospel than they had ever heard, and he wanted their full attention (plus, he did not want to be cursed; see Gal. 1:8–9).

Paul's gospel is the gospel regarding God's **Son,** born of a physical mother, making him fully human; conceived by the **Spirit of holiness,** making him fully divine and sinless; and raised by a father who was a **descendant of David,** qualifying him as well as part of the royal lineage in Israel. It is the gospel of **Jesus Christ our Lord,** Paul said, the Lord who by the power of God conquered death and the grave. What good news would there be in a gospel that is based on "bad news"—the news that the promised Messiah was killed, and his kingdom apparently with it? It is therefore the resurrection of Christ that puts the "good" in the good news. Be assured, Paul said—the gospel you are going to hear from me is the gospel that "I received" (1 Cor. 15:3).

1:5–6. Verse 5 is perhaps the most pregnant proposition in the entire letter, for it contains the seeds of Paul's entire spiritual life and ministry as a believer and apostle. **For his name's sake** reveals Paul's ultimate motivation in preaching the gospel. His further references to the name of God in Romans betray the depth of his concern that the life, death, and resurrection of Jesus Christ be vindicated: the name of God was blasphemed among the Gentiles (Rom. 2:24, quoting Isa. 52:5; Ezek. 36:22). God wanted his saving name proclaimed throughout the earth (Rom. 9:17, quoting Exod. 9:16) because "Everyone who calls on the name of the Lord will be saved" (Rom. 10:13, quoting Joel 2:32). The ultimate role of the name of God in the earth is to be the object of reverence and praise (Rom. 15:9, quoting 2 Sam. 22:50; Ps. 18:49).

Why, therefore, did Paul receive **grace and apostleship** from God? **For his name's sake . . . to call people from among all the Gentiles to the obedience that comes from faith.** It is instructive, and perhaps convicting, to see how Paul turns to the Old Testament to explicate the gospel message. The average Christian today does admirably when he or she refers to the death, burial, and resurrection of Jesus Christ, the benefits of which are appropriated by faith. But the understanding of God's salvific intent for the world in the Old Testament is beyond the pale of most believers.

Remember: when Paul, and the Old Testament writers, refer to "the Gentiles" or "the nations," they are referring to the whole world. As Jews, they were looking beyond themselves to everyone else. The Gentiles are "the world" which John 3:16 says, "God so loved" (including the Jews, of course). It is obvious at the very start of this letter that Paul has "the world" in his sights, and he wants the Roman believers to catch his vision.

Deftly, he weaves them into the universal scope of the gospel by saying that they are among the Gentiles **who are called to belong to Jesus Christ.** Paul is building his case for going beyond Rome to Spain and the "ends of the earth" (Acts 1:8). Follow the reasoning: "I, Paul, am a voluntary bondservant of Christ, called by Christ **to call people from among all the Gentiles to the obedience that comes from faith.** You Romans are an example of what I must do elsewhere, for **you also are among those who are called to belong to Jesus Christ.** I belong to Christ as a slave, as do you. If we partner together in the extension of the gospel, I can be supported as I go on to Spain and you can continue to spread the gospel in Rome. A harvest is prepared among the nations and in Rome" (1:13).

Thus Paul concludes the most lengthy introduction of himself and his ministry to be found in any of his letters. If there is a sobering admonition from the life and testimony of the apostle to the Gentiles, it is this: "What is our purpose in life, and from whence comes that purpose?" Perhaps we have thought our purpose is to be the best pastor, or the most life-changing teacher, or the most careful scholar, or the most able administrator we could be. All of those are worthy means to that which is the only worthy goal: the proclaiming of the gospel among the nations for his name's sake.

Much of the church today, especially the church in the West, does not see the vast portions of the world which do not praise the name of the Savior. Paul saw those near him (Rom. 10:1) and those who were far from him (Rom. 15:28). He will shortly explain to the Roman believers how spiritual blindness can come upon those who do not respond obediently to the grace and faith they have received. May all who teach the Word of God, and especially the Book of Romans, have eyes to see as Jesus saw (Matt. 9:36) and to respond as Paul responded.

B Paul: Committed to the Romans (1:7–15)

SUPPORTING IDEA: *Truth has its ultimate application in the lives of people.*

Paul's transitional reference to the Roman believers in verse 6 is the first stone in what is a bridge between himself and his explanation of the universal application of the gospel: "Here is who I, Paul, am (1:1–6) an apostle sent to the nations; here is who you Roman believers are, Jews and Gentiles who have embraced the gospel concerning Christ (1:7–15); and beyond us both lies the rest of the world for whom Christ died, a world desperately in need of the gospel (1:18–3:31). Rome can be a gateway for me, a launching pad, as I push further west with the gospel—if we unite our hearts and abilities in partnership in the gospel" (15:24).

1:7. In another profound link between himself, his vision, his mission, and the church in Rome, Paul now refers to the believers in Rome by the most sacred title possible: **saints.** He had already told them in 1:1 that he was "set apart for the gospel," and even this language could tempt the average believer to view Paul in a different class—more spiritual, more committed, more disciplined in spiritual matters. Some so-called "super-apostles" had already begun to throw their weight around in the church in Corinth (not likely any of the original Twelve), and Paul no doubt battled the tendency of some to elevate him beyond where he saw himself—as nothing apart from the grace of God (2 Cor. 11:5; 12:11).

In calling the believers in Rome **saints**, Paul is saying that they also are set apart as holy, as spiritual, as called by God to the highest levels of privilege, and thereby responsibility, imaginable. Twenty-nine times in eight of his epistles Paul referred to believers as saints. If there ever was a critical concept that would link Paul's "set-apartness" with the Corinthians' "set-apartness," this was it.

Saints is actually the adjective for "holy" (*hagios*). Saints are therefore "holy ones." The two-stage process of holiness is often reversed, resulting in putting the proverbial cart before the horse.

The first stage of holiness is positional; it is something believers are declared to be because of their position in Christ (Eph. 1:4). Because of our positional holiness, we are able to become holy in practice, progressively more so as we mature in Christ (1 Thess. 4:7). In this verse, Paul is focusing on the believer's positional holiness. An understanding of the Old Testament root concept will help. *Qodesh* was the Hebrew word signifying "holy," but like many words in the vocabulary of Israel it was adapted from the Semitic culture. It basically meant something that was set apart for a particular use. Cultic temple prostitutes were referred to by this root word because they were set apart for religious purposes (Gen. 38:21).

Our revulsion in thinking of a prostitute as "holy" is an example of our thinking of the second stage of holiness before understanding the first. Knives, tables, lamps—all the articles of the tabernacle and temple worship in Israel were called "holy" because they were set apart for sacred use. Think of it: one minute a knife is ordinary, the next it is holy, all on the basis of being declared holy (set apart for special use) by the priest.

Perhaps the most striking example of the ordinary becoming holy is when God said dirt was holy. When Moses approached the burning bush on Mount Horeb, God told him to remove his sandals "for the place where you are standing is holy ground" (Exod. 3:5). The dirt "here" was holy; the dirt "over there" was not. Why? Because the dirt "here" was set aside as the meeting place between God and man. When the meeting was over, the dirt was no longer holy.

So when Paul calls the Roman believers **saints**, what is he saying? He wants them to know that, regardless of how they view themselves, how unimportant they may think themselves to be in the grand scheme of things, they are as "holy" as Paul himself is. Paul is a saint, and they are saints. Paul has been set apart to accomplish God's goal of spreading the gospel to the nations, and so have the Romans. It has nothing to do with spiritual giftedness, the office one does or does not hold, one's education or appearance, one's wealth or poverty, or one's outward manifestations of spirituality. Rather, "holiness"—total dedication to the service of God and his purposes—is a positional reality for every believer, like it or not!

1:8–10. Paul reveals that he has heard that the "sainthood" of the believers in Rome is not positional only. They have acted upon their "set-apartness" to become faithful witnesses for Christ. All over the known Christian world the church in Rome is being talked about because of their faith. Who would be surprised at there being a church in Jerusalem, the spiritual capital of the Mediterranean world? No one—it would be expected. But in Rome, the capital of the pagan world, there is a thriving community of Christian believers? This was something to talk about, and people were spreading the word.

You can understand Paul's genuine pleasure and thanksgiving as expressed in verse 8. Because he has his heart set on taking the gospel into pagan lands where no one has been before, he is eager to come and meet and fellowship with these believers who know how to thrive spiritually in the heart of the Roman Empire! His prayers have been frequent that God would open the way for him to visit the church in Rome.

What do people in your sphere of influence hear about your church, your Bible study group, your mission organization—or about you? Much is said about Christians and their ministries today. Word spreads rapidly about increased attendance, about innovative programs, about multimedia presentations, about new facilities, about conferences and seminars. But how often does one hear about a church that is known for its faith, as were the Christians in Rome? Even if one takes the less objective rendering of *pistis* (faith) in verse 8, and suggests that it refers simply to the Christian beliefs of those in the Roman church, it is still a commendation of note.

How many times does the secular world look at a church or organization and say, "That group really seems to have a genuinely spiritual life; they seem like what real Christians ought to be." It is no wonder that Paul wanted to get to Rome as quickly as he could to meet these believers whose **faith [was] being reported all over the world.** And no wonder he continued to pray for them diligently. Perhaps he prayed, "Lord, keep their faith and their fire alive. May they be the catalyst for a powerful outreach into the nations of the world!" Are you praying that for your church, your organization, your study group, your family—for yourself?

1:11–13. The other reasons Paul wanted to visit the church in Rome was for mutual edification and, as always, for reaping a harvest of souls. Paul's sense of propriety (his spiritual maturity and discernment) are quickly apparent as he revealed his longing to visit the Roman church. Remember—this was not a church that Paul planted. Somehow (we do not know how) the church began and prospered without the apostle Paul ever having been there or having communicated with it outside of verbal messages perhaps being sent by travelers.

It would have been tempting for a lesser leader to convey the "I'll take it from here" attitude—to seek to barge into a prosperous situation and assume that everyone would immediately promote him to the top of the pyramid. Paul was wiser. Not only does he want to impart **some spiritual gift** to them (v. 11), he wants to be encouraged by them as well (v. 12). Verse 12 is no quick correction of a *faux pas* in verse 11. Nor does verse 11 convey a desire to come into their midst and, on call, display the "things that mark an apostle—signs, wonders and miracles" (2 Cor. 12:12). Paul knows that only the Godhead dispenses spiritual gifts (*charismata;* Rom. 12:6; 1 Cor. 12:11; Eph. 4:11), so neither is he coming to impart spiritual gifts to believers. He is coming simply to be used in whatever way God might choose to use him to help strengthen the church in Rome—that you may be established by **some spiritual gift** (v. 11), not "that I may establish you."

And, he is coming to be strengthened himself. John Stott captures the heart of the apostle that is so evident in these verses:

> [Paul] knows about the reciprocal blessings of Christian fellowship and, although he is an apostle, he is not too proud to acknowledge his need of it. Happy is the modern missionary who goes to another country and culture in the same spirit of receptivity, anxious to receive as well as give, to learn as well as teach, to be encouraged as well as to encourage! And happy is the congregation who has a pastor of the same humble mind! (Stott, p. 57)

Finally, Paul was patient and content with the will of God. Do not forget that Paul was a "servant of Jesus Christ" (1:1). He said without embarrassment or hesitation that he had planned often to go to Rome but had **been prevented.** By what? Evangelism **among the other Gentiles?** Satanic opposition (1 Thess. 2:18)? The daily pressure of his "concern for all the churches" (2 Cor. 11:28)? A quick perusal of 2 Corinthians 6:3–10 and 11:23–33 shows that Paul had more than enough to occupy his time. But he also had more than enough faith in his Master's plan for his life and agenda than to become discontent over his desires not being met.

It is impossible for Paul's heart to stay beneath the surface. Like a spiritual artesian well, his desire to preach the gospel to the Gentiles bubbles to the surface of its own accord. He longs to come to Rome in order to reap a spiritual harvest there **just as I have had among the other Gentiles.** In this seemingly casual reflection, Paul tells us who he is. Likewise, in our seemingly casual comments and reflections to others we reveal our heart of hearts as well. What we talk about, what we do in our free time, what we read, what we watch on television, where we venture on the Internet—the small "comments" about ourselves that we make day after day—reveal who we are. Paul was a man in the grip of the gospel. Wherever he went, whoever he was with, whatever his agenda, his priority remained the same—tell the world about Jesus.

1:14–15. Almost as a footnote—perhaps wondering if the believers in Rome would be puzzled by his passion—he explains **why [he is] so eager to preach the gospel also to [those] who are at Rome** (v. 15). It is because he is in debt to Jesus Christ for a price he can never repay. It is a profoundly humbling realization to note that the world's greatest theologian and apologist, an amazingly gifted man, never got over the fact that God loved him so much that the Son of God died to pay the price for his sins. The words of the bond-servant noted earlier from Deuteronomy 15:12–17 come back to mind here, as if Paul is saying to Christ, "I am well off with you; I do not want to leave."

When one realizes that Jesus Christ has paid an infinite debt that secures one's life and welfare for eternity, it is to the shame of the church that there are not millions of apostle Pauls roaming the earth looking for one more person to tell about the gospel of the grace of God. What does it say about our understanding of the gift of God that so many feel no indebtedness, no obligation, to Christ at all? Paul's attitude was, "If I am the only one who senses this indebtedness, that changes nothing. I am still indebted. And as long as there is one person left on earth to whom the invitation to eternal life has not been issued, then I am not a free man. I will remain a bondservant of Christ until the last lost sheep has been brought into the fold."

Greeks (the educated, the intellectuals, the sophisticated) and **non-Greeks** (the uneducated, the lower class, the barbarians), **wise** and **foolish**—there were no beginning and ending points on the scale of who Paul felt obligated to reach. His use of a figure of speech (a merism, citing the extremes in opposite directions to indicate a totality; see Ps. 139:8–9) shows the breadth of his vision for the gospel. Paul's perspective should become "the characteristic of a Christian's life once this level of spiritual honor and duty becomes real. Quit praying about yourself and spend your life for the sake of others as the bondservant of Jesus. That is the true meaning of being broken bread and poured-out wine in real life" (Chambers, *My Utmost*, July 15).

Ⓒ Paul: Convinced of the Power of the Gospel (1:16–17)

SUPPORTING IDEA: *Truth produces conviction and courage in those who believe it.*

Paul now comes to the climax of his introductory greeting to the church at Rome, and in it states what is for him the theme of the letter and his life. We have said in this commentary that the theme of Romans is the power of the gospel. By that, we mean that it is the controlling idea in Paul's approach to the grand scheme of salvation. Without the gospel, and without the power that the gospel *is* (not the power that the gospel *has*), there can be no salvation, no deliverance, no life. Everything that God wants for us is to be found in the gospel, and Paul is going to spend the rest of his letter explaining every facet of it.

So far, the apostle has said this: "(1) I am called by God to spread the gospel; (2) I am thankful for and encouraged by what the gospel has produced in the lives of you in Rome; and (3) I want to come and join you—for your benefit and mine—as we continue to proclaim the gospel in Rome and as I prepare to push ahead into the nations beyond you." Then, he gives them the reason for his unquenchable confidence and energy in his calling—a confidence he wants to spread among the Romans as well: "(4) Am I ashamed to come to the most powerful city in the world and proclaim our gospel? No, because the power of God will cast in stark relief the "power" of man; the gospel will reveal the righteousness of God amidst the unrighteousness of man. And everyone now lost in Rome and the world that embraces the gospel will be saved—as we have been! That is why I am not ashamed of the gospel!"

1:16–17. John Stott recounts a comment made by Scottish theologian James Stewart concerning this passage: "There's no sense in declaring that you're not ashamed of something unless you've been tempted to feel ashamed of it" (Stott, p. 60). We think of Paul as invincible, yet he was human. Jesus anticipated that his followers might one day be ashamed to identify with him (Mark 8:38), and Peter soon confirmed that prediction by denying him three times in one night (Matt. 26:75). Even Paul himself confessed to arriving in Corinth in "weakness and fear, and with much trembling" (1 Cor. 2:3) so plainspoken did he see himself as compared to the eloquent and sophisticated Greeks. And yet Paul, in truth, was never ashamed of his Savior. He spoke before royalty, rabbis, rulers, and rabble—to him, it made no difference. As he is about to demonstrate to the Romans in subsequent chapters, all are in need of the gospel.

Paul's confidence turns on three occurrences of *gar* ("for" or "because") in these two verses. The first is untranslated in the NIV, but should be, as it provides the transition from his earlier statement of eagerness: "I am so eager to preach the gospel also to you who are at Rome [*for*] **I am not ashamed of the gospel,** *because* **it is the power of God** . . . *for* **in the gospel a righteousness from God is revealed** (vv. 15–17; emphasis added).

Paul is giving the Roman believers a paradigm for life that the contemporary church desperately needs to understand: *nothing will display the righteousness of God (and thereby his person and glory) to a needy world like the message of the gospel.* Not surprisingly, it is a paradigm that Paul drew from the Old Testament and applied to the believers in Rome. We can draw on both instances and apply it to our benefit today.

So much has been written by commentators and theologians on these verses that "it is not easy to summarize, let alone to systematize, the debate" (Stott, p. 61). What is the meaning of the **righteousness from God**— attribute, action, or advantage? And what does it mean that righteousness is **by faith from first to last?** And does *ho de dikaios ek pisteos zesetai* mean **the righteous will live by faith** or "the one who is righteous by faith will live"? Good questions all, and best answered with a look at the context from which Paul draws his final phrase **(the righteous will live by faith)**, and the context to which he is applying and addressing it (the believing community of Christians in Rome).

In verse 17, Paul quotes something God said to the prophet Habakkuk (Hab. 2:4; also quoted in Gal. 3:11; Heb. 10:38–39). God's statement was one of comfort to Habakkuk, who was at his wits' end with God. First, wickedness was rampant in Israel and God seemed oblivious to it, moving Habakkuk to rail against God in a series of complaints (Hab. 1:2–4). Second, when God said he was going to use a nation more wicked than Israel (the Babylonians) to punish Israel, this produced cries and complaints of injustice from the prophet (Hab. 1:12–2:1). It might be said that Habakkuk was embarrassed, ashamed of God's inaction and his choices.

Paraphrased, God's answer to Habakkuk was this: "I am about to reveal something to you, Habakkuk, that I want you to record so that a herald may go and proclaim it (Hab. 2:2). It is a revelation of my righteousness, and will put to rest your fears of inaction and injustice. In the meantime—until my righteousness is revealed—you who are righteous are to trust me, to live by faith. There is nothing you can do to 'fix' the situation. You will have to live by faith, not by sight, until what I have written is accomplished" (Hab. 2:4).

Now, fast forward to A.D. 57. Paul is writing to a community of Christian believers living in the most powerful city in the world. Just three years prior to his letter, the reign of the Roman Emperor Claudius (ruled A.D. 41–54) had ended. Claudius had banished all Jews from Rome around A.D. 49–50 because of the continuing disruptions "instigated by Chrestus" (a misspelling of "Christ," scholars agree; recorded by the historian Suetonius in *Claudius*, 25). Obviously, the disruptions were not led by Christ in person, but were perhaps instigated by debates over his person. Claudius ended the disruptions by driving all Jews (including those who had come to believe in Christ; see Acts 2:10) out of Rome. Paul met Aquila and Priscilla for the first time in Corinth, where they settled as expatriates from Rome (Acts 18:1–2). Supposedly, when Claudius's reign ended, Jews were allowed to return to Rome. But the banishment no doubt had an unsettling, disruptive, and persecutorial effect on the young body of believers in Rome.

Unfortunately, this was just a foretaste of what Rome would give to the church in years ahead. Paul himself would suffer a martyr's death at the hands of Nero along with multitudes of believers during Nero's reign. Could the believers in Rome have wondered where God was in the midst of their suffering under Claudius? Could they have been embarrassed, even ashamed, as Habakkuk had been, that God was seemingly doing nothing to rescue them? Could they have felt powerless to act, wanting to do something but not knowing what to do?

Paul had read Habakkuk, and he knew that the Roman believers needed a revelation from God—some good news in the midst of their confusion. And so he writes verses 16 and 17 to them: the **gospel** is God's good news and Paul is the herald who is **not ashamed** of the circumstances or of God. Why? Because God's **righteousness** is **revealed** in the gospel! The pagan power of Rome (like the pagan nation of Babylon in Habakkuk's day) is no match for the **power of God** which is the gospel, Paul says. Do not think that God's power is absent—it is here in the gospel! And God's righteousness will be revealed against all manner of sin everywhere. In the meantime, the righteous must live by faith. Rather than thinking you are powerless to change Rome, the gospel gives you the power of God to change lives.

Now fast forward to the end of the second millennium A.D. In a day when Western civilization is said to be in its "post-Christian" phase, believers can feel powerless to effect the cultural trends and tides that bring constant pressure to bear. What the church needs today is what Habakkuk needed in 600 B.C. and oppressed believers needed in A.D. 50—a herald with a revelation of good news from God! The gospel is that revelation, and Paul's letter to the Romans is the tablet upon which it is written. But where are the heralds? They are meant to be every believer who knows that **the righteous will live by faith** regardless of the circumstances.

As Paul will soon explain, every person whom you pass on the street today is in need of the good news of the gospel. Whether an unbeliever oppressed by sin who is trying to create his or her own salvation, or a believer oppressed by the world who feels powerless living amidst unrighteousness. For both, the righteousness of God is revealed in the gospel, and for now, those who would be righteous will find life by faith.

The bottom line to history is that God will judge all human affairs: the Babylonians, Habakkuk, the Romans, Paul, the church, you, me—all will be judged. His righteousness will balance human actions. The message of the gospel—the message of Romans—is that we do not have to wait for the end of history to discover the effects of God's righteous judgment. His righteousness (his judgment) is revealed in the gospel. Paul will show convincingly in Romans that all have sinned and stand under the condemnation of God, and that the gospel reveals that fact now. Therefore, since man can know today of his sin and impending judgment, he can accept today God's righteousness in place of his own unrighteousness and be saved (therefore, the **righteousness from God** is an attribute, an action, and an advantage).

In addition, the gospel vindicates God's name today (see Rom. 1:5). As God heralded his righteousness to Habakkuk (Hab. 2:2) but did not execute it upon the Babylonians until years after Habakkuk's death, so the gospel heralds the righteousness of God today. **For his name's sake** (1:5), Paul says, he was given grace to proclaim the gospel among the Gentiles. Let the Romans laugh at "Chrestus," the common carpenter from Galilee. We will not be ashamed because the gospel of Christ reveals the true righteousness of God which transforms the "righteousness" of the Romans from laughter to lament. God's name may be mocked, but it is also vindicated—through the gospel.

Finally, Paul is proclaiming in Romans 1:16–17 a fresh insight into the truth of Isaiah 55:11: "So is my word that goes out from my mouth: It will not return to me empty, but will accomplish what I desire and achieve the purpose for which I sent it." This gospel does not *contain* the power of God. It *is* the power of God to everyone who believes it and lives in it (*ek pisteos eis pistin*; **by faith from first to last**), **first for the Jew, then for the Gentile.** Starting with Israel, the gospel is flowing to the nations, and Paul is inviting the Romans to partner with him in that proclamation of power.

> **MAIN IDEA REVIEW:** *Paul is identified by commitment to his calling, commitment to people, and commitment to the gospel.*

III. CONCLUSION

Prepared for "Come What May"

Paul wrote Romans near the end of his third missionary journey (about A.D. 57). He had already written Galatians, 1 and 2 Thessalonians, and 1 and 2 Corinthians, addressing significant problems that had arisen among churches he had planted. Following Romans, all of his remaining letters were written from prison (Ephesians, Colossians, Philemon, and Philippians in his first Roman imprisonment; 2 Timothy in his second Roman imprisonment) except for 1 Timothy and Titus—two letters written to two young church planters in Ephesus and Crete. In six of his letters (2 Corinthians, Philippians, Colossians, 1 and 2 Thessalonians, and Philemon) Paul lists Timothy as coauthor. Standing in the midst of all these letters is Romans, Paul's magisterial monograph to the power of the gospel of Jesus Christ.

Dictated by the apostle Paul to Tertius (Rom. 16:22), Romans is a systematic overview of the content of the gospel that Paul had been preaching for more than a decade. It was his longest and most important epistle up to that time in his ministry, and thus deserved his most lengthy and detailed introduction. What Paul was about to say to the Romans demanded credibility, and the first seventeen verses of chapter 1 provide it.

Paul established himself as a lover of God and God's Son Jesus Christ, a lover of the Roman believers and their faithfulness to God, and a lover of the gospel of God which saved him, the believers in Rome, and anyone who would accept it. One cannot help but wonder if something else was occupying the apostle's mind as he set forth the introduction to this grand epistle. He was aware of the persecution in Rome under Claudius which resulted in the expulsion of Jews from Rome.

He was also aware that danger awaited him in Jerusalem, his immediate destination to deliver the relief funds raised by the Macedonian churches. He knew that the unbelieving Jews in Jerusalem might seek to harm him upon his return (Rom. 15:30–31), as it would soon be specifically prophesied over him by Agabus (Acts 21:10–11). Had he received other indications, signs from the Lord, that he needed to commit to writing the revelation of the mystery of the gospel which God had delivered to him before heading into perilous places?

We have no indication of that; to suggest so is to speculate. But it is not idle speculation. Paul had completed his evangelization of the "known" world (the Eastern Mediterranean regions), and was preparing to move into the "regions beyond" (2 Cor. 10:16). If he had suffered the kinds of persecutions and dangers that he had among the civilized, what must await him among the uncivilized? Would not now be a good time to prepare a record of the gospel and send it to the Roman church where he hoped to soon arrive (Rom. 1:15; 15:23–33)? If he made it to Rome, the letter would have prepared the church to receive him and assist him on his way to Rome. If he never made it to Rome, the letter would be in the hands of a large and thriving church which could disseminate it to others (remember, the Jerusalem church had been decimated by persecution at this time, hence Paul's trip to deliver funds to relieve their suffering).

In a matter of months from when Paul finished Romans, as he journeyed to Jerusalem, the prophet Agabus came to where Paul was staying at Philip the evangelist's house in Caesarea (Philip the father of four daughters who were prophetesses; Acts 21:8–9). There he prophesied that the Jews in Jerusalem would seize Paul and hand him over to the Gentiles. Though all present pleaded with Paul not to go to Jerusalem, he answered them, "Why are you weeping and breaking my heart? I am ready not only to be bound, but also to die in Jerusalem for the name of the Lord Jesus" (Acts 21:13).

This conviction was not new for Paul. Everything he did was for "[Christ's] name sake" (Rom. 1:5), including whether to live or die. At the time of this prophecy, and Paul's response, Romans was probably in the hands of the church in Rome via the hands of Chloe (Rom. 16:1–2). Paul knew in his heart that his life was more settled than it had ever been. Churches were planted and thriving. The truth of the gospel had been written down and was at that moment being heralded to the churched and unchurched in Rome (cf. Hab. 2:2). And he awaited only one thing: "The Lord's will be done" (Acts 21:14). As it turns out, Paul made it to Rome. From Jerusalem to Rome he preached to kings and counselors, and ultimately suffered there—again, for the name of Jesus (Acts 9:15–16).

Paul's identity, by which he introduced himself to the Romans, stood him in good stead to the end. May those of us who read Romans today receive it as, in a manner of speaking, the last will and testament of a man who loved God, God's people, and God's gospel to the end. May we do our inheritance from him the justice it deserves.

PRINCIPLES

- A person's identity will be revealed in what is said and done.
- A heart for God will be revealed ultimately in a heart for people.
- A heart for people will be revealed in a heart for the gospel.
- The stronger one's purpose and calling, the more effective one will be.
- The loftier one's public position, the lower one's private perspective should be.
- A life calling should be based on eternal values and truth.

APPLICATIONS

- What do my words and actions reveal about my identity?
- Who are the people in whom I am building a love for God and the gospel?
- How am I proving my love for the gospel message?
- How would I describe my life's purpose and calling?
- What evidence is there that I am comfortable with the role of a bondservant of Christ in my public ministry?
- Do my priorities in life and ministry reflect values that are true and eternal?

IV. LIFE APPLICATION

Belief Determines Identity

Two identities of the apostle Paul can be traced to what he believed at two different periods of his life. His preconversion identity—an admirer of God, a champion of the letter of the law, a purveyor of bad news, a persecutor of the church—stands in contrast to his postconversion identity—a worshiper of God, a champion of the Spirit, a herald of good news, a builder of the church. The difference is in what he believed before and after encountering the grace of God in Christ. Having not met the Roman believers personally, he wanted them to know who he was. He used the introduction to his letter to convey his love for God, love for them, and love for the gospel committed to him by Christ.

Martin Luther, the instigator of the Protestant Reformation, also displayed two different identities during two different periods of his life. Listen to his pregrace self-description: "I hated that word, 'justice of God' . . . the justice by which God is just and by which he punishes sinners and the unjust . . . I was a sinner with an extremely troubled conscience . . . I hated the just God who punishes sinners . . . I grumbled vehemently and got angry at God . . . I was raging with wild and disturbed conscience . . . I badgered St. Paul about that spot [concerning the justice, or righteousness, of God] in Romans 1." Now witness the transformation of a miserable monk into a contented Christian: "All at once I felt that I had been born again and entered into paradise itself through open gates . . . I saw the whole of Scripture in a different light . . . I exalted this sweetest word of mine, 'the justice of God,' with as much love as before I had hated it with hate. This phrase of Paul was for me the very gate of paradise" (Luther, pp. 421–428).

What changed Martin Luther's identity? His encounter with the grace of God in Christ which then changed his thinking, just as it changed Paul's. Every believer's identity should be changing daily as well. If we have embraced the gospel of Jesus Christ, we have embraced the power of God, for the gospel is the power of God. No one can remain unchanged who has received the grace of God in the gospel and walks in it "by faith from first to last" (Rom. 1:17).

In both the apostle Paul and Martin Luther we have living, breathing displays of the truth of 2 Corinthians 5:17: "Therefore, if anyone is in Christ, he is a new creation; the old has gone, the new has come." So radical was the change in Paul's life that if someone had come to his door and asked for Saul of Tarsus, Paul would have been justified in responding, "He no longer lives here. In fact, he does not live in this city, or in this country. In fact, he no longer exists!" Or if when Dr. Martin Luther walked into one of his classrooms to teach his students, and they greeted him—"Good morning, Dr. Luther"—he would have been justified in ignoring their greeting, as if the person they remembered and were addressing no longer even existed.

The apostle to the Gentiles, and the leader of the Protestant Reformation, did not exist before their respective conversion experiences! How do we know? Because no churches were planted in the Mediterranean region, and the established church in Europe was not disrupted by debates over the truth of Scripture. The two men identified as the human agents of the two greatest religious revolutions in history only became those agents as a result of their conversions to Christ.

In Luther's case, it was the truth of Romans 1:17 that gradually began to awaken his heart to the fact that his righteousness before God was imputed to him by God, not as a result of his own works. When he realized that truth—the very truth that Paul explained to the believers in Rome—he looked around him and saw that Christendom in Europe in the early sixteenth century, at least within his Roman Catholic church, was vastly out of line with Scripture. Romans 1:17 became like a plumb line by which he gauged the theological foundation of the church. When he held the plumb line up, and saw that little was consistent with it, he could not restrain himself. And only by the gallant aid of his friends did he escape with his life—a life he was prepared to sacrifice for the truth, if necessary, just as the apostle Paul was (Acts 21:13).

The record of these two men, and the identity that flowed from what they believed, is a challenge for every believer today to consider. While God may not have called each of us to be "the apostle to the Gentiles," or to lead a reformation that transforms Western civilization, he has called us to something. The question is, Has our conversion to Christ made us new creatures practically, for the sake of the kingdom of God, as well as positionally? Do we so identify with God, with his people, and with his gospel that it is as if our old person no longer exists? Do those who know us as teachers of the Word of God become more aflame for the fulfillment of the Great Commission of Christ as a result of our teaching? Do they sense that for us teaching the Bible is not a job, not a source of pride, not a labor, but a means to an end—a way to connect with the heartbeat of our missionary God?

May your heart grasp afresh the vision that consumed the apostle Paul, the missionary-apostle to the Gentiles. May those you are currently teaching so sense your love for God, your love for them, and your love for the gospel that they are caught up afresh, or maybe for the first time, with a hunger to extend the gospel, the power of God, to those who have not heard!

V. PRAYER

Heavenly Father, thank you for the apostle Paul. May his servanthood, his leadership, and his love for eternal and heavenly things capture our hearts as we study this epistle in the weeks ahead. Create in your church a fresh commitment to take the gospel to the ends of the earth. Form an identity in us that reveals this commitment to everyone we meet. Amen.

VI. DEEPER DISCOVERIES

A. Calling (1:1)

Paul was "called to be an apostle" by and for Jesus Christ (see the discussion of "Apostle" below). His call was definite, particular, and unequivocal, which raises the question of calling in the spiritual life for "average" Christian: should believers expect to be called by God to a particular ministry or task in the body of Christ?

At least three "calls" can be identified in the New Testament: a call to salvation (Acts 2:39; Rom. 1:5–7; 8:30; 1 Cor. 1:9; Gal. 1:6); a call to God's kingdom purposes and plans (Rom. 8:28; 11:29; 1 Cor. 7:15,17,24; Gal. 5:13; Eph. 1:18; 4:4; Col. 3:15; 1 Thess. 4:7; 2 Tim. 1:9); and a call to ministry (Rom. 1:1; 1 Cor. 1:1). This last call is the one by which Paul knew he was to be an apostle. Interestingly, though Paul said he was called (Gr. *kaleo*, the most common word for "call," e.g., Rom. 1:1) to be an apostle, his "calling" from Christ to apostleship is less exact linguistically *in situ*. For instance, he was "appointed" or "chosen" (Acts 26:16; Gr. *proxeirezomai*) by Christ, "sent" (Acts 26:17; Gr. *apostello*) by Christ, and "called" or "summoned" (Acts 13:2; 16:10; Gr. *proskaleomai*) by Christ to new fields of ministry. His conclusion after these experiences was that God had "called" (Rom. 1:1; Gr. *kaleo*) him to be an apostle.

Paul obviously believed his apostleship was a gift from God (Eph. 4:11). In light of his other teachings on spiritual gifts being given to every member of the body of Christ (Rom. 12:3–8; 1 Cor. 12), believers should listen for God's "appointments, sendings, or summonings" to use the gift(s) he has given. At the very least, every believer should assume that God has equipped (called) him or her to a specific ministry in the body of Christ based on the distribution of spiritual gifts. It is not necessary to assume that there will always be a specific geographic "calling." Like Paul, we should minister where we are until we conclude (Acts 16:10) that God is specifically directing elsewhere.

B. Apostle (1:1)

Paul identifies himself as one "called to be an apostle" (Rom. 1:1). The word *apostle* is from the verb *apostello,* which itself is from the union of *apo* (from, away from, from a distance), and the primitive verb *stello* (to prepare, arrange). Therefore, to prepare from a distance became "to send," from which derived the noun, "one sent." Therefore, the meaning of apostle is a "sent one."

Three categories of apostles appear in the New Testament. First, Christ himself is "Jesus, the apostle and high priest whom we confess" (Heb. 3:1). This designation is consistent with his having been sent from the Father (John

17:18; 20:21), and forms the basis of his subsequent sending of the apostles. Second, the original twelve disciples were ultimately designated by Jesus to be apostles (Mark 3:14; Luke 6:13), Matthias being added to the group after Pentecost to replace Judas (Acts 1:21–26). In the choosing of Matthias we find the only statement of the qualifications of an apostle: one who has been with the Eleven during the ministry of Christ, from the time of John's baptism of Jesus until the ascension. He also had to be a witness to the resurrection.

Third, these qualifications set up the question as to the use of the term to describe others who lived during the apostolic age but were not present with Jesus during his ministry. Paul obviously falls into this category, as do James, the halfbrother of Jesus (Gal. 1:19; 2:9), Barnabas (Acts 14:4,14), Andronicus and Junias (Rom. 16:7), and possibly Timothy and Silas (1 Thess. 1:1; 2:6).

Paul was obviously a witness to the resurrected Christ on the road to Damascus, and there is little question that his designation as an apostle was authentic. The best summary of Paul's apostolic credential is found in Acts 26:15–18 where a number of key words are important: Christ "appeared" to Paul, "appointed" him as a "witness," and "sent" (*apostello*) him to do the same things that Jesus did in his own ministry—"open their eyes and turn them from darkness to light, and from the power of Satan to God, so that they may receive forgiveness of sins and a place among those who are sanctified by faith in me." This commissioning is so clear as to be irrefutable.

Paul always maintained a humble posture concerning his apostleship, never getting over the fact that the very one he persecuted had chosen him to bear his name before the Gentiles. Though his position as an apostle carried authority (2 Cor. 10:8), Paul preferred to identify with the weakness of Christ's sufferings (2 Cor. 13:4) and the "foolishness" of the gospel (1 Cor. 1:18,23). Because of his humility, some suggested he was no apostle at all (1 Cor. 9:2; 2 Cor. 11:5; 12:11).

Apostles are mentioned in the context of gifts given to the church (Eph. 4:11). Since one or more of these gifts are supported elsewhere in the New Testament as ongoing offices (e.g., pastor-teacher), some suggest that apostles have continued as well. Others differentiate between the office of apostle (those of the apostolic age given special ability and power by Christ; 2 Cor. 12:12), and the role of apostle (church planting, leadership authority, etc.). Others suggest on the basis of Ephesians 2:20 that apostles and prophets were only for the foundation period of the church and should not be expected to continue past that foundational (first-century) period.

C. Gospel (1:2,9,16)

Two aspects of the gospel message converge in the use of *euangelion* (gospel or "good news"), *euangelizomai* (to preach the good news), *kerusso* (to preach or proclaim), and *didasko* (to teach). The gospel is not only the good news of the life, death, and resurrection of Jesus Christ for sinners; it is the good news of the kingdom of God. The second part of the gospel is unknown to many believers.

Twentieth-century evangelicalism, having cut its eye-teeth on a dispensational or historic premillennial eschatology, have all but relegated theological discussions of the kingdom of God to a future millennial event. Many Christians use the phrase "the kingdom of God" in a very general sense but have no sense that it is part of the "good news," the gospel. The gospel that Christ preached was the good news of the kingdom of God (Matt. 4:23). When he sent his disciples out to preach, it was to preach about the kingdom of God (Luke 9:2); so they went and preached "the gospel" (Luke 9:6).

Paul, however, clearly says that the gospel he received was that Christ died for our sins, was buried, was resurrected on the third day, and appeared to more than five hundred witnesses (1 Cor. 15:1–8). And yet Luke tells us that Paul's message included "testifying to the gospel of God's grace" (Acts 20:24) and "preaching the kingdom" (Acts 20:25). When in house arrest in Rome, his message consisted of two parts: the kingdom of God and the person of the Lord Jesus Christ (Acts 28:23,31). He "preached" (*kerusso*) the kingdom, but he "taught" (*didasko*) about the Lord Jesus Christ. This follows the pattern set by the evangelist Philip who "preached the good news (*euangelizomai*) of the kingdom of God and the name of Jesus Christ" (Acts 8:12). Further, Paul makes it clear the kingdom of God is very much a present reality as well as a future one (Rom. 14:17; 1 Cor. 4:20; 6:9).

The good news we have to share is twofold: the kingdom of God (light) has irrupted into the midst of the kingdom of Satan (darkness) and all true believers have been transferred into God's name by virtue of the salvation won by the Son of God, who came to defeat Satan and destroy his works (Col. 1:13–14; 1 John 2:7). It is this kingdom—a kingdom of righteousness, peace, joy, and power in the Holy Spirit (Rom. 14:17; 1 Cor. 4:20)—that Paul was so passionate to spread the good news about. To proclaim a gospel that allows only the forgiveness of sin without entrance into the kingdom of God (and all its attendant blessings) is like giving a person the key to a new home but never allowing him or her to enter it. May the gospel we preach be the good news of the kingdom and of the Lord Jesus Christ.

VII. TEACHING OUTLINE

A. INTRODUCTION

1. Lead Story: What Was Driving Columbus?

2. Context: The year is A.D. 57, and the apostle Paul is nearing the end of his third missionary journey. He spends three months in Corinth where he writes the letter to the church in Rome. He has established churches in Asia Minor, Galatia, and Macedonia that are thriving and reaching others. But the church in Rome he did not plant, and has never visited. He has wanted to visit the church in Rome on numerous occasions, but has never gone there. Upon leaving Corinth, he plans to return to Jerusalem to deliver a financial gift from the churches in Macedonia to the struggling and persecuted believers in Jerusalem. He gives evidence at the end of his letter to the Roman church that perilous times may lie ahead for him, but he reassures the believers in Rome that he still intends to visit them. In fact, he tells them that he wants them to aid him as he takes the gospel to Spain. The letter he writes to the believers in Rome is his longest, his most systematic, and contains the longest introduction of himself found in any of his letters.

3. Paul's purpose in writing is to introduce himself to the church at Rome and to lay a foundation for a partnership with them to spread the gospel to the far reaches of the known world—Spain and beyond. After his trip to Jerusalem, he plans to visit them and spend time in ministry with them in Rome before leaving for Spain. This letter, which they will have had time to read and digest before his arrival, will be a theological education for them. If the church is going to partner with him in spreading the gospel to Spain, they must know the heart of the gospel and the heart of the apostle to the Gentiles. The first seventeen verses of Romans 1 is our introduction to both.

B. COMMENTARY

1. Paul: Called by God (1:1–6)
   - a. Paul's identity (1:1)
   - b. The gospel's identity (1:2–4)
   - c. The Romans' identity (1:5–6)
2. Paul: Committed to the Romans (1:7–15)
   - a. He identifies them as saints (1:7)
   - b. He thanks God for their faith (1:8–10)
   - c. He longs to spend time with them (1:11–13)
   - d. He is indebted to them and all people (1:14–15)
3. Paul: Convinced of the Power of the Gospel (1:16–17)
   - a. The gospel is the power of God (1:16)
   - b. The gospel reveals the righteousness of God (1:17)

C. CONCLUSION: BELIEF DETERMINES IDENTITY

VIII. ISSUES FOR DISCUSSION

1. For how many churches is the spread of the gospel a recognizable priority? What would be the identifying characteristics of a church for which the spread of the gospel was a top priority?

2. How do most Christians define "the gospel"? If the gospel is indeed "the power of God," how should that power be demonstrated among those who have embraced the Christian gospel? In what ways is the power of God evident in the church today as recognized by surrounding society?

3. How many churches have reports being spread about their faith and their Christian testimony as did the church in Rome? Why do not more churches enjoy this kind of reputation? What kinds of Christian virtues and practices would commend a church to its surrounding community and society at large?

4. Based on the amount of personal evangelism that takes place, many believers seem to be ashamed of the gospel. Why is this true? What must happen for believers to gain confidence in "the power of God" that will bring salvation?

Romans 1:18–32

Everyone Needs the Gospel

I. **INTRODUCTION**
Eyes Are Not the Key to Seeing God

II. **COMMENTARY**
A verse-by-verse explanation of the chapter.

III. **CONCLUSION**
The Master Clock
An overview of the principles and applications from the chapter.

IV. **LIFE APPLICATION**
Harmony in Idolatry
Melding the chapter to life.

V. **PRAYER**
Tying the chapter to life with God.

VI. **DEEPER DISCOVERIES**
Historical, geographical, and grammatical enrichment of the commentary.

VII. **TEACHING OUTLINE**
Suggested step-by-step group study of the chapter.

VIII. **ISSUES FOR DISCUSSION**
Zeroing the chapter in on daily life.

"*W*hat happened was this ... They traded the glory of God who holds the whole world in his hands for cheap figurines you can buy at any roadside stand."

Eugene Peterson

Romans 1:18–32

IN A NUTSHELL

*H*aving stated the theme of his letter—the power of the gospel—Paul moves immediately to begin substantiating the need for the gospel. Just as the Jews would be held accountable for God's specific revelation to them through the Law, God holds the rest of humanity (the Gentiles) accountable for his general revelation to them through creation. As the gospel reveals the righteousness of God, so the rejection of God's general revelation reveals, and subjects humanity to, the wrath of God.

Everyone Needs the Gospel

I. INTRODUCTION

Eyes Are Not the Key to Seeing God

*T*he nineteenth-century evangelist Dwight L. Moody, attending a meeting in London, was struck by the power and earnestness of the speaker to whom he was listening. He was all the more intrigued when he discovered the speaker was blind. Moody met the man after the service to learn his story: "He told me that he had been stricken blind when very young. His mother took him to a doctor and asked him about her son's sight. 'You must give up all hope,' the doctor said. 'Your boy is blind, and will be forever.' The mother took her boy to her bosom and cried, 'Oh, my boy, who will take care of you when I am gone? Who will look after you?' forgetting the faithfulness of the God she had taught him to love.

"This blind man became a servant of the Lord, and was permitted to print the Bible in twelve different languages, printed in the raised letters, so that all blind people could read the Scriptures themselves. He had a congregation, my friends, of 3,000,000 people [the estimated number of blind worldwide in Moody's day] and I think that blind man was one of the happiest beings in all London. He was naturally blind, but he had eyes to his soul, and could see a bright eternity in the future. We pity those who have not their natural sight; but how you should pity yourself if you are spiritually blind" (*Heritage,* p. 1018).

Moody's encounter with a blind saint illustrates perfectly the point to be made by the apostle Paul in Romans 1:18–32—eyes are not the key to seeing. Paul will demonstrate in this section of his letter to the church at Rome that people with perfectly good eyesight have looked all around the world and never seen what is plainly evident—the signs pointing to the existence of God. Creation boldly declares the glory of God, as the psalmist puts it (Ps. 19:1), through what God has made—and yet the natural human tendency is to look at the evidence and suppress it, offering the excuse that he never saw it at all.

It is important to understand why Paul is pointing this out to the Roman believers. We have said that he is writing to the Romans to prepare them for his visit, to develop a partnership with them for his future missionary endeavors to Spain and beyond, and to present to them the most thorough statement of the gospel of Jesus Christ that has been recorded—for use by the church in Rome, Macedonia, or in any other region where the gospel would spread. He has just told them that the gospel is the power of God for the salvation of everyone who believes (Gentiles and Jews alike; Rom. 1:16) because the gospel reveals the righteousness of God.

The logical question the believers in Rome might ask is, "Why does the righteousness of God need to be revealed?" Paul's answer will be, "Because the wrath of God has already been revealed against those who have suppressed his glory. Proclaiming his own righteousness is God's response to his wrath."

As noted by John Stott, Paul works with four "revelations" in making the transition from Romans 1:1–17 to Romans 1:18–32 (Stott, pp. 70–71). Noting them in reverse order helps to understand the big picture of Paul's purposes as he writes to the believers in Rome:

- First, God reveals his glory in creation (which mankind suppresses; Rom. 1:18–20)
- Next, God reveals his wrath toward mankind (because of man's suppression of his glory; Rom. 1:18).
- Next, he reveals his righteousness in the gospel (as an act of grace and mercy to provide escape from his wrath; Rom. 1:17)
- Finally, he reveals his power in the gospel (to save those among humanity who deserve his wrath but who are willing to receive his grace; Rom. 1:16).

The church in Rome was surrounded by a paradox. On the one hand, the Roman Empire, and the capital city of Rome specifically, was among the most sophisticated cultures in the world. On the other hand, it was one of the most depraved cultures as well. If Hellenism had elevated the spirit of man, then Rome had elevated the soul of man. Rome was rank humanism at its worst. Every appetite was fulfilled, no desire was left unmet, and no sin was left uncommitted. What Paul is about to write to the church in Rome will clearly demonstrate that suppressing the knowledge of God and elevating the knowledge of sin does not spare man from the wrath of God. His letter will allow believers to recognize that their ability to "see" God was not because they did not deserve God's wrath, but because they believed the gospel—the power of God for salvation.

In this opening section of his argument, Paul demonstrates three things: the revelation of the wrath of God (vv. 18–20); the reasons for the wrath of God (vv. 21–23); and the results of the wrath of God (vv. 24–32). While most commentators suggest that Paul is dealing here with the sins of pagans, or the Gentiles, it must be remembered that the Gentiles, biblically speaking, are the entire human race minus Israel. In Romans 1:18–3:20, Paul points out that every person stands under the wrath of God, but for different reasons. Gentiles (the human race), because they have rejected God's general revelation in creation, and Jews (2:1–3:8) because they have acted contrary to God's specific revelation to them, the Law. For this reason, the next chapter in our commentary is titled "Even Jews Need the Gospel." This title conveys that it is not just the non-Jew who has incurred the wrath of God, but Jews as well. Paul summarizes both arguments in 3:9–20, concluding that "all have sinned and fall short of the glory of God" (3:23).

The importance of this portion of Paul's letter cannot be underestimated. If the believers in Rome did not believe that all people everywhere, including themselves, deserved God's wrath, there would be no motivation to take the gospel to their Roman neighbors or to the barbarians in Spain after Paul arrived. Neither would there be motivation for praise and worship of God to which Paul would call them later in the letter (11:33–12:2).

That has not changed in our day. There can be no doubt that the complacency concerning world evangelization which so characterizes the Western church is in part due to the absence from the pulpits of the truth of Romans 1–3. It has been well said by many that bad news is what makes good news good! While some in eighteenth-century New England may have criticized Jonathan Edwards for his hard line in "Sinners in the Hands of an Angry God," all would rejoice in the spiritual harvests that resulted in the Great Awakening that followed his preaching.

As you teach your students or congregation the truths of Romans 1, may the glory of the gospel—the power of God for salvation—shine ever more brightly as the reality of the need of humankind is rediscovered.

II. COMMENTARY

Everyone Needs the Gospel

> **MAIN IDEA:** *Because humankind has chosen to reject the clear evidence of God's existence and rule, God has allowed the human race to demonstrate to itself exactly how devastating life can be when lived in rebellion against God.*

A Revelation of the Wrath of God (1:18–20)

> **SUPPORTING IDEA:** *God is justified in revealing his wrath against the human race because it has suppressed the evidence for his existence and failed to worship him as the Creator God.*

1:18. The reason the righteousness of God "is revealed, a righteousness that is by faith from first to last" (1:17), is because the **wrath of God is being revealed from heaven against all the godlessness and wickedness of men.** Paul uses the exact same word (*apokaluptetai*, from whence comes "apocalypse," or "revelation") in both verses to connect righteousness and wrath. In both words, the revelation of which Paul speaks is a present passive form, indicating that the revelation is continual and that it is being done by God.

Both revelations are intentional, not accidental, incidental, arbitrary, or circumstantial.

There should be no doubt about the close connection between the theme of Paul's letter to the Romans as stated in 1:16–17 (the power of the gospel, a gospel in which righteousness is revealed) and the declaration of his wrath in 1:18. The connection is weakened in the NIV because of the failure to translate the first word in verse 18, the conjunction "for" (*gar*). The reason God is calling Paul (and the church at Rome and the church today) to preach the gospel in which his righteousness is revealed is because humanity in general has suppressed God's truth and righteousness. C. K. Barrett's translation of 1:18 communicates the essence: "A clear signal of the revealing of God's righteousness is the fact that his wrath is being revealed from heaven against all the ungodliness and unrighteousness of men who, by their unrighteousness, *hold the truth imprisoned*" (Barrett, p. 32; emphasis added). What sinful human beings think they can suppress, God has chosen to spread through the foolishness of preaching, of which Paul is not ashamed to be a part (Rom. 1:9,16; 1 Cor. 2:4; Gal. 2:7; Titus 1:3). This fact is at the heart of Paul's subsequent questions in Romans 10:14: "How, then, can they call? And how can they believe? And how can they hear with someone preaching to them?" As long as the truth is suppressed by sinful men, no one will hear it!

To fail to grasp this connection is to fail to understand the urgency of Paul's mission and message, both in his day and in ours: left to the will of human beings, the truth would only be suppressed (witness the former activities of the apostle himself!). Therefore, God breaks in, redeems some for himself, reveals the truth to them, and sends them out in the power of the Holy Spirit to preach the truth to others. This is the heart of the Great Commission which Paul was fulfilling: to gospelize (evangelize) the world.

God's wrath is against those who suppress the truth, whether Jew or Gentile. God's gospel (1:1) is for those who stand under his wrath, whether Jew or Gentile (3:23). At the exact same time that his wrath is being revealed (present passive indicative) his righteousness is being revealed (present passive indicative) in the gospel. It is his wrath, in fact, that makes his righteousness so obvious. But without the preaching and teaching of the doctrine of his wrath, it is impossible to see the fullness of his righteousness.

There is actually one fundamental, underlying reason for the wrath of God being revealed against man: man suppresses (again, present tense) the truth about God. In the case of those Paul is discussing here—pagans who have not had the benefit of God's revealed will through the Law and Prophets—the truth they are guilty of suppressing is that truth revealed about God in creation (v. 20). Nothing is more evident about the heart of God than his desire for fellowship with those created in his image. God wants humankind to know him!

He has revealed himself in creation generally, and specifically through the verbal revelations given to Israel for the benefit of the whole world (Gen. 12:3). Therefore, when that which he purposely reveals for our benefit is suppressed, it is of the greatest offense. And to be sure, the suppression is not accidental; rather, it is very much intentional. In fact, the suppression of the truth about God by mankind is described with the same word which Paul and the writer to the Hebrews exhorted believers to forcefully hold *to* the truth about God (1 Cor. 11:2; 1 Thess. 5:21; Heb. 3:6,14). Paul would never counsel anyone to hold to the truth of God casually. Therefore, this word (*katecho*) means to "hold fast, firmly," or, in a negative sense, "restrain" (2 Thess. 2:6–7, NASB).

One of the most stinging rebukes Jesus Christ ever delivered was to those Pharisees who, having taken away the "key to knowledge" were preventing others from entering the kingdom (Luke 11:52). The Pharisees had become blind guides of the blind (Matt. 15:14). Instead of being stewards of the truth of God, revealing his glory and his promises and provisions to Israel and the nations, the Pharisees had become blind to the truth and were causing blindness in others besides. So perverted does suppressing the truth become that it reverses itself completely. Instead of championing the truth and leading others into it, those who suppress the truth ultimately applaud the devolution into sin by others (Rom. 1:32). No wonder Jonathan Edwards saw "Sinners in the Hands of an Angry God!"

But what is this anger, this wrath of God that Paul says is being consistently revealed from heaven (Paul mentions wrath eleven times just in Romans)? Surely one of the most maligned of God's characteristics, his wrath, is not like the wrath of man. Humanly speaking, wrath calls to mind the severest form of anger, and anger produces images of those we know who demonstrate carnal, fleshly anger. We then apply that human tendency to God, and judge him for his wrath the same way we judge those in our lives who vent their wrath upon us. But nothing could be further from the truth.

God's wrath may be thought of in two broad categories, one being the expected result of the other. There is a wrath of God that will be demonstrated during a period of time at the end of earth's history when God judges sin and sinners. Paul speaks of that wrath in Romans 2:5, calling it "the day of God's wrath" (see also Col. 3:6; 1 Thess. 1:10; Rev. 14:19). It is when his righteousness, the same righteousness revealed in the gospel, will be realized by those who have not benefited from the realization of his righteousness in the death of Christ. By the end of history the wrath of God will have been brought to bear upon the sins of every person.

Those for whom Christ bore the wrath of God on Calvary's cross will not experience the final outpouring of his wrath. But this point-in-time wrath of God is not the wrath Paul is referring to in this verse, though it is the logical result of it as viewed on a space-time continuum.

The wrath Paul refers to here is "the holy revulsion of God's being against that which is the contradiction of his holiness" (Murray, p. 35). Some have, and will always, object to God being "angry." The difference (and it makes all the difference) between God's anger and ours is that ours will always be compromised by sin whereas his flows from a sinless nature. That is not to say that a man or woman cannot express a form of "righteous" anger or indignation, but it is to say that it will never be *totally* righteous, whereas God's is. In fact, it is actually easier to think of God's wrath as an expression of what he is: love (1 John 4:8,16).

God's constant emotion toward those created in his image is love, but his love becomes severe in the face of sin. Even in the human realm, we would question the love of a father for a child who did not react "angrily" if that child were abused by another—or even if that child were abusing himself in sin. C. E. B. Cranfield puts it well: "His wrath is not something which is inconsistent with his love: on the contrary, it is an expression of his love. It is precisely because he loves us truly and seriously and faithfully that he is wroth with us in our sinfulness" (Cranfield, p. 29). Therefore, God's love flows toward the human race continually.

The love of God is like a river of emotion flowing from his heart toward his creation. Whether that river is the "quiet waters" that bring refreshment (Ps. 23:2) or the "mighty waters" that rise against sin (Ps. 32:6) is the difference between his love and his wrath.

1:19–20. Paul continues his opening statement with a summary **since.** The word here (*dioti*) is a combination of two common conjunctions: *dia* (on account of) and *hoti* (because). It has the sense of "in as much as" or "in light of the fact that." Therefore, "in light of the fact that God has made knowledge about himself plain to everyone," Paul says, he is justified in exercising his wrath toward humankind for suppressing that knowledge.

In the most elementary of human terms, this is not a case of a father who chastens his teenager for something that he never even told him to do. Rather, this is a case of the teenager leaving school, and all the way home seeing billboards, street signs, flashing marquees, signs on buses, bumper stickers, airplanes pulling message banners—"Billy, don't forget to set the garbage out for the trash truck!" Then, when he gets home, there are phone messages, e-mail messages, and television commercials reminding him of the same thing. That is how plainly God has made knowledge of himself available to the human race, Paul says.

That which God has made known to humanity is **his eternal power and divine nature.** That is the external part of his self-revelation. But in addition to demonstrating externally (those are like the billboards and signs Billy's father put up), God has even caused man to understand internally what is seen externally (this would be like the characteristics of responsibility and integrity that Billy had learned from living in his parents' household for six-teen years). So both externally and internally, God has provided sufficient insight through his creation—remember, Paul is discussing the Gentiles, those who have no special revelation from God as did the Jews—for humans to know he exists, and sufficient internal motivation to understand that what they are seeing is the handiwork of God.

Interestingly, Psalm 19 uses terminology akin to propositional, verbal testi-mony (the kind of revelation Israel received from God) to describe how the creation speaks of the Creator: "The heavens declare . . . the skies proclaim . . . they pour forth speech . . . . There is no speech or language where their voice is not heard. Their voice goes out . . . their words to the ends of the world" (Ps. 19:1–4). Paul will shortly say to Israel that they are thoroughly accountable to God because of the specific nature of his revelation to them. Likewise, God is saying that all mankind has been spoken to specifically enough to be account-able to God—**so that men are without excuse.**

Paul is making a case for the gospel: its power, God's righteousness which it reveals, and the necessity for taking it to the farthest parts of the earth, beginning with Spain. To make his case he must explain that all people are under the wrath of God. This he has done in 1:18–20 in a summary fashion. He now proceeds to provide details on the specific reasons for God's wrath and the results of his wrath.

Ⓑ Reasons for the Wrath of God (1:21–23)

SUPPORTING IDEA: *Instead of worshiping its Creator, the human race descends into idolatry and worships the creation.*

1:21. "Idolatry" is a familiar word to use in the context of biblical discus-sions. But while we may be conversant with the idea of idolatry, we are not as well schooled on what it means to be an idolater—or the spiritual ramifica-tions of idolatry. Paul spells it out in three short verses.

Idolatry is worship, and at the heart of worship is the attribution of glory. When people "exchanged the glory of the immortal God for images made to look like mortal man and birds and animals and reptiles" (v. 23), they moved into idolatry. It is for the exchange of glory that God's wrath is revealed. The Hebrew word for glory, *kabod,* means "weight." If something had weight in the Old Testament, it had worth or value. In fact, it was not until after Israel's return from captivity in Babylon that the use of coins became prominent as a medium of exchange. Up until that time, value was determined by weight of silver or gold (a *shekel*) or some other valued commodity (leading to admoni-tions against using dishonest scales or balances when doing business: Prov. 11:1; 16:11; 20:23). Therefore, the heavier something was the more valuable it was, or the more "glory" it had.

The glory of God is the measure of the weight, or worthiness, or value of God. Worship, or "worthship," was to be ascribed only to him because nothing had more glory or value than God. Because the glory of the Lord was matchless—"Who among the gods is like you, O LORD? Who is like you—majestic in holiness, awesome in glory, working wonders?" (Exod. 15:11)—to give worship to anything else would be to suggest a comparison between the object worshiped and God. In light of God's infinite worth (glory), no earthly comparison can do justice to the offense generated by giving worship to any thing or any person besides God.

Only two categories of "entities" exist in the biblical universe: Creator and created. And these two are separated by an infinite gulf of worth, or glory. Granted, of all the created things, man has more weight (worth, glory) than all the rest of creation (Ps. 8:3–9, esp. v. 5). But even so, the glory of man is not the same as the glory of the One who made man (Ps. 8:1). Humankind's rightful place, in all its appropriate glory among the creation, is looking "up" into the face of the Creator, ascribing ultimate glory to him. When a human being looks "horizontally" at another human, or "down" (on the scale of glory) to a plant or animal, he is worshiping something that has no more—indeed less—worth than he or she does.

1:22–23. This exchange of glory is the theft of glory in no uncertain terms, and could not be more "foolish" (v. 21). Humans began ascribing "worthship" to other humans, or to **birds and animals and reptiles**, when "their foolish hearts were darkened" (v. 21). Literally, **they became fools** and became idolaters. If "stupid is as stupid does," then "foolish is as foolish does" as well. Idolatry is a sign of moral and spiritual depravity (the baseline of foolishness), a sign of the rejection of the glory and prominence of God.

For such foolishness the wrath of God is revealed, Paul says. The glory of God is the "heaviest" thing in the universe. To assign, through worship, the glory of the Creator to a part of the creation is to turn moral and spiritual sensitivity upside down. And such upsetting of the spiritual order of things has dreadful repercussions.

Ⓒ Results of the Wrath of God (1:24–32)

> **SUPPORTING IDEA:** *Because immorality springs from idolatry, a holy God is justified in revealing his wrath against the unholy practices of the human race.*

So far, Paul has said that the wrath of God is revealed against humanity in light of the suppression of truth about God. When people act as if they do not know the truth about God ("The fool says in his heart, 'There is no God'" Pss. 14:1; 53:1), then their hearts become increasingly dark and they move to idolatry. And because idols cannot speak or write, and there is no revelation to govern the people, idolatry always results in immorality ("Where there is no revelation, the people cast off restraint," Prov. 29:18). The sin of the human race is getting ever more specific: first, the suppression of truth. Then, the specific sin of idolatry.

Now, Paul will catalog the specific sins that characterize the lives of those who suppress the truth about God and exchange his glory for the glory of a part of the creation. (Note: as you go through this last section, think about Rome and the people Paul was writing to. Also think of where you live and what you observe about mankind's descent away from God into sin. See if you think Paul's assessment of the human tendency to sin is accurate and provides justification for his saying that the wrath of God is being revealed from heaven.)

We said above that the wrath of God that Paul discusses here is not the judgment-type wrath that will come at the end of human history. Rather, there is an ongoing, dual manifestation of his wrath, revealed in their bodies (vv. 24–27) and in their souls, or minds (vv. 28–32). It becomes obvious that what begins as a willful choice in the realm of the spirit (idolatry, vv. 21–23) ultimately manifests itself in body and soul as well.

1:24–27. Some commentators make much of the threefold occurrence of **God gave them over** (vv. 24,26,28) to construct a three-part outline of the remainder of Romans 1. However, this seems forced in light of the clear unity of verses 24–27 and its topic of sexual immorality compared against the catalog of additional sins in verses 28–32. Therefore, rather than listing three distinct ways or reasons by which **God gave them over**, it is more natural to see the first two occurrences (vv. 24,26) as being repetitive for emphasis, with the final "giving over" standing by itself as indicative of a different category.

Both in the present verses, and in verses 28–32, it is important to understand what it means that **God gave them over**. First, note the causality indicated in both verses 24 and 26. Verse 24 begins with **Therefore** (*dio*) and verse 26 with **Because of this** (*dia touto*). Verse 24 follows Paul's statement that human beings have exchanged the glory of God for the "glory" of created beings, and verse 26 follows his assertion that the truth of God has been exchanged for a lie.

Rather than fine-tuning the differences between these two exchanges and their resulting, respective retributions, a more general conclusion is acceptable: humankind has, as an act of the will, chosen to replace the glory of God and the truth of God with lies that justify idol worship and unbridled moral license. As a result of these choices, God has given the human race over to the pursuit of a life based on idol worship (whether outright or subtle) and philosophies built on their own moral and speculative preferences.

When God "gives them over," is it passive or active? That is, does he merely step out of people's way and allow them to pursue those things which depravity dictates ("He [God] ceased to hold the boat as it was dragged by the current of the river" [Frederick Godet, *in loc.,* cited by Moo, p. 111]), or does he take an active role in moving them deeper into a downward cycle of sin "like a judge who hands over a prisoner to the punishment his crime has earned"? (Moo, p. 111). Certainly, both the human and divine elements are present in Scripture.

In the Old Testament, God handed over Israel's enemies to her for their intentional destruction (Exod. 23:31; Deut. 7:23–24) and reversed the situation at other times by handing over Israel to her enemies (Lev. 26:25; Josh. 7:7; Judg. 2:14; 6:1,13). These military examples are particularly instructive since God's passively stepping out of the way and allowing war to take its inevitable result might or might not have accomplished his will or purpose. In fact, examples exist of the exact opposite of what one might have expected to happen militarily. In these cases, the active "giving over" of God is the only explanation (see, for example, the defeat of 185,000 Assyrians [2 Kgs. 19:35], and the victory of Ai over Israel [Josh. 7:3–5]). The case of Job being given into the hands of Satan is another example of God's active involvement (though in this case not for purposes of retribution; Job 1:12; 2:6).

Another clear picture arises from Paul's use of the same word (*paradidomi*) that he uses in Romans 1. In 1 Corinthians 5:5 Paul decides that a believer in the church at Corinth needs to be delivered over to Satan "so that the sinful nature may be destroyed and his spirit saved on the day of the Lord." This involved not a passive standing aside by Paul and the leaders of the church (allowing the man to remain a part of the fellowship), but the action of expelling him from the fellowship, delivering him to the realm of the devil. In the closest parallel found to Paul's words in Romans 1, Ephesians 4:17–19 discusses Gentiles who have arrived at the same depraved state as Paul describes in Romans. But in Ephesians, he says that they "have given themselves over to sensuality" (*paradidomi,* Eph. 4:19), which certainly involves active, not passive choices on their parts.

It is best to conclude that God takes an active involvement in giving people over to the desires of their hearts. Certainly they are responsible for their choices, and in some sense God may be viewed as allowing sin to take its normal course. But in the end, God's giving those who bear his image over to sin is an active process on his part, whether for reform or for retribution or both. As has been well stated, "the punishment of sin is sin."

And to what did God give them over? To **sexual impurity for the degrading of their bodies with one another.** Note that the giving over was in the context of **the sinful desires of their hearts.** The sin was present in the heart before it was manifested in the body. Paul's reference in verse 24 is a general statement of sexual immorality that resulted from idolatry, amplified in verse 26. One of the most shocking discoveries of modern archaeology has been the evidence of unbridled immorality associated with pagan worship practices. In any culture, the character of worshipers is a good indicator of the character of the worshiped. When gods are created with connections to sexual activity (such as fertility gods and goddesses), then sexual activity by worshipers is what is deemed necessary to placate the god. In general, Paul says, idolatry will ultimately lead to immorality.

But then Paul moves to the most graphic evidence of the complete inversion of the spiritual and therefore moral compass of the human species. It is not just sexual immorality to which God has given them over, it is sexual inversion and perversion. Homosexuality was rampant in the Roman Empire (fourteen of the first fifteen emperors practiced homosexuality; Hughes, *Romans*, p. 44), and represented perhaps the greatest offense to Jewish sensibilities. As Jewish and Gentile believers in the church in Rome looked around their society, they would have seen homosexuality practiced and encouraged at every turn.

It seems that Paul has chosen homosexuality as the nadir of sinful expression because of its complete reversal of God's natural order. Some forms of sexual immorality (perhaps that referred to in v. 24?) at least falls within the natural order of male-female relations. But homosexuality (vv. 26–27) so totally moves out of the realm of what is natural that it indicates a total throwing off of the revealed will and design of God. It is as if those practicing it have said, "There is no order, reason, or logic associated with anything. We are free to experiment and create at will. We have become as gods, creating new orders and practices of our own."

Homosexuality, while perhaps not the most hurtful of sins (as say, compared to murder), is certainly the ultimate in arrogance and sinful rebellion against the order of God. It is frightful to consider what happened to the Roman Empire after reaching a point of immorality, which championed homosexuality (not tolerated, but championed), and then to look at modern cultures which have devolved to a similar place morally.

Paul's last words in verse 27—**received in themselves the due penalty for their perversion**—are the most frightful of all. What is the penalty? Is that penalty delivered culturally as well as individually? How many innocents suffer as a result of the error of others? And yet the penalty of homosexuality is not inevitable. Paul says that practicing homosexuals (along with some others) will not inherit the kingdom of God, but *former* homosexuals can (1 Cor. 6:9–11). When homosexuals, or any other person, is washed, sanctified, and justified "in the name of the Lord Jesus Christ and by the Spirit of our God" (v. 11), then they are freed, at least eternally, from the **penalty for their perversion**.

1:28–32. Finally, **since they did not think it worthwhile to retain the knowledge of God, he gave them over to a depraved mind.** Knowledge is retained in the mind, and sinful humankind has decided it is not worthwhile to retain the knowledge of God. This must refer to thoughts about God, the function of the conscience, the mental evaluations that even a pagan goes through about who and where God is and how one may know him. When people do not pursue these God-given internal and external evidences (see Eccl. 3:11; Acts 17:23–31), they gradually develop minds characterized continually by depravity—as in the days of Noah: "Every inclination of the thoughts of [man's] heart was only evil all the time" (Gen. 6:5). It is characteristic of a depraved mind to reverse the importance of everything, including evil and its origin.

Jesus Christ had this discussion with his disciples after talking to the religious leaders in his day. The Pharisees thought if they kept the exterior of their lives "clean" through religious ritual that the inner condition of their heart would be hidden. But Jesus said that it was their heart (the inner man) that actually determined what would appear on the outside, and that it was impossible to stop it. The heart, he said, is the source of all evil thoughts and actions (Mark 7:20–23).

Paul is saying essentially the same thing here. The inner motivations of humanity are depraved and result in outward behavior. The list of depraved behaviors and practices defies certain categorization as did most "vice lists" common in the moral literature of Paul's day (see similar lists in the New Testament in Matt. 15:19; 1 Cor. 5:10–11; 6:9–10; 2 Cor. 12:20; Gal. 5:19–21; Eph. 4:31; 5:3–4; Col. 3:5,8; 1 Tim. 1:9–10; 2 Tim 3:2–4; 1 Pet. 2:1; 4:3). But Moo has found what logical and linguistic handles do exist, translating them as follows:

1. *The first four are general in focus:* "filled with all manner of unrighteousness, evil, greed, wickedness."
2. *The next five revolve around envy and its consequences:* "full of envy, murder, strife, deceit, malice."
3. *The last twelve cover slander (two), arrogance (four), and then six related by form more than by content:* "gossips, maligners, haters of God, proud, arrogant, overbearing, devisers of evil, disobedient to parents, without understanding, without faithfulness, without affection, without mercy" (Moo, pp. 118–119).

Paul, writing to those who undoubtedly knew of his past as a persecutor of Christian believers, concludes with what must have been a difficult thing to write (except that Paul never had any difficulty in exulting in the grace of God that saved a sinner like himself). He points out that those who act with depraved indifference are worthy of death—and know they deserve to die (Rom. 6:23). Yet they continue! And not only do they continue in the same acts, **but also approve of those who practice them** (1:32).

It was Paul, the zealot, who had stood by and watched the stoning of Stephen, the church's first martyr, in Jerusalem. He did not watch passively, rather he "was there, giving approval to his death" (Acts 8:1), "guarding the clothes of those who were killing him" (Acts 22:20). Granted, Paul's "approval" was small. He was only one person on that day who approved of the murder of a man. But as a result of his small piece of the puzzle being added to all the other pieces of the puzzle of persecution that day, "a great persecution broke out against the church at Jerusalem, and all except the apostles were scattered throughout Judea and Samaria" (Acts 8:1). It is possible that giving approval to sin can, in the long run, result in even greater condemnation.

Consider the attitude toward members of the black race in the post-emancipation Southern United States. How many lynch mobs were made up of people who would never have committed the sin of murder themselves individually, but by standing on the edge of the crowd gave tacit approval to what was taking place? By being there, they were helping to foment an environment of intolerance and racism and hatred. Had they been evil enough to commit the murder themselves, that would have been sinful. But to help create an environment where others are emboldened to sin, resulting in the deaths of many more, may even deserve greater condemnation.

One can only cringe at the "wrath of God" that awaits those public officials in government who, by passing legislation which not only does not restrain evil but in fact encourages it, have made it possible for millions to yield to the temptation to sin. It is true that many, weak in conviction, conscience, and caring, will not sin when they think that public sentiment is against them. But remove the restraints of moral imperatives, and sin multiplies. One of the responsibilities of leadership is to encourage righteousness and thereby restrain sin (see Rom. 13:1–7).

Paul concludes this section with a point to which he adds a counterpoint beginning with 2:1. Those who sin and approve others who do are obviously guilty and deserving of the wrath of God. But what about those who do not approve of the sin of others, those who make moral judgments about the sins they see around them? Are they as deserving of the wrath of God? Paul will answer that question next.

MAIN IDEA REVIEW: *Because humankind has chosen to reject the clear evidence of God's existence and rule, God has allowed the human race to demonstrate to itself exactly how devastating life can be when lived in rebellion against God.*

III. CONCLUSION

The Master Clock

In the town hall in Copenhagen stands the world's most complicated clock. It took forty years to build at a cost of more than a million dollars. It has ten faces, fifteen thousand parts, and is accurate to two-fifths of a second every three hundred years. The clock computes the time of day, the days of the week, the months and years, and the movements of the planets for twenty-five hundred years. Some parts of that clock will not move until twenty-five centuries have passed. While enormously impressive, and while the clock would serve faithfully for more than the lifetime of any person alive, the two-fifths of a second it loses every three hundred years are a problem. By what perfect standard shall the clock be reset every three hundred years?

The atomic age has come closer to solving the problem. The cesium-atom clock is used to define the second, the basic unit of time of the International System of Units. Cesium-133 atoms are bombarded with microwave radiation which generates energy within the atoms. The frequency levels associated with the energy generation are used to calculate time to an accuracy level of about plus or minus one second in one million years. Well, that is closer than the Copenhagen clock, but still not the perfection we are looking for.

The interesting thing about even the most precise clocks is that they are all dependent on something else for setting the correct time. No man-made clock can set, and keep, perfect time on its own. There has to be a reference point by which time is set. Whether it was the sun in 3,500 B.C. that was the reference point for the earliest shadow clocks, or the energy levels of atoms in the twentieth century, everyone recognizes that the universe—God's creation—is the standard reference point for life on earth.

While we have made progress in keeping better time over the centuries, we have actually just succeeded in discovering smaller reference points—from the sun to atoms. We have not succeeded in eliminating the reference points and becoming independent of the creation in which we exist. Nor, Paul argues in Romans 1, have we succeeded in becoming independent of the Creator.

Paul might walk into the most sophisticated atomic energy laboratory in the world today and ask the question of the scientists who are setting the cesium-atom clock: "How do you know the atoms are vibrating consistently in response to the microwave radiation to which you are subjecting them? And who do you think is responsible for that consistency?"

It is Paul's contention in Romans 1 that the evidence of a grand plan for the universe is everywhere around us. A clock in Copenhagen with thousands of moving parts, or an atomic clock with vibrating atoms, is like a child's Tinker-Toy set compared to the intricacies of the universe. Any clock maker who is not struck with the fantastic plan that keeps the universe's moving parts on schedule has done what Paul describes in Romans 1—he or she has suppressed the knowledge of God's "eternal power and divine nature"

(v. 18). All creation points to the existence and presence of a Creator God, so clearly that God holds all people responsible for the knowledge.

By his propositional statements, Paul wants the believers in Rome to know that God's plan now is to reveal his righteousness through the preaching of the gospel because people have suppressed the revelation of his righteousness in creation. All they need do is look around them in Rome—or recall the rumors they have heard about the barbaric hordes beyond the Empire's boundaries—to know that the human race has completed the cycle Paul has described for them: know the truth, suppress the truth, replace the truth with idolatry, allow idolatry to justify immorality, and choose to live in depravity—and encourage others to live there—even though you know it is wrong. Spirit, body, and soul—the human race has progressed from knowing the truth to living in depravity.

The righteousness of God has been replaced by the depravity of man among the nations, but Paul is in the process of revealing through the preaching of a righteousness-revealing, power-to-save gospel. It is this gospel message, and the foundational truths that underlie it, that he wants the believers in Rome to understand and become partners with him in spreading.

PRINCIPLES

- God's wrath (his holy response to depraved sin) is being revealed constantly against ungodliness and wickedness.
- God's eternal power and divine nature have been sufficiently revealed by God in creation to make all human beings accountable for knowledge of him.
- No person on earth at any time in history can be excused from accountability for knowing about God.
- Humankind in general has substituted the worship of idols for the worship of God because idol worship justifies (allows) immorality.
- Homosexuality represents an inversion of the natural order, is sin, and carries with it a penalty for those who practice it.
- Depravity of mind manifests itself in the outward behaviors of those who have suppressed the knowledge of God.

APPLICATIONS

- Is there anything in my life which could justifiably incur the wrath of the holy God of Scripture?
- If creation is enough to make people accountable, what additional spiritual advantages do I have that make me even more accountable to God?

- Is there any contemporary "idol" in my life? Anything to which I have given loyalty and devotion which should be directed solely to God?

- Do my views on sexual immorality and sexual perversion align with those of Romans 1?

- From Paul's list of depraved behaviors, are there any that ever appear in my life as a believer in Christ? What does this tell me about the state of my mind?

IV. LIFE APPLICATION

Harmony in Idolatry

The hundred-year-old church in a bedroom community of a major metropolitan area had just realized a windfall. A commercial real estate developer had offered them a staggering sum of money for the property their church was built on. The city sprawl was headed their way and he was putting together parcels of land for a huge shopping mall and office park complex. Realizing that the money would allow them to construct a new facility which would better attract and minister to the many young families moving into the area, a majority of the church voted with the leadership to accept the developer's offer. That, as it turned out, was the easy part. They almost needed to build two new facilities.

As a committee of members reflecting the church's varied age groups began meeting to plan for the new facility, it quickly became apparent that two points of view would predominate. They older members of the committee, many of whom had grown up in the church and financed its last half-century of ministry, wanted to construct a very traditional new building—like the old one, only a bit larger. "The old design has worked for years. Why change it?" they said. The younger members of the committee felt that a more contemporary facility would move the church into its next period of growth by providing multiuse facilities for worship, recreation, education, and community outreach—plus its modern design would reflect a progressive mentality to be complemented by a commitment to biblical values.

As the congregation began to hear rumors of the conflict, words such as "senseless," "faithless," "heartless," and "ruthless" surfaced over the phone, over backyard fences, and in whispers in the church hallways. What was happening to Harmony Community Church? Nothing that a fresh reading of Romans 1:18–32 would not reveal. Starting at the end of the chapter and moving back to verse 18, one discovers that "senseless, faithless, heartless, [and] ruthless" are words Paul uses to describe the ultimate impact of idolatry in a human being. Though Paul wrote this chapter to describe the process that has thrown the entire human race into a depraved, lost condition, the process can be discovered even in a body of Christian believers. Harmony Community Church was experiencing the results of idolatry.

When the glory and worship of God is replaced by the glory and worship of a created thing, an idea, another person, a goal—a preference for a new church's design—the potential exists for depravity to get the upper hand. William Law, the eighteenth-century English cleric and theologian, put it this way: "Hence also has arisen another species of idolatry, even among Christians of all denominations; who, though receiving and professing the religion of the Gospel, yet worship God not in spirit and truth, but either in the deadness of an outer form, or in a pharisaical, carnal trust in their own opinions and doctrines." Idolatry becomes the toe-hold of carnality and depravity regardless of how "Christian" the idolater is. Another English theologian, Charles F. D. Moule, said, "Idolatry is an attempt to use God for man's purposes, rather than to give oneself to God's service."

The members of Harmony Church were using the construction of a building for God to promote their own agendas rather than submitting their agendas to God's service. Has this happened in your spiritual life, in your marriage, in your friendships, in your ministry, in your church? Paul is going to address later in his letter to the Roman believers some attitudes and activities that had the potential to become full-blown conflicts between the Jewish and Gentile believers in the church in Rome (Rom. 14). Having demonstrated the source of carnality in Romans 1, he has headed off excuses that may have been offered in defense of disunity in the church.

What about your life, relationships, or church? Have you defended actions or attitudes that Paul relates to depraved carnality in Romans 1? If so, at the beginning of your study of Romans, now is the time to exchange the worship of any idol for the worship of the true and living God. As Paul wanted the Romans to see, so he wants us to see—the world will never be reached by a church that looks more like the unsaved than the saved.

V. PRAYER

Heavenly Father, please reveal to us any way, from small to large, in which we have suppressed the knowledge or practice of the truth about you. If we have substituted the glory of anything for your glory, please forgive us. If we have used you to advance our own agendas instead of revealing your glory, please forgive us. Help us to experience and reveal your righteousness to a lost world by living out the power of your gospel. Amen.

VI. DEEPER DISCOVERIES

A. The Wrath of God

For teachers using this commentary, the most important "classroom" issue surrounding the wrath of God is definition—from God's point of view. People see petulance and anger displayed consistently in society, and so naturally think that God's anger and wrath are the same as what they see around them. Because the potential for outbursts of wrath is high in the human dimension, and because most of those outbursts are of the "unrighteous" variety (based on selfish or carnal motives), people are uncomfortable and insecure with the whole concept of wrath emanating from a loving God.

A key verse in this regard is James 1:20: "For man's anger does not bring about the righteous life that God desires." The same word (*orge*) is used here as is used for God's wrath in Romans 1:18, but James clearly separates the two. The wrath of man does not produce righteousness, therefore it is unrighteous. And yet the very same word applied to God parallels his righteousness: "God is a righteous judge, a God who expresses his wrath every day" (Ps. 7:11). Wrath is a manifest part of God's righteousness, whereas it is an evidence of our *un*righteousness.

The key to understanding God's wrath (and taking it out of the realm of emotion, impulse, and arbitrariness) is judgment. Paul says in Romans 2:5, "You are storing up wrath against yourself for the day of God's wrath, when his righteous judgment will be revealed." Wrath comes as a result of judgment (a decision), and judgment comes as a result of comparison with a standard. Therefore, God's wrath is always a function of his having judged something against the standard of his righteousness or his established order.

There are three ways (times) in which God judges and exercises wrath: first, on a continual, present-tense basis, as described in Romans 1. Second, on an incidental basis through the agency of earthly or heavenly agents and means: angels (2 Sam. 24:17); Israel (Ezek. 32:9–31); the Gentile nations (Isa. 10:5–6); forces of nature (Judg. 5:20); even snakes (Num. 21:6); civil rulers (Rom. 13:4); and his Son (Ps. 2:5–12). Third, at the end of history when his wrath will be exercised permanently and finally against all manner of wickedness, human and angelic (Rom. 2:5; 1 Thess. 1:10; Rev. 6:16–17). The reasons for the exercise of his wrath are generally two: to maintain and/or restore order (either natural or spiritual), and retribution against those who have violated God's order willfully without repentance.

God's wrath (his judgment against violations of his standards) is not issued quickly. Scripture is clear that "the LORD is compassionate and gracious, slow to anger . . . nor will he harbor his anger forever" (Ps. 103:8–9; see also Exod. 34:6; Num. 14:18; Neh. 9:17; Pss. 86:15; 145:8; Joel 2:13;

Jonah 4:2; Nah. 1:3). God's wrath is deliberate and is always measured against a righteous standard, which is the primary characteristic that sets it apart from the wrath of man. The wrath of God flows out of, and is always exercised to accomplish, the righteousness of God.

B. The Lost Condition of Those Who Have Not Heard the Gospel

No question is asked more in the context of Romans 1 than, "What about the innocent people in Africa who have never had a chance to hear the gospel? Isn't God unfair for judging them?" Besides the fact that the gospel is spreading and the church of Jesus Christ is growing faster in Africa today than in many parts of the world, there are other problems with this question.

First, Romans 1 does not say anything about the wrath of God coming upon those who do not believe the gospel. It says the wrath of God is revealed against godlessness and wickedness. Second, God is never "unfair" or "fair." These are words used in human conversation which do not apply to God. God is righteous and just, not fair, according to Scripture. So the answer to the question, "Isn't God unfair for judging them?" is "No." The task is to determine why his judgment is just.

First, no one who has never heard of Jesus Christ will ever be judged for not believing in him (Rom. 10:14). God would certainly be unjust if he judged someone for something they never had the opportunity to do. Second, it is clear from Scripture that God has established testimony to himself in nature, the created order (Rom. 1:20; Ps. 19; Acts 14:16–17). Third, the testimony is plain (Rom. 1:19), having been made plain by God himself. Fourth, humans choose to hold down the knowledge of God that they have been given rather than embracing it and seeking more (Rom. 1:18). Therefore, what "the innocents" are being held accountable for is what they were given, and they were given enough light about the existence of God to seek him, but they choose not to do so (Rom. 3:12). Because God is just, there will be degrees of punishment for unbelievers who are judged (Eccl. 12:14; Matt. 11:22,24; 12:36; Luke 8:17; 12:2–3,47–48; 20:47; Rom. 2:5–7,16; Rev. 20:12–13).

Therefore, God is just and righteous in his judgments of those who have not heard of Christ or had a chance to respond to the gospel. Those who have heard the gospel clearly and still refused to believe will suffer a greater judgment than those who have not.

C. General Versus Special Revelation

It is helpful for students and all Christians to understand the difference between general and special revelation, and to know in which category Paul's words in Romans 1:18–20 belong. General revelation refers to the self-revelation of God that is available to all human beings "in general," while special revelation refers to those irruptive events in history when God breaks into the natural order of things and reveals himself specially or specifically in terms of content, means, or audience. It can also be said in summary that general revelation is not normally salvific or efficacious whereas special revelation is.

Paul, in Romans 1, refers to a knowledge of God that the entire human race has. Therefore, the knowledge of God he discusses falls into the category of general revelation. The specific kind of general revelation he refers to—that which may be discerned about God from creation—is one of several types of general revelation outlined by Millard J. Erickson (*Christian Theology*, Vol. 1, pp. 154–155).

1. *Nature.* This is the locus of general revelation referred to by Paul in which evidence of God's existence can be discerned from creation (cf. Ps. 19). Whether the intricacies of a flower, the grandeur of a sunset, the miracle of birth, or the order of the heavenly bodies, nature is a panoramic display of the glory of God.

2. *History.* This locus of general revelation gets better as hindsight increases, but with more than five thousand years of recorded history to work with, the perspective of history begins to afford evidence of a master plan. Often the survival of the nation Israel, especially when compared to other ancient nations, is offered as evidence of a divine plan.

3. *Man himself.* The moral impulse mentioned by Paul in Romans 1:32 ("Although they know . . . that those who do such things deserve death") is an indication of a moral thread in man absent from the rest of creation. The tendency of people groups to create moral codes, be they ever so distinct and disparate, is evidence of a moral imperative in the universe since man represents the highest part of the created order.

4. *Man's religious nature.* Man consistently worships, giving rise to the question, "Who is man innately driven to worship?" It is suggested that deep within man is a search for the connection to his and her Creator.

Contrasted with these general evidences of the existence of God are various categories of special revelation, given not to everyone but to groups or individuals for specific reasons (though the "revelation" may have been recorded and ultimately shared with others). In essence, special revelation is verbal communication whether delivered and received as speech, writing, dreams, visions, or other forms. The essence is something special that is communicated from God to the recipient. (The following points are summarized from Grudem, *Systematic Theology*, pp. 47–50.)

1. *The Word of God as a Person: Jesus Christ.* John 1:1,14 says that Jesus Christ, as a man, was the word of God. Thus he became the fullest and clearest form of special revelation from God (Phil. 2:5–11; Col. 2:9).

2. *The Word of God as Speech by God.* Examples of this category of special revelation are God's decrees (by which things happen; Gen. 1:3; Ps. 33:6; Heb. 1:3); God's words of personal address (by which he speaks to people personally; Gen. 2:16–17; Exod. 20:1–3; Matt. 3:17); God's words through humans (by which others speak for him; Deut. 18:18–20; Jer. 1:9); and God's words in written form (the Bible; this category contains all of the special revelation contained in the above categories, plus other revelation "inspired by God" for the benefit of those who read and obey the Bible).

The mystery explained and entrusted to the apostle Paul by Jesus Christ is an example of special revelation (words of personal address) that Paul then communicated to others and which, under the inspiration of God, was incorporated into the Bible. Both general and special revelation are the self-revelation of God to the human race, the former to heighten man's wonder of God, the latter to heighten his worship of God.

D. The "Men" (1:18)

While Paul's argument in Romans 1:18–20 is clear theologically, it is less clear exactly who Paul is talking about—those against whom the wrath of God is being revealed. That is, is Paul thinking of the population of Rome as he writes? Certainly Rome qualified in terms of wickedness to serve as an example of "the godlessness and wickedness of men." Yet that would place strictures on applying the truth of the passage to all the human race. But if it applies to all, how is the wrath being revealed? In cycles? To all men at all times?

While we cannot speak with certainty about what was in the apostle's mind as he composed Romans 1, a study that pays dividends in this regard is to discover the parallels existing between Romans 1 and Genesis 1–3, the narrative of the Creation and Fall of humans. Could Paul have been linking the revelation of the wrath of God to man's fall into sin in Eden, making his summary in Romans 1 a theological introduction to Romans 5 where he plainly connects man's sin to the sin of Adam? Note the parallels between the Genesis and Romans 1 accounts: "creation of the world" (1:20); "birds and animals and reptiles" (1:23); "images" (1:23; cf. the "image of God" in Gen. 1:27); man's plain knowledge of God (1:19,21); man's desire to become wise but fall into foolishness (1:22); the desire to function independently of God (1:21); the exchange of truth for a lie (1:25); and the knowledge that sin and rebellion result in death (1:32). (cf. Stott, pp. 70–71 for a fuller discussion).

The common elements in the Genesis and Romans accounts seem to add support to the view that Paul is taking his reference point all the way back to the beginning. This suggests that the wrath of God—his righteous indignation and revulsion at the violations in his created and moral order—has been being revealed since Genesis 3.

VII. TEACHING OUTLINE

A. INTRODUCTION

1. Lead Story: Eyes Are Not the Key to Seeing God

2. Context: Paul has stated in Romans 1:16–17 that he is not ashamed of the gospel. It is the power of God for salvation, and in it the righteousness of God is being revealed. We could say that the righteousness of God is being re-revealed through the preaching of the gospel. In Romans 1:18–32 Paul explains that the glory and truth about God has been so suppressed by mankind that it is having to be re-revealed to the human race in the form of the preaching of the gospel. And while the gospel is being preached, the wrath of God is being revealed against those who, by their suppression of the knowledge of God, do not know him and keep others from knowing him as well.

3. Transition: Because of the dramatic descriptions Paul gives of those who suppress the knowledge of God, we might be tempted to exempt ourselves from his text. But the pattern which leads people to become the objects of God's wrath is a subtle one: first idolatry, then immorality, then brash invincibility. Every believer needs to heed the description of the human race's descent into sin and see if Paul's words apply.

B. COMMENTARY

1. Revelation of the Wrath of God (1:18–20)
   a. Revelation "for" (1:18)
   b. Revelation "since" (1:19–20)

2. Reasons for the Wrath of God (1:21–23)
   a. Not glorifying the Creator (1:21)
   b. Glorifying the creation (1:22–23)

3. Results of the Wrath of God (1:24–32)
   a. Depraved in body (1:24–27)
   b. Depraved in mind (1:28–32)

C. CONCLUSION: HARMONY IN IDOLATRY

VIII. ISSUES FOR DISCUSSION

1. What are some of the ways that unbelieving people suppress the truth about God? Is the church ever guilty of suppressing certain parts of God's truth? In what ways?

2. Imagine yourself walking onto the stage of history with no prior knowledge of God, the Bible, or the gospel. What evidences of the existence and presence of God do you think you might discern? What do unbelievers say about those evidences that seem so clear to you?

3. What are the biggest idols that the church is tempted to worship personally or corporately today? How many of those idols are also worshiped by the unbelieving culture that surrounds the church? What warning does Romans 1 offer about where idol worship leads?

4. If homosexuality is the strongest evidence of the ultimate inversion of God's natural order, where do most Western cultures stand today in honoring God's designs? What does that say about the likelihood of the wrath of God being revealed against them?

5. How can the power of the gospel affect the depraved condition of those described in 1:29–32? What hope could you offer one who has spent a lifetime suppressing the knowledge of God and failing to worship him (see 1 Cor. 6:9–11)?

Romans 2:1–3:20

Even Jews Need the Gospel

I. INTRODUCTION
From Cannibals to Polynesians—The Law of the Heart

II. COMMENTARY
A verse-by-verse explanation of the chapter.

III. CONCLUSION
Face-to-Face with Reality

An overview of the principles and applications from the chapter.

IV. LIFE APPLICATION
Dead Men's Bones

Melding the chapter to life.

V. PRAYER
Tying the chapter to life with God.

VI. DEEPER DISCOVERIES
Historical, geographical, and grammatical enrichment of the commentary.

VII. TEACHING OUTLINE
Suggested step-by-step group study of the chapter.

VIII. ISSUES FOR DISCUSSION
Zeroing the chapter in on daily life.

Quote

"*Indeed*, I think that even if it were possible, nobody should try to escape God's judgment, for not to come to God's judgment is not to come to improvement, to health or to a cure."

Origen

Romans 2:1–3:20

IN A NUTSHELL

Paul turns from his consideration of the spiritual condition of the Gentiles—the human race in general—to the spiritual condition of the Jews—his chosen people in particular. The question to be answered in this section is, Will the Jews escape the scrutiny of God because of their privileged position of being God's chosen people? The answer: No. Because of their privilege, they have more responsibility, and will be judged accordingly.

Even Jews Need the Gospel

I. INTRODUCTION

From Cannibals to Polynesians—The Law of the Heart

*M*issionary-anthropologist Don Richardson was hardly ready for the story that his Yali friend Erariek was about to tell him, a story that provided yet another example of the truth of Scripture. Erariek, a member of a Stone Age tribe in central New Guinea, related how his brother, Sunahan, and a friend were attacked by a neighboring tribe while they were harvesting food in their garden. Sunahan's friend was hit by arrows as the two tried to flee the attacking cannibals. Their mission that morning had been to harvest food for a meal, not become the meal!

Instead of running back on the trail that led to their village on a ridge above the garden, Sunahan and his friend made a dash across the garden area toward a low stone wall. Just before they reached the wall, more arrows killed Sunahan's friend. Sunahan, on the other hand, leaped over the wall and stood behind it, baring his chest and laughing at his attackers. Not a single arrow was fired at Sunahan as he stood behind the low wall, and his attackers fled as members of the Yali tribe rushed from the village to avenge the death of their friend.

Amazed that Sunahan was not killed, Richardson asked Erariek why the marauders did not fire arrows at him when he stood there brazenly tempting them. "Sunahan was standing *inside* the stone wall," Erariek explained. "The ground inside that stone wall is what we Yali call an *Osuwa*—a place of refuge. If the raiders had shed one drop of Sunahan's blood while he stood within that wall, their own people would have punished them with death when they reached home. Likewise, although Sunahan held weapons in his hand, he dared not release an arrow at the enemy while standing within that wall. For whoever stands within that wall is bound to work violence against no man!"

Richardson shifts the scene to the Polynesian paradise of Hawaii. A sacred precinct called *Pu'uhonua-o-honaunau* is believed to have been built around A.D. 1500 by King Keawe-ku-i-ke-kàai. It originally was a temple with a ten-foot-high stone wall around it, much of which still stands today on the western shore of Hawaii about six miles south of the monument commemorating the death of English explorer Captain James Cook. But *Pu'uhonua-o-honaunau* was no ordinary temple. It was a place of refuge for "defeated warriors, noncombatants, or taboo breakers" who reached its safety ahead of their pursuers. Getting inside King Kiawe-ku-i-ke-kàai's ancient wall was no game of hide-and-seek. It meant saving one's life! Any fugitive who entered found a shelter provided for him. A garden and grove of coconut palms provided food, and a spring bubbled with fresh water. Amazingly, *Pu'uhonua-o-honaunau* was only one of a network of twenty such "cities of refuge" scattered throughout the Hawaiian island chain.

Anyone familiar with the Old Testament is already wondering at the connection between the *Osuwa* in New Guinea, the *Pu'uhonua-o-honaunau* in Hawaii, and the "cities of refuge" in Israel. The connection, Richardson believes, is another evidence of the Gentiles (everyone except the Jews) showing "that the requirements of the law are written on their hearts, their consciences also bearing witness" (Rom. 2:15). Remember what God commanded Moses to do when they entered the promised land? They were to designate six of the Levites' towns to be cities of refuge, "so that anyone who has killed another accidentally can flee there" (v. 15 of Num. 35:6–34; see also Josh. 20:1–9). The basic moral premise was protection of the accused until proven guilty or innocent. In a region where blood revenge and retaliation was the norm, indeed where next of kin were *expected* to carry out immediate revenge, the cities of refuge provided a haven until civil systems of justice could be set up in the promised land.

Where did the cannibals of New Guinea and the Polynesians of Hawaii learn to provide a place of refuge for those fleeing retaliation? We do not know, of course, with any certainty. But the basic moral premise—that a person fleeing for his or her life should have an opportunity for protection from vengeance-seeking enemies—obviously reflects the law of God as revealed in Israel's civil code. And, it may well serve as a wonderful example of how "justice," be its execution ever so primitive or unrefined, is rooted in the human heart as the "right" goal to pursue.

Paul continues in Romans 2:1–3:20 to demonstrate that the righteousness of God is being justifiably revealed against the unrighteousness of humans. Having proved in 1:18–32 that the human race as a whole has suppressed the knowledge of God and moved from idolatry to immorality to "invincibility" against God (knowing they are doing wrong but doing it anyway regardless of the consequences; v. 32), he now turns to the Jews. In his discussion of the Jews' standing before God, he will make clear to them that God's judgment (not salvation, but judgment) will be on the basis of his law—and everyone has his law. Some have it written down "on paper" (the Jews), others have it written on their hearts (the Gentiles; everyone besides the Jews).

This section of Romans comes as a wake-up call to the church in Rome. In essence, Paul's message is the same as that given by James: "Anyone, then, who knows the good he ought to do and doesn't do it, sins" (Jas. 4:17). For Jewish believers, it removes their assumption of privilege and special treatment as the recipients of the law. For Gentile believers, it reminds them that God's law has been written in their hearts from the beginning—no excuses! Finally, it brings back into perspective the theme of Paul's letter to them—the power of the gospel to reveal the righteousness of God in the face of the unrighteousness of humankind. If the letter to the Romans stopped at the end of this section, the church would have reason enough to know that every person on earth needs the gospel. It is up to the church today to get the gospel to them.

II. COMMENTARY

Even Jews Need the Gospel

> **MAIN IDEA:** *Paul is making a case to the Roman believers that the whole world needs the gospel, and has demonstrated that Gentiles deserve God's wrath. Lest Jews think they will escape God's judgment by their privileged position, he now shows that they also need the gospel as a result of failing to obey God's law.*

Prologue: How God Judges (2:1–16)

> **SUPPORTING IDEA:** *Because the concept of Jews needing the gospel will be controversial to his Jewish readers, Paul transitions from Gentile judgment to Jewish judgment with a statement on how God judges.*

The first three chapters of our commentary on Romans provide an overview of the need of the human race—righteousness before God. Paul takes a deductive approach by stating up front his mission and message—to proclaim the power of the gospel to make people right with God (1:16–17). He then follows up his premise with evidence to support it. Because there are only two categories of people in the world, Gentile and Jew, his evidence has two halves. The first half, that Gentiles are guilty of sin before God, he presented in 1:18–32. In this chapter of our commentary, we study the second half of Paul's evidence. Not only are Gentiles (the human race in general) in need of attaining the righteousness of God; so are Jews—the "exception" in the human race as God's chosen people.

It needs to be stated up front: this can be a complicated section of Scripture to work through. It can easily appear to the reader (undoubtedly, some whom you teach will ask about this) that Paul contradicts himself concerning the role of "works" (e.g., "It is those who obey the law who will be declared righteous"; 2:13). In addition, his discussion of the Jews can seem to have more than one perspective (e.g., Is there an advantage to being a Jew? Yes [3:1] and No [3:9]). Therefore, we will take a deductive approach and clarify at the outset some things that Paul is saying in this section of Romans. Rather than building a case inductively, we will state the conclusions, then offer the evidence. Hopefully, with the top of the puzzle box in front of us, the pieces of the puzzle will fall into place more easily.

Here are some things Paul is, and is not, saying in Romans 2:1–3:20. He is *not* saying that . . .

- Salvation is by works.
- Works are a means of salvation *in lieu* of hearing and responding to the gospel message.
- "The heathen" who have not heard the gospel can be saved in a manner differently from those who have heard.
- Jews and Gentiles (Gentiles who have never heard the gospel) are equally responsible before God.

He *is*, on the other hand, saying that . . .

- Judgment, not salvation, is the focus in this section.
- Increased privilege brings increased responsibility, which brings harder judgment.
- Judgment is based on works.
- Works are judged on the basis of light received.
- God's standard for judgment—the righteousness of God—is the same for everyone.
- Everyone, Jew and Gentile alike, is guilty before God of unrighteousness. Gentiles have violated the law written on the heart, while Jews have violated the law given specifically to them by God.

Having stated those conclusions up front will make it easier to identify them in the midst of Paul's text.

2:1. Note the transition Paul makes between discussing the unrighteousness of the Gentiles (people in general; 1:18–32) and the unrighteousness of the Jews (2:17–3:8). The last thing he mentions in 1:32 is that people's minds are so depraved that they, in a manner of speaking, boast about their sin. Not only do they sin willingly (knowing they will be judged for it); they encourage and approve of others doing the same. It would be hard to describe boastful, sinful arrogance much more plainly. Yet there is another kind of boasting that is just as sinful: the kind that the Jews were guilty of. They boasted in and bragged about their privileged relationship to God (2:17).

Mentioning the concept of "boasting" at least thirty times in his epistles, Paul never yielded to the temptation to boast in himself. Rather, he knew that, like the guilty tax-gatherer who stood in stark contrast to the boastful Pharisee in Jesus' parable (Luke 18:9–14), there was only one thing that he would ever be able to boast in—the mercy and grace of God (1 Cor. 1:31; 13:4; 2 Cor. 1:12; 10:17; 11:30; 12:5,9; Gal. 6:14; Eph. 2:9). While it is not likely that Luke's gospel had been written by the time Paul wrote Romans, Luke's introduction to Jesus' parable about self-righteousness fits Paul's emphasis perfectly: "To some who were confident of their own righteousness and looked down on everybody else, Jesus told this parable" (Luke 18:9). Jesus' parable stands as a paradigm for understanding Paul's transition from the guilt of the human race (Gentiles) to the guilt of the Jews.

	Jesus' Parable (Luke 18:9–14)	Paul's Argument (Rom. 1:32–2:29)
Directed to	"To some who were confident . . ." (the Jews; 18:9).	". . . you who pass judgment on someone else . . ." (2:1).
Subjects	A Pharisee (Jew) and a tax collector (a Jew who worked for the Romans, therefore considered as a pagan, Gentile, sinner).	Gentile sinners (1:32) with self-righteous Jews (2:17).
Contrast	Jews who were "confident of their own righteousness and looked down on everybody else" (18:9).	Jews who "rely on the law and brag about" their relationship to God (2:17) and "pass judgment on someone else" (2:1).
Comparison	". . . other men—robbers, evildoers, adulterers—or even . . . this tax collector" (18:11).	Those filled with "wickedness, evil, greed and depravity . . ." (see 1:28–32).
Jewish Standards of Righteousness	"I fast twice a week and give a tenth of all I get" (18:12).	". . . rely on the law . . . your relationship to God . . . instructed by the law . . ." (see 2:17–20).
Gentile Standards of Righteousness	"God, have mercy on me, a sinner" (18:13).	". . . their consciences also bearing witness, and their thoughts now accusing, now even defending them" (2:15).
God's Response	". . . this man, rather than the other, went home justified before God" (18:14).	". . . the one who is not circumcised physically and yet obeys the law will condemn you" (2:27).
Conclusion	". . . a man is a Jew if he is one inwardly; and circumcision is circumcision of the heart, by the Spirit, not by the written code. Such a man's praise is not from men, but from God" (Rom. 2:29).	

Paul is going to follow Jesus' lead in demonstrating that it is not external religious righteousness, but inner spiritual righteousness, that is of primary importance to God. Therefore, as he concludes chapter 1 by describing those who sin blatantly and willingly (and pass judgment approvingly on others who likewise sin; 1:28–32), he issues a warning to any who would pass judgment *disapprovingly* as if they themselves are not guilty of sins: **you who pass judgment on someone else . . . are condemning yourself, because you . . . do the same things** (2:1). Following this warning (**You, therefore, have no excuse;** 2:1), Paul will describe three ways in which God judges, whether he is judging the human race (Gentiles) or his chosen people (Jews). He judges according to truth (2:2–4), works (2:5–11), and light received (2:12–16).

Before proceeding with Paul's explanation of how God judges, a word is in order about who Paul is addressing in Romans 2:1–16. He obviously begins addressing Jews in 2:17, and has been addressing Gentiles in 1:18–32. We have said that these two "classes" encompass all of humanity, so there cannot be a third group. Therefore, Paul is addressing anyone who judges another, whether Jew or Gentile. Some commentators set this section aside as Paul's words to the "Moralists," but it is most likely that he is thinking of Jewish moralists in the church at Rome who think themselves less sinful than their Gentile fellow-believers (and certainly less than their Roman fellow-citizens!).

The **you** in verse 1 is the fictional "you" common to the diatribe format Paul uses in Romans. Engaging a fictional, yet representative, opponent was an accepted way to present, and counter, opposing points of view. Because his fictional opponent is more likely Jewish than Gentile, 2:1–16 is included here with Paul's discussion of Jewish accountability (2:17–3:8). (For an illuminating discussion of how some moral [unbelieving] Gentiles might have been tempted to agree with Paul about their more "sinful" relatives [whom Paul has just described in 1:28–32], and how Paul might have had them in mind as well as moralizing Jews, see Bruce, pp. 82–83.)

2:2–4. To anyone who is tempted to moralize about another's life, Paul has a series of warnings beginning in verses 2–4. The essence is, God does not play favorites with people (2:11). It is as if his priority is not judging people; it is "judging" three things: truth (vv. 2–4), works (vv. 5–11), and light (vv. 12–16). Running the risk of misrepresenting God's love for individuals, we could even say that God does not look at "who" is being measured against the standards of truth, works, and light (Jew or Gentile); he simply looks at how those three elements have been manifested and honored among his creation and judges accordingly (i.e., righteously).

First, God judges according to **truth.** Since **we know** (common literary form to indicate understood agreement) that God is **truth** (John 14:6; 16:13; 17:17) and bases his judgment **on truth,** it would be hypocritical for anyone to think that God's true judgment would apply partially rather than impartially. Was this not at the heart of Jesus' consistent denunciation of the

Pharisaical hypocrisy he encountered among the Jews in his day? His simple word of warning was, "Do not judge, or you too will be judged" (Matt. 7:1). He uses the key descriptive word that Paul implies—"hypocrite" (Matt. 7:5)—when referring to those who judge others of sin when they themselves commit the same or worse sin (a plank versus a speck; Matt. 7:4).

Whether the Jews in Rome were intimately familiar with the teachings of Jesus or not, there was a classic illustration of hypocrisy from their own history which should have come immediately to mind. Second Samuel 12:1–14 tells the story of Nathan's confrontation of David after his triple sin of adultery, murder, and hypocrisy. Most importantly, note who instigated the revelation of David's hypocrisy: the Lord (2 Sam. 12:1). It was not Nathan's standard of truth that was violated, but God's. And as is so often true in cases of hypocritical judgment, David knew the truth when he heard it. The rich man in the story Nathan told was outrageous in his unrighteousness, and David responded appropriately with anger (2 Sam. 12:5; cf. Rom. 1:18).

So it was not David's judgment against the rich man that was wrong (nor were the Pharisees wrong in noting the speck in another's eye; Matt. 7:3), *it was David's judgment of another while knowingly tolerating the same sin in his own life!* That is hypocrisy—and Paul says God will have none of it. If he judges the Gentiles, he will judge the Jews the same way. That is the heart of judging on the basis of truth.

Lastly, Paul reminds his "opponents" (those who think it acceptable to judge others) that hypocrisy is really **contempt for the riches of his kindness, tolerance and patience.** While the Jews may have wondered why God was so tolerant with Gentiles, the truth is that he is tolerant with them as well. They had failed to recognize that **God's kindness** is not careless oversight (as in failing to note sin), but is careful oversight (as in leading sinners **toward repentance**). **Contempt** is not overlooked by God forever. "As God has made everything with a certain measure, weight and number, so also his patience has certain limits," said Origen. And as the fourth-century A.D. writer (called by Erasmus) Ambrosiaster warned, one day "he who thought that the longsuffering of God's goodness was something to laugh at will not hesitate to beg for mercy." Truth has only one lens through which it looks and judges. Any who think that God views them differently than other sinners is hereby warned by Paul to think differently.

2:5–11. Another indication that Paul is writing primarily with Jews in mind is his quoting of the Old Testament to make his point: "**God 'will give to each person according to what he has done'**" (Ps. 62:12; Prov. 24:12). Here, he says that, in addition to judging righteously on the basis of truth, God will judge on the basis of works—**what** each person **has done.** Do not forget our initial deductions at the beginning of this chapter. The issue here is not salvation—it is how God evaluates all people: on the basis of truth, works, and light. The point he is making here is that God shows no partiality or favoritism when he judges the human race. Salvation is always by faith, not by works (Eph. 2:8–9).

Paul is not contradicting himself in Romans 2; rather, he is contradicting those who would wonder why God does not judge the really wicked Gentiles of the world. His response is that those who themselves are going to be judged ought not to be judging others.

The same wrath that Paul said is currently (present tense) being revealed against the "godlessness and wickedness of men" (1:18) is being stored up by the moralizers **for the day of God's wrath, when his righteous judgment will be revealed** (2:5). Wrath is being revealed as people are given over (1:24,26,28) to increasingly sinful practices as their sin is judged. But one day, a final, external judgment will be revealed when God will judge each person for what he or she has done in life.

Paul uses the opposite ends of the spectrum of righteousness to illustrate his point in verses 6–11:

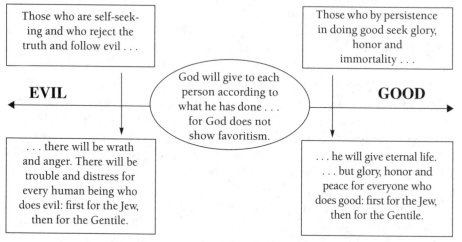

Those who are self-seeking and who reject the truth and follow evil . . .

Those who by persistence in doing good seek glory, honor and immortality . . .

EVIL

God will give to each person according to what he has done . . . for God does not show favoritism.

GOOD

. . . there will be wrath and anger. There will be trouble and distress for every human being who does evil: first for the Jew, then for the Gentile.

. . . he will give eternal life. . . . but glory, honor and peace for everyone who does good: first for the Jew, then for the Gentile.

It is obvious that there is no person who has lived completely at either end of the spectrum—totally evil or totally good—which is how we know that Paul is creating a hypothetical example to make his point. Certainly no one is totally righteous, and though all people are "wholly defiled" and "wholly inclined to all evil" (to quote the Westminster Confession of Faith), no one is as evil as he or she could possibly be.

Therefore, all people are somewhere on the spectrum between points just shy of either end. All have sinned (Rom. 3:23), and God **'will give to each person according to what he has done.'** This "giving" will occur on **the day of God's wrath, when his righteous judgment will be revealed.** On the other hand, God's righteous judgment would require that if anyone did persist in

doing good, seeking **glory, honor and immortality** (that is, they never sinned), he would grant them **eternal life**.

For all, church father Chrysostom's words are ominous: "Paul deprives those who live in wickedness of any excuse and shows that it is from factiousness and carelessness that they fall into unrighteousness [see 2:8]. . . . Their fall is voluntary; their crime is not of necessity." *Not of necessity*. By the time Paul gets through Romans 6, and then concludes Romans 8, it will become obvious that "crime is not of necessity." But where "crime" exists, God **does not show favoritism**.

2:12–16. Finally, in addition to truth and works, God will judge according to the light a person has received. In simple terms, this means that God's righteousness will not allow him to hold anyone responsible for what they never possessed. Paul has already told us that every person possesses knowledge of God, "since what may be known about God is plain to them, because God has made it plain to them" (1:19). Specifically, "his eternal power and divine nature" have been made known to every person, "so that men are without excuse" (1:20). Therefore, everyone will be held accountable for the knowledge of God that exists in the created world.

But remember—Paul began this section warning Jewish moralists not to view themselves as less likely to be judged than wicked Gentiles. Now he is about to burst their bubble of privilege in shocking fashion! He is about to tell them that a Gentile—a heathen barbarian who does not have the law, who has no personal relationship with God, who is ignorant of God's statutes—could be judged less harshly than a Jew! The reason for this goes to the very heart of why the Jews were confused: they tended toward the view that judgment was on the basis of possession (of the law, of privilege, etc.), whereas God says that judgment is on the basis of practice—how faithful we are to what we possess.

A Jew (or any person) with great access to the word and will of God, but who practices none of it, will be held far more accountable than a Gentile (any person) who possesses a minimal amount of information about God but who practiced faithfully what he or she knew. This was one of the new realities of the kingdom of God, of the mystery of the uniting of Jew and Gentile into one body, that the Jewish believers in Rome were going to have to get used to. God's chosen people were no longer "chosen" to be treated differently than Gentiles.

Here is how Paul makes his argument (again, he is using "either/or" categories for the sake of argument: either you have the law [Jews] or you do not [Gentiles]; and "law" should be interpreted as "specific revelation of the righteous will of God," not so much the complete corpus of the Mosaic Law code):

- Verse 12: Gentiles will not be judged by the law; Jews will.

- Verse 13: Possessing the law really is not the issue anyway; it is obeying the law that forms the basis of judgment in God's sight.
- Verses 14–15: Note: after all, the Gentiles (those without specific written revelation of God's will) prove they in fact have the will (law) of God because they do what God desires on the basis of their conscience. God counts their actions as righteous whether their motivation is the written law or the law written on their heart.
- Verse 16: **This will take place** (the declaring of men righteous; end of v. 13) on the judgment day when the truth about men's hearts is revealed by God.

Therefore, if one has an abundance of light about God (the Jews), judgment will be based on this abundance of knowledge about God. If one has a paucity of light about God (the Gentiles), then judgment will be based on very little knowledge (relatively speaking) about God. No one will be judged for light they did not receive; everyone will be judged for light they did receive.

One of the most startling and clear examples of the basis of Gentile judgment versus Jewish judgment is found in Amos's prophecy against Israel. Six wicked Gentile nations surrounding Judah and Israel are condemned by God through the prophet:

- Aram (Damascus, Amos 1:3–5), for brutally attacking Gilead (Israel) (1:3).
- Philistia (Gaza, Amos 1:6–8), for selling Israelite captives into slavery to Edom (1:6).
- Phoenicia (Tyre, Amos 1:9–10), for selling Israelite captives into slavery and breaking a covenant of brotherhood (1 Kgs. 5:1,12; 16:30–31).
- Edom (Amos 1:11–12), descended from Esau, for attacking his "brother with a sword" (descendants of Jacob).
- Ammon (Amos 1:13–15), for brutalizing the women of Gilead (Israel).
- Moab (Amos 2:1–3), for desecrating the body and burial site of the king of Edom.

Then, Amos prophesies judgment against Judah as well, but note the cause:

Judah (Amos 2:4–5), "Because they have rejected the law of the LORD and have not kept his decrees, because they have been led astray by false gods, the gods their ancestors followed."

Clearly, the basis of Judah's judgment is totally different than the surrounding Gentile nations. Judah is judged for disobeying the laws of God, while the Gentiles are judged for disobeying the laws of humanity and decency. Should the Gentiles have known better? Yes, according to Romans 1:19–20 and 2:14–15. Therefore, the Gentile nations are judged on the basis of the law in their heart and conscience, and Judah (the Jews) are based on the written, revealed law of God. (Israel, the ten northern tribes, the target of the bulk of Amos's prophecy, has her sins detailed in the remaining seven chapters of the book—and they are of every sort. But clearly, Israel would be judged on the same basis as Judah—the revealed, written word of God.)

Romans 2:1–16 is almost like a parenthesis in Paul's overall argument. He left off in 1:32 talking about the Gentiles' sins, and picks up in 2:17 with the Jews' sins. The sixteen verses in between are like a giant set of scales that will bring into balance what Paul is about to tell the Jews in 2:17–3:8. His Jewish audience in the church in Rome is not likely to be wildly enthusiastic about what they are about to hear. But again, it is part of his ministry to take the gospel—**my gospel**—to the Gentiles. The Jews have to understand the new economy of God, and be just as thankful for the grace and mercy of God as the Gentiles, if they are to be enthusiastic about helping Paul get the gospel to them.

Mounce well summarizes Paul's calling the gospel **my gospel**: "Paul's attachment to the gospel was profound. . . . [it] remained at the very center of his ministry of reconciliation. . . . In a day when so much preaching has sold its birthright for a pot of psychological porridge, the need for renewed focus on the essential gospel has never been greater. The gospel is to be *your* gospel. God has entrusted it to *you* (2 Cor. 5:19)" (Mounce, p. 97).

While 2:1–16 is brief and parenthetical, we have given it extra discussion because of its critical role in connecting Jews and Gentiles in their need for the gospel. What Paul has to say now to the Jewish believers will require less explanation because of the groundwork he has already laid.

B God's Accounting for Jewish Judgment (2:17–3:8)

SUPPORTING IDEA: *Paul outlines Jewish assets, liabilities, and what is truly profitable to God before detailing the bottom line: who is really a Jew in God's sight.*

An accounting paradigm seemed a natural one within which to analyze Paul's words concerning Jewish accountability before God. After all, one can almost hear them say, "How do you figure that, Paul?!" He moves back into the diatribe format (begun in 2:1) in order to engage a fictional, self-righteous Jewish questioner. Do not forget—Paul had been a self-righteous Jew himself (Phil. 3:4–6). He knows *exactly* how they think, and focuses in immediately on the assets and liabilities of their position.

2:17–20. The positive side of the Jewish ledger was strong. Paul lists eight advantages to being a Jew—eight "boasts" by which they thought God's judgment of them would not be as harsh as the Gentiles:

Verse 17:

1. They were the Jews! They were God's chosen people, his *only* chosen people, the "apple of his eye" (Zech. 2:8). This must count for something!

2. They **rely on the law.** Had God chosen any other people to reveal his will to at Sinai? Their religious reverence for the law betrayed the hope they put in their possession of it.

3. They **brag** about their **relationship to God.** Different from idols of wood and stone, Israel's God was their Father (Isa. 63:16; Mic. 3:11).

Verse 18:

4. They **know his will.** Israel could, it is true, say that they knew the will of God. They were the only ones with special revelation from him (Exod. 4:22).

5. They **approve of what is superior.** Dietary laws, lifestyle restrictions, worship instructions—the Jews had a narrower view of life than their neighbors; a view they deemed superior (Gal. 1:14).

6. They are **instructed by the law.** Psalm 119 extols the merits of God's decrees as those which direct the steps of man. The Jews relished God's instructions (so much so that they made up hundreds of decrees to go along with his, eventually preferring theirs over his; see Matt. 23).

Verses 19–20:

7. They are convinced they **are a guide for the blind, a light for those who are in the dark, an instructor of the foolish, a teacher of infants.** Indeed, they were called by God to be such to the nations of the world (Isa. 42:6; 49:6).

8. They **have in the law the embodiment of knowledge and truth** (see Ps. 19:7–9).

It is understandable, while not excusable, how Israel could be tempted to think of themselves as better than the rest of humanity. In terms of privilege and possession, they did have a chosen place. In terms of practice, however, they failed as frequently as the Gentiles. In that fact is found the Jewish liabilities.

2:21–24. Jewish liabilities can be outlined as cleanly as their assets by just imagining the opposites. That is, the behavior their privileged position should have produced was not how they lived. Paul calls them to account for the discrepancy:

- They taught others, but did not teach themselves.
- They preached against stealing, yet stole.

- They preached against adultery, but committed adultery.
- They abhorred idols, but stole from pagan temples.
- They bragged about the law, yet dishonored God by breaking it.

The upshot of their behavior was the most terrible of results: **God's name is blasphemed among the Gentiles because of you.** While not a direct quote, Paul builds this statement on two references (Isa. 52:5; Ezek. 36:22) from the most terrible period in Israel's history, the exile and captivity of her people. The name of God that was so holy to the Jews that they would not even pronounce it was being dragged through the dirty streets of the pagan world like a bad joke. "All day long my name is constantly blasphemed," the Lord said through Isaiah (52:5). Three different times, Ezekiel recounts, God had not judged Israel when they came out of Egypt to keep his name from being profaned in the eyes of the nation (Ezek. 20:9,14,22). Though they deserved judgment, he withheld it and patiently tried to teach them his ways so that the surrounding nations would not ridicule his name because of his people. Finally, however, his patience ran out, and he sent the nation into exile—which caused his name to be blasphemed (Ezek. 36:20–21).

But then, to redeem the glory of his name, God prophesied through Ezekiel that he would judge the nations that captured Israel, but not for Israel's sake—"for the sake of my holy name, which you have profaned among the nations where you have gone" (Ezek. 36:22). But then note God's ultimate, missionary purpose in judging Israel's oppressors: "I will show the holiness of my great name, which has been profaned among the nations, the name you have profaned among them. *Then the nations will know that I am the* LORD, *declares the Sovereign* LORD, *when I show myself holy through you before their eyes*" (Ezek. 36:23; emphasis added).

For God, for Ezekiel, and now for Paul, there was a missionary purpose in keeping the name of God holy—*that the nations will know that Yahweh, Israel's God, is the* LORD! Do not miss the significance of this for the Jewish believers in Rome: "Yes," Paul is saying to the Jews, "the Gentiles have sinned and deserve God's judgment. But from Abraham on it has been my purpose to use you to save the Gentiles from their sins. But *your* sins are so blatant that the Gentiles laugh at my name! How can I ever redeem them when it is you who need redemption! Your sins are as judgment-worthy as theirs. No, yours are *more* worthy of judgment than theirs, because you are supposed to be their light. And when you allow your light to go out, how great is the darkness in which they remain!"

The late theologian-apologist Francis Schaeffer saw a worrisome connection between Paul's words to the Jews and the contemporary American church:

Again we must admit, this is surely how God looks at much of Christendom today. Claiming to be under the umbrella of Christendom, claiming to have some sort of special blessing because the bells ring in the cathedrals, because in the United States great numbers of people go to church, and yet we commit blasphemy against God as we turn from the clear teaching of His Word. It is a sober truth and we must face it: if we have the Bible, if we enjoy all the blessings it brings, and yet by our lives bring shame upon God's name, we are guilty of the greatest irreverence. . . . When the man with the Bible treats it as an external thing only, it causes the man without the Bible to dishonor the God of the Bible. Surely, then, the man with the Bible is justifiably under God's wrath" (Schaeffer, p. 61).

2:25–27. Paul now reveals in the simplest of terms the true profit in being a Jew: **observe the law.** Paul had already written to Galatian proselytes that "every man who lets himself be circumcised . . . is obligated to obey the whole law" (Gal. 5:3). This was, of course, not a surprise, if not a reality. Circumcision was the "sign of the covenant" (Gen. 17:11) between Abraham, and his descendants, and God. As the participants cut off their foreskin, so were they admitting willingness to be cut off from God should they fail to meet the stipulations of the covenant. Israel's failure throughout her generations was to substitute the "sign of the covenant" with the keeping of the stipulations—obedience to the law. Indeed, God warned through Jeremiah that being circumcised in the flesh, as many of Israel's neighbors were, would protect no one from judgment—including his own people Israel (Jer. 9:25–26).

Therefore, **circumcision has value if you observe the law.** But if you have been physically circumcised, yet fail to keep the law, **you have become as though you had not been circumcised.** So critical is the observance of the law that the Gentiles (those **not circumcised physically**) who [obey] **the law** will condemn the Jews who, though circumcised physically, are lawbreakers! True spiritual profit, in God's eyes, is found in obedience to him. Assets of access to God are canceled by liabilities of license with God's words. There is profit only in obedience. If these implications and hints have not been sufficient to make Paul's points, his next words will go straight to the bottom line.

2:28–29. A true Jew cannot be determined by line of sight—it is not a matter of externalities. **A man is a Jew if he is one inwardly.** This also was not new, if not forgotten. From the time of the choosing of Israel's second king (the first one who followed after God's own heart), God has looked differently than man looks. When Samuel *saw* Jesse's son Eliab, he thought, "Surely the LORD's anointed stands here before the LORD" (1 Sam. 16:6). What did Samuel see that made him think Eliab was to be the new king?

Apparently not what God was looking for: "Do not consider his appearance or his height, for I have rejected him. The LORD does not look at the things man looks at. Man looks at the outward appearance, but the LORD looks at the heart" (16:7).

And in Jesus' day, the Jews were still living life externally: "Everything they do is done for men to *see*" (Matt. 23:5; emphasis added). From banquet and synagogue seats to the size of phylacteries and tassels to being noted and greeted as "Rabbi" in the marketplace, the Jews lived large on the outside but small on the inside (see Matt. 23:5–7). Unfortunately for them, the inside is where God looks.

Four things, Paul says, will allow us to recognize a true Jew in God's sight:

1. He does not emphasize outward and external signs (v. 28).
2. His heart has been circumcised (revealed before God) (v. 29).
3. The Spirit's knife ("the word of God"; Heb. 4:12) has performed the circumcision on the heart (v. 29).
4. God's praise drowns out the "praise" of men (v. 29).

Continuing the diatribe format which he began in 2:1, Paul now moves to raise and answer the objections which he knew would flow from his Jewish readers in Rome. After all, he has just dismantled the superstructure of Jewish religion—in the name of the gospel.

3:1–8. In behalf of his Jewish readers, Paul raises four legitimate objections to what he has just written:

1. *Verses 1–2:* What is the point in being a Jew at all? By the time Paul finishes his letter to the Roman believers, he will have listed a number of advantages, or benefits, of being a Jew. He begins the list here, but does not finish it until 9:4–5. Here he names **first of all** the benefits: the Jews **have been entrusted with the very words of God.** Paul wants to counteract the thinking that the disobedience of the Jews has destroyed their privileged place. It has not! They are still the recipients of God's special revelation. Their failure to walk according to their calling (cf. Eph. 4:1; Phil. 1:27; Col. 1:10; 1 Thess. 2:12) did not negate their privilege of having been the earthly repository and steward of the revelation of God's words to mankind. This was, indeed, the first of all their advantages.

2. *Verses 3–4:* Second, Paul's fictitious objectors ask whether God's judgment on their faithlessness would not make God faithless as well. After all, it was God who promised to be faithful to Abraham's descendants. Is God not now being unfaithful? Stott paraphrases the objection to highlight Paul's use of words related to *pistis* (faith), showing Paul's play on words: "If some to whom God's promises were entrusted (*episteuthesan,* v. 2) did not respond to them in trust (*epistesan,* v. 3a), will their lack of trust (*apistia*) destroy God's

trustworthiness (*pistis*, v. 3b)? If God's people are unfaithful, does that necessarily mean that he is?" (Stott, p. 96).

Paul's outburst—**Not at all!**—betrays his outrage at the thought that anyone could suggest God being unfaithful. Even their greatest king, David, was willing for himself to be judged a sinner and God **proved right** when he pronounced judgment (Ps. 51:4). In fact, God's pronouncement of judgment, as his covenant declared he would, is a sign of his faithfulness.

The next two objections (vv. 5–6 and vv. 7–8) are actually of the same category, but will be noted separately because of their differing emphases. They both suggest the following syllogism:

Major premise: When God forgives sinners, his grace is manifested.

Minor premise: I am a sinner.

Conclusion: The more I sin, the more opportunity for him to manifest his grace.

Certainly not! (v. 6) Paul says with energy. God does not need the willful sin of man to demonstrate his "divine nature" (Rom. 1:20). His righteousness and his glory are his to demonstrate in other ways.

3. *Verses 5–6:* If God warranted man's sin in order to display his own righteousness, then how could he be just in judging the world—the whole point of Paul's letter up to this point? Such an argument could only arise out of a **human argument** (a "depraved mind"; Rom. 1:28).

4. *Verses 7–8:* Along the same (illogical) lines, if people's propensity to lie only makes God's truthfulness stand out more clearly, and thus his glory, why are people condemned for something that glorifies God? To answer in modern terms, Paul would say that the end does not justify the means. Getting to the right place (God's glory) the wrong way (by man's sin) can never be justified. As to those who suggest such a thing, Paul says, **their condemnation is deserved.**

Having fully established that the Jews, as well as the Gentiles, stand under the judgment of God's righteous standards, Paul asks a concluding question about the status of Jews before God.

C Epilogue: Who God Judges (3:9–20)

SUPPORTING IDEA: *Paul's uses his summary of Jewish accountability before God to remind his readers that all—Jews and Gentiles alike—have demonstrated their unrighteousness before God.*

3:9. In his diatribe format, the answer to Paul's final response coming from his fictitious questioner could be challenged as contradictory to his answer in 3:1. Paul has said that there are advantages to being a Jew (Rom. 3:1–2), but that those advantages do not include being excused from judgment. Therefore, the Jews ask, **Are we any better?** to which Paul replies, **Not** at all! Well, if advantages do not mean we are better off, then what do they mean? The advantage to being a Jew is access to God's special revelation and the blessings that come from responding obediently to it. But being better off (in the sense that Paul knew the Jews would be asking)? No, because Jews are going to be judged by the same righteous standards as Gentiles—and in fact, more scrupulously because of their advantages!

Paul's declaration that both Jew and Gentile alike are **all under sin** is only the first of three declarations about who God judges. The other two witnesses are the Old Testament and the law itself. As if concluding this section of his epistle in a courtroom, Paul brings compelling evidence to show the Jews that *all*—everyone in the world—is guilty of sin and will be judged accordingly.

3:10–18. The second witness, beside the apostle himself, is the Old Testament. The corpus of special revelation which formed the Jews' advantage (Rom. 3:1–2) turns out to be the strongest witness against them. From the Psalms, Isaiah, Ecclesiastes, and Proverbs come the seminal thoughts that Paul "quotes" in order to show the Jews one thing: the texts which God committed to them for the purpose of being a light to the Gentiles have now been turned upon them. It is as if someone grabbed their sword out of their hand—the sword by which they were to fight their way through the darkness of this world—and killed them with it. Not with anger or vitriol does Paul bring the testimony of Scripture against them. In fact, even if they had been manifestly successful at obeying God for all their generations, the verses he cites would still be true. It is just that he would not have to be hurting them by reminding them; they would have been humbled by the reality of their own sin and would not have needed the apostle to the Gentiles to call them to account.

"Righteous" Jews or unrighteous Jews, **all have turned away . . . there is no one who does good, not even one.** That is true generally, and it is true specifically: **throats . . . tongues . . . lips . . . mouths . . . feet . . . eyes** are all guilty, going their own way. The senses and sensibilities of humans—both Gentile and Jew—have validated the Word of God.

3:19–20. Paul declared that all have sinned (3:9). The Old Testament declares that all have sinned (3:10–18). And finally, the law declares that all have sinned (3:19–20). **The law** here has a dual reference in Paul's words. First, it simply refers to the verses he has just quoted, showing that the law speaks **to those who are under the law.** Paul is not asking the Jews to give heed to the sacred writings of some other religion, but to their own. If you claim these writings, he says, then receive their claim upon your life. Do not own them without letting them own you. Receive their verdict without objection.

Second, however, Paul says that the law's purpose is to let you know that the law cannot make you righteous. Rather, it is **through the law [that] we become conscious of sin.** In other words, when the law says, "Do this or that," it is really saying, "You can't do this or that." The law wants you to know that you are guilty of not being able to keep it, and that your righteousness will never have its source in the law. The law tells you of your unrighteousness; the gospel tells you of the righteousness of God.

Paul has concluded his words concerning his beloved kinsman (Rom. 10:1–3). He has brought the church at Rome to the point where they understand that they are unrighteous (Jew and Gentile), the Romans are unrighteous, the "barbarians" in Spain and beyond are unrighteous, that **there is no one righteous, not even one** (3:10). He is now ready to tell them who is righteous—God alone—and more importantly, how a bridge may be built upon which they may move from their unrighteousness to the righteousness of God. This he will do beginning in 3:21—"a righteousness from God . . . has been made known."

> **MAIN IDEA REVIEW:** *Paul is making a case to the Roman believers that the whole world needs the gospel, and has demonstrated that Gentiles deserve God's wrath. Lest Jews think they will escape God's judgment by their privileged position, he now shows that they also need the gospel as a result of failing to obey God's law.*

III. CONCLUSION

Face-to-Face with Reality

Christian writer Walter Wangerin, Jr., eloquently expresses the heart of what Paul wants the believers in Rome to understand about their relationship to God: "My wife is . . . a mirror. When I have sinned against her, my sin appears in the suffering of her face. . . . The passion of Christ . . . is such a mirror. Are the tears of my dear wife hard to look at? Well, the pain in the face of Jesus is harder. . . . Nevertheless, I will not avoid this mirror! . . . for this is the mirror of dangerous grace, purging more purely than any other" (Rowell, *Quotes & Idea Starters,* Baker Book House, 2000 p. 37).

How often we avoid the mirror! Much of our society today lives as Dostoyevsky chronicled in *The Brothers Karamazov:* "If God does not exist, everything is permissible." By avoiding the mirror of God's truth, we act like the deceived man imagined by James the apostle who looks in the mirror of God's word and goes away, immediately forgetting what he saw (Jas. 1:22–24). Everything becomes permissible; nothing is prohibited. But as much as we might want to deny the realities of sin and unrighteousness— as much as the believers in Rome might not have wanted to hear about their sin—Paul delivers to us no such luxury. Paul is a realist, and the truth is that all have sinned. Our spouse, our friends, our loved ones know we have sinned. We see it in their faces. And we would see it in the face of our God if we would look into his Word—that mirror that reflects not only who we are but who he is, and who we can become in him.

But agreeing with Paul, with the Old Testament, with the law of God is our first step. Agreeing that we have sinned is all God needs to know to show us the depths of his grace. Agreeing that *all* have sinned is all *we* need to know to become Paul's partner in the power of the gospel.

Humorist Garrison Keillor is probably right when he summarizes the contemporary perspective on truth: "Sometimes you just have to look reality square in the face and deny it!" That may work for the weight you have gained, the grades you have made, or the lack of money you have saved—for a while. But the truth will always win out, because "all truth is God's truth" (Frank Gaebelein and Arthur Holmes). As a teacher, be an example of realism and truth to your students by embracing what Paul, the Old Testament, and the law of God say about you. Then, encourage your students to do the same. Together, you and your students can become a powerful witness to the life-saving truth you have just studied: agreeing with God about our unrighteousness prepares us to receive his righteousness.

Faces around us may reflect our sin, but Helen Lemmel wrote of a face that we can look at and find a glory and grace in which our sin fades away—not because we deny it, but because we accept the reality of it, and the reality of the grace that forgives it:

Turn your eyes upon Jesus,
Look full in His wonderful face,
And the things of earth will grow strangely dim
In the light of His glory and grace.

PRINCIPLES

- There is no excuse for passing judgment about another person's sin.
- Being impatient with God about another's sin shows contempt for the patience he shows toward me and my sin.
- God shows no favoritism in his judgment of sin.
- Obeying the will of God is more important than knowing the will of God.
- I am accountable before God for what I know about God.
- Hypocrisy incurs the judgment of God.
- Spirituality is evaluated by God internally more than externally.

- No human being naturally hungers after God and is responsible for not hungering.

APPLICATIONS

- Who are the people whose sin I tend to judge? What excuse do I use to justify my judgment?
- Have I confessed the contempt for God's patience with me which my judgment of others produces?
- What categories do I tend to place people in which indicates that I view them (judge them) differently? Why do I show this kind of favoritism?
- What are the areas of God's will that I know, but do not currently practice?
- What spiritual practices or principles have I recently taught to others that I myself am not practicing? How does God evaluate my hypocrisy?
- If people could see my private, spiritual center (my heart), would they find it consistent or inconsistent with my public, external behavior?
- How often recently have I expressed thanks and praise to God for creating a hunger in me for himself?

IV. LIFE APPLICATION

Dead Men's Bones

Commissioned in 1936, the R.M.S. Queen Mary was the most awe-inspiring ocean-going vessel in the world. She was 1,019 feet long, at 81,237 tons displaced twice the tonnage of the Titanic, had 12 decks (the promenade deck was 724 feet long), and carried 1,957 passengers attended by a crew of 1,174. Transformed from a luxury liner to a troop transport in World War II, she carried 765,429 members of the military to and from the European war zones. The Queen Mary was retired from regular passenger service in 1967 after making 1,001 Atlantic Ocean crossings, and is presently harbored in the port of Long Beach, California. Even today, her magnificent and gleaming exterior cuts a beautiful profile against the blue waters of the Long Beach harbor. But when the Queen Mary was retired from active passenger service, it was discovered that part of her gleaming exterior was hiding something far less attractive and substantial.

The Queen Mary's three elliptical smokestacks—36 feet long, 23 feet wide, and ranging from 70 down to 62 feet in height—were made of sheets of steel over an inch thick. During her decades of service, at least 30 coats of paint had been applied to the massive smokestacks, forming a shell around the steel interior. But when the smokestacks were removed for maintenance after her decommissioning, it was discovered that they were nothing but shells. When lifted off the liner and placed on the docks, they crumbled! Over the years, the thick steel of which they had been made had turned to rust from long exposure to heat and moisture. The beautiful exteriors of the smokestacks revealed a rusty, crumbly interior that spoke not of beauty and elegance but of deterioration and decay. The external appearance was hiding the internal reality.

While the Queen Mary's inconsistencies between outward maintenance and inward deterioration were not purposeful, Jesus encountered a situation in Jerusalem where the same inconsistency seemed to be no accident. The Pharisees' lives had apparently become like the Queen Mary's smokestacks—gleaming on the outside, rusty on the inside. "Hypocrites," Jesus called them (Matt. 23:25–28). They were like dishes that were polished until they shone on the outside, but inside had the grease and crumbs from yesterday's feast festering and attracting flies. They were like the tombs outside the city wall that camouflaged the resting places of dead people's bones with coats of bright whitewash. Gleaming on the outside, gruesome on the inside.

These whitewashed tombs were especially interesting, an unwitting image of the walking tombs which the Pharisees themselves had become. The Old Testament warned against coming in contact with the body of a dead person; one could be declared unclean simply by walking over or bumping into the tomb or grave of the deceased. Therefore, in order to keep people from becoming defiled by contact with the dead, tombs were often whitewashed to make them more visible, and therefore avoidable, at night. In other words, the resting place of the dead got a gleaming white exterior to prevent people from becoming unclean by accidental contact.

Based on Jesus' assessment, guess who else should have been whitewashed to prevent people from being defiled by their presence? The Pharisees had become like the Queen Mary's smokestacks and like whitewashed tombs—looking good on the outside, but inside was a different story. The smokestacks could not help their condition, and the dead did not ask for their spanking-white burial boxes. But the Pharisees worked hard at their hypocrisy. They knew that what they were doing was double-minded.

Paul says the Jews, the most privileged people spiritually on earth, had become spiritually hypocritical. And he said that God's name was being blasphemed among the Gentiles because of it (Rom. 2:24). The Romans in Jerusalem in Jesus' day did not take God seriously because they did not see anything in God's people to take seriously. Do the "Romans" of our day feel the same? If the multiple coats of Sunday-go-to-meeting paint were stripped from us, would there be steel or rust underneath? Do people today want to whitewash us so they can avoid us when they see us coming? How will we ever complete the task that Paul was trying to complete—spreading the gospel to a needy world—if our exterior is covering a crumbling and decaying interior?

V. PRAYER

Heavenly Father, forgive us for the places in our lives where we have focused on the exterior and ignored the interior. Forgive us for not living up to the light you have given us. Forgive us for causing your name to be blasphemed on account of our hypocrisy. And help us, Lord, not to judge. Help us to be grateful for your patience toward us. And help us to agree with you about the reality of our unrighteousness so we may agree with you about your righteousness. Amen.

VI. DEEPER DISCOVERIES

A. Judgment (2:1–3)

Paul speaks of two kinds of judgment in this section of Romans: man judging man and God judging man. In the commentary, we have already noted the inappropriateness of people passing uncharitable or hypocritical judgment on others, and Jesus' stern warnings against the same. The primary reason that people are not to judge other people is because there is one Judge who will judge all things: "There is only one Lawgiver and Judge, the one who is able to save and destroy. But you—who are you to judge your neighbor?" (Jas. 4:12). Since there is one Judge over all, what right does a human being have to take on that role? James's Jewish epistle fits perfectly with the words of the patriarch Abraham who pled with God to distinguish between the righteous and wicked before judging Sodom: "Will not the Judge of all the earth do right?" (Gen. 18:25).

It is God as "Judge of all the earth" to whom Paul refers in Romans 1–2. But when does God judge Gentiles and Jews? And how are believers to be judged? As noted in the commentary, the judgments Paul refers to in Romans 2 are judgments to determine punishment, not judgments to determine salvation. It is this distinction which makes it clear that Paul's emphasis on works is not the determinant for salvation, which is always by grace through faith (Eph. 2:8–9). Even believers will be judged on the basis of their works, but for the purpose of determining rewards, not punishment.

Some students of Scripture (primarily holding to an amillennial or post-millennial view of eschatology) see one future judgment in which Jesus Christ (Acts 10:42; 17:31) will judge every person who has ever lived. That judgment will be on the basis of works, motives, thoughts, and words.

Believers, on the basis of that judgment, will receive varying degrees of rewards; unbelievers, varying degrees of punishment (Ps. 62:12; Jer. 17:10; Matt. 11:20–22; 12:36; 16:27; 25:35–40; Rom. 2:12–16; 2 Cor. 5:10; 1 Pet. 1:17; Rev. 20:12; 22:12). Spiritual rewards appear to await those who respond faithfully to the will of God while on earth (Matt. 5:11–12; 6:19–21; Luke 19:12–27; 1 Cor. 3:10–15).

Other students of Scripture (primarily holding to a premillennial view of eschatology) would separate the judgments of believers from that of unbelievers. Believers would appear before the judgment seat of Christ vis-a-vis the rapture of the church (1 Cor. 3:10–15; 2 Cor. 5:10), and then the rest of humanity would appear before Christ at the Great White Throne judgment of Revelation 20:11–15.

B. Conscience (2:15)

"Let your conscience be your guide." This over-used aphorism is often employed when no other guidance is available. But is the conscience intended to be a guide for anyone, and especially for believers? While the Old Testament offers little data on the conscience, there is definitely a "consciousness" or awareness of right and wrong—from the very beginning. Adam and Eve hid from God in the Garden of Eden (Gen. 3:8), and even Cain gave some indication by his countenance that his anger was guilt-related (Gen. 4:6). Other indications exist of people wanting to maintain guilt-free feelings concerning their actions—what we call a "clear conscience" (Gen. 20:5–6; 1 Sam. 24:5; 25:31; Job 27:6).

In the New Testament, Paul developed the concept extensively, using the word which referred in common Greek to the guilt or discomfort experienced by those who knew or believed they had done wrong (*syneidesis*). In Romans 2:14–16 he says that the conscience exists in every person at a very basic level as an internal moral compass. He goes so far as to state that the rejection of the direction of that compass is serious enough to constitute grounds for judgment. But that is for an unbeliever, one without the Word of God or the Spirit of God. What happens to the conscience when a person becomes a believer?

It should be kept clear (meaning it still exists) by avoiding sin (2 Cor. 1:12; 1 Tim. 1:5,19; 3:9). The rejection of the guide of the conscience can result in the harming of faith (1 Tim. 1:19). Because the moral sensibilities of a believer are to be more precise than those of an unbeliever, the conscience must be in a state of development (1 Cor. 8:1–13; 10:23–11:1). Care should be taken that the conscience not be corrupted by false teaching (1 Tim. 4:2; Titus 1:5), another indication that the conscience must be trained and developed. The only way to obtain and maintain a clear conscience is through the cleansing of the blood of Christ that forgives sin and removes guilt (Heb. 9:14; 10:22).

While the conscience exists universally, and is the primary guide to right and wrong for the unbeliever, the conscience should be in a constant state of "sanctification" and development to maturity. The Holy Spirit and the Word of God are the primary sources of guidance for the believer (John 16:13–15; 2 Tim. 3:16), and as the believer is trained to discern good and evil (Heb. 5:14) the conscience can play a role in "gray areas" where the Word and the Spirit are not explicit.

VII. TEACHING OUTLINE

A. INTRODUCTION

1. Lead Story: From Cannibals to Polynesians—The Law of the Heart
2. Context: Paul is in the process of laying the foundation for the gospel in the minds of the believers in Rome. For good news to be good, the bad news has to be revealed. And the bad news in the early chapters of Romans is that all have sinned, Jew and Gentile alike. The good news is going to follow immediately in Romans 3:21 where Paul will reveal that a righteousness of God is available to those who have no righteousness of their own.
3. Transition: In Romans 1:18–32, Paul showed clearly that the human race was receiving the wrath of God because of its sin. Sensing that the tendency of some Jews might be to say, "They deserve it," Paul now shows that the Jews are part of the human race and deserve God's judgment as well. Paul sets about to clearly define the difference between privilege—what the Jews had—and practice—what they lacked. God shows no partiality—"Even Jews Need the Gospel."

B. COMMENTARY

1. Prologue: How God Judges (2:1–16)
   a. The temptation to judge (2:1)
   b. God judges according to truth (2:2–4)
   c. God judges according to works (2:5–11)
   d. God judges according to light received (2:12–16)
2. God's Accounting for Jewish Judgment (2:17–3:8)
   a. Jewish assets (2:17–20)
   b. Jewish liabilities (2:21–24)
   c. True profit before God (2:25–27)
   d. The Jewish bottom line (2:28–29)
   e. Jewish objections answered (3:1–8)
3. Epilogue: Who God Judges (3:9–20)
   a. Paul says: "All have sinned" (3:9)

b. The Old Testament says: "All have sinned" (3:10–18)

c. The law says: "All have sinned" (3:19–20)

C. CONCLUSION: DEAD MEN'S BONES

VIII. ISSUES FOR DISCUSSION

1. What impact does a judgmental attitude by the church toward society have on our ability to spread the gospel in our societies? How should the church distinguish between right and wrong in culture without sacrificing the ability to influence the culture for Christ?

2. What is the condition of the "corporate conscience" of the church in America? How much guilt do average Christians carry around with them about past or present deeds, motives, or words? What impact does a less-than-clear conscience have on the power and health of the church as a whole?

3. Where are the biggest inconsistencies between what the contemporary church believes and what it practices? What are some examples? What impact does this inconsistency have on evangelism?

4. How do Paul's words on the moral and spiritual state of humanity affect the role of government and society to create a moral environment in which to live? Is it true that "you can't legislate morality," or is it a matter of whose morality is going to be legislated?

Romans 3:21–31

Righteousness: What the Gospel Offers

"*If* there be ground for you to trust in your own righteousness, then all that Christ did to purchase salvation, and all that God did to prepare the way for it, is in vain."

Jonathan Edwards

Romans 3:21–31

 IN A NUTSHELL

*P*aul has conclusively demonstrated in Romans 1:18–3:20 that everyone in the human race, both Jew and Gentile, is unrighteous. The Jewish believers in Rome needed to understand that their heritage and privileges did not translate into righteousness before God, and all the believers in Rome needed to understand the condition of the whole human race—guilty, unrighteous—in order to understand Paul's missionary passion. "But now," Paul says, the good news comes. Man is unrighteous, but God has revealed in the gospel how unrighteous man can become righteous before God: through faith in Jesus Christ.

Righteousness: What the Gospel Offers

I. INTRODUCTION

The Business of God

*O*ne of the oldest and most respected business periodicals in America is *Forbes Magazine*. Founded in 1917 by B. C. Forbes, the original business magazine has become the flagship of a modern business publishing company operated today by the founder's grandsons. *Forbes* is respected for many reasons, not the least of which is its conservative fiscal and economic approach to the global economy.

But *Forbes* garners respect from readers for another reason. It is perhaps the only prominent business publication that highlights the enduring value of truths from the Bible. On the editorial page masthead one finds a quote from Proverbs: "With all thy getting get understanding" (4:7, KJV). And on the last page of each issue is found a collection of quotations from famous individuals on topics relating to "the business of life." Prominent on that page in each issue is a different text from the Bible, chosen from favorite passages sent in by *Forbes* readers.

The business quotes that have appeared on the final page of *Forbes* are collected in a massive volume titled *The Forbes Book of Business Quotations: 14,173 Thoughts on the Business of Life*. A total of 368 topics (from "Ability" to "Zeal") are commented on by writers, business moguls, churchmen, politicians, humorists, and other famous spokespersons of the human family. Make that 367 topics—for there is one topic in this massive compendium embellished and illustrated by no human wisdom: the topic of "righteousness."

Whether by design or by default, *The Forbes Book of Business Quotations* lists no "human" entries under "Righteousness" save eight passages of Scripture (Pss. 15:1–2; 92:12–13; Prov. 16:8–9; 29:2; Isa. 3:10–11; Jer. 22:13; Hos. 10:12; 2 Tim. 4:7–8). The starkness of this category's supporting materials is striking. While other Scripture verses are sprinkled throughout the volume under various topics, "Righteousness" is the only topic totally illustrated by Scripture verses. It is as if the editor agreed with the apostle Paul's assessment of the human condition in Romans 3:11— "There is no one righteous, not even one."

And if there is no one righteous, how could anyone say anything worthwhile about "righteousness"? Men and women can comment intelligently, helpfully, and humorously about "Anger," "Humility," "Obligations," "Purpose," "Tolerance," and "Work"—and a whole host of other interesting human topics. But "Righteousness"?

According to the apostle Paul, for a human being to speak authoritatively about righteousness would be like an irate person commenting on anger, a destitute person commenting on wealth, or an arrogant person commenting on humility. In those cases, one would simply find a calm person, a rich person, or a humble person to speak to those subjects. Unfortunately, one cannot find a righteous person to comment authoritatively on righteousness. The very condition of humankind—total, complete, pervasive, unrighteousness—disqualifies us at the outset.

What if one only had *The Forbes Book of Business Quotations* by which to live one's life? The verses it quotes on righteousness do well in suggesting how to *act* righteous, which is good for our life on earth. But how does one attain a righteous standing before God, which is what we need to know for our life beyond this earth?

For answers to that question, Romans 3:21–31 (and Paul's ensuing illustrations and discussion) is our only source of hope. We are devoting an entire chapter in our commentary to these eleven verses since they are the core of the answer to the most important question any person could ever ask: "But how can a mortal be righteous before God?" (Job 9:2). Job asked, but could not answer, that question. The world's wisest people, even in our modern day, cannot answer that question. The only person who can answer that question is God. Thankfully, he inspired the apostle Paul to record the fundamental truths about man's movement from unrighteousness to righteousness in the passage we are about to study.

Man has expertise in many areas of life and business, but righteousness is not one of them. Righteousness is the business of God. F. F. Bruce cites the Roman poet Horace, who criticized writers of tragedies in his day for introducing a god into the plot to solve some knotty problem. Martin Luther, Bruce notes, "took up [Horace's] words and applied them to the forgiveness of sins: here, [Luther] said, is a problem that needs God to solve it. True, for sinful man cannot solve it, though he desperately needs a solution to it" (Bruce, p. 96). It is God's solution to a knotty theological and practical problem which Paul presents in Romans 3:21–31: How can God remain just while at the same time justifying the unjust?

II. COMMENTARY

Righteousness: What the Gospel Offers

MAIN IDEA: *Because the human race is completely unrighteous, the instigation for providing righteousness had to come from God. God satisfied his own standards of righteousness by offering a righteous sacrifice (his Son) for the sins of humankind. Every person who embraces by faith what God has done can be declared righteous in his sight.*

Commentators are unanimous in their ascriptions of importance to the eleven verses we are about to study. C. E. B. Cranfield calls this pericope the "centre and heart of the whole of Romans 1:16b–15:13" (Cranfield, p. 68). Robert Mounce elevates its significance one level higher, saying it is "generally acknowledged to be the most theologically important segment of the entire New Testament" (Mounce, p. 114). But it is Leon Morris who perhaps most accurately captures its significance, suggesting that it may be "possibly the most important single paragraph ever written" (Morris, p. 173; cited by Stott, p. 109).

Morris is probably correct given the nature of what it reveals: a solution to the breach between God and man that occurred in the Garden of Eden. A solution had been hinted at in the Old Testament, but then it was a remedy revealed only to the Jews. The Gentiles, the vast majority of the human race, had been going through religious rites and incantations for centuries trying to get in touch with God and curry his favor. And now Paul reveals how and why it is possible for man to stand justified before God.

But to grasp the impact of what Paul is about to tell the Romans, we must remember where and to whom he is writing. The Jews had been convinced for centuries that their heritage stood them in good stead with God, and what their heritage did not cover, their works of righteousness would (Paul has just finished explaining the fallacy of their thinking).

Gentiles, on the other hand, had no specific knowledge of the true God. Rome was a city filled with temples to gods of every sort. Even the Roman emperors were considered divine. And because Roman gods were man-made, they tended to operate in the image of humans, meaning they were untrustworthy, capricious, and required constant placation. Sacrifices were made to Gentile gods to waylay their anger, to woo their affections, and to win their favor. There was no particular rhyme or reason—not to mention justice or righteousness—associated with the Gentile gods. There was only the will and emotion of the gods to which the Gentiles responded as best they could.

Therefore, both parties—Jews and Gentiles—would be coming to Paul's words about God's righteousness out of "theologically dysfunctional" backgrounds. The Jews would be shocked at the idea that they needed righteousness and that the Gentiles qualified to receive God's grace on an equal footing with themselves. The Gentiles would be shocked to discover that the true God would offer anything free—that he would provide his own sacrifice and turn away his own wrath; and that once turned away, it would stay away.

In relating the following passage of Scripture—one of the most theologically profound, yet conceptually simple, in all the Bible—to the postmodern, post-Christian world, today's teacher is not far from Paul's dilemma with his audience in Rome. Many students will find it hard to believe they have done anything to deserve the wrath that Paul says God has taken it upon himself to turn away. Others with a religious view of God will find it hard to believe that righteousness can be received freely, without religious qualification and effort. Still others will be shocked to learn of grace—that Bible-only doctrine which says "I love in spite of" instead of "I love because of."

The Vanity Fair to which Pilgrim Paul wrote is not totally removed from the Vanity Fair where you teach. This passage of Scripture has the answer for the self-righteous (all have sinned), the self-sacrificing (God provides the sacrifice), the self-condemning (all can receive righteousness), and the self-sufficient (boasting is excluded).

May this most important paragraph ever written become second nature to you. May the one who is both just and justifier reveal to you in fresh ways the depths of the riches of his grace in Christ Jesus. And may the heart of the apostle cause your heart to be renewed with a passion to reveal the righteousness of God to every person who has yet to see it.

A Righteousness: Made Known in the Old Testament (3:21)

> **SUPPORTING IDEA:** *The righteousness revealed at the present time is the same righteousness revealed in former times.*

3:21. Paul got the bad news over with first in his letter to the Romans. From 1:18 through 3:20 he painted a drastic, but accurate and realistic, picture of the spiritual and moral condition of the human race. **But now** he begins to paint a picture that is altogether different and better. "But now" is one of Paul's favorite contrasting conjunctions. Sixteen times in his epistles he uses the *nuni de* construction to bring his readers up sharply and prepare them for a contrast, and many of those times the NIV renders it as here, **but now** (e.g., Rom. 6:22; 7:6; 15:23; Eph. 2:13; Col. 1:22). Good cases can be made for Paul thinking temporally ("but now in this age of righteousness, beginning with the death of Christ") or logically ("but now, in stark contrast to the unrighteousness of humankind, the righteousness of God has been made known"). Both aspects contain truth.

The logical use could not be more obvious, but the temporal element is present in Paul as well; see 2 Corinthians 6:2 where he refers to the "day of salvation" that has come in Christ (cf. *idou nun . . . idou nun*—"I tell you, now . . . now" with *nuni de,* **but now**). Either way, **but now** lets his Roman readers know that Paul is shifting to a new theme. And what a theme it is!

In Romans 1:17, Paul said that "in the gospel a righteousness from God is [being] revealed." This is a present tense, ongoing reality. Whenever and wherever the gospel is preached, "a righteousness from God is revealed" through the proclamation of the death and resurrection of Christ. Here, he picks up the theme of **a righteousness from God** again, but this time says that it **has been made known**. Here Paul uses the perfect tense, pointing to an action in the past with results continuing into the present—without doubt he refers to the death of Christ. Since the death of Christ, God's righteousness **has been made known**—but **apart from law**. Before the death of Christ, God's righteousness was revealed according to law, as it was law which revealed the righteous standards of God ("And if we are careful to obey all this law before the LORD our God . . . that will be our righteousness"; Deut. 6:25). But now it is revealed **apart from the law.**

Reformed scholar John Murray stresses the absence of the law in the present manifestation of God's righteousness: "When Paul says 'without the law' the absoluteness of this negation must not be toned down. He means this without any reservation or equivocation in reference to the justifying righteousness which is the theme of this part of the epistle. This implies that in justification there is no contribution, preparatory, accessory, or subsidiary, that is given by works of law. . . . To overlook this accent is to miss the central message of this epistle. To equivocate here is to distort what could not be more plainly and consistently stated" (Murray, p. 109).

However, Paul himself will say at the end of this section that, even now, "we uphold the law" (3:31)—but not as a means of justification. He told the Galatians that the law was "put in charge to lead us to Christ" but that "now that faith has come, we are no longer under the supervision of the law" (Gal. 3:24–25). The problem with righteousness being revealed according to law is that no one could attain to the righteousness that the law required (see Rom. 9:30). In other words, "all have sinned" (3:23).

Yet even in the Old Testament, the righteousness of God was revealed apart from the law, and both **the Law and the Prophets testify** accordingly. The church father John Chrysostom pointed out that "Paul does not say that the righteousness of God has been *given* but that it has been *manifested,* thus destroying the accusation that it is something new. For what is manifested is old but previously concealed. He reinforces this point by going on to mention that the Law and Prophets had foretold it" (Bray, p. 99).

The Law and the Prophets was common parlance for the entire Old Testament. Jesus used the phrase (Matt. 5:17; 7:12; 22:40; Luke 16:16; 24:27,44) as did Luke (Acts 13:15) and Paul on other occasions (Acts 24:14; 26:22; 28:23). **The Law** referred to the first five books of Moses, and **the Prophets** to everything else (the major and minor prophets as well as the historical books and "the Writings"—the wisdom literature; Matthew even refers to a quote from Psalm 78:2 as being "spoken through the prophet"; Matt. 13:35). But how did **the Law and the Prophets testify** to the righteousness from God that **has** [now] **been made known?**

In the next chapter, Paul will use Abraham as an example of a "Gentile" who found righteousness from God apart from the law. Abraham serves as the linchpin of his argument that righteousness comes only by faith (see also Gal. 3:6–25). Abraham's experience with God is the practical example of everything that Paul is so meticulously laying out in Romans 3–4. Paul, in essence, is lecturing in the courtroom of justice, explaining exactly how it is possible that what we see in Abraham's life could take place.

Remember—Abraham was a pure-bred Gentile when he met God (as was everyone in the world; there were no Jews before Abraham!), devoid of faith and devoid of righteousness. When God led him from his home in Ur of Mesopotamia, Abraham had little to go on but faith. Blind faith actually, since he had no idea where God was taking him. But as his relationship with God developed (430 years before the law was given, Paul tells us in Gal. 3:17), he learned to trust, to believe God.

And so we find in Genesis 15:6 the essence of the Pauline argument: "Abraham believed the LORD, and he credited it to him as righteousness." There is **righteousness from God** being revealed (credited) apart from the law, "through faith" (v. 22). For Abraham, it was not "faith in Jesus Christ" (v. 22) at that point. But as the Law was given through Moses, and it became obvious that the sacrifices prescribed by the law had to be repeated annually, that the forgiveness God granted for sin was in anticipation of a better sacrifice to come.

The Prophets also testified of a righteousness apart from the law. One of Paul's theme verses (Rom. 1:17) quotes Habakkuk 2:4: "The righteous will live by his faith." Not "by the law," but "by his faith." Peter, when speaking to the Gentiles in Cornelius's house, said that "all the prophets testify about [Christ] that everyone who believes in him receives forgiveness of sins through his name" (Acts 10:43). There it is again: the prophets talking about faith as a means to forgiveness. Perhaps Peter had Isaiah 53:11 in mind: "After the suffering of his soul, he will see the light of life and be satisfied; by his knowledge my righteous servant will justify many, and he will bear their iniquities." Or perhaps he was thinking of the prophecy of Isaiah concerning the child, the son that was to be born, upon whose shoulders the government would rest, whose kingdom would manifest justice and righteousness forever (Isa. 9:6–7).

Righteousness by faith, righteousness in a person, was a consistent, if not totally understood and detailed, theme of the Old Testament prophets. And Paul is telling the Gentile and Jewish believers in Rome that his gospel is the gospel that brings to fruition that righteousness from God first proved by the law, then revealed by the prophets—the righteousness that can only come by faith.

B Righteousness: Comes Through Faith (3:22–24)

> **SUPPORTING IDEA:** *Because all have sinned, all can be justified freely by God's grace through Jesus Christ.*

In verses 22–24, Paul introduces a thought so contrary to Jewish and Gentile sensibilities as to be scandalous—an example of the clash of kingdoms at its best. The idea that the wicked could be **justified freely** was unheard of, not only in Rome but also in Israel. The iron-booted authority of Rome not only condemned the guilty but probably a lot who were innocent as well. But the eye-for-an-eye heritage of Paul's Jewish readers would likewise be brought to attention by his forthcoming words (though there were sufficient examples of grace and mercy in the Old Testament, e.g., David the king, had they been desirous of incorporating it into their worldview).

"Acquitting the innocent and condemning the guilty" (Deut. 25:1; see also Exod. 23:7) was the norm in Israel. If the guilty party was acquitted, it was often because an official had been bribed (Isa. 5:23). Paul's gospel was bringing an entirely new way of administering justice. Since everyone is guilty (Rom. 2:10), everyone deserves to be condemned in order for God to be just. God would become as unrighteous as the guilty if he overlooked their sins and did not condemn them. But what the world did not count on was a God who was both just *and* a justifier of the guilty. No one goes free without the penalty being paid. It is just that no one imagined that the judge would also pay the price.

Think of the millions upon millions of people in our world today who labor under consciences burdened by guilt. We know they do because Paul has told us their thoughts accuse them (Rom. 2:15) when they break God's laws. And think of the mental machinations they must go through, contemplating what to do about that which they have done wrong (we can know how they think because it is how we thought before receiving God's pardon). And then think what this guilt-removing gospel of grace could do to liberate them from the present and eternal penalties of sin!

When the heart of Paul's gospel, which is found in these three verses, becomes ever clearer in the eyes of teacher and preacher, there will be no end to the setting free of captives. Paul knew it, and wanted to free the spiritual captives not only in Rome but in Spain and beyond. And he wanted all who read his letter to the Romans to join him in revealing the **righteousness from God** which can become the righteousness man so desperately longs for and needs.

3:22. First, Paul says that **faith** is the key to receiving God's righteousness. Do not forget to connect this verse, and what Paul is declaring, with his original statement about the "righteousness from God" in 1:17. Think of it this way: "For in the gospel a righteousness from God is revealed, a righteousness that is by faith (1:17) . . . [and by the way, all are in need of this righteousness, whether Jew or Gentile (1:18–3:20)] . . . **This righteousness from God comes through faith in Jesus Christ to all who believe (3:22).**"

That is the essence of what Paul has said in Romans so far. Looked at another way:

I am writing, and coming to visit you, to minister the gospel to you.

The gospel reveals what the world needs more than it needs anything else: righteousness. The human race has forfeited its own righteousness (more about that in Romans 5) and can only look to God to regain righteous standing before him.

Contrary to the sanctimonious attempts of the Jews, and the bungled religiosity of the Gentiles, the only way to gain this righteousness is by faith in Jesus Christ. Forget everything else—faith is the key to standing on righteous ground before God.

And who can receive this righteousness? **All who believe. There is no difference.** We know that this is true when we look ahead to the closing chapters of the redemption story and see people "from every nation, tribe, people and language, standing before the throne and in front of the Lamb" (Rev. 7:9; see also 5:9; 14:6). The church of Jesus Christ should be the greatest force in the world for breaking down racial and ethnic barriers—and often it is. Unfortunately, the stories of the love of God pulling down centuries-old walls of division often go unheard. Instead, the news is filled with years of strife between Protestants and Catholics in Northern Ireland, or uneasy truces between black and white Christians in the American South. But Paul says that **there is no difference.** None is better than another. All receive righteousness the same way, **through faith in Jesus Christ.**

All men and women are made equal by three things: first, our equality in need (all are guilty). Second, our equality in what we receive (redemption is one gift; the same for all). Third, our equality in how we receive redemption (by faith; everyone receives it the same way). Equality in Christ represents a radical message from one who formerly prided himself on his rung on the ladder of racial respectability.

Combining Paul's words here (and in Rom. 10:12 and 1 Cor. 12:13) with those in Galatians (3:28), Colossians (3:11), and John's in Revelation (5:9;

7:9; 14:6), here are the differences common in Paul's day which the gospel ignores: Jew, Gentile, circumcised, uncircumcised, barbarian, Scythian, slave, free, male, female, language, ethnicity, racial stock, and tribe (people group). To these, we could add the differences that have become important in our day: weak, powerful, educated, uneducated, rich, poor, economically developed, economically deprived, sophisticated, or plain. Why do none of these distinctives matter in the eyes of God?

3:23. Note Paul's declaration, **For all have sinned and fall short of the glory of God.** The English bishop, Handley Moule, perhaps has put Paul's words in the most telling way of all: "The harlot, the liar, the murderer, are short of [God's glory]; but so are you. Perhaps they stand at the bottom of a mine, and you on the crest of an Alp; but you are as little able to touch the stars as they" (Stott, p. 109). The great deception, of course, comes when those on the Alps fail to see that their microcosmic advantage over their fellows in degrees of behavior removes their feet not an inch from the corrupt moral ground that they, and the worst sinner, stand on together.

Failure in a moral sense is the cause for righteousness having to come from God, according to Paul here. Jews and Gentiles have "all sinned" (aorist tense; a snapshot in time of the condition of the human race) and continue to **fall short** (present tense; a moving picture, a film, a video showing the continual failure of man to reflect the glory of God). When Paul says here that **all have sinned** (*pantes . . . hemarton*), he uses the same Greek words as he does in 5:12 when discussing the entrance of sin into the world through Adam, the father of the human race: "all sinned" (*pantes hemarton*).

To separate the two aorist phrases (both describe conditions), think of the 3:23 **all have sinned** as an "Activity Aorist" and the 5:12 "all sinned" as an "Adamic Aorist" (these are not in your Greek grammar!). In light of Paul's present tense **fall short** in 3:23, and in light of his just-concluded recitations of the actual sins of Jews and Gentiles, it seems that the **all have sinned** in 3:23 is a picture of mankind's sinful characteristics. The 5:12 "all sinned," on the other hand, seems to be a picture of mankind's inherited character as a sinner. In other words, by 5:12 Paul will have said that as descendants of Adam, mankind *is* a sinner and proves it by sinning. All of which causes him to **fall short of the glory of God.**

The concept of "falling short" of the **glory of God** is a good description of our modern Western cultures. The verb (*hustereo*) has root meanings of "come late," "be behind," "come short," deriving from the adverb for "latter" or "later." In other words, the image here is not one of absence, but one of always being behind. For the schedule-driven and time-warped modern, it is not difficult to conceive of what it means to constantly "be behind" in life's activities. We are in the race; we just do not ever win.

This image suggests something of what it means to **fall short of the glory of God.** Regardless of what we do we never seem to catch up to the **glory of God;** we are always behind. Meaning, because of our sin ("Adamic Aorist"), our sins ("Activity Aorist") constantly cause smudges to appear where glory should shine through. God's image, to be continually reflected in the earth through the creatures that bear its glory, is defaced and marred. Try as we might—good works, noble thoughts, kind gestures—we might as well, as Bishop Moule put it, be standing in the Alps trying to touch a star. We will always fall short. (On the glory of God in man see Gen. 1:26–28; Ps. 8:5–6; Isa. 43:7; Rom. 8:29; 1 Cor. 11:7; Eph. 4:24; Col. 3:10; Heb. 2:5–9; 1 John 3:2.)

It is the **all** of verse 23 that levels the playing field of the gospel. Since **all have sinned,** then all need justification. And since all need justification, all can have it—but only one way: **through faith in Jesus Christ.** John Wesley summarized well Paul's words up to this point: "Ye are saved (to comprise all in one word) from sin. This is the salvation which is through faith. This is that great salvation foretold by the angel, before God brought his first-begotten into the world: 'Thou shall call his name Jesus, for he shall save his people from their sins.' And neither here, nor in other parts of Holy Writ, is there any limitation or restriction. All his people, or as it is elsewhere expressed, 'all that believe in him,' he will save from all their sins; from original and actual, past and present sin, 'of the flesh and of the spirit.' Through faith that is in him, they are saved both from the guilt and from the power of it" (*Heritage,* p. 201).

3:24. The key to receiving God's righteousness—a righteous standing in his sight—is faith. The cause for God's having to provide righteousness for humankind is moral failure on our part. And now, Paul reveals the cost to those who are justified—it is provided free: **[we] are justified freely by his grace.**

What is free for us was not free for God, for we are justified **through the redemption that came by Christ Jesus.** The price God paid for our justification was incalculable, in that it involved the sacrifice of his Son. And it is also an offense to the human ego, as Oswald Chambers has observed: "There is a certain pride in people that causes them to give and give, but to come and accept a gift is another thing. I will give my life to martyrdom; I will dedicate my life to service—I will do anything. But do not humiliate me to the level of the most hell-deserving sinner and tell me that all I have to do is accept the gift of salvation through Jesus Christ" (Chambers, *My Utmost,* Nov. 28).

What does it mean that we **are justified?** It does not mean that God looks at me "just-as-if-I'd" never sinned. Hortatory hokum at best, it is bad theology at worst that drastically discounts what God has done in Jesus Christ. When God justifies—declares righteous—a guilty sinner, two things happen:

negatively, the sinner is declared no longer guilty of sin. Positively, the sinner is declared righteous. Not *made* righteous, but *declared* righteous. God cancels out the debt of guilt that is on the sinner's account and then credits righteousness to his or her account. Both actions must take place for justification to occur. To say that, once justified, God looks at sinners as if they had never sinned, discounts the worth of the sacrifice God offered to forgive our sin.

Charles Swindoll explains it this way: after a day of dirty yard work, a hot shower and a bar of soap renders one clean. It is tempting to say, "'Ah, it's just as if I'd never been dirty.' But that would not have adequately conveyed the power and the value of the water and soap. Better to look in the mirror and say, 'I was filthy and now I'm clean'" (Swindoll, p. 327). All one need do is look back in the first two chapters of Romans to realize exactly how much sin was cancelled and how much grace is required to declare sinners righteous. John Newton had it right in "Amazing Grace," when he marveled at the grace that "saved a wretch like me."

Paul uses forms of "justification" more than twenty times in Romans and Galatians. It is at the heart of the gospel. And the heart of justification is the crediting of one person's righteousness to the account of another. When Paul illustrates justification in Romans 4, he will use forms of the word "credit" ten times in that one chapter alone to drive home the point that our justification is a free gift. The righteousness of God, specifically that of his Son Jesus Christ, has been credited to the account of all who believe in him and what he accomplished by his death and resurrection. Why did God have to transfer the righteousness of Christ to our account? Because we have none of our own. We are totally unrighteous; Christ is totally righteous.

Everett Harrison explains why we are **justified freely by his grace** and illuminates the bankrupt nature of our own accounts. **Freely** is *dorean*, an adverb from *dorea*, a gift. Interestingly, *dorean* is used in John 15:25 when Jesus is characterizing those who hate him: "They hated me without reason (*dorean*)." When Paul says that we are **justified freely**, he is saying that we are "justified without reason" insofar as reasons that exist in the sinner. "God finds no reason, no basis, in the sinner for declaring him righteous. He must find the cause in himself" (Harrison, p. 42). Justification "expresses the judicial action of God apart from human merit according to which the guilty are pardoned, acquitted, and then reinstated as God's children and as fellow heirs with Jesus Christ" (Boice, *Galatians,* p. 449).

The motivation for God's justification of guilty sinners is **grace**. As has been rightly said, "If mercy is not getting what we do deserve, grace is getting what we don't deserve." Blaise Pascal said that "grace is indeed needed to turn a man into a saint, and he who doubts it does not know what a saint or a man is" (Ward, p. 130). Only grace could declare an unrighteous sinner righteous. The well-worn phrase, "But for the grace of God, there go I" regains its strength when one understands that the person who said it first was watching guilty criminals going to their death on the gallows. Perhaps John Bradford, the sixteenth-century English Protestant martyr, had Romans 3:24 in mind when, watching the death march, he said, "But for the grace of God there goes John Bradford" (Ward, p. 88).

The grace of God in our salvation was when God interrupted the death march, took us out of line, and took our place. As Deitrich Bonhoeffer reminds the church, "Grace is costly because it costs a man his life, and it is grace because it gives a man the only true life" (Ward, p. 205).

Justification comes through **redemption that came by Christ Jesus.** Fortunately, "redemption" was a term not lost on either Jews or Gentiles, for it was a term of the slave market. Historians believe that the population of first-century Rome was probably more than half slaves, so Gentiles in the church at Rome understood **redemption**—the process whereby a slave's freedom is purchased for a ransom price. For the Jews, in addition to having statutes governing the redemption of slaves (Lev. 25:47–53), their entire salvific history was bound up in their redemption out of slavery in Egypt (Exod. 15:13; Deut. 7:8; 9:26; 13:5 15:15; Neh. 1:10; Pss. 77:15; 78:42; Isa. 43:1; Mic. 6:4). What was new for both classes of humanity was that there is a slavery that all people are subject to for which there is only one ransom price.

Jesus himself confronted the Jews on this issue when they declared they were no one's slaves: "Jesus replied, 'I tell you the truth, everyone who sins is a slave to sin'" (John 8:34). This is the redemption that the gospel proclaims—freedom from slavery to sin purchased by the ransom price of Christ's own death.

Righteousness: Demonstrates God's Justice (3:25–26)

SUPPORTING IDEA: *God justifies the wicked by being both the judge and the sacrifice for sin.*

Paul's concern now is to answer the question, "How can God himself be called righteous, or just, if he simply declares the wicked righteous?" And it is a good question. The same God who seems to be holding sinners accountable for their wickedness appears not to be holding himself accountable with the same consistency. Imagine if a judge arbitrarily decided to pronounce a group of guilty lawbreakers innocent and reinstated them as members in good standing of the community. That judge would be guilty of the same inconsistency (injustice) that God could be accused of if he did a similar thing. Is that what he did when he "justified freely" those who sinned? It is Paul's purpose to demonstrate that while God is indeed **the one who justifies**, he is also **just** in doing so.

3:25a. Few passages of Scripture have had more ink spilled over them by theologians than Romans 3:25a. Critical commentaries are filled with the technical discussions that revolve around the meaning of the word *hilasterion*, translated in the NIV as "sacrifice of atonement," and in other translations as "propitiation" (e.g., KJV, NASB, NKJV). In our "Deeper Discoveries" section, we will comment on some of the finer points of this discussion, but here stay focused on the bigger picture, which is the role of the *hilasterion* in God's justifying of sinners. When God **presented** Jesus Christ as a *hilasterion*, "he did this to demonstrate his justice" (v. 25b). There is the crux of the issue raised in the question outlined above—the need to explain how God can justify sinners and remain just himself.

Here is the heart of the matter: when Paul calls Christ a *hilasterion*, he uses a Greek word which the translators of the Greek version of the Old Testament used more than twenty times to translate the Hebrew *kapporeth*. The *kapporeth* was the covering of the ark of the covenant in the holy of holies in the tabernacle and temple. As outlined in Leviticus 16, the high priest was to take the blood of the sacrificial bull (v. 14) and goat (v. 15) and sprinkle it on the cover of the ark of the covenant (*kapporeth*) in order to make atonement (*kipper*) for himself, his household, and the people. The ark of the covenant contained the tablets of the Ten Commandments representing God's moral and righteous standards which had been broken. But when the sacrificial animals were killed and their blood sprinkled over the cover of the ark, the broken laws of God were atoned for by the death of the animals instead of the death of the Israelites.

Leviticus 17 goes on to point out two critical factors: first, life is in the blood, and second, God initiated the sacrifice (v. 11). Therefore, God took it upon himself to initiate the exchange of life by the shedding of blood: the life of a "sinless" animal for the life of a sinless human.

When Paul then says that Christ became a *hilasterion*, he could be saying that Christ became the "mercy seat" (Heb. 9:5 NASB; "atonement cover," NIV) or he could be using the term simply to represent the atoning sacrifice (or propitiation) for our sins since in the tabernacle the sprinkling of sacrificial blood "turned away" (propitiated) the wrath of God. In either case, it is clear that Christ became the sinless sacrifice prefigured by the Old Testament sacrifices. And the effect on God's standards of righteousness? His standards were totally satisfied, allowing him to free those (redeem those) who were slaves in the marketplace of sin.

F. F. Bruce summarizes nicely by noting, "Paul has thus pressed into service the language of the lawcourt ('justified'), the slave-market ('redemption') and the altar ('expiation,' 'atoning sacrifice') in the attempt to do justice to the fullness of God's gracious act in Christ. Pardon, liberation, atonement—all are made available to men and women by his free initiative and may be appropriated by faith" (Bruce, pp. 101–102).

By believing in (having faith in) the efficacy of **his blood**, and the covering of God's broken law, a sinner is able to appropriate (have applied to his or her account) the righteous standing (the sinlessness) of the sacrifice, **Christ Jesus.** Do not forget that "the wrath of God is being revealed from heaven" (Rom. 1:18), and now that wrath has been propitiated, or turned away. God's wrath has been turned away from those who deserve it to one who did not deserve it.

Paul now anticipates another question: Why did God do this at this time?

3:25b. He did this to demonstrate two aspects of **his justice**—the first here and the second in verse 26. First, in order to avoid a charge of unrighteous mercy (inconsistent justice) arising from the past when sins had gone unpunished, or when sins were punished on a temporary basis. The Old Testament sacrifices were temporary and symbolic, not permanent and eternally effectual (as Heb. 9 points out). But now God has vindicated his mercy, because all the **sins committed beforehand**, temporarily and symbolically atoned for, have now been permanently atoned for—and justice has been served and demonstrated.

3:26. Second, he did it . . . to be just and the one who justifies, and in so doing reveals his own righteous character. This is the final answer to the question of God's own justice (righteousness). If he had forgiven sin without a sacrifice, the charge of injustice would be valid. But because a sacrifice was made for sin—and because he himself initiated and provided the sacrifice— he is both **just and the one who justifies those who have faith in Jesus.** The righteousness of God that demanded a payment for sin is demonstrated by his own provision of the payment.

Paul uses diatribe again in verses 27–30 to illustrate why God's justice leaves man totally in his debt, as Francis Schaeffer illustrates:

> Our faith has no saving value. Our religious good works, our moral good works, have no saving value because they are not perfect. Our suffering has no saving value. We would have to suffer infinitely, because we have sinned against an infinite God; and we, being finite, cannot suffer infinitely. The only thing in all of God's moral universe that has the power to save is the finished work of Jesus Christ. Our faith merely accepts the gift. And God justifies all those who believe in Jesus (3:26). If all this is true, then verse 27 is certainly an understatement. (Schaeffer, p. 81)

Ⓓ Righteousness: Excludes Boasting (3:27–31)

SUPPORTING IDEA: *When sinners are justified by God's grace, there is no room to boast except in God and his righteousness.*

3:27–28. Paul enters into dialogue again with an imaginary opponent who is struggling with the idea that humans can contribute nothing to their own salvation. There is no room to boast when one is given a gift. **Faith**, in simple terms, is simply saying "Yes" to God's gift of redemption and justification through Christ. **Faith** is agreeing with God that his plan of salvation is the one that saves. It is absolutely incongruous for a person to have **faith** and then boast about **observing the law** as an instrument of salvation. It would be the same as receiving a valuable birthday present and then insulting the giver by insisting on paying for it yourself. Once the item was paid for by you, it ceases to be a gift. Only when it is totally paid for by another, and received by you "by 'Yes' alone" (by faith alone), is it a gift. Only at that point is boasting excluded.

The believer who insists on boasting that something he or she has done has contributed to salvation has not understood Paul. For he maintains **that a man is justified by faith apart from observing the law.** If there is any boasting to be done, it is only in the one who gives the gift.

Martin Luther gave his opponents in the church further cause to persecute him when he added the word "alone" to his translation of verse 28 into German. "Alone" is not in the Greek text and it certainly does not violate the spirit of Paul's words. But when Luther wrote that **a man is justified by faith** "alone" (*sola fide* in Latin), he created one of the three great rallying cries of the Reformation: *sola fide* (faith alone), *sola gratia* (grace alone), and *sola scriptura* (Scripture alone). Interestingly, when John Wesley encountered Luther's commentary on Romans in 1783, in the dark hours of his own pilgrimage to genuine faith, he recounts, "I felt I did trust in Christ, Christ alone for salvation." So Luther's, and ultimately the Reformation's, focus on a singular object (Christ) and a singular instrument (faith) of salvation ultimately served the church well.

3:29–30. Boasting is also excluded by the unity of the salvation God offers. That is, his salvation is for everyone who believes. The **same faith** that is the instrument for the justification of the Gentiles is the instrument for the justification of the Jews—and vice versa. How inappropriate is it to boast about achieving something that has been given as a gift to the whole human race? The boaster ends up embarrassing himself and revealing his lack of understanding of the gift that has been provided.

3:31. Finally, boasting is excluded by the law itself. While this may sound contradictory on the surface, here is the point: it is the law which shows people that they have failed in all points to be righteous, forcing them to the conclusion that they must accept righteousness as a free gift of God. The law says, "You have nothing to boast in and I can prove it!"—and then proceeds to name all the places in which we have failed morally. Therefore, the free "gift of God" (Rom. 6:23) is the only way that we can attain salvation, and it took the law to reveal it. Therefore, the law serves the gospel by removing all boasting about how one might be saved.

As a result, Paul says, **we uphold the law.** No less a giant in the faith than Augustine instructed Martin Luther in upholding the law:

> Through the Law God opens man's eyes so that he sees his helplessness and by faith takes refuge to His mercy and so is healed. . . . The Law was given, in order that we might seek after grace. Grace was given, in order that we might fulfill the Law. It was not the fault of the Law that it was not fulfilled, but the fault was man's carnal mind. This guilt the Law must make manifest, in order that we may be healed by divine grace. (Luther, p. 77)

Religious rituals and ceremonies can be insidious temptations to divert people from the path of salvation by faith. The monk Martin Luther, constrained by self-imposed limitations in every area of life, faced many temptations, not the least of which was the temptation to view righteousness as something of his own doing: "As wealth is the test of poverty, business the test of faithfulness, honours the test of humility, feasts the test of temperance, pleasures the test of chastity, so ceremonies are the test of the righteousness of [by] faith" (Ward, p. 99). Fortunately for the sake of the gospel, Luther, like Paul, by the grace of God broke free from a salvation by works and embraced the truth of redemption and justification by grace through faith in Jesus Christ.

MAIN IDEA REVIEW: *Because the human race is completely unrighteous, the instigation for providing righteousness had to come from God. God satisfied his own standards of righteousness by offering a righteous sacrifice (his Son) for the sins of humankind. Every person who embraces by faith what God has done can be declared righteous in his sight.*

III. CONCLUSION

The Penalty Must Be Paid

Cliff Barrows, the long-time song leader at Billy Graham Evangelistic Association crusades, tells a story about how his children learned to appreciate the price that Jesus paid for their sins. When they were small, the children persisted in doing something that they had been forbidden to do. Mr. Barrows told his children that if they violated the standard again, they would be disciplined for their actions. Upon returning home, a saddened father discovered that his children had yet again disobeyed their father. But the thought of spanking them overcame him.

"I just couldn't discipline them," he said. "Bobby and Bettie Ruth were very small. I called them into my room, took off my belt and then my shirt, and with a bare back I knelt down at the bed. I made them both strap me with the belt ten times each. You should have heard the crying. From them, I mean. The crying was from them. They did not want to do it. But I told them the penalty had to be paid and so through their sobs and tears they did what I told them . . . . I must admit I was not much of a hero. It hurt. I have not offered to do that again. It was a once-for-all sacrifice, I guess we could say, but I never had to spank those two children again, because they got the point. We kissed each other. And when it was over we prayed together" (Swindoll, pp. 543–544).

In Romans 3:21–31 Paul demonstrates how God can remain righteous while he declares guilty sinners righteous. How can he be just and a justifier of the wicked? It can only be done if the price for their wickedness is paid. Just as no slave can be redeemed out of the bondage of slavery for sin without the payment of a ransom price, so no sinful human being can be released from the guilt of sin without a penalty for that sin being paid. Cliff Barrows declared his own children "righteous" after the penalty for their sin had been paid. But he did not spank the family dog or cat. He did not recruit an innocent neighbor to come in and take his children's punishment. Rather, he stooped down to their level and received upon himself the penalty that they deserved. And this, Paul says, is what God in Christ has done for us.

"What do righteousness and wickedness have in common? Or what fellowship can light have with darkness?" Paul asked in 2 Corinthians 6:14. A righteous God and his unrighteous creation cannot fellowship together. They will be forever separated by an unbridgeable chasm created by sin. But when God took the initiative and bridged the gap, fellowship was restored. Just as Cliff Barrows kissed and prayed with his children after initiating and receiving in himself the penalty for their sin, so we can have fellowship with God through faith in the one who paid the penalty for our sin.

While "righteousness and wickedness" have nothing in common, "righteousness and righteousness" have everything in common. When a believer is declared righteous by a righteous God through the atoning sacrifice of Jesus Christ, the two can be united in a righteous and eternal fellowship.

PRINCIPLES

- Securing right standing before God is a central theme of Scripture throughout the Old and New Testaments.
- The cross of Christ has always been the ultimate object of genuine saving faith.
- Because all people obtain an unrighteous standing before God the same way, they must obtain a right standing before God the same way: through faith in Christ.

- Right standing before God is obtained freely by God's grace or not at all.
- Without the shed blood of Christ, there would have been no atonement for sin.
- There is a judicial basis for the exercise of God's mercy.
- Because we receive, rather than achieve, right standing before God, boasting is excluded.
- The law is the servant of the gospel by pointing out the human inability to achieve right standing before God by one's self.

APPLICATIONS

- When I see the people around me, do I see them in terms of their standing before God?
- Do I ever misplace my personal faith, directing it to any thing or any person other than Christ's work on the cross?
- Have I ever watered down the gospel by suggesting to others that there is a way to please God outside of faith in Christ?
- Does receiving God's grace as a free gift cause my pride to rebel?
- How often do I meditate on the infinite price that Jesus Christ paid by willingly shedding his own blood to secure my salvation?
- Am I willing to absorb the cost of wrongs done to me by others so that I might extend mercy to them?
- Is my right standing before God a source of pride, or humility, for me?
- When I encounter standards which, in my flesh, I do not want to obey, do I allow them to motivate me to seek God's enabling to do the right thing?

IV. LIFE APPLICATION

Awakening in Aldersgate

Two centuries after Martin Luther fanned into flame a spark of faith that ignited the Protestant Reformation in Germany, two brothers at Oxford University in England were struggling to find the reality of faith in Christ. Charles Wesley and his friends, later to be joined by John Wesley, met regularly together as a group that came to be called "the Holy Club." Their purpose was religious, their activities commendable in every way. They engaged in public and private good works, the study of sacred literature, mutual accountability, and deeds of generosity toward others, all apparently to make better their chances for salvation.

The Wesley brothers left Oxford in 1735 on their most serious attempt yet at good works—to preach the gospel in America as chaplains to the settlers and missionaries to the Indians in the primitive region. After two years, thoroughly discouraged, they returned to England. The only positive reflection with which they returned was of the vitality of the faith of some Moravians they encountered on their journey.

Back in London, on May 24, 1738, John Wesley begrudgingly attended a Moravian meeting in Aldersgate Street where the leader was reading from Martin Luther's preface to his commentary on Romans. From John Wesley's own journal comes his testimony: "About a quarter before nine, while he was describing the change which God works in the heart through faith in Christ, I felt my heart strangely warmed. I felt I did trust in Christ, Christ alone, for salvation; and an assurance was given me that he had taken away *my* sins, even *mine,* and saved *me* from the law of sin and death." Wesley later recounted how he felt he had exchanged "the faith of a *servant*" for "the faith of a *son,*" realizing that he could never do enough works to receive salvation but that he must receive it as a gift from God.

Lest any should doubt whether Luther's spark had found dry tinder in the heart of Wesley, listen to the words Wesley preached just twenty-five days later on June 18, 1738, in the chapel at St. Mary's, Oxford University:

> For this reason the adversary so rages whenever "salvation by faith" is declared to the world; for this reason did he stir up earth and hell: to destroy those who first preached it. And for the same reason, knowing that faith alone could overturn the foundations of his kingdom, did he call forth all his forces and employ all his arts of lies and calumny to affright that champion of the Lord of hosts, Martin Luther, from reviving it. Nor can we wonder thereat; for as that man of God observes, "How would it enrage a proud strong man armed to be stopped and set at nought by a little child coming against him with a reed in his hand?" (*Heritage,* p. 205)

Martin Luther was like a little child with a reed who enraged the adversary of the gospel in the sixteenth century by proclaiming *sola fide*—salvation by faith alone. A reformation was begun, and was continued by the Wesleys, Whitefield, and others after them, proclaiming the heart of the gospel from Romans 3:21–31. The question now is whether the gospel of the apostle Paul that awakened the heart of John Wesley will awaken and quicken the heart of those who study Romans today?

As a teacher, will you allow the simplicity of the gospel—salvation through faith in Christ—to be the heart of what you teach? And will you fan the spark of salvation by faith in the hearts of your students? Some may be like Luther and Wesley, laboring under the yoke of servanthood, seeing God as a taskmaster who counted their good works, always bringing a report that they had not yet done enough to be saved. Others may just be beginning to grasp the kingdom reality that in God's economy there is no work for salvation but only faith. And still others may have already entered into that Wesleyan experience of "sonship," receiving gratefully that gift that only sons and daughters can receive.

As a teacher, with the Word of God in hand and the Spirit of God in heart, you are in the enviable position of potentially igniting a reformation of faith where you live and minister. Your pulpit, your lectern, your counseling room can be a modern day Aldersgate as you read Romans to hearts ready to be awakened! Seize the moment, and unleash on a needy world a new generation of Wesleys who see that "Christ, Christ alone" is their only hope.

V. PRAYER

Heavenly Father, I ask that the reality of your gift of salvation by grace through faith in Christ may plumb unreached depths of praise and gratitude in my own heart. Thank you, Lord Jesus Christ, for descending to the depths of my need and taking upon yourself the penalty and punishment for my sins. May you give me such understanding and humble appreciation for your gospel that those who hear my teaching will be compelled to discover and embrace the Christ of Romans, and share his gospel with others. Amen.

VI. DEEPER DISCOVERIES

A. Justification (3:24)

Justification is the doctrine for which Romans is most famous—and rightly so. Paul uses some form of the verb *dikaioo*, "to declare righteous," fifteen times in Romans (and the noun form, *dikaiosis*, twice) compared to twelve other usages in his other epistles combined. Several distinctives concerning justification should be noted in order to be faithful to the sense in which Paul uses it.

First, justification means "declare or pronounce righteous," not "make righteous." That is, the word is a forensic term from the courtroom which declares legal standing, not a moral term from the counseling room which declares ethical standing. It is obvious that every justified believer has not been completely morally transformed; they are still sinners. It is the suggested contradiction between God's declaring righteous those who are still in some ways morally unrighteous that has caused erroneous understanding of justification. In the New Testament, moral transformation and development is an issue of sanctification, not justification. Justification declares one righteous in the sight of God because of a choice of the will of God in a moment.

Sanctification through the Word of God and the Holy Spirit motivates the will of the believer to choose that which is consistent with the righteousness of God over time.

Second, justification does not mean forgiveness. Forgiveness is akin to pardon, which is the taking away or removing of a debt or penalty. Justification is a positive action that credits with a new status. Stott cites two helpful sources: Marcus Loane indicates that forgiveness says, "You may go; you have been let off the penalty which your sin deserves." Justification says, "You may come; you are welcome to all my love and my presence." Also, theologian Charles Hodge stated, "To condemn is not merely to punish, but to declare the accused guilty or worthy of punishment; and justification is not merely to remit that punishment, but to declare that punishment cannot be justly inflicted . . . Pardon and Justification therefore are essentially distinct. The one is the remission of punishment, the other is a declaration that no ground for the infliction of punishment exists" (Stott, p. 110). First Corinthians 6:11 is a helpful verse for viewing justification in the context of salvation along with forgiveness and positional sanctification.

Third, the ground of justification is in God, not man. It is clear from Romans 1:18–3:20 (specifically 3:10–18) that the unrighteousness of the human race would never allow anyone to be declared righteous on the ground of his or her own merit. Therefore, the ground of righteousness must be found outside man, which means God. It is the merit of Christ which becomes the ground of any person's justification. Paul uses the term "in Christ" to picture the believer as being identified with the righteousness of Christ. In spite of our sin, "there is now no condemnation for those who are in Christ Jesus" (Rom. 8:1). In spite of our sin, "if anyone is in Christ . . . the old has gone, the new has come!" (2 Cor. 5:17). In spite of our sin, we have "been given fullness in Christ" (Col. 2:10). This is further reason for why Paul says that all boasting is excluded.

B. Sacrifice of Atonement (Propitiation) (3:25)

The Greek word for sacrifice of atonement, as mentioned in the commentary section, is *hilasterion*. Besides its use in Romans 3:25 it occurs elsewhere in the New Testament only in Hebrews 9:5 where it is rendered "the atonement cover" in the NIV. It is a technical term taken from the Old Testament, referring almost always to the cover of the ark of the covenant. *Hilasmos* is a related word, meaning "propitiation," and is used in 1 John 2:2 and 4:10. The verb *hilaskomai* means "to make propitiation" and occurs in Luke 18:13 ("have mercy") and Hebrews 2:17 ("make atonement for").

The question surrounding this word in Romans 3:25 regards its meaning and how that meaning is to be reflected in the English (or other) languages.

The primary question is whether Paul intended to picture Christ as the sacrifice (as a perfect lamb), the place of sacrifice (as the mercy seat, or cover of the ark), and the priest (by offering himself) all at the same time. His statement in 3:25 that God "presented him" as a *hilasterion* argues for taking mercy seat as the meaning since Paul is comparing Christ as a public "mercy seat" to the mercy seat in the tabernacle which was concealed in the holy of holies and seen only by the high priest. Others feel that, in spite of Christ's having been compared to other inanimate objects (door, vine, water, bread, etc.), the complicated picture of focusing several salvific images in one word is beyond what even the theologian Paul would have done.

In addition, the question of propitiation and appeasement versus expiation is an issue. A minority of theologians feel that appeasement, and to a lesser degree propitiation, attributes pagan characteristics to God, suggesting rage and anger which must be satisfied by a sacrifice. They would prefer expiation (forgiveness) instead. This incorrect view of propitiation fails to account for the wrath of God which is clearly set forth by Paul in the early chapters of Romans—a wrath grounded in righteousness, not personal arbitrariness. When God is propitiated by the sacrifice of Christ, his justified wrath is immediately turned away once and for all. The one-time nature of the *hilasterion* argues for propitiation as the correct view.

The majority of evangelical commentators follow either the NIV ("sacrifice of atonement") or the NASB and other translations (propitiation) in translating *hilasterion*. This reflects their view that Paul did not picture Christ as the mercy seat (the covering of the ark) but as the atoning sacrifice by virtue of his blood being shed.

C. The Relationship of Redemption, Propitiation, and Justification

These three key words are crucial to the theological import of Paul's argument in Romans. Yet a failure to keep the subject and object of each distinct from the others can lead to error. James M. Boice has presented in graphic form the relationship between the three terms that is valuable enough to reproduce as a teaching aid. It is taken from his commentary on Romans (Boice, 1:380–382).

Simply put, the Son propitiates the Father by turning away the Father's wrath toward the believer's sin. The Son also redeems the believer by paying the price with his own blood for his or her redemption from slavery to sin. And the Father justifies believers by declaring them righteous on the basis of the death of Christ as the payment for sin. This "Salvation Triangle" (Boice's term) clearly illustrates the relationship between these three great theological concepts in Romans 3:21–31.

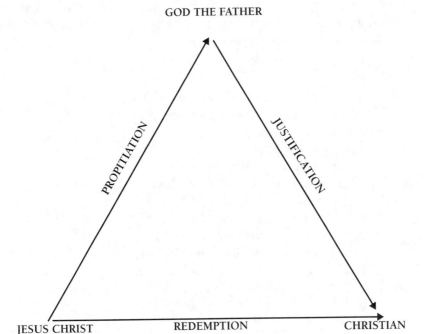

GOD THE FATHER

PROPITIATION

JUSTIFICATION

JESUS CHRIST   REDEMPTION   CHRISTIAN

VII. TEACHING OUTLINE

A. INTRODUCTION

1. Lead Story: The Business of God

2. Context: Paul is working his way through an in-depth presentation of the gospel to the believers in Rome. In 1:18–3:20 he presents conclusive evidence that God is justified in revealing his wrath against the human race because all, Jew and Gentile alike, are guilty of suppressing the knowledge of him that they have been given. This is the first step in a presentation of the good news of the gospel—acknowledging the bad news that man has sinned and deserves the judgment of God. Having concluded his presentation of the "bad news," Paul now turns to the "good news"—the remedy to the terrible spiritual condition of all people.

3. Transition: Paul provides his own transitional phrase, "but now" in 3:21, to move from the unrighteousness of humankind to the righteousness of God. What fate awaits a human race toward whom the righteous wrath of God has been directed? The only solution is for his wrath to be "turned away"—directed elsewhere—lest the human race perish. It is this remarkable solution which Paul undertakes to

explain in the next eleven verses of Romans. God took it upon himself to turn his wrath away from those who deserve it, and turn it in a most unexpected direction!

B. COMMENTARY

1. Righteousness: Made Known in the Old Testament (3:21)
2. Righteousness: Comes Through Faith (3:22–24)
    a. Faith is the key (3:22)
    b. Failure is the cause (3:23)
    c. Free is the cost (3:24)
3. Righteousness: Demonstrates God's Justice (3:25–26)
    a. Justice explains sacrifice (3:25a)
    b. Justice vindicates mercy (3:25b)
    c. Justice reveals character (3:26)
4. Righteousness: Excludes Boasting (3:27–31)
    a. Boasting excluded by faith (3:27–28)
    b. Boasting excluded by unity (3:29–30)
    c. Boasting excluded by the law (3:31)

C. CONCLUSION: AWAKENING IN ALDERSGATE

VIII. ISSUES FOR DISCUSSION

1. What are the subtle, invisible "walls" within the church of Jesus Christ that reveal there are still "differences" in how we view one another? (See v. 22.) Compare and contrast the difference between how God sees people and how people see people.
2. What are the three most glaring ways that Christians as a whole (the church at large) continue to fall short of the glory of God? How can we bring glory to God even in our failures?
3. What is the difference between "free grace" and "cheap grace?" How can believers avoid cheapening the grace of God that comes to them freely?
4. What norms in a modern, prosperous society can influence the way believers think about performing to earn the grace of God? How can these temptations lead to subtle forms of spiritual "boasting?"

Romans 4:1–25

Faith: What the Gospel Requires

I. INTRODUCTION
The Power of a Picture

II. COMMENTARY
A verse-by-verse explanation of the chapter.

III. CONCLUSION
Abraham Lives!

An overview of the principles and applications from the chapter.

IV. LIFE APPLICATION
How to Amaze Jesus

Melding the chapter to life.

V. PRAYER
Tying the chapter to life with God.

VI. DEEPER DISCOVERIES
Historical, geographical, and grammatical enrichment of the commentary.

VII. TEACHING OUTLINE
Suggested step-by-step group study of the chapter.

VIII. ISSUES FOR DISCUSSION
Zeroing the chapter in on daily life.

"*M*aking grace believable to the contemporary reader is the almost insurmountable problem of the novelist who writes from the standpoint of Christian orthodoxy."

F l a n n e r y   O ' C o n n o r

Romans 4:1–25

IN A NUTSHELL

*R*omans 4 serves as an illustration for the truth presented in Romans 3, culminating in verse 28: "A man is justified by faith apart from observing the law." To prove his point, Paul calls on the most revered figure in Judaism, Abraham, and demonstrates that Abraham was justified (declared righteous) by God on the basis of faith, not works.

Faith: What the Gospel Requires

I. INTRODUCTION

The Power of a Picture

If Flannery O'Connor thought that explaining grace is difficult for modern writers (see her quote at the beginning of this chapter), think of the challenge the apostle Paul had! Fortunately for Paul, he knew well the teaching traits of the two wisest teachers the world has ever known: Solomon and Jesus. No one came close to their pedagogical prowess for wisdom, brevity, the turn of a phrase, and the ability to draw—and keep—a crowd. And the one thing they did best (see below), Paul employs in Romans 4.

God had given Solomon (at his request; 2 Chr. 1:10–12) "wisdom and knowledge" to govern the people of Israel, in addition to great wealth, riches, and honor. As it turned out, "Solomon's wisdom was greater than the wisdom of all the men of the East, and greater than all the wisdom of Egypt." The fame of his wisdom "spread to all the surrounding nations," probably in the form of his three thousand proverbs and more than a thousand songs. He taught not only about human life, but about botany, biology, and zoology. Kings in every country sent representatives to listen to Solomon's wisdom (see 1 Kgs. 4:30–34). The queen of Sheba came herself from Arabia to test Solomon with hard questions, and "nothing was too hard for him to explain to her" (2 Chr. 9:2). She got twice what she expected (2 Chr. 9:6).

Unlike Solomon, Jesus used a two-pronged approach to teaching: words and works. His miracles obviously attracted large crowds, but there is plenty of evidence to indicate that his words furrowed brows all over Israel; people had never heard a teacher like Jesus, and they hung on his every word (in no small part because they loved to see him confound those who prided themselves as the teachers of Israel; e.g., Matt. 23:13,15,23,25,27,29,34). The authority with which Jesus spoke was in sharp contrast to the authority present in their own teachers (Matt. 7:29). They would gather in large numbers from all over Judea, and from as far away as Tyre and Sidon, to hear him teach (Luke 6:17–18) and heal. When he taught in the temple courts, the Jews were amazed at his words and wondered, "How did this man get such learning without having studied?" (John 7:15).

There is no question that Solomon and Jesus were master teachers. And if there is one technique that stands as a common denominator for both, it is the use of comparison. A simile—the use of "like" or "as" to compare unlike things; the known illuminating the unknown—was their favorite tool. For instance, Solomon said that a man without self-control is *like* a city whose walls are broken down (Prov. 25:28). Everyone in Solomon's day immediately knew the dangers posed by a city with broken-down walls, whereas the moral dangers of a lack of self-control were more abstract. So the dangers of the known (broken down walls) illumines the dangers of the lesser known (an intemperate person).

Similarly, Jesus said that the kingdom of God was *like* many things: a sower of good seed, a mustard seed, yeast, hidden treasure, a merchant, and a fishing net—all well-known in his day (Matt. 13). The kingdom of God, as Jesus was presenting it, was unknown; so he used the known to cast the light of understanding on the unknown. The use of similes was (and is) a powerful teaching tool. When one can point to a concrete example to shed light on an abstract concept, understanding is aided.

While Paul does not use "like" or "as" to introduce Romans 4, he is on the same pedagogical path as Solomon and Jesus. He has just concluded what many commentators believe is the most important part of Romans, or the New Testament, or world literature (depending on who you ask; see the "Introduction" to the last chapter). And it is not easy material, given the content and the audience. First, this was all new to the Gentiles. They were the fresh-scrubbed recruits to this movement called "the Way" (Acts 9:2), and Paul laid the gospel out for them step-by-step. But neither was it easy for the Jews, Paul's own religious kin. They were hearing things in Romans 1–3 that perhaps furrowed their brows like Jesus' teaching did the brows of their Jerusalem brethren years before.

Like every good teacher or preacher, Paul needed an illustration—a concrete example of what it means to be justified by faith apart from the works of the law (his topic in Rom. 3). It had to have the authority of God, and it had to appeal to both Gentiles and Jews. And it had to prove—absolutely—that justification and righteousness come by the instrumentality of faith. Abraham was perfect! He was a Gentile—a pagan Chaldean—who was credited with righteousness as a result of his faith, and who then became the most revered faith-and-father-figure in Jewish history. His credibility was along the lines of "Abraham said it, I believe it, and that settles it" in Israel.

So Romans 4 is where Paul presents his concrete illustration of justification by faith. The known (Abraham) is the illuminator of the unknown (how a person is justified before God apart from the works of the law, whether Jew or Gentile). By showing how Abraham was credited with righteousness by faith, Paul wants the Roman believers to learn that the gospel—in which the righteousness of God is revealed—requires faith, not works, as a response.

II. COMMENTARY

Faith: What the Gospel Requires

MAIN IDEA: *Abraham established the priority of faith over works for every Jew or Gentile after him who sought righteousness from God.*

A Abraham: The Forefather of Faith (4:1–8)

SUPPORTING IDEA: *Both Abraham and his descendant, King David, enjoyed the status of righteousness solely by believing God.*

Paul's setup for chapter 4 of Romans begins in 3:28: "For we maintain that a man is justified by faith apart from observing the law." The "we" is an editorial/apostolic "we" that without question carried weight. But Paul knew that there was a far weightier voice that could speak to this issue than his, and he invokes this voice in 4:1. As if he knew what the British lexicographer Samuel Johnson would one day say—"Example is always more efficacious than precept"—Paul proceeds to use Abraham as his prime example of righteousness by faith.

4:1–3. The most influential voice in Judaism was the voice of "father Abraham," so Paul suggests to his readers that they poll the patriarch on the matter of faith: **What then shall we say that Abraham, our forefather, discovered in this matter** [the matter of faith versus works]? The testimony of the founder of the faith would have far-reaching importance.

From Jesus' interaction with the Jews it was plain just how revered Abraham was in the nation of Israel. On one occasion, the Jews were about to give Jesus the "Abraham-is-our-father" defense when he cut them off in mid-whine, saying, for all practical purposes, "Prove it: act like Abraham and you can call him your father" (see John 8:39). On another occasion, the Jews suggested to Jesus that he was making himself out to be greater than the greatest person in Israel, Abraham. "Who do you think you are?" they asked Jesus, implying that no one is greater than "our father Abraham" (John 8:53).

Acknowledging Abraham's rightful place in Israel's Hall of Fame, Jesus himself pictured the patriarch as the one who received a poor beggar in paradise when he died (Luke 16:22) and who rebuked the rich man who cried out from hell for mercy (Luke 16:25). All persons considered, Abraham's experience with God would be the perfect illustration for Paul to use with the believers in Rome. The Jewish believers would be obligated to yield to Abraham's precedent-setting example because he was the father of their previous faith. And the Gentile believers would have no reason *not* to yield to his authority. Though not physical descendants of Abraham, they clearly would be aware of his role in the development of the Jewish-Christian faith that Paul was writing about.

Though he does not use the same words here, Paul told the Galatian believers in his letter to them that God "announced the gospel in advance to Abraham" (Gal. 3:8). Paul makes the same argument in Romans 4 (absent the use of the word *gospel*) to prove that the gospel he is preaching is the same gospel that Abraham received (in Gen. 12:3) and believed: all people on earth will be blessed through Abraham's faithfulness to God.

In verse 2 Paul says that Abraham could have boasted if he had been declared righteous for his works—**but not** boasted **before God.** Paul's point (which he had already made in Rom. 2:10–18) is that God justifies no one on the basis of works because no one's works are righteous—period. The implication is that only by faith could Abraham have been justified by God. And **what does the Scripture say?** Paul quotes Genesis 15:6 to prove that Abraham was counted as righteous when he **believed God.** The church father Origen, in his *Commentary on the Epistle to the Romans,* reasoned it syllogistically (brackets added):

"This is a rhetorical argument, which goes like this:

[MAJOR PREMISE:] Someone who is justified by works has nothing to boast of before God.

[MINOR PREMISE:] But Abraham did have something to glory in before God.

[CONCLUSION:] Therefore he was justified by faith and not by works" (Bray, p. 109).

Genesis 15:6 is profoundly important in developing a theology of salvation, which is obviously why Paul uses it here. Think of Abraham's situation at the time of his interaction with God in Genesis 15. As far as we know, his experience with God had been minimal. He had somehow been called (led) from his home and pagan background in Ur (or was Abraham a worshiper of the one true God in Mesopotamia, like the monotheistic Melchizedek, king of Salem, whom he was soon to encounter in Canaan?), and several years later ended up in Canaan where he received promises from God about future blessings.

After a less-than-noble sojourn in Egypt, Abraham and his wife and household returned to Canaan, where he rescued his nephew Lot from marauding kings. But even then he demonstrated a level of integrity that foreshadowed the nature of his heart—he refused to profit illegitimately from his victory over the kings (Gen. 14:21–24). After this, the Lord spoke to him and confirmed the promise of multitudinous descendants—as many as the stars in the sky—and **Abraham believed God, and it was credited to him as righteousness.**

Thomas à Kempis, the fifteenth-century German writer, could have been thinking of Abraham when he wrote, "What is required of you is faith and a sincere life, not loftiness of intellect or deep knowledge of the mysteries of God." Abraham was doubtless intelligent, but just how deep could his knowledge of the mysteries of God have been at the time he placed his faith in his word? He believed God on the basis of what he knew of God at that point. Somehow, as Andrew Murray learned, "Faith expects from God what is beyond all expectation" (cf. Eph. 3:20) (Ward, p. 184).

Simple faith resulted in righteousness being credited to Abraham. Nearly two millennia after Abraham, Paul tells the Romans that righteousness comes the same way for them and for all who hear the gospel—including us, who read his letter nearly four millennia after Abraham. God is indeed the same "yesterday and today and forever" (Heb. 13:8).

4:4–5. The line of demarcation between wages and gifts is work. When one **works**, he or she gets what is deserved—wages come **as an obligation**. When one does not work, there is no **obligation** to be given anything. Anything that is received originates in grace and is delivered **as a gift**. Such is **righteousness** from God. Man's work has been faulty (unrighteous); therefore, there is no **obligation** to be "paid" with a wage—**credited as righteousness**. If we are **credited** with **righteousness**, it is only because we have believed God's assessment of our situation and his promises and received righteousness as a gift.

4:6–8. If Abraham, the father of Israel, sets the precedent for this early in the Book of Genesis, David, the king of Israel, later confirms it in the psalms. Note Paul's words in verse 5: "God who justifies the wicked." We do not normally think of **the wicked** when we first think of David, Israel's shepherd-king. But do not miss Paul's point: for the first two chapters of Romans he discusses the wicked in detail, and now is going to give us an example of a wicked person who was justified by faith. But **David? David** who defeated Goliath, who honored a demonized king Saul, who kept his promises to Jonathan, who danced and worshiped before the Lord, who wrote Israel's greatest hymns?

Yes, **David.** Just as with Abraham, Paul is choosing another of Israel's most beloved (the meaning of "David" in Hebrew) forefathers to show that not even those in the Hall of Fame have enough works to justify them before God.

Paul's quotation from David is from Psalm 32, a liturgical psalm of thanksgiving for God's discipline that led to confession and forgiveness. Many Bible students suggest this psalm is tied to David's sordid situation with Bathsheba and Uriah, her husband (see Ps. 51 for another post-Bathsheba psalm). David lusted after Uriah the Hittite's wife, used regal authority to procure her, committed adultery with her, deceived Uriah, and arranged for his murder (2 Sam. 10–12). See if you think any of the terms Paul used to describe the wicked in Romans 1:28–31 could apply to this web of sin spun by Israel's "beloved": "greed," "envy," "murder," "deceit," "arrogant," "invent ways of doing evil," "faithless," "heartless," and "ruthless."

If anyone sinned seriously, David did. But if anyone had enough works in his righteousness account to offset his sin and receive righteousness as an obligation, David did as well (that is, if sort-of-righteous was God's standard, which it is not). Apparently, God credited **righteousness** to **David** (Rom. 4:6) because his **transgressions are forgiven**, his **sins are covered**, and **the Lord will never count against him** anything he had done. But on what basis? We know it was **apart from works**, because the only thing David did was to agree with God (exercise faith) about what he had done and how he must be forgiven—as a gift of God's grace.

When Nathan the prophet came to David and exposed David's sin and duplicity, David said, "I have sinned against the LORD." As soon as David agreed with God by faith, Nathan said, "The LORD has taken away your sin" (2 Sam. 12:13). Whether it was his sins with Bathsheba and Uriah that he refers to in Psalm 32 or some other sin, David confirms the prophet's pattern in his own words: "I acknowledged my sin to you and did not cover up my iniquity. I said, 'I will confess my transgressions to the LORD'—and you forgave the guilt of my sin" (Ps. 32:5). Then follow in his psalm the words quoted by Paul on the blessedness of receiving **righteousness apart from works**.

Abraham and David—from the mouth of two witnesses (and Paul makes three; see Deut. 17:6; 19:15; Matt. 18:16; 2 Cor. 13:1; 1 Tim. 5:19; Heb. 10:28) comes the fact that, under the old covenant and the new covenant, man is justified only one way before God: by faith. About this time in Paul's letter to the Romans, those Gentile believers hearing it for the first time were probably itching to ask Paul a question. He takes the words right out of their minds: "Is this blessedness only for the circumcised, or also for the uncircumcised?" (v. 9). Like a good teacher, Paul says, "I'm glad you asked."

B Abraham: The Father of *All* Who Have Faith (4:9–17)

SUPPORTING IDEA: *Because Abraham was called and credited with righteousness while a Gentile, it is clear that both Gentiles and Jews are justified the same way: by faith.*

4:9–11. It is now Paul's task to answer the question that he has posed in behalf of his readers (this is not so much the jousting of diatribe as much as Paul directing his presentation by raising and answering reasonable questions which his readers will have). In verse 10, Paul goes directly to the bottom line and asks, concerning Abraham's being credited with righteousness, **Was it after he was circumcised, or before?** That is the critical question. If

Abraham was **circumcised**—a work of obedience—before he was credited as righteous, then it could be argued he was declared righteous on the basis of works. If he was declared righteous before he was circumcised, then his **righteousness** would be purely a result of **faith**. As soon as he asks, Paul answers: **It was not after, but before!** Therefore, Abraham was justified on the basis of faith alone.

However, that is not the answer to the first question Paul raised (or at least only an indirect one demanding reasoning from his readers). The first question was, Is justification by **faith** for the Jews (the **circumcised**) alone, or for Gentiles **(the uncircumcised)** as well? Paul's answer is, since Abraham was justified by **faith** before he was **circumcised**, then justification by faith is for the uncircumcised. Since the "uncircumcised" are the Gentiles, justification by faith is for Gentiles as well as Jews. A brief overview of Abraham's circumstances will make this clear—keeping in mind one critical factor: *Abraham was justified by faith as a human being, not as a Gentile or a Jew! This establishes faith as the standard for all human beings.*

Before the rite of circumcision was instituted (signifying that Abraham and his descendants would become a peculiar people unto God, i.e., the Jews), there were only human beings in the world. Abraham met God, trusted God, and was declared righteous by God on the basis of his faith. After that, he and his descendants were marked by circumcision as a sign and seal of their "set-apartness" to God. At that point only did there become two categories of people: Jews, and everyone else (Gentiles; the Heb. is *hagoyim*, "the nations"). Here is how it happened:

Genesis 6–8	Worldwide flood destroys all except eight people: Noah, his three sons, and their wives.
Genesis 9–10	Noah's sons and their wives repopulate the earth.
Genesis 11:1–26	Abraham (Abram) descends from Noah's son Shem. Abraham's father's (Terah) family resides in Ur in southern Mesopotamia (modern Iran).
Genesis 11:27–32	Terah moves his household northwest to Haran (modern Syria) in anticipation of settling in Canaan. Terah dies in Haran.
Genesis 12:1–8	God calls Abraham to leave Haran and go to Canaan. There he makes promises to him about his and his descendants' future.
Genesis 12:9–14:24	Abraham sojourns in Canaan, Egypt, and the Negev.
Genesis 15	God makes promises to Abraham about his descendants (vv. 4–5) *and declares Abraham righteous when Abraham trusts in those promises* (v. 6).

Genesis 16	Ishmael, an "illegitimate" son, is born to Sarah's maid Hagar, when Abraham was 86 years old (v. 15). The implication is that Abraham was 85 when he was declared righteous since Ishmael was apparently conceived and born after the promise of a son to which Abraham responded in faith (15:4–6).
Genesis 17	Rite of circumcision instituted as a sign and seal of God's promise and Abraham's faith-response (v. 11). This is when Abraham is 99 years old and Ishmael is 13 (17:1,24–25). *Therefore, if Abraham was 85 years old when declared righteous, justification occurred 14 years before he was circumcised at age 99.*
Then, skipping forward to . . .	
Exodus 20	The law is given, *430 years after the giving of the promise* (Gal. 3:17). The 430 years is from Exodus 12:40, and is the number of years Israel was enslaved in Egypt. (The Greek version of the Old Testament, the Septuagint, indicates that 435 years was the period of time Israel was in Egypt *and in Canaan,* which would then amount to a span from Abraham to the giving of the Law. However, the actual number of years from Genesis 15 to Exodus 20 would be considerably more than 435. Paul's point in Galatians is not chronology, but theology: the promise given to Abraham was not just for him and his immediate descendants, and was not replaced by law at Sinai. If it had been only for Abraham and been fulfilled in his lifetime, the Law would have superceded it as a separate agreement. But since Abraham's inheritance of land, seed, and blessing [Gen. 12:1–3] were not completely fulfilled in his lifetime [nor 430 years later] the promise still stands and is not abrogated by the giving of the law at Sinai. The law and its works does not set aside the promise and its faith as the basis of man's relationship with God.)

The upshot of Abraham's relationship with God is that he was declared righteous before he was circumcised. He "became a Jew" by being circumcised fourteen years after God declared him righteous. Therefore, **he is the father of all who believe but have not been circumcised, in order that righteousness might be credited to them.** When God chose an instrument by which people could be found righteous in his sight, faith was the instrument, declared through a man named Abraham. When Abraham, fourteen years later, became the father of a new family of humans (his descendants) who would have a special purpose in his plan, God did not institute a new basis for the relationship between Abraham and his descendants (the Jews). Faith remains the human instrument required for justification in God's sight, whether for Jews or Gentiles.

At least one member of the church in Rome understood what Paul was writing and spread the apostolic doctrine in his own later writings. Clement, the bishop of Rome (active around A.D. 90–100), wrote, "It is through faith that Almighty God has justified all that have been from the beginning of time" (Ward, p. 2).

4:12. The conclusion of Paul's answer to the question in verse 9 is that Abraham **is also the father of the circumcised . . . who also walk in the footsteps of the faith that our father Abraham had before he was circumcised.** What God showed Abraham before calling him into a unique relationship with himself—that faith is the response to God that justifies a person in God's sight—did not change because of circumcision. When Abraham became the first Jew, he became so as a result of his faith first, and circumcision second. Therefore all of Abraham's descendants who would walk **in the footsteps** of their forefather would have to walk by faith first.

As Paul told the Galatians, "Understand, then, that those who believe are children of Abraham" (Gal. 3:7). And, as he will tell the Romans later, "In other words, it is not the natural children [of Abraham] who are God's children, but it is the children of the promise who are regarded as Abraham's offspring" (Rom. 9:8). Judaism, with its rituals and requirements, was a framework, a skeleton, which needed a heart of vibrant faith. If the heart of faith was missing, Jews (or any person) were nothing more than "whitewashed tombs, which look beautiful on the outside but on the inside are full of dead men's bones" (Matt. 23:27).

That takes care of the relationship of faith and circumcision, but what about faith and the law as far as Abraham was concerned? In the chart of the growth of Abraham's relationship with God (above), the last item noted is the giving of the law—"430" years after the giving of the promise.

4:13–15. It is clear from Paul's next comments that not only does faith take priority over circumcision, but faith takes priority over law as well. F. F. Bruce notes, "If circumcision had nothing to do with Abraham's justification by God, with all the promised blessings that accompanied it, the law had even less to do with it" (Bruce, p. 108). Circumcision was instituted only fourteen years after Abraham was declared righteous, whereas 430 years (Gal. 3:17) had passed before the law was instituted. As noted in the chart above, Paul expands on this topic in detail in Galatians 3, making the point that the law did not replace the promise. The promise continues beyond Abraham, beyond the Hebrew slaves in Egypt, and beyond the giving of the law at Mt. Sinai.

One of Paul's phrases in verse 13 needs explanation: **heir of the world.** When understood, it emphasizes even more the power of the promise that God gave Abraham, and that he received by faith. Nowhere in any of the various iterations of God's promises to Abraham does God promise Abraham that he or his descendants would become **heir[s] of the world** (see Gen. 15:5–21; 17:4–8; 18:18–19; 22:17–18). Geographically, he was promised the land of Canaan as an inheritance (Gen. 12:1; 13:14–15,17; 15:7; 17:8; 28:4; 35:12), a land which would stretch from "the river of Egypt to the great river, the Euphrates" (Gen. 15:18). Neither was he promised that he would rule over domains encompassing all the world's peoples, though he was promised that he would be the father of "many nations" (Gen. 17:4–6). So what of the promise **that he would be heir of the world?**

Several things may be noted. First, the promise in Genesis 12:3 specifies that "all peoples on earth will be blessed through you." In that sense, God gave Abraham a promise of a "blessed world"—a world that through Abraham's innumerable seed would become a heritage of blessing for him. Second, Abraham's descendants (plural) are likewise to be viewed in the singular, as Paul says in Galatians 3:16,19: "'And to your seed,' meaning one person, who is Christ." This recalls the familiar King James language of the *protoevangelium* ("first gospel") in Genesis 3:15 where God says to the serpent, "I will put enmity between . . . thy seed and her seed; it shall bruise thy head, and thou shalt bruise his heel."

Therefore, the messianic implications of the promise are clear when Christ is seen as the Seed of Abraham. Christ will indeed exercise universal rule over the earth in the future, and in that way fulfill the promise to Abraham universally. Finally, the spiritual ramifications of those who are Abraham's children by faith "inheriting the earth," and reigning with Christ, are clear (Matt. 5:5; 2 Tim. 2:12; Rev. 5:10; 20:4,6; 22:5). Paul may simply, by the inspiration of the Holy Spirit, be expanding the realm of fulfillment beyond what the original recipient of a promise or prophecy saw or understood—a phenomenon not uncommon in biblical prophecy.

The eschatological definition of the promise is not Paul's intent in this verse. Rather, he is making sure that his readers know that the promise to Abraham (however it is interpreted or ultimately fulfilled) did not come through law. And while the Mosaic Law can always be seen lurking in the background in these discussions (and Paul clearly refers to it chronologically in Gal. 3:17), the point here is that promises do not come through the instrument of law. **Faith has no value** if promises are received on the basis of law.

Stott explains that law and promise are incompatible realms of instrumentality. Both have their place, but they cannot coexist in the same domain: "Law-language ('you shall') demands our obedience, but promise-language ('I will') demands our faith. What God said to Abraham was not 'Obey this law and I will bless you', but 'I will bless you; believe my promise'" (Stott, p. 131). Law, in principle and by design, **brings wrath,** but **where there is no law there is no transgression.**

Paul means here that if a promise is made on the basis of law, it would never be fulfilled. Why? Because **law** reveals **transgression,** and **transgression** demands the **wrath** of God. The first time Abraham or one of his descendants sinned (if the "promise" was based on law), God's wrath would be unleashed and the benefits of the promise would be retracted. But where the inheritance **of the world** is based on promise instead of law, **there is no transgression**. That does not mean there is no sin; it simply means that **there is no transgression** being watched for as a basis for annulling the blessings of the promise. But what then does God do with the sins of those to whom the promise is made? How can he fulfill the promise even if those to whom the promise is made continue to fail?

4:16–17. Paul's answer is the overall theme of the Bible: the promise will be fulfilled by grace through faith (Eph. 2:8–9). In fact, the only way that God could guarantee that Abraham and his descendants would become a great nation, that Abraham's name would be great in the earth, that he would be a blessing, that those who bless him and his descendants would qualify to be blessed, and that all the peoples on earth would be blessed by God (Gen. 12:1–3) was for God, by his grace, to promise that it would happen! **Therefore, the promise comes by faith, so that it may be by grace and may be guaranteed to all Abraham's offspring**—both to those who are Abraham's physical descendants and believe and to those who are his descendants by faith.

Just as the Jews might have held to "Abraham said it, I believe it, and that settles it," Paul is now saying that "God promised it, Abraham believed it, and that settles it." As God continues to forgive, by his grace, the failures of Abraham and his descendants, the promise remains in effect. Should God "change his mind" (which he will not; Num. 23:19; 1 Sam. 15:29) and switch from grace to law, the "promise" would be annulled. When God told Abraham that he had made him "a father of many nations" (Gen. 17:5), that was a guarantee that the promise was a promise to be fulfilled by grace through faith.

What kind of faith did it take for Abraham to hear that promise from God and believe, at his and Sarah's age, that **nations** would one day come from his loins? He had to believe that God was one who **gives life to the dead and calls things that are not as though they were.** In that way, Abraham foreshadowed the New Testament definition of faith: "being sure of what we hope for and certain of what we do not see" (Heb. 11:1). Abraham had to be "fully persuaded" (Rom. 4:21).

Paul makes reference here to the deadness of Abraham's and Sarah's reproductive abilities. The God who gives life to dead things and calls into existence that which is not was the God who was speaking to Abraham. The God who, *ex nihilo* (out of nothing), created the heavens and the earth by speaking them into existence was the God who was speaking to Abraham. It is one thing to hear the accounts of creation as they were passed along by Noah and his sons after the flood, and to be amazed at what creation must have been like. But now Abraham was being challenged to let God do his creative work in him and his wife. This was different!

All his life, Abraham had hoped for a son, and he finally reached a point where he was sure it would not happen. He had never seen his own progeny, and was probably certain that he would never see it. But now, he was being asked to hope again and to see for the first time. He was being asked to believe God.

Ⓒ Abraham: The Father of the "Fully Persuaded" (4:18–22)

SUPPORTING IDEA: *Abraham was forced to walk by faith, not by sight, and trust God to fulfill his promises.*

4:18–19. In pre-flood days, Abraham and Sarah would have been considered adolescents at age 100 and 90 (Gen. 17:17). But in the day in which the Lord came to Abraham to tell him how the promise would be fulfilled, Sarah was "worn out" and Abraham was "old" (Gen. 18:12). Sarah was not worn out from childbearing, for she had never given birth. Her womb had been barren her entire life (Gen. 11:30). Paul said her womb was **dead** and that Abraham's body **was as good as dead.** Think of what it would mean for a couple approaching the century mark to be told that **many nations** were yet to spring forth from them when they had never had a single child together! Nevertheless, God said, **So shall your offspring be.**

So what did the father of faith do? First, he surveyed the possibilities and options. **He faced the fact** that this was not going to happen naturally. Given his and Sarah's track record for conception, and the weakness of their respective faculties, there would have to be another option. As he looked around him, there was only one other option: God would have to supernaturally cause Sarah to conceive. Next, **without weakening in his faith** in the face of challenging options, he committed himself to God's ability. He exercised faith. He became certain that what he could not see would one day be—not because of any strength or ability on his or Sarah's part, but because God had said it. Abraham placed his entire confidence in one thing: the word (promise) of God.

4:20–22. In spite of odds that would have attracted every unbelieving dollar in town, Abraham **did not waver through unbelief regarding the promise of God, but was strengthened in his faith and gave glory to God.** When we see that Abraham was **strengthened in his faith,** we are prone to view "wavering through unbelief" as the opposite; i.e., having weak faith instead of strong faith. But it is not that at all. **Waver** here is *diakrino,* which means to act as a judge, to pass judgement, to decide or determine. The point is that he did not allow **unbelief** to put him in a judgment mode where, like a trial judge or jury, he would weigh the evidence and make his decision.

"What are the chances of God pulling this promise off?" a judge might ask. "Let's examine the evidence." We've never seen God do anything like this before; we are obviously past child-bearing age; we would be the laughing stock of the neighbors even if God did do it; Sarah might die giving birth at her age; God could somehow engineer a greater good by not delivering us a son; and on and on and on in the school of "How Many Reasons Can We Think of Not to Believe God?" That is exactly what Abraham *did not* do—turn into a judge who critiques at the human level the possibilities of God succeeding in doing what he promised.

So what did he do? He became **fully persuaded that God had the power to do what he had promised.** And what persuaded him? In verse 20 Paul says that Abraham **was strengthened in his faith.** "Was strengthened" or "grow strong" is *endunamoo,* to make powerful. This verb is from the same root as the familiar *dunamis,* or power. Now look at verse 21: Abraham became **fully persuaded that God had [the] power**—the *dunatos,* the power or ability—to perform. In other words, Abraham's faith was empowered by contemplating God's power! The more Abraham looked at who he was and who God was, the more empowered—**fully persuaded**—he became that God was able to do that which he had promised.

And therein lies the secret of faith: *faith is always strong or weak depending on how we perceive the object of our faith.* Is the God to whom we look weak in our eyes? Then we will have weak faith. Is our God strong in our eyes? Then our faith will grow strong accordingly. There was nothing in Abraham that gave him strong faith, but there was everything in God that gave him strong faith. **This is why "it was credited to him as righteousness."** Why? God responded to Abraham's response to him. When God saw that Abraham viewed him as a powerful God—all the way back in Genesis 15:6 where Abraham first believed God's promise—he credited that "perspective of power" (faith) to Abraham as righteousness.

Abraham, in so many words, said to God, "I believe you, Lord. I believe you are powerful enough to do what you have said. Though I am powerless, you are powerful, and I will rest in that. I will live not in light of what I can see but in light of what you have said." That is faith. When God saw that in Abraham, he said, "Abraham, your faith has united us. We are one in our perspective on the present and the future. I forgive all your sins, and receive you into my presence. Your status, because of your faith-response to me, is one of righteousness. Your faith has become the standard by which the rest of the human race can know me as well. Any who believe as you have believed will be righteous in my sight."

Thankfully, the "any who believe as Abraham believed" includes those to whom Paul wrote. Like Abraham, God asks us to believe in his ability to bring life out of death—but in a totally different way.

Ⓓ Abraham: The Father of Those Who Believe in "Resurrection" (4:23–25)

SUPPORTING IDEA: *Just as Abraham trusted God to bring life from his and Sarah's "dead" bodies, so those who trust in Christ and his resurrection from the dead will be justified by faith.*

4:23. Little did Moses know that when he penned Genesis 15:6 he was writing it for and about others in addition to Abraham. There was a much greater resurrection on the horizon of history than the resurrection of human reproduction in Abraham's and Sarah's bodies. But what God did for them was only a picture of what he was going to do for the entire human race. The outcome of faith would be the same—justification in God's sight—but the demonstration of God's power would be different. In fact, the demonstration of power that God gives the world to believe in today is the greatest display of power the world has ever seen.

4:24–25. Paul says that **God will credit righteousness** to anyone in the world today who believes **in him who raised Jesus our Lord from the dead.** This is the same exercise in faith that Abraham was asked to participate in. Compare the similarities and the differences:

	Abraham	Us
Object	God and his promises about the future (descendants and blessings)	God and his promises about the future (forgiveness of sin, eternal life)
Evidence	God's power manifested in resurrecting an aged couple's reproductive ability	God's power manifested in resurrecting his Son
Perspective	Abraham had to look forward in complete faith to an event that had not happened.	We have the opportunity to look back to an event that has already happened and is historically verifiable.
Result	Faith results in Abraham being credited with righteousness	Faith results in our being credited with righteousness

Abraham was asked to believe what he had never seen. We are asked to believe what many witnesses have seen and verified. It is easy to see why Abraham is a prime example of faith in Hebrews 11, and why Paul pictures him as the "father" of faith. God never disparages those who see and believe, but believing and seeing by faith somehow receives his special attention. Remember Jesus' words to "doubting" Thomas? When Thomas insisted on evidence that Jesus had been resurrected, Jesus accommodated him. But then Jesus delivered this "Abrahamic-style" principle: "Because you have seen me, you have believed; blessed are those who have not seen and yet have believed" (John 20:29).

There are four classes of people in the world regarding faith:

1. Those who believe without seeing (includes Abraham and others who may have been asked by God to trust him by faith alone).

2. Those who believe after seeing (includes any who receive clear presentations of the gospel, including evidence of the resurrection of Christ, and believe).

3. Those who do not believe after seeing (those who hear and see clear evidence of the power of God, or the gospel, but will not believe; could include those who "see" evidence of God in general revelation but suppress the truth; Rom. 1).

4. Those who have yet to hear the postresurrection gospel message.

If those who believe without seeing are blessed, what are those who see and do not believe (cf. John 6:36; 10:25–26,38)? And what of those who have not had the opportunity to believe in Paul's gospel message? Paul understood what a triumph of faith Abraham accomplished by taking God purely at his word *before the fact.* Now, *after the fact of Christ's resurrection,* people today have the opportunity to receive the same justification by faith that Abraham received. In other words, Paul's perspective seems to be this: "We have the evidence in hand to show the world that the God of Abraham, the God of power, wants to grant justification to those who believe that Christ is risen! Our task is to get the message to them, giving them the opportunity to believe."

Finally, Paul summarizes the two sides of the salvation coin: Christ was **delivered over to death for our sins,** but then he was **raised to life for our justification.** What's the difference? The sacrificial atonement for sin was accomplished through the death of Christ (Rom. 3:25), and the approval of God was manifested in the resurrection. Christ's resurrection set his death apart from all other human deaths (e.g., the two thieves who died with him but who were not resurrected). Anyone could die claiming to be a sacrifice for the sins of the world. The test would be their resurrection.

This is similar to the time Jesus told the paralyzed man that his sins were forgiven. When the teachers of the law criticized him for taking the place of God by forgiving sins (and rightly so, unless Jesus was God!), he (as later with Thomas) accommodated their skepticism: "'But that you may know that the Son of Man has authority on earth to forgive sins . . . .' He said to the paralytic, 'I tell you, get up, take your mat and go home'" (Mark 2:10–11). The man "got up" (was "resurrected") and walked home.

That was a microcosm of what happened in Christ's death and resurrection: the forgiveness of sins validated by resurrection. As happened on that ordinary, dusty day in Israel—"This amazed everyone and they praised

God"—it can happen again today. As the hymn writer tells us, "As Thou hast been [for Abraham], Thou forever wilt be [for all who share his faith]" (*Great Is Thy Faithfulness,* Thomas O. Chisholm, brackets added).

May God give us grace to boldly proclaim the death of Christ **for our sins,** and the resurrection of Christ **for our justification,** so that Abraham's family of faith may continue to grow, making him the "heir of the world" (Rom. 4:13)! Though we do not see him face to face today, as we spread his gospel he can be "unseen but not unknown":

> Jesus, these eyes have never seen
> That radiant form of thine;
> The veil of sense hangs dark between
> Thy blessed face and mine.
> Yet though I have not seen, and still
> Must rest in faith alone,
> I love thee, dearest Lord, and will,
> Unseen but not unknown.

(Ward, p. 187)

MAIN IDEA REVIEW: *Abraham established the priority of faith over works for every Jew or Gentile who wants to be counted as righteous in the sight of God.*

III. CONCLUSION

Abraham Lives!

Though the patriarch Abraham has gone to his reward with the Lord, his faith continues to live in his spiritual children—those who believe in God as he did. While the object and direction for our saving faith is the death and resurrection of Jesus Christ, we still need faith to live every day. In fact, it was a temporal need that was at the heart of Abraham's faith in God. He and Sarah needed a son through whom they could begin to create a human heritage, a people separated unto God for his purposes. The faith of Abraham needs to be exercised daily by believers who have needs for which looking to God is their only answer.

But how many people would willingly put themselves into positions *requiring* such faith? One who did was George Müller, the German-born minister of the nineteenth century. After a profligate youth and life-changing conversion to Christ, Müller moved to London, where he involved himself in a variety of ministries. Eventually, he was drawn to Bristol, England, where he began ministering to the multitudes of orphan children in the vicinity.

Starting with only a few children, he eventually had two thousand under his care, accommodated in a large spread of houses and buildings.

Müller's ministry might not have gained such attention except for the way in which it was financed. He made no requests for funds at all, but simply committed his needs to God in prayer. Müller himself lived without financial or material assets, but trusted for all things in the provision of the one whom he believed had promised to meet all of his needs. By Müller's own testimony, there were times when he would have no food with which to feed the orphans under his care. But acting by faith, he would prepare the table, set the children at their places, and then wait upon God's provision. Invariably, provision would arrive—a delivery, a knock at the door, an unexpected gift. George Müller was a man who, like Abraham, placed his faith in the God who promised he would provide.

"Faith does not operate in the realm of the possible," Müller wrote. "There is no glory for God in that which is humanly possible. Faith begins where man's power ends" (Rowell, p. 60). He also wrote that "the vigour of our spiritual life will be in exact proportion to the place held by the Bible in our life and thoughts" (Ward, p. 184). Was this not the secret to Abraham's faith—the place God's word held in his life and thoughts? Abraham believed what God said (believed that he would keep his word), and that faith was credited to him as righteousness. George Müller believed what God said in his Word (e.g., "And my God will meet all your needs according to his glorious riches in Christ Jesus," Phil. 4:19) and rested in his faith. And while it was Müller's faith in the death and resurrection of Christ that resulted in his justification (Rom. 4:25), it was undoubtedly his faith in God and his word which resulted in God's continual honoring of his faith through material provision.

Does Abraham live today? Yes—through the legacy of faith that he left all who are his descendants in faith. But as the pundit would say, there is "belief" and then there is "belief." May the belief of the Abrahams and George Müllers in the kingdom become the belief of the rest of us as well. God is waiting for many more to step forward and take him at his word.

PRINCIPLES

- Attaining righteousness by grace as a gift through faith results in boasting—but boasting in God.
- There is nothing anyone can do to attain righteousness before God on their own.
- Works that glorify God are always preceded by faith.
- Faith is a "human" instrument; not a Gentile or Jewish instrument. Anyone wanting to know God may do so by faith.
- Abraham's true descendants are those who know God by faith.

- True faith has God's words and actions (his character and power) as its basis.

APPLICATIONS

- Has anyone recently heard me boasting of anything except that which God by grace has supplied?
- Can I identify anything in my life or ministry that I am tempted to think gives me standing before God (other than my faith in Christ)?
- Have I ever clouded the gospel message in any way that makes it less than totally available to anyone at any time by faith alone?
- Have I allowed the sole category of "faith in Christ" to dissolve all other categories and barriers into which the church sometimes places groups of believers?
- Is my faith weak because of a lack of intimacy and experience with God's character and his power?

IV. LIFE APPLICATION

How to Amaze Jesus

Would you like to amaze and astonish Jesus? There are two ways to do it—one is recommended, the other is not. There are only two times when the Gospels record Jesus being "amazed" or "astonished" (Gr. *thaumazo*) at something, and, amazingly, both have to do with faith.

On one occasion (see Luke 7:1–10), a Roman centurion's servant was sick and lay dying. The centurion, a Gentile, asked some Jewish elders to go and bring Jesus to heal the sick servant. Upon hearing about the centurion's need, Jesus agreed to go. When Jesus was on the way, he met friends of the centurion who approached Jesus with a different message. Yes, the servant was still sick, and yes, the centurion still requested Jesus' healing mercy for his servant. But now the message was, "But say the word, and my servant will be healed" (v. 7).

The centurion had apparently thought better of his original request. He, apparently a humble man (see vv. 4–5), was embarrassed that he had asked Jesus to walk all the way to his home. His new message to Jesus revealed profound understanding: "Authority is not bounded by geography. Your word, Jesus, will be just as effective whether you are here or there. I understand authority; my soldiers do what I say. I do not understand the nature of your authority, exactly how it works, but I know that you have authority. Just say the word from where you are, and I am confident my servant will be healed."

When Jesus heard this, "*he was amazed . . . and said, 'I tell you, I have not found such great faith even in Israel'*" (v. 9; emphasis added). Jesus responded to the centurion's faith, for when the centurion's friends returned to his house, they found the servant well. Faith exercised on the basis of character ("I know you want to heal") and power ("I know you can heal") brought the centurion the answer he sought. Does this prove Paul's point in Romans 4 that anyone with the faith of Abraham can receive God's blessing, whether Jew or Gentile? Apparently so. Was Jesus amazed at the centurion's faith, or amazed that the physical sons of Abraham ("even in Israel") had no such faith?

Upon returning to his hometown, Nazareth, on one occasion, he encountered a great deal of skepticism and hostility from the hometown folk (Mark 6:1–6a). To put it bluntly, "they took offense at him" (v. 3), which they probably lived (or died) to regret. So great was their dishonor of Jesus (so scant was their faith), "He could not do any miracles there, except lay his hands on a few sick people and heal them" (v. 5). In some mysterious way, the hands of the Son of God were partially tied by the shallowness of his Jewish friends' faith. Jesus was apparently ready and willing to do great things for them (were there people in Nazareth sick unto death who could have been saved?), but could not. Once again, the issue of faith prompted amazement in Jesus, only this time "he was amazed at their lack of faith" (v. 6a).

Apparently, great faith amazes Jesus—both the presence of it and the absence of it. A Gentile soldier had great faith, and Jesus did great things. A community of Jews had little faith, and Jesus did little things. In another of the ironies of Scripture, God uses a Gentile to demonstrate once again that the faith of the father of the Jews is available to anyone. And, he showed that being a physical descendant of Abraham, a Jew by birth, does not guarantee a person the blessings of God. The critical factor to which God responds is faith. The critical factor which amazed the Son of God was finding it or not finding it.

Since Jesus is amazed at both ends of the faith spectrum—great faith and little faith—it appears that he must be constantly shaking his head in amazement for one reason or the other as he surveys the life of his people. If he came into your study, classroom, pulpit, church, business, or home, for which reason would Jesus be amazed, and to what degree? Would he be awed at your faith, or would he be awed at the lack of it? What evidence, one way or the other, would he find in your prayer journal? In your checkbook? In your notes on your dreams and visions for the future?

"When the Son of Man comes, will he find faith on the earth?" (Luke 18:8). When our faith is like Abraham's and the Roman centurion's, we will be "fully persuaded" (Rom. 4:21) that what God says he will do, he fully intends to do. We are going to amaze Jesus one way or the other. Let us purpose to amaze him with great faith.

V. PRAYER

Heavenly Father, thank you that you have placed no restrictions on my access to you except that I would believe you. Thank you for father Abraham and the pattern of faith he established. Thank you that through his faith, your blessings have come to me. Increase my faith, O Lord. May you search me out when you need a faithful servant to accomplish a task for you on earth! Amen.

VI. DEEPER DISCOVERIES

A. Works (4:2,4,6)

Three times in Romans 4, Paul uses the word *works,* and it occurs nine times in the epistle as a whole. Because the term *works* is used frequently in Christian discussions ("We're saved by grace, not by works"; "I see no good works in her life; is she really saved?"), it will be helpful to identify the way Paul is using the term in the passages studied in this chapter of the commentary.

When discussing works in relation to Abraham (Rom. 4:2), Paul obviously cannot be referring to "works of the [Mosaic] Law" since, as we have seen, the law came hundreds of years after Abraham lived. Therefore, the works referred to in Romans 4 are the larger category of works, deeds, efforts, or strivings which human beings might undertake in order to gain favor with God. These could certainly include the specific works or deeds mandated by the Mosaic Law, whether the Decalogue (the moral law) or the civil and religious statutes. Often in the Old Testament, the prophets condemned religious works and deeds which were either mandated by the Law or otherwise had legitimate spiritual purposes, but which were being done in a context of sin or carnality (1 Sam. 15:22–23; Isa. 1:11–17; 58:1–14; Hos. 6:6; Amos 5:21–27; Mic. 6:6–8; Mal. 2:13–14; 3:6–12). Those kinds of works—religious works accomplished for the purpose of gaining approval from God—were also expressly condemned by Jesus (Matt. 23).

Circumcision was another type of "work" which came long before the Mosaic Law and which, over time, began to be a status symbol of righteousness. But as Paul demonstrates, circumcision was given to Abraham after he was declared righteous by God. But it clearly was a point of confusion in the Christian community as Paul mentions it twenty-one times in Romans alone and forty-six times in all of his epistles. It was a "work" with value, but not in relation to salvation. It was a cultural work that identified the Jewish race, not that saved them.

Lastly, though Paul does not discuss this in Romans 4, works in the New Testament are an expected outgrowth of being a new creature in Christ—works of service. These kinds of works clearly have nothing to do with obtaining salvation, but are an outgrowth of a new set of kingdom priorities by which a believer lives his or her life. The clearest evidence of this is Ephesians 2:8–10 where Paul says we are not saved by works (v. 9), but that there are good works which God has prepared for us to do (v. 10). Works do not save us, but works become an outgrowth of our salvation (for other mentions of this category of works in the New Testament see Eph. 4:12; 1 Tim. 2:10; 5:10,25; 6:18; Heb. 10:24; Jas. 2:14,18,20,26; 3:13; 1 Pet. 2:12; Rev. 2:2,19).

Acts of religious service or human kindness, while having value for the good they accomplish, have no value in dealing with sin. Only an atoning sacrifice can deal with the sin question, and only the resurrection of Christ from the dead proved that he was the atoning sacrifice that God accepted. To seek the result that Christ's death provided (salvation) by our own works would be to negate the perfect works of Christ on our behalf.

B. Circumcision (4:9)

Circumcision of the male sexual organ was practiced widely among Semitic peoples, of which the Hebrews were a part. It is not certain when and where the practice began universally (it is also practiced by other cultures), though there is clear biblical testimony that the rite was instituted for Abraham and his descendants in Genesis 17:10–14. Circumcision was to be the sign of the covenant between God and Abraham. Hebrew terminology for making a covenant was to "cut" a covenant. In Genesis 15, as an act of solemnization of the portion of God's promises to Abraham recorded there, animals were cut apart. Normally, both parties to the covenant walked between the cut-apart animals signifying their willingness to have the same done to them should they break the covenant (in Gen. 15, only God walked between the pieces since the covenant was unconditional).

It is possible that the circumcision rite in Genesis 17—the cutting of the male foreskin—played a similar role, especially in light of the promises made to Abraham by God at that time. The promises specifically dealt with Abraham's progeny: "I will . . . greatly increase your numbers"; "I have made you a father of many nations"; "I will make you very fruitful"; "I will make nations of you" (Gen. 17:2,5,6).

Given Abraham's age and limited reproductive capability, it is possible that the cutting of his reproductive organ was a way for him to cast himself totally upon the ability of God to make him a father. In doing so, every male descended from Abraham would be permanently reminded by their own circumcision that their very existence was a result of the power and promise of God directed toward their forefather Abraham. There is no biblical evidence to support that idea other than the traditional understanding of "cutting" as part of the covenant ratification, and the unique connection between the nature of the promises of God to Abraham in Genesis 17 and the male sexual organ.

By the time of the monarchy in Israel, circumcision had become a symbol of religious pride. Non-Israelites were referred to as the "uncircumcised," and the internal, spiritual covenant dynamics of which circumcision was a seal were being neglected. Thus the prophets, probably Jeremiah first, introduced the concept of the circumcision of the heart as being the true circumcision (Jer. 4:4; 9:26; Ezek. 44:7,9; though see Deut. 30:6). This was not to replace external circumcision but to point to the reality for which circumcision stood: a heart commitment. Paul even says in Romans 2:29 that "circumcision is circumcision of the heart, by the Spirit, not by the written code."

Circumcision in the early church was a problem. Because most early converts were Jews, a question quickly arose as to whether new Gentile converts had to be circumcised. Effectively, did Gentile converts need to become Jews before becoming Christians in order to be fully "initiated" believers? Leaders of the church in Jerusalem apparently felt in the affirmative about circumcision (Acts 11:2), while Paul, the apostle to the Gentiles, was opposed. Peter was apparently on the fence for a little while (Gal. 2:11–21).

The Jerusalem Council dealt with this and other Jewish issues, and decided that circumcision was not a requirement for inclusion in the covenant promises in Christ (Acts 15). Though it was no longer a theological issue, it was still very much a cultural one as evidenced by Paul's circumcision of Timothy before taking him on an evangelistic mission in an area populated by Jews (Acts 16:1–4).

VII. TEACHING OUTLINE

A. INTRODUCTION

1. Lead Story: The Power of a Picture
2. Context: Picture Romans 3:21–4:25 as Paul making and illustrating the key point in Christian theology. In 3:21–31 he says that righteousness has been made known by God to man to solve the problem of man's lack of righteousness. That righteousness is based on the atoning death of Jesus Christ on the cross, and is credited to the account of sinful people only one way—through faith in Christ. Then, in chapter 4, Paul illustrates the truth that righteousness comes only through faith by appealing to the experience of the father of Israel, Abraham.

3. Transition: Paul proves that righteousness comes only by faith by showing that God credited righteousness to Abraham before he had been circumcised or the law had been given. Therefore, there was nothing that Abraham had done that could have merited God's favor other than what he did in response to God's promises: he believed God. And that belief (faith) was credited to him as righteousness.

B. COMMENTARY

1. Abraham: The Forefather of Faith (4:1–8)
   a. Abraham: The precedence of faith (4:1–5)
   b. David: The confirmation of faith (4:6–8)
2. Abraham: The Father of *All* Who Have Faith (4:9–17)
   a. Faith and the uncircumcised (4:9–11)
   b. Faith and the circumcised (4:12)
   c. Faith's priority over law (4:13–15)
   d. Faith that brought forth many nations (4:16–17)
3. Abraham: The Father of the "Fully Persuaded" (4:18–22)
   a. Faith hopes in the promise (4:18–19)
   b. Faith trusts in the power (4:20–22)
4. Abraham: The Father of Those Who Believe in "Resurrection" (4:23–25)
   a. Abraham's belief in "resurrection" resulted in righteousness (4:23)
   b. Our belief in *the* resurrection results in righteousness (4:24–25)

C. CONCLUSION: HOW TO AMAZE JESUS

VIII. ISSUES FOR DISCUSSION

1. What does it mean to you to "believe God"? What personal illustrations can you offer from your own life of success, or failure, in trusting in God?
2. What is society's overall impression of the "supernatural" nature of Christianity? What evidence is there that the church is accomplishing things that would not happen except by the power of God?
3. In your opinion, in what areas would God want the body of Christ to trust him more; to live more by faith?
4. What are the ultimate negative repercussions in your own life when you fail to exercise strong faith in God?
5. If the church is to fulfill the Great Commission, to extend the gospel of Christ to all peoples, in what areas will greater faith be required? In what ways has a lack of faith played a part in not having fulfilled the Great Commission even after two thousand years?

Romans 5:1–21

Peace: What the Gospel Produces

I. **INTRODUCTION**
Peace, Peace, When There Is No Peace

II. **COMMENTARY**
A verse-by-verse explanation of the chapter.

III. **CONCLUSION**
Something You Cannot Help,
Something You Can
An overview of the principles and applications from
the chapter.

IV. **LIFE APPLICATION**
It Takes One to Paint One
Melding the chapter to life.

V. **PRAYER**
Tying the chapter to life with God.

VI. **DEEPER DISCOVERIES**
Historical, geographical, and grammatical enrichment of the commentary.

VII. **TEACHING OUTLINE**
Suggested step-by-step group study of the chapter.

VIII. **ISSUES FOR DISCUSSION**
Zeroing the chapter in on daily life.

"*G*od cannot give us happiness and peace apart from him-self, because it is not there. There is no such thing."

C . S . L e w i s

Romans 5:1–21

I N A N U T S H E L L

*H*aving proven that justification before God comes only through faith, Paul now reveals the result of justification: peace with God. What the first Adam lost in the Garden of Eden, the second Adam has restored. Now any who seek peace with God may have it.

Peace: What the Gospel Produces

I. INTRODUCTION

Peace, Peace, When There Is No Peace

*T*he human quest for peace is never-ending. Ever since Cain lifted his hand against his brother Abel (Gen. 4), peaceful coexistence has been little more than a fleeting ideal. There is a reason for that, of course, and it is not that people do not want peace. It is just that they want it on their own terms—terms which, of course, conflict with other peoples' terms.

Take the radical Black Muslim leader Malcolm X, who said in 1963, "Be peaceful, be courteous, obey the law, respect everyone; but if someone puts his hand on you, send him to the cemetery. That's a good religion." Be peaceful until someone invades your space; then do what you have to do to keep the peace. The poet W. H. Auden thinks the gender of the peacemakers is the key: "I see little hope for a peaceful world until men are excluded from the realm of foreign policy altogether and all decisions concerning international relations are reserved for women, preferably married ones." A survey of history would suggest there is more to it than that.

Men have made valiant efforts at peace through the years which everyone believed would be successful. For example, American President Jimmy Carter hammered out the Camp David Accord between Egyptian president Anwar al-Sadat and Israeli prime minister Menachem Begin in 1978. This accord was to help resolve differences between the descendants of Ishmael and the descendants of Isaac which began thousands of years earlier. And other peace agreements between the descendants of these two ancient combatants followed: Israel's Yitzhak Rabin and the Palestinian Liberation Organization's Yasir Arafat in 1993; Israel's Rabin and Jordan's King Hussein in 1994; Rabin and Arafat again in 1995; Israel's Benjamin Netanyahu and Arafat in 1996; and on and on.

Gerry Adams, the president of Ireland's Sinn Fein political party, and himself a leader/participant in the Protestant-Catholic conflicts in Northern Ireland, has it right when he says, "Making peace, I have found, is much harder than making war." Difficulty has not precluded attempt, however. Following "The Great War," World War I, so shocked was the world community at the carnage inflicted upon the world by itself that it formed the League of

Nations in 1919 as a means of preventing a similar war from ever taking place again.

During the 1930s the league failed to prevent a number of aggressive actions by expanding nations, including Hitler's repudiation of the Versailles Treaty that ended World War I. Following World War II (a non-verbal comment on the effectiveness of the League of Nations), the United Nations was formed for the purpose of maintaining international peace and security—which, of course, it has been unable to do during its tenure on the world stage. As the prophet of old predicted, man will always cry, "Peace, peace . . . when there is no peace" (Jer. 6:14; 8:11).

Even those who claim to worship the same Prince of Peace, such as the Catholics and Protestants in Northern Ireland, find that peace escapes them. But there is one realm in which peace is available and attainable at any time, by any person, and that is peace in God's domain. Paul introduces Romans 5 with a revolutionary statement: "We have peace with God."

Peace with God is what the gospel of Jesus Christ produces in the lives of those who embrace that gospel. And peace with God, Paul wants his readers to know, is the most fundamental peace there is. All other peace in the world has its basis in peace with God—which is the fundamental reason why peace will never be permanent in the human realm until all human beings embrace the rule of God. While the hippie and anti-war counter-culturists in the 1960s may have wanted us to "Give Peace a Chance," they would have been wiser to acknowledge that peace between people has little chance before peace with God is established. And the good news of the gospel message is that peace with God has been established! All that remains is for every person to enter the kingdom of God where peace is the norm.

Romans 5 will reveal that peace has blessings and a basis. In fact, the basis for peace is what Paul has been presenting in Romans through the end of chapter 4: peace with God is possible because the wrath of God has been deflected. God's wrath (Rom. 1:18) has been satisfied by the atoning sacrifice offered by his own Son, Jesus Christ (Rom. 3:25). His justice has been demonstrated and satisfied in the same event (Rom. 3:26), and he is at peace. All this is to say that peace with God depends on his being at peace with us, not our being at peace with him.

The idea that sinful humankind would find some fault in sinless God upon which to base hostility toward him is, of course, unthinkable. But the idea that sinless God has found fault in sinful humans, which fault has aroused his indignation, is thoroughly biblical, beginning in Genesis 3 and continuing in Romans 1 and 2. Therefore, it is God who needed to announce peace, which he has done.

To use the analogy so powerfully portrayed by C. S. Lewis in *The Chronicles of Narnia*, Aslan, the lion-king, is no longer "on the move."

Tremors could be felt throughout Narnia when Aslan was afoot and seeking his enemies. Conversely, a palpable peace invaded his kingdom when he was at peace. Thus is the nature of the kingdom of God. Those who choose to accept the God-King's announcement of peace, secured by Jesus the Lion of Judah, may enter into his peace—and enjoy the benefits thereof.

In this next chapter of Romans, Paul mentions some of the benefits of peace with God and goes into great detail about the basis of peace—how it was lost and how it was regained through justification by faith. If we were to move the message of Romans 5 into our modern culture, we might cast it in terms of the slogan gracing T-shirts and bumper stickers throughout the Southern United States: "If mama ain't happy, ain't nobody happy!" But conversely (and happily for those in "mama's" domain), when mama is happy, then everybody else can be happy.

At the risk of using any human example to illumine a divine activity, the metaphor has value. It is impossible for anyone in God's domain to be "happy" unless God himself is "happy." But when God is satisfied, is at peace, then his peace becomes that which pervades his domain, allowing for peace to be enjoyed by all. In fact, one day when the earth is filled with none except those who have accepted his perfect peace, the whole earth will be at peace—even the animal kingdom (Isa. 11) and the creation itself (Rom. 8). Remarkably, a foretaste of that age of peace is available to all who receive his provision of peace by placing faith in Jesus Christ.

II. COMMENTARY

> **MAIN IDEA:** The answer to life's most important question—How can one have peace with God?—is to be declared just in God's sight. Paul explains the benefits and the basis of finding peace with God.

Peace: What the Gospel Produces

A The Benefits of Peace with God (5:1–11)

> **SUPPORTING IDEA:** Access to God, hope in the future, knowing the love of God, being saved from the wrath of God—all this and more are benefits of finding peace with God.

Before beginning our study of Romans 5, it will be helpful to summarize how and why Paul has arrived at this point in his letter. "Therefores" in Pauline literature usually signify a turning point, and that is certainly true at the beginning of chapter 5 (see also Rom. 1:24; 2:1; 3:20; 4:16; 5:12; 6:4,12; 8:1,12; 9:16,18; 11:22; 12:1; 13:5,10; 14:13,19; 15:9,17).

We have said that Paul's letter to the church at Rome is about the gospel that is the power of God for salvation to everyone who believes (1:16). Paul has gone to great lengths to demonstrate that the whole world is worthy of, and stands under, the present and future wrath of God. Gentiles are guilty before God for violating his standards, as are Jews. But God has responded to the need of humankind by justifying—declaring righteous—the wicked in a way that preserves his own innate righteousness: God sent forth his own Son to become a propitiatory sacrifice for the sins of the whole world. This gift of grace nullifies any other means by which the wicked might try to achieve right standing before God, such as works of the law or flesh. Indeed, the only way one is able to be declared righteous is to do nothing—nothing except *receive* through faith the gift of God just as Abraham did.

So far, the gospel which Paul is declaring says that all the world has sinned; God has provided a solution whereby the penalty of sin is carried out but upon Another offered as a sacrifice; and the benefits of the sacrificial atonement may be received by faith, canceling out the debt of sin. Sinful human beings can be justly declared righteous by accepting the gift of righteousness offered by a Judge who remains righteous throughout the process—a just justifier of the wicked, a notion unheard of in Rome's pagan pantheon. This takes us through Romans 4, bringing us to the fifth of Paul's "therefores" in Romans 5:1. What point is he about to make in chapter 5?

We can safely say that, had Paul ended his letter to the Romans at the end of chapter 4, the church in Rome could have been assured of their own salvation and had adequate information to spread the gospel to others. That is, the core of the gospel message is complete by the time Paul arrives at Romans 5:1. "Therefore," he turns, as he does in other epistles, to the "practical" side of the gospel after a didactic, theological section (cf. Eph. 4:1; Col. 3:1; Gal. 5:1; 1 Thess. 4:1; 2 Thess. 3:1).

Students of Romans have long agreed that the major turning point in Romans for that purpose is at chapter 12, verse 1, where the believer is exhorted to present himself or herself to God as a living sacrifice in light of all God's mercies (detailed in and through Romans 1–11). This is certainly the major turning point in the book. But Paul's turning point at Romans 5:1 is a marked one nonetheless: **Therefore, since we have been justified through faith, we have peace with God through our Lord Jesus Christ.** This profound theological statement summarizes everything that has come before.

Peace with God is what the gospel produces in the life of the person who receives the gospel message. It is as if Paul wants to take the next exit off the theological superhighway he has been on and say, "Let's rest for a moment and consider what we have just discussed. Let's talk first about the blessings which accrue to the one who receives the gospel. Then I want to explain to you an amazing body of truth about how we lost our peace with God to begin with, and how it was recovered. You will see that the spiritual condition of the entire human race has been a function of the actions of two men. It is really quite simple when you see it." Following that "pit stop" in chapter 5, you will see Paul fire up his engines of diatribe again in Romans 6:1 and begin tackling more of the thorny issues of the mystery that is the gospel: "What shall we say, then? . . ." and off he goes!

So Romans 5:1–21 is a bit of a rest, where the benefits and basis of justification by faith are explored under the rubric of **peace with God.** We will use **peace with God** as a paradigm to study Paul's words in chapter 5 because of its all-encompassing nature. **Peace with God** is not one of the benefits of justification by faith—it is *the* benefit; a synonym, if you will. It is the greatest need of the human race, for if any person has **peace with God,** all other needs will be met (see further on the meaning of **peace** under the 5:1 discussion below). And this truth brings us to a final reflection on Romans 5 and the gospel.

In one context or another, Paul refers to "peace" in his letters almost fifty times. Surely it was not lost on this linguist-theologian that the original context of the term *gospel* was one of war and peace. A "gospel" was originally the reward given to the messenger who bore the good news of victory in battle. Eventually, the word signified the message itself—the good news of victory and peace. How appropriate then for Paul to follow four chapters of explaining the core of the gospel to declare that **we have peace with God!**

Has this part of the gospel message been lost in modern evangelism? Most often, the gospel is "explained" rather than "proclaimed" to needy people. Instead of proclaiming what God has already done ("It is finished," John 19:30) by establishing the basis for peace between himself and the human race, we focus on the non-Christian's sins and what *they* must do. In fact, God has already done it! The good news of the gospel is that God has won the battle and peace is at hand. It is a *proclamation* first, an *invitation* second (if needed).

Picture a herald going throughout a parched land, ringing a bell and shouting that provision has been made to save the people from starvation and thirst. The "invitation" to come and receive the provision never needs to be made. All thirsty and starving people need to hear is that food and drink are just over the next hill and they will follow (witness the crowds that followed Jesus).

In that sense, the gospel is a proclamation of peace to billions of people worn down by a lifetime spent at war. The analogy fails when we realize that many people do not know they are in a war; thus Paul's words in Romans 1–4, explaining the "tension" (the war) between God and humankind. People know they are wounded, they just do not know it is because they have been in a spiritual war. But when people do realize that "life is war," the proclamation of the gospel—**we have peace with God**—becomes like a cool drink to a parched pilgrim. As the prophet Isaiah said, "Come, all you who are thirsty, come to the waters" (Isa. 55:1).

Romans 5 is a poignant moment in Paul's epistle, for it begins with a message that goes straight to the heart of the gospel: the cessation of hostility by God toward man. All who desire peace with God may have it by simply changing their minds about the current state of affairs and accepting the announcement of peace. When a herald approaches from a distant land and proclaims, "We have peace!"—what has changed for the residents of the homeland? Only their minds. They have not seen the war; they have not struggled hand-to-hand with the enemy; they have not witnessed the surrender—*but they believe the gospel message that the war is over. They change from a status of being at war to being at peace.*

As you teach this chapter of Romans, make sure that you proclaim, as well as explain, the gospel! The battle really is over. Those who believe that report—that good news, that gospel—will have **peace with God through our Lord Jesus Christ.**

5:1. When Paul says **therefore**, he is preparing to draw together the two key truths which have occupied his attention in the letter so far: the need for justification by God (Rom. 1:8–3:20) and the means of justification ("faith," Rom. 3:21–4:25). **Since we have been justified** implies the need and the exercise of the solution. Perhaps the most telling turn of style in this verse could be easily overlooked: his use of **we** instead of "you" or "they." In the first four chapters of Romans, "you" or "they" occurs (in English) seventy-seven times, while "we" occurs only fifteen times, and many of those are editorial uses. The significance of his change to first person language in Romans 5:1 is that he is now addressing content which applies to those who **have been justified**—believers in Christ—as opposed to those who needed to be justified—the pagan, the religious moralizer, and/or the Jew addressed in previous chapters.

Romans 1–4 explains the condition of the wicked and how they can be declared righteous by God. Romans 5–12 addresses those who, while still sinners, have been declared righteous by God through faith in Jesus Christ. That obviously includes Paul and the believers in the Roman church—thus the switch to **we.**

Though the critical commentaries may be consulted by the teacher for a fuller discussion, several points concerning a textual problem in verse 1 are worth noting. Depending on the context in which the teacher is working, this textual problem can serve as a helpful illustration for students of the complexities of Bible translation and the factors involved in decision-making by translators:

1. *The problem:* Should Romans 5:1 read "we have" peace with God, or "let us have" peace with God? This question arises because of the presence of both readings in ancient Greek manuscripts. Which represents the original?

2. *The significance:* "We have" states an objective fact (**we have peace with God**) while "let us have" is an exhortation to pursue a subjective experience of **peace with God** based on the reality of being **justified through faith**. Both have merit theologically. The former is a position, the latter is an experience. The former says we have peace, the latter says we should pursue peace.

3. *The facts to consider:* The forms of the Greek word in questions differ by only one letter. "We have" is *exomen* (present active indicative, first person plural), while "let us have" is *exōmen* (present active subjunctive, first person plural). The similarity of the two forms could have contributed to confusion by a scribe at some point when copies of Romans were made. Or there may have been a theological bias for one form or the other by someone at some point in the history of the transmission of Paul's letter to the Romans. When the evidence from the copies of ancient Greek manuscripts is weighed, more ancient copies contain "let us have" than "we have." However, the most important factor to consider is context. Which form better fits the context in which it occurs?

4. *The decision:* On the basis of context, the English translations with the widest readership today have adopted the indicative ("we have") rather than the subjunctive ("let us have"). Paul's argument in Romans 5 is propositional, not exhortative. He is stating what is true in light of our justification. The chapter does not contain verbs in the subjunctive mood; rather, the indicative mood is the standard (cf. v. 11, "we have now received reconciliation"—present active indicative).

Some translators have tried to incorporate both senses: the NEB has "let us continue at peace with God" while Phillips's translation reads "Let us grasp the fact that we have peace." The KJV, NASB, NKJV, and NIV all read **we have peace**. For a contemporary twist, the popular translation by Eugene H. Peterson, *The Message,* says, "By entering through faith into what God has always wanted to do for us—set us right with him, make us fit for him—*we have it all together* with God because of our Master Jesus" (emphasis added to show his rendering of the words in question). Having it all together with God is definitely a propositional synonym for being at peace with him!

The New Testament is filled with places where ancient manuscripts differ, but rarely do the differences carry the theological and practical import of this example. Do we, or do we not, have peace with God on the basis of being **justified** in his sight **through our Lord Jesus Christ**? Given Paul's references to the wrath of God in Romans 1–4 (1:18; 2:5,8; 3:5; 4:15)—references which leave no doubt as to the propositional reality of wrath!—it seems clear that Paul is now saying that the most profound legal transaction in the history of the universe has changed wrath to **peace**. When God the judge declares those who place faith in Christ innocent, they immediately are at **peace** with him. On such profound declarations are built the securities, and thus the practices, of the Christian faith.

What is this **peace** we possess? Commentators agree that the Greek word *eirene* is best understood in the New Testament by its use in the Septuagint (Greek translation of the Old Testament) to translate the Hebrew *shalom*. While *shalom* is generally thought of as "peace," its meaning is much broader and deeper. Its semantic range covers "completeness, soundness, welfare, peace" (*Brown, Driver, and Briggs* Hebrew lexicon), issuing in narrow renderings such as friendship, tranquility, contentment, health, wealth, safety, soundness, and wholeness.

This is not to say that all of these shades of meaning are present in Romans 5:1, defining the peace which the believer has with God. But it is to illustrate the depth of the concept in the mind of a Jewish writer like Paul. If he had been writing Romans in Hebrew, *shalom* is probably the word he would have used. In fact, in Ecclesiastes 3:8, *shalom* is used as the opposite of war—a fitting analogy to Paul's use of peace as the replacement of wrath, and for the roots of "gospel" in the glad tidings of the cessation of war. To refer back to Eugene Peterson's rendering of Romans 5:1, peace means having it all together with God.

Here, and usually in the New Testament, **peace** is not first a reference to an internal state or feeling (e.g., "peace of mind" in 2 Cor. 2:13 is actually "rest in my spirit;" not a translation of *eirene*). Instead, **peace** is "external and objective," a condition "in which all the hostility caused by sin has been removed. It is to exist no longer under the wrath of God" (Mounce, p. 133). But what is the normal result of the cessation of wrath or conflict? Surely it is the enjoyment of the reality of peace, which certainly, and legitimately, leads to feelings of security and comfort. As C. K. Barrett has stated, **peace** "is reflected in the *feeling* of peace and security which man enjoys when he knows that he is reconciled to God" (Barrett, p. 102).

What a contrast **peace with God** must have been to the *pax Romana* (Roman peace) under which the Roman Christians were living! Begun under the first emperor Augustus (63 B.C.–A.D. 14; made emperor in 29 B.C.), the *pax Romana* was three hundred years of relative peace and prosperity enjoyed in the Roman Empire. While Roman peace was nearly ninety years old when Paul wrote Romans, it was not always a time of peace for Christians. While "peace with Rome" was unstable and insecure for believers, **peace with God** was settled. Regardless of the unsettled nature of life as a persecuted—or at best tolerated—religious minority in the Roman Empire, Christians in Rome were assured by Paul that their **peace with God** was a settled fact.

One of the ironies of history is that Augustus, under whose reign the *pax Romana* began, is also the emperor who called for the census that sent a poor Nazarene carpenter and his wife to the city of David to be counted (Luke 2:1–7). While in Bethlehem, Joseph and Mary became the parents of Jesus, who "himself is our peace" (Eph. 2:14). It would take one who *is* peace to say, "Peace [*eirene*] I leave with you; my peace I give you. I do not give to you as the world gives. Do not let your hearts be troubled and do not be afraid" (John 14:27). From objective truth flows subjective experience as much today as during the *pax Romana*.

Martin Luther, in a sermon on Romans 5, said that "peace with God" presents a remarkable antithesis:

- The righteous man has peace with God but affliction in the world, because he lives in the Spirit.
- The unrighteous man has peace with the world but affliction and tribulation with God, because he lives in the flesh.
- But as the Spirit is eternal, so also will be the peace of the righteous man and tribulation of the unrighteous.
- And as the flesh is temporal, so will be the tribulation of the righteous and the peace of the unrighteous (*Heritage*, p. 96).

As hindsight has proved, and spiritual foresight should have expected, the man-made *pax Romana* was little more than a blink in the eye of history. The lesson for the present from the church of the past is to combine 1 Timothy 2:1–2 with Romans 5:1. Pray for those in authority so that we "may live peaceful and quiet lives" ("peaceful" is actually *eremos*, tranquil), but for true peace (*eirene*) look only to God.

5:2a. The first benefit that Paul mentions flowing from peace with God is **access** to the presence and reality of God himself. For a human picture of what it means *not* to have access based on peace, consider David's tumultuous days in the court of Saul. David would enter the king's presence to serve the king, but on more than one occasion had to flee for his life, narrowly evading the sharp point of Saul's spear. Saul plotted against David to have him killed, and eventually hounded David all over the dusty Judean countryside "as a flea—as one hunts a partridge in the mountains" (1 Sam. 26:20).

Is this the access, based on peace, that one expects from the head of a kingdom? As a loyal servant of the king (loyal to the end, to his credit), David's access to Saul was dictated first by the king's daily moods, then by the king's desire for murder. What began as a relationship of grace turned into a grappling by Saul for power and control (read the whole story in 1 Sam. 18–26).

The picture that Paul paints for the Christians in Rome is one of complete, unhindered **access** to God because we have peace with God. Because our peace with God is through our Lord Jesus Christ, Paul says in Ephesians 3:12 that "in him and through faith in him we may approach God with freedom and confidence." The writer to the Hebrews echoes the same truth when he says we may "approach the throne of grace with confidence" (Heb. 4:16).

In no way is the truth of our access to God more graphically illustrated than in the ripping apart of the gigantic curtain, or veil, which blocked access to the Holy of Holies in the Jerusalem temple. Not only was the veil designed to block access to God's holiness; it also separated God from human sinfulness. But when Christ died on the cross, paying the penalty for the sin which prevented access to God personally, "the curtain of the temple was torn in two from top to bottom" (Matt. 27:51). The writer to the Hebrews says that the curtain was a picture of Christ's body being torn to provide access to God (Heb. 10:20), after which it is possible for us to "draw near to God with a sincere heart in full assurance of faith" (Heb. 10:22).

What is the **grace in which we now stand**, to which we have **gained access by faith?** Of the six times Paul mentions **grace** in Romans 5, this instance stands alone from the other five. They occur in the second half of the chapter, most notably in the context of the "gift of God" (5:16). And the gift? It is the "gift of righteousness" (5:17) and "eternal life in Christ Jesus our Lord" (6:23). In other words, the overarching **peace with God**—the *shalom* of God—has allowed us to **stand** in the place of righteousness, eternal life, and salvation by **grace** (see Eph. 2:8). Can you imagine being able to enjoy these positional blessings if we did not have peace with God?

5:2b–4. Because we have peace with God, and have received the gift of salvation by grace, we also enjoy the benefit of security—living life in the present in light of the hope and certainty of the future. Not only does life in the present have unknown factors over which we have little or no control, but also there is the factor of our own sinfulness. Paul stated earlier in this letter (3:23) that "all have sinned and fall short of the glory of God." And yet here he says that "this grace in which we now stand" gives us hope of reclaiming, now in part but completely in the future, the **glory of God** which we were created by God to reflect.

Every human being was created to be a walking billboard, a living display of the **glory of God.** Like a neon sign bereft of glowing gas, the human frame apart from God stands lifeless and unanimated, displaying nothing except the closed-for-business look of an abandoned storefront. Pieces of evidence can be found to indicate a former glory, but not enough to see it today. Therefore, Paul says, having been "justified," resulting in peace with God, the **hope** that we have in manifesting the **glory of God** brings us joy! He will expand on this theme in even greater detail in chapter 8, verses 18–25.

It is not only the position we have—standing in the grace of God—but it is also our experience which produces hope in us. Paul's words here have become some of the most memorable in the history of Christian writing. The Christian can rejoice in suffering because suffering ultimately produces hope. In what other worldview or religion in the world can it be said by the adherents that suffering produces hope? Without Paul's complete formula for hope, it does appear preposterous to believe that one could suffer and rejoice in the midst of it because of the hope it gives. How can this be? Suffering leads to hope because . . .

- suffering produces perseverance;
- perseverance produces character; and
- character produces hope.

While the NIV translates *thlipsis* here as **sufferings,** in this context the better rendering is the NASB's "tribulations." More often than not, Paul's use of *thlipsis* refers to tribulations or afflictions suffered in behalf of the ministry of the gospel. And so what is he saying—that simply suffering for the sake of the gospel produces hope? Not in and of itself. Hope arises out of a willingness to persevere in the things of God in spite of tribulation, which **perseverance** results in proven **character.** Not just **character,** but proven **character.** *Dokime* has the sense of a character that has been tested and found approved, as had the Macedonians (2 Cor. 8:2, where "severe trial" combines *dokime* and *thlipsis*), the Corinthians (2 Cor. 9:13), and Timothy (Phil. 2:22).

There is suffering in life, to be sure, but there is also suffering for the sake of the gospel and for the kingdom of God. We are not approved by God for bearing up under the sufferings of living in a fallen world, sufferings which all endure. Rather, we are approved by God, and enjoy the hope of realizing the **glory of God** when we persevere through afflictions that are brought because of our relationship with Christ.

The Corinthians were reminded by Paul that "our light and momentary afflictions [*thlipsis*] are achieving for us an eternal glory that far outweighs them all" (2 Cor. 4:17; see also Rom. 8:18; 2 Thess. 1:5). Paul and Barnabas reminded the churches they visited that "we must go through many hardships [*thlipsis*] to enter the kingdom of God" (Acts 14:22). It is "by perseverance," Charles Spurgeon said, that "the snail reached the ark."

Hope derives from persevering through afflictions wherein we prove to ourselves that we are Christ's and because we are Christ's we shall share in the **glory of God** in the future! The person who falls away from faith in the moment of suffering for Christ is the person who has failed to offer proof that he or she is standing in the grace of God. No one in the modern era epitomizes a life committed to standing for Christ more than Dietrich Bonhoeffer. In the face of persecution, imprisonment, and ultimately death by order of

Heinrich Himmler himself in April 1945, the German pastor failed to silence his voice of Christian conscience against Nazi atrocities.

Bonhoeffer lived out in his life what he had encouraged others to believe: "Suffering, then, is the badge of true discipleship. The disciple is not above his master. Following Christ means *passio passiva*—suffering because we have to suffer. That is why Luther reckoned suffering among the marks of the true Church, and one of the memoranda drawn up in preparation for the Augsburg Confession similarly defines the Church as the community of those 'who are persecuted and martyred for the gospel's sake'. . . . Discipleship means allegiance to the suffering Christ, and it is therefore not at all surprising that Christians should be called upon to suffer" (Swindoll, pp. 548–549).

5:5–8. "Hope deferred makes the heart sick," Proverbs 13:12 tells us, "but a longing fulfilled is a tree of life." Some things we **hope** for in life do not come to pass. When that happens, disappointment sets in. Disappointment produces discouragement; discouragement, unproven character; unproven character, despair. How does the Christian know that he will not one day be sick of heart? How does the believer know that one day she will not have suffered in vain? First the answer, then the two proofs, says Paul.

The answer is that we are the recipients of God's love for us ("the love of God;" subjective genitive; not "our love for God," an objective genitive), and hope that is based on God's love does not disappoint. Why? Two proofs: one subjective, the other objective.

The subjective reason is that **God has poured out his love into our hearts by the Holy Spirit, whom he has given us.** Significantly, this first mention of the Holy Spirit in Romans in relation to the life of the believer comes in the context of justification by faith. This means at least three things (Stott, p. 142): first, if you have been justified by faith, you have received the Holy Spirit. Second, the giving of the Holy Spirit is connected with the act of justification, meaning that all who are justified have experienced the Holy Spirit's presence. Third, the Holy Spirit bears witness to the believer's spirit that God loves him or her.

This last point, the subjective reason by which the believer knows that **hope does not disappoint,** is said a different way by Paul in Romans 8:16: "The Spirit himself testifies with our spirit that we are God's children." No child who is loved by its father has any doubt that the father is trustworthy; any doubt that the hope directed toward the father will not one day be a "tree of life." And the Spirit tells us—in our heart—that we are children of God.

Objectively, Paul goes on, God has already proved his love for us, in that **while we were still sinners, Christ died for us.** It is unnatural to think that one person would volunteer to die for another, even if that person was good or righteous. But who would die for an enemy? At the time when **we were still powerless** to help ourselves—strapped to the executioner's block, guilty as charged, about to die—Jesus Christ stepped forward and took the place of us, his enemies! In a godless culture, "What's Love Got to Do With It?" is a valid question. But in God's world, in Paul's day and in ours, love has everything to do with it. The Holy Spirit tells us continually of God's love for us (**poured out** is perfect tense of *ekchunno;* past action with continuing results), and points our thinking back to the space-time reality of that love—the day Jesus Christ sacrificed himself for his enemies.

5:9–11. To complete the enumeration of the benefits of peace with God, Paul declares that we are saved—now and forever. A number of contrasts in verses 9–10 make his point:

Saved Now (v. 9)	Saved Forever (v. 10)
Justified: declared free of guilt and righteous in God's sight, once and for all.	Reconciled: put an end to the hostilities between warring parties, allowing for ongoing relationship.
Justified by his blood.	Reconciled through the death of his Son.
Saved from wrath.	Saved through his life.

Here, salvation has both a "now" and a "not yet" aspect. For the one who has placed faith in Christ, justification, based on Christ's shed blood as a substitutionary sacrifice, guarantees that he or she will never experience the wrath of God. Jesus Christ experienced that wrath in the believer's place. Paul is primarily speaking eschatologically regarding wrath (**shall we be saved**; future tense); the wrath of eternal judgment that will be poured out upon all those who reject his free offer of the gift of grace. The believer is here and now **saved from God's wrath through him.**

While justification is a forensic term, establishing the legal basis upon which the believer is freed from sin, **reconciliation** is a relational term. When two parties are **reconciled,** it means they are no longer hostile toward one another. Whatever had been a matter of difference between them has been removed. They have **reconciled** their differences and are prepared to move into the future together. Both justification and **reconciliation** are accomplished through the death of Christ, but the former focuses on death while the latter focuses on **life.** It is for that reason that Paul says in verse 10 that **having been reconciled,** we shall be **saved through his life!**

Christ's death as a sacrifice was different from the Old Testament sacrifices for many reasons, not the least of which is that he did not remain dead. It is through his resurrected **life** that we are saved today, tomorrow, and forever. Not only did he come back to life after being our sacrifice; he came back to life in order to be our high priest: "Because Jesus lives forever, he has a permanent priesthood. Therefore he is able to save completely those who come to God through him, because he always lives to intercede for them" (Heb. 7:24–25). Jesus serves (present tense) as a high priest in the true tabernacle in heaven (Heb. 8:1–2) so that "if anybody does sin, we have one who speaks to the Father in our defense—Jesus Christ, the Righteous One" (1 John 2:1).

Justification did not bring about perfection in our lives; only a status, a standing, of perfection in God's sight. Those justified still sin, and the reason we will be saved in spite of our sins (the reason our sins do not become an offense to the Father and create a condition of "irreconciliation") is because Jesus Christ continually intercedes for us with the Father, applying the benefits of his death in the heavenly tabernacle. Is it any wonder that Paul says **we also rejoice in God?** Through the death and the life of Jesus Christ, we have received, and we maintain, reconciliation with God. His death is the basis of our justification and reconciliation; his life is the basis of our sanctification and our ultimate salvation. Being justified, reconciled, sanctified, and glorified is better than living a long life anticipating the wrath of God. Every believer has cause to rejoice in what God has done **through our Lord Jesus Christ.**

Such are the benefits of peace with God. It now seems that Paul was ready to conclude this portion of his letter to the Romans with a brief summary statement about how death and sin were overcome by the justification "that brings life for all men" (Rom. 5:12,18). Instead, he appears to interrupt himself and pen one of the most profound theological treatises in the history of the church. He sets forth in great detail the basis for justification by faith— how sin entered the world and destroyed the peace man had with God, and how sin was removed (paid for) so that peace with God (and life for man) might be restored.

Before looking at Paul's treatise in detail, let us examine the bigger picture of the second half of Romans 5. In essence, verses 12–19 form one long conditional sentence interrupted in the middle by a lengthy explanation of both the subordinate clause and the main clause. Here is how it works:

Subordinate clause: **Just as sin entered the world through one man, and death through sin, and in this way death came to all men, because all sinned** (v. 12). It is the *hosper* (**just as**) at the beginning of verse 12 that makes this a conditional clause. It begs for a main clause to complete its thought! But the main clause does not come until six verses later in verse 18.

Main clause: **So also the result of one act of righteousness was justification that brings life for all men** (v. 18). The *houtos kai* (**so also**) picks up the thought begun with **just as** in verse 12 and completes it in verse 18. Therefore, the heart of Romans 5:12–21 is a conditional scenario: **Just as . . . so**

also. There is obviously more to it than that, but that is the structure of Paul's argument.

The next step is to ask and answer, **Just as** "what"? and **so also** "what"? To continue our use of the peace of God as Paul's overall thought in this chapter, here is what he will say in ever-expanding levels of detail:

1. **Just as** Adam . . . **so also** Jesus Christ.
2. **Just as** Adam disobeyed God . . . **so also** Jesus Christ obeyed God.
3. **Just as** Adam disobeyed God and lost peace with God . . . **so also** Jesus Christ obeyed God and restored peace with God.
4. **Just as** Adam disobeyed God and lost peace with God for all who are physically related to him . . . **so also** Jesus Christ obeyed God and restored peace with God for all who are spiritually related to him.

That is where Paul is headed in this last section of chapter 5. It is essentially a contrast between Adam (the first Adam) and Jesus Christ (the second Adam). One final note: structurally, it helps to note where Paul broke off his conditional clause (the protasis) and where he picked up again with the main clause (the apodosis). Here is how the section works:

Verse 12: **just as** . . . (the protasis).

Verses 13–17: Paul interrupts his conditional sentence to contrast Adam and Christ.

Verse 18: Paul realizes he left his protasis way back in verse 12, so he repeats the protasis (the condition) again in verse 18 in order to pick up his original thought, and completes it with the apodosis (the main clause), both in verse 18. This is the sentence he started to deliver in verse 12 before he decided to go into more detail in verses 13–17. So, in verse 18 we have **just as the result of one trespass was condemnation for all men, so also the result of one act of righteousness was justification that brings life for all men.**

In a sense, verse 18 is the Book of Romans through chapter 4: condemnation (Rom. 1–3) and justification (Rom. 4). This section of Romans 5 has been greatly debated for twenty centuries of church history because it deals with who is guilty before God and why, and who is saved by God and how. Did Paul really interject this section into Romans on an impulse, as the structure might suggest? Probably not—unfinished and interrupted sentences are not unheard of in his writing (cf. Eph. 3:1). But the manner in which he starts over in verse 18 suggests that he recognizes that he left his readers a good ways back and needed to catch them up. Perhaps this is one of the clearest instances of the Holy Spirit carrying a human writer along to accomplish divine purposes (2 Pet. 1:21) while not overshadowing the human process of writing.

Romans 5:12–21 is not an easy passage of Scripture to diagram. All the teacher need do is review the commentaries to come away thoroughly discouraged about being able to outline this section of Scripture for his or her students. In keeping with the purpose of this commentary series—to help teachers communicate truth to students—we will focus on easily identifiable markers in this section which highlight the apostle's main point: to contrast what Adam did with what Christ did, which reveals the reason for justification which provides the peace with God we enjoy. *Christ's act reversed Adam's act and provided a basis for God to justify those who, by faith, switch their identify from Adam to Christ and regain their peace with God.* That is the heart of Romans 5:12–21.

Warren Wiersbe has noted three words used by Paul which highlight his theme (Wiersbe, p. 53). After noting these and their significance we will proceed to look at the verses which illustrate his theme through comparison and contrast.

One. This word appears in the Greek text of Romans 5:12–21 twelve times. The English reader of the NIV sees it a total of thirteen times in that translation. That is, on average, more than one occurrence per verse for this section of ten verses. Why the many uses of this term? Theologians use the term *solidarity* ("a union of interests, purposes, or sympathies among members of a group"—*American Heritage Dictionary*) to account for Paul's purpose in stressing unity with the use of "one."

Two types of solidarity are presented in Romans 5:12–21: the solidarity of the whole human race with Adam, and a new solidarity of those who are in Christ. For Paul, nested as he was in Hebrew thought and culture, the idea of corporate personality, or spiritual solidarity, was not a new thought. Terminology which refers to Israel, a nation of individuals, as a person or single entity (the same for the church being referred to as the body of Christ) is evidence of solidarity, or corporate personality. That is what Paul is doing in Romans 5:12–21—demonstrating how mankind is in solidarity with Adam, and the effects of that, then revealing a new solidarity in Christ which overcomes and overlaps with the solidarity of Adam ("overlaps" because not all of the effects of our solidarity with Adam, e.g., physical death, are removed by solidarity with Christ).

Post-enlightenment Westerners, worshipers at the shrine of individualism, are not as familiar with solidarity as were ancient cultures. But we are familiar with the language of solidarity, expressed most memorably in our age in John Donne's seventeenth meditation in his *Devotions upon Emergent Occasions:*

> No man is an island, entire of itself; every man is a piece of the continent, a part of the main; if a clod be washed away by the sea, Europe is the less, as well as if a promontory were, as well as if a manor of thy friends or of thine own were; any man's death

diminishes me, because I am involved in mankind; and therefore never send to know for whom the bell tolls; it tolls for thee. (referenced by Bruce, p. 120)

While singers-songwriters Paul Simon and Art Garfunkel tried to convince a lost-in-space generation in the 1960s that "I am a rock, I am an island, and a rock feels no pain," they were wrong. Paul is about to demonstrate that the whole human race has felt the pain of one man's sin precisely because no man is an island. Conversely, when Paul says that all believers are "one in Christ" in Galatians 3:28, he is expressing the other half of the solidarity coin.

Reign. This verb is used five times by Paul in this section (Rom 5:14,17,21). Couple this term with the presence of two main characters, Adam and Christ, each of which represents a contrasting solidarity, and immediately a plot presents itself. Since there can be only one who reigns, which will it be? The first Adam or the second Adam? Death or life? It will be one of Paul's purposes in this section to show that the life brought by the second Adam, Jesus Christ, has displaced the spiritual death brought by the first Adam.

Many/many (much) more. The adjective "many" (*polus*) and the comparative "much more" (*pollo mallon*) appear a total of six times in the passage (vv. 15,17,19). Something is obviously being compared in quantity, depth, capacity, extent, effectiveness, impact—compared somehow—which provides another clue to Paul's purpose. One of the main characters' reign is going to redound far more, and perhaps effect more people, than the reign of the other.

With these key terms in mind, let us now look verse-by-verse at what makes peace with God possible.

Ⓑ How Peace with God Was Lost: A Study in Comparison (5:12–14)

SUPPORTING IDEA: *Peace with God for the human race was lost when the first man, Adam, lost his relationship with God through disobedience.*

5:12. This is the key verse in the whole section, especially the phrase **because all sinned.** Paul seemed to anticipate the centuries of dialogue and debate—even disagreement—that would take place over his words **because all sinned.** It is following these words that he breaks off his sentence and pens verses 12–17 to offer the needed supporting materials.

Paul clearly says that **sin entered the world through one man,** meaning Adam. Genesis 3 demonstrates Adam's leadership (not Eve's; cf. Luke 3:38; 1 Cor. 11:3; 1 Tim. 2:13) and fatherhood of—and thus responsibility for—the human family. **Death** came **through sin**—again, clear from Genesis. In chapter 3 Adam died spiritually, and in Genesis 5:5 he died physically. It is the spreading of **death through sin**, and death spreading **to all men, because all sinned,** that is difficult. But the point is made here by Paul that when Adam sinned, he lost peace with God. Somehow, that sin spread to all people descended from Adam since **all sinned,** which means that everyone in the human race lost their peace with God as well.

5:13–14. Three options have been presented for how all sinned. First, Paul could mean that "all sinned" as he said they did in Romans 3:23: "All have sinned and fall short of the glory of God." In that context, Paul is talking about individual sins, and in 5:12 he would mean that because all have sinned like Adam sinned (whether by tendency or example), all have died like Adam died. The primary problem with this position is set forth in verses 13–14: sin is only known as a result of transgressing the law; **sin is not taken into account where there is no law.** In spite of there being no revealed law of God **from the time of Adam to the time of Moses,** people still died. Therefore, "all sinned" does not mean that they committed individual sins (though they did) as a basis for judgment since there was no revealed standard from **Adam to . . . Moses.**

A second meaning for "all sinned" could be that all inherited from Adam a tendency to sin (a sin nature) and knowingly sinned by violating the moral code of God written on the heart (Rom. 2:15) and thus died. The chief problem with this view is that those who are not morally accountable, such as infants and the mentally infantile, die without having knowingly violated any standard of God, written or unwritten. Whether humans have inherited a sin nature from Adam is not questioned; we have. The question is whether this is the basis for Paul's words "death came to all men, because all sinned" (v. 12).

The only way to account for those who died from **Adam to . . . Moses,** and those who die without moral knowledge of sinning, is the third view: that when Adam sinned, *humanity* (the basic meaning of Heb. *'adam*) sinned in him. This is confirmed by Paul in 1 Corinthians 15:22 where he says, "in Adam all die." Likewise, in Romans 5:8 Paul said that "while we were still sinners, Christ died for us." How could Christ die for the actual sins of those who had not yet been born? Finally, in Romans 5:18 Paul will say even more plainly that "the result of one trespass was condemnation for all men," period.

Paul's whole argument in this section of Romans is based on headship: Adam, as the head of the human race, sinned and God saw in Adam the whole human race as guilty. Conversely, the second Adam, Jesus Christ, is the head of a new spiritual race. Christ did not sin, and God saw in Christ's innocence all who unite themselves to him by faith as likewise innocent. Our being declared guilty in Adam is no more on the basis of our "sins" than being declared innocent in Christ is on the basis of our "not sins." In both cases, headship is the cause. Those who think it unjust of God to lump them into Adam's sin might consider whether they should think it just for God to lump them into Christ's righteousness.

Whether from Adam to Moses or from Moses to now, Paul says that the human race lost its peace with God as a result of guilt inherited from Adam. Thankfully, we were not left in that state; our peace with God has been won back for us by the second Adam, the explanation of which Paul now begins.

◉ How Peace with God Was Recovered: A Study in Contrasts (5:15–21)

SUPPORTING IDEA: *Peace with God was recovered the same way it was lost—by the actions of one man. Jesus Christ appeared as the "second Adam" to gain through obedience what Adam lost through disobedience.*

5:15. This section is called "A Study in Contrasts" because Adam and Christ actually did two different things, but in a similar sense (contrasts based on suggestions in Wiersbe, pp. 55–57). Adam's act of sin caused the human race to become guilty before God; Christ's acts of obedience (his years of daily obedience plus his final act of sacrificial obedience) created the potential for all human beings to have their guilt erased before God. Therefore, their actions and results are contrasted (in five ways) instead of compared.

First, Paul contrasts the sin of Adam with the gift of Christ. Paul's focus regarding Adam's sin is that "death came to all men" (v. 12) as a result. Therefore, if all Christ's obedience did was to reverse what Adam lost, then all would simply live forever and not die. But **the gift** (of righteousness; see v. 17) **that came by the grace of the one man, Jesus Christ,** resulted in **much more.** In fact, in the earlier part of this chapter, Paul highlights what some of the **much more** is: peace, access to God, hope in the future, eternal life. All that the grace of God brings to humankind is what came through the **gift** that Christ procured.

5:16. Next, Paul contrasts the timing of Adam's condemnation with the timing of the gift of Christ's righteousness. This is another aspect of the "much more" of the gift of righteousness mentioned in the previous verse. Here is Paul's argument: God's **judgment** of Adam followed only **one sin and brought condemnation.** But after thousands of years of history and billions of sins committed by multiplied millions of people, God still, by his grace, gave the human race the gift of **justification** (righteousness) through the death and resurrection of Christ. Speaking colloquially, how much "more better" is that?

5:17. Third, Paul contrasts the reign of death with the reign of life. Adam's kingdom of life was short-lived. Whatever amount of time he spent in the Garden of Eden prior to sinning was the extent of his kingdom of life. After he sinned, death reigned in his world and all of his descendants died: "Adam . . . died . . . . Seth . . . died . . . Enosh . . . died . . . Kenan . . . died . . . Mahalalel . . . died . . . Jared . . . died . . . Enoch . . . died . . . Methuselah . . . died . . . Lamech . . . died . . . Noah . . . died" and so on (Gen. 5:1–32; 9:28). Quite a legacy, in a manner of speaking. One need only fast forward a few thousand years and insert his or her parents' or grandparents' names in the list to see that the reign of death continues. But the new reign, the reign of the One who *is* life (John 14:6), Jesus Christ, has come through his obedience to God.

Paul says that Christ "must reign until he has put all his enemies under his feet. The last enemy to be destroyed is death" (1 Cor. 15:25–26). That is why the believer in Christ reigns with Christ, for the believer does not fear death. The believer in Christ knows that because the reign of "death has been swallowed up in victory" (1 Cor. 15:54), we can join Paul in mocking death: "Where, O death, is your victory? Where, O death, is your sting?" (1 Cor. 15:55). Not only do we live and reign with Christ now positionally; we will one day reign with him literally (2 Tim. 2:12; Rev. 22:5).

Once these verses on the reign of death through Adam versus the reign of life through Jesus Christ take root in the heart of the believer, Paul's exhortation in Romans 6:12 becomes much easier to understand: "Do not let sin reign in your mortal body so that you obey its evil desires." Having been rescued from the reign (dominion, realm, kingdom) of death and brought into the reign of life, why would anyone want to go back? (Col. 1:13–14).

5:18–19. Fourth, the one trespass of Adam is contrasted with the one act of righteousness of Christ. Many Bible students have gotten off track theologically in this section because of Paul's language. If these two verses were taken out of the context of Romans 5:12–21, it would be easier to justify a misinterpretation. Paul appears to make a clear parallel in verse 18 between Adam's **one trespass** and the **condemnation for all men** which resulted from it, and Christ's **one act of righteousness** that **brings life for all men**. Likewise in verse 19, it could appear that because **the many** (all humankind) **were made sinners** that **the** (same) **many** (all humankind) **will be made righteous**. The result? Universalism—the doctrine that just as Adam's disobedience caused all to die, Christ's obedience will cause all to live. All were lost, but all have been found.

While the *carte blanche* version of universalism (all were lost, but all will be saved, no exceptions) has been espoused by some more liberal Bible readers, another form has been expressed by conservative interpreters—universalism with a twist. This modified version of viewing Romans 5:12–21 makes this comparison:

The traditional, orthodox view of Romans 5: "All are lost except those who intentionally accept Jesus Christ as Savior and Lord."

The modified universalism: "All are saved except those who intentionally reject Jesus Christ as Savior and Lord."

The modified view ends up with some saved and some lost, but for different reasons than the orthodox view. The great masses of humanity who have not either accepted or rejected Jesus Christ because the gospel has never been presented to them are saved in the modified universalism view on the basis of Romans 5:18–19. The motivation for presenting the gospel changes from a decision to challenge the unsaved to accept the gospel and be saved (they are already saved) to one of accept the gospel and reap the benefits of knowing God's grace. If people hear about Christ and the grace of God and reject it, then they are lost. If they hear and continue, then they reap the benefits of the grace of God and "remain saved."

The most obvious fault with any universalism view, even one who tries to make people responsible for accepting what they hear, is verse 17: "how much more will *those who receive* God's provision of grace . . . reign in life" (emphasis added). The whole issue of solidarity in these verses (not to mention the rest of the testimony of Scripture, e.g., John 3:16) is to make it clear that those in solidarity with Christ are a new race, a subset, of the human race which is dead because of sin. Paul is not referring to the entire human race flip-flopping from death to life the day Christ was resurrected from the grave. Nor is he talking about everyone flip-flopping from death to life except those who specifically choose to stay dead by rejecting the grace of God once they hear about it. He is talking about headship. The **all** of the first Adam is not the same as the **all** of the second Adam. The Adams are different, therefore the "manys" and the "alls" are different.

Both death and life were the result of one act: one an act of sin, the other an **act of righteousness**. The condemnation of the former and the blessing of the latter flow to all who are "in" their representative head. All human beings are in Adam physically, so all die. But not all human beings are in the second Adam spiritually, so not all live. Those descendants of the first Adam for whom "there is now no condemnation" are those who are in the second Adam, "in Christ Jesus" (Rom. 8:1). And the way a descendant of the first Adam gets to be "in" the second Adam is by receiving "God's abundant provision of grace" (Rom. 5:17; see also John 1:12; Acts 2:38; 1 Tim. 1:16).

5:20–21. Finally, Paul contrasts law with grace. Content-wise, this is ground the apostle has already covered (Rom. 3:20–31). But he summarizes the place of the **law** in the discussion in anticipation of one of his readers asking, "What about the law?" In other words, he has already said that those living from Adam to Moses (those without the law) are as guilty as those living after Moses. Jews saw the giving of the law, and its corollary impact on the moral, civil, and ceremonial aspects of the nation, as the single most important distinctive of their nation. And Paul seemed to be saying that it was irrelevant in the current discussion. "Not so," Paul will say. **The law was added so that the trespass might increase.** But the law did not make anyone more or less righteous, because all sinned in Adam.

But the law did do this: by making the **trespass . . . increase**, it became a vehicle for demonstrating the "much more" of the **grace** of God to overcome the sin which the law revealed. This aspect of Paul's final section of Romans 5 is a fitting conclusion to his treatise comparing Adam and Christ. Nothing is greater than the grace of God. As the hymn writer has put it,

> Marvelous grace of our loving Lord,
> Grace that exceeds our sin and our guilt,
> Yonder on Calvary's mount outpoured,
> There where the blood of the Lamb was spilt.
>
> Grace, grace, God's grace,
> Grace that will pardon and cleanse within;
> Grace, grace, God's grace,
> Grace that is greater than all our sin.

—Julia H. Johnston

MAIN IDEA REVIEW: *The answer to life's most important question—How can one have peace with God?—is to be declared just in God's sight. Paul explains the benefits and the basis of finding peace with God.*

III. CONCLUSION

Something You Cannot Help, Something You Can

Warren Wiersbe has drawn a beautiful set of summary contrasts between the first and second Adam, and in doing so points out one thing that we cannot help, and one thing that we can:

Adam came from the earth; Jesus is the Lord from heaven.

Adam was tested in a garden, surrounded by beauty and love; Jesus was tempted in a wilderness, dying on a cruel cross surrounded by hatred and ugliness.

Adam was a thief, and was cast out of Paradise; Jesus turned to a thief and said, "Today you will be with me in paradise."

The Old Testament is the book of the generations of Adam and ends with a curse (Mal. 4:6); the New Testament is the book of the generations of Jesus Christ and ends with "no more curse" (Rev. 22:3) (Wiersbe, p 58).

No one can help being born in Adam. Every human being bears the guilt of Adam as a result of their first birth. But everyone can help *staying* in Adam. By virtue of the second birth (John 3:7)—placing faith in Jesus Christ—we can be "in Christ" forever. In Christ is where we will discover the "much more" of the grace of God.

PRINCIPLES

- Peace with God is based on something God has done, not how I feel.
- There is no time when I do not have access to God.
- Tribulation has a purpose in God's plan for my life.
- If no one else ever does, God loves me and has proved it to me.
- What I have gained in Christ is far more than what I lost in Adam.
- My sins are another way of measuring the grace of God.

APPLICATIONS

- Do I allow my circumstances to blind me to the peace I have with God?
- Do I fail to call upon God even though I have constant access to him?
- Do I welcome tribulation for Christ's sake and welcome its purpose in my life?
- When was the last time I felt self-pity because I thought no one loved me?
- Do I ever envy the non-Christian, thinking they have more than I ever will?
- Do I use my failures as a motivation to praise God for his grace?

IV. LIFE APPLICATION

It Takes One to Paint One

Rembrandt Harmenszoon van Rijn, known to the modern world simply as Rembrandt, knew of what he painted. One of the most famous artists in post-Reformation Europe, Rembrandt was raised in a devoutly Reformed home in Holland. By the age of 25, his portraits were among the most acclaimed in Holland. While he painted secular subjects as well as biblical ones, his art gradually became separated from other Protestant and Catholic painters who portrayed biblical and ecclesiastical scenes from an unrealistic, mythological perspective.

Rembrandt's deep theological understanding of the helplessness of man before a holy God pushed him to paint realistically. His own wife and son, as well as street people and beggars, became his models for paintings with biblical themes. He went so far as to include himself as one of the enemies of God in his painting of *The Raising of the Cross.* He painted himself into this piece as one of those lifting the cross, helping to crucify his own Savior. The painful, sinful, and needy state of humanity—indeed, the state of his own condition—he refused to conceal.

Toward the end of his career, he was confronted even more with his own sinfulness. When his wealthy wife died, and he was threatened by her will from losing her estate if he remarried, he instead took a common-law wife, his housekeeper, and even bore a child with her. His immoral actions brought him into conflict with the Reformed Church in Amsterdam. This fact, plus financial difficulties ultimately ending in bankruptcy, again brought into stark relief his status of a sinner before God.

When Rembrandt painted one of his last great works in 1662, *Return of the Prodigal Son,* he painted his own confession of faith that prodigal sons of a heavenly Father can only find forgiveness and reconciliation under the gentle touch of his hand. When the father of the prodigal received the kneeling penitent in Rembrandt's painting, Romans 5:8 was illustrated—"God demonstrates his own love for us in this: While we were still sinners, Christ died for us." If it takes a prodigal to paint a prodigal, it surely takes a returned prodigal to paint a reconciling father. While not everyone can apply paint to canvas with the skill of Rembrandt, our very lives are canvasses nonetheless. God would paint his reconciling message in us for all the world to see.

The peace of the prodigal son is ours in Christ. The reconciling love of the Father is ours to receive and share with others. May God help us to live in the benefits of his peace, and be ambassadors of his reconciliation to a yet-to-return prodigal world.

V. PRAYER

Heavenly Father, I praise you today that I have peace with you. Thank you that your wrath is no longer directed at my sins because of the Lord Jesus Christ taking my place in your sight. Please remind me by the promptings of your Holy Spirit to avail myself of the benefits of your peace. And may I always have the spiritual integrity to thank you for giving me, through Jesus Christ, so much more both now and for eternity, than I ever gave up by leaving Adam! Amen.

VI. DEEPER DISCOVERIES

A. Reconciliation (5:10)

Reconciliation (*katallage*) and reconcile (*katallasso, apokatallasso, diallasso*) are powerful words for New Testament theological insight. They have clear secular attestation which provides helpful insight into their sacred use. In addition, reconciliation at the theological level is a rare work of God which is also committed to man through the message of reconciliation. The occurrences of the words in the New Testament are rare enough to allow thorough study.

"For pagans and Christians alike, *reconciliation* is the action of reestablishing friendship between two persons who are on bad terms, to replace hostility with peaceful relations" (Spicq, 2:262). Non-theological uses of the words occur in the New Testament as follows: exhortation to bring peace between (reconcile) two individuals, one of whom has a complaint against the other (Matt. 5:23–24); exhortation to try and put away the complaint (reconcile) of an official toward a citizen lest it result in a jail sentence (Luke 12:58); Moses' attempt to bring peace between (reconcile) two Israelites who were fighting (Acts 7:26); command to a deserted wife to remain unmarried or be remarried to (be reconciled to) her former husband (1 Cor. 7:11). The goal is always the reestablishing—not the initial establishing—of peace between warring parties.

This carries over into the theological uses, and especially in the context of Romans 5 where the reestablishing of once-held-but-lost peace between God and man is the focus. Theologically, God takes the initiative in reconciling sinful humankind to himself (2 Cor. 5:19). Having done this initially (Rom. 5:10–11), God then commits the message of reconciliation to those who are reconciled in order that they may seek the reconciliation of others (2 Cor. 5:19). We become ambassadors of Christ, ambassadors of reconciliation (2 Cor. 5:20).

The distinction must be kept clear between our ability to reconcile (which only God has) and our ability to implore others to be reconciled (to accept the reconciliation God has accomplished and now offers). Reconciliation is the work of God, representation the work of man. Even the creation and the physical universe will be reconciled to God on the basis of the putting away of sin at the cross of Christ (Col. 1:20). The ultimate goal of the believer's reconciliation to God is holiness—free from accusation of sin, and free from the stain of sin as well (Col. 1:22).

B. First and Second Adam (5:14)

While the term "second Adam" is not found in Scripture, "last Adam" is, referring to Christ (1 Cor. 15:45). Since there were only two "Adams," the first and the last, "second Adam" has been used as a synonym for the biblical "last Adam." Paul makes a clear connection between the two in Romans 5:14, saying that the first Adam "is a pattern of the one to come." "One" here does not refer to "the Adam to come," but to Christ. Nonetheless, it is clear from Paul's further contrast between the two in Romans 5:15–19 and in 1 Corinthians 15:45–49 that the paradigm of comparing Adam and Christ was a comfortable, and perhaps common, one in the apostolic period.

Perhaps Paul drew his inspiration from Luke's understanding of the temptation experience of Jesus in the wilderness (Luke 4:1–13). Though the written version of Luke's gospel account was probably not complete and in circulation when Paul wrote Romans and 1 Corinthians, the two had spent enough time together during the missionary journeys for Luke to have influenced Paul's thinking about the first and second Adam. When Luke did write his gospel narrative, he tellingly linked the two. The last verse of Luke 3 identifies Adam as "the son of God" (Luke 3:38). Three verses later (Luke 4:3), Luke has Satan identifying Jesus as the Son of God, clearly linking the first Adam and the second stylistically and theologically.

But it is the contrasts and parallels of the temptation experience itself that so closely identifies the two "Adams": paradise versus wilderness; satisfied versus "starving"; tempted by Satan in both accounts; tempted by the lust of the flesh, the lust of the eyes, and the pride of life in both accounts; disobedience to the Word of God versus adherence to the Word of God; yielding to temptation versus resisting temptation; banished by angels versus ministered to by angels (Matt. 4:11); fall from righteousness versus established in righteousness.

Clearly, the early church (Matthew as well as Luke) saw the temptation experience of Christ as being the Garden of Eden revisited—but under the harshest of conditions, making Christ's victory all the more profound. In his victory, the second Adam regained dominance over Satan which the first Adam gave up in Eden.

C. Universalism (5:18)

Universalism, extending back to the earliest centuries of the church, is the erroneous belief that ultimately all human beings will be restored back to a right relationship with God for eternity. Some universalists have held that this occurs at death, some after a time of punishment. But ultimately, all will be restored. In addition to a misreading of the passages under consideration in this chapter (Rom. 5:18–19), universalists have appealed to verses such as Ephesians 1:10 and 1 Corinthians 15:22. Their most impassioned plea is a logical one, not a biblical one: since all were lost in Adam, all will be restored in Christ. While bearing the weight of logic, the premise does not bear the weight of language. "All" does not always mean "all without exception."

In Peter's quotation of Joel's prophecy on the day of Pentecost (Acts 2:17; Joel 2:28–32), Peter does not mean that at Pentecost the Holy Spirit was poured out on all people in the world. Rather, it is clear from the early part of Acts 2 that "representatives" of all the world is meant: people regardless of nation, age, race, etc. Likewise, when Luke says that "all the Jews and Greeks who lived in the province of Asia heard the word of the Lord" (Acts 19:10), he did not mean every living human being; rather, he meant Jews and Greeks representing all the parts of the province of Asia (see also Acts 1:1,19; 2:47; 3:9,11 and many other verses in the New Testament).

Other reasons why the "all = all" correlation does not work in the case of salvation are:

1. Because all people are physically linked to Adam does not mean that all people are automatically spiritually linked to Christ. Being physically linked to Adam required no choice; being spiritually linked to Christ requires a choice (John 1:12).

2. Romans 5:17 makes "receiving" a qualification for reigning.

3. New Testament warnings against wrath and judgment would be meaningless in the face of universalism even for those who hold to punishment followed by restoration. The New Testament does not support the concept of temporary punishment (purgatory).

4. Justification follows faith, not death (Rom. 4:1). In fact, what follows death is judgment, which does not bode well for those anticipating universal restoration (Heb. 9:27).

D. How Many Will Be Made Righteous? (5:19)

Though universalism is not taught in the Scripture, Romans 5:12–21 gives ample reason to anticipate that the number of saved will be large. John Stott gives reasons to anticipate that the number of saved will ultimately be much larger than the number lost (Stott, p. 159–160):

1. *Paul's use of kingdom terminology in Romans 5:12–21.* The use of *basileuo,* to reign, is connected to *basileia* (kingdom) and *basileus* (king). The upshot of Paul's use of this term is to say that the kingdom of life in Christ will triumph over and reign over the kingdom of death of Adam. It would be hard to imagine the kingdom of grace being less than, instead of much more than, the kingdom of sin and death for all eternity.

2. *Paul's use of superlative language. Perisseuo* (abound, exist in abundance; vv. 15,17) and *hyperperisseuo* (to super-abound, exist in greater abundance; v. 20) are Paul's way of saying how much better

are the effects of Christ's works than Adam's. He breaks the one-to-one connection between Adam's work and Christ's work with these words; they are not used to describe any part of Adam's works. Therefore, whereas death came to all through Adam, what comes through Christ abounds, even super-abounds. One thing passed to all through Adam—death. Many things super-abound to believers through the unlimited grace of grace. And the super-abundance is not just to individuals. The grace of God abounds to the human race in far greater measure than death passed to every human being. The whole of salvation, in a sense, is greater than the sum of its parts.

3. *Paul's use of* a fortiori *reasoning (reasoning that is logically more certain than another).* Paul's "how much more" is his way of saying that it just makes sense that the Son of God will save more than a mere man (Adam) lost. Though Adam lost all the human race, "how much more" of them will the grace of God reach than it will not reach. "God is superior to man, grace to sin, and life (God's free gift) to death (sin's wage)" (Stott, p. 160).

Stott concludes: "The deliberate use of these three models of speech (kingdom, superlative and *a fortiori* language) surely justifies the conclusion that the work of Christ will in the end be seen to be much more effective than the work of Adam; that Christ will raise to life many more than Adam will drag to death; and that God's grace will flow in more abundant blessings than the consequences of Adam's sin" (Stott, p. 161). He goes on to cite John Calvin, who said, "It is granted that Christ is much more powerful to save than Adam was to destroy," and Reformed theologian Charles Hodge, who theorized, "We have reason to believe that the lost shall bear to the saved no greater proportion than the inmates of a prison do to the mass of the community" (Stott, p. 161).

VII. TEACHING OUTLINE

A. INTRODUCTION

1. Lead Story: Peace, Peace, When There Is No Peace

2. Context: Chapter 5 marks a transition point in Paul's letter to the church at Rome. In chapters 1 through 4, his primary form of address was "you" and "they," referring to those who needed to understand the gospel. In fact, the letter to Romans could end with chapter 4 and contain a complete presentation of the gospel. But now Paul turns his attention to those who have received, and believed, the gospel message.

3. Transition: When a person places faith in Jesus Christ, and is justified (declared righteous) in God's sight on the basis of that faith, what difference does it make? The primary difference is that the person enters into a new realm—the realm of peace with God. What had once been a relationship marked by the wrath of God directed toward sin is now a relationship based on the cessation of hostility. The believer regains the peace, through the work of Christ on the cross, that Adam had and lost in the Garden of Eden. Paul's purpose in Romans 5 is to explain the benefits of peace with God, and explain its basis by comparing the disobedience of Adam with the obedience of Christ.

B. COMMENTARY

1. The Benefits of Peace with God (5:1–11)
   a. The promise of peace (5:1)
   b. Access to God (5:2a)
   c. Viewing the present in light of the future (5:2b–4)
   d. Experiencing the unconditional love of God (5:5–8)
   e. Saved now and forever (5:9–11)
2. How Peace with God Was Lost: A Study in Comparison (5:12–14)
   a. From Adam to the present (5:12)
   b. From Adam to Moses (5:13–14)
3. How Peace with God was Recovered: A Study in Contrasts (5:15–21)
   a. The sin of Adam contrasted with the gift of Christ (5:15)
   b. The timing of Adam's condemnation contrasted with the timing of Christ's righteousness (5:16)
   c. The reign of death is contrasted with the reign of life (5:17)
   d. The one trespass of Adam contrasted with the one act of righteousness of Christ (5:18–19)
   e. Law contrasted with grace (5:20–21)

C. CONCLUSION: IT TAKES ONE TO PAINT ONE

VIII. ISSUES FOR DISCUSSION

1. How does "peace with God" translate in the believer's life into the practical realm of living? Should those who have "peace with God" also manifest a greater sense of personal peace, contentment, or tranquility in their daily lives? Why or why not?
2. If it is true that tribulation leads to perseverance, character, and hope, why are we so averse to experiencing tribulation? How can Christians develop a "long view" toward life, incorporating the reality of

tribulation and suffering as a contributor to spiritual formation and godliness?

3. How should the example of Christ dying for us while we were sinners (Rom. 5:8) impact our relationships with other people?

4. Powerlessness was our condition when Christ died for us. What forms of power do we personally, or the church corporately, try to accumulate in today's culture? What deception is there in the accumulation of power as a means to godliness?

Romans 6:1–23

How the Gospel Delivers from Sin

"*It* is absurd ... for those who are called to reign with Christ to choose to be captives to sin, as if one should throw down the crown from off his head and choose to be the slave of a hysterical woman who comes begging and covered in rags. ... How is it that sin can reign in you? It is not from any power of its own but only from your laziness."

C h r y s o s t o m

Romans 6:1–23

I N   A   N U T S H E L L

Having completed five chapters on the need for and basis of justification, Paul now turns to the power of the gospel to change lives. The believer's identification with the death, burial, and resurrection of Christ, provided through justification, means the believer is no longer a slave to sin, but serves a new master—the righteousness of God.

How the Gospel
Delivers from Sin

I. INTRODUCTION

The "Mad Monk" Who Lived Like the Devil

*I*n his commentary on Romans, F. F. Bruce makes reference to a figure from church history who illustrated the problem of antinomianism—the casting off of moral restraint in order to experience more of God's grace and forgiveness (Bruce, p. 127). This tragic character, dubbed the "Mad Monk" by many in his day, would be a chief contributor to the 1917 Bolshevik Revolution in Russia which ushered in seventy years of atheistic materialism. A closer look at his life reveals the theological bankruptcy of antinomianism and why Paul responded so strongly to the charges against him in Romans 6:1–2.

Grigory Yefimovich Novykh (1872–1916) was born into a peasant family in Siberia, Russia. Illiterate in spite of attending school, he acquired the nickname "Rasputin"—Russian for "debauched one"—because of his flagrantly licentious and immoral lifestyle. Undergoing a religious conversion of some sort at age eighteen, he ended up at the monastery of the Khlysty (Flagellants) sect. This group had historical roots of operating outside traditional ecclesiastical structures, but Rasputin perverted their teachings into pure antinomianism: one draws closest to God when feeling "holy passionless" and arrives at that point through sexual exhaustion and prolonged debauchery.

Leaving the monastery without becoming a monk, he wandered thousands of miles through Europe and the Middle East, arriving eventually at Jerusalem. He gained a reputation as a holy mystic with the ability to heal the sick and tell the future. Arriving back in St. Petersburg in 1903, he was welcomed by clerical leaders and eventually introduced into court circles (in spite of his odoriferous propensity for never bathing).

Emperor Nicholas II and his wife Alexandra were taken with Rasputin, especially because of his healing effects on their only son Alexey, the future czar of Russia. The child was a hemophiliac, and Rasputin saved his life on one occasion by stopping his bleeding when doctors were unable to do so. This "miracle" endeared Rasputin to the royal family and gave him increased powers of influence with them. They saw him in the courts as a humble and holy religious peasant with powers from God. Outside the court, he continued to earn his nickname, attending orgies and religious services with equal devotion.

Through his belief that physical contact with his body produced healing effects, Rasputin seduced young women repeatedly and continued in all manner of immoral behavior. Rumors of an affair between Rasputin and the emperor's wife, Alexandra, even circulated. Counselors to the emperor insisted on Rasputin's removal, but the emperor failed to do so under the influence of his wife.

When Nicholas II left St. Petersburg to command Russian troops at the beginning of World War I, Rasputin became chief advisor to Alexandra, who had been left in charge of Russia's internal affairs. His influence resulted in a series of disastrous clerical and governmental appointments, causing increasing dissent among Russians suffering at the hands of the autocracy. A group of extreme conservatives, some related to the czar, and all holding influential positions, plotted in December 1916, to kill Rasputin as a way to end his deleterious influence on the Russian nation. This they accomplished in late December, but it was too late. The Bolsheviks, seizing the opportunity to capitalize on the negative perception of the emperor, revolted in 1917.

The God who was missing from the life of the Empress's closest advisor in 1916 was officially driven completely out of Russia beginning in 1917. Was antinomianism the cause of the Bolshevik Revolution in Russia? No. But there can be no way to estimate the damage done to a government (irrespective of its other weaknesses) by a man who proffered spiritual power on one hand and lived like the devil on the other.

In Romans 6, Paul twice raises and refutes the charge of antinomianism (vv. 1,15). His answer is simple: a true Christian cannot live in sin because he or she is dead to sin. The believer is no longer the servant of sin but the servant of righteousness. The chapter is spent explaining how a believer in Jesus Christ can have died to sin and been made alive to righteousness. In that explanation is the answer to the charge that Paul, or any other true believer in Christ, could possibly be an antinomian.

Now that the believer is justified through faith in Christ (Rom. 1–4), how then shall he or she live (Rom. 6–8)? In this first of three chapters on the "making holy" (sanctification) of the believer (Rom. 6–8), Paul talks about how the believer is delivered from sin by the power of the gospel. The first fourteen verses show how the grace of God has united us with Christ in his death, burial, and resurrection, and the last nine verses reveal how we are made servants of righteousness.

II. COMMENTARY

How the Gospel Delivers from Sin

> **MAIN IDEA:** *When the believer in Christ is reckoned by faith to be dead, buried, and resurrected with Christ, he or she ceases to be the servant of sin and becomes the servant of righteousness.*

Ⓐ An Objection to the Grace in the Gospel (6:1–2)

> **SUPPORTING IDEA:** *Grace is not a license to sin because the recipient of grace has died to sin and can no longer live in it.*

6:1. The Greek word *diatribe,* from which derives our "diatribe," is not a biblical word. But its parent, *diatribo,* occurs eight times in Acts, always with the meaning of "remain" or "spend time" (e.g., Acts 12:19; 14:3,28). How did we get from "spending time" to "diatribe"? *Diatribo* derives from *dia* (through, by means of, because of, for the sake of) and *tribein* (to rub hard, to make a path). It referred to spending time at something or wearing away at something, and then was applied to spending time at discourse or study. A diatribe, though having a negative connotation today of a bitter denunciation or discourse, was in the Greek world a respectable format for learning: spending considerable time at discourse and dialogue, wearing away a subject until it has been completely examined.

For his part, Paul upholds the classic definition of diatribe in Romans. He uses the method of creating fictional opponents who raise one-verse objections to what he is teaching, then wears them down with a chapter-length answer (see Rom. 3:1,3,5–9,27–31; 4:1–3,9–10). He picks up the diatribe format again in verse 1, anticipating a question to something he has just written in 5:20: "But where sin increased, grace increased all the more." He can hear his detractors: "What kind of gospel is this you are proclaiming, Paul? A gospel that requires us to do nothing to prove we are the chosen of God? Nothing, that is, except believe? If our good works count for nothing, and our sinful deeds cause the grace of God to be revealed more, then why do not we **go on sinning so that grace may increase?**"

It is not necessarily a bad question; rather, it is a question born out of ignorance. It is a question that anyone who was having a mystery explained to him in detail for the first time would ask (Rom. 11:25; 16:25; Eph. 3:3–9; 6:19). If anything, this chapter of Romans is about "knowing." Twice Paul affirms things "we know" (vv. 6,9—though even here, there may be a slight dig by the apostle in the sense of "you do know, don't you?"), and twice he asks them outright, "Don't you know?" (vv. 3,16). Then a fifth instance "commands" that the Roman believers go further than just knowing—they must calculate and credit themselves as the possessors and beneficiaries of certain knowledge (*logizomai*, present middle imperative; v. 11).

So when Paul enters back into the diatribe mode in v. 1 (and again in v. 15), he does so not as a bitter denunciation. He does so as one who, with the Thessalonian believers, was "like a mother caring for her little children" (1 Thess. 2:7). As a mother would want her children to know—even possess and act on—the truth, so Paul wants that for the Roman church. What is his answer to the question?

6:2. His answer is *me genoito!* **By no means!** No one ever accused Jewish mothers of not speaking the truth when it needed speaking, and here Paul plays that role. Fourteen times in his epistles (ten times in Romans alone), he uses this phrase to separate truth from error. Depending on the context, the NIV becomes a thesaurus for *me genoito:* "Not at all!" (Rom. 3:4,31; 9:14); "Certainly not!" (Rom. 3:6; 7:7); "By no means!" (Rom. 6:2,15; 7:13; 11:1); "Never!" (1 Cor. 6:15); "Absolutely not!" (Gal. 2:17; 3:21); "May I never" (Gal. 6:14). Every rookie seminary student loves to see *me genoito* on a Greek vocabulary quiz because there are so many ways to get it right!

But as history (and the "Mad Monk") demonstrates, there are many ways to get theology wrong, and Paul does not want the church in Rome to be in error over such a critical area of truth as sin and grace. **By no means!** gets their attention, which is followed by the answer that he spends the rest of the chapter explicating ("detailed, learned, and lengthy exploration or analysis"—*American Heritage Dictionary*): **We died to sin; how can we live in it any longer?**

The tenses of the two verbs in his answer explain Paul's answer clearly: **We died to sin** (aorist tense; past action, viewed as a single, completed act), therefore **how can we live in it any longer?** (future tense; ongoing, repeated action in the future). The NIV's **how can we live in it** does not convey the future tense, and therefore set up the contrast with the aorist tense **(we died)** as well as the NASB's "How shall we who died to sin still live in it?" Eugene Peterson's *The Message* is even more graphic: "If we've left the country where sin is sovereign, how can we still live in our old house there? Or did not you realize we packed up and left there for good?"

The sense is this: "Something permanent happened to you in the past. Therefore, how could you think that something contrary to that past act could possibly be right for the present and the future? You **died to sin.** Therefore, how could you think (and ask) whether it would glorify God for you to "go on sinning so that grace may increase" (v. 1)? It is good for God's grace to be revealed more and more, but not if it happens as a result of something that is contrary to God's clearly revealed will in the past—your death **to sin.**" Certainly Paul anticipated his reader's next question: "Died to sin? What do you mean that we 'died to sin'?"

B   The Death of Christ Was a Death to Sin (6:3–7)

> **SUPPORTING IDEA:** *The believer in Christ is united with Christ in his death so that the sin nature might be done away with.*

Paul said in Romans 5:12 that "sin entered the world through one man, and death through sin, and in this way death came to all men, because all sinned." Then he said that in the same way that all were made sinners by one man's actions, "the many will be made righteous" (5:19) by another man's action. The solidarity of mankind in sin was replaced by a new solidarity (for those who would receive it)—a solidarity of righteousness in Christ. Part of the human race—all who have exercised faith toward God—would become a "faith race" and find a new solidarity in Christ. The reason that this is possible is that *Christ died a death to sin for all humankind.* His death—a death brought on by the guilt of Adam's sin—was to be a death for all who want to be free from sin. That is what Paul means when he says that the Roman believers had "died to sin" in Christ. And that is what he explains in Romans 6:3–7.

First, he reminds them that their baptism pictured the death of Christ (6:3–4), and then he explains that the purpose of Christ's death—and their death in Christ—was to be free from sin (6:5–7).

6:3–4. Paul reminds the Roman believers (**don't you know?**) of the meaning of their baptism. It is unfortunate that many modern believers in Christ can read these two verses and wonder if Paul is speaking metaphorically or figuratively about baptism— referring to some baptism of which they are unaware and with which they have had no experience. Granted—there is more than one kind of baptism mentioned in the New Testament and, yes, most of them are figurative. For instance, John the Baptist said that, whereas he baptized with water, Jesus Christ was coming to baptize with the Holy Spirit and with fire (Matt. 3:11; John 1:33). Jesus himself confirmed the coming baptism by the Holy Spirit (Acts 1:5), and the fire appeared as well (Acts 2:3).

In addition, Paul said there is a non-water baptism by which the Holy Spirit places (immerses?) every believer into the body of Christ (1 Cor. 12:13). Even the Israelites, Paul said, were somehow baptized "into Moses" as they were engulfed by the cloud and (seemingly) by the Red Sea (1 Cor. 10:2).

But in this case, Paul is referring to literal water baptism, and in a way that is unfortunately not emphasized when modern believers are baptized. Several important truths concerning baptism should be noted here: First, Paul is making the assumption that all the believers in Rome had been baptized. When he says **all of us who were baptized into Christ Jesus,** he is not referring to all the believers who had been baptized as opposed to all the ones who had not. He is referring to **all** believers as opposed to non-believers who had not been **baptized into Christ Jesus.** Baptism does not appear to be an optional event in the Christian experience as it is for many modern believers.

Not only is baptism not optional, the New Testament, especially the Book of Acts (see, e.g., Acts 9:18 and "Deeper Discoveries"), gives ample evidence that baptism occurred in the immediate context of faith-conversion. This is almost unheard of in contemporary Christendom. Often weeks, months, even years will pass between the time a person becomes a believer in Christ and his or her baptism. In modern Christianity, the primary emphasis is placed upon the intellectual event of "believing," which is completely consistent with the post-Enlightenment environment of rational intellectualism. However, in the New Testament, equal emphasis appears to be placed on the physical—repenting and being baptized (Acts 2:38), accompanied by exhortations, warnings, and teachings that baptism without faith is a dead work; that baptism must be, as the Anglican catechism says, "an outward visible sign of an inward spiritual grace."

Not only did baptism happen, and happen in the immediate context of conversion, it meant something! Here is a test which any teacher can use: before teaching the content of Romans 6:3–4, take a poll of the believers in the setting where you are teaching to determine how many of the believers have in fact been baptized, and what the average amount of time was that elapsed between conversion to Christ and baptism (you will likely be surprised). Then, have some people share their understanding of the meaning of baptism. See how many people can explain baptism in the terminology Paul uses in Romans 6:3–4.

You will likely not be surprised—but shocked! Most modern believers have not been taught the theological significance of baptism, nor do they know the important place baptism has as a symbol to be used by the Holy Spirit in their conscious minds and imaginations to help them live lives free from the mastery of sin (in the same way that the bread and cup are symbols which stimulate and motivate the believer to worship and holiness vis-à-vis the Lord's Supper).

All believers should know and unite around the truths concerning baptism that Paul presents in these verses. To not understand the connection between baptism and freedom from sin is to miss a critical link between Romans 1–5 (justification based on the life, death, burial, and resurrection of Christ) and Romans 6–8 (living sanctified lives based on the imputation of the efficacy and merit of the life, death, burial, and resurrection of Christ).

The shortest version of Paul's message in verses 3–4 is to reverse the order:

Verse 4b: Jesus Christ's act of obedience by going to the cross—and his subsequent resurrection—was an act of solidarity in behalf of a human race that had inherited a permanently fatal sentence of death from father Adam (Rom. 5:12,19). His purpose was to provide **a new life** for all who would, by faith, identify with him and his act of obedience to **the glory of the Father.**

Verse 4a: When Jesus Christ died on the cross and was resurrected on our behalf, he provided a faith-focus for the believer. Just as those who looked upon the bronze serpent in the wilderness were saved (Num. 21:8–9), so any who look upon the cross of Christ are saved today (John 3:14–15). We were not crucified and buried; Christ was. But when we are baptized as believers-in-what-he-did, we are baptized into—immersed in, made partakers of—[his] death in order that . . . **we too may live a new life.**

Verse 3: "**Don't you know** this?" Paul seems to be saying. "Don't you know that you died to sin when you believed in Christ who died to the condemnation of sin that was yours? When you were baptized, you **were baptized into his death.**"

Remember: these statements of Paul's are in answer to the question of his fictional opponent, "Shall we go on sinning?" (v. 1). He is answering, in essence, by saying that your baptism proves that you died to sin: *"How can you possibly continue in something to which you died?"* The believer who has died to sin has also been raised to **live a new life.** Sin was the old life, and your baptism means you agreed to be identified with a new life. *How can you possibly think of leaving your new life and going back to your old life?*

Baptism in the New Testament—and we are living in the era of the New Testament—is as close to getting saved by works *without doing so* as one can get. This is why some have misinterpreted verses in the New Testament and suggested that there is a connection between physical baptism and spiritual regeneration. There is not! Salvation is by faith alone. But when Peter says, "Get up, be baptized and wash your sins away, *calling on his name*" (Acts 22:16; emphasis added) and "baptism that now saves you" (1 Pet. 3:21), it is not difficult to see the parallels between faith and baptism—but like railroad tracks, they remain parallel, never converging. Paul's words to the Philippian jailer connect the two more clearly: "Believe in the Lord Jesus, and you will be saved . . . then *immediately* he and all his family were baptized" (Acts 16:31–33; emphasis added).

The reason for the immediacy of baptism following conversion is because of what Paul explains in Romans 6:3–4. Baptism puts the believer physically, emotionally, and spiritually in touch with the object of his or her faith—the person and work of the Lord Jesus Christ who was crucified for them, in the following manner:

Paul's final words of verse 4—**we too may live a new life**—are the focus of his continuing explanation in verses 5–7: the purpose of death is to be freed from sin; to live a life no longer enslaved to the power, shame, and judicial guilt of sin, but a life "enslaved" to righteousness.

	Jesus Christ	Believer
Death	A submission of the will to the Father's plan; a choice to die; death on a cross.	Agreement of the will with the Father's judgment: "I deserve to die and accept God's just decision and his merciful provision;" the point of conversion by faith for the believer.
Burial	The experience of being covered by death in a tomb or the "earth." Christ took upon himself the sins of the world but in death was separated from sin as a master or condemner. Sin has no power over the dead.	Waters of baptism "cover" the believer as a picture of burial in a tomb or the earth. As Christ was separated and freed from the sins of the world in death, so the believer is symbolically freed from sin as a master.
Resurrection	Christ was resurrected from the dead to a "new life."	As the believer comes out of the waters of baptism, **a new life** is begun.

6:5–7. Again taking Paul's words in reverse order will bring his argument into quick focus:

Verse 7: **Anyone who has died has been freed from sin.** This is a plain, literal statement; its simplicity has caused many to miss its power. ($E=mc^2$ seems simplistic. It is not simplistic, but it is *simple*. Einstein would have suggested the difference between the two was nothing less than "atomic.") Why are there no stone walls crowned with barbed wire, no K-9 corps, no towers with search lights, no armed guards patrolling the perimeters of . . . cemeteries? Because the possibility of illegal activity by the "residents" of these underground dwellings is zero. Why? Because the dead have been **freed from sin.** They are free from the temptation of it. They are freed from the committing of it. They are freed from the guilt of it. And they are freed from punishment for it. They are **freed from sin.** That is easy to understand for the dead, but Paul is talking about the living.

Verse 6: Believers have been **crucified with him** (Christ) so that we might enjoy, while living, the same benefit that the dead enjoy—freedom from sin. Only one thing can free a person from the temptation, commission, guilt, and punishment of sin—death! But all would agree that death is a high price—the ultimate price—to pay. Paul knew it. That is why he cries out, personifying one with no hope who realizes that death is the only exit from sin, "Who will rescue me from this body of death?" (Rom. 7:24). Note his word—*rescue*. Sin is a one-way journey to death. The only way to be freed from it is to allow it to take its natural course—death—or be rescued. "Thanks be to God," he says, because "Jesus Christ our Lord" has *rescued* us from the dominion of darkness and brought us into the dominion of righteousness (Rom. 7:25; Col. 1:13).

Verse 5: The benefit of being **united with him . . . in his death** is that **we will certainly also be united with him in his resurrection.** Unlike those in the cemetery who have died in ages past, the believer is resurrected immediately following his or her death with Christ. Again, this is the picture gained through baptism. We die, then we live.

A few points need to be made to clarify what Paul is expressing. First, the analogy between dead people and living people being freed from sin breaks down at an obvious point. It is impossible for people in cemeteries to sin; the same cannot be said for believers in Christ. Here is the difference: those who have identified with the death and resurrection of Christ still have the potential for sin, but they no longer have the *obligation* to sin. Paul will explain in detail further in chapter 6 the difference between being a slave to sin and a slave to righteousness. One is obligated to obey a master, but believers are no longer **slaves to sin.** Therefore, believers are not obligated to "obey its evil desires" (Rom. 6:12). Identifying with Christ through faith and baptism does not free the believer from the possibility of sin, but it does free the believer from the obligation to sin.

Second, there are three key clauses in verse 6 that succinctly define Paul's point in this section:

1. **Our old self was crucified with him.** It was not our capacity to sin that died with Christ, but our **old self.** The capacity to sin still lives, but our old life does not. The life of "transgressions and sins, in which you used to live when you followed the ways of this world and of the ruler of the kingdom of the air," by which we gratified "the cravings of our sinful nature" and followed "its desires and thoughts"—that life died with Christ (Eph. 2:1–3). The life we lived as "sexually immoral . . . idolaters . . . adulterers . . . male prostitutes . . . homosexual offenders . . . thieves . . . greedy . . . drunkards . . . slanderers . . . swindlers"—that life died with Christ (1 Cor. 6:9–10). "That is what some of you were," Paul says. "But you were washed . . . sanctified . . . justified in the name of the Lord Jesus Christ (1 Cor. 6:11; see also Eph. 4:22; Col. 3:9)

2. **The body of sin** has been **done away with.** The body of sin here refers to our proclivity to sin. But it has not been **done away** in the sense of being eradicated. *Katargeo* is broadly translated. It can mean everything from "abolish" to "fade away" to "render powerless." *Katargeo* is built from *kata* ("according to") and *argeo* ("to be idle"), the latter word being a combination of the negative prefix *a* and the noun *ergon* ("work," "deed," or "result"). Therefore, *argeo* is the negation of work or activity or deeds or results. But negation by eradication or negation by the removal of power? The whole thrust of Paul's argument demands "negation by removal of power." Why

would he, in verse 13, exhort the Roman believers not to offer themselves to sin if they did not have the potential to do so? Therefore, the inclination to sin has not been eradicated, but it has been rendered powerless when we walk in God's power.

3. We are **no longer . . . slaves to sin.** This is how the **body of sin** has been rendered powerless. A freed slave can stand directly in the presence of his or her former master, look the master in the eye, and ignore every command. Is there a temptation based on history and precedent to ask with trembling voice, "How high?" when the former master says "jump!"? Of course there is; old habits die hard. But there is neither the obligation to jump nor to ask "how high?" There is the complete freedom to turn and walk away. The reason is because we have been **freed from sin** (v. 7)—and this is the key term which ties this truth to the preceding five chapters of Romans.

Guess what Greek word is behind **freed from sin?** It is Paul's old standby, *dikaioo*—to justify, to pronounce righteous. The term that forms the bedrock of the gospel in Romans 1–5, to justify, is here translated in the NIV as **freed.** We have been "justified" from our sins (*dedikaiotai;* perfect passive indicative; we are the recipients of an action in the past which has results continuing into the future). We have been "declared righteous" in spite of our sins. We have been declared "free to go" because the price for our sins has been paid by another. We are no longer under the dominion of sin, of darkness, whose only way out was death. We have been rescued by another (Col. 1:13) who went down the road of death for us, freeing us from the obligation, the control, the guilt, and the penalty of both Adam's sin and our own sins.

When prisoners are released from bondage, or a slave is emancipated, they have to go somewhere—and so it is with the believer in Christ. If we have been freed "from" sin, what have we been freed "to"? The ancient father, Cyril of Jerusalem, summarized it well in his *Catechetical Lectures:* "As Jesus died in taking away the sins of the world, that, by doing sin to death, he might rise in righteousness, so too, when you go down into the water and are, in a fashion, entombed in the water as he was in the rock, you may rise again *to walk in newness of life*" (Bray, p. 155; emphasis added).

Ⓒ The Resurrection of Christ Was a Resurrection to Life (6:8–10)

SUPPORTING IDEA: *The believer in Christ is united with Christ in his resurrection so that he might live to God.*

6:8–9. Both here and in verse 5, when Paul says "if," he is saying "since" ("*ei* with 'the indicative of logical reasoning'"; Moo, p. 377). His opening statement in this verse could be translated, "Since it is true that we died with

Christ, we believe that we will also live with him" (Moo, p. 377). By his use of grammar, Paul wants the Roman believers (and us) to know that we have **died with Christ,** and that given that fact, **we will also live with him.** Life with him, life lived "to God" (v. 10), is what the believer is freed from sin "to." We can no more not live with Christ, than Christ cannot live to God. If God raised Christ, we are also raised with him.

And what is this living **with him?** It is nothing short of the transformation of our lives, our sanctification. Think of those who actually did **live with him** in person. Were their lives not radically altered? Did Peter, James, John, and the others not discover a measure of life, a way of life, that they had never known? A life that became so precious to them that they were willing to die for its promulgation? What believer today, given the opportunity and a clear vision of this new life, would not want to live with Jesus? Who would not want to have him as a friend, a teacher, a counselor, a protector?

If we could boil the theological concept of sanctification down to a manageable phrase, would it not be "living with Jesus"? Granted, not all who lived with Jesus were sanctified. But none who wanted to be made holy were left unholy; none who wanted to follow him were turned away; none who wanted to **live with him** were told they could not. And so it is for us, Paul says. **If we died with Christ, we believe** (*pisteuo;* we have faith, confidence, surety) **that we will also live with him.**

The reason for our confidence is his resurrection. As Paul told the Corinthians, "If Christ has not been raised . . . you are still in your sins . . . [and] we are to be pitied more than all men" (1 Cor. 15:17–19). But he was raised; and because he was raised **he cannot die again; death no longer has mastery over him.** And because it does not have mastery over him, it does not have mastery over us, because we died and were raised with him. **Has mastery** is present active indicative of *kurieuei,* from *kurieuo,* to exercise lordship over. **Death** has no ongoing position of lordship over the Lord, nor over those who are the Lord's. Christ submitted to the reign of death (Rom. 5:21) once for those on whom death had a claim. But having done it once, he will never do it again.

6:10. Christ died **once for all** (aorist tense; one completed act), but **the life he lives** (present active indicative; ongoing, continuous action), **he lives to God** (see Heb. 7:27; 9:12,26,28; 10:10; 1 Pet. 3:18; Rev. 1:18). What were we freed to do? To live with Jesus, to live to the glory of God. That is as certain a reality as the death and resurrection of Christ himself. "If Christ were to die again, it follows that those who have died with him and who will be raised with him will also die again along with him! Therefore, the apostle makes it clear that Christ will never die again, so that those who will live with him may be sure of having eternal life" (Origen; quoted in Bray, p. 161).

The question at this point is not one of "What?" but of "How?" How does this actually become a reality in the life of the believer? Fortunately, the key is not new ground. In fact, it is ancient ground, the ground upon which Abraham stood in Genesis 15:6, to which Paul refers in Romans 4:3.

D Christ's Death and Resurrection Are Imputed to the Believer (6:11–14)

SUPPORTING IDEA: *Just as sin and death have no mastery over Christ, the believer can be free from the mastery of sin by faith.*

It is at this very point in our understanding of New Testament theology that a whole series of familiar verses will begin to take on better sense and meaning. Verses such as John 3:3 (the concept of being "born again"), 2 Corinthians 5:17 (the concept of becoming a "new creation" in Christ), and Galatians 2:20 (the concept of myself no longer living but Christ living in me) are mysteries to most believers. They sound like ideas that Scripture writers use to describe the Christian experience, but which might be more at home in a fantasy or fiction work. In other words, they are good word pictures, but are not intended to be embraced as literal truth. And in a sense, they are not "literal."

Nicodemus asked Jesus if a person would (literally) enter a second time into the womb in order to be born again (John 3:4). The answer was and is "No." But word pictures, metaphors, are intended to reveal a truth that is concrete. So there are figures of speech involved. But many Christians have a hard time believing that the truth behind the figure is true truth—that I have (somehow) been born again, am (somehow) a new creation, and (somehow) have Christ living his life in me. The same could be said about Paul's current discussion: the fact that we have died with Christ, have been raised with him, and are no longer under the mastery of sin. Paul's explanation of how we incorporate the truth of Romans 6 into our lives will help incorporate other hard-to-manage truths of Scripture as well.

To experience the freedom from the mastery of sin that Paul is teaching, there are three things the believer must do: count (v. 11), cut (v. 12), and consecrate (v. 13), followed by a conclusion (v. 14).

6:11. In the simplest of terms, Paul says that the way we are to experience what Jesus experienced (**in the same way** that he is free from sin to live to God) is to **count yourselves dead to sin but alive to God. Count yourselves**—so far, this has been something that God has done to us, and now Paul says we are to do it to ourselves. For instance, in Romans 4:3 Paul says that "Abraham believed God, and it was credited to him [counted to him] as righteousness." That forms the basis of Paul's argument in Romans 4 that God likewise will credit righteousness to the account (**count yourselves**) of those who exercise faith like Abraham did.

The word is *logizomai* which can mean "to count," "to credit," "to think." In the numerous times Paul uses the word in his epistles, the NIV translates it with the following semantic range: "think" (Rom. 2:3; 2 Cor. 11:5; 12:6; Phil. 4:8), "regard" (Rom. 2:26; 9:8; 14:14; 1 Cor. 4:1), "maintain" (Rom. 3:28), "credit" (Rom. 4:3,4,5,6,9,10,11,22,23,24; Gal. 3:6), "count" (Rom. 4:8; 6:11; 2 Cor 5:19), "consider" (Rom. 8:18,36; 2 Cor. 10:7; Phil. 3:13), "keep a record" (1 Cor. 13:5), "reason" (1 Cor. 13:11), "claim" (2 Cor. 3:5), "expect" (2 Cor. 10:2), "realize" (2 Cor. 10:11), "hold" (2 Tim. 4:16). Anyone who ever doubted the richness of the English language will appreciate the depth and variety of terms used to translate a single Greek word.

Logizomai is from *logos*, an idea embodied in a word (or, in the case of Christ, a person). *Logizomai* here is present middle imperative, a command to be carried out upon oneself: count yourselves. In essence, *logizomai* says that words have meaning. When believers in Christ arrive in heaven one day, they will see Abraham. Why? Because God declared that Abraham was righteous. What God said had meaning, and the results of it will be shown when we arrive in heaven and see Abraham, just like God said. In the same way, if God says those who have died and been raised with Christ are **dead to sin**, they *are* **dead to sin**.

This is not a word game, or a matter of positive thinking. It is a matter of conforming our minds and renewing our minds (Rom. 12:2) to the truth from God's perspective. It is a matter of believing (and coming to understand experientially) that when God speaks truth . . . because his words are alive they bear fruit and produce results (Isa. 55:11; Heb. 4:12). God's words change things (Mark 4:39) and people (Mark 2:9–12). So when God says that the believer in Christ is dead to sin as a result of identification with the death and resurrection of Christ, that person has, in fact, been changed from being a person alive to sin to being a person dead to sin.

Because words are how we communicate and think, and because different words will strike a responsive note in different people different ways, the entire semantic range of a concept like *logizomia* is helpful to meditate upon:

Logizomai	[that is . . .]	that this is true.
count yourselves . . .	think for yourselves, regard yourselves as, maintain for yourselves, credit your-selves, consider yourselves, keep a record for yourselves, reason with yourselves, claim for yourselves, expect for yourselves, realize for yourselves, hold onto for yourselves . . .	. . . dead to sin.

6:12. Based on what we have embraced as true about our newfound status regarding sin, Paul commands (imperative of *basileuo*) us not to **let sin reign in your mortal body so that you obey its evil desires**. We are to cut our ties to sin. This command, coupled with the command to "count yourselves" in the previous verse, proves without doubt that the old self that was crucified with Christ was not the sin nature. Rather, it was the previous sinful lifestyle. Paul warns the believer here to cut the ties to the previous sinful lifestyle. Christ submitted himself to the reign (*basileuo*) of sin when he died in order that "grace might reign through righteousness" (Rom. 5:21). How could a believer allow sin to **reign** and **obey its evil desires** when Christ has already submitted to the reign of sin in death?

6:13. Finally, we are to consecrate ourselves to God and **offer the parts of [our] body to him as instruments of righteousness**. Offer (*paristemi*) brings the language of sacrifice and worship to mind quickly. Romans 12:1 is an obvious parallel, where Paul says to "offer your bodies as living sacrifices . . . [which is] your spiritual act of worship." Another illuminating use of this word is in Matthew 26:53, where Christ says that, if needed, the Father "will at once put at my disposal (*paristemi*) more than twelve legions of angels." The predominant use of this word in the New Testament is to refer to "bystanders"—i.e., those who are constantly there by the side as a backdrop. The sense seems to be to come and stand alongside God, offering what you have to him as **instruments of righteousness**. We are to be at his disposal for the purposes of righteousness—body, mind, will, emotions, spirit. Paul is preparing to expound the whole concept of "offering" in verses 15–20 in terms of who one is enslaved to. It is all a matter of mastery—whether sin or righteousness is the master.

6:14. In conclusion, Paul reminds the Roman believers that the gospel they are hearing about is a gospel of grace. For those under the law, sin is the master, simply because the law has no power to enable one to resist sin. Law does an excellent job of pointing out failure, but it cannot empower one to keep from failing. Only one thing can: **grace**. Paul had already told his readers that **grace** will reign through righteousness to bring eternal life (Rom. 5:21), and the time for that in the individual's life is once the identification with Christ's death and resurrection has been made. Once the identification with Christ is made, it is the constant flow of grace into the life of the believer that "teaches us to say 'No' to ungodliness and worldly passions, and to live self-controlled, upright and godly lives in this present age" (Titus 2:11–12).

An extended word from F. F. Bruce is helpful on the whole matter of death to sin:

Is it a legal fiction, or an exhortation to pull ourselves together and make a new start, a good resolution to do better in the future? . . . Is this just an exertion of the will, or an effort of the imagination? No, it is not. It is something that has proved its reality in the lives of many, and such people have no difficulty in understanding what Paul means. For the God of whom he speaks is the living God, and when men and women present themselves to him, to be used in his service, he accepts them as his servants and gives them the power to do his will. The Christ of whom Paul speaks is the Christ who truly died and rose again, and in the lives of those who put their trust in him "He breaks the power of cancelled sin." (Bruce, p. 133)

E The Believer Is Emancipated from Sin and Enslaved to Righteousness (6:15–19)

SUPPORTING IDEA: *When the believer is the servant of righteousness, he or she is free from the control of sin.*

The second half of this chapter of Romans serves as an illustration of the first half. In verses 1–14 Paul teaches the principle that the gospel frees the believer from the power of sin when the believer reckons himself or herself dead to sin and raised to a new life of righteousness. As a result of that truth, Paul exhorts the believer in verse 13 to offer the parts of his or her body to God as instruments of righteousness. To illustrate that exhortation, Paul will use the analogy of slavery in verses 15–23.

6:15. This is the second time in this chapter that Paul uses the diatribe format to raise and answer the same question: Does not grace allow for the throwing off of all moral restraint? The pattern here is the same as in the earlier part of the chapter: proclaim grace (5:21); raise the objection (6:1); answer the objection (6:2–14). Here the pattern is: proclaim grace (6:14); raise the objection (6:15a); answer the objection (6:15b–23). There is little difference between the two objections. As for his answers, Paul answers the first one theologically and the second one illustratively. It was Augustine who best summarized the principles Paul expounds in these chapters when he said, "Love and do as you please" (Augustine, cited by Bruce, p. 133).

6:16. Before looking at the details of Paul's analogy, it is helpful to note in verse 19 his stated reason for using slavery as an analog: **because you are weak in your natural selves.** In other words, he begins the analogy here in verse 16, and then offers in verse 19 his reason for using it. In essence, he is simply doing what any good teacher will do to aid understanding—finding a point of common ground with his students that will move a concept (death to sin) from the abstract realm to the concrete.

Slavery would have been a good analogy to almost any audience Paul addressed in his day, as it was a widespread practice (cf. Paul's letter to Philemon). But slavery was particularly apropos to his audience in Rome because of the number of slaves in the city. It has been estimated that perhaps the majority of the population of Rome was comprised of slaves of one sort or the other. Certainly some, if not many, of the believers in the Rome church were slaves. Therefore, Paul's analogy would immediately be understandable to them. They would either be slaves against their will (e.g., prisoners of war), or voluntary slaves (more on the order of household servants who indentured themselves to a household for the purposes of welfare or survival).

Interestingly, Paul will address both kinds of servants in this passage, though the "voluntary" servant is his primary focus. Based on what he wrote in Romans 5, everyone is born a "slave to sin"—without choice of will. His primary focus here, however, is the death to sin that allows the voluntary offering of oneself to another master for service.

Paul picks up a key word from verse 13—"offer." In verse 13, he told the Roman believers to offer themselves to God for purposes of righteousness. Implicit in the offering, he says here, is slavery. Regardless of who you offer yourself to, you become a slave of the one you serve. If I offer myself to God, but obey sin, then I am a slave of sin, not of God. So in answering the objection raised in verse 15—"shall we sin because we are not under law but under grace?"—the answer is "no" because you will become the slave of sin, not of God, if you do. And that **leads to death**. If you are a Christian, and continue to sin because you know God's grace will forgive you, you have in reality become a slave **to sin**.

On the other hand, obeying God means you are a slave to **obedience, which leads to righteousness**. The inconsistency of this is to illustrate what was taught in the first half of the chapter: the believer has died to sin in Christ; how and why would one submit himself to a master to whom he or she had died? (Note Paul's juxtaposition of sin and obedience in this verse. We might have anticipated him saying "or to righteousness, which leads to life," so as to parallel **death** with life, instead of **or to obedience, which leads to righteousness**. Apparently in Paul's mind the opposite of sin is obedience to God; therefore, anyone who sins cannot be said to be obeying God as his or her master.)

6:17. Paul commends the Roman believers for, in practice, fulfilling what he has been explaining to them in principle: obeying **the form of teaching to which [they] were entrusted**. Two things are worthy of note here. One is **the form of teaching**. It is easy to forget that first-century believers did not have "Bibles" as we refer to them today—convenient, codified collections of the canon of Scripture. The Old Testament existed on scrolls in synagogues, and the New Testament was being written. Instead of written copies of Scripture, oral tradition was the means for transferring history and teaching from one place, or one generation, to another.

The Oriental practice of oral tradition has never been illustrated as dramatically as it was in Alex Haley's monumental fictionalized chronicle, *Roots* (1976). Haley, a modern African-American, traced his family roots back hundreds of years to his homeland, Africa, and ended up in a village in an area where his ancestors apparently lived. Because there were no written historical or genealogical records in which he could search for the name of his ancestor, Kunta-Kinte, he had to sit and listen to a village elder recite from memory the lengthy genealogies of the tribe. In the midst of the scores of the names the elder was reciting—so-and-so begat so-and-so—Haley suddenly heard the name of his ancestor, Kunta-Kinte. He knew he was home!

The oral genealogies the elder recited were of the same style as the genealogies and lists found in Genesis 4, 5, 10, 11; 1 Chronicles 1–9; Ezra 2, 8; Nehemiah 7; Matthew 1; and Luke 3. Genealogies, history, and eventually moral and ethical codes (cf. the Decalogue, the Ten Commandments, as a summary of the entire Mosaic Code, which was eventually summarized by Jesus in just two commandments; Exod. 20:1–17; Deut. 5:1–21; Matt. 22:36–40) were all first codified in forms easily transferred by language before writing became widespread.

There is evidence from ecclesiastical history that, even in the early days of Christianity when writing was common (but "publishing" was still laborious, so copies were limited), that the corpus of Christian teaching was in verbal form which could be easily transferred and taught to new converts. Liturgical denominations today still "catechize" new and young converts with a question-and-answer format which teaches them the basics of the faith in a form easily understood and remembered.

In their attempt to avoid the dangers of rote worship through the repetition of written or memorized liturgies, many modern (independent, nondenominational) evangelical churches have cut themselves off from the historic precedent and continuity of the past by failing to expose their members to the great creeds of the Christian church—even theological summaries given by Christ himself such as "the Lord's Prayer." Many adult Christians today, having grown up in liturgical churches as young people where they memorized the Apostles' and Nicene Creeds, find the **form of teaching** of those historic statements coming back to them readily when they attend churches where the creeds are used.

There is a comfort and security in declaring, testifying, confessing out loud the same things that millions of other believers in generations past have confessed—that "I believe in God the Father Almighty, Maker of heaven and earth, and in Jesus Christ" (the Apostles' Creed), or "I believe in one God the

Father Almighty, Maker of heaven and earth, And of all things visible and invisible" (the Nicene Creed), or the words of other equally orthodox creeds of the church. Certainly these creeds were not **the form of teaching** to which Paul referred, as they were not formulated until hundreds of years after Paul wrote Romans. But there was *some* **form of teaching** that the Rome believers were adhering to. On other occasions, Paul makes reference to teachings and traditions that were extant in the church in some corporal form, and the **teaching** he refers to here is undoubtedly of the same kind (see 1 Cor. 11:2; 15:3; 1 Thess. 4:1; 2 Thess. 2:15; 3:6; 2 Tim. 1:13).

Whatever the content of the **teaching** was that the Rome believers had received, it was apostolic and Paul was pleased with their adherence to it. They perhaps did not know, until they had the benefit of hearing the words of Romans 6, that they had been **slaves to sin**—but they had been. Just as Paul used Romans 5 to explain the basis of justification (which he had presented in Rom. 4), so here he is using the second half of chapter 6 to illustrate (using the analogy of slavery) the truths presented in the first half of the chapter.

The second thing to note in this verse can easily be overlooked by careless reading. Paul does not refer to the "form of teaching which was entrusted to you." Rather, he says **the form of teaching to which you were entrusted**. Paul had had the gospel committed to him by God (1 Tim. 1:11) and he, in turn, had committed it to Timothy and others (1 Tim. 6:20; 2 Tim. 1:14). But not to the Romans. In fact, he committed the Romans to it! C. K. Barrett has the best insight on what Paul is doing here: "One expects the doctrine to be handed over (the verb—*paradidonai*—is used for the transmission of traditions; 1 Cor. xi. 23; xv. 3) to the hearers, not the hearers to the doctrine. But Christians are not (like the Rabbis) masters of a tradition; they are themselves created by the word of God, and remain in subjection to it" (Barrett, p. 124).

6:18. Not only were the Roman believers entrusted to the word of God; they were made **slaves to righteousness**. When they offered themselves to Christ (v. 15), they became the **slaves** of Christ, and to the righteousness which is the opposite of the sin to which they had died.

6:19. Here is Paul's "analogy apology" referred to above under verse 16. He hates to put spiritual truth into such worldly form as slave terminology since the analogy is imperfect (referring to freedom in Christ as "slavery"). He makes the same exhortation here as in verse 13, but now in the terminology of the slave world. Instead of offering **the parts of your body in slavery to impurity**, offer them to your new master, Christ, as slaves of righteousness.

The third-century Christian father Origen wrote eloquently about the differences there should be when a believer dies to the master (which is) sin and submits to the master (which is) righteousness, **leading to holiness**:

Paul . . . requires the same zeal from the convert as was present in him as a sinner. Once your feet ran to the temples of demons; now they run to the church of God. Once they ran to spill blood; now they run to set it free. Once your hands were stretched out to steal what belonged to others; now they are stretched out for you to be generous with what is your own. Once your eyes looked at women or at something which was not yours with lust in them; but now they look at the poor, the weak and the helpless with pity in them. Your ears used to delight in hearing empty talk or in attacking good people; now they have turned to hearing the Word of God, to the exposition of the law and to the learning of the knowledge of wisdom. Your tongue, which was accustomed to bad language, cursing and swearing has now turned to praising the Lord at all times; it produces healthy and honest speech, in order to give grace to the hearers and speak the truth to its neighbor. (Origen, cited in Bray, p. 170)

⬛ The Benefit of Death to Sin Is Eternal Life (6:20–23)

SUPPORTING IDEA: *The wages of sin is death, but the gift of God is eternal life.*

6:20–23. In the last four verses of this chapter, Paul asks the believers in Rome to think about the quality and direction of their lives before coming to know Christ and their lives since. Compare, if you will, the benefits of each. Never one to sugarcoat or beat around the proverbial bush, Paul asks them (and us) directly: **What benefit did you reap at that time from the things you are now ashamed of?** The "benefit" of being **slaves to sin . . . free from the control of righteousness,** was **death!** Because "no one can serve two masters" (Matt. 6:24), when they were **slaves to sin,** they could not be controlled by righteousness—and sin results in death (v. 23).

Conversely, when they died to sin and became **slaves to God,** they would be free from the control of sin—and righteousness leads to **eternal life.** Because sin is deceptive, and because it is the "old self" (the former way of life; v. 6) that has died, not the "body of sin" (the capacity to sin; v. 6), the Christian has to be exhorted to remember to what he or she has died (sin) and to what he or she now lives (righteousness).

In today's modern world of materialism, even mature believers can be tempted to think there are benefits in the life of slavery to sin. Asaph, the ancient psalmist, warned the faithful of Israel about the deception of sin and wickedness, and its ultimate end—destruction (death; Ps. 73:18–19). But at any given moment, the wicked appear prosperous, to have no struggles, to be healthy and strong, and to be "free from the burdens common to man; they are not plagued by human ills" (Ps. 73:5). So what if they are a tad prideful and arrogant? They are carefree and continue to increase in wealth (see Ps. 73:3–12).

It was not until the psalmist "entered the sanctuary of God" that he "understood their final destiny" (Ps. 73:17). Whereas their end was destruction, the psalmist realized in God's presence that his end was to be with God forever—eternal life: "Yet I am always with you; you hold me by my right hand. You guide me with your counsel, and afterward you will take me into glory . . . God is the strength of my heart and my portion forever" (Ps. 73:23–26).

It would be difficult to find a better passage of Scripture to illustrate the truth of Paul's concluding verse to the first six chapters of Romans: **For the wages of sin is death, but the gift of God is eternal life in Christ Jesus our Lord.** We have earned death as our wages as Adam's children; we have received as a gift of God's grace the privilege of being rescued from solidarity with the first Adam to solidarity with the second Adam. He died; we died. He was raised; we were raised. He lives to God; we live to God. He will live forever; we will live forever with him.

> **MAIN IDEA REVIEW:** *When the believer in Christ is reckoned by faith to be dead, buried, and resurrected with Christ, he or she ceases to be the servant of sin and becomes the servant of righteousness.*

III. CONCLUSION

Know Who You Are

The Duke of Windsor, who would have been crowned King Edward VIII of England, died on May 28, 1972, before acceding to the throne. A BBC television program on that same night reviewed the main events of his life up to that point. In a clip that was included from a previous filmed interview, the Duke of Windsor reflected on his upbringing as the Prince of Wales: "My father [King George V] was a strict disciplinarian. Sometimes when I had done something wrong, he would admonish me saying, 'My dear boy, you must always remember who you are'" (Stott, pp. 187–188).

In this chapter, the apostle Paul wants believers in Rome (and beyond) never to be guilty of the fate of the Israelites: "My people are destroyed from lack of knowledge" (Hos. 4:6). Four times in chapter 6, Paul focuses on "knowing" (vv. 3,6,9,16). He wants the believers in Rome to know who they are, and then let that knowledge be reflected in their behavior. If a future earthly king could be called to account for his behavior on the basis of who he was, how much more should the believer in Christ—destined to rule and reign over far more than an earthly kingdom—be certain of whom he or she is and act accordingly?

The Duke of Windsor could trace his lineage back centuries in England's history in order to discover who he was. To discover who he or she is, the believer in Christ has two lineages to trace: one as old as history itself, the other as young as the believer is old. First is the lineage that goes all the way back to Adam, discussed in Romans 5. That lineage insured that we were slaves to sin, destined for death. But the other lineage is only one generation old. It is the lineage the believer establishes when he or she identifies by faith with the death, burial, and resurrection of Jesus Christ. At that moment, there is a death to sin, the identity that produced behavior to be ashamed of (v. 21). The believer is given a new identity, a new lineage, a new heritage—that of Jesus Christ himself. He is transferred to a royal household (1 Pet. 2:9) and begins the process of being made ready to reign with Christ forever (Rev. 5:10; 20:6; 22:5).

Do you—as well as those you teach—know who you are? Your identity is bound up in one of two lineages, the first or the second Adam, and you serve one or the other of two masters: sin, or obedience leading to righteousness. The gospel has come to deliver us from sin and to give us eternal life in Christ Jesus our Lord.

PRINCIPLES

- Sin is never needed in order to demonstrate grace.
- Baptism is not a ceremony; it is an ordinance that illustrates profound theological truth.
- The believer, through identification with Christ, died to sin and was raised to new life—by faith.
- The believer's life after coming to know Christ should be different than before coming to know Christ.
- The believer in Christ is not obligated to sin.
- Holiness is the goal of the believer's life.
- Eternal life is the benefit of death to sin and life in Christ.

APPLICATIONS

- Is there a "controlling" sin in my life that I commit willingly because I am counting on God's grace to forgive me?
- Have I been baptized as a believer in Christ? If I am responsible for baptizing others, do I make sure they are instructed in the theological implications of baptism as soon as possible after their conversion?
- Do I rest in faith alone as the cause of my having a life free from the control of sin?

- What differences are there (the difference between wickedness and righteousness) in my life since coming to know Christ?
- Do I use the words "I can't help myself" in describing my sin (or allow others whom I am counseling to use them)?
- Am I content with pursuing holiness, or do I envy the wicked?
- Have I thanked God today for the gift of eternal life that he has provided in Jesus Christ?

IV. LIFE APPLICATION

Don't You Know You Are Free?

Because of Abraham Lincoln's Emancipation Proclamation, slaves throughout the United States were legally free as early as the first day of 1863. But what was legally true did not become a reality for most of the slaves until much later. The vast majority of the African-American population had never known anything in America but slavery. Shelby Foote, author of an acclaimed three-volume history of the Civil War (*The Civil War: A Narrative*), described the phenomenon of slaves who were free but did not know it:

> The word spread from Capitol Hill out across the city, down into the valleys and fields of Virginia and the Carolinas, and even into the plantations of Georgia and Mississippi and Alabama. "Slavery Legally Abolished!" read the headlines, and yet something amazing took place. The greater majority of the slaves in the South went right on living as though they were not emancipated. That continued throughout the Reconstruction Period.

> The Negro remained locked in a caste system of "race etiquette" as rigid as any had known in formal bondage. Every slave could repeat, with equal validity, what an Alabama slave had mumbled when asked what he thought of the Great Emancipator whose proclamation had gone into effect. "I don't know nothin' 'bout Abraham Lincoln 'cept they say he sot us free. And I don't know nothin' 'bout that neither." (cited by Swindoll, p. 525)

What was a tragedy to begin with—that human beings were made the subjects of masters who kept them in cruel bondage—was made doubly so by the slaves' lack of knowledge and understanding that they had been set free by an emancipator. If a person with the power, authority, and willingness to set the captives free does so, it makes little difference to the captives until they know that their freedom has been decreed—and know what it means to live in that freedom.

Proclaiming freedom in Christ from sin is precisely Paul's burden in Romans 6. Don't you know that when you were baptized, you were baptized into Jesus Christ's death (6:3)? Don't you know that you were crucified with him (6:6)? Don't you know that Christ is no longer under the mastery of sin, and neither are you (6:9)? Don't you know that whoever you offer yourselves to, you will be enslaved to (6:16)?

All the slaves freed by Lincoln had to do was to offer themselves to "freedom" as their new master and they would have been free indeed. All the believer in Christ needs to do to be free from the mastery of sin is offer himself or herself to God as a slave of righteousness. The African-American slaves were free from bondage and did not know it. Many Christian believers have been freed from the mastery of sin but do not know it. Paul's message in Romans 6 is to declare that the gospel of Jesus Christ is an emancipation proclamation from the mastery of sin.

> So send I you to take to souls in bondage
> The word of truth that sets the captive free,
> To break the bonds of sin, to loose death's fetters
> So send I you, to bring the lost to me.

—E. Margaret Clarkson, "So Send I You," 1954

V. PRAYER

Heavenly Father, may the Holy Spirit illumine the eyes of my heart to see my identity with the death, burial, and resurrection of your Son, Jesus Christ. May I never see baptism again without seeing the price he paid for me, so that I might be seen by you as having died to sin and been raised to new life. I offer my body to you afresh as an instrument of righteousness. I offer myself to you afresh as a slave to obedience. Thank you for the gift of eternal life. Amen.

VI. DEEPER DISCOVERIES

A. Antinomianism (6:1,15)

The most compelling evidence that antinomianism existed as a problem in the church long before Martin Luther labeled it is found in 1 Corinthians 5–6. Antinomianism, the view that it is not necessary for Christians to acknowledge or abide by the moral law of God since they are under grace, had caused serious immorality to take root in the church at Corinth. Though it was not as bad as the antinomianism practiced by the Adamite sect in North Africa (they called their church "Paradise" and worshiped in the nude in honor of Adam), it still required Paul's intervention and correction.

A member of the church was allowed to live in an immoral relationship (apparently) with his stepmother (1 Cor. 5:1). There also seemed to be a measure of pride on the part of the Corinthians, as if this "liberty" represented a measure of spiritual enlightenment or maturity on their part. Paul took immediate and drastic action to correct the heresy: "When you are assembled . . . hand this man over to Satan, so that the sinful nature may be destroyed and his spirit saved" (1 Cor. 5:4). The logical reason for rooting out sin is that "a little yeast works through the whole batch of dough" (1 Cor. 5:6), meaning that if the license was not revoked quickly, the entire Christian community would look like the non-Christian community out of which they had been redeemed.

In addition to incest, the members of the church were suing one another in civil courts (1 Cor. 6:1–11) as well as engaging in all sorts of sexual immorality (1 Cor. 6:12–20). Other admonitions of the apostle Paul for Christians to flee evil desires (2 Tim. 2:22), flee idolatry (1 Cor. 10:14), and put off the former way of life (Eph. 4:22) make sense only when there is a moral imperative to maintain purity and holiness.

Antinomianism has not had serious, mainstream adherents in the modern era of the church. It has surfaced primarily in relation to the question of whether the law should serve as the moral basis for Christian living as opposed to the moral commands of the New Testament alone, and whether the law of God should be used as a motivation in evangelism as opposed to the grace of God.

B. Baptism (6:3–4)

The Book of Acts provides helpful insights into the immediacy of baptism following conversion. The modern church has separated belief and baptism into separate events, whereas the conversion experience in Acts was almost a single, hyphenated event: believe-and-be-baptized. Note the following verses:

- Acts 2:38: "Repent and be baptized."
- Acts 2:41: "Those who accepted his message were baptized."
- Acts 8:12: "But when they believed Philip . . . they were baptized."
- Acts 8:36–38: "'Why shouldn't I be baptized' . . . and Philip baptized him."
- Acts 9:18: "Immediately . . . he could see again. He got up and was baptized."
- Acts 10:47–48: "'They have received the Holy Spirit' . . . . So he ordered that they be baptized."
- Acts 16:14–15: "The Lord opened her heart to respond . . . . she and the members of her household were baptized."

- Acts 16:31–33: "'Believe in the Lord Jesus' . . . then immediately he and all his family were baptized."
- Acts 19:4–6: "On hearing this, they were baptized."
- Acts 22:16: "What are you waiting for? Get up, be baptized and wash your sins away."
- In addition to Acts, the accounts of the Great Commission place significant emphasis upon baptism.
- Matthew 28:19: It is interesting that the assumed part of the Great Commission instructions is "faith." It is not mentioned, but is an understood element of "make disciples." Baptism, however, is given explicit presence in the instructions.
- Mark 16:16: "Whoever believes and is baptized will be saved, but whoever does not believe will be condemned." Here is an example of belief and baptism being a "single" event, so much so that baptism is not even mentioned in the negative half of the statement. It is assumed to be part of "believing."

While it is clear, especially from Romans, that salvation is a result of faith, it is also clear that the process of identifying with Christ through baptism had a much higher priority in the salvation scheme than it seems to have in the contemporary church.

C. Catechism (6:17)

While catechism is not a scriptural term, it derives from *katecheo*, to instruct, a word which occurs a number of times in the New Testament (Luke 1:4; Acts 18:25; 21:21,24; Rom. 2:18; 1 Cor. 14:19; Gal. 6:6). A "catechumen" (from the passive participle of *katecheo*) early on became one who was "catechised," or instructed in religious matters.

Paul's reference to a "form of teaching" certainly suggests some format of basic instruction that the believers in Rome had received prior to their receiving this epistle. There is no extant evidence of what form that teaching might have taken. By the time of post-Acts church history, there is evidence that catechisms, though not necessarily in question-and-answer form, were in use to instruct new believers prior to their joining the church through baptism. When infant baptism became widespread in the sixth century, prebaptism catechisms were adapted and used as instructional tools in the church to "disciple," or train believers in the rudiments of the faith. Some have suggested that the Book of 1 Peter is representative of catechismic teaching, being directed to believers who were scattered away from Jerusalem (1 Pet. 1:1) and therefore in danger of being without sound teaching.

D. "In Christ" (6:11,23)

One of Paul's most often-used terms (eighty-six times in his epistles) occurs eleven times in the Book of Romans (twice in ch. 6; vv. 11,23). While it is used in ways that are easy to understand, such as falling asleep in Christ (i.e., dying as Christians; 1 Cor. 15:18), or simply referring to those in Christ as believers (Gal. 2:4), in Romans 6 "in Christ" is closely tied to our identification with Christ through justification by faith. In Galatians 2:17, Paul ties justification together with being "in Christ."

Based on everything Paul has taught in Romans 1–5, it is clear that the only way a person can be "alive to God" (Rom. 6:11) is through the intermediation of Jesus Christ. Because humankind is sinful, separated from God, dead in trespasses and sin, men and women cannot be alive to God on their own. They must have righteousness imputed to them, and they must identify with the death and resurrection of Christ on their behalf as Paul describes in Romans 6. Therefore, when he says, "count yourselves dead to sin but alive to God in Christ Jesus" (v. 11), he is saying "count yourselves . . . alive to God through the impartation of righteousness to you as a result of your identity-by-faith with the death, burial and resurrection of Christ."

Taking this understanding and applying it to perhaps the most well-known verse which uses "in Christ" (2 Cor. 5:17) renders the following understanding: "Therefore, if anyone is in Christ (a recipient of the impartation of righteousness through having identified by faith with the death of Christ), he is a new creation." Being a new creation means being in Christ, and this means having received the status of justification through the exercise of faith in the work of Christ on one's behalf.

VII. TEACHING OUTLINE

A. INTRODUCTION

1. Lead Story: The "Mad Monk" Who Lived Like the Devil
2. Context: In Romans 5, Paul explained that when Adam died, all human beings died, but when Christ died for all human beings, all had the potential for new life. The grace of God reigned over the sin of Adam, bringing eternal life through Jesus Christ. But this raises the question: If Adam's sin brought the demonstration of God's grace, should we go on sinning so that grace will be revealed all the more?
3. Transition: Paul uses Romans 6 to explain that the death of Christ to the penalty of sin also meant the death of all who believe in him to the practice of sin. By identifying with the death, burial, and resurrection of Christ, believers have been freed from the obligation to sin.

They should now choose to present themselves to a new master, righteousness, which will lead them on the path to holiness.

B. COMMENTARY

1. An Objection to the Grace in the Gospel (6:1–2)
    a. The question (6:1)
    b. The answer (6:2)
2. The Death of Christ Was a Death to Sin (6:3–7)
    a. Baptism pictures the death, burial, and resurrection of Christ (6:3–4)
    b. The purpose of death is to be freed from sin (6:5–7)
3. The Resurrection of Christ Was a Resurrection to Life (6:8–10)
    a. Resurrection breaks the mastery of death (6:8–9)
    b. Death is once; life is forever (6:10)
4. Christ's Death and Resurrection Are Imputed to the Believer (6:11–14)
    a. Count yourself dead to sin, alive to God (6:11)
    b. Cut your ties to sin (6:12)
    c. Consecrate your life to righteousness (6:13)
    d. Conclusion: Sin has no mastery over those under grace (6:14)
5. The Believer Is Emancipated from Sin and Enslaved to Righteousness (6:15–19)
    a. The objection repeated (6:15)
    b. Offering oneself is the equivalent of enslaving oneself (6:16)
    c. Offering oneself to righteousness leads to holiness (6:17–19)
6. The Benefit of Death to Sin Is Eternal Life (6:20–23)
    a. The "benefit" of sin is death (6:20–21)
    b. The benefit of holiness is eternal life (6:22–23)

C. CONCLUSION: DON'T YOU KNOW YOU ARE FREE?

VIII. ISSUES FOR DISCUSSION

1. How do churches in general treat baptism with regard to timing and instruction related to its meaning? What difference would it make in the lives of new believers if Paul's explanation in Romans 6 were taught?
2. Does the average believer see conversion to Christ as leaving (dying to) one life and beginning (being raised to) a new life? If not, what meaning of conversion is being communicated?
3. What level of moral latitude do contemporary Christians give themselves, trusting in God's grace to forgive? How does a Christian know

when he or she is taking inappropriate advantage of the grace of God versus being trapped unintentionally in sin?

4. Besides the gift of eternal life, what benefits can you cite in your life that have come as a result of your dying to sin and becoming a servant of righteousness? Why are these benefits better than the "benefits" of the wicked?

Romans 7:1–25

How the Gospel Delivers from Law

I. **INTRODUCTION**
A Wretch Like John and Paul

II. **COMMENTARY**
A verse-by-verse explanation of the chapter.

III. **CONCLUSION**
Face-to-Face with Death

An overview of the principles and applications from the chapter.

IV. **LIFE APPLICATION**
Signs of Living Under Law

Melding the chapter to life.

V. **PRAYER**
Tying the chapter to life with God.

VI. **DEEPER DISCOVERIES**
Historical, geographical, and grammatical enrichment of the commentary.

VII. **TEACHING OUTLINE**
Suggested step-by-step group study of the chapter.

VIII. **ISSUES FOR DISCUSSION**
Zeroing the chapter in on daily life.

"*W*hen it is a question of our justification, we have to put away all thinking about the Law and our works, to embrace the mercy of God alone, and to turn our eyes away from ourselves and upon Jesus Christ alone."

John Calvin

Romans 7:1–25

IN A NUTSHELL

*I*n Romans 6, Paul proved that grace is not a license to sin. In this chapter, he proves that law is not a synonym for sin. To the contrary, law is a good thing as it reveals the sinfulness of the capacity that resides in every person. Deliverance from the sinful condition that the law reveals is found in Jesus Christ.

How the Gospel
Delivers from Law

I. INTRODUCTION

A Wretch Like John and Paul

"*W*retch" is one of those words that sounds like what it means. *Wretch.* It sounds bad just to say it. The noun form is bad enough—a wretch—but the verb form is even worse—to wretch—the definition of which this discussion will leave to the imagination. The adjective—wretched—attributes the qualities of the noun to a person, place, or thing. Somehow this hard-sounding word—*wretch*—was used by two very mature and famous Christians to describe themselves, both at the height of their maturity. Understanding why will provide insight into the understanding of Romans 7.

John Newton is well known as the author of *Amazing Grace,* perhaps the most famous hymn in Christendom. In it, of course, he says, "Amazing grace, how sweet the sound, that saved a wretch like me." Though many moderns, tipping their hat to the purveyors of sensitivity and self-esteem, have excised "wretch" from Newton's hymn and replaced it with less offensive terms, nothing but "wretch" will do. If the hymn writer himself were alive today, he undoubtedly would insist on leaving the hymn just as he wrote it. No one knows better than himself what a wretch had been found by God's amazing grace. To downplay the "wretchedness" of the one found is surely to diminish the "amazingness" of the grace that seeks and finds.

Another hymn writer a generation after Newton, Charlotte Elliot, was afflicted with the same "poor self-esteem." In *Just As I Am,* she describes herself as "tossed about with many a conflict, many a doubt, fightings within and fears without . . . poor, wretched, blind." Once we get to Romans 7:24, we will discover that it is the moderns who have the esteem problem, not the ancients. No less a pillar of faith than the apostle Paul found himself beset with conflicts in the inner man to the point of bewailing his own wretchedness.

But what was it that caused Newton to see himself as a "wretch" who was found by God's grace? What would bring any person to consider himself or herself as "sunk in deep distress, sorrow, misfortune, or poverty; a miserable, unhappy, or unfortunate person; a poor or hapless being"? (*The Oxford English Dictionary*). John Newton's pre-Christian life certainly would qualify. Following his sea-captain father to a sailor's life, he was tossed out of the British Royal Navy for his rebellious ways. Ending up in West Africa, he worked for a slave trader where he himself was basically enslaved and vilely mistreated. One chronicler described him as "a wretched looking man toiling in a plantation of lemon trees in the Island of Plaintains . . . clothes had become rags, no shelter and begging for unhealthy roots to allay his hunger."

Escaping the island in 1747, Newton was washed overboard while drunk in a violent storm. He was saved only when another sailor harpooned him and pulled him back aboard! It was that near-death experience, and the lingering message of Thomas à Kempis's *The Imitation of Christ,* that turned him to God. Though a Christian, he continued for six more years as the captain of a slave ship, a practice he then gave up and ultimately crusaded against. He went back to England and entered the pastoral ministry, becoming well-known for his preaching and his hymns.

There is much fodder for the mill of wretchedness in John Newton's life. Rebel, profligate, drunkard, slave trader—enough wretchedness is there for many a hymn about the grace of God. But interestingly, there is a part of John Newton's story that aligns him with the apostle Paul's sense of wretchedness—that inner conflict that goes on in the life of every person who "knows the good he ought to do and doesn't do it" (Jas. 4:17).

John Newton had a Christian mother who dreamed and prayed that one day her son would become a preacher of the Word of God. Because she died when John was a child, she did not live to see her dreams realized or her prayers answered. But one has to believe that, in the years she had with him, this godly woman instilled in her son a sense of "the way he should go" (Prov. 22:6). Surely, throughout all the years of Newton's ungodly activities, a conflict was raging within him. As he compared his behavior with his mother's teachings, how many of Paul's words in Romans 7 could have been Newton's: "I do not understand what I do" (v. 15). "I have the desire to do what is good, but I cannot carry it out" (v. 18). "The evil I do not want to do—this I keep on doing" (v. 19).

As we will see, Paul wrote his words describing his life as a believer in Christ (though as a persecutor of Christians in his preconversion days, Paul, like John Newton, had things in his past to bewail). In Newton's case, we tend to think of him as writing only about his profligate, slave trading days. But he was undoubtedly cognizant in his later years that his preconversion wretchedness did not disappear upon the exercise of his faith in Christ. The awareness of the utter sinfulness of sin is a mark of maturity in the Christian believer, while the denial of sin's pervasiveness is a sign of immaturity.

Romans 7 is a wake-up call to those who think that the Christian life is all sweetness and light. It is, as both John Newton and the apostle Paul can testify, a life of victory; but it is a victory won out of conflict. The ability to conform the hand (what I do) with the heart (what I want to do) is part of the tension of the "now, but not yet" that is characteristic of the Christian life in this present age: we are freed from sin, but still must wrestle with its unrelenting presence. One day the conflict will cease. But for now, Paul says we are rescued moment-by-moment by "Jesus Christ our Lord."

Paul wrote this chapter to prove that we are not rescued by the law. We do not defeat sin by obeying the law. Sin loves the law! Sin gains strength from the law! Trying to defeat sin by the law is like throwing "Brer Rabbit in 'de briar patch"—nothing could be more comfortable. The law is what reveals sin because it reveals the righteousness of God. The law is good and the law is godly—and shows us that we are neither. And thus is born the conflict of profligates-turned-preachers named Newton and persecutors-turned-preachers named Paul. And thus is born the conflict that rages in the heart of every maturing Christian.

In this chapter, Paul explains how the power of the gospel delivers us from the conflict that the law hands us. When the law condemned John Newton, the former slave-trader traded his slavery to the law of sin for slavery to God's law (Rom. 7:25)— just as any believer can do today.

II. COMMENTARY

How the Gospel Delivers from Law

MAIN IDEA: *The mature believer in Jesus Christ is not one who never struggles to obey God. Rather, the mature believer is one who has been released from the law's condemnation and made free to serve its requirements by dying to the law through Jesus Christ.*

This chapter of Romans is about law in general more than the Mosaic Law in particular, though that is certainly included in Paul's application. Law, in one form or the other, is mentioned thirty-five times in the chapter; the Holy Spirit is mentioned once (v. 6). By contrast, Romans 8 refers to the Holy Spirit more than twenty times, the law only four times. One of the dangers in interpreting these two chapters of Scripture is to view them linearly, as if chapter 7 deals with law (pre-Christian, the Old Testament), and chapter 8 deals with the Spirit (Christian, the New Testament).

The best way to view them is to remember that Paul did not write his letter with chapter and verse notations. While these markers help us keep track in our reading and study of God's Word, they sometimes complicate things by their artificial lines of demarcation. It helps to view both chapters 7 and 8 as a whole. Both are written for mature Christians, but describe different aspects of the Christian life.

Taken separately, Romans 7 seems to view the Christian life from a defeatist perspective while chapter 8 views it victoriously. The purpose of this contrast is to show that Christians can be defeated by the law and the sin it reveals if they do not remain identified, moment-by-moment, with the death and resurrection of Jesus Christ; if they do not accomplish the law's goals **in the new way of the Spirit, and not in the old way of the written code** (Rom. 7:6).

Romans 7 is a continuation of a teaching begun in Romans 5:20. In chapter 5, Paul says that justification and peace with God have come through Jesus Christ (5:1), and that the law was added that sin might increase (5:20) making justification by faith alone all the more praiseworthy. But where sin increased, grace increased all the more (5:20); there is no sin or amount of sin larger than the grace of God. Two questions, or objections, to this teaching are raised and answered by Paul. First, grace is not a license to sin (Rom. 6:1–2 and the remainder of ch. 6). Second, just because the law reveals sin does not mean that the law is bad, or sinful (Rom. 7:7, and the rest of ch. 7). The law is good in that it reveals sin; but the law becomes an intolerable yoke if one tries to eliminate sin by obeying the law.

Paul's point in the chapter is to show how the gospel can free anyone from the yoke of slavery to the law and its condemnation of sin. Just as justification is not accomplished through the law (Rom. 6:14), neither is sanctification accomplished through the law (Gal. 5:18).

Ⓐ The Believer's Death to Law: an Illustration (7:1–6)

> **SUPPORTING IDEA:** *Just as the death of a husband frees a wife to remarry, so the believer is not free to be united to God until he or she is dead to the law.*

7:1. Paul makes consistent and timely use of illustrations in his teaching (cf. Abraham in Rom. 4 and slavery in Rom. 6). In this regard, he follows in the footsteps of Solomon and Jesus, the masters of the use of the common to illustrate the sublime. Verses 1–6 of this chapter contain an illustration that bridges chapters 6 and 7. The concept of "death" looks back to Romans 6 (eighteen references), while "law" looks forward to the bulk of chapter 7. His presentation of the illustration follows perfect deductive form: the principle to be illustrated (v. 1), the illustration (vv. 2–3), and the application of the illustration (vv. 4–6).

The principle Paul states applies to law in general: **law has authority over a man only as long as he lives.** Literally speaking, law is "lord over" (*kurieuo*; see also Rom. 6:9,14; 14:9) a person only while that person is alive.

This concept was discussed in detail in the last chapter based on Paul's statement in Romans 6:7: "Anyone who has died has been freed from sin." Just as dead people are not tempted to sin, so they are free from the demands of the law. Therefore, Paul is picking up the principle from chapter 6 and redirecting it in chapter 7: physical death frees one from the temptation to sin *and* the authority of the law.

Those to whom Paul is writing could connect easily with the concept of law's authority. The Gentile believers in the Roman church were used to the imperial law of Rome being an iron boot on their neck. If there was one thing Rome was not, it was soft on law. To Rome's credit, justice *de jure*—justice according to law—be it ever so malevolently applied by the emperor *du jour*, became a building block of Western civilization. The Jewish believers in Rome, on the other hand, came from the tradition of *Torah*—the Jewish law handed down by God to Moses on Mt. Sinai.

While the law went through periods of neglect in Israel, on the whole Israel venerated the law. Even today when Jewish men gather at the Western Wall in Israel, the scrolls are lifted high as the supreme revelation of God to his chosen people. So law was not a foreign concept to Paul's audience in Rome; they knew the law ended with the last breath of the one under the law.

7:2–3. Paul uses marriage to illustrate the principle of law applying only to the living. It is interesting to note Paul's assumptions concerning the sanctity and permanence of the marriage relationship. To be sure, his point here is not to teach about marriage as he does in 1 Corinthians 7:1–15 or Ephesians 5:22–33. Rather, his whole point in using marriage as an illustration is based on the assumption that his audience agrees with the biblical teaching on the permanence of marriage. There is even an assumption on his part that some in Rome who might be ignorant of the biblical paradigm for marriage would agree with the *human* (natural) *law* that says when two people join together, it is for life.

Did all in Rome live that way? Certainly not. Did all in the church live that way? Probably not. And all in the church today certainly do not live that way. But Paul's goal here is not to pursue that end. Rather, while teaching directly on one thing (the law) he affirms another thing (the marriage bond).

In the case of his illustration, marriage, Paul's point is that laws governing marriage are null and void when the marriage union is broken by the death of one spouse. Death is the only thing that frees one from the lordship of law in marriage. D. M. Lloyd-Jones cites four ways that Paul's use of marriage as an illustration relates to the subject of law (cited by Boice, 2:721–722):

1. *A woman who is married to a man is under the authority of that man.* Whether natural law (e.g., Rom. 1:26–27) or a law given specifically by God, laws represent authority. Law cannot be abandoned by per-

sonal choice. A wife could not leave her husband and marry another man while her first husband was still living.

2. *The subjection of a wife to a husband in marriage is a lifelong subjection.* The illustration of marriage as a permanent union illustrates the permanence of law. Law represents authority, and that authority is permanent. The marriage vows are a perfect example of this permanence: "Till death do us part."

3. *In spite of the permanent nature of this relationship and the resulting authority, there is nevertheless the possibility of entering into another relationship.* This is the key point Paul wants to make in his illustration: death is the only thing abrogating the authority of law. He repeats the key element in the breaking of the marriage bond in verse 2 and in verse 3: **but if her husband dies . . . But if her husband dies.** In this case, the law is honored and upheld—glorified, if you will—by what appears to be a violation of the law, a second marriage. Paul is laying the groundwork here to answer the objection that the gospel of grace sets aside the law; nullifies it; abrogates it; makes it useless. Paul is proving that it is the law that gives the gospel of grace power and authority. He is going to show that when believers die to the "sinful passions aroused by the law" (v. 5), they are free to be united with another. That is the law. And without that law, there is no skeleton upon which to build a new creature in Christ Jesus (2 Cor. 5:17).

   It is worth noting at this point that Paul is giving an illustration here, not presenting an allegory. The difference is this: an illustration has one point, an allegory many. Paul presents an allegory in Galatians 4:21–31, where his language is full of phrases such as "the women represent"; "This is Hagar"; "Hagar stands for . . . and corresponds to"; "Jerusalem . . . is our mother"; etc. In an allegory, almost every piece of the story makes a point. Not so with an illustration. Interpreters, especially the allegorical interpreters arising out of the Alexandrian School in Egypt in the first few centuries of the Christian era, have tried in vain to make Paul's application in verses 4–6 fit the illustration in verses 2–3. But there is only one point to be made: death nullifies marital unions.

4. The object of the new relationship is "that we might bear fruit to God" (v. 4). Paul is going to demonstrate, by applying the illustration to believers, that no one bears fruit to God by way of the law. The only way to "bear fruit to God" is to get out of the relationship with the law and into a relationship with Jesus Christ.

7:4–6. Stuart Briscoe tells of his experience as a raw recruit in the Royal Marines during the Korean Conflict. His company was under the supervision of a particularly intimidating sergeant major who dictated how life was going to be for the young soldiers. Briscoe did not realize exactly what a dominant force the sergeant major had become in his life until the day he was discharged from the Marines. On that day, he knew he was a "free" man. No more orders; no more drills; no more "Yes, SIRS!" In spite of what he knew, the first time he encountered the sergeant major after walking out of the discharge office as a free man, he still popped to attention—until he realized he did not have to. He was "dead" to the sergeant major.

So he relaxed in his new identity, and approached the sergeant major as a "former" Marine—casual and comfortable. Regardless of how his former superior may have disliked Briscoe's new posture and attitude, he was powerless to do anything about it. Briscoe had been discharged from—Briscoe had died to—the sergeant major and his laws (Hughes, *Stories*, pp. 248–249).

So, my brothers, you also died to the law through the body of Christ . . . in order that we might bear fruit to God, Paul continues. It is time now for him to apply the illustration from marriage to the life of the believers in Rome. Whether seeking new life in a new marriage, or new life after time in the Marines, only one thing will release one *from* the old and *unto* the new—death to the old. It is obvious that Paul's analogy does not flow point-for-point, and that he did not intend it to. To strain at making dot-to-dot connections between his illustration and his application will result in frustration. Remember simply that in verse 4, he isolates the key point of the marriage illustration: death **to the law** is necessary in order for one to be joined to Christ.

And how do we die **to the law?** This is obviously a reference back to Romans 6:2–7 where Paul used baptism as a picture of the death, burial, and resurrection of the believer with Christ—all by faith reckoning (Rom. 6:11). While Romans 6 dealt with our death to sin, Romans 7 deals with our death to the law. The "Aha!" for the believer comes in discovering that death to one is death to the other. Paul will say later in chapter 7 that he would not have known what sin was if the law had not told him what was sin (Rom. 7:7). The law sets the standard, reveals that we have failed to meet the standard, produces guilt over the failure, and condemns to death. In Romans 6, we die to the penalty of sin since Christ died in our place and we died with him. In Romans 7, we die to the law that is always there, continually revealing the sin we commit. By dying to the law we die to the guilt it produces. By dying to sin we die to the penalty the law dictates. The gospel delivers the believer from sin and from the law.

John Stott suggests a number of helpful parallels between the two chapters (Stott, p. 194):

	Romans 6	Romans 7
Freedom	. . . from sin	. . . from the law
Death	. . . to sin (6:2)	. . . to the law (7:4)
Union	. . . with Christ's death (6:3)	. . . through the body of Christ (7:4)
Freed	. . . from sin (6:7,18)	. . . from the law (7:6)
Shared	. . . in Christ's resurrection (6:4–5)	. . . with him who was raised from the dead (7:4)
We now	. . . live in newness of life (6:4)	. . . serve in newness of Spirit (7:6)
Our fruit	. . . leads to holiness (6:22)	. . . is borne to God (7:4)

Not only are there parallels between chapters 6 and 7; there are also contrasts between the "then" and "now" of the Christian experience:

	Then	Now
Romans 6	"When you were slaves to sin" (6:20)	"But now . . . you have been set free from sin" (6:22)
Romans 7	"When we were controlled by the sinful nature" (7:5)	"But now . . . we have been released from the law" (7:6)

Note that in both chapters, the "former" condition was slavery to, and control by, the propensity to sin. The solution to that in chapter 6 is to be freed from sin through the death of Christ; the solution in chapter 7 is to be freed from the law through the death of Christ. Therefore death—identification with the death of Christ—is the only way to be freed from sin and the law. This is the point of Paul's illustration.

There is a clear purpose in our dying to the law—**that we might bear fruit to God** (v. 4). This is contrasted by Paul with the prior relationship we were in—married to the law—in which **sinful passions . . . bore fruit for death** (v. 5). To use a purposely dramatic illustration, suppose a marriage union had produced only stillborn children because of a genetic predisposition in one of the partners. Then, due to the death of the spouse with the abnormality, the healthy spouse remarries. At once, the new couple begins to bear fruit in the form of healthy children. It took death to bring about a situation whereby the healthy spouse could begin to bear "fruit" in the form of healthy children.

Likewise, Paul said in Romans 6:21–22 that "the things you are now ashamed of (which you did when controlled by sin) . . . those things result in death." But as a result of being united to God through Christ, the result is eternal life. In chapter 7, he says that **we bore fruit for death** (v. 5).

Paul's presentation in this section is based on covenantal language. Under the old covenant, God's kingdom—the source of life for all who would enter it—was instituted. The invitation was given through Moses for the people of Israel to choose life over death: "See, I set before you today *life* and prosperity, *death* and destruction" (Deut. 30:15; emphasis added). "This day I call heaven and earth as witnesses against you that I have set before you *life* and *death*, blessings and curses. Now choose *life*, so that you and your children may live" (Deut. 30:19; emphasis added). Continuing under the new covenant, Jesus' introduction of the kingdom included the offer of life: "The thief comes only to steal and *kill* and destroy; I have come that they may have *life*, and have it to the full" (John 10:10; emphasis added). From his death, new life came, just as he taught from the evidence of nature: "Unless a kernel of wheat falls to the ground and dies, it remains only a single seed. But if it dies, it produces many seeds" (John 12:24). From death comes fruit, as Paul wrote to the Corinthians: "We always carry around in our body the *death* of Jesus, so that the *life* of Jesus may also be revealed in our body. For we who are alive are always being given over to *death* for Jesus' sake, so that his *life* may be revealed in our mortal body" (2 Cor. 4:10–11; emphasis added).

Death was the ultimate end of all who would not die to their sin and choose life; those who would not die to their own kingdom's agenda, and choose the life found in God's kingdom. Every person, as Paul tells the Galatians, bears fruit unto death ("the acts of the sinful nature," Gal. 5:19–21) or unto life ("the fruit of the Spirit," Gal. 5:22–23). Against the fruit of the Spirit, "there is no law."

Paul concludes this section with a statement which serves as a launching pad for the rest of the chapter: **we serve in the new way of the Spirit, and not in the old way of the written code** (v. 6). Under the old covenant, the written law continued, year after year, to hold people under its condemnation. It led to the death of thousands upon thousands of sacrificial animals, culminating in the death of the sinless lamb of God, Jesus Christ. There is now a **new way**, the **way of the Spirit**, by which man lives. Paul could easily have jumped from this statement to his statement in Romans 8:1. He introduces **the new way of the Spirit**, which he then calls "the law of the Spirit of life" in Romans 8:2. From there, he begins expounding on how the Holy Spirit is the key to the believer's ability to live the **new way**, the way of life.

But he knows that his statement in Romans 7:6 is going to cause questions, especially among the Jewish believers in Rome. If the law represents the **old way**, that must mean it has no value; or perhaps it was sinful and evil to begin with if it has been replaced by **the new way**. It is to this potential misunderstanding that Paul turns his attention before moving on to teach about the Holy Spirit in chapter 8.

But Paul is going to accomplish more than one thing in verses 7–25. He is going to answer the objection about the irrelevancy of the law, but in doing so he is going to add a piece to the sanctification puzzle which has so far been missing at a detailed level: the reality that, though we have been freed from the *control* of sin, we have not been freed from the *contest* with sin. This he will do in two steps. First, the value of the law (Rom. 7:7–13); second, the believer's conflict with the law and the sin it reveals and stimulates (Rom. 7:14–25).

B The Value of Law (7:7–13)

SUPPORTING IDEA: *God uses a holy thing (law) to reveal an evil thing (sin) so that a necessary thing (death) might result in the most important thing (life).*

While chapter 6 of Romans defends grace (Rom. 6:1,15), chapter 7 of Romans defends law (Rom. 7:7,13). Paul makes sure that the believers in Rome understand that the law is not sinful, is not the cause of sin, and is not discarded in light of "the new way of the Spirit" (Rom. 7:6).

7:7. Paul sets out first to demonstrate the value of the law. Granted, it is "the old way" (v. 6), but his fictional questioner would have us believe that the law is sin. Paul brings his typical energy to bear on the response: the law is **certainly not** sin (see notes on Rom. 6:2, *me genoito*). He then details the first of five ways that the law is valuable. Just as a black speck is made "visible" against a pure white background, so is sin made visible by the purity of the law. The law reveals what was there all along, but was "invisible" since everything around it was the same. In a world of "black" sins, individual acts of sin are unknown until a pure white standard is introduced. Immediately all the individual acts of sin become visible.

Paul illustrates his point by using coveting as an example: **I would not have known what coveting really was if the law had not said, "Do not covet."** Had Paul coveted before he became aware of the law that said, **Do not covet?** Yes. But the law named his sin and made him accountable for it. No longer could he say (if he ever did), "I didn't know I was coveting!" This first benefit of the law assumes "responsibility" on the part of the sinner, that the sinner would have a knowledge of his or her sin. In the spirit of Galatians 3:24–25, the law was a "tutor" (NASB) to lead us to a higher plane, the plane of faith. "Now that faith has come, we are no longer under the supervision of the law" (Gal. 3:25). Faith in Christ is "the new way of the Spirit"; the law is "the old way of the written code."

How did we get to the "new way"? By the "written code," the law (Rom. 7:6). The law continues to have that value today. No one comes to Christ in faith, even today, without a clear recognition of his or her sin—the personal yoke of guilt we bear for having violated the righteous standards of a holy God.

Before going further into this section of chapter 7, the identity of "I" must be established. Pages in the critical commentaries are taken up with discussions concerning who Paul is talking about in verses 7–13 (see "Deeper Discoveries" at the end of this chapter). Some reading the chapter in plain English might wonder what the discussion is all about, and we must wonder if the Roman believers stopped the reader of Paul's letter at this point and asked, "Who is Paul referring to when he says, 'I'? Is he referring to himself? To Adam and the human race? To Israel? To himself as a carnal believer?" While it is true that Paul's letters at times taxed even his fellow apostles when it came to understanding (2 Pet. 3:16), sound hermeneutics demands that the plainest meaning be taken unless there are objections which cannot be overcome (the doctrine of the perspicuity of Scripture).

Therefore, when Paul says **I would not have known**, we assume he is referring to himself, and then by extension any other human being who has sinned and come to a knowledge of his or her sin. The best assumption to be made concerning the entirety of Romans 7:7–25 is that it is divided into two sections (as mentioned above): the value of the law and the conflict with the law. Again, this is easily the plainest way to view the past tense verbs in verses 7–13 and the present tense verbs in verses 14–25. He seems to be referring to his past experience in coming to a realization of sin through the law in verses 7–13, and his ongoing experience in wrestling with what the law continues to reveal in him in verses 14–25. In both cases, the law is "good" (vv. 12,16).

In the first case, the law aids in his salvation; in the second, the law aids in his sanctification. Neither the law nor sin disappear from the believer's life after the salvation experience. Their presence creates the conflict, the birth pangs, if you will, which cause us to "groan inwardly as we wait eagerly for our adoption as sons, the redemption of our bodies" (Rom. 8:23). If the apostle Paul was led to Christ by the law (Rom. 7:7–13), and wrestled with the law's revelation of his still-alive sin nature even as a mature believer (Rom. 7:14–25), it is probable to view both experiences as normative.

Therefore, Paul is writing plainly about himself in Romans 7. Though we tread carefully here, there is a sense in which Romans 7 parallels Romans 5 in presenting a picture of solidarity. Adam was an individual who sinned, and all sinned in him. Christ was an individual who obeyed, and "all" (by faith) obeyed in him. Paul was an individual who came to grips with his sin through a knowledge of the law, *and though his actions were not representative of the human race,* they are a picture of what every person who comes to faith in Christ experiences. Paul's words are his personal testimony, given to explain the conflict and struggle with sin that every believer experiences. This understanding will serve as a framework upon which we will hang additional insights as we go through the remainder of the chapter.

7:8–9. Next, Paul says that the law reveals the human proclivity to sin. Why is this of value to the spiritual seeker? Because it settles, once and for all, the absolute moral bankruptcy of the human condition. Not only does law reveal sin; it primes the pump of sin. All human nature needs to know is that something is off limits for it to want to embrace it. The value in this is that it causes us to cry with Isaiah, "Woe to me! . . . I am ruined! For I am a man of unclean lips, and I live among a people of unclean lips, and my eyes have seen the King, the LORD Almighty" (Isa. 6:5). Isaiah saw the glory of the Lord himself; we see and hear his glory through his law. In either case, we are ruined when it comes to our own righteousness. The glory of God's character, revealed in his law, is our undoing.

Listen to Oswald Chambers's take on what Paul is saying in verse 9: "The moral law does not consider our weaknesses as human beings; in fact, it does not take into account our heredity or infirmities. It simply demands that we be absolutely moral. The moral law never changes, either for the highest of society or for the weakest in the world. It is enduring and eternally the same. The moral law, ordained by God, does not make itself weak to the weak by excusing our shortcomings. It remains absolute for all time and eternity. If we are not aware of this, it is because we are less than alive. Once we do realize it, our life immediately becomes a fatal tragedy. 'I was alive once without the law, but when the commandment came, sin revived and I died' (Rom. 7:9, NKJV)" (Chambers, *My Utmost*, December 1).

C. S. Lewis's literary and spiritual mentor, George MacDonald, expressed similar sentiments: "The immediate end of the commandments never was that men should succeed in obeying them, but that, finding they could not do that which yet must be done, finding the more they tried the more was required of them, they should be driven to the source of life and law—of their life and His law—to seek from Him such reinforcement of life as should make the fulfillment of the law as possible, yea, as natural, as necessary" (Lewis, p. 26).

Both Chambers and MacDonald are one in heart with the apostle. Paul discovered in his own life that **when the commandment came, sin sprang to life and I died.** Or, to use Chambers's words, Paul's life became a "fatal tragedy." Not only does the law not make exceptions for the weak, it does not make exceptions for the strong, which is what Paul was. Remember that Paul was "as for legalistic righteousness, faultless" (Phil. 3:6). Paul probably had in mind here not only the Ten Commandments and the 613 additional commands, but the myriad of Pharisaical "traditions" which were required of zealous Jews (Mark 7:4,8–9; Gal. 1:14). But his law-keeping did not excuse Paul. The deeper into the law Paul got, the larger were its leaps as sin sprang to life. Sin came to life and Paul died. That was exactly what was supposed to happen, since it put Paul (and humankind) at the mercy of God.

Speaking of being at the mercy of God, another reason to suggest that Paul is using his own experience as a picture of the human condition is the way his language mirrors precisely the experience of Adam in the Garden of Eden. Adam was **alive apart from law** when first placed in the garden by God. But as soon as God told Adam the one thing he could not do (Gen. 2:16–17), **sin, seizing the opportunity afforded by the commandment, produced in [Adam] every kind of covetous desire.**

Had Adam coveted the fruit of the tree of the knowledge of good and evil before the prohibition was given? He may have looked at it like any other tree in the garden, but looking is not coveting—because **apart from law, sin is dead.** Coveting is a sin, looking is not. But once the prohibition was given, looking, stimulated by the prohibition, became coveting—**when the commandment came, sin sprang to life and [Adam] died.** It is this death—and the realization of it by the spiritually deceased—that becomes the third value of the law.

7:10–11. Continuing the parallel Paul could be drawing with Adam's experience in the Garden, Paul identifies the law's third value. When God gave Adam the command not to eat of the tree of the knowledge of good and evil, it was to ensure his life, for "when you eat of it you will surely die" (Gen. 2:17). Paul's words could easily have been Adam's in retrospect: **I found that the very commandment that was intended to bring life actually brought death.** What happened in the Garden of Eden after the command was given to Adam? Satan, **seizing the opportunity afforded by the commandment, deceived me, and through the commandment put me to death.** Obviously, Paul has not stated his intention to use Adam's example as a parallel of his own, so we are not looking for exactness (it was Eve who was deceived, not Adam; 1 Tim. 2:14. Also, it was not Satan who put Adam to death, but sin, just as Paul states in his own case).

The point of the suggested parallel is that Paul's experience mirrors Adam's, and "everyman's," in the way the law reveals death. The truth is that "the soul who sins is the one who will die" (Ezek. 18:20). Sin is empowered by the commandment of the law, so the **commandment put me to death.** The objection of the sinner at this point is the same as the child who protests to his parent, "If you hadn't told me not to cross the street, I wouldn't be getting a spanking!" Adam, Paul, and all of us protest to God, "If you hadn't told me not to covet, I wouldn't be dead!" But tell us he did, and dead we are.

"And the value of discovering we are dead is?" the unconvinced will ask. The value is that we are put out of our misery—the misery of guilt and shame. By being declared dead, we can be made alive again: "You were dead in your transgressions and sins" (Eph. 2:1), but "when you were dead in your sins . . . God made you alive with Christ. He forgave us all our sins" (Col. 2:13).

7:12. The fourth value is that the law reveals the nature of the Lawgiver. The troublemaker in the death scenario is not the law, but the sin nature, on which Paul is about to pull back the curtain in the second half of the chapter. But here he brings to a conclusion his essential answer to the objector who had asked, "Is the law sin?" (v. 7). Because the law comes from a holy, righteous, and good God, the law itself must reveal those same characteristics, which it does. Is there an unholy commandment to be found among God's laws? No, because God is holy (Lev. 19:2). Is there an unrighteous commandment to be found among God's laws? No, because God is righteous (Dan. 9:14). Is there an evil commandment to be found among God's laws? No, because God is good (Mark 10:18).

7:13. A final question reveals the fifth value of the law. Paul poses it as a "yes or no" question: "Did the law (a good thing), **become death to me?**" We could ask it another way in order to invite his answer: "*How* did something holy, good, and righteous make me dead?" As Paul has already said, the law kills no one. Rather, it is sin which kills. The law enters the room, sin springs to life, and we die (v. 9). What the law does, which is of great value to us, is reveal the utter sinfulness of sin. Or, as Paul says, the law came **so that through the commandment sin might become utterly sinful.** Paul spares no effort to reveal the purely contemptible nature of sin—the sin to which the believer was enslaved before dying with Christ (Rom. 6), and the sin to which the believer is no longer enslaved but still does battle against (Rom. 7:14–25). Sin takes a holy, righteous, and good thing—the law—and uses it for unholy, unrighteous, and evil purposes.

Consider a modern example: we hear on our news channel of an adult who has tricked (deceived) a small, innocent child into participating in the most lewd and perverse forms of sexual activity. We recoil at the horror of it! How could anyone so evil use someone so blameless for such a perverted purpose? In a similar way—but much worse—sin uses the law of God for a perverted purpose—the spiritual death of a human being.

At the conclusion of this section of Paul's presentation, we must remind ourselves of the title of our chapter: "How the Gospel Delivers from Law." After the above discussion on the value of the law, a final legitimate question would be, "If the law has so much value, why do we need to be delivered from it?" The answer lies in the inextricable intertwining of law and sin. Paul said it best in verses 5 and 6: "we were controlled by the sinful nature" and its passions which were "aroused by the law . . . . But now, by dying to what once bound us" (the propensity to sin), "we have been released from the law."

In other words, if we had no inclination to sin, we would simply obey the law of God and find life. But because of our sin, the law brings death, not life. Therefore, the good news of the gospel is that we have been delivered from the condemnation of the law by dying to the propensity that once controlled us.

C The Believer's Conflict with Law (7:14–23)

SUPPORTING IDEA: *Delighting in God's law internally and obeying God's law externally will remain a source of conflict for the believer in this life.*

7:14–17. Paul begins his shift in emphasis from the past tense to the present tense in this verse. In this entire section (7:14–25), he says the same thing in several different ways (**it is sin living in me**, v. 17; "it is sin living in me," v. 20; "the law of sin at work within my members," v. 23). Like a prism, he splits a ray of truth into its component parts, allowing the whole to be seen in light of its parts. If Paul's point in this section were to be summarized in one verse, Galatians 5:17 would likely be it: "For the sinful nature desires what is contrary to the Spirit, and the Spirit what is contrary to the sinful nature. They are in conflict with each other, so that you do not do what you want." As we have already seen, the Spirit is absent from this discussion save for the reference in verse 6 where Paul contrasts the era of the written code with the new way of the Spirit. That conflict continues to be his theme in the remainder of Romans 7.

At the outset, it must be noted that, just as the debate was joined in 7:7–13 concerning the identity of the "I" in those verses, so the debate rages on here. The primary thorn in the flesh of interpreters is verse 14 itself, where Paul says he is **unspiritual, sold as a slave to sin**. After all, was not the point of Romans 6 to say that the believers "used to be slaves to sin" but were now "slaves to righteousness" (Rom. 6:17–18)? Verse 14, along with verses 18 and 24, make it difficult for many to believe that Paul is describing his experience as normative for the Christian life.

Some interpreters (e.g., Stott, pp. 209–211) see Paul writing as a believer, but as an Old Testament, or pre-Pentecost, believer who does not have the benefit of the Holy Spirit's presence and power. Still others reject the notion that Paul is writing from the perspective of spiritual regeneration; that 7:14–25 describes the experience of an unregenerate person (e.g., Moo, pp. 445–451).

Appealing once again to the plainness of Scripture, it is entirely credible to take Paul's words at face value in describing his present Christian experience (and thus what is likely to be the experience of all believers). The key to understanding Paul's perspective is the ability to hold in tension seemingly conflicting points of view in the present eschatological age in which we live. What is true *positionally* for the believer may not always be true *practically* in his or her experience. Seemingly, if we are no longer slaves to sin, we would never sin again; perfectionism would be achieved.

But in all the times when Paul chastised sinning believers such as the Corinthians and the Galatians, he never accused them of not being Christians. He called them weak, immature, childish—but not unregenerate. Paul understood the tension between positional truth and practical expression. Thus, in his own life, he could bemoan the intense realization of the pull of sin and its constant assault on the members of his body and its use of the law to provoke him to sin, while at the same time confess that "in my inner being I delight in God's law" (v. 22). No unbeliever delights in God's law. According to Paul, unbelievers view God's truth as foolishness, not a source of delight (1 Cor. 1:18–27; 2:14).

Consistent with Jewish thought, Christian eschatology recognizes that the present age is not the age to come; there is a difference between the two (2 Cor. 1:22; 5:5; Eph. 1:21; 1 Tim. 4:8; Titus 2:12). One does not begin when the other ends; rather, they overlap. George E. Ladd's writings on the kingdom of God best illuminate the "tension" in which we now live (see, e.g., his *The Gospel of the Kingdom,* 1959, esp. ch. 2). The inclusion of the kingdom of God into the kingdom of Satan vis-à-vis the ministry of Jesus has created conflicting kingdoms for a period of time until the kingdom of God is consummated and fills the earth. It is the conflicting period of time that accounts for the tension between the desire to do right and the temptation to do wrong. *We do not achieve on earth the perfection we will enjoy in heaven.*

Romans 6, 7, and 8 should not be viewed in a linear fashion, as if the believer moves from one to the other.

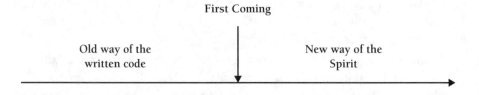

Rather, all are true for the believer, all the time (except for Rom. 7:7–13, which pictures the preconversion person's relationship with the law). And they take place in the tense period of overlap illustrated below:

During this period of overlap, the believer occupies a position described by C. K. Barrett:

> It is of the essence of Christian life that men are *simul justi, simul peccatores,* at the same time righteous and sinners. They are righteous in Christ, sinners in themselves (or, in Adam). Because Christ is now hidden from men's eyes in heaven until his *parousia,* the holiness and righteousness of Christians, which are not their own but his, are hidden, and the body of sin is all too clearly visible. . . . [The believer] is, and he is not, free from sin; he lives, and he does not live, for God; he is at the same time a righteous man and a sinner. This ambiguous personal position reflects the eschatological situation. The Age to Come has dawned, in the life, death, and resurrection of Jesus; but the present age has not passed. The two exist uneasily side by side, and Christians still look earnestly for the redemption of the body (8:23), knowing that they have been saved in hope (8:24). (Barrett, pp. 120–121, 142–143)

Paul had been a Christian approximately twenty-five years when he wrote the letter to the Romans. Why do we think that Paul should have walked in perfection, or even in victory, every moment of his own spiritual experience? Remember, he had no one to lean on and learn from. How long would it have taken him to make the radical transformation from living life under the law to living life under grace (Rom. 6:14)?

Throughout his apostolic ministry, Paul was painting a picture of the dawning of a new age while trying to sit back and enjoy the sunrise himself. Who does not know mature believers today who continue to wrestle with sin and identify with Paul's experience, while at the same time remaining submitted to the Holy Spirit in their life? Rather than being a picture of an unbeliever, Romans 7:14–25, together with Romans 8, pictures the believer who has been positionally delivered from the law but who, experientially, lives in the tension of the "now but not yet."

It probably is true that in the lives of most earnest Christians the two conditions Paul described [the struggle of Romans 7 and the victory of Romans 8] exist in a sort of cyclical advance. Recognition of our inability to live up to our deepest spiritual longings (ch. 7) leads us to cast ourselves upon God's Spirit for power and victory (ch. 8). Failure to continue in reliance upon the power of the Spirit places us once again in a position inviting defeat. Sanctification is a gradual process that repeatedly takes the believer through this recurring sequence of failure through dependency upon self to triumph through the indwelling Spirit. (Mounce, pp. 167–168)

And it is not just with regard to the law that we find this tension. Anders Nygren has noted the consistency of tension in describing sanctification all the way through chapters 6 through 8 of Romans (noted by Mounce, p. 168). We can illustrate it this way:

	We are . . .	Yet we . . .
Romans 6	free from sin	must battle against sin
Romans 7	free from the law	are not free from its criteria for righteousness
Romans 8	free from death	long for the redemption of the body

Seeing the tension that exists in all realms of our sanctification makes the second half of Romans 7 easier to understand. The first contrast Paul draws between himself and the law is that the law is **spiritual** (good, holy, righteous) but that he is **unspiritual**. When he looks at the law and sees that it contains what he should do, and then looks at himself doing what he does not do, he does not **understand**. That is more a statement of consternation than confusion, for Paul clearly understands: **it is no longer I myself who [does the opposite of the law], but it is sin living in me.** Does Paul *have* to commit the sin that the law sets before him vis-à-vis its commands? No—he has been rescued from the obligation to obey sin and disobey the law, as he will testify in verses 24–25. But the conflict is there, and it presents itself in two ways.

7:18–20. First, Paul does what is not desired, "those things which [he] ought not to have done" in the words of the Anglican confession. When Paul says, **What I do is not the good I want to do; no, the evil I do not want to do—this I keep on doing,** his words must be measured against his life for interpretation. Had Paul not done much that he desired to do in obedience to Jesus Christ? Had he not suffered greatly for the sake of the spread of the gospel, nearly losing his life on more than one occasion? Certainly there is evidence that Paul did much of what he wanted to do. What then of his words?

He is speaking of the sinful capacity that lives in him still. If it were up to Paul (or to us), we would do only what the law wants us to do. Yet we **keep on doing** the opposite. Paul does not mean that he does only evil, or that he does more evil than good, but that the conflict with evil is one that keeps on (present active indicative of *prasso*). The lure of sin is not dead though we have died to it. It will not die during "this present age" until we die physically. Only in "the age to come" will we be free from doing those things which we ought not to do.

Not only does Paul do what is not desired; he does not do what is desired.

7:21–23. Here Paul uses the law motif to illustrate from another angle the conflict he experiences. Two laws are mentioned: **the law of my mind** (his desire to obey God's law), and **the law of sin** (that which wars against the law of his mind). He states a principle by which these two laws conflict with one another: **when I want to do good, evil is right there with me.** All of us can identify with the apostle's succinct summary of the spiritual experience.

Not only Paul, but all believers, have "left undone those things which we ought to have done." And as the Anglican confession rightly concludes ("there is no health in us"), Paul is about to explode with his own spiritual diagnosis.

The Believer's Deliverance from Law (7:24–25)

> **SUPPORTING IDEA:** *The only deliverer from the law's condemnation is Jesus Christ our Lord.*

One of the results of the gospel is that it delivers us from the condemnation of the law. "Of what use then is the Law? To lead us to Christ, the Truth—to waken in our minds a sense of what our deepest nature, the presence, namely, of God *in* us, requires of us—to let us know, in part by failure, that the purest efforts of will of which we are capable cannot lift us up even to the abstaining from wrong to our neighbor" (George MacDonald, in Lewis, p. 20).

The law did its perfect work in the apostle Paul, reviving his soul (Ps. 19:7a). It convicted him of his sin and showed him that the only deliverance for him was Jesus Christ. No wonder Paul could call the law a "tutor to lead us to Christ, that we may be justified by faith" (Gal. 3:24, NASB). That is exactly what the law did for him. Once delivered from the law, Paul was able to serve the ends of the law—righteousness—in the power of the Holy Spirit (Rom. 7:6).

Paul summarizes the entire chapter—the conflict of the believer that causes him or her to remain dependent upon the Spirit—in the final verse. When it is Paul the believer talking, he makes himself **a slave to God's law**. But when his sinful capacity speaks out, he is **a slave to the law of sin**. As mentioned in this chapter earlier, it is a shame that chapter divisions in our Bibles cause us to "stop" at certain points in the consideration of the text. While this is a logical point in the flow of Paul's thought for a pause, Romans 7 and 8 should be read together. Immediately, Paul moves from wretchedness to victory in declaring that the law of the Spirit of life in Christ Jesus has set him "free from the law of sin and death" (Rom. 8:2). The gospel is indeed good news, delivering the believer from death by law to life by grace through the Spirit.

> **MAIN IDEA REVIEW:** *The mature believer in Jesus Christ is not one who never struggles to obey God. Rather, the mature believer is one who has been released from the law's condemnation and made free to serve its requirements by dying to the law through Jesus Christ.*

III. CONCLUSION

Face-to-Face with Death

It is not uncommon for commentators to suggest what might have been in Paul's mind when he cried out, "What a wretched man I am! Who will rescue me from this body of death?" (Rom. 7:24). "Wretched" we understand, but what is the "body of death" from which he wants to be rescued? A most gruesome picture is that presented by the Roman poet Virgil (70–19 B.C.), with which his audience in Rome might well have been familiar (noted by Bruce, p. 147). In Book Eight of the *Æneid,* Virgil's epic poem that chronicles the wanderings of Aeneas after the fall of Troy, the horrific cruelty of the Etruscan king Mezentius is told. To punish and torture his living captives, Mezentius tied them face to face with decomposing corpses of those killed in battle, leaving them bound together until the living captive died. Virgil's poetic presentation does little to soften the horror of such a fate:

> The living and the dead at his command
> Were coupled, face to face, and hand to hand,
> Till, chok'd with stench, in loath'd embraces tied,
> The ling'ring wretches pin'd away and died.
> —Virgil's *Æneid*, Book Eight

What did Paul call himself—a "wretched man"? What did Virgil call those locked in the embrace of death—those "ling'ring wretches"? Surely no word other than "rescue" would fit both scenes. And if Paul had Virgil's epic in mind, then this image of "body of death" suddenly puts the gospel's deliverance from the law in a new and more serious light.

The modern believer can know little of what Paul knew of being rescued from the yoke of the law. People like Paul were practically genetically coded to view the keeping of the law as the highest spiritual good. Then, after believing, teaching, and practicing that for years, Paul is thrown to the ground on a highway to Damascus and told that he has to change his worldview. Paul was to discover that the law which he had embraced as a lover was suddenly transformed in his arms to a decomposing set of standards that was killing him—and he could not break free from it! But unlike Mezentius's corpses who killed the living, Paul the living was turning the law into something evil. It was Paul's sin that was driving the life out of the law. His proclivity to sin was not only killing him, but it was turning the law from something pure and noble into something rotten and lifeless.

The body of death from which Paul needed rescuing was his propensity to sin which had turned the law into his executioner. But rather than dying a slow and putrid death, Paul was rescued by the Lord Jesus Christ. Jesus cut the ropes and set the Pharisee prisoner free. Jesus died the death to which the law had condemned Paul, allowing Paul to live the life that the keeping of the law promised. And the same is possible today. No one needs to remain bound to the law—"thanks be to God" (Rom. 7:25).

PRINCIPLES

- The believer cannot be committed to the law and to Christ at the same time.
- To be controlled by the pull of sin is to be continually stimulated by the law to sin.
- To be released from the law is to serve the goals of the law (righteousness) in a new way: by the Spirit.
- The law is good in that it reveals what separates us from God: our sin.
- Sin, not that which reveals sin, is the source of spiritual death.
- The Christian life is a lifelong challenge of aligning heart and hand for God's glory.

APPLICATIONS

- Am I a spiritual adulterer? Have I truly died to the demands of the law (which I cannot keep) in order to rest in a righteous union with Christ (who kept the law for me)?

- Is there a sin which continually defeats me? Am I focusing more on the law against that sin than I am on Christ?
- How have I seen righteousness realized in my life by focusing on the Spirit's help instead of the letter of the law?
- Have I thanked God recently for his righteous standards that reveal my need for him?
- Do I ever blame God, and his righteous standards, for my sin instead of taking responsibility for my sin?
- Am I prepared to be engaged in spiritual conflict for the rest of my life? Do I accept the reality of the power of sin in my outward self?

IV. LIFE APPLICATION

Signs of Living Under Law

All cultures, in some way, acknowledge standards, rules, or laws by which the society operates. Regardless of their source, their morality, or the consistency of their application, people recognize law. Ray Steadman offered four evidences that all people everywhere live under law of some kind (cited by Boice, 2:719):

1. *We are proud of our achievements.* The standards we reach point to those who have reached higher standards than ours and those who have fallen short of us. Because the law reveals failure, "one of the first marks of a person who is living under the law is that he is always pointing out how well he is doing" in order to divert attention from failure.

2. *We are critical of others.* Just as cheaters are most offended by being cheated, so we are critical of others in the areas of our own failures. Because our failures make us insecure, we seek security be creating insecurity in others through criticism.

3. *We are reluctant to admit our own failures.* We boast when we want others to know that (in our opinion) we have met or exceeded the requirements of "the law" (or at least have not fallen short as much as others). This is the opposite. We hedge about our failures and mistakes, only reluctantly admitting them, because we know that some law stands over us in judgment. The very fact that we seek not to reveal our failures is evidence that we believe standards exist that we failed to satisfy.

4. *We suffer from depression, discouragement, and defeat.* When our societies, our families, or our personal lives suffer defeat and failure, one of our first inclinations is to issue new "laws." Our human nature is immediately inclined to think that legislation of some sort is the answer to our failure. It is a fruitless and hopeless cycle. We (societies,

families, individuals) break the laws we have, which throws us into confusion and depression. We then think the problem is with the laws, so we enact new ones. We then fail to keep those, which throws us even deeper into despair. If, we think, we could only discover better, higher, more numerous, more pointed laws, we would be able to keep them successfully.

Given the inclination of the human race to create, enact, wrangle over, revise, and be terrorized by "law," is it any wonder that Paul the apostle proclaimed a gospel that had as one of its foundation stones, "we have been released from the law" (Rom. 7:6)? And is it any wonder that this gospel was met with resistance? Why, the absence of law strips sinful humanity of any reason to boast or to engage in self-pity! And it also strips the sinful human nature of a reason to sin, since apart from law, sin is dead (Rom. 7:8).

Are you, or those you teach, caught up in law of one sort or the other? When we move from "the old way of the written code" to "the new way of the Spirit" (Rom. 7:6), something wonderful happens: "all things are lawful" (1 Cor. 10:23, NASB). Think of it! All things are lawful! But before disobedience turns liberty into license, remember also that, under the leadership of the Holy Spirit ("the new way of the Spirit"), "not all things are profitable . . . not all things edify" (1 Cor. 10:23, NASB).

Determine today to discover where in your life law is being abused by your ever-present capacity to find life on your own terms, and reidentify if necessary with the death and resurrection of Jesus Christ. The gospel you believe has delivered you from sin (Rom. 6) and has delivered you from law (Rom. 7). To be free of one is to be free of both. Before moving to Romans 8 where you will learn to be free from death as well, get in step with the new way of the Spirit.

V. PRAYER

Heavenly Father, thank you for delivering me from a law I could not keep, a law that had already condemned me to death. Thank you for allowing your Son, Jesus Christ, to fulfill the demands of the law for me that I might be free to live by the Spirit. And thank you for the strength of your Spirit by which I persevere in the daily struggle against sin. Thank you for rescuing me from the body of death to which I was bound. Amen.

VI. DEEPER DISCOVERIES

A. Marriage, Divorce, Adultery (7:1–3)

As discussed in the commentary, Romans 7:1–3 is not primarily a teaching on marriage, divorce, or adultery. Paul simply uses marriage law as an illustration of the authority of law. Yet it never fails that the teacher expounding these verses will get questions on these very sensitive areas—especially in the modern era when the church at large fares little better than the culture in general in maintaining healthy marital relationships. Following are the key Scriptural passages dealing with these topics:

- Genesis 2:24: The cornerstone of the doctrine of marriage in Scripture.
- Exodus 20:14; Deuteronomy 5:18: Prohibition of adultery.
- Exodus 20:17; Deuteronomy 5:21: Prohibition against the coveting of another man's wife. Evidence also for monogamy as the standard in marriage.
- Leviticus 21:7, 14; 22:13; Numbers 30:9: Evidence of the permissibility of divorce in the Old Testament, although not justification for it (cf. Matt. 19:8).
- Deuteronomy 22:22–24; John 8:3–7: Punishments for adultery in Israel.
- Deuteronomy 24:1–4: Provision for a bill of divorce in Israel.
- Ezra 9:2; 10:3, 16–17: Instance of wholesale divorce following the return from Babylon when Ezra forced Israelite men to put away their foreign wives in order to maintain spiritual purity in the nation.
- Malachi 2:16: God's attitude toward divorce.
- Matthew 5:27–30: Adultery of the heart.
- Matthew 5:31–32: Governance of divorce; prohibition of remarriage of the divorced; exception to the prohibition of divorce (5:32; see also Matt. 19:9).
- Matthew 19:3–99; Mark 10:2–12; Luke 16:18: Jesus' teaching on marriage, divorce, adultery.
- 1 Corinthians 7:1–16: Paul on marriage, divorce, remarriage.
- 1 Timothy 5:14: Permission for young widows to remarry.

B. Law, Commandments (7:12)

When Paul says that the law and commandments are holy, righteous, and good (Rom. 7:12), he is reflecting the Israelite heritage that elevated the law above all else. The very idea that someone might suggest that the law is sin (Rom. 7:7) was an affront to any Jew, especially a rabbinically trained Jew like Paul. How could anything that was sin be "more precious than gold" and "sweeter than honey" (Ps. 19:10)?

The most concentrated sources for examining the place of the statutes and commands of God in Israel are Psalm 19:7–11 and Psalm 119 in its entirety (all 176 verses). Psalm 119 employs eight different Hebrew terms in referring to the words of God: law, statutes, precepts, commands/commandments, laws (all of which are found in Ps. 19:7–11, though occasionally with different English renderings), decrees, word, and promise. Psalm 119 displays a level of reverence for the commands of God in Israel that is unparalleled in ancient or modern legal literature.

Israelites had stringent responsibilities regarding the law of God. They were to know it (Exod. 33:12–13), love it (Ps. 119:47,97), observe or keep it (Deut. 4:1,6; 29:9), teach it in their families (Deut. 4:9–10), and keep it in their hearts (Deut. 11:18). One of the most wonderful aspects of the promised (and fulfilled) new covenant through Jeremiah was that the law would be in the mind and written on the heart (Jer. 31:33; cf. Heb. 8:10). Any study of Romans 7 will be greatly enhanced by a meditative reading of Psalm 119 and other passages dealing with God's law in the Old Testament. Having done so, the perverseness of sin as presented in Romans will be brought into even sharper contrast with the holiness, righteousness, and goodness of the law.

C. Perfectionism (7:14–23)

The question of sin in the life of the believer comes to the fore in Romans 7. Many feel Paul could not be writing as a believer due to his apparent inability to control the powers of sin in his life. This raises the theological question of "perfectionism" in its various forms. Perfectionism is the doctrine that it is possible in this life to attain a position of not sinning; not free from the temptation to sin, but free from yielding to the temptation to sin (most perfectionists would differentiate sins by mistake from sins of choice, and say that perfectionism does not rule out sins by mistake, or unwitting sins).

Perfectionism is a part of the discussion of sanctification, which is Paul's primary concern in Romans 6–8. Historically and generally speaking, perfectionists have been of the Arminian persuasion with its emphasis on the freedom of the will. They suggest that through the grace of the Holy Spirit it is possible to arrive at a point where one chooses not to sin again. They cite various Scriptures such as Matthew 5:48; Ephesians 4:13; 1 Thessalonians 5:23; Hebrews 13:20–21; and 1 John 3:4–6 as evidence for their position.

Students of the Reformed persuasion do not allow the perfectionist position as a possibility in Christian sanctification. They cite Paul's experience in Romans 7 as a primary proof (though it has been noted that not all agree about Paul's spiritual condition in Romans 7). Another key antiperfection passage is 1 John 1:8–10 where John says we lie if we say we have no sin. They would also say that John's words in 1 John 3:4–6 do not support the perfectionist position due to the present tenses of the verb forms. John is talking about continuing, habitual sin in 3:4–6 as proof that one does not belong to Christ, not occasional sins.

Finally, antiperfectionists would cite all the warnings against sin in the New Testament as evidence that sin is a distinct possibility, with instructions for discipline implying a distinct probability. Perfectionists would counter that warnings and provisions for sin among Christians do not invalidate the goal and possibility of not sinning.

All Christians can agree on the goal of perfectionism: not sinning. The danger of perfectionism is creating further guilt and shame among those seeking the perfection plane but failing to reach it. The danger of antiperfection teaching is too casual an attitude toward sin and its consequences.

D. "I" (7:7–13,14–23)

The commentaries are filled with discussions on the identity of the "I's" in Romans 7:7–13 and 14–23. For instance, Douglas Moo gives a helpful presentation of four defendable positions concerning the "I" of 7:7–13 (Moo, pp. 424–427):

1. Paul is speaking autobiographically, with variations on when and how Paul was awakened to the requirements of the law (Rom. 7:9).
2. Paul is speaking of Adam specifically (many early church fathers), or of all people in corporate solidarity with Adam (later and contemporary interpreters).
3. Paul is speaking of Israel. This view would then have Paul addressing Jews still under the Mosaic Law in verses 14–23.
4. Paul is speaking of no one in particular and everyone in general. This view has Paul using figurative language to describe the confrontation between God and every person.

C. E. B. Cranfield mentions seven possible identities for the "I" in 7:14–23 (Cranfield, pp. 156–157):

1. Paul is speaking autobiographically as a Christian.
2. Paul is speaking autobiographically, referring to his preconversion status and written from that perspective.
3. Paul is speaking autobiographically, referring to his preconversion status but now written with Christian understanding.
4. Paul is writing about and from the perspective of the non-Christian Jew.
5. Paul is writing about the non-Christian Jew as seen by a mature Christian.
6. Paul is writing about the Christian who is fighting the spiritual battle in his own strength.
7. Paul is writing about the experience of all Christians generally, including the most mature who still wrestle with sin and the demands of the law.

Other helpful discussions of Paul's perspective in Romans 7 may be found in the commentaries by Stott, MacArthur, and Schreiner.

VII. TEACHING OUTLINE

A. INTRODUCTION

1. Lead Story: A Wretch Like John and Paul
2. Context: Paul, having begun with Romans 6, is now in the middle of a three-chapter presentation on the sanctification of the believer. In Romans 6, the believer is declared free from sin; in Romans 7, the believer is declared free from the law; and in Romans 8, the believer will be declared free from death and free to live in the Spirit.
3. Transition: Paul begins chapter 7 with an illustration that proves that any law has authority only over the living; those who have died are dead to the demands of law. Then, to prove that the law is still valuable, he demonstrates how the law reveals sin—sin that remains alive as a source of conflict in the believer. Only one person can deliver the believer from the demands of the law—Jesus Christ our Lord.

B. COMMENTARY

1. The Believer's Death to Law: an Illustration (7:1–6)
    a. The principle (7:1)
    b. The illustration (7:2–3)
    c. The application (7:4–6)
2. The Value of Law (7:7–13)
    a. Law reveals sin (7:7)
    b. Law reveals the human proclivity to sin (7:8–9)
    c. Law reveals death (7:10–11)
    d. Law reveals the nature of the Lawgiver (7:12)
    e. Law reveals the sinfulness of sin (7:13)
3. The Believer's Conflict with Law (7:14–23)
    a. Spiritual versus unspiritual (7:14–17)
    b. Doing what is *not* desired (7:18–20)
    c. Not doing what *is* desired (7:21–23)
4. The Believer's Deliverance from Law (7:24–25)

C. CONCLUSION: SIGNS OF LIVING UNDER LAW

VIII. ISSUES FOR DISCUSSION

1. What parallels can be drawn between our resistance to civil laws and our resistance to the laws of God? Cite examples of laws (civil and religious) we are loathe to keep, and explain why we believe we can justify our exemption from them.

2. Explain the difference between bearing fruit for God and bearing fruit to death (Rom. 6:4–5). Where do nonreligious acts fall, e.g., community service? Into how many realms of the believer's life should bearing fruit for God extend?

3. Give examples from your own experience of behavior which came to life with energy once you learned there was a prohibition against that behavior. How did you handle the situation?

4. How does the organized church, by its corporate practices and structure, hinder the process of believers learning to live free of the condemnation of law? What should the church's attitude and practice be about laws and commandments at the corporate level?

Romans 8:1–39

How the Gospel Brings New Life in the Spirit

I. INTRODUCTION
Great, Greater, Greatest

II. COMMENTARY
A verse-by-verse explanation of the chapter.

III. CONCLUSION
The True Meaning of Freedom

An overview of the principles and applications from the chapter.

IV. LIFE APPLICATION
Conquering the Conquerors

Melding the chapter to life.

V. PRAYER
Tying the chapter to life with God.

VI. DEEPER DISCOVERIES
Historical, geographical, and grammatical enrichment of the commentary.

VII. TEACHING OUTLINE
Suggested step-by-step group study of the chapter.

VIII. ISSUES FOR DISCUSSION
Zeroing the chapter in on daily life.

Quote

"*The* Christian life is essentially life in the Spirit, that

is to say, a life that is animated, sustained, directed and

enriched by the Holy Spirit. Without the Holy Spirit true

Christian discipleship would be inconceivable, indeed

impossible."

John Stott

Romans 8:1–39

I N   A   N U T S H E L L

Paul's three-chapter treatise on sanctification (Rom. 6–8) concludes with chapter 8. The conflict between the Holy Spirit and the propensity to sin presented in chapter 7 is here answered with the
presentation of another "law" (principle)—the law of the Spirit of life
through Christ Jesus. Paul explains the "new way of the Spirit" (Rom.
7:6) and reveals the benefits of the new life the Spirit gives.

How the Gospel Brings New Life in the Spirit

I. INTRODUCTION

Great, Greater, Greatest

$\mathcal{L}$inguistic scholars and historians could probably explain to us how degrees of intensity developed in human language. We use the three levels of intensity of adjectives and adverbs without thinking of their official labels which we learned in long-forgotten grammar lessons: the absolute or positive degree (e.g., happy), the comparative degree (happier), and the superlative degree (happiest).

With some things, it is easy to assign one of the three labels. Take buildings for instance. When it was completed in 1931, the Empire State Building in New York City was the world's tallest building at 1,250 feet. It was tall, taller, and tallest. Now, however it is only tall, since several buildings have surpassed it in height: the Sears Tower in Chicago is 1,453 feet tall, and the World Trade Center in New York City is 1,348 feet tall. At the time of this writing, the title of tallest goes to the Petronas Twin Towers in Malaysia which stand at 1,482 feet tall (taller than the second tallest, the Sears Tower, by only 29 feet).

The glory of the Twin Towers will be short-lived, however, since a tower presently under construction in Chongqing, China, will top out at 1,499 feet. It will be bested in 2001 by a yet taller building in Shanghai, China, the Shanghai Financial Center, which will stretch another ten feet and hold the record at 1,509 feet. Not to be outdone, New York real estate mogul Donald Trump wants to take a giant leap heavenward by constructing a 1,791-foot-tall building in New York City to house the New York Stock Exchange.

With concrete and steel, it is always easy to tell what is tall, taller, and tallest. However, use another set of terms—good, better, and best—and you quickly move from the objective to the subjective. Which of the world's tallest buildings is the "best" building? At that point, bring your lunch and prepare for a long debate between architects, tenants, engineers, and city-dwellers. In cases of subjective matters, the superlative is in the heart of the beholder.

Moving the discussion from buildings to books, which book of the Bible would you say is the greatest? Which chapter? Which verse? Which word or phrase? While the Bible is objective in many ways (we can measure the longest and shortest books, chapters, and verses), applying subjective measurements like "greatest" is far more difficult. And, of course, it is a matter which cannot be (and need not be) decided. Every reader is entitled, at any given stage of the spiritual pilgrimage, to cast a vote for what he or she feels is the greatest portion of Scripture. James Boice recalls how, after anointing Romans 8 as the greatest chapter of the Bible in a sermon, a friend pointed out to him that he had already given that label to Hosea 3 in a previously published book. He fell back on D. Martyn Lloyd-Jones' dictum that the greatest book of the Bible should always be the one being studied or taught at that moment (Boice, 2:782–783).

It is interesting that, given the allowance for freedom and subjectivity in determining great, greater, and greatest portions of Scripture, we have arrived at the chapter of Scripture which many call the greatest, which is part of the book that many call the greatest, and which contains the verse that many call the greatest. The book is, of course, Romans. The chapter is 8. And the verse is 28. For reasons heretofore enumerated, Romans could legitimately be called the greatest book in the Bible. But why chapter 8? The Lutheran Pietist leader Philipp Jakob Spener (1635–1705) said it most poetically—if the Bible was a ring and the Book of Romans its precious stone, chapter 8 would be "the sparkling point of the jewel." But the American Charles G. Trumbull (1872–1941), editor of *The Sunday School Times*, perhaps said it most thoroughly:

> The eighth of Romans has become peculiarly precious to me, beginning with 'no condemnation,' ending with 'no separation' [originally noted by Swiss commentator F. Godet (1812–1900)] and in between, 'no defeat.' This wondrous chapter sets forth the gospel and plan of salvation; the life of freedom and victory; the hopelessness of the natural man and the righteousness of the born again; the indwelling of Christ and the Holy Spirit; the resurrection of the body and blessed hope of Christ's return; the working together of all things for our good; every tense of the Christian life, past, present, and future; and the glorious, climactic song of triumph, no separation in time or eternity "from the love of God which is in Jesus Christ our Lord." (Boice, 2:782)

Robert Mounce's more contemporary assessment equals Trumbull's in ardor:

> With chap. 8 we arrive at what may be called the inspirational highlight of the Book of Romans. Here the apostle is swept along in a wave of spiritual exaltation that begins with God's provision of the Spirit for victory over the old nature, breaks through the sufferings that mark our present existence, and crests with a doxology of praise

to the unfathomable love of God revealed in Christ Jesus. Nowhere in the annals of sacred literature do we find anything to match the power and beauty of this remarkable paean of praise. Although the pinnacle of this exalted prose awaits our arrival at verses 28–39, the earlier sections provide the setting against which the culminating truths will break forth with an even greater brilliance. We are not dealing here with mere theology. As Paul wrote, his pen gave evidence that he was caught up in an experience of profound worship and spiritual adoration. (Mounce, pp. 173–174)

It would be difficult to argue with either Trumbull's or Mounce's assessment of Romans 8, whether one calls it the greatest chapter in the Bible or not. Perhaps it is so well loved because it addresses human beings' greatest sense of need—the need for protection, security, and safety. Paul has just succeeded (in Rom. 6–7) in stripping away two appealing sources of security for human beings: sin and legalism. Many people go in one direction and define themselves by their sins; many others go in the opposite direction and define themselves by their attempts at sinlessness. The majority are adrift between the two poles, using the oars of pleasure and pride to go in circles as they seek a safe port in the storm of life.

But Paul has said that we can, by dying both to sin (Rom. 6) and to the law (Rom. 7), have a new identity in Jesus Christ—which sounds good in theory, but it needs to be fleshed out for practice. That is the purpose of the eighth chapter of Romans. Paul reveals that, while we have to "reckon" our death and resurrection with Christ to be true (Rom. 6:11), the key to living it is not a matter of reckoning. Rather, it is a matter of being controlled by the Holy Spirit, who ushers us into the family of God.

If Romans 8 is the greatest chapter in the Bible, it is because it tells the believer that he or she is a child of God whose life is totally overshadowed by the protective hand of a loving, heavenly Father. While the last two verses in the chapter are profound—[nothing] can **separate us from the love of God that is in Christ Jesus our Lord**—it is verse 28 that so succinctly applies that love to the life we have been left to live on earth. Verse 28 says that God has a purpose in everything that happens to those who have done what Paul described in Romans 6 and 7. Throwing away the crutches of pleasure and pride could leave one vulnerable to pain and suffering. But Romans 8:28 says that vulnerability has been replaced by a confidence in the purposes of God—everything works together for the believer's good.

While engineers can measure the heights of skyscrapers with extreme accuracy, believers can measure their personal peace and security fairly accurately as well. And for centuries, numerous other chapters of Scripture notwithstanding, the eighth chapter of Romans has perhaps introduced more believers to the new way of life in the Holy Spirit, a way leading to a new life of peace and security in God, than any other chapter in the Bible. All would agree that Romans 8 is a great chapter in the Bible. Many people would go further and claim that it is greater than most. Still others, because of the message of the new way of life in the Spirit, believe it is the greatest of all.

II. COMMENTARY

How the Gospel Brings New Life in the Spirit

> **MAIN IDEA:** *The gospel of Jesus Christ makes possible a brand new way of life for the believer—life lived abundantly in and through the power of the Holy Spirit.*

A The New Way: Freedom from Condemnation (8:1–4)

> **SUPPORTING IDEA:** *Because believers died with Christ, the law has no more power to condemn the believer for violation of God's standards.*

The first seventeen verses of Romans 8 detail the freedoms of believers who have died both to sin and to the law—the new way of life in the Spirit: freedom from condemnation, from control by the sinful disposition, and from fear of separation from God. Verses 18–39 then describe the three bases of the new life in the Spirit: the promises of God, the purposes of God, and the protection of God.

8:1–2. Paul's **therefore . . . now** (Gr. *ara nun*, occurring together for emphasis) occurs this way only here in Paul's epistles. Coupled together, the two particles call attention to a turning point in Paul's epistle (see 5:1 and 12:1 for other major turning points signified by **therefore**). The question is, Upon what point is Paul turning his presentation of the gospel? Is he saying **therefore** based on all of Romans 1–7 that precedes 8:1? This is not likely in light of his turning point in Romans 5:1. Rather, it seems more likely that specifically, **therefore** is based on 7:1–6, and generally on Romans 6–7.

Here is why: we noted in the last chapter that 7:1–6 is actually an illustration for Romans 6. Also, we said that Paul's argument could have proceeded directly from 7:6 to 8:1 since 7:7–25 serves only as an aside to answer Jewish objections about the role of the law. Because it turned out to be a rather lengthy aside, it appears to be integral to the argument. But it is integral as a subtext, not the main text. The main text of Paul's argument can be seen most clearly by skipping from 7:6 directly to 8:1: "But now, by dying to what once bound us, we have been released from the law so that we serve in the new way of the Spirit, and not in the old way of the written code" (7:6). **Therefore, there is now no condemnation for those who are in Christ Jesus** (8:1).

Granted, Paul picks up the reference to "Jesus Christ our Lord" in 7:25 with his reference to **Christ Jesus** in 8:1. But the flow of his argument is clearly to summarize all of Romans 6–7 by saying that those who have died to sin and the law **in Christ Jesus** (6:8,11,23; 7:6) are now free from the condemnation incurred by living under the same. F. F. Bruce points out that **condemnation** (*katakrima*) probably should more accurately be thought of as "penal servitude," i.e., the results of **condemnation** (Bruce, p. 151). **Condemnation** in a legal sense is the opposite of justification, but Paul is not saying here that we are justified (i.e., "not condemned"). He is in a point in his argument where he is discussing the freedom that comes from being **in Christ Jesus**. Therefore, if we have been set **free from the law of sin and death**, then we no longer are slaves to sin and death (see Rom. 6:15–23). We no longer have any term of punishment or servitude to fulfill as a result of being declared "guilty" (see *katakrima* in Rom. 5:16,18). Fittingly, Eugene Peterson (*The Message*) calls **condemnation** "a continuous, low-lying black cloud" which Paul says no longer hangs over us.

In Christ Jesus and "in Christ" occur 119 times in Paul's epistles. The other epistles add only four additional occurrences (none in Acts and the Gospels). It is fitting that the apostle who received the revelation of the mystery of the union of Jew and Gentile into one body should coin a phrase to describe those incorporated into one body by that union. The body is, of course, the body of Christ, the church (Rom. 12:5; 1 Cor. 12:12,27; Eph. 4:12; Col. 1:24). But it is not the membership of all Christendom's organized churches. Rather, the body of Christ is that mystical body made up of those who have died together with Christ through faith, and have been made "one with him in spirit" (1 Cor. 6:17). Not only is there **no condemnation** [penal servitude] **for those who are in Christ Jesus,** they also are . . .

- redeemed (Rom 3:24),
- alive to God (Rom. 6:11),
- possessors of eternal life (Rom. 6:23),
- free from the law of sin and death (Rom. 8:2),
- members of one spiritual body (Rom. 12:5),
- sharers in Christ's work (Rom. 16:3,9),
- sanctified (1 Cor. 1:2),
- recipients of grace (1 Cor. 1:4),
- secure in death (1 Cor. 15:18),
- bold to speak the truth (2 Cor. 2:17),
- new creatures (2 Cor. 5:17),
- free (Gal. 2:4),
- justified (Gal. 2:17),
- recipients of the blessings given to Abraham (Gal. 3:14),
- sons of God (Gal. 3:26),

- one with others regardless of race, gender, or social condition (Gal. 3:28),
- recipients of every spiritual blessing in heaven (Eph. 1:3),
- seated in the heavens (Eph. 2:6),
- created for good works (Eph. 2:10),
- brought near to God (Eph. 2:13),
- partakers with Jews of the promises (Eph. 3:6),
- forgiven by God (Eph. 4:32),
- encouraged (Phil. 2:1),
- at peace (Phil. 4:7),
- provided for (Phil. 4:19),
- anticipating the resurrection of our bodies (1 Thess. 4:16),
- overseen by providence (1 Thess. 5:18),
- alive (2 Tim. 1:1), and
- saved (2 Tim. 2:10).

Interestingly, none of the above blessings could be true if we were under **condemnation** by God. But being **in Christ Jesus** means we are **free from the law of sin and death** which blocked our way to every other blessing which is ours in Christ. The **law of the Spirit of life** which Paul says has set us free from the **law of sin and death** is more of a principle, or controlling power, than a law (cf. Rom. 7:23). This **law of the Spirit of life** "like a strong wind, has magnificently cleared the air, freeing you from a fated lifetime of brutal tyranny at the hands of sin and death" (Peterson, *The Message*). The third-century Greek father Origen commented that "the law of the Spirit of life is the same thing as the law of God. . . . For to serve the law of God and to be under the law of the Spirit is to serve Christ. To serve Christ is to serve wisdom, which is to serve righteousness, which is to serve truth and all related virtues" (Bray, p. 201).

Before leaving this section, note should be made of the significant textual problem in verse 1. The phrase "who walk not after the flesh, but after the Spirit" appears in Romans 8:1 in the KJV. Because it appears only in later Greek manuscripts, and is identical to the same phrase in verse 4, most commentators agree that the phrase in verse 1 is a copyist's error and should not be included in the text. The commentary by Boice gives a helpful explanation of how the error could have been made (Boice, 2:792).

8:3–4. When a prisoner is freed from condemnation and penal servitude, he or she is freed to something else. Regardless of where the prisoner ends up, at the moment of release he or she has been freed to life. Such is the transition from verses 1–2 to 3–4. If verses 1–2 are about position (freed from servitude to sin and death), then verses 3–4 are about practice—free to live **according to the Spirit**. It is here that Paul moves beyond his summary statement of chapters 6 and 7 (Rom. 8:1–2) and continues his treatise on sanctification—the position of holiness (set-apartness) which is ours in Christ which forms the basis of our becoming holy in practice. These four verses are not unlike the position/practice parallel found in Ephesians 2:8–10: "by grace you have been saved, through faith . . . to do good works."

All along, it was God's intent that **the righteous requirements of the law might be fully met** [fulfilled] in his people: "See, I set before you today life and prosperity, death and destruction. For I command you today to love the Lord your God, to walk in his ways, and to keep his commands, decrees and laws; then you will live and increase, and the Lord your God will bless you in the land you are entering to possess" (Deut. 30:15).

When the Ten Commandments were repeated in Moab, Moses told the people to "learn them and be sure to follow them" (Deut. 5:1). "They are not just idle words for you," he said later, "they are your life" (Deut. 32:47). Unfortunately, a perfect set of requirements was given to an imperfect people. This was not a mistake on God's part; rather, it was part of a glorious plan to bestow grace and mercy on those who needed it most—those who had become enslaved by the nature they inherited from Adam and which had been revealed by the law.

So the law had two purposes: to provide life and to reveal the death in man—man's sinful nature. Because the law had no power of its own, it could not overcome the power of sin in humankind. But in a sinless person, the law could be fulfilled since a sinless person has his or her own spiritual power by which to keep the law. What God did in Christ Jesus to overcome the dilemma of a perfect law being given to imperfect people was to send **his own Son in the likeness of sinful man to be a sin offering**. God condemned sin in order that the righteous requirements of the law might be fully met in us.

How did God condemn sin? Here, the NASB probably reads more accurately than the NIV. The NIV says that God **condemned sin in sinful man**. Literally, the text says that God "condemned sin *in the flesh*" (*en te sarki*). In whose flesh? The NASB says that God sent "His own Son in the likeness of sinful flesh and . . . condemned sin in the flesh," drawing a parallel between how Christ came and where sin was condemned. In light of Old Testament sacrificial parallels, as well as Paul's argument, it seems that this rendering is more sensible. Man's sin was condemned in Christ's flesh. Though it is unstated by Paul, it is obvious that he is drawing a contrast between **sinful man** and righteous Christ. The fact that Christ knew no sin was why he could receive unto himself the penalty for man's sin and credit man with his own righteous standing before God: "God made him who had no sin to be sin for us, so that in him we might become the righteousness of God" (2 Cor. 5:21).

To return to the Old Testament roots of the necessity for the **requirements of the law** to be kept by those who would live, Christ **condemned sin** for that very purpose. **In order that** (*hina* plus aorist subjunctive denoting purpose) we might be credited with having kept the law, the one who kept the law perfectly sacrificed himself for us—those **who do not live according to the sinful nature but according to the Spirit.**

Paul's point is not that Christ's condemning of sin is valid only for those who walk in the Spirit, as if walking in the Spirit were a condition to be met in order to receive the benefit of Christ's work. He is using the phrase to refer to believers in Christ; those who died and were raised with Christ. Christ came in our **likeness** so that he might fulfill the requirements of the law. "If Christ had not taken on our nature, he could not have been one of us. On the other hand, had he become completely like us (i.e., had he sinned), he could not have become our Savior" (Mounce, p. 175).

This is, of course, the great mystery of the *kenosis* (from Gr. *kenoo*, to empty), whereby Christ "made himself nothing (emptied himself), taking the very nature of a servant, being made in human likeness" (Phil. 2:7; see also Heb. 2:14–17). He became human, yet remained divine. It was not that his divinity made him unable to sin; rather it was his keeping of the requirements of the law in the power of the Spirit (John 3:34) that made him able *not* to sin. Christ's fulfilling of the **righteous requirements of the law** made our justification and salvation possible, which made the presence of the Spirit in us a reality, which makes it possible for us to keep God's standards.

Did God expect that we would keep the requirements of the law having been filled with the Spirit? That apparently was the intent of the new covenant promises in Jeremiah 31:33 (see Heb. 8:11–12), and seems as well to be Paul's intent as expressed later in Romans: "The commandments . . . are summed up in this one rule: Love your neighbor as yourself. . . . Therefore, love is the fulfillment of the law" (Rom. 13:9–10).

Freeing believers from sin and death means that they are also free from being controlled by the power of sin in our members.

B The New Way: Freedom from Control by the Power of Sin (8:5–14)

SUPPORTING IDEA: *Though the power of sin is still present, the Holy Spirit frees the believer from being controlled by what this appetite desires.*

8:5–8. Here, in different language, is Paul's contrast between the deeds of the flesh and the fruit of the Spirit in Galatians 5:19–23. He lists the deeds and the fruit in Galatians; here he explains from whence they arise. The mind of a human being can be set upon only one thing—either the desires of the flesh or the Spirit. The new way of life in the Spirit makes it possible for the mind of the believer to be set upon **what the Spirit desires.** Here is what Paul states, implicitly and explicitly, about the two kinds of people he is describing:

	Those Who Live in Accordance with the Flesh	Those Who Live in Accordance with the Spirit
What they think about doing	Minds are set on the desires of the flesh	Minds are set on the desires of the Spirit
Ultimate end	Leads to death	Leads to life and peace
Attitude toward God	Hostile toward God	Receptive toward God
Attitude toward God's standards	Does not submit to God's law	Seeks to fulfill God's law
Ability to keep God's standards	Unable to submit to God's law	Able to submit to God's law
Ability to please God	Cannot please God	Able to please God

Paul is not defining two categories of people here: Christians versus non-Christians, or Spirit-filled Christians versus "carnal" Christians. Rather, he is using the opposite extremes of the spectrum to illustrate two ways of living life in God's world. One way is to live it according to the desires and directives of the flesh, a way that produces hostility toward God and ultimately death. The other way is to live life according to the desires of God as revealed and empowered by his Holy Spirit, a way that leads to life and peace.

James Boice recounts a story from the life of the English abolitionist, William Wilberforce, that illustrates the vacuum of spiritual understanding manifested by those who are devoid of the Spirit. Wilberforce, a strong Christian, had tried unsuccessfully to get his friend, William Pitt the Younger, the prime minister of England, to go and hear the great British preacher Richard Cecil. Pitt was a nominal Christian only, a church member, and Wilberforce thought the preaching of Cecil might awaken saving faith in his friend's heart.

Finally agreeing to go with Wilberforce, Pitt attended Cecil's preaching service where the two sat under a powerful and wonderful presentation of the truths of God. Wilberforce was sure that his friend Pitt would sense the truth and embrace it wholeheartedly. But as they left the service, Pitt turned to Wilberforce and said, "You know, Wilberforce, I have not the slightest idea what that man has been talking about." Boice concludes by saying, "Clearly, Pitt was as deaf to God as if he were a physically dead man" (Boice, 2:808–809).

This is Paul's point. A person with his or her mind set upon the things of the flesh cannot "accept the things that come from the Spirit of God, for they are foolishness to him, and he cannot understand them, because they are spiritually discerned" (1 Cor. 2:14). All one has to do is look around societies and cultures to see the results of living life with the mind set on only that which the flesh desires. The result is not life and peace—it is death and destruction. But that is the easy observation to make, the one down at the far end of the spectrum. What about those who claim to be Christians who yet manifest many of the same characteristics as those who make no such claim? What are we to do with the indicators from contemporary polls that suggest the practices of "Christians" are often not much more spiritual than those who live in and of the world? Paul is about to suggest a serious implication.

8:9–11. There is an "awful" (awe-inspiring) connection between the presence of the Holy Spirit in a life and the manifestation of the Spirit's control. In essence, Paul says, **if the Spirit of God lives in you,** you will be controlled **by the Spirit.** That does not mean believers will not quench the Spirit, for they will (1 Thess. 5:19). Nor does it mean that believers will not grieve the Spirit, for they will (Eph. 4:30). Nor does it mean that one in whom the Holy Spirit dwells cannot sin, for he or she surely can. But it does mean that a person in whom the Holy Spirit dwells should be manifesting the control of the Spirit.

As in the case of William Pitt, the English prime minister, it is possible to be a sterling church member without having the presence of the Holy Spirit in one's life. And without **the Spirit of Christ,** one does not belong to Christ, i.e., one is not a Christian.

Beginning in verse 10, Paul presents an amazing set of contrasts concerning the **body** and the **spirit** of the believer. First, **your body is dead because of sin.** But, he continues, **if Christ is in you . . . your spirit is alive because of righteousness.** Finally, if your spirit has been made alive (you have been made righteous), **the Spirit of him who raised Jesus from the dead . . . will also give life to your mortal bodies** (which had previously died due to sin). The mortal body of the believer, in which dwells a quickened human spirit, will also be raised from the dead. The same **Spirit** that **raised Christ from the dead** will also raise those believers from the dead in whom the Spirit now dwells (see also 1 Cor. 6:14; 2 Cor. 4:14; 1 Thess. 4:14).

The presence of the Spirit inside the believer is a critical factor. The Spirit's presence determines whether a person is a true believer. The Spirit's presence regenerates the human spirit. And the Spirit's presence will one day regenerate the believer's mortal body. Corrie ten Boom offered an insight into this marvelous truth: "I have a glove here in my hand. The glove cannot do anything by itself, but when my hand is in it, it can do many things. True, it is not the glove, but my hand in the glove that acts. We are gloves. It is the

Holy Spirit in us who is the hand, who does the job. We have to make room for the hand so that every finger is filled" (Rowell, p. 82).

8:12–14. Perhaps the most important implication of the fact of the Spirit's control is that we are assured of being made children of God. This idea comes as a conclusion to one thought and an introduction to the next. Paul concludes his words about freedom from control of the sin nature by saying that we have an obligation to **put to death the misdeeds of the body . . . because those who are led by the Spirit of God are sons of God.** That fact—the sonship of the believer—leads Paul into his next major section on the security of the believer in the new way of the Spirit.

Here, however, Paul begins by saying that believers are under obligation—but **not to the sinful nature.** Rather, our obligation is to the Spirit. The believer is indwelled by the Spirit; the believer's spirit has been regenerated by the Spirit; and the believer's body will be resurrected from the dead by the Spirit. That puts the believer under an obligation to **put to death the misdeeds of the body.** What believer, understanding the implications of the presence of the Spirit that Paul has just enumerated, could feel the slightest freedom to indulge the sinful desires of the flesh? We are under a holy obligation. And if we do not put to death **the misdeeds of the body?** It is a sign that no obligation to do so is felt, which is a sign of the lack of the presence of the Spirit, which is a sign that **you will die.**

This is not a "lose-your-salvation" verse—put to death the deeds of the flesh and you will live, indulge the deeds of the flesh and you will die. Rather, it is a "big-picture" verse, indicating what should be the natural outcome in the life of one who has the presence of the Spirit: an obligation to be holy, to manifest one's sanctification in righteous behavior.

The obligation to practice righteousness consistent with our spiritual position is a clear call in the New Testament:

- Romans 6:13: "Do not offer the parts of your body to sin."
- Colossians 3:5: "Put to death . . . whatever belongs to your earthly nature: sexual immorality, impurity, lust, evil desires and greed, which is idolatry."
- Galatians 5:24: "Those who belong to Christ Jesus have crucified the sinful nature with its passions and desires."
- Mark 9:43–47: "If your hand causes you to sin, cut it off. . . . And if your foot causes you to sin, cut it off. . . . And if your eye causes you to sin, pluck it out."

But the most compelling reason of all to live lives of holiness is because we have been adopted into a holy household—**because those who are led by the Spirit of God are sons of God.** There is a better way, Paul is saying, and that way is to enter wholeheartedly into fellowship with the Father who is holy. One senses that Paul could have been writing about many contemporary believers when he makes this transitional statement. How many Christians today—genuine believers in whom the Spirit dwells—are not putting to death **the misdeeds of the body?** A great many, it would appear. And how many are living on the edge of the family of God, never having taken the steps to move into close fellowship with the Father and his other sons and daughters?

If one has been living a rough and undisciplined life, and is suddenly thrust into the presence of mannered and dignified people, there is an instant **obligation** (for most people) to correct their behavior. It is the same when we move into intimate relations with the family of God, beginning first with the Father and then with his children. Those professing believers who fuel the polls which make the church more like the world than like Jesus Christ have missed an important **obligation**—the **obligation** to **put to death the misdeeds of the body**—an obligation is easy to miss on the outskirts, hard to miss at the table of fellowship.

Paul's hint at sonship is now exploded into its full glory by the apostle in the final of his three freedoms: freedom from the fear of separation from God. When one begins to enjoy the role of heir, the insecurities which fed much of our fleshly disposition begin to disappear, and the **misdeeds of the body** with them.

C The New Way: Freedom from Fear of Abandonment (8:15–17)

SUPPORTING IDEA: *The Holy Spirit testifies with believers' spirits that they will be forever the children of God.*

8:15–16. Paul declares that believers are children of God in whom there should be no fear. What is the fear that Paul says has been removed by the presence of the Spirit of God? Essentially and psychologically, it probably comes closest in our modern era to the codependent person or the addict getting well. Oftentimes people fear losing what has provided their identity for a significant period of time. Just as a former smoker has to learn what to do with his or her hands when nervous or in a social setting, so the new believer fears a new relationship as a child of God. The void left by the absence of sin will be filled by the Spirit and works of righteousness in time, but there is an initial fear. Several passages of Scripture provide insight:

1 Corinthians 2:12: "We have not received the spirit of the world but the Spirit who is from God, *that we may understand what God has freely given us*" (emphasis added). Do nonbelievers, those who have the "spirit of the world," live in fear of God and of the unknown? Yes, in their heart of hearts. They fear death, hell, judgment, eternity, punishment—not to mention tomorrow and what it might take from them. You will not find fear being discussed on talk shows, but you will find it being covered up through frantic forays into

materialism, sex, substance abuse, depression, and other denial-oriented diversions. When the children of God recognize their position, instead of being afraid of life and God, their eyes are open to what God has freely given them.

2 Timothy 1:7: Instead of "a spirit of timidity" (fear), we have been given the Holy Spirit, who is love, power, and self-discipline. Rather than living in fear of life and what it may hold, the Holy Spirit's love, power, and self-discipline through us gives us a whole new perspective on life.

Matthew 7:9–11: Children of God do not receive booby prizes or gag gifts from their Father. Even evil fathers know how to give appropriate gifts to their children; how much more will the "Father in heaven" give his children good gifts?

Paul himself provides the best illustration. Instead of a spirit of fear, we have received a spirit of **sonship**, or adoption. Adoption is a strictly Pauline metaphor, one common to him and his readers in Rome, due to the practice of adoption in the Roman Empire. Paul says in Ephesians 1:5 that adoption is a sovereign act of God, the result of his predestined pleasure and will. In Galatians 4:5–7, he repeats much of what he says in our Romans text, with one important addition: "That we might receive the full rights of sons" (Gal. 4:5). Therein lies the heart of sonship, or adoption. One who was not a natural son is adopted by a father and given every legal right of sonship held by the natural sons. He is made an heir of the father, and given equal standing (often a more privileged standing) with the father's natural progeny.

Because Paul does not expand the metaphor in detail, the careful expositor will not do so either, pushing cultural aspects of Roman adoption into the realm of sanctification. But the key point—legal standing as a child of God— is fully represented by Paul's adoption metaphor: Jesus Christ is God's (only) natural Son and believers are adopted into the family of God and made "heirs of God and co-heirs with Christ" (Rom. 8:17).

As an adoption record in a court of law receives a stamp, seal, or signature verifying its authenticity, and validating the adoptee's rights from that day forward, so the believer is given a seal by God. The Holy Spirit is given to believers to be a "deposit, guaranteeing what is to come" (2 Cor. 1:22). "Having believed," Paul says, we were "marked in [Christ] with a seal, the promised Holy Spirit" (Eph. 1:13). In Romans Paul says that the Holy Spirit plays a unique role, testifying with the spirit of the believer that **we are God's children.** By the presence and power of the Spirit, we call out to God in a personal way—**Abba, Father.** The Spirit gives us that liberty in our spirits because we know from him **that we are God's children.**

Variant forms of the Aramaic **Abba** can be heard in the Israeli and Arab marketplaces of today as young children call to their fathers in the hustle and bustle of the crowded market. **Abba,** or "daddy," represents the familiar cry of the heart from one who knows who the father is. Because it is the Spirit of God who is given to believers, the heart of the child is linked with the heart of the Father in permanent intimacy.

But the believer is not just a child of God, but an heir of God as well. Being a child means that I have a family now; being an heir means I am included in the family forever.

8:17. No more dramatic validation of our status as **co-heirs with Christ** can be found than that which came through the Son's own request to the Father. First, Christ told his Father that he had given the disciples the glory that had been given to him (John 17:22). The purpose of that was that the unity (solidarity) of believers with Christ might be evident to all the world, and that the Father's love for believers was the same as his love for the Son (John 17:23). Finally, Christ asked the Father: "I want those you have given me to be with me where I am, and to see my glory, the glory you have given me because you loved me before the creation of the world" (John 17:24). Christ offers to share his own inheritance, his glory, with those whom the Father has given to him, meaning the disciples and all who would believe in him.

But there is a "catch." Coheirs will share in glory only in the same manner in which the heir achieves glory. In the case of Christ, it was through suffering. The NIV's **if indeed** is not a condition in the Greek text, but rather a fact—adopted coheirs share in *all* the inheritance of the son. If suffering is the son's portion, then it will likewise be the portion of the adopted coheirs. But Paul never shrunk from this inheritance in his own life, and encourages the believers in Rome to view their past, present, and future sufferings for the cause of Christ as part of their sonship.

If the son learned obedience through suffering, so will the adopted sons (Heb. 5:8). If the son carried around in his body the persecutions of the public, so will the adopted sons (2 Cor. 4:10). If the son grew weak under persecutions without losing heart, so are the adopted sons called to do likewise (2 Cor. 4:16). It is conformity to the son that the adopted sons are gaining day by day as we "are being transformed into his likeness with ever-increasing glory" (2 Cor. 3:18). We are called to **share in his sufferings in order that we may also share in his glory.**

D A New Life: Based on the Promises of God (8:18–25)

SUPPORTING IDEA: *The believer's new life as a child of God has a firm foundation in God's promises and plans for his children.*

Paul's whole premise in chapters 6–8 of Romans is that the "new way of the Spirit" (Rom. 7:6) results in a new life for the believer. The old life was a life of slavery and servitude to sin, law, and death. Now, having died with

Christ and been given the Holy Spirit, believers have a new life. We are free "to serve" not in the "old way of the written code" (Rom. 7:6) but in freedom and liberty. We are able to fulfill the requirements of the law through the power of the Spirit, not through the powerlessness of the law itself.

The new life we have been given in the Spirit is based on three things: the promises of God (Rom. 8:18–25), the purposes of God (Rom. 8:26–30), and the protection of God (Rom. 8:31–39).

8:18–21. The first promise is that of future glory. Perhaps no truth is so glaringly absent from the understanding of most Christians than the truth, and the implications thereof, that this world is not our home. When it finally settles into the heart and mind of the believer that we are "aliens and strangers in the world" (1 Pet. 2:11; cf. also Heb. 11:13; 1 Pet. 1:1), many things change. Our **present sufferings** will be viewed against a backdrop of future glory that relegates today's difficulties to insignificance by comparison. In fact, "The whole creation is on tiptoe to see the wonderful sight of the sons of God coming into their own," as J. B. Phillips put it (Mounce, p. 184).

In some unexplained sense, the entire creation's subjection to **frustration** awaits the glorious revelation of the **children of God**, at which time **the creation itself will be liberated from its bondage to decay and brought into the glorious freedom of the children of God.** Surely this is the "new heavens" and "new earth" of which the prophets and apostles wrote (Isa. 65:17; 66:22; 2 Pet. 3:13) and which John the apostle even beheld (Rev. 21:1).

The curse to which the Creator subjected his creation (Gen. 3:14,17) will finally be lifted when the coheirs inhabit the glorious new heavens and new earth (Rev. 22:3). When the curse is lifted, the creation will once again be an Edenic environment suitable for the image-bearers of God to inhabit and to reflect the Creator's glory. At present, the creation reflects the curse of sin; when sin is finally removed from the children of God, the creation will spring forth in glory.

8:22–23. The future will be glorious for the believer because of the full realization of what we have only a taste of at present—**our adoption as sons, the redemption of our bodies.** The **firstfruits of the Spirit** (cf. Exod. 23:19; Lev. 23:9–14; 2 Cor. 1:22; 5:5; Eph. 1:13–14; 4:30) is the down payment, the certainty, we have from God that one day we will enter into our full inheritance as children of God. But now we, and the earth with us, groan painfully until that day.

Or do we? How many believers today **wait eagerly** for their adoption as children of God? How many have grown used to the cacophony we call life on planet earth? How many Christian hearts break over the tragedy and despair present in the lives of so many in our world? We, even the church, have so effectively distanced ourselves from the **groaning** of the **creation** that we forget that we live in the midst of a curse. It is as if we have taken the anesthesia intended for the mother laboring to give birth in the next room. The results of the curse are in our very presence, but we fail to hear it. Any believer who does not **groan inwardly** and **wait eagerly** for his or her adoption has a shallow understanding of the present condition and future hope God has provided for his children.

The **firstfruits of the Spirit** makes it possible for us to be "hard pressed on every side, but not crushed; perplexed, but not in despair; persecuted, but not abandoned; struck down, but not destroyed" (2 Cor. 4:8–9). "We do not lose heart . . . for our light and momentary troubles are achieving for us an eternal glory that far outweighs them all" (2 Cor. 4:16–17). "We know that the one who raised the Lord Jesus from the dead will also raise us with Jesus" (2 Cor. 4:14)—coheirs receive the same resurrection as the heir—the **redemption of our bodies**.

Do we groan in the interim? Yes—we groan and are burdened! (2 Cor. 5:2,4). But in our groanings we have the **Spirit**, "guaranteeing what is to come" (2 Cor. 5:5). One day, many believers who enter into the fullness of their **adoption** as children of God will look back and wonder how they could have felt so at home in a world so full of groaning.

8:24–25. Finally, there are promises for patience rewarded. Paul never intended to communicate to the Romans that their lives as believers were easy. In fact, he took great pains in this portion of his letter to be brutally honest with them. We live in a cursed world; we groan; we are in labor pains; we long for the redemption of our bodies. The one thing that living in this world requires is patient **hope**. In fact, from the moment of our salvation, **hope** became our watchword because we were saved by faith (Eph. 2:8–9), and faith sees nothing. But "faith is being sure of what we hope for and certain of what we do not see" (Heb. 11:1). All who live by faith are called to be "imitators of those who through faith and patience inherit the promises" (Heb. 6:12, NASB; e.g., Abraham, Heb. 11:12–15), and that includes those to whom Paul writes. That patience will be rewarded when the children of God enter into the full measure of their adoption.

🇪 A New Life: Based on the Purposes of God (8:26–30)

SUPPORTING IDEA: *As a child of God, the believer will ultimately realize God's purposes of conforming believers to the image of Jesus Christ.*

This section of Paul's epistle contains the verse mentioned in the introduction to this chapter—verse 28. It forms the core of the believer's confidence that his or her new life is based on the purposes of God. Surrounding that core verse are other elements of truth related to it: we discover and surrender to God's purposes in prayer (vv. 26–27), and we recognize God's purposes in conforming us to the image of his Son, Jesus Christ (vv. 29–30).

8:26–27. Hope sustains and helps the believer through the present times of suffering. **In the same way,** the Spirit helps and sustains the believer **in weakness,** specifically through the ministry of prayer. The advocacy role of the Spirit was promised by Jesus, and this is part of the fulfillment of those promises (John 14:16,26; 15:26; 16:7). Paul's description of the Spirit's role in prayer is one of the most intimate glimpses we have in all of Scripture of the inner workings of the Godhead. When we are weak and trembling, confused about the purposes of God in our sufferings or our confusion, **the Spirit himself intercedes for us with groans that words cannot express.** The Father searches our heart, "not to know what [our] conscious prayers are, but to find out what the prayer of the Holy Spirit is" (Chambers, *My Utmost,* Nov. 8).

In language we cannot understand, the Father searches the human heart, the abode of the Spirit, to hear the Spirit's prayer. When the Father hears his will being prayed by the Spirit **(because the Spirit intercedes for the saints in accordance with God's will),** then the Father and Spirit are in perfect harmony for the purposes of God to be accomplished in the believer through the instrument of prayer.

Who has not bent the knee before the Father and been at a loss for words? How often does the mind of man fall short in discerning the purposes of God? Yet how often do we rise from a season of wordless prayer to have our hearts refreshed, our hope renewed, and our faith rewarded, knowing that the Spirit has prayed and the Father has heard? Thank God for the ministry of the Holy Spirit, who intercedes to bring the purposes of God to fruition.

8:28. The purposes of God are the most important reality in the spiritual life. The purpose (*prothesin*) of God's will is what controls everything (Eph. 1:11) in light of eternity (Eph. 3:11). God **called** us to a holy life on the basis of his purpose and grace, and it is that purpose to which we have been **called** that verse 28 invites our submission (God's calling here is not the calling of the many in Matt. 22:14, but the effectual calling to salvation of Rom. 11:29; 1 Cor. 1:9; Eph. 4:4; 1 Thess. 2:12; 2 Tim. 1:9; and 1 Pet. 2:9).

Our new life in the Spirit is based on God's good purposes for our lives, and that includes suffering. The suffering (v. 17) and groaning (v. 23) that Paul has been discussing is what is in view in verse 28. When we find ourselves in trying circumstances in life, we can **know that in all things God works for the good of those who love him, who have been called according to his purpose.** Read literally, it is easy to see why some consider this the greatest verse in Scripture. It tells us that nothing happens outside of God's plan for our good.

An important grammatical question clarifies the role of God in accomplishing his purposes. "All things" can be taken either as the subject (as in KJV; "all things work together"), or as the object (NIV [adverbial], "in all things God works"; NASB [direct object], "God causes all things to work"). As the subject, "all things" are in control, and while they end happily, they do so seemingly in and of themselves. When God is the subject, he causes (*sunergei,* from *sunergeo,* to work with) all things to work together for good. In other words, there is no doubting the outcome's ultimate good. Lest we translate according to our theological preferences, it must be noted that (a) there is not a compelling grammatical reason to translate one way or the other (see the commentaries for minor possible reasons), and (b) the meaning is not radically altered with either translation.

It should probably be agreed with Moo that the plainest rendering of the text is that of the KJV ("all things work together for good"), but that "it does not finally matter all that much" between the choices mentioned above (Moo, p. 528). The reason is that **God** and **his purpose** are the controlling elements of the verse. Paul is clearly subordinating **all things** to the **purpose** of God, regardless of how the verse is written.

8:29–30. These two verses explain what God's purpose is in his calling to salvation, and how it is accomplished. First, the purpose: that there might be **many** who would be **conformed to the likeness of his Son.** God was not satisfied to have a family with an "only child." Indeed, the entire human family, all the descendants of Adam and Eve, were to have been his family, walking in fellowship with him for eternity. But since the rebellion of man, it has been his purpose to redeem a family for himself out of the fallen race.

Second, his method: from our perspective, God adopted us as spiritual orphans into his family, so that **his Son . . . might be the firstborn among many brothers.** That is the metaphor for what God did behind the scenes to accomplish his purpose. That "behind the scenes" activity is called by scholars the *ordo salutis,* the order of salvation. How did God save those whom he adopted into his family? Five of the key actions are listed in these verses, and they are highlighted in the list below. Since the Reformation, the following list has generally represented the agreement of the majority on the way God has provided Christ with **many brothers** (taken from Boice, 2:916):

1. *Foreknowledge:* God's setting his love upon (choosing) those who would be conformed to his Son's image (Amos 3:2 [cf. KJV "known" with NIV "chosen"]; 1 Cor. 8:3; Gal. 4:9).

2. *Predestination:* God's determining the destiny of those upon whom he has set his love.

3. *Calling:* God's effectual call from death to life those upon whom he has set his love (cf. the calling forth of Lazarus in John 11).

4. *Regeneration:* God's quickening, making alive, the spirit of those who are called so that they can believe.

5. *Faith:* God's gift of faith (Eph. 2:8–9) exercised by the regenerate.

6. *Repentance:* The turning from sin of those who have believed (this step is often combined with faith into a step of faith-repentance, or repentance and faith).

7. *Justification:* God's declaring as righteous those who have repented and believed.

8. *Adoption:* God's inclusion of the justified in the family of God.

9. *Sanctification:* God's work through the Holy Spirit to conform those in the family of God into the image of his Son.

10. *Perseverance:* God's insuring that those who are effectively called complete their pilgrimage of faith.

11. *Glorification:* God's fulfillment of his purposes—the making of fallen sinners into the image of his Son, Jesus Christ, for eternity.

While these passages have generated much heated discussion over the years (primarily concerning the meaning of **foreknew** and **predestined**), there is one key element which, if overlooked, gives rise to confusion, but if observed, gives focus to the passage. That key element is **God** himself: God has a "purpose" (v. 28), God **foreknew,** God **predestined,** God **called,** God **justified,** and God **glorified** (though future, glorification is written here in a "prophetic past tense"). This passage is all about God, not man! God is the adopter, humans are the adoptees. God is designing, engineering, and accomplishing his salvific purpose in the earth, quite apart from the interference and influence of men and women (as hard as that is for Type-A moderns to accept).

In light of this overarching oversight of the Father God over his family, how should that make the believer feel? Or, to use Paul's words, "What, then, shall we say in response to this?" (Rom. 8:31).

F A New Life: Based on the Protection of God (8:31–39)

SUPPORTING IDEA: *As a child of God, the believer is secure that nothing in the universe can separate him or her from the love of God.*

There are three bases for the protection that the believer can depend on from God—protection based on precedent (8:31–32), based on legal standing (8:33–34), and based on the love of God (8:35–39).

8:31–32. Beginning in verse 31, there are five critical questions asked by the apostle that lend a sub-structure to the entire final section of verses 31–39. The first two questions deal with precedent:

Question 1: **If God is for us, who can be against us?** This question is a good theoretical one, but certainly a practical one for Christians living in Rome in the first century. Remember Paul's ultimate mission to and through the Romans as laid out in the introduction and first chapter of this commentary. His heart was to see the believers in Rome partner with him to launch a missionary effort into Spain and the regions beyond. How successful could one man, even all the believers in one city, be in such an undertaking, especially in light of combustible Roman opposition? In light of the verses Paul has just written, it would seem clear that those whom God intends to save will be saved, the opposition of humankind notwithstanding. Since salvation turns on the will of God, not the will of man, opposition to God from the human realm is not really an issue (see also Exod. 3:12; Isa. 41:10; Hag. 1:13; Pss. 56:9; 118:6; Isa. 8:10; Jer. 20:11; Heb. 13:6).

Chrysostom pointed out centuries ago that even those who oppose God end up glorifying him: "Yet those that be against us, so far are they from thwarting us at all, that even without their will they become to us the causes of crowns, and procurers of countless blessings, in that God's wisdom turneth their plots unto our salvation and glory. See how really no one is against us!" (cited by Moo, p. 539).

Question 2: **He who did not spare his own Son, but gave him up for us all—how will he not also, along with him, graciously give us all things?** It seems hard to deny the background of the Abraham and Isaac story here as a model for Paul's argument (Gen. 22:1–19). Because Abraham did not withhold his son, his only son, Isaac, God blessed him with everything else that he could be blessed with. The logical argument in that scenario could also have been Paul's prompting: it is illogical to conceive that God would give his most treasured "possession"—his only Son—to secure the salvation of sinners, and then not also give all else that is necessary to bring that salvation to completion.

The precedents God has already established—by demonstrating in Paul and the believers in Rome that no one can thwart his salvific ends, and by giving the best he had to give—provide good reason for believers to rest in God's protection. Precedent is critical in any legal setting, but Paul's next two questions deal with the legal standing of believers before God.

8:33–34. *Question 3:* **Who will bring any charge against those whom God has chosen?** This question is raised as a defense of what Paul taught in Romans 3:21–5:21 concerning justification—the legal position of believers before God. All have sinned, all fall short of the glory of God, but all (who believe) are justified freely by God's grace through the redemption that came by Christ Jesus. As the judge, God was perfectly just in paying the penalty for and declaring "free to go" the unjust (Rom. 3:23–26). As a result, no charge can be brought against **those whom God has chosen** (foreknown, predestined, called, *justified,* and glorified).

Should a Roman emperor seek to bring a charge against a believer in Rome for worshiping a king other than Caesar, that charge would have no effect in the eyes of God. Should Satan seek to bring a charge against the elect of God in order to discredit their faithfulness, such a charge would go unregistered. God has already brought all the charges which could possibly be brought against the believer to the bar of justice and declared them erased: "Having canceled out the certificate of debt consisting of decrees against us and which was hostile to us; and He has taken it out of the way, having nailed it to the cross" (Col. 2:14, NASB). Therefore, **Who will bring any charge against those whom God has chosen?** (for the Old Testament background on God's defense of his chosen, cf. Isa. 50:8–9; 52:13–53:12; Zech. 3:1–5).

Question 4: **Who is he that condemns?** If no charge can be brought against the elect of God, then certainly no condemnation can be brought against them either. Again, Paul is summarizing what he has taught previously: "Therefore, there is now no condemnation for those who are in Christ Jesus" because of having been set free through Jesus Christ from the law which condemns us from our sin (Rom. 8:1–2). Isaiah spoke prophetically of a day when God's elect would condemn those who accused them: "'No weapon that is formed against you will prosper, and every tongue that accuses you in judgment you will condemn. This is the heritage of the servants of the LORD, and their vindication is from Me,' declares the LORD" (Isa. 54:17, NASB).

Continuing the legal motif which insures our freedom from charges and condemnation, believers have their own divine advocate who continually defends them before the bar of heavenly justice (1 John 2:1; Heb. 4:14–16).

8:35–39. *Question 5:* **Who shall separate us from the love of Christ?** In this final section, Paul asks his final question in the first verse of the section and answers it in the last:

Q.: What can separate the believer from God's love? (v. 35)

A.: *Nothing* can separate the believer from God's love. (v. 39)

Paul (knowingly? unknowingly?) takes on the prophet's mantle in verse 36 as he quotes from Psalm 44:22 to demonstrate that there will always be opposition to God's people and the work of God in the world. The world is cursed; it is an antagonistic environment; it is under the control of the evil one (1 John 5:19). There will be many natural and supernatural attempts made to convince the believer that he or she has been separated from the love of God. (Paul knows that nothing can separate us from the love of God, but he also knows that it can *appear* that we have been separated from the love of God. He wants to dispel both notions.)

Paul himself will become like a **sheep to be slaughtered** within a few short years under the brutal hand of the Roman emperor Nero. He could have included "Roman emperors" in the list in verses 38–39, but that would probably seem trivial to Paul—like a gnat bite or a speed bump on the highway to heaven. Let us not consider **trouble or hardship or persecution or famine or nakedness or danger or sword. . . . No, in all these things we are more than conquerors through him who loved us.** Rather, let us consider the giant spectrums of impediments to our remaining in God's loving care:

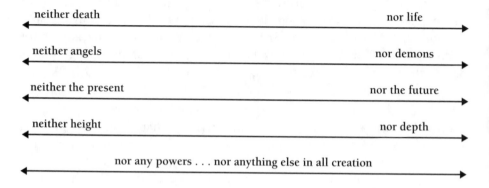

neither death	nor life
neither angels	nor demons
neither the present	nor the future
neither height	nor depth
nor any powers . . . nor anything else in all creation	

Paul was a man of unshakeable confidence in the love of God. He feared neither the tangible hardships of life (see his experiences in 2 Cor. 6:3–10; 11:16–33) nor the intangible fears that creep into the consciousness of any normal person. Am I suffering for a reason? What if I wake up on the other side of death and discover I have been fooled? What if I do not wake up on the other side of death? Where will the love of God be then? All normal saints have considered these questions, and Paul is just bold enough and confident enough to get them out on the table and answer them. He wanted the Romans to deal with them, and wanted third-millennium believers to deal with them as well. His answer then, and his answer now, is that **[nothing] will be able to separate us from the love of God that is in Christ Jesus our Lord.**

MAIN IDEA REVIEW: *The gospel of Jesus Christ makes possible a brand new way of life for the believer—life lived abundantly in and through the power of the Holy Spirit.*

III. CONCLUSION

The True Meaning of Freedom

John Chrysostom (A.D. 347?–407), eventually patriarch of Constantinople, earned the moniker "golden-mouth" because of his eloquent sermons against the lavish excesses of his day. This earned him no favor with Roman authorities, and when he was brought before the Roman emperor he was threatened with banishment if he remained a Christian. Chrysostom's reply to the emperor reflects the insight of one who understands that true freedom in life comes with freedom in the Spirit and security in the love of God:

> "Thou canst not banish me for this world is my father's house."
>
> "But I will slay thee," said the emperor.
>
> "Nay, thou canst not," said the noble champion of the faith, "for my life is hid with Christ in God."
>
> "I will take away thy treasures."
>
> "Nay, but thou canst not for my treasure is in heaven and my heart is there."
>
> "But I will drive thee away from man and thou shalt have no friend left."
>
> "Nay, thou canst not, for I have a friend in heaven from whom thou canst not separate me. I defy thee; for there is nothing that thou canst do to hurt me." (cited by Hughes, p. 171)

Chrysostom understood what Paul wanted the believers in Rome to understand—that once we are liberated from the condemnation of sin and death, we are truly free. Nothing else matters—not geography, not possessions, not relations, not life or death. When we have condemnation and judgment lifted from our shoulders, we escape into the mental, emotional, and spiritual freedom that we created to live in. Indwelt by the Spirit, we enter into the life and peace that only can be experienced by those who have come to know freedom through Christ.

Is Romans 8 the greatest chapter in the Bible? If it is not, it could only be because another portion states its message even more clearly, for the message of chapter 8 is surely the greatest: for those who are in Jesus Christ there is freedom from condemnation and all its attendant fears, and a new life in the Spirit that guarantees our ultimate and eternal glorification in the presence of God.

PRINCIPLES

- In Christ, I am free from any condemnation.
- In Christ, I have kept the righteous requirements of the law.
- In Christ, I am obligated to be led by the Spirit.
- In Christ, I am a child of God and a coheir with Christ.
- In Christ, I will be redeemed from this cursed creation.
- In Christ, I am certain of my eternal glorification.
- In Christ, I fear nothing either in or out of this world.

APPLICATIONS

- Do I harbor a sense of shame or a guilty conscience about things for which I know I have been forgiven?
- Does my practice (behavior) match my position of righteousness?
- What practices are there in my life that I do not believe are led by the Spirit?
- As an adopted member of the family of God, how would I evaluate my contribution as a family member?
- How consistently do I rely on my future redemption to serve as an antidote to the frustrations of living in a cursed world?
- What practical difference should the promise of future glorification make on my present physical, mental, and emotional capabilities?
- What do I fear—and why, in light of the promises of God?

IV. LIFE APPLICATION

Conquering the Conquerors

At its greatest extent, the Roman Empire reached as far north as the British Isles, into Europe as far as modern Germany, eastward throughout Asia Minor, and around the eastern Mediterranean rim south throughout North Africa. The Romans were conquerors and builders in the tradition of the world's greatest empires. In fact, they were the greatest empire yet to cast a shadow across the plain of human history. And yet Paul, in his letter to the Roman believers in A.D. 57, said that Christians were "more than conquerors." Little did the Christians in the world's mightiest city, in the heart of the Roman Empire, know how they were about to be called upon to be "more than conquerors."

As the Romans, over time, embraced the worship of many gods inherited from surrounding peoples—Isis, Dionysus, Mithras, Cybele, and others—they also offered official recognition to long-standing religions such as Judaism. Since the days of Julius Caesar, Judaism had been allowed to exist in the Roman Empire as a minority sect which seemed not to cause harm—witness the coexistence of Roman rule and Jewish rule in Jerusalem as evidenced in the Gospels and Acts. But when Christian missionaries fanned out from Jerusalem with the gospel in the A.D. 30s they headed straight for the Jewish quarters in Roman cities—especially Rome—and began making converts. As evidenced from Paul's closing in Romans 16, there were many believers in Rome with whom he was on a first-name basis.

For nearly thirty years Roman officials looked upon Christianity as a variant sect of Judaism, and paid it little heed. But as Christians became more numerous, and tension between Jews and Christians increased (witness the Roman historian Tacitus's record of a conflict among the Jews in Rome regarding one "Chrestus," probably a reference to Christ), officials began to recognize that Christianity was different from Judaism, and that it was gaining in influence. Public and official opinion began to turn against Christianity, and in A.D. 64—seven years after the writing of Romans—it took an ugly turn.

On July 19, a fire swept through Rome, raging for seven days, destroying ten of the fourteen wards in the city. Many felt that Emperor Nero was responsible, using it as a form of urban renewal, since he grabbed prime real estate after the fire on which to build his own new palace. To turn the tide of negative opinion from himself, Nero blamed the Christians in Rome. For the next four years, until Nero's death in A.D. 68, Christians were persecuted, impaled on poles and used as torches, thrown to ravenous dogs in the arenas, and made to spill their blood over Rome and much of the empire. Even Paul and Peter were killed during this period of persecution.

But who conquered whom in that tragic period of persecution? We need only to look around the world today and see a worldwide church—and no Roman Empire—to answer the question. Apparently, the words that Paul wrote in Romans 8 had taken root during the seven years between his letter and the start of Nero's persecution. The "persecution," "danger," and "sword" (Rom. 8:35) of Nero were not enough to conquer the church of Jesus Christ. The church turned out to be more than (their) conquerors!

What did the Roman believers think of Paul's words when they first heard them read in a meeting of the church? Did they think Paul was warning them about a coming persecution? What do we think about his words when we read them today? Could a time come today when the church of Jesus Christ will undergo persecution such as Nero's? The modern church needs to learn from the church at Rome how to conquer the conquerors. Paul did not write Romans 8 as an exercise in theology, but as instructions for how to live free from the fear of being separated from the love of God—regardless of what test may come. If we are not ready to light up the modern skies with the flame of our faith, then we have not yet internalized Paul's message.

V. PRAYER

Heavenly Father, how I thank you for the freedom and security I have in you! You have made it possible for me to have a clear conscience at the end of the day, and to awaken to a life free from fear each morning. By giving your Son for my salvation, you have proven that you are willing to give all that is necessary for my life both now and for eternity. In gratitude to you, may your Spirit who lives in me find my mind set on what he desires that I may be more than a conqueror today. Amen.

VI. DEEPER DISCOVERIES

A. Providence (8:28)

"Providence" is a nonbiblical term used in Christian discourse to refer to a very biblical concept. Romans 8:28 is one of several key passages used to support the doctrine of providence. The closest we have in biblical Greek to a word for "providence" is *pronoeo,* to foresee, have regard, provide, have respect for. It consists of *pro-* (before), and *noeo,* to perceive, think, consider. Therefore, the concept of looking or providing ahead of time is behind the concept of our English word *providence* (see 1 Tim. 5:8 for the use of *pronoeo* closest to our meaning for providence, and Rom 12:17 and 2 Cor. 8:21 for other uses).

To quote the Westminster Confession of Faith (V. i), "God, the great Creator of all things, doth uphold, direct, dispose, and govern all creatures, actions and things, from the greatest even to the least, by His most wise and holy providence, according to His infallible foreknowledge, and the free and immutable counsel of His own will, to the praise of the glory of His wisdom, power, justice, goodness and mercy." In shorter terms, providence describes God's use of his knowledge, plan, and power to fulfill his purposes for all of his creation, including humankind.

Many wonderful examples of God's providence exist in Scripture (Joseph's time in Egypt, Gen. 50:20; the separation of Jacob's family from the Egyptians so that they might develop into a nation, Gen. 43:32; 46:34; God's use of and judgment of Assyria, Isa. 10:6–7,12; the crucifixion of Christ, Acts 2:23; 4:27–28). Other statements ensure us that God is watching over all of his creation at all times (Matt. 6:25–34; Acts 14:17; 17:22–30; Rom. 1:18–23).

Several points regarding providence must be maintained clearly:

1. *Providence absolves no person of responsibility.* We cannot sin and expect God to clean up after us. Though Pharaoh played a role in manifesting the glory of God, he was still held accountable by God.

2. *Providence is not deism or fatalism.* God is intimately involved in caring for his creation in order to accomplish his purposes. "Whatever will be, will be" is not synonymous with providence.

3. *Providence is centered in Christ, not in us.* Although Romans 8:28 is a verse of great comfort, and Paul does say that God's activity is "for the good of those who love him," something larger than individuals is

happening within the scope of providence. All of God's providence is directed toward the goal of establishing his Son over all things forever (Ps. 2). Thus, that which is for our good is ultimately for the good of God's kingdom, of which we are a part as believers. We must not allow God's providence to become self-centered; it is for our good, which is directed toward his glory. This is the mystery of providence: how God can direct his activities for the good of every one who loves him while at the same time exercising his providence at a corporate level for all of creation.

B. Foreknowledge (8:29)

Foreknowledge is a biblical term meaning "to know ahead of time." Its verb form (*proginosko*) and noun form (*prognosis*) occur a number of times in the New Testament. God foreknew that Christ would be crucified (Acts 2:23); God foreknew those he predestined to be glorified (Rom. 8:29–30); God foreknew the nation of Israel (Rom. 11:2; see also Amos 3:2); believers are elected to salvation according to the foreknowledge of God (1 Pet. 1:2); Christ was foreknown (chosen; appointed) by God before the foundations of the world (1 Pet. 1:20).

The theological issue regarding this term in Romans 8:29 is its meaning in relation to predestination. Paul says that "those God foreknew he also predestined" to be saved. In simplest terms, the Reformed (Calvinistic) branch of the church believes that foreknowledge is the equivalent of choosing (the view taken in this commentary), which is followed by "pre-destining" (setting their destiny in place); the Arminian branch of the church believes that God's foreknowledge refers to his ability to look down through the corridors of time and see who would respond to faith and who would not, and predestining to eternal life those whom he saw would believe.

It is certainly consistent with Scripture that foreknowledge is first in Paul's list, since God's foreknowledge stands over and above all else. Because he is over all things (Isa. 57:15), and years are but as moments to him (Ps. 90:4), he is able to declare "the end from the beginning and from ancient times things which have not been done, saying, 'My purpose will be established, and I will accomplish all My good pleasure'" (Isa. 46:10, NASB). What he has known from all eternity is what must occur.

The chief problem with the Arminian view, in light of the clear declaration of Scripture that no one seeks God (Rom. 3:9–18), is to answer how any could have been seen by God to turn toward him. Even if he is the author of their turning by the gift of faith (Eph. 2:8–9), he would have had to choose the recipients of the faith-gift since some clearly have not turned. He ultimately has to be the source, by his choosing, of those he predestines to believe.

C. Predestination (8:29)

Predestination is from the Latin *praedestinare,* to foreordain. The Greek term behind predestination is *proorizo,* which occurs six times in the New Testament (Acts 4:28; Rom. 8:29,30; 1 Cor. 2:7; Eph. 1:5,11). *Proorizo* consists of *pro-* (before), and the word from which we get "horizon," *horizo,* to mark off by boundaries; to determine. Even from these etymological roots, one gets a sense of predestination's meaning.

People react negatively to predestination, though most of what they are reacting negatively against is foreknowledge. It is the "choosing" of God that bothers people, and that choosing is found in foreknowledge. While we cannot relieve the tension (it is bound up in "his pleasure and will" [Eph. 1:5]), we can determine clearly what God predestined believers to do or be. Romans 8:29 says that we were predestined "to be conformed to the likeness of his Son," and Ephesians 1:5 says that we were predestined "to be adopted as [God's] sons through Jesus Christ." These two statements are the same, in that Romans 8:29 goes on to say that Christ was "the firstborn among many brothers." Those he foreknew, God marked out a place for (predestined; drew a horizon line of inclusion) in his family.

James Boice discusses three objections people have to the doctrine of predestination (Boice, 2:924):

1. *It makes salvation arbitrary and God a tyrant.* Tyrants do not display mercy, which is what God did by choosing some to be saved who deserved to be lost. Arbitrariness is not consistent with a predetermined plan (Eph. 1:11) which is unknown to us.

2. *It denies human freedom.* Predestination actually restores human freedom to some who were sold as slaves to sin (no human freedom to choose righteousness).

3. *It destroys the motivation for evangelism.* God predetermines the means as well as the ends. Evangelism is part of his plan to accomplish his predetermined will.

D. Perseverance (8:30)

While the term "perseverance" (*hupomone*) occurs in the New Testament, it is not used in the same way that it is used theologically to describe Paul's teaching in Romans 8:30. Theologically, perseverance refers to the truth that those whom God foreknows, predestines, calls, and justifies will be glorified in the end. None will fall away; none will be lost.

The primary objections to the doctrine of perseverance are based on Scripture passages that seem to indicate that some who began in faith did not end in faith. If this were true, it would negate the doctrine of perseverance. Some of these passages are Mathew 13 and 25; Romans 11:20–21; 1 Corinthians 9:27; Galatians 5:4; Philippians 2:12; Hebrews 2:1–3; 6:4–6; 2 Peter 1:10; 2:1–2.

The primary reason to hold to the doctrine of perseverance (in addition to Scriptural evidence such as John 6:39; 10:27–28; Phil. 1:6; 1 John 2:19) is what Paul says in Romans 8:29–30. What consistency would there be in God's foreknowing, predestining, calling, justifying—and then leaving to chance the ultimate end of that which he had foreordained should happened? So certain is Paul of the ultimate glorification of the believer that he speaks of it in the past tense ("he also glorified").

VII. TEACHING OUTLINE

A. INTRODUCTION

1. Lead Story: Great, Greater, Greatest
2. Context: The context for this passage is the last chapter in Paul's major section of the epistle on sanctification (chs. 6–8). He closes this chapter with a profound statement on the sovereignty of God (Rom. 8:28–39) which he will use as a springboard to launch into the next chapter on God's sovereign dealings with the nation of Israel.
3. Transition: Having been set free from slavery to sin (Rom. 6) and having been emancipated from the law (Rom. 7), the Christian is now shown a new way of life—life in the Spirit of God, which brings ultimate peace and security.

B. COMMENTARY

1. The New Way: Freedom from Condemnation (8:1–4)
   a. Because the Spirit has set us free from sin and death (8:1–2)
   b. Because the requirements of the law have been met in us (8:3–4)
2. The New Way: Freedom from Control by the Power of Sin (8:5–14)
   a. Control of the Spirit means life and peace (8:5–8)
   b. Control of the Spirit means a regenerated body and spirit (8:9–11)
   c. Control of the Spirit means life as sons of God (8:12–14)
3. The New Way: Freedom from Fear of Abandonment (8:15–17)
   a. Believers are children of God (8:15–16)
   b. Believers are heirs of God (8:17)
4. A New Life: Based on the Promises of God (8:18–25)
   a. Promises of future glory (8:18–21)
   b. Promises of realized adoption (8:22–23)
   c. Promises of patience rewarded (8:24–25)

5. A New Life: Based on the Purposes of God (8:26–30)
   a. Purposes discovered in prayer (8:26–27)
   b. Purposes based on calling (8:28)
   c. Purposes based on ultimate Christlikeness (8:29–30)
6. A New Life: Based on the Protection of God (8:31–39)
   a. Protection based on precedent (8:31–32)
   b. Protection based on legal standing (8:33–34)
   c. Protection based on the love of God (8:35–39)

C. CONCLUSION: CONQUERING THE CONQUERORS

VIII. ISSUES FOR DISCUSSION

1. What is the evidence in the life of a person who has his or her mind set on what the flesh desires? What is the evidence of having one's mind set on what the Spirit desires?

2. If the evidence of the Spirit is fruit (behavior; Gal. 5:22–23), and the presence of the Spirit is required for genuine Christianity, why does not the church put more emphasis on fruit in determining who is or is not a true believer in Christ? What would be the dangers of such an emphasis? Where is the balance?

3. How many Christians live their lives as people who are "more than conquerors"? What does this phrase mean on a day-to-day level rather than just an eternal level? What are the kinds of threats to experiencing God's love that believers face today in which they should be "more than conquerors"?

Romans 9:1–29

Israel's Past Is Consistent with the Gospel

Quote

"Though justice be thy plea, consider this,

That in the course of justice, none of us

Should see salvation."

Shakespeare

Romans 9:1–29

 I N A N U T S H E L L

If nothing can separate the called of God from God's love (Rom. 8:39), why is God's chosen nation, Israel, cut off from his love? Could the same thing happen to a believer in Christ? And why are not more Jews believers in Christ if they are the chosen nation? Paul begins a three-chapter aside on the nation of Israel to explain their spiritual condition: past (Rom. 9), present (Rom. 10), and future (Rom. 11). In this chapter, Paul explains that salvation is not a function of lineage or merit, but of God's merciful election.

Israel's Past Is Consistent with the Gospel

I. INTRODUCTION

It's My Vineyard and I'll Pay What I Want To

In every metropolitan area, a common site is the "labor pool." This is the place in the community where the unemployed gather in hopes of being offered work for the day by a local employer. The jobs are usually for the day only, at a set hourly wage determined by the employer, and they can begin early or late in the day—whenever someone looking for workers happens to appear.

Imagine this scenario: a group of laborers congregates early in the day hoping to be offered work. An employer comes by at 9:00 A.M., selects several men, and transports them to his farm, agreeing to pay them $100 for the day's work. At noon he goes back and secures another group and takes them to the farm, and does the same thing at 3:00 P.M. Then, at 5:00 P.M., when the day is almost over, he returns to the labor pool and gets a final group that he takes to the farm.

Around 7:00 P.M., when the day's work is completed, the men line up for their pay. The first group has worked ten hours, the second group seven hours, the third group four hours, and the last group only two hours. The foreman pays them beginning with the last group first, and they receive $100 for their two hours' work. The word quickly spreads back through the line that the wage has been greatly increased! The last group hired worked only two hours and received $100, or $50 per hour. Those in the first group, who had labored through the heat of the day, quickly calculate that, at $50 per hour, they would receive $500 for their day's work! What a windfall!

But when the other groups are processed through the pay line, they all receive the same as the last group hired—$100 for the day. The workers in the first group are outraged: "We worked five times as long as the last group did, yet they received the same wages as we did. That's not right! We should receive more!"

Calmly, the owner of the farm replys: "What's not right about your wages? You agreed to work for me for $100, and I have paid you $100. What is unjust about that?" While the first group stammered for a reply, he went on: "What I choose to do with my money is really not your concern. As long as I am just with you, I can be as generous as I see fit with anyone I want to."

The seasoned Bible student will recognize that this modern tale is based on a story Jesus told in Matthew 20:1–16. The purpose of the story as it came from Jesus was to illustrate that, in the kingdom of God, "the last will be first, and the first will be last"—to illustrate that things in the kingdom of God often work diametrically opposite to the way things work in the human kingdom. But this parable—illustrating the intersection of justice and generosity (mercy)—bears directly on Paul's presentation in Romans 9.

Bearing in mind the hermeneutical principle of not forcing more upon a parable than it will bear, consider the elements of this story (the primary difference between our parable and Jesus' is that Jesus' vineyard owner took *all* who were available each time he went to seek more workers. Our farmer chose the ones he wanted each time he returned). Jesus' parable was not about salvation, but in both parables justice and generosity are kingdom principles which Paul deals with in Romans 9: the large pool of laborers, who have no "right" to work, are completely at the mercy of an outside employer to change their destiny for the day. The employer has the means to prosper them and accomplish his own purposes as well, so he has the privilege of choosing, from the larger pool, those whom he desires to hire.

The employer pays what he stated to the first group, so he is just. He pays what he wants to pay to the last group, so he is generous. He is also merciful (not giving what is deserved). Grace is receiving what we do not deserve; mercy is not receiving what we do deserve. In the case of the last group of workers, they did not receive what they deserved (they deserved an hourly wage commensurate with the first group); they received much more! So the employer was not only just; he was generously merciful at the same time.

How does this apply to Paul's point in Romans 9? The apostle's last statement to the Roman believers was that nothing will be able to separate God's chosen ones from the love of God in Christ (Rom. 8:39). And yet, undoubtedly in the minds of many believers, there was an apparent contradiction in Paul's words. What about Israel? They were God's chosen people and were obviously, for the most part, outside of the love and blessings of God. If God chose Israel, had he now "unchosen" them? And if he changed his mind about Israel, could he also change his mind about us? Not only did the fear of losing the protection of God's love raise its ugly head, but this proved to be an opportunity for Paul to answer another question which had no doubt been posed often to him: Why were there so many unbelieving Jews? If they were God's chosen people, why did not more of them embrace the Messiah God gave them?

The next major portion of Paul's epistle is spent answering these questions. Indeed, this block of chapters (9–11) is an aside of sorts. Paul could have easily moved from the semidoxology of Romans 8:37–39 to the exhortation of Romans 12:1, and maintained perfect continuity in his epistle. With the close of his section on sanctification (chs. 6–8), the next logical thing for him to say is, "Therefore, I urge you, brothers . . . to offer your bodies as living sacrifices" (Rom. 12:1). Instead, he diverts to a lengthy explication of Israel's past, present, and future so as to provide the needed insight on the personal salvation—as well as security—of the believers in Rome. He arrives at the same place at the end of chapter 11 as he did at the end of chapter 8—a glowing statement of praise for God's salvation and mercy in choosing and calling any to salvation when all are undeserving.

Unless one understands the union of justice and mercy, one will struggle with God's plan of salvation which elects only some to be saved. This lack of understanding is evident when many contemporary believers read the parable of Matthew 20:1–16. Because we are such creatures of our modern world's economy (a day's wage for a day's work; labor unions which guarantee workers' "rights," retirement plans, job security, maternity/paternity leave, etc.), we chafe at the idea that everything we get from God comes by way of his mercy, and we especially chafe at the idea that some might get his blessings who are not half as "deserving" as we are.

Romans 9, the first of Paul's three chapters concerning Israel (and ultimately all believers), introduces mercy as the core concept in election (Paul concludes with mercy in 12:1), and explains why it appears that God has been unfaithful (he has not) in light of the small number of Israelites who have believed.

II. COMMENTARY

Israel's Past Is Consistent with the Gospel

MAIN IDEA: *Neither lineage nor merit is a factor in salvation, but election as mediated by God's justice and mercy.*

A The Gospel: The Intersection of Responsibility and Sovereignty (9:1–5)

SUPPORTING IDEA: *Responsibility and sovereignty work together to bring salvation through the gospel.*

John Stott cites numerous commentators who have struggled with the placement and interpretation of Romans 9–11 in the epistle (Stott, pp. 261–262). A simple comparison of the subject matter in chapters 8 and 9 reveal striking parallels that make it obvious what Paul is doing: he is continuing his exposition of God's processes of salvation, only now with direct reference to Israel. At least seven themes that he touched on in chapter 8 are interpreted in light of Israel's marginal response to the gospel:

	Romans 8	Romans 9
Adoption/Sonship	verse 15	verses 4,26
Glory	verses 18,21	verses 4,23
Purpose of God	verse 29	verse 11
Foreknowledge/Election	verse 29	verse 11
God's Children	verses 14,16	verse 8
Calling of God	verses 28,30	verses 12,24
Cut off/Separation from God	verse 39	verses 22,28,29

If foreknowledge, election, adoption, sonship, and all the other truths of salvation through the gospel are true (ch. 8), why do they not appear to be true for Israel (ch. 9)? Rather than raise this question with the diatribe format that he has used previously in the letter, Paul enters directly into the answer. Apparently, his passionate response to an obvious question drives him immediately into revealing his heart— confirmed by the **Holy Spirit**. His pointed answer to the assumed question—"Did God not keep his word to Israel?"—comes in verse 6: "It is not as though God's word had failed." But prior to giving that answer, Paul's heart bursts forth in a display of passion for the lost unrivaled in Christian literature.

In the first five verses of chapter 9, Paul is going to give evidence of both sides of the salvation process: the human side and the divine side. While God is ultimately and sovereignly over salvation (cf. God as the subject of the five key verbs in 8:29), part of his purposes includes the human factor (responsibility) in not only spreading the gospel but in believing the gospel. The human side (responsibility) is revealed in verses 1–3, and the divine side (sovereign election) in verses 4–5.

9:1–3. Paul is so struck at the end of chapter 8 with the powerful and protecting love of God—and the fact that most of Israel has not experienced that love making it seem as if God had not kept his promises to Israel—that his love for his nation bursts out in a display of brokenness that would shame most who claim to have a "burden for the lost." Fearing it may appear that he has no concern for the lost condition of most Jews in light of God's sovereign oversight of salvation, he confesses his **sorrow and unceasing anguish** over Israel's spiritual condition. His concern is not sentimental, traditional, or fleshly—rather, it is a concern validated by **the Holy Spirit**. Paul demonstrates the valid role that the **conscience** can play in the spiritual life when it has been shaped and disciplined in spiritual maturity (Heb. 5:14).

Paul is acknowledging the great chasm that existed between God's original plan for Israel—"You will be for me a kingdom of priests and a holy nation" (Exod. 19:6)—and the recent and present reality—"The chief priests and the elders of the people came to the decision to put Jesus to death" (Matt. 27:1). What had happened? How did the nation that was to act like a conglomerate of priests end up being led by priests who put their own Messiah to death?

The truth of this reality broke the apostle Paul's heart all the more because he had been one of the most ardent persecutors of Jesus and his Way. Paul had experienced a radical transformation, but he knew that the vast majority of Israel had not. Nowhere is this seen in sharper contrast than Acts 9. "Breathing out murderous threats against the Lord's disciples," Paul "went to the high priest and asked him for letters to the synagogues in Damascus" so that he might take any believers found there "as prisoners to Jerusalem" (Acts 9:1–2; see also 22:19; 26:11). Eighteen verses later, Paul "began to preach in the synagogues that Jesus is the Son of God" (Acts 9:20). It is no surprise that "all those who heard him were astonished" at his salvation and transformation as he continued to "baffle" the Jews living in Damascus (Acts 9:21–22).

From that point on, Paul—the apostle to the Gentiles (Rom. 11:13)—made the Jewish synagogues of Asia Minor and southern Europe his first stop in preaching the gospel (Acts 13:5,14; 14:1; 17:1–2,10,17; 18:4,19; 19:8). Why? Because the Jews were his brothers, his kinsmen (Acts 13:26,38; 22:1; 23:1,5–6; 28:17), and his heart ached for their salvation.

One wonders if Paul ever outlived the grief he must have felt about stirring up so much hatred against Christ among the leaders in Israel. Forgiveness cleanses the conscience, but it does not remove the regret. In that spirit, Paul declares his willingness to be **cursed and cut off from Christ** for the sake of his brother Israelites. The strongest imprecation in the Greek language—*anathema* (eternally condemned; see Gal. 1:8–9)—is what he declares himself willing to be if only Israel could be saved.

Once before, when Israel rebelled against God at Sinai, its leader had offered his own life in return for God sparing theirs (Exod. 32:32). Both then, and in Paul's case, the human side of salvation is seen: the responsibility to intervene in every manner possible to save the lost, and the responsibility of the lost to believe. Because God has ordained human involvement in the salvation equation, Paul goes about it as if it all depended on him. Why else would he risk his life on numerous occasions, and enter into arguments and debates and dialogues in synagogues and marketplaces to try to persuade unbelievers to believe the gospel?

9:4–5. But there is another side of the gospel, and that is the side of God's sovereign election; his unconditional choosing. Israel was begun through a man whom God chose out of the human pool in the Chaldees, Abram by name. When his descendants reached nationhood size (rag-tag though they were), he plucked them out of the backwaters of obscurity in Egypt and made them his nation at Sinai. If anyone can find a condition within Abram or Israel to justify God's choosing, it would be the first time. God did not choose Israel because of anything in Israel (Deut. 7:7), but because of something in himself—purposeful love and mercy.

The evidence of his choosing is plentiful: **adoption as sons . . . divine glory . . . covenants . . . the law . . . temple worship . . . promises . . . patriarchs . . . the human ancestry of Christ.** God sovereignly bestowed on Israel all of this and more. Along the way, however, many (from the human perspective) had not acted responsibly in responding faithfully to God's gifts. They had wandered outside of the covenant provisions and so were not experiencing the covenant blessings. This raises the question Paul is seeking to answer in this chapter: *Has God failed to keep his word to Israel?* How does one mesh human responsibility to believe and remain faithful with God's sovereign choice which, according to Romans 8:30, leads to glorification at God's initiative? For the believers in Rome, this raises the question of whether God will remain faithful to his promises to them; whether they, having believed the gospel, will be glorified in the end.

The key to understanding how God works in human salvation is to understand how he has worked, and is working, in the salvation of Israel (recall the parallels between individual salvation in Romans 8 and the salvation of Israel in Romans 9 as outlined in the chart above). The full picture of God's working in Israel will be painted over three chapters by Paul, signed with his doxology of praise in 11:33–36. But in the remainder of chapter 9, Paul will explain the history of how God chose Israel, and who is Israel and who is not. Seeing that, it will be clear that God has remained perfectly true to his word.

B The Gospel Has Always Been Based on Election (9:6–13)

> **SUPPORTING IDEA:** Even as far back as Abraham, God's good news of salvation (the gospel) has always been the outworking of God's choice.

9:6–9. In verse 6 is the controlling principle for understanding election: **Not all who are descended from Israel are Israel.** Paradoxical in nature, this simple sentence is the clearest evidence for election. Paul will illustrate the truth in this paradox in two ways: first, by showing that the gospel (here we use the term broadly in the sense of God's announcement and promise of salvation's blessings) has never been based on heritage, lineage, or pedigree

(9:6–9); and second, by showing that the gospel has never been based on merit (9:10–13).

Israel is the name given to Jacob, Isaac's son, when he wrestled with the angel of God and submitted to the purposes of God in his life (Gen. 32:22–32). Paul is going to show that, like a funnel, the channel for the blessings of God promised to Abraham got narrower and narrower in the first three generations of Jews. Just because one was a descendant of Abraham did not mean that one was an inheritor of the promises of God to Abraham. Initially this was true because Abraham had two sons—Isaac through Sarah, and Ishmael through Hagar, Sarah's maid. But the promise had been given to Sarah's child, not Hagar's: **It is through Isaac that your offspring will be reckoned.**

Though Ishmael's descendants grew numerous as God promised (Gen. 16:10; 25:12–18; the modern Arab nations, generally speaking), they were not the inheritors of the promises given to Abraham. It is not the physical descendants of Abraham who are God's children, but those who have received (and are walking in) the promise made to Abraham. The modern equivalent of this truth might be, "It is not the children of Christian parents who are Christians; it is those who have personally embraced Christ as Savior and Lord who are Christians." Paul had already said as much just a few verses earlier in chapter 8 ("those who are led by the Spirit of God are sons of God"; v. 14) and in chapter 4 ("the promise comes by faith"; v. 16).

Though Paul has clarified this earlier in Romans (4:9–17), it deserves repeating here: Paul is not saying that salvation comes only to the descendants of Abraham, Isaac, Jacob, and his twelve sons. Rather, he is saying that salvation (election; see Rom. 9:11) is based on promises, but that the promises of salvation do not flow along lines of heredity. Rather, they flow along lines of faith. He is simply making the point at this early stage of his exposition of election that God chose Isaac and did not choose Ishmael. This truth establishes God's practice of election in Israel from the very beginning.

9:10–13. While the promise of salvation was not made on the basis of lineage, neither was it made on the basis of merit, or good works. **Isaac** was chosen instead of Ishmael, and Isaac married **Rebekah**, who gave birth to twin boys. At first, it would seem that both the boys—**Jacob** and **Esau**—would be chosen by God since they were both the sons of **Isaac** through whom salvation promises were flowing. Not so. **Before the twins were born or had done anything good or bad,** Rebekah was told that **the older will serve the younger** (see Gen. 25:23). And why was **Jacob** chosen over **Esau**? So that **God's purpose in election might stand.**

This is the same purpose that Paul referred to earlier when referring to "those . . . who have been called according to his purpose" (Rom. 8:28). In accordance with Deuteronomy 29:29—"The secret things belong to the LORD our God, but the things revealed belong to us and to our children forever, that we may follow all the words of this law"—not all has been revealed about the purposes of God. Here are some things we do know from the perspective of New Testament revelation:

- His purpose is set, is based on foreknowledge, and included the death of his own Son (Acts 2:23).
- Individuals apparently serve God's purpose during their lifetimes, as did David (Acts 13:36).
- Believers are called according to God's purpose, and God causes all things in their lives to meld with his purpose (Rom. 8:28).
- Part of God's purpose involves displaying his power and proclaiming his name in all the earth (Rom. 9:17).
- God's purpose requires some noble vessels and some common ones (Rom. 9:21; 2 Tim. 2:20).
- God has a plan by which his purpose is worked out, which includes the choosing of individuals to fulfill certain parts of his purpose through his predestined plan (Eph. 1:11).
- God's purpose is eternal and is accomplished through Jesus Christ (Eph. 3:11).
- God works his will, to include even our actions, in and through us to accomplish his purpose (Phil. 2:13).
- Believers are saved and called to a holy life on the basis of nothing in themselves but because of God's purpose enacted through grace (2 Tim. 1:9).
- God's purpose is unchanging in nature (Heb. 6:17).

Admittedly, these verses do not tell us all we would like to know about the purpose of God in general or, specifically, **God's purpose in election.** But it does tell us how his **purpose in election** is carried out—by choice. That is not a profound revelation; all purposes are carried out on the basis of choices and decisions. But here Paul is affirming God's right to choose in order to accomplish his purpose—not only his purpose leading to the death of his Son as a sacrifice for sin, but all other of his eternal purposes as well.

The language used by God—**Jacob I loved, but Esau I hated** (see Mal. 1:2–3)—is poetically comparative, not absolute. Rachel was loved by Jacob more than Leah (Gen. 29:31–33; cf. Deut. 21:16–17), and Christians are to "hate" their parents and other family members, even their own life, in comparison to their love for Christ (Luke 14:26; cf. Matt. 10:37). The focus in all these instances is not on the "not chosen"—how could God *hate* Esau? How unloving for Jacob to *hate* Leah! Imagine being asked by God to *hate* your parents! Rather, the focus is on the chosen—Jacob preferred Rachel (for his own reasons); God chose Jacob (for his own reasons); we choose Christ over all others. The "not chosen" are not chosen according to purpose, not according to hate.

So what has Paul said so far? These three things:

1. The nation of Israel was chosen as a people through which his blessings would flow to the world (Gen. 12:1–3; Amos 3:2).
2. Within that people, God's purpose resulted in additional choices (elections) being made which involved individuals.
3. God's word (promises) has not failed. The elect Israel within national Israel still are recipients of his promises.

The way we know that we have interpreted Paul correctly so far is by reading what happens next. In Romans 9:14, Paul returns to the diatribe format, allowing the fictional objector the opportunity for cross-examination.

ⓒ The Gospel Has Always Been Based on Justice and Mercy (9:14–18)

SUPPORTING IDEA: *The two complementary parts of salvation through the gospel are God's justice and his mercy.*

Paul is hit immediately with the charge of portraying God as unjust. The key to understanding why God is not unjust in his purpose of election is to understand that election is based on one thing: the mercy of God (Rom. 9:16). Paul will explain two things about mercy: first, justice is not negated by mercy (9:14–15), and second, mercy is not negated by choice (9:16–18).

9:14–15. Is God unjust? This question has been raised before by Paul's antagonists. Interestingly, the first time Paul was accused of making God unjust for condemning sinners (Rom. 3:5), and now he is accused of making God unjust for saving sinners (Rom. 9:14)! This alone is evidence enough of humankind's basic problem: in our natural state, we simply resist the ways of God. We do not like it when he judges, and we do not like it when he saves.

That contradiction returns us to the point that Paul made earlier in the epistle that "all have sinned and fall short of the glory of God" (Rom. 3:23). Humans, Paul said in Romans 3:10–18, are not righteous, do not understand or seek God, have turned away and become worthless, lie and practice deceit, murder, and cause ruin and misery. This puts us all, proverbially, "at the mercy of God." Is justice negated by mercy? Absolutely not. Justice is served in the condemnation of all according to our sins. If God, in his mercy, chooses to extend mercy to some to accomplish his purpose of bringing salvation to many, justice has still been served to all by condemning their sin to begin with.

Recall the opening illustration that contained two examples of mercy. Out of the pool of unemployed workers, it is not unjust for the farmer to choose some to work and not others. Nor is it unjust for him to pay what was agreed upon to some and pay others a higher amount. In neither case is justice negated by mercy. Rather, as Monikka Mannau, a Bangladeshi Christian, has said regarding the foundational parable of Jesus, "Such was the justice and mercy of the owner of the vineyard that the needs of the men and their families meant more to him than the concept of payment for work done. At the end of the day, all [the chosen] were paid the same" (Ward, p. 290).

Neither is it unjust for God to choose some in the nation of Israel to receive his promised blessings and others not to receive them. As God spoke to Moses, "I will have mercy on whom I have mercy" (Exod. 33:19). Moses was the only one to see God's glory on a personal basis. Was it unjust for God to choose Moses? No, it was an evidence of **mercy** and **compassion** according to his purpose for Moses, for Israel, and for the whole world.

There is something uniquely divine about **mercy**. We see human beings exercise **mercy** occasionally, but it is only because of the image of God upon us. Animals do not exercise **mercy**, nor does Satan. And left to our own, neither do humans. Yet how quick we are to apply "justice!" The Spanish novelist, Miguel de Cervantes, author of *Don Quixote,* had it right when he said, "Among the attributes of God, although they are all equal, mercy shines with even more brilliance than justice" (Ward, p. 115). No one deserves to be chosen, to be made holy (set apart) and once again fit for God's purpose. God's purpose in election is totally a function of the divine action called **mercy**.

9:16–18. But even if we agree that justice is not negated by **mercy**, we must go farther and recognize that **mercy** is not cancelled out by choice. That is, our tendency is to think that if God looks out over the pool of condemned humans, and chooses one for this purpose and another for that, it must be on the basis of something he sees in that person (we think that about God because it is usually how we choose). That would make his choice not motivated by mercy in the purest sense, but by something redeemable—some characteristic, some cause, some condition—in the person. Wrong again, Paul says. **It does not, therefore, depend—**"It?" What does "It" refer to? Paul must be referring to "God's purpose in election" (v. 11). Therefore, we hear Paul saying, **[God's purpose in election] does not, therefore, depend on man's desire or effort, but on God's mercy.**

No one desires or makes an effort to be chosen by God ("no one seeks God"; Rom. 3:11). God did not see in Abraham a desire to be chosen for the purpose of God. God did not notice effort in Isaac and laziness in Ishmael and forsake the latter as a result. God did not look in Rebekah's womb and see honesty in Jacob and trickery in Esau and choose accordingly. If anything, in the case of these two, he saw the opposite—and chose Jacob anyway according to his purpose. God does not choose (elect) on the basis of any condition or cause in a human being. He chooses on the basis of his purpose. And because his choice results in not giving the chosen what they deserve, his choice is merciful.

As F. F. Bruce points out, "If [God] were compelled to be merciful by some cause outside himself, not only would his mercy be so much the less mercy, but he himself would be so much the less God" (Bruce, p. 178).

But there is a flip-side to **mercy**—the hardening of the heart. This is another often misunderstood aspect of God's purpose in election. Fortunately, Paul provides both a picture and an example of how a heart is hardened. The picture is in 2 Thessalonians 2:2–11, where Paul is explaining the future role of the man of lawlessness who is destined to appear on the world stage. The man of lawlessness is innately evil, proclaiming himself to be God. That is his character, his essence. But, Paul says, something is "holding him back, so that he may be revealed at the proper time." His power, in fact, "is already at work" but is being restrained. When that restraint is lifted, Paul says, the lawless man's power will be fully manifested "in all kinds of counterfeit miracles, signs and wonders, and in every sort of evil." The full manifestation of his evil will be evident when God's restraint is removed.

God did not make the lawless man evil. Rather, he is mercifully restraining his evil for a time. But when the restraining grace of God is revealed, the full force of his evil will be manifested. His heart will be totally hardened at that point.

This teaching of Paul about the man of lawlessness is consistent with another lawless man that he uses as an example of the flip-side of mercy. If mercy (election) is not giving people what they deserve, then the hardening of the heart is simply allowing what they deserve to run its full course. The hardening of the heart is, in that sense, pure justice. Pharaoh is Paul's example in Romans 9. Exodus tells us that in some cases Pharaoh hardened his own heart (Exod. 7:13,22; 8:15,19,32; 9:34–35), and in other cases God hardened Pharaoh's heart (Exod. 4:21; 7:3; 9:12; 10:1,20,27; 11:10; 14:4,8,17).

In reality, God's hardening of Pharaoh's heart was much like the future man of lawlessness—simply stepping aside and letting evil and arrogance run its course. As Leon Morris has pointed out, "Neither [in Pharaoh's case] nor anywhere else is God said to harden anyone who had not first hardened himself" (cited by Stott, p. 269). This same action on God's part is pictured by Paul in Romans 1 as "giving them over." Those who persisted in exchanging the glory of God for idols were ultimately given over to their sexual impurity, shameful lusts, and depraved minds "to do what ought not to be done" (Rom. 1:24,26,28).

Paul's conclusion to mercy as the basis for election is simple: **God has mercy on whom he wants to have mercy, and he hardens** (i.e., does not have mercy on by leaving in their sinful state) **whom he wants to harden.** It is still the choice that bothers us; why would God choose some to show mercy and not choose others? Warren Wiersbe reminds us that God's holiness demands justice, but his love manifests mercy: "God is holy and must punish sin; but

God is loving and desires to save sinners. If everybody is saved, it would deny His holiness; but if everybody is lost, it would deny His love. The solution to the problem is God's sovereign election" (Wiersbe, p. 104).

Ⓓ The Gospel Has Always Been Based on God's Sovereignty (9:19–29)

SUPPORTING IDEA: *In the final analysis, salvation is the out-working of the sovereignty of a just and loving God.*

Like dominos in a row, Paul's last assertion brings yet another objection—that man is blameless if God is the one who "fails to choose." That is, if God's purpose is satisfied by not electing some, why does God then still blame the nonelect for their status and hold them in judgment? Paul answers according to God's sovereignty (vv. 20–21) and God's glory (vv. 22–24) and then calls on two Old Testament saints for confirmation—Hosea (vv. 25–26) and Isaiah (vv. 27–29).

9:19. When the objection is voiced, it shows a striking misunderstanding: **For who resists his will?** In reality, those judged by God are not held by him in judgment for resisting his will for them to be saved. Rather, they are acting entirely in accord with his will, with their choice, and with his justice. Picture the flow of God's action, before any mercy is exercised, as a river. His justice sees that all people are flowing in the direction of judgment. That is his will because it is consistent with his justice. None in the flow of that river are resisting his will because there are none who seek God. It is the flow (the purpose) of his will that is carrying them along, and all are acting in concert with his will, not resisting his will. God is not standing on the banks crying out for them to turn to him and be saved, only to discover that they are resisting his will. When his purpose for some changes, and his hand of mercy is extended to them, they are given a new heart, a clean heart, and are saved willingly. The not-chosen do not remain where they are against either their own will or God's will. Therefore, none resist his will.

Passages of Scripture such as 2 Peter 3:9 would seem to contradict the notion that none resist his will ("He is patient with you, not wanting anyone to perish, but everyone to come to repentance"). God is patient in working out his will, and his patience may give the appearance of his waiting and hoping in anticipation of just one more person becoming one of the elect. As humans are wont to do, we immediately think of God's actions from our own frame of reference, e.g., that of a parent and a recalcitrant child. When a mother instructs her four-year-old to eat his vegetables, and he refuses, he is resisting her will. She then adopts the "I can sit here longer than you can" strategy, hoping that he will change his mind, eat his vegetables, and end the stand-off. This is *not* what 2 Peter 3:9 is suggesting.

Some believe that, in a general way, it is God's will that all of the human race come to repentance, but that specifically he knows this will not happen. At that point what God desires comes into conflict with what actually takes place; not a likely solution. Rather, it is better to see God as patient, waiting for the fullness of time in which all of the elect of God are brought to repentance. God can **blame us** because our lack of repentance is our own choice, is consistent with our will, and ultimately with his.

9:20-21. Not only are none resisting his will, but from the perspective of God's sovereignty, it is totally inappropriate for human beings to object to the Creator's will (choices). In a day when authority figures in general get little respect (though often deservedly so), it is hard for moderns to grasp the idea that there could be somewhere in the universe an absolute Authority. Even if it is given that such an Authority exists, it is well within the purview of the fallen human nature (modern or ancient) to question that authority—indeed, to shake a fist in the face of that authority (obviously this is not a modern problem alone, or Paul would not have been dealing with it in his letter to the Roman believers).

To illustrate the inappropriateness of talking back to God, Paul uses well-known imagery from the Old Testament of the potter and his clay (Isa. 29:16; 45:9; 64:8; Jer. 18:1-10; see also Isa. 10:15). Like most general analogies in Scripture, Paul is making a single, primary point here: God is the Creator, and we are the creation. It really is acceptable for God to be God. The creation's inability to comprehend the Creator's choices does not, *ipso facto,* imply error on the part of the Creator. Rather, it simply validates the gap between the mind of the Creator and the mind of the creation.

Even Paul's potter/clay illustration has been misused by modern objectors who would suggest that the pots being made by the potter for **common use** are crying out all the while to the potter, begging to be made into pots for **noble purpose.** They are not. To see the potter as the malevolent force in this illustration is to see God as an uncaring, arbitrary potter of human figurines who praises himself for the beauty of some and resigns others to a dusty shelf. It is imperative to remember that both pots come from the **same lump of clay**—common clay, as in pots made for **common use.** The mercy-based miracle is that God could take common clay and *transform* it into something for his **noble purpose.** No pot left in its common state is left there against its will. No one resists God's will in their nonelection; rather, they fulfill it. It is totally within bounds for God to sovereignly mold common clay for his **noble purpose.** It is totally out of bounds for anyone to question the potter's action.

9:22-24. Paul continues his answer to the objection posed in verse 19, but this time his answer goes to the revelation of God's glory rather than his sovereignty. While there are some parallel themes in these two verses, they can be difficult to sort out. Here is the logical order of what Paul is saying (remembering that the last thing Paul has said is that the potter has the right to use the same lump of clay for both noble and common purposes; v. 21):

1. As a sovereign, God could have demonstrated at any time his **wrath and power** against **objects of . . . wrath—prepared for destruction** ("prepared" in v. 22 is not the same verb as "prepared beforehand" in v. 23; the former is *katartizo*, meaning according to completeness, made ready or perfect, fully trained; the latter is *proetoimazo*, to prepare, get ready, or make ready beforehand. The implication is that the **objects of his wrath** in v. 22 are made complete, or brought to their perfect end, by destruction, whereas **objects of his mercy** in v. 23 are made ready by God, ahead of time, for glory. The former implies a natural result; the latter implies an interruption, a change, a preparation that is causative to change one's status).

2. However, instead of revealing his **wrath** and **power**, God used **great patience** in dealing with them.

3. **He did this** (patiently postponed his wrath) in order to **make the riches of his glory known** (which he bestowed) upon **the objects of his mercy** (the elect). ("Upon" differs from the NIV in verse 24. It makes more sense that *epi* here is "upon" (NASB) instead of "to" (NIV). The change from "to" to "upon" changes the reason for God's acting patiently:

"To" makes **the objects of his mercy** the object of his demonstration of patience. How does his patience toward **the objects of his wrath** reveal glory to those who are already **the objects of his mercy**, and thereby already know his glory?

"Upon" makes **the objects of his wrath** the object of his demonstration of patience. Here, he wanted **the objects of his wrath** to see **the riches of his glory** which was bestowed "upon" **the objects of his mercy**. In other words, rather than destroying the nonelect immediately, he bears with them patiently in order that they might see the riches of his glory as revealed in his actions toward **the objects of his mercy**.

God's dealing with Pharaoh in the Book of Exodus is a prototype for God's patience as described by Paul. How many times could God have justifiably struck down the ruler of Egypt because of his insolence? Yet, in order that Pharaoh might see the glory of God in redeeming the least of the land of Egypt, he allowed Pharaoh to live. Pharaoh witnessed the plagues, the pillar of fire, the parting of the Red Sea, the granting of miraculous powers to his adopted Hebrew son, and most of all, the redemption (think "calling" in Rom. 8:30) of a people so despised in Pharaoh's sight that the Egyptians would not even eat with them (Gen. 43:32; 46:34).

The identification of **us** in verse 24 is a matter of discussion. The NIV treats the last part of verse 22 and all of verse 23 as separate from the narrative which begins in verse 22 and ends in verse 24. That is, the NIV reads (beginning in v. 22) **the objects of his wrath . . . even us, whom he also called** (v. 24). That makes **us** to be believers who were once **objects of his wrath** but who were called by him to be glorified (see "calling" in Rom. 8:28–30). Most interpreters, however, take **us** to follow and be identified with **objects of his mercy** in verse 23. In either case, the truth is that from both Jews and Gentiles **objects of his mercy** have been called to reveal his glory to **the objects of his wrath.**

But Paul wants his readers to know this is not new theology. In the final verses, he appeals to Hosea and Isaiah to show that God has always had objects of mercy and objects of wrath.

9:25–26. Paul uses the context of Hosea 2:23 and 1:10 to demonstrate his adoption of those who are far from him. These verses only introduce a subject on which Paul will give great detail in chapter 11—the adoption of Gentiles into covenant blessings, and the regathering to himself of many in Israel who were far from him.

The original context of the Hosea passage is God's spiritual restoration of the nation of Israel, when he will pour out his mercy upon a people who were not his people spiritually. They were his people ethnically, but not spiritually; by heritage, but not by heart. Here, Paul uses the spiritual restoration of Israel as an example of God's mercy. He is a loving, forgiving God who reveals his glory to objects of his wrath by extending his love to the objects of his mercy. In fact, Paul will use this same argument in Romans 10:19 and 11:11 to prove that God's extension of love to Gentiles was used to make unbelieving Jews envious, angry, and jealous enough to return to God. When the objects of his wrath (unbelieving Jews) saw the riches of his glory upon the objects of his mercy (Gentiles; see Rom. 9:23), they returned to God.

9:27–29. While Paul uses Hosea to show that God's mercy is wide enough to include Gentiles, he now uses Isaiah to show that God's justice is focused enough to exclude some in Israel. This returns us to the original point of this chapter: How can we know that God will keep his word to us since it appears that he broke his word to Israel? We have already stated that the misconception in this question is that ethnic Israel is the same as spiritual Israel, which Paul says in 9:6 they are not: "Not all who are descended from Israel are Israel." Here Paul explains how the number was shrunk so drastically—why only a **remnant** in Israel are really Israel (he will explain "why" in Rom. 9:30–33).

The original promise to Abraham was that Israel would be like "the sand on the seashore" (Gen. 22:17). Yet because of God's **sentence** of judgment on Israel for her sin, **only the remnant will be saved.** In fact, even in God's judgment is his mercy found: **Unless the Lord Almighty had left us descendants** (God had promised a permanent heritage of descendants), **we would have become like Sodom . . . [and] Gomorrah.** Apparently, in God's sight, all had sinned and come short of the glory of God (Rom. 3:23), meaning that all deserved to die, as did **Sodom** and **Gomorrah.** But because God had mercy on a **remnant** through whom the Messiah and blessings to the rest of the world would come, Israel did not perish.

Therefore, "It is not as though God's word had failed." He has been faithful to his promises to Israel, in fact more than faithful. He has shown mercy where only judgment was deserved. But because he has been faithful, the believers in Rome may know that God will likewise be faithful to them.

> **MAIN IDEA REVIEW:** *Neither lineage nor merit is a factor in salvation, but election as mediated by God's justice and mercy.*

III. CONCLUSION

Lord, Have Mercy On Me

The Orthodox tradition of Christianity has for centuries preserved what is called "The Jesus Prayer," a model of humble and contemplative simplicity in worship before God. Though longer and shorter versions of the prayer have been used at different times, the most often recorded form is, "Lord Jesus Christ, Son of God, have mercy on me, a sinner." This prayer certainly has scriptural support—for its brevity (Matt. 6:7–8), its Christ-centeredness (John 14:13–14), and its recognition of our continual need for repentance and forgiveness (God's mercy) in spite of our sin (1 John 1:8–9).

Several times in the Gospels, those seeking the mercy of God cried out in words similar to the Jesus Prayer. Near Jericho on one occasion, a blind man was sitting by the side of the road as Jesus approached. Upon learning that Jesus of Nazareth was passing by, he called out, "Jesus, Son of David, have mercy on me!" (Luke 18:38). On another similar occasion, ten lepers stood at a distance and called out to Jesus, "Jesus, Master, have pity (mercy) on us" (Luke 17:13). In a story Jesus told, a guilty tax collector stood at a distance from the temple in Jerusalem to pray. So aware was he of his guilty condition that he would not even raise his eyes to heaven. In typical mourning behavior, he beat his breast and prayed, "God have mercy on me, a sinner" (Luke 18:13).

The interesting thing theologically about the Jesus Prayer is, when it is a sincere and penitent request for mercy, it can be prayed only by those to whom mercy has already been extended. According to Paul, no one seeks mercy (pardon, forgiveness, compassion) from God in and of himself or herself. Mercy is extended to the called of God to awaken in them a spiritual hunger and desire, and from that awakening comes a cry for "more mercy, Lord!" It is a prayer for what has already been received—which is not a problem. We pray for love, having received love; for grace, having received grace; for patience, having received patience; for compassion, having already received compassion. It is only consistent that when we pray for mercy, it is because God's mercy has awakened our need for more.

The unbeliever may ask, "If I pray sincerely for mercy, does that mean I've already received mercy from God? Mercy I did not ask for? Does that mean I am becoming a Christian? What if I do not want to be a Christian? What if I just want God to fix this unfair situation I am in right now?" Some who cry for mercy may indeed be crying for justice—which should give reason for pause. As R. C. Sproul has said, "Don't ever ask God for justice—you might get it. We may see non-justice in God, which is mercy, but we never see injustice in God" (Hughes, p. 245). Asking God for justice will result in judgment, for that is what his justice requires. Asking God for mercy is a wiser tack. "If we refuse mercy here, we shall have justice in eternity," wrote the Anglican Bishop Jeremy Taylor (1613–1667; Hughes, p. 245).

In the final analysis, the elect of God are those who ask for, and receive, mercy from God. The American preacher and journalist Henry Ward Beecher summarized it well: "The elect are whosoever will, and the non-elect, whosoever won't" (Ward, p. 162).

Not a moment should be spent worrying about whether one is of the elect or not. Rather, when one senses a need for the mercy and grace of God, it should be asked for, if a prayer as simple as the Jesus Prayer is all one knows how to do. That simple prayer received an answer from God when it was prayed by hurting and shameful people in Jesus' day, and it will receive his answer today. God is prepared to grant the riches of his glory to all who call out to him.

PRINCIPLES

- God's word has never failed.
- Spiritual life is not inherited as a legacy.
- Spiritual life is not given as a reward for merit.
- Spiritual life comes through the purpose of God in election on the basis of God's mercy toward sinners.
- Submission, not questioning, is the appropriate posture of humans before God.

APPLICATIONS

- Is there a need in my life to which God's Word speaks, for which I am having difficulty believing him?

- Am I relying on any spiritual inheritance—parents, church, denomination, my own prior spiritual achievements—to bring authenticity to my spiritual experience?
- Have I been deceived in any way into thinking that God chose me for salvation because of my personal attributes or merit?
- Have I grown complacent about my responsibilities in evangelism in light of God's sovereign election?
- Do I have a clear understanding of the difference between respectfully reasoning with God and disrespectfully challenging his authority?

IV. LIFE APPLICATION

I Like What You Have Done, But . . .

A company specializing in printing and computer graphics ran a popular television commercial in 1999 that epitomized marriage in the 1990s—the decade that made bicoastal marriages and prenuptial agreements part of the common parlance. The commercial opened with a stylish young couple having dinner in a fashionable restaurant. It appeared that the woman was about to tell her boyfriend that the relationship was over, when he pulled out a stack of full color, computer-generated flip charts. "Wait," he pleads, "until you see these. This first chart graphs the rapid growth of my feelings for you since we've been together. And this next one shows my estimated earning potential over the next thirty years. And here is a composite image of what our child would probably look like."

"I like what you've done here, Roger," the woman says, obviously impressed, as she flips back through the charts. It looks as if the credentials he has presented have won the day—and his beloved's heart. It appears she may give him the marital nod after all based on his persuasive credentials and attributes. The message of the commercial? It could not be plainer, as the announcer closes it out: "Sometimes what you say is not as important as how you say it."

In addition to modern marriage proposals, think of all the other ways that modern societies teach us to think in terms of credentials and qualifications. Entire businesses have sprung up in recent years around the sole task of interviewing for and winning a desired job. These companies handle everything from designing your résumé to dressing you appropriately to drilling you on interview techniques—all for the purpose of enhancing your attributes and qualifications. From the days of grade school, when we learn that we either do or do not have much to offer based on whether we are chosen first, middle, or last in the ritual of dividing up for recess kickball games, to the modern world of corporate—and matrimonial—competition, life is about how much we can bring to the table.

Let us go back to the table at the fancy restaurant, and consider another kind of marriage proposal. In this case, you are the bride, and the prospective groom, whom you really hope is going to ask you to marry him, is at the table with you. Consistent with your cultural conditioning (remember the fellow in the commercial?), you begin painting the rosiest picture possible in order to win the confidence of your suitor. Just as you are pulling out your computer-generated flip charts, he gently holds up his hand and interrupts you: "While I appreciate all you have to offer me and our future relationship, I knew you and chose you to be mine before you had any of those things. I have chosen you, not because of what you bring to me, but because of my love for you. All you need do is say yes to my choosing." Such is the choice of God in election.

One of the reasons we react so suspiciously to the doctrine of election is because of what Paul says in Romans 9:16: "[God's choosing] does not, therefore, depend on man's desire or effort, but on God's mercy." We are the bride of Christ, and God arranges our marriage to him based on his mercy, not on our desire or effort. Likewise, his nonchoice of others is based not on their lack of desire or effort, but on his sovereign justice. Therefore, God's choice in election—and his nonchoice—are in both cases a function of his sovereign will.

How then does he choose? We do not know how his mercy and justice inform his choice. But it is okay for us not to know. The reason we cannot figure out how he would choose purely on the basis of mercy and justice is because we cannot figure out how *we* would choose solely on that basis. And when we cannot conceive of how we would do something, we likewise cannot conceive of God doing it. This is creating God in our image, the fundamental root of human dysfunction.

The same anger we felt on the playground in being not chosen by a team captain, the same wave of resentment we felt when rejected by a romantic interest, and the same crushed esteem we experience in being passed over for a job opportunity—these are the same emotions we transfer to God at the thought of his choosing some and not others. In the doctrine of election, the one thing that God gives humans to focus on—that sets his election apart from playgrounds, matrimony, and the workplace—is the simplest part of all: whosoever will may come (John 7:37–38).

V. PRAYER

Heavenly Father, I praise you today that I can call you "Father." Thank you for choosing me to know you. Thank you for including me in your eternal family. May your Holy Spirit continually remind me that I stand in your love not by my desire or my effort, but by your mercy alone. Help me to honor you by reflecting your glory, so that those who are yet to be touched by your mercy may see your love. Amen.

VI. DEEPER DISCOVERIES

A. Reprobation (9:13)

Not a biblical term in the sense that it is used in theology today, the English word *reprobation* is from *reprobatus,* the past participle of Latin *reprobare,* to reprove. It refers to the active condemnation to hell of the nonelect as punishment for their sins, as opposed to his passively "passing over" the nonelect, leaving them in their sins (often referred to as "double predestination"). Among "modern" theologians, John Calvin gave an early and detailed treatment of reprobation in his *Institutes* (III.23.1ff.), calling it a "horrible" doctrine, yet one that could not be avoided from the plain teaching of Scripture. The example of Jacob and Esau (Rom. 9:13) is cited as a prime example of reprobation, where even before their birth, one is elected to blessing and the other consigned to judgment.

A key issue wrestled with at the Synod of Dort (1618–1619) in the Netherlands, in addition to reprobation, was the relationship of the decrees of election and reprobation to the eternal decrees of God. Did God decree man's election and reprobation before or after the fall of man into sin? Two positions have been maintained since:

Infralapsarianism (Latin for "after the fall) adherents cite the following order for the decrees of God:

1. The decree to create the world and its inhabitants
2. The decree to allow the fall into sin
3. The decree to save some of the fallen (election)
4. The decree to not save the rest (reprobation)
5. The decree to provide a Savior for the elect
6. The decree to send the Holy Spirit to effect salvation among the elect.

Supralapsarian (Latin for "before the fall") adherents would move the decrees to election and reprobation before the creation. No normative position has been taken within orthodoxy. Of those who discuss the issue, more favor the infralapsarian view.

B. Hardening of the Heart (9:17–18)

The question arises with the hardening of the heart as to whether it is permanent, leading to damnation. In the case of Pharaoh, the context of Paul's discussion certainly seems to imply that it is. Mercy and hardening, mentioned in verse 18, certainly seem to run parallel to mercy and compassion in verse 15, and the context of the entire chapter is about the mercy that leads to salvation. Therefore, hardening would appear to be the opposite, leading to condemnation. Douglas Moo comments:

> It seems, then, that this text, in its context, provides important exegetical support for the controversial doctrine of "double predestination" [see above on Reprobation]: just as God decides, on the basis of nothing but his own sovereign pleasure, to bestow his grace and so save some individuals, so he also decides, on the basis of nothing but his own sovereign pleasure, to pass over others and so to damn them. . . . God's hardening is an act directed against human beings who are already in rebellion against God's righteous rule. God's hardening does not, then, *cause* spiritual insensitivity to the things of God; it maintains people in the state of sin that already characterizes them. This does not mean . . . that God's decision about whom to harden is based on a particular degree of sinfulness within certain human beings; he hardens "whomever he chooses." But it is imperative that we maintain side-by-side the complementary truths that (1) God hardens whomever he chooses; (2) human beings, because of sin, are responsible for their ultimate condemnation. Thus, God's bestowing of mercy and his hardening are not equivalent acts. God's mercy is given to those who do not deserve it; his hardening affects those who have already by their sin deserved condemnation (Moo, pp. 598–600).

Moo's position is that God's hardening (condemnation) comes as a result of God's leaving people in their state of sin. Other, more strict, interpreters would say that God's hardening (before the fall) consigned certain individuals to their state of sin. In either case, hardening appears to result in permanent condemnation (the hardening and restoration of Israel notwithstanding; see Rom. 11:7,25, and Rom. 12 in this commentary).

C. Evangelism and the Sovereignty of God (9:18)

Critics of the doctrine of election often suggest that it destroys the motivation for evangelism. After all, if "God has mercy on whom he wants to have mercy, and he hardens whom he wants to harden" (Rom. 9:18), what point is there in our trying to persuade people one way or the other? None other than Jonathan Edwards, the eighteenth-century New England pastor and theologian, evangelized directly from texts such as Romans 9:18. Never was there a stronger teacher of the doctrines of sovereign election and predestination, yet never was there a more passionate evangelist. From Edwards's sermon on Romans 9:18 come these five points of application to the hearer:

1. From this we learn how absolutely we are dependent on God in this great matter of the eternal salvation of our souls.
2. We should adore the absolute sovereignty of God with great humility.

3. If you are saved, you are to attribute it to sovereign grace alone and give all praise to God, who alone makes you differ from another.

4. Learn how much cause you have to admire the grace of God, which has stooped to save you.

5. We may make use of this doctrine to guard those who seek salvation from two opposing extremes—presumption and discouragement.

On this last point, Edwards speaks to the one who has not yet embraced the mercy of God:

> Do not presume upon the mercy of God, and so encourage yourself in sin. Many hear that God's mercy is infinite and therefore think that, if they delay seeking salvation for the present and seek it [later], that God will bestow his grace upon them. But consider that, though God's grace is sufficient, yet he is sovereign and will use his own pleasure whether to save you or not. If you put off salvation till [later], salvation will not be in your power. It will be as a sovereign God pleases, whether you shall obtain it or not. Seeing, therefore, that in this affair you are absolutely dependent on God, it is best to follow his direction in seeking it, which is to hear his voice today: "Today if ye will hear his voice, harden not your heart."
>
> Beware also of discouragement. Take heed of despairing thoughts, because you are a great sinner, because you have persevered so long in sin, have backslidden, and resisted the Holy Ghost. Remember that, let your case be what it may and you ever so great a sinner, . . . God can bestow mercy upon you without the least prejudice to the honor of his holiness, which you have offended, or to the honor of his majesty, which you have insulted, or of his justice, which you have made your enemy, or of his truth, or any of his attributes. Let you be what sinner you may, God can, if he pleases, greatly glorify himself in your salvation. (Boice, 3:1095–1098)

James Boice comments on Edwards' words:

> Brothers and sisters, that is the way to do evangelism. It is not what the hard hearts of sinners want to hear. They want to be told that God owes them something, or at least that their destinies are in their own hands. But even if they hate and heap scorn on these doctrines, that in itself may be a beginning in the matter of their salvation. For it shows that they have at least understood the truth, though they may still be rejecting it. And they cannot accept it until they understand it.
>
> Fight against it as you wish, it is still truth: God will be glorified in your destiny one way or another, in your salvation or in your

eternal damnation. But if you have begun to see that, it may be an important first step in the surrender of your own will and great pride, and the discovery of God's mercy in Christ, which is the only thing that has ever saved anyone. (Boice, 3:1095–1098)

D. Remnant (9:27)

An Old Testament term applied to a believing portion of the nation of Israel, it is used only twice in the New Testament to refer to Israel, both times in Romans (9:27; 11:5). The use here is a quotation from Isaiah (10:22–23) who named his first son Shear-Jashub, "a remnant will return" (Isa. 7:3). Romans 9:29, a quotation of Isaiah 1:9, probably also refers to the remnant of Israel. The remnant of Israel is a key theme in the Book of Isaiah (10:20–22; 11:11,16; 28:5; 37:4,31–32).

A remnant is a piece, or a portion, and was used theologically to refer to that portion of the nation of Israel that God would grant faith to in order that the nation might remain alive as promised to the patriarchs. Even in Elijah's day, the remnant of faithful in Israel numbered only seven thousand (1 Kgs. 19:18), and an undoubtedly smaller remnant survived the Assyrian invasion with Hezekiah (Isa. 37:4). While Paul in Romans 9 does not speak of the remnant in Romans in terms of election, the remnant has always been identified as the elect (faithful) of God. At the very least, the remnant is a key illustrative point for the believers in Rome as to why it appears that God had not been faithful to all of Israel (Rom. 1:6).

Most importantly, the remnant will reappear in Romans 11 as that portion of Israel chosen by God's grace (11:5). The remnant will survive in the face of the hardening of the rest of Israel (11:25) until the full number of Gentile elect are saved, at which time "all Israel will be saved" (11:26).

VII. TEACHING OUTLINE

A. INTRODUCTION

1. Lead Story: It's My Vineyard and I'll Pay What I Want To

2. Context: In Romans 8, Paul completed three chapters on the subject of sanctification. If he had moved directly to chapter 12, covering exhortations and applications for Christian living, we would not have been surprised. But Paul, ever the thorough teacher, goes further. He wants believers to understand that their salvation and sanctification are sure in spite of the fact that most of God's chosen people were separated from him. An understanding of how God elects to salvation is required in order to have confidence in God's promises.

3. Transition: Paul knows that his fellow Israelites are lost and without God, and his heart breaks. But he knows that it is not God's fault. While God sovereignly chose Israel to be his chosen people, each Israelite must in turn choose God—and that choosing comes only as a response to the outreach of God's mercy toward individuals. God is both just and merciful. Illustrating these attributes in the nation of Israel not only provides understanding about the chosen people's spiritual status, but provides security for the believer who wants to trust the promises of God.

B. COMMENTARY

1. The Gospel: The Intersection of Responsibility and Sovereignty (9:1–5)
    a. The recognition of responsibility in the gospel (9:1–3)
    b. The recognition of sovereignty in the gospel (9:4–5)
2. The Gospel Has Always Been Based on Election (9:6–13)
    a. The gospel has never been based on lineage (9:6–9)
    b. The gospel has never been based on merit (9:10–13)
3. The Gospel Has Always Been Based on Justice and Mercy (9:14–18)
    a. Justice is not negated by mercy (9:14–15)
    b. Mercy is not negated by choice (9:16–18)
4. The Gospel Has Always Been Based on God's Sovereignty (9:19–29)
    a. The objection to election (9:19)
    b. The answer from God's sovereignty (9:20–21)
    c. The answer from God's glory (9:22–24)
    d. An illustration from Hosea (9:25–26)
    e. An illustration from Isaiah (9:27–29)

C. CONCLUSION: I LIKE WHAT YOU HAVE DONE, BUT . . .

VIII. ISSUES FOR DISCUSSION

1. What are the most problematic aspects of the doctrine of election to the average Christian? Why has the average Christian never heard a sermon from the pulpit on the doctrine of election?
2. What are the practical benefits of what the believer learns from Romans 9? Particularly, what do you learn about God? What do you learn about salvation? What do you learn about humankind?
3. What is the general level of trust most Christians have in God and his promises? How does the church's history of suffering, even martyrdom, affect the average believer's perspective on God's sovereign oversight of his church?

Romans 9:30–10:21

Israel's Present Illustrates the Gospel

I. INTRODUCTION
Good News, Bad News

II. COMMENTARY
A verse-by-verse explanation of the chapter.

III. CONCLUSION
A Prodigal People
An overview of the principles and applications from the chapter.

IV. LIFE APPLICATION
How Beautiful Are the Feet
Melding the chapter to life.

V. PRAYER
Tying the chapter to life with God.

VI. DEEPER DISCOVERIES
Historical, geographical, and grammatical enrichment of the commentary.

VII. TEACHING OUTLINE
Suggested step-by-step group study of the chapter.

VIII. ISSUES FOR DISCUSSION
Zeroing the chapter in on daily life.

"How ow odd / of God / to choose / the Jews"

William Norman Ewer

"But not so odd / as those who choose / a Jewish God, / but

spurn the Jews."

Cecil Browne

(in reply to Ewer)

Romans

9:30–10:21

IN A NUTSHELL

*I*srael's present spiritual condition—both in Paul's day and in ours—can be described in one word: unbelief. And in her unbelief, Israel serves as an illustration of the gospel message, a gospel that must be believed to be received. In chapter 9, Paul presented divine election as one side of the coin of Israel's unbelief. In this chapter, Paul presents Israel's responsibility as the other side of her own unbelief.

Israel's Present Illustrates the Gospel

I. INTRODUCTION

Good News, Bad News

*T*he great evangelical preacher, Donald Barnhouse, related an insightful story about a young man who applied for a job with Western Union delivering telegrams. Fortunately, a position was available—Could he start right away? the manager wanted to know. "Well," said the boy, "there's one thing I must warn you about before I get started. I am psychologically so constituted that I cannot stand any scene of unhappiness. I'm only willing to deliver good news. Birth announcements, that's fine. Congratulations for success, fortunes that have been received, promotions, acceptance of marriages—all the joys and bliss news, that I will deliver. But sickness and death and failure and all of that, that's alien to my nature. I just won't deliver them." It did not take the manager very long to say, "I guess I'm still looking for the one that's gonna fill this job, because this responsibility requires that you also announce bad news" (Swindoll, p. 321).

Such is the case with the gospel of Jesus Christ. There is good news, but there is also bad news. We have said that the theme of the letter to the Roman believers is the gospel that is the power of God for salvation (Rom. 1:16). Paul has already made it imminently clear in the early chapters of Romans that, as Adrian Rogers is wont to say, "It's the bad news that makes the good news good." In the early chapters of Romans (esp. chapter 3), Paul made it clear that "all have sinned and fall short of the glory of God" (Rom. 3:23). Following that bad news, he moves to the good news in chapters 4 and 5—though all have sinned, all can be justified (declared free of sin's power and penalty) through faith in Jesus Christ.

That is indeed good news, and to illustrate how good it is, Paul takes the next three chapters (6–8) to explain how the gospel sets the believer free from sin and the law and releases him into a new life in the Spirit. As we said earlier, Paul could have then closed the "good news/bad news" part of the letter and moved directly on to chapter 12 to begin fleshing out the practical ramifications of the power of the gospel within the context of life in the body of Christ. Alas, there is more bad news/good news to deal with first, which is Paul's focus in chapters 9–11.

The bad news is that Israel—represented at Rome by a number of Jewish believers in Christ—has for the most part not inherited the spiritual blessings associated with her honored position in the plan of God. Paul knew this fact could easily cause believers to doubt the word of God to them. If God did not keep his promises to Israel, why should we expect him to keep his promises to us? Does the good news of the gospel not apply to Israel?

Paul takes three chapters to cycle from the bad news to the good news regarding Israel, and in doing so raises higher than ever before the curtain that has concealed the mystery of God's ways in salvation. Chapter 9 uses Israel's past to show that God's sovereign election is consistent with the gospel, and that his election of only a remnant of Israel to believe accounts for the smallness of faith in the nation. Chapter 10 transitions from the past to the present and shows that, sovereign election notwithstanding, Israel's own failure to believe God has resulted in her condition of unbelief. As Paul says in Romans 10:16, "Not all the Israelites accepted the good news." That is the bad news; but there is good news coming—and that is Paul's topic in chapter 11.

But in chapter 10, we find that Paul is a man willing to deliver the bad news along with the good. And he is a man unafraid of theological conundrums. In chapter 9, there is divine sovereignty in election. In chapter 10, there is human responsibility in faith. How are the two to be reconciled? Some have constructed systems and paradigms by which to give mental relief to all who suffer from theologically-induced tension headaches. Not the great Charles Simeon of nineteenth-century Cambridge:

> When I come to a text which speaks of election, I delight myself in the doctrine of election. When the apostles exhort me to repentance and obedience, and indicate my freedom of choice and action, I give myself up to that side of the question. . . . As wheels in a complicated machine may move in opposite directions and yet subserve a common end, so may truths apparently opposite be perfectly reconcilable with each other, and equally subserve the purposes of God in the accomplishment of man's salvation. (Stott, p. 278).

We might say that Simeon, as one who lived in a time when the Calvinist-Arminian controversies were raging in England, rose each day as an Arminian and retired each night as a Calvinist. He, along with the apostle Paul and all who hold the sovereignty-responsibility question in correct tension, worked to spread and proclaim the gospel as if it depended on him, but at the end of the day rested in the complete sovereignty of God to bring about the ultimate purposes of God in election and salvation.

The responsibility side of the sovereignty-responsibility antinomy is Paul's focus in Romans 10. He uses Israel's present condition of unbelief ("present" referring not to a specific time period, but generally from the time of Israel's rejection of Christ until her regathering at the end of the age discussed in Romans 11) to illustrate the gospel. In principle, the gospel has been made abundantly clear and available, though some, from a human perspective, choose not to believe. Most of Israel is in that category today. Again, that is the bad news. The good news is that, though Israel has rejected her Messiah, "whoever believes in him shall not perish but have eternal life" (John 3:16)—including whoever in Israel.

II. COMMENTARY

> **MAIN IDEA:** *Israel's present state of unbelief is due to her lack of acceptance of the good news of salvation by faith.*

Israel's Present Illustrates the Gospel

A Israel's Present Condition: Unbelief Through Zeal Without Knowledge (9:30–10:4)

> **SUPPORTING IDEA:** *Israel's zeal without knowledge led to the pursuit of righteousness based on merit.*

9:30–31. Romans 9:30–33 could have been covered in the last chapter dealing with Israel's past, as they are included in our Bible chapter divisions as the last four verses of chapter 9. But it seems that Paul's question—**What then shall we say?**—is a giant leap in his discussion from the past tense to the present. Not only does he move from discussing Israel's past as far back as the patriarchs, but he also shifts gears in his argument. In chapter 9, he addressed the issue of why so few Israelites had actually come to faith in Christ by appealing to divine election. God's sovereign choices, beginning with Abraham, have governed the development of his plan of salvation from the beginning.

At this point in our study of Romans, and especially as we enter more deeply into Paul's discussion of Israel in Romans 9–11, it is important to remember two things: Paul's calling and ultimate goal in life, and that which fueled his understanding of his calling. These two things have everything to do with our understanding of Romans 9–11. Paul's calling was to be the apostle to the Gentiles (Rom. 15:16–18). For a Jewish zealot like Paul, this amounted to so much heresy, so blind had the nation of Israel become to her original commission from God. When "something like scales fell from Saul's eyes, and he could see again" (Acts 9:18) following his blinding conversion, this was symbolic of the removal of spiritual blindness which had rested upon Israel for generations (see Matt. 13:14–15 and Isa. 6:9–10 for now; more on this in the next chapter).

It is no coincidence that when Paul was given his sight again, he "saw" (was told by Christ) that, as a Jewish believer in Israel's Messiah, it was his job to fulfill what was Israel's original calling from God since the days of Abraham: to take the blessings of God to all the peoples of the earth. To make a long story short, Israel was blessed to be a blessing. First explained to a "Gentile" named Abram (who became the first Jew), God said, "I will make you into a great nation and I will bless you . . . and all peoples on earth will be blessed through you" (Gen. 12:1–3). What Israel had lost sight of through the generations was that they were to be a missionary light to the rest of the inhabited earth. And they had failed completely in their calling.

Consider Bob Sjogren's contemporary paraphrase of God's words to Abram in Genesis 12:1–3:

> God looked down and saw 70 distinct groups of people [*the author is referring here to the post-Flood people groups listed in the Table of Nations in Genesis 10*], and He loved every one of them equally. He wanted to reach out to all of them with the blessing of redemption. He could have spoken the Gospel to each of them separately, but He chose not to. He chose to use mankind to reach mankind, in order to prepare mankind in the process to rule and reign for eternity.
>
> So, He picked out one man and said to him, "Abe, I want to bless you. In fact, I want to bless your socks off. I want to pour My grace upon you. I want to give you My word. I want to give you My Holy Spirit. I want to be your God, and I want you to be My people. The reason that I want to bless you, Abram, is that I love you, but also I want you to turn around and pass My blessings to all those 70 other groups of people that I formed at the tower of Babel, because I love them, too.
>
> "Now Abe, you're not to just sit around in a nice easy chair saying, 'Oh, thank the Lord, I'm blessed.' You're to reach out to those other peoples and tell them what I'm telling you" (Sjogren, pp. 28–29).

Telling the rest of the world what God had told them was precisely what Israel had failed to do. And the result of their failure was plainly obvious by Paul's day: spiritual blindness and unbelief. It is a bit easier to understand Paul's compassion for his fellow Israelites (Rom. 9:1–5) when we understand what Paul understood—that blind people do not know they are blind. Even when they are told they are blind, they have no reference point (sight) by which to understand their blindness. Paul knew that it was the unmerited grace of God that chose him out of a blind people and granted him the gift of spiritual sight.

The same thing that happened to Abraham happened to Paul. Paul was not made the head of a nation, granted. But he was pulled out of darkness and given sight in order to take that sight to others. Was Paul on task? He was indeed, having seen both sides of the spiritual equation. To paraphrase the Hollywood siren who said that she preferred wealth over poverty, Paul might have said, "I've been blind, and I've had sight, and sight is definitely better."

The heart of Paul's teaching about Israel (the good news) will come in Romans 11. But for now, Paul is explaining to his readers in Rome how Israel had come not to believe in what God had promised and provided. His first point was in chapter 9, that "not all who are descended from Israel are Israel" (Rom. 9:6). This is God's divine and sovereign election in narrowing the channel of blessing by which the nations of the world would hear the good news of God's salvation. In our present chapter, Paul will answer the question we cited above: **What then shall we say?**

If God's election has resulted in only a remnant of believers in Israel (people like the Old Testament prophets, Jesus' twelve disciples, the 120, then a large number of Jewish believers who populated the postresurrection church), what are we to make of this? Why did God "elect" there to be so few if such a huge task was at hand—the task of evangelizing (blessing) the entire world's population with the knowledge of God? The answer lies in the fact of Israel's disobedience to God's command. That is not to say that God's election of Israelites decreased in direct correlation to the increase in her disobedience. Election is based in eternity, not in time (Eph. 1:4), and not on human performance. But it is to say that the divine antinomy between election and responsibility is seen clearly in Israel's election and her disobedience.

As we will show when studying Romans 11, Israel's spiritual blindness resulted from her disobedience. The election and preservation of a remnant in Israel by grace (Rom. 11:5–6) was evidence of the "partial hardening" (Rom. 11:25) that came with her blindness. Instead of being judged and destroyed, they were blinded and a remnant preserved who understood that they were a channel of blessing to the rest of the world.

In fact, Paul is writing to part of that Jewish remnant, preserved in the church at Rome. He wants them to understand the critical links between grace, election, belief, blindness, and the calling of God. These chapters represent a monumental effort on Paul's part to restore the vision and calling of God to the "Israel of God" (Gal. 6:16)—those of faith who are descended from Abraham and those Gentiles who are grafted into God's purposes by grace (Rom. 11). The missionary mandate of God is the most ancient mandate given to the people of God, whether Jew or Gentile. Paul is on a mission to fulfill that mandate in his lifetime and wants the church at Rome to partner with him in that task.

Therefore, we pick up Paul's discussion of Israel's present unbelief with his last words in chapter 9, where he draws a conclusion relative to the present based on Israel's prior history. And Paul's conclusion is this: God's electing activity in Israel is clearly illustrated by the fact that the Gentiles, **who did not pursue righteousness**, obtained it, **but Israel, who pursued a law of righteousness, has not attained it.** What an irony! This would be comparable to a professional gold miner going to the field with all the latest high-tech prospecting tools, laboring diligently according to form, and finding nothing, and a lazy, drunken town bum stubbing his toe on a rock in the trail which turns out to be part of a mother lode that makes him fabulously wealthy. One was searching for everything, but found nothing; the other was searching for nothing, but found everything. Such was the case with Israel and the Gentiles.

The evidence of God's intent to fulfill his purposes in election in blessing the nations could not be clearer. The character sketch Paul presents in 2 Timothy 3:1–5 makes it clear that salvation has come to the Gentiles through election by grace alone (Eph. 2:8–9; Rom. 11:5–6): lovers of self, lovers of money, boastful, arrogant, revilers, disobedient to parents, ungrateful, unholy, unloving, irreconcilable, malicious gossips, without self-control, brutal, haters of good, treacherous, reckless, conceited, lovers of pleasure rather than lovers of God, holding to a form of godliness.

The Gentiles Paul describes here—those who **did not pursue righteousness**—are the same people he describes in 2 Timothy who were not "lovers of God" (2 Tim. 3:4) These are people who, if they ever experienced salvation, would do so by salvation finding them, not by them finding salvation. And indeed salvation found them. But why?

9:32–33. Where Israel failed was in pursuing righteousness **not by faith but as if it were by works.** Paul has discussed this thoroughly already in his letter (the difference between righteousness attained by works versus faith), and here he makes only a passing reference to the core problem in Israel by way of introducing verses from Isaiah which bridge the past and present. No less than fifteen times in this section of Romans does Paul quote passages from the Old Testament to show that the unbelief which characterized Israel in the past has persisted into the present. Interestingly, Paul does not simply cite the passages from a historical perspective; he cites them and then reapplies them to the milieu in which Israel exists at his time of writing. Throughout this chapter, we will cite these passages in a uniform format so as to compare their original context with Paul's use of them with reference to "modern" Israel.

As evidence of Israel's lack of **faith,** Paul cites two verses from Isaiah (8:14; 28:16), combining them into one verse in chapter 10. (See chart on next page).

Israel had certainly stumbled over Jesus Christ and his claims to Messiahship; so much so that they crucified him. Both Paul and Peter apply the

Original Context Isaiah is warning Israel and Judah not to rely on Assyria for help but to trust in the Lord. God is like a stone or rock in their path. If they don't embrace him (have faith in him) they will stumble over him.	Isaiah 8:14 And he will be a sanctuary; but for both houses of Israel he will be a stone that causes men to stumble and a rock that makes them fall. And for the people of Jerusalem he will be a trap and a snare.	Romans 9:33a See, I lay in Zion a stone that causes men to stumble and a rock that makes them fall,	Paul's Application Paul, as was apparently commonly accepted, applies these references to the stone to Christ, meaning that Israel has stumbled over what was clearly in her path—her own Messiah.
Isaiah is pronouncing a "woe" on Israel (Isa. 28:1) for her injustice and unrighteousness. God will use his standards as a cornerstone on which to build a sure foundation.	Isaiah 28:16 See, I lay a stone in Zion, a tested stone, a precious cornerstone for a sure foundation; the one who trusts will never be dismayed.	Romans 9:33b and the one who trusts in him will never be put to shame.	Here Paul does not duplicate the "stone" reference, but only quotes the last part. Israel in his day was dismayed for having not trusted in Christ the cornerstone.

Old Testament references to "stone" and "cornerstone" to Christ (cf. 1 Pet. 2:4–8), and in doing so they follow his lead. Jesus quoted Psalm 118:22 ("The stone the builders rejected has become the capstone;" Luke 20:17) and Isaiah 8:15 ("Everyone who falls on that stone will be broken to pieces, but he on whom it falls will be crushed;" Luke 20:18) in referring to himself. Immediately upon hearing Jesus refer to himself this way, the teachers and chief priests tried to arrest him because they knew he was making himself out to be God (to whom the passages referred in the Old Testament) and because they knew he was referring to them as those who were about to be broken and crushed (Luke 20:19).

Paul's citation of these verses is a way to demonstrate that the Jews had yet to embrace and build on the stone which God had provided to be the foundation of their **faith**, the Messiah Jesus Christ. Rather than receive a "righteousness that is by faith" (Rom. 9:30), the Jews stumbled over Jesus and were being crushed under the weight of their own unrighteousness.

10:1–4. If anyone ever doubted whether God's sovereign election to salvation was somehow outside the pale of human responsibility and activity, verse 1 will forever erase that doubt. Paul, the teacher of sovereign election in Romans 9, now testifies that his prayer to God is that Israel might be saved. If election is settled in eternity past, how can prayers in the present have an impact on election's outworking? Paul does not seek to explain away the tension, though post-Pauline theologians attempt to (God ordains not only the ends but the means by which the ends are achieved, e.g., **prayer** for the salvation of the lost).

The best way to learn theology is to watch the apostle Paul in action. Did he believe only a remnant of Israel had been saved? Yes (Rom. 9:27). Did he believe that **prayer** for Israel's salvation was still his responsibility? Yes (Rom. 10:1). Paul's constant ministry for the saved, as well as the unsaved, was a ministry of **prayer** (Rom. 1:10; 2 Cor. 13:7; Eph. 1:15–23; 3:16–17; Phil. 1:4; Col. 1:3,9–10; 1 Thess. 1:2–3; 2 Thess. 1:3,11–12; 2 Tim. 1:3; Phlm. 1:4,6). Likewise, he tried to inculcate his readers with the importance and urgency of **prayer** for all types of needs (Rom. 15:30–31; 2 Cor. 1:11; Eph. 6:18–20; Col. 4:3–4; 1 Thess. 5:17,25; 2 Thess. 3:1–2; 1 Tim. 2:1; 5:5). There was nothing in Paul's doctrine of sovereignty, election, or predestination that could not, and should not, be touched by **prayer.**

Without a doubt, Paul's prayer for Israel was that what had been taken away from them—spiritual discernment and **knowledge** (see Isa. 6:9–10)—would be restored to them. He knew they were not carefully rejecting the claims of Christ, as if they knew something that he did not. They were stumbling over Christ because of spiritual blindness. It was as if they were walking down a path on a moonless night and stepped on the tail of the Lion of Judah who was lying in their way. They never even knew what hit them. Thus is the nature of spiritual blindness.

They did not lack **zeal**; they lacked **knowledge** (not "head" knowledge, *gnosis,* but "real" knowledge, perception, or recognition, *epignosis*). As a result of their lack of **knowledge**, their zeal became misguided. Interestingly, **zeal** (*zelos*) is most often translated "jealousy" in Paul's epistles, context making the difference. But in its essence, zeal *is* jealousy, and it can be in a healthy sense. Paul is saying that because the Jews lacked spiritual perception, their jealousy was for their religious traditions rather than the things of God. And Paul should know, as that is what he was zealous/jealous for (Acts 22:3; 21:20; Gal. 1:13–14; Phil. 3:6).

One of the most intriguing statements ever made by Christ is his words to the "experts in the law" in Luke 11:52, where he castigates them for having "taken away the key to knowledge (*gnosis*)." What was the key that was taken away that kept knowledge locked up in Israel? The Scriptures themselves provide few certain clues. Was it the repentance preached by the prophets (Luke 11:47–51)? Was it the fear of the Lord (see the NIV translation of Isa. 33:6)? If Jesus' immediate audience, the experts in the law (scribes; Luke 11:46,52) are his specific audience, then perhaps a right understanding of the law (the Old Testament) is what the scribes had taken away from the people of Israel. Not only did they themselves lack true knowledge, but they were preventing everyone else from gaining it as well (Luke 11:52b). Not only did they fail to recognize Jesus as the Messiah, but they failed to point him out to the nation.

Of all people, the scribes should have seen the fulfillment of the Old Testament messianic prophecies in Jesus. Is it any wonder that Paul quotes more passages from the Old Testament in Romans 10 than in any other passage of similar length in his writings? He wants the church at Rome to know that the Scriptures have been clear for generation after generation about God's plan and how to live in step with it. The fact that Israel was out of step was due to their failure to believe, not God's failure to make it clear.

The specific knowledge they lacked was that **righteousness . . . comes from God**, not from themselves. As the **end of the law**, Christ made it possible for **everyone who believes** to attain a righteous standing before God. As the **end** (*telos*) **of the law**, Christ was its fulfillment (Matt. 5:17; Rom. 10:4), not its chronological termination (Rom. 6:15). However, it was his fulfillment of the law's requirements, and his resulting confirmation in righteousness, that cast the law aside as a tormentor of all who bore the guilt of not keeping it.

Ⓑ The Instrument of the Gospel Is Personal Faith (10:5–13)

> **SUPPORTING IDEA:** *Israel's spiritual heritage has always been based on a personal faith response to God's revelation.*

10:5. Paul begins a lengthy section on the necessity for gaining **righteousness** through faith, not through the **law**. In doing so, he contrasts two different sets of instructions from Moses to Israel. Moses on **righteousness** by **law** (from Leviticus) and Moses on "righteousness" by "faith" (v. 6; from Deuteronomy).

Paul quotes Leviticus 18:5 as a reminder of what he has already thoroughly presented as impossible—the attainment of righteousness by the law:

Original Context	Leviticus 18:5	Romans 10:5	Paul's Application
If Israel wants to live, she must obey from the heart all of God's commands, including the commands for sacrifice which would cover her unwitting sins. Obedience to the law was the path to life.	Keep my decrees and laws, for the man who obeys them will live by them. I am the LORD.	Moses describes in this way the righteousness that is by the law: "The man who does these things will live by them."	Paul has already made it clear that human weakness (sin) was the law's downfall. No one has kept the law, therefore no one has gained life through the law.

The law as a source of life before God was not disputed, even by Christ. When an expert in the law asked him what must be done to inherit eternal life, Jesus quizzed him on his understanding of the **law**. When he replied correctly that we are to love God and love our neighbor (Deut. 6:5; Lev. 19:18), Jesus replied, "You have answered correctly. Do this and you will live" (see Luke 10:25–28). In the economy of the old covenant, keeping the "holy, righteous and good" law (Rom. 7:12) was the source of life (Deut. 6:25). The problem was that no one could keep it, necessitating a permanent redemption from the curse of the law (Gal. 3:10–14).

10:6–11. Yet even when the law was the standard for spiritual life, God did not make it difficult for Israel to exercise obedience to it. He did not hide the law from Israel, nor did he fail to forgive them when they failed to keep it. God made it abundantly clear to Israel what they were to do to live. Paul makes a creative application of several Old Testament passages at this point to prove that, just as God made his will abundantly clear to Israel in the Old Testament, he is making it abundantly clear to Israel "today." He applies passages originally intended to demonstrate the nearness of the law to show the nearness of **the word of faith we are proclaiming:**

Original Context	Deuteronomy 30:12–14	Romans 10:6–8	Paul's Application
Moses' conclusion to the "blessings and curses" section of Deuteronomy (Deut. 28–30) concludes with his admonition that "what I am commanding you today is not too difficult for you or beyond your reach" (Deut. 30:11). To the extent that any faithful Israelite wanted to obey God's laws, God had made his will perfectly clear and accessible to them.	It is not up in heaven, so that you have to ask, "Who will ascend into heaven to get it and proclaim it to us so we may obey it?" Nor is it beyond the sea, so that you have to ask, "Who will cross the sea to get it and proclaim it to us so we may obey it?" No, the word is very near you, it is in your mouth and in your heart so you may obey it.	But the righteousness that is by faith says, "Do not say in your heart, 'Who will ascend into heaven?'" (that is, to bring Christ down) "or 'Who will descend into the deep?'" (that is, to bring Christ up from the dead). But what does it say? "The word is near you; it is in your mouth and in your heart," that is, the word of faith we are proclaiming.	Building on the Old Testament theme of "accessibility to the will of God," Paul substitutes Christ and the gospel (the word of faith) for Moses' references to the law. No Jew (or any person) would be able to complain that the will of God (righteousness by faith in Christ) was hidden. The transition from law to faith was as plain as the initial standard of law had been in Deuteronomy.

The next three verses (9–11) deal with **the word of faith.** Verse 9 says what it is; verse 10 explains it; verse 11 offers assurance of its veracity based on a promise from the Old Testament.

The word of faith is not a word in the literal sense, but is a "message"— essentially a condensed summary of the gospel. It is the message that a person must receive in order to become a Christian. Specifically, in the case of Israel, it is a message that hits at the heart of their religious beliefs. **Jesus is Lord** is thought to be the oldest Christian confessional statement, and as such was a clear expression of the deity of Christ. **Lord** (*kurios*) was the Greek word used in the Septuagint (Greek translation of the Old Testament) to translate the Hebrew *Yahweh*, the personal name of God, sacred to the Jews.

For a Jew to **confess** . . . "Jesus is Lord" would be to ascribe deity to Jesus of Nazareth, the very source of the Jewish outrage that led to his crucifixion in Jerusalem. There is no mistaking Paul's intent in formalizing the requirement for salvation when speaking of a Jewish nation locked in unbelief (though the same formula of faith existed for Gentiles; see 1 Cor. 12:3; Phil. 2:11). Jesus was the "stone" which Israel had stumbled over just twenty-five years earlier in Jerusalem, the stone that was still squarely in the middle of their path.

But confessing **Jesus is Lord** is not the whole gospel. In fact, it is the outward, public manifestation of a heart-held belief. Thus comes the other half of the **word of faith**, affirmation that Christ had indeed been resurrected from the dead. The resurrection was an essential part of apostolic preaching in the early days of the gospel ministry (Acts 2:31–32; 3:15; 4:10; 10:40; 17:32), and became a central part of Paul's teaching to the churches (Rom. 1:4; 4:24–25; 6:4–5,9; 7:4; 8:11,34; 1 Cor. 6:14; 15:4,7,12–17,20,29; 2 Cor 4:14; 5:15; Gal. 1:1; Eph. 1:20; Phil. 3:10; Col. 2:12; 3:1; 1 Thess. 1:10; 2 Tim. 2:8). It is interesting to compare the apostle Paul's consistent emphasis upon the resurrection as a validating factor for the Christian faith. Indeed, if there is no resurrection, there is no Christianity.

Paul would have the church remember the centrality of the resurrection in the gospel, and orders his words in a helpful A-B-B-A format (possibly) to aid retention as well as teach correct theology:

A *Confess:* If you *confess* with your mouth, "Jesus is Lord,"

B *Believe:* and *believe* in your heart that God raised him from the dead, you will be saved.

B *Believe:* For it is with your heart that you *believe* and are justified,

A *Confess:* and it is with your mouth that you *confess* and are saved.

What the heart believes, the mouth confesses. Contrary to the famous drill sergeant credo, "Where the head goes, the body follows," Paul's creed is consistent with that of James, the Lord's half brother. Belief and confession are like faith and works—the truly saved will always ultimately manifest a complementary expression of their new life in Christ. Faith can give way immediately to confession as it did with the apostle Paul (Acts 9:20–22), or it may come slowly as with some Jewish leaders who believed in Jesus but were bound by fear (John 12:42). Ultimately, however, Jesus himself indicates that confession of our faith is a requirement, even in the face of impending persecution (Matt. 10:32–33).

Paul's language here has confused some people over what one must do to be saved. Ultimately, there is only one thing: believe (Gen. 15:6). But here Paul says two "things" must be done: *confess* that Jesus is Lord and *believe* in the resurrection. But other passages would suggest that repentance, baptism, being born again, entering the kingdom, and having faith are all required. They are and they are not. They are in the sense that every true Christian will have done them all. They are not unless the one element—faith—is present.

The point is that if we confess, repent, are baptized, believe, and (try to) enter the kingdom in the flesh—as Israel had done—it will be to no avail. All of those things must be done, but they must be done *believing,* or not done at all. And in that sense, faith (belief) is the core. The thief on the cross (Luke 23:42–43) had time only to believe, but by doing so he entered the kingdom. But anyone in whom faith springs up and begins to bear fruit will have done "all the above" as a testament to his or her salvation.

Paul's paralleling of justification with salvation is not a word game or a play on words. We are **justified** by our belief in the person and work of Christ (represented here by the resurrection), but we are **saved**—confirmed in our faith and carried to the portals of the kingdom of God—by the outworking of our faith (here represented by confession). One cannot choose justification (belief) without salvation (confession), or vice versa. Unless God's providence directs otherwise (witness the thief), the normal Christian life is lived under the power of both.

Finally, Paul comes full circle on his quotation from Isaiah 28:16 in Romans 9:33 by citing again the last part of verse 16. To stumble over the stone which is Christ is to fall into unbelief; to embrace the stone (**believe** and **confess**) is to have security forever:

Original Context	Isaiah 28:16	Romans 10:11	Paul's Application
Being "dismayed" in Isaiah is a picture of confusion, hopelessness, captivity, starvation, trouble, and despair. Trust in the Lord is the antidote to all these conditions.	So this is what the Sovereign LORD says: "See, I lay a stone in Zion, a tested stone, a precious cornerstone for a sure foundation; the one who trusts will never be dismayed."	As the Scripture says, "Anyone who trusts in him will never be put to shame."	Paul changes the wording of the verse by inserting "him." It does not alter the meaning of the verse, but applies trust in the rock (Yahweh) of the Old Testament to Christ in the New Testament.

10:12–13. Paul has finished comparing righteousness by the law with righteousness by faith. The evidence is that, just as in the Old Testament when God made his will readily available to Israel so that they might embrace it and live by it, so God has made his will available "today." And his will for everyone, **Jew and Gentile**, is faith in Christ. Here Paul concludes with a promise from the Old Testament, from Joel 2:32:

Original Context-	Joel 2:32a	Romans 10:13	Paul's Application
Joel's original "everyone" seems to refer to the "all people" detailed in Joel 2:28, people without regard to age or gender (see Num. 11:29; Gal. 3:28). The primary application does not seem to include Gentiles, but everyone in Jerusalem (Joel 2:32b).	And everyone who calls on the name of the LORD will be saved.	for, "Everyone who calls on the name of the Lord will be saved."	Paul follows Peter's lead (Acts 2:21) in expanding Joel's prophecy to "Jews and all . . . who live in Jerusalem" (Acts 2:14), and "all who are far off" (Acts 2:39; cf. Eph. 2:12–13). Peter says God calls those who call on him (Acts 2:39b).

Given Paul's clear teaching that all, without exception, have sinned (Rom. 3:23), it is only consistent that God's salvation should come to all (Rom. 3:22). Remembering that the mission of Israel was to receive salvation from God and then be "a light for the Gentiles" (Isa. 42:6; 49:6; Luke 2:32; Acts 13:47; 26:23) also substantiates the expansion of Joel's prophecy to include the Gentiles. This is another example of the Old Testament prophets not fully realizing the extent of what they wrote, which necessitated the revealing of the mystery of Jews and Gentiles being brought together in one body, the mystery given to the apostle Paul (Rom. 1:5; 11:25; 16:25; Eph. 3:3,6,9).

Though Paul does not use the word, Joel's prophecy was a promise (Acts 2:39). In this section directed at Israel's unbelief, Paul is promising Israel that the gospel is accessible to them; they can believe it; it will save them forever—they will be saved if they call on the name of the Lord. The irony of this entire passage is that while the task was originally to get the Gentiles included in what Israel was given, now the tables have turned. It is Israel who needs to be included in what the Gentiles are readily accepting. Paul will delve into this irony—and reveal the reason for it—in the next chapter.

🄲 The Vehicle of the Gospel is Proclamation (10:14–15)

SUPPORTING IDEA: *The salvation scenario begins with a preacher's proclamation and ends with personal profession of faith.*

All this talk of salvation to Jews and Gentiles reexposes Paul's true heart. In the first few verses of his long letter to Rome, he declared his mission "to bring about the obedience of faith among all the Gentiles, for His name's sake" (Rom. 1:5, NASB). His desire to enlist the church at Rome as a partner in his task is the primary reason for his lengthy epistle—making sure that they understand the gospel he has been called to declare. But the gospel is not just for the Gentiles; it is for the Jews as well. It serves us well to hearken back to the objection he is laboring to answer: "Has God's word to Israel failed?" (see Rom. 9:6). His answer is No! All Israel has to do to regain the blessings of her heritage is believe—"Everyone who calls on the name of the Lord will be saved" (Rom. 10:13). But calling on the name of the Lord does not happen in a vacuum. Paul outlines for the believers in Rome how God saves people. It is not through the evidence of his handiwork in creation (Rom. 1:20). It is not through works or the law (Rom. 9:32). Rather, it is through the preaching of the gospel.

10:14a. Calling requires faith. **How . . . can they call on the one they have not believed in?** In the Old Testament, calling on the name of the Lord was a metaphor for worship and prayer (Gen. 4:26; 12:8; Ps. 116:4). No one can call out to God who has not believed in him.

10:14b. Faith requires hearing. **And how can they believe in the one of whom they have not heard?** More than anything else, this question is the crux of all missiological activity since the first century. God has ordained that people have to hear (or read, or otherwise understand the content of) the word of God in order to be saved. One who knows the gospel must communicate it to one who does not know it.

10:14c. Hearing requires preaching. **And how can they hear without someone preaching to them?** Since no other media except the human voice was of practical value in spreading the gospel in the first century, **preaching** is Paul's method of choice. And yet, in the media-rich day in which we minister, has anything replaced preaching as the most effective way to communicate the gospel? We thank God for the printed page, and even for cutting-edge presentations of the gospel circling the globe on the internet. But it is still the human voice that cracks with passion, the human eye that wells with tears of gratitude, and the human frame that shuffles to the podium, bent from a lifetime of service to the gospel, that reaches the needy human heart most readily. Hearing may not *require* **preaching** in person today, but it always benefits from it.

10:15. Preaching requires sending. **And how can they preach unless they are sent?** Even when his servants were unwilling (e.g., Jonah), God has been sending the message of salvation to the ends of the earth from the beginning. Paul, a "sent one" (apostle, *apostolos*), was sent to the Gentiles, and he needed the church at Rome to help him. But he also wanted them to be available for God to send them. There were many, many Jews in Rome who were still stumbling over the stone in the path of salvation. How would they ever call on the name of the Lord unless someone is sent? Paul wants the church at Rome to get in step with those who have borne good news to Israel before, most specifically those who brought the good news of their deliverance from captivity in Assyria:

Original Context	Isaiah 52:7	Romans 10:15	Paul's Application
"Good news" in its earliest contexts was that of victory in battle. In Isaiah it is deliverance from captivity in Assyria (cf. Isa. 52:4, 11–12), a type of the coming deliverance from sin.	How beautiful on the mountains are the feet of those who bring good news, who proclaim peace, who bring good tidings, who proclaim salvation, who say to Zion, "Your God reigns!"	And how can they preach unless they are sent? As it is written, "How beautiful are the feet of those who bring good news!"	Just as the "good news" was delivered to Israel in the Old Testament, so it still must be delivered in Paul's day. It is a different gospel—a better one—of permanent deliverance from captivity to sin.

Six key terms, taken in reverse order, summarize God's plan for taking the good news of the gospel to those in need: send, preach, hear, believe, call, saved.

Ⓓ The Assumption of the Gospel Is Personal Responsibility (10:16–21)

SUPPORTING IDEA: *Unbelief is the result of the choice not to believe.*

With a final barrage of scriptures from the Old Testament, Paul proves his point that, in spite of sovereign election from God's side of the equation, Israel is in a state of unbelief by her own choice. Personal responsibility is part of the ministry of the gospel, both in delivering it and in choosing whether or not to receive it. God's responsibility was to get "the gospel" to Israel; it was Israel's responsibility to act on it.

10:16–18. Unfortunately, **not all the Israelites accepted the good news** (the obvious implication being that some did—the remnant; cf. Rom. 9:27; 11:5,25). Paul uses a situation in Isaiah's day to illustrate:

Original Context	Isaiah 53:1	Romans 10:16	Paul's Application
Isaiah was proclaiming good news of salvation to Israel (Is. 52:7,10) but at the same time was questioning whether any would believe.	Who has believed our message and to whom has the arm of the LORD been revealed?	For Isaiah says, "Lord, who has believed our message?"	Paul's application of this verse is the same as Isaiah's, just a few centuries later. Israel once again was hearing the good news, but not believing.

The apostle John agreed with Paul's assessment of Israel's condition. Even though the Israelites saw Jesus' miracles with their own eyes, "they still would not believe in him" (John 12:37). John then says this was in fulfillment of Isaiah 53:1, just as Paul did. Paul then reiterates what he said in verses 14–15, that faith can only come through hearing **the message, and the message is heard through the word of Christ. The word of Christ** here is perhaps best taken as "the spoken words about Christ," referring to the preaching of the gospel. **Word** is *rhema,* the uttered or spoken word as opposed to *logos,* the revealed word as expression of thought. A. T. Robertson has *christou* as an objective genitive (Robertson, 4:390), yielding "the spoken message about Christ."

Is it possible that Israel did not hear—either in Isaiah's day, in Jesus' day, or in Paul's day? Paul answers as if the answer would be obvious to anyone who cared to look: **Of course they [heard]**—and he uses another Old Testament quote to prove it, with another fresh application:

Original Context	Psalm 19:4	Romans 10:18	Paul's Application
In its direct application, this psalm supports Paul's contention in Romans 1:20 that creation proves the existence of God.	Their voice goes out into all the earth, their words to the ends of the world. In the heavens he has pitched a tent for the sun,	Their voice has gone out into all the earth, their words to the ends of the world.	Paul uses the "voice" of creation as an analogy for how the gospel has spread to the end of the (Jews') world.

If we parallel Paul's argument in Romans 1:20 with his argument here (Ps. 19:4 being the common element between the two), then just as all people everywhere "are without excuse" (Rom. 1:20) concerning the existence of God, so Jews everywhere are without excuse concerning the existence of their Messiah and his work. Having answered a first objection to Israel's lack of responsibility, Paul answers a second.

10:19–20. Did Israel not understand? Paul calls Moses and Isaiah to the witness stand to show, by way of logical deduction, that Israel cannot claim an inability to understand God's will through his message. The point that both of them make is this: if the Gentiles, who are not a formally constituted people, who have no spiritual background and training, and who neither seek after nor ask for God, can understand God's good news, surely Israel could have—and can!

Original Context	Deuteronomy	Romans 10:19	Paul's Application
Deuteronomy 32 contains the Song of Moses, where Moses speaks for God about Israel's spiritual future. Numerous Gentile peoples, devoid of spiritual understanding, would still "understand" the will of God and discipline Israel.	32:21 They made me jealous by what is no god and angered me with their worthless idols. I will make them envious by those who are not a people; I will make them angry by a nation that has no understanding.	Again I ask: Did Israel not understand? First, Moses says, "I will make you envious by those who are not a nation; I will make you angry by a nation that has no understanding."	Paul is not simply reciting history by quoting Moses. He is provoking envy in Israel by reminding them that God has used those with no understanding in his elective purposes, whereas Israel is rejecting God's purposes.

Original Context	Isaiah 65:1	Romans 10:20	Paul's Application
God is answering a prayer of Isaiah to return to rebellious Israel. Those to whom God reveals himself appear to be Israelites who had formerly rejected God.	"I revealed myself to those who did not ask for me; I was found by those who did not seek me. To a nation that did not call on my name, I said, 'Here am I, here am I.'"	And Isaiah boldly says, "I was found by those who did not seek me; I revealed myself to those who did not ask for me."	Paul once again (cf. his use of Hos. 1:10; 2:23 in Rom. 9:25–26) applies passages dealing with Israel to God's inclusion of the Gentiles in his salvation purposes.

Paul had earlier in Romans (2:19–20) accused the Jews of boasting about being "a guide for the blind, a light for those who are in the dark, an instructor of the foolish, a teacher of infants" and yet "God's name is blasphemed among the Gentiles" because of them (Rom. 2:24). This is his very point in these verses. Those who had been given understanding in every conceivable way by God, both under the old covenant and the new covenant, were now being shown to be the foolish ones. Those whom the Jews had accused of being foolish and infants—the Gentiles—were now coming into fellowship with the God of Israel in spite of their lack of spiritual sophistication. In terms of the opportunity for understanding, Israel had no excuse for her unbelief.

10:21. Paul cites one final verse and applies it to Israel's "current" situation in the exact same manner as it was originally written:

Original Context	Isaiah 65:2	Romans 10:21	Paul's Application
Isaiah 65:1–7 is an awful condemnation of Old Testament Israel's spiritual practices and attitudes. Verse 2 summarizes God's perspective on his attempts to reach them.	All day long I have held out my hands to an obstinate people, who walk in ways not good, pursuing their own imaginations.	But concerning Israel he says, "All day long I have held out my hands to a disobedient and obstinate people."	There are parallels between the arrogance of Israel in Isaiah's day and the Pharisees' arrogance in Paul's day. God was still holding out his hands to a disobedient people.

The context of this final passage cited by Paul reveals the spiritual pride, resulting in disobedience, that was the hallmark of Israel up through Paul's day. In Isaiah's day, the leaders of Israel thought they were too good to associate with others (Isa. 65:5), the "sinners" of their day. Remarkably, they displayed this same attitude in Jesus' day (Matt. 9:11; Luke 7:39; 18:9–12). Those sinners, the downtrodden in Israel and Gentiles without spiritual understanding, were the very ones who were finding their way into the kingdom of God by faith in Christ. All the while, Paul's heart, reflecting the heart of God, was breaking over the unbelief of God's chosen people.

> **MAIN IDEA REVIEW:** *Israel's present state of unbelief is due to her lack of acceptance of the good news of salvation by faith.*

III. CONCLUSION

A Prodigal People

The beloved story of the prodigal son (Luke 15:11–32) offers insights into the lamentable condition of the nation of Israel—and specifically, God's relationship to Israel as will be revealed in Romans 11. While Jesus did not tell the story of the prodigal as an illustration of Israel's woes, the father in the story sets the stage for the question Paul asks in Romans 11:1: "Did God reject his people?" It might appear that he has, echoing the objection first raised by Paul in Romans 9:6 concerning the faithfulness of God and his promises.

In the story, a son, who apparently has every advantage of prosperity and security that a wealthy father could provide, decides to squander what he is destined to receive. And mind you, what he is given is purely by grace, for the father is under no obligation to divide his estate between his two sons before his death. But he does, allowing what he probably knows is going to be a wanton spree of wasteful living by the son. The son takes his position, privilege, and possessions in hand and heads out on his own, becoming a total embarrassment to the father and his family. Should we think that no word filters back from the "distant country" where the son has gone? That the father is living in complete ignorance of his son's activities? That the father is not tempted to go and plead with his son to change his ways?

We do not know how long the father waited chronologically, but it was long enough for the son to have "spent everything" he had. The father allowed the son to sink deeper and deeper into the mire of his own making, until he had nothing. Even the food that the pigs ate began to look appealing. Here he was, a Jewish son of privilege, beginning to admire what the Gentiles among whom he lived possessed. Even the Gentiles' pigs lived better than he was at the moment.

We could ask, along with Paul in Romans 11:1, "Did the father reject his son?" And answer just as Paul did: "By no means!" The father, in his wisdom, waited until the son's hardness of heart had run its course; waited until the son "came to his senses" (Luke 15:17). We know that the father's heart was still full of love for his son because of the watch he kept for him. "But while he was still a long way off, his father saw him and was filled with compassion for him; he ran to his son, threw his arms around him and kissed him" (Luke 15:20).

Israel, for centuries, has been in a "distant country," both geographically and spiritually, from her father. She is "still a long way off," but that does not mean that her father is not looking for her return. The discordant spiritual note on which Romans 10 ends will find resolution and harmonious conclusion as Paul moves into the next chapter. We will find the reasons why God, in his wisdom, let Israel leave home, and the evidence that Israel, while "still a long way off," will one day return. Most of all, it will be clearly demonstrated that, chapter 10 notwithstanding, God has not rejected his people.

Paul continues, in painstaking and heartbreaking detail, to inform the church at Rome about the gospel. He is committing to writing things that, as far as we know, had never been revealed to the human race about the divine plan of God for the human race. Whether the Roman believers understood not only the magnitude, but the privilege, of what they were receiving from Paul is unknown. How they responded to it is unknown. Perhaps from our perspective of history we have a better appreciation than they would from their vantage point of history-in-the-making.

But here is the question for the church today: Do we realize the magnitude and privilege of having the curtain raised by Paul on the stage of world history? Do we stand in awe at even what our limited understanding can grasp of the ways and works of God in dealing with the human race? Or have we resigned such affairs to the domain of scholars in ivory towers, thinking them irrelevant to the church at large?

It needs to be asked daily, "How can they hear without someone preaching to them" (Rom. 10:14). Paul went to bed at night praying and dreaming about those in Spain and the regions beyond who had yet to hear the gospel. About whom do we pray and dream? Do we stand, like God the father and the father of the prodigal, with outstretched hands to a disobedient and obstinate people? Are we praying and dreaming about the salvation of a spouse, a loved one, a neighbor, a coworker, an unreached people group, a country?

If not, then we have become more like the prodigal's older brother, more like the leaders of Israel in Isaiah's day, more like the Pharisees in Paul's day. We have become smug in our spiritual condition, proud of where we stand, and too good to reach out to and associate with those who do not yet know the love of the father. These verses in Romans 9–11 are not about theology (though they are theological). They are not about doctrine (though they are doctrinal). They are not about pedagogy (though they are pedagogical). They are about lost people—*a* lost people, to be specific, God's chosen people. When our hearts beat with Paul's over the lostness of Israel and the Gentiles, we will have received all the gospel that he is giving. We need to live in these chapters until that day dawns.

PRINCIPLES

- Pursuing spiritual ends by works leads to stumbling and falling.
- Church leaders should have a passion for the lost.
- Zeal is dangerous unless properly informed and directed.
- Anyone who believes and confesses Christ can be saved.
- The gospel must be sent and proclaimed for people to be saved.
- God's grace is more persistent than obstinance and disobedience.

APPLICATIONS

- Is there any spiritual work in which I am currently involved which makes me vulnerable to stumbling and falling because of the absence of faith?
- If passion is contagious, how likely are those I lead to be infected with a passion for winning the lost?
- Assuming I am zealous for the kingdom of God, is my zeal properly informed and directed at kingdom goals?
- Is there anyone whom I have concluded is beyond being saved?
- Do I see my errands, my trips, my daily movings about as opportunities to deliver the gospel to those who may not have heard?
- Are my hands outstretched to an obstinate or disobedient one with whom I associate? If not, why not?

IV. LIFE APPLICATION

How Beautiful Are the Feet

As we opened, we close with help from Donald Grey Barnhouse, one-time pastor of the Tenth Presbyterian Church in Philadelphia. He was told a story by a missionary in western Africa that illustrates the heart of one who is gripped by a passion for spreading the gospel (condensed from Boice, 3:1249–1251):

It seems that an African man who had become a radiant Christian believer was also afflicted by the dreaded elephantiasis disease. This loathsome condition hardens and enlarges the flesh of the lower legs and feet so that they often appear as solid columns of flesh from the knees down, sometimes twelve to fifteen inches in diameter. It is a painful and restrictive condition, making simple walking a laborious challenge. But the man was so appreciative of the grace of God that had come into his life that he thought nothing of the pain of his condition. He went from hut to hut in his west African village, sharing the good news of the gospel, knowing that none could believe unless they heard the gospel. He shuffled and hobbled on his afflicted limbs day after day until all had heard the good news.

Once he had evangelized his entire village, he began a painful, daily trek to a village two miles distant, not being able to bear the thought that some were there who had not heard the gospel of the grace of God. He would start early in the morning and walk to the nearby village, go from hut to hut, then walk home. This process he repeated until every hut in that village had received the good news of the gospel.

With no one else to tell about Christ, he asked his pastor and the missionary about going to the next closest village, a larger village located ten miles from his own. They both discouraged him from considering the journey, given his condition. But one day, his relatives awoke to find him gone. It was not until later that the full story came out, related by the inhabitants of the distant village.

It took him until noon to traverse the ten-mile distance to the village, and when he arrived, his leathery stumps were bloody and swollen. Not wasting time even to eat, he spent the rest of the day in the village going from hut to hut telling people about the grace of God. The sun was setting when he set out for his own village. Somehow he made it through the pitch-black jungle, falling upon the missionary's porch at midnight. The missionary, who was also a doctor, summoned help and they lifted the poor, semi-conscious man into the dispensary. The doctor related later how his own tears mingled with the salve with which he bathed the beautiful feet of this wounded gospel messenger. Without counting the cost to himself, this man lived out the words of the apostle Paul, "And how can they hear without someone preaching to them?" (Rom. 10:14). Feet that in the eyes of the world could best be described as horrific had become the beautiful feet of one who brings the good news (Rom. 10:15).

It is ironic that many Christians, who go to great lengths to dress their feet in the world's latest fashion, have not the beauty of a diseased African saint who could not rest until all within his reach had heard the gospel. How beautiful are our feet? How beautiful are the feet of the church of Jesus Christ at large? May we be people of passion more than fashion as we take the good news of the gospel to a waiting world.

V. PRAYER

Heavenly Father, thank you for not pulling back your outstretched hands until I responded to your gospel of salvation. Thank you that your grace and forgiveness were sufficient to include me in your kingdom. My prayer is to echo Paul's, that Israel might be saved. Pour out your Spirit and your mercy upon your chosen people, that they may begin turning to you. Make me a messenger of the gospel to them, and to all who have yet to believe. Amen.

VI. DEEPER DISCOVERIES

A. The Use of the Old Testament in the New Testament

As mentioned in the commentary, this chapter of Paul's letter to the Romans has more quotations from the Old Testament than any other single chapter in his collection of epistles. Some guidelines for understanding the use of the Old Testament in the New Testament would be helpful for this chapter and for chapter 11, where Paul will continue his dependence upon passages dealing with God and Israel. (The following draws heavily on "The Old Testament in the New Testament," found in Elwell, *Dictionary of Biblical Theology*, pp. 582–585, which is recommended for further study.)

First, some statistics: the fourth edition of the United Bible Societies' Greek Testament (1993) lists 343 Old Testament quotations in the New Testament, as well as no fewer than 2,309 allusions and verbal parallels. The books most used are Psalms (79 quotations, 333 allusions), and Isaiah (66 quotations, 348 allusions). In the Book of Revelation, there are no formal quotations at all, but no fewer than 620 allusions.

Second, styles of usage: first-century literary forms and function generally governed the framework of how New Testament writers used the Old Testament. Common styles included *midrash*, an expanded narrative with interpretive comments inserted (e.g., Stephen's speech in Acts 7:2–53); *pesher*, where Old Testament texts are connected with contemporary events (e.g., Acts 2:16; Rom. 10:8); and *gezerah shawa*, where two or more verses using the same word in different parts of the Bible are interpreted in the light of each other (e.g., Heb. 4:3–7).

The most critical (and controversial) part of understanding the use of the Old Testament in the New is when New Testament authors seem to give new meanings to Old Testament passages. This is seen several times in Romans 10 when Paul applies to the Gentiles something originally written to Jews, or when he applies to the gospel something originally describing the nonverbal testimony of creation to the existence of God. The key element in this interpretive freedom is, of course, based on the increased revelation given to New Testament writers.

It is clear from the New Testament that mysteries were written about in the Old Testament which were not understood by their authors. For example, Paul is the apostle to whom is revealed the mystery of Jew and Gentile united in one body by faith in Christ. Other examples include Matthew's greater understanding of Old Testament messianic prophecies in light of the revelation of Christ, the use by the author of Hebrews of quotations from the Psalms having to do with the Davidic kingship that he applies to Christ, and John's use of prophecies from Isaiah and Ezekiel in describing the new heavens and earth and the temple. All of these are examples of "Aha!" experiences that the gift of hindsight brings to the Old Testament.

Paul's use of the Old Testament in Romans 9–11 is one of the best examples of expansion and fulfillment (not reinterpretation) of the Old Testament. It is hard to imagine Moses and Isaiah disagreeing with Paul's use of what they wrote had they been alongside the apostle and had his perspective.

B. The "Word of Faith" (10:8)

The phrase occurring in Romans 10:8, "word of faith," has given rise to an entire movement in Christendom referred to by many as the "Word of Faith Movement." It is based on a supposed understanding of the Greek word *rhema,* and the dynamics associated with it, in the New Testament.

The chief word used for "word" in the New Testament is *logos,* which occurs 330 times. It is a derivative of the most common word for "speak," *lego.* *Rhema* occurs much less frequently: sixty-eight times in the New Testament, eight times in Paul's epistles, and four times in Romans, all in chapter 10 (vv. 8 [twice], 17,18). While the two words can be similar in meaning, *logos* refers more often to an idea or a concept, while *rhema* is most often used of a message spoken or written that is intended to suggest a consequence or a result. If *logos* is static, then *rhema* is dynamic. Thus, when Paul uses the word in Romans 10, he uses it in all four instances to refer to the gospel, the message of faith in Christ. The *rhema* is more than just the concept of faith in Christ; it is the message about Christ intended to produce faith in the hearer. It is a word of faith that is "near you . . . in your mouth and in your heart" (10:8), designed to result in faith in those who hear (10:17).

From this concept of a word that produces results has sprung the belief in the "Word of Faith Movement" in "speaking into existence" that which faith conceives. "What you believe, you can receive" has become a creed of the "Word of Faith Movement." The fact that Jesus said that man does not live on bread alone "but on every word [*rhema*] that proceeds out of the mouth of God" has suggested to some that the promises of God are to become reality for us as we speak forth that which God has spoken forth. These ideas, coupled with Paul's teaching on "confession" in the same context (Rom. 10:9–10), added the dimension of "positive confession" to the word of faith. If we have not experienced what the *rhema* of God has promised, we are to confess that it is ours by a word of faith until God's *rhema* is actualized in our existence.

While commendable for its emphasis on faith, this movement has been criticized for its dependence on the writings of E. W. Kenyon (1867–1948), who incorporated a metaphysical view into his biblical teachings. Kenyon believed that the spirit world controls and shapes the physical world, and that the Christian should speak that which he or she wants to occur. Speaking it with sufficient words (*rhema*) of faith will cause the physical world to conform to the spiritual (faith) world. This obviously moves the believer into the realm of God, who spoke into existence the creation from nothing. Not surprisingly, proclaiming Christians as "mini-Gods" is another outgrowth of this movement. The writings of Kenyon are the foundation upon which modern "Word of Faith Movement" teachers base much of their teaching—teachers such as Charles Capps, Kenneth Hagin, Kenneth and Gloria Copeland, and Fred Price.

C. Antinomy

Throughout the section of Romans where Paul deals with the past, present, and future of Israel, the facts of God's sovereignty in election and man's responsibility to believe come face to face with one another. Theologians and philosophers refer to such a "conflict" of ideas as an antinomy (from Gr. *anti*, against, and *nomos*, law). Norman Geisler points out that the word *antinomy* is used in two ways: first, to refer to an *actual* contradiction, paradox, or antithesis; something which is absurd or impossible; second, to an *apparent* contradiction, "as in the mysteries of the Christian faith." In this sense, an antinomy is something that goes beyond reason, but against reason. It is not irrational, but transrational (see Geisler, *Encyclopedia*, p. 28).

In the case of divine election and human responsibility, the Bible clearly says that both are true; therefore, there is no contradiction. The apparent contradiction comes only from the human point of view. What must be remembered is that these truths are not human in origin, but divine. Because something appears contradictory to the human mind only means that a human would not have designed it that way, not that it is false. What originates in the mind of God may be reasonable to humans and it may not. When it is not, it must be remembered that both God's ways and his thoughts are higher than ours (Isa. 55:8–9).

D. Lordship Salvation (10:9)

Paul's statement that confessing "Jesus is Lord" (along with believing) has given rise to the term "Lordship salvation"—the view that there is only one Christ, one that is both Savior and Lord, and that a believer cannot accept Christ as Savior without also submitting to his lordship as well. In this view, a Christian and a disciple are synonymous, not separate. Spiritual growth and maturity is a sign of new life, and if there is no growth or maturity it is an evidence of the absence of life. The historic view of the Christian church has been "Lordship salvation," or, more simply, salvation by faith in the Lord and Savior Jesus Christ (the "Lordship salvation" term was coined by adherents of the opposite view).

The opposite view—that a person can become a Christian simply on the basis of belief in the facts of Christ's life, death, and resurrection, without any change in life or outward manifestation—is actually the newer view. It flourished through a body of Christians called Sandemanians, or Glasites, which flourished from 1725 until around 1900 in England and the United States. Robert Sandeman, the son-in-law of John Glas, the founder of the group, held that mere assent to the work of Christ is all that is necessary for salvation. His position was in reaction to a book by James Hervey, *Theron and Aspasio* (1755), a Calvinistic evangelical work that Sandeman alleged made faith a work of man by which man earns salvation.

In the United States, variations of this view have been popularized in the twentieth century primarily by those who are concerned with "frontloading" the gospel with the conditions of discipleship. A balance is needed here that acknowledges the lordship and authority of Jesus without making 100 percent surrender to him (who of us has truly attained this?) a condition of salvation.

VII. TEACHING OUTLINE

A. INTRODUCTION

1. Lead Story: Good News, Bad News
2. Context: Romans 9–11 is a section that is crucial to understanding, and maintaining confidence in, the gospel promises of God. At the end of chapter 8, Paul said that nothing could separate the believer from the love of God in Christ. In chapters 9–11, he is proving that Israel is not separated from God, appearances notwithstanding. The sovereign interplay between divine election and human responsibility is working out the preservation of a remnant of believers in Israel, to whom God's promises stand, while the Gentiles are being brought into his body at the same time. The result of God's plan is that "all Israel will be saved, as it is written" (Rom. 11:26).
3. Transition: In chapter 10 of Romans, Paul follows his presentation of election in Israel's past (chap. 9) with her present condition of unbelief. He maintains that for all people, but Israel in particular, they must believe the gospel, the gospel must be preached to them, and they must accept personal responsibility for having not believed the gospel.

B. COMMENTARY

1. Israel's Present Condition: Unbelief Through Zeal Without Knowledge (9:30–10:4)
    a. The difference between Israel and the Gentiles (9:30–31)
    b. Where Israel failed (9:32–33)
    c. The danger of zeal without knowledge (10:1–4)
2. The Instrument of the Gospel Is Personal Faith (10:5–13)
    a. Righteousness through the law (10:5)
    b. Righteousness by faith (10:6–11)
    c. The promise of righteousness by faith (10:12–13)
3. The Vehicle of the Gospel Is Proclamation (10:14–15)
    a. Calling requires faith (10:14a)
    b. Faith requires hearing (10:14b)
    c. Hearing requires preaching (10:14c)
    d. Preaching requires sending (10:15)
4. The Assumption of the Gospel Is Personal Responsibility (10:16–21)
    a. Israel received the gospel (10:16–18)
    b. Israel is responsible for her lack of understanding (10:19–20)
    c. Israel chose not to believe the gospel (10:21)

C. CONCLUSION: HOW BEAUTIFUL ARE THE FEET

VIII. ISSUES FOR DISCUSSION

1. Given your personal experience in churches you have attended, how burdened is the church today for the salvation of Israel? How well informed is the average believer about where Israel fits in the present and future of God's salvation story?
2. Considering all the Christian preaching that goes on in the world today, how much of it is in the spirit of Romans 10:14–16? That is, how much preaching is preaching to the lost? How clearly has the church separated its two tasks of proclaiming the gospel to the lost (evangelism) and teaching the Bible to the saved (edification)? What evidence of strategic planning and thinking do you see on how to reach the lost?
3. Does a deceived church know it is deceived? How easy would it be for the Christian church to fall into the same sin as Israel (spiritual pride) and find God turning to "lesser" groups to accomplish his purposes (e.g., to what part of the body of Christ has God turned in recent years to launch the most aggressive missionary outreaches in history)? How can the church protect itself from spiritual pride?

Romans 11:1–36

Israel's Future Vindicates the Gospel

"*F*rom first to last, and not merely in the epilogue, Christianity is eschatology, is hope, forward looking and forward moving, and therefore also revolutionizing and transforming the present."

Jürgen Moltman

Romans 11:1–36

IN A NUTSHELL

*P*aul's seemingly discouraging assessment of the past and present of Israel's spiritual life now changes tempo to an upbeat prediction about her future—all Israel will be saved!

Israel's Future Vindicates the Gospel

I. INTRODUCTION

The Bible in a Word

*F*or the last two centuries, a story has been told that is a fitting introduction to Paul's topic in Romans 11. Frederick the Great, king of Prussia from 1740 to 1786 (Prussia occupied the territory of modern-day northern Germany and Poland), asked for proof that the Bible is true in a discussion with his court chaplain. Frederick, under the influence of the atheistic French philosopher Voltaire, had become skeptical of Christianity and of the reliability of the Bible. His words to the chaplain supposedly were, "If your Bible is really true, it ought to be capable of very easy proof. So often, when I have asked for proof of the inspiration of the Bible, I have been given some large tome that I have neither the time nor desire to read. If your Bible is really from God, you should be able to demonstrate the fact simply. Give me proof for the inspiration of the Bible in a word."

One word to prove the reliability of the Bible? What would you have said if faced with the same challenge? Love? Sin? Grace? Guilt? Conscience? Surely the best one-word defense of the Bible's reliability would be a theological word, something that probed the depth of the intellect and touched the center of the soul. While perhaps equipped to offer a profound term for the king's consideration, the chaplain resorted to what was plain and obvious—something that all the world could see.

"Your Majesty, it is possible for me to answer your request literally," the chaplain replied. "I can give you the proof you ask for in one word."

Amazed, the king asked, "What is this magic word that carries such a weight of proof?" he asked.

"Israel," the chaplain said. Frederick the Great of Prussia responded only with silence (story told in Boice, 3:1375–1376).

Indeed, Israel is considered to be nothing less than a miracle as far as nations are concerned. The detailed records we have of this nation are beyond that of any other. We know when the nation was founded, why, and by whom. We have a detailed written record of her ancient and modern history, and focused accounts of things experienced by her people during her decentralized history between the ancient and modern eras. Her homeland is the same as it has been for thousands of years. Her language is still intact.

And her religion, while only a minority practice it faithfully today, is unchanged in its tenets as laid out in its original source documents.

Those facts would be remarkable by themselves, and in fact suggest that the nation has had smooth sailing which has allowed its continuity and provided longevity over the centuries. Nothing, of course, could be further from the truth—and therein lies the miracle. Israel has not survived as a nation *because* of her fortunes; she has survived *in spite of* her fortunes. Consider the primary points in Israel's history (ancient dates from the NIV Study Bible "Old Testament Chronology" chart):

- 2100 B.C.: Abram heeds God's call and moves from Mesopotamia to Canaan; the nation is begun with Abram.

- 1876 B.C.: Abraham's seventy descendants go from Canaan to Egypt to escape a famine; they are enslaved by the Egyptians for nearly four hundred years. During this time they become a people numbering perhaps two million.

- 1446 B.C.: God redeems his people from slavery and establishes them as a nation at Mt. Sinai by giving them a complete civil, liturgical, and moral code of laws by which they are to govern themselves. The land of Canaan, promised originally to Abraham, is to be their home forever.

- 722 B.C.: The ten northern tribes of Israel are decimated by the Assyrians, with a large portion of the population carried into captivity in Assyria. Most never return to their homeland.

- 586 B.C.: The capital of the nation, Jerusalem, is destroyed by the Babylonians, and the population of the two southern tribes is carried into captivity in Babylon. The land and the nation lie fallow for seventy years.

- 538–432 B.C.: Groups of exiles return from Babylon and rebuild Jerusalem. The nation endures four hundred years of conflict and infighting.

- A.D. 70: The capital, Jerusalem, is destroyed by the Romans. Most of the population flees their homeland, seeking safety in parts of Asia Minor and Mesopotamia.

- A.D. 70–1940: The nation is deconstituted, scattered primarily throughout Europe and Asia. Jerusalem and the homeland are the scene of scores of military conflicts, and are ruled off and on by Turks, Muslims, and Western powers—but not Israel.

- A.D. 1940s: The Holocaust in Nazi Germany (and other pogroms in Eastern Europe and Russia) results in the death of millions of Jews.

- A.D. 1948: The Zionist movement receives permission from the United Nations to reestablish Israel as a nation in her homeland.

By 1967 Israel has regained control of Jerusalem and the main portions of her promised homeland.

- A.D. 1948–present: Millions of Jews from all over the world return to their ancient homeland, with more arriving each year. The nation is reconstituted and functions once again, four thousand years after its founding, as a major player in world affairs.

It is obvious from the above chronology that Israel could have vanished from the world's stage many times in the course of her history. The fact that she has not is what caused Frederick the Great's chaplain to cite "Israel" as his one-word justification for the Bible's truthfulness and reliability. No other nation extant at the time of Israel's founding has survived what she has survived: genocide, removal for nearly two millennia from the homeland, persecution, the repeated destruction and rebuilding of the capital city. Israel's existence could be classified as miraculous, but in truth only God does miracles. How do we know that it is God who is behind Israel's continued recoveries from near-extinction?

Out of hundreds of Scripture references pertaining to God and his relationship to and plan for Israel, perhaps God's words through Jeremiah say it best:

> This is what the LORD says, he who appoints the sun to shine by day, who decrees the moon and stars to shine by night, who stirs up the sea so that its waves roar—the LORD Almighty is his name: "Only if these decrees vanish from my sight," declares the LORD, "will the descendants of Israel ever cease to be a nation before me." This is what the LORD says: "Only if the heavens above can be measured and the foundations of the earth below be searched out will I reject all the descendants of Israel because of all they have done," declares the LORD (Jer. 31:35–37).

From those promises, it would seem that as long as the sun, moon, and stars continue making their appointed rounds, and until the universe is mapped and the center of the earth is explored, Israel will never cease to be a nation. Thus is revealed that the same person that is behind all legitimate miracles is behind the miracle of Israel: God. Israel's existence after four thousand years is one of the greatest testimonies that the words the Bible credits to God are indeed his. But Israel's miraculous story is not over yet.

Referring back to the above chronology, about the time Paul was writing his letter to the Romans (A.D. 57) Israel was in a state of national disarray. An initial period of persecution of Jewish believers, in which Paul participated, occurred after the resurrection of Christ. Many Jews fled throughout Asia Minor. Then, only thirteen years later, the boot heel of Rome came down on Jerusalem in the person of the Roman general Titus, and the nation was formally conquered. The questions Paul addresses in Romans—"Has God gone back on his word to Israel?"—were legitimate even in A.D. 57, and begged for an answer in A.D. 70. Though Paul was martyred in A.D. 67/68, Titus's crushing of Israel in A.D. 70 would not have caused Paul to change what he wrote to the Roman believers in A.D. 57. He knew the promises of God, and knew that Israel's future was as predictable as her past was observable.

Therefore, in Romans 11, Paul brings to a conclusion his three-chapter summary on the salvation history of Israel. He is demonstrating to the believers in Rome that the gospel has been at work in Israel—past, present, and future—just as it is presently at work among the Gentiles. Most importantly in chapter 11, he is going to prove that God's word to Israel has not been rescinded—that Israel's greatest day of salvation is still ahead. What seems to be a reduction in the number of Israelites who are sharing in covenant blessings is the result of unbelief in Israel. Israel's unbelief caused God to allow a partial hardening to come over the nation so that the blessings of salvation might be taken directly to the Gentiles by God's messengers (like Paul), a task originally assigned to Israel. Then, when the full number of the Gentiles has come in (to the kingdom of God), "all Israel will be saved" (Rom. 11:26).

The Bible is not a fortune-telling book, but it is a fact-telling book. Israel has a past, present, and a future as a nation. The person who denies the facts of Israel's future, as laid out in Romans 11, would be as foolish as one who denied the facts of her past and present.

II. COMMENTARY

Israel's Future Vindicates the Gospel

MAIN IDEA: *The gospel, the power of God unto salvation for the Jew first and then for the Gentile, will be dramatically vindicated by events in Israel's future.*

A God Has Always Preserved the Elect in Israel (11:1–10)

SUPPORTING IDEA: *Paul in the New Testament, and the remnant of Israel in the Old Testament, proves that God has not rejected his chosen people.*

11:1. Of the fourteen times Paul uses the exclamation **by no means!** (*me genoito*), ten of them are in the epistle to the Romans (in addition to this verse see 3:4,6,31; 6:2,15; 7:7,13; 9:14; 11:11. See also this commentary on Rom. 6:2 for more details on *me genoito*). The frequency of this phrase in Romans is evidence of the controversial nature of Paul's content. Usually it is in response to the objections or questions of a fictional objector whom Paul's diatribe format calls forth. But here, Paul is asking and answering his own question so as to continue the treatment on Israel which began in Romans 9:1.

Specifically, his statement that God is continually holding out his hands to "a disobedient and obstinate people" (Israel; Rom. 10:21) begs the question, **Did God reject his people?** Paul uses himself as "Exhibit A" to prove that God did not **reject his people.** The fact that Paul, **an Israelite . . . a descendant of Abraham . . . from the tribe of Benjamin** (cf. Phil. 3:5), is also an apostle of Jesus Christ, sent to deliver the mystery of the gospel to the Gentiles, proves that God has not abandoned Israel! If Paul were the only Jew on earth who believed in Jesus Christ, it would be proof positive that God had not rejected his people.

Paul's statement is more than a piece of evidence in an argument. It is a confirmation of what he has been teaching about election. In other words, no one comes to faith in Christ by happenstance. If a person does not believe in Christ, it is evidence of the hand of God in divine, sovereign election, and if someone does believe in Christ, it is likewise evidence of the hand of God. The fact that many Jews had not believed in Christ is evidence that they were not the elect of God. But the fact that Paul has believed means he was foreknown, predestined, called, justified, and glorified (Rom. 8:29–30). And if God called Paul, a Jew, it is obviously evidence that God has not abandoned the Jews.

The fact that God has never totally rejected the Jews is evident from Paul's spiritual life, but it can also be proved from the darkest days of Israel's history.

11:2–4. Paul lends further support to the idea that foreknowledge by God is synonymous with choosing, not simply with knowing in a cognitive sense. Here, Paul implies that for God to **reject** his people would be to "unchoose" them or "unknow" them. We might paraphrase Paul's words this way: "God did not reject what he selected." Eugene Peterson's *The Message* puts it this way: "God has been too long involved with Israel, has too much invested, to simply wash his hands of them."

Paul's argument is based on an understanding of foreknowledge. To rightly understand what it means that God **foreknew** Israel is to also know that Israel could not have been rejected by God (i.e., had his promises to her broken). The clearest text on the meaning of foreknowledge pertaining to Israel is Amos 3:2a: "You only have I chosen of all the families of the earth." The Hebrew for "chosen" in this verse is *yada'*, to know (rendered also this way by NASB), which is paralleled in the New Testament by *ginosko*, to know, and *proginosko*, to foreknow, used by Paul in Romans 11:2.

Yada' means to know conceptually, by experience, and even by sexual contact. It can imply close familiarity and intimacy, and can approximate the most-used Hebrew word for "choose," *bahar*. In Amos 3:2, the obvious implication is that, if Israel is the only nation on the earth that God knows intimately, it is because he chose them as the people to whom he would reveal himself. This is consistent with his choosing and calling of Abraham, whose descendants make up the nation. *The New International Dictionary of New*

Testament Theology says concerning *yada'*, "When God knows a person (Jer. 1:5) or a people (Amos 3:2) he chooses or elects him. This knowledge, understood as election, is gracious and loving . . . but it demands a personal response" (p. 2:395).

Israel's lack of personal response (at least the response God was looking for) is evident in Deuteronomy 9:24: "You have been rebellious against the LORD ever since I have known (*yada'*) you." The NASB translates it more literally as, "You have been rebellious against the LORD from the day I knew you." This could easily be translated "from the day I chose you" to give it the same sense as Amos 3:2—the intimate relationship that God had in mind for his chosen people Israel.

The upshot of this discussion is that when Paul says in Greek that God **foreknew,** Amos says in Hebrew that he "chose." And Paul says that God has not rejected that which he has chosen to be his own. This verse carries the same meaning as the permanence of marriage in Genesis 2:24 as interpreted by Jesus in Matthew 19:5-6. A man and a woman choose each other, come together ("know" each other intimately), and do not separate from each other after that. The covenant bond between God and Israel is a model for the covenant loyalty between a man and a woman. The key Old Testament word for loyalty in covenant is *hesed* (loyal love), most closely paralleled in the New Testament by *agape* (unconditional love). It is this covenant loyalty that causes God not to reject his people Israel.

Paul cites one of the clearest statements of God's preservation of a remnant of Israelites through whom his covenant blessings would continue to flow by pointing out the experience of **Elijah.** At a time when Elijah thought he was the only prophet left in Israel, God assured him that neither he nor the nation had been forsaken: **I have reserved seven thousand who have not bowed the knee to Baal** (see 1 Kgs. 19:18). Undoubtedly a round number (cf. 2 Sam. 8:4; 1 Kgs. 19:18; 2 Kgs. 24:16; 1 Chr. 29:4; 2 Chr. 15:11; 30:24; Job 1:3; Rev. 11:13), seven thousand represented the divine designation of the faithful part of the nation Israel which God had preserved and who had not entered into Baal worship (meaning that the majority of the nation had).

It is important to point out the differences in the two circumstances in Israel's history—in Elijah's day and in Paul's. To compare the two once again points out God's sovereign involvement in election:

	The question:	The answer:
Elijah's Day	Has not Israel rejected her God? (1 Kgs. 18:22; 19:10,14)	No, I have reserved a remnant that has been faithful (1 Kgs. 19:18)

	The question:	The answer:
Paul's Day	Has God rejected his people Israel? (Rom. 11:1)	No, there is a remnant chosen by grace (Rom. 11:5)

Regardless of the perspective from which one views the situation—whether from God's or from man's—the answer is the same: God will fulfill his sovereign purposes in salvation by remaining faithful to his promises and by preserving a remnant in Israel. It is the remnant in the Old Testament to which Paul gave testimony first. He now turns to Israel in the New Testament era.

11:5–6. Just as God preserved a **remnant** of faithful believers in Israel during Elijah's day (as he had done throughout the nation's history; the example with Elijah is cited by Paul as a clear example), so God is preserving a remnant in the nation of Israel even as Paul writes. He had already explained earlier in Romans that election in Israel was based neither on heritage (both Ishmael and Isaac were descendants of Abraham, but only Isaac received the promise; Rom. 9:6–9) nor on merit (while Jacob and Esau were in the womb, before either had done anything good or bad, Jacob was chosen over Esau; Rom. 9:10–13).

Heritage and merit (works) were the two most lofty ideals among religious Jews—the fact that they were descendants of Abraham and zealously kept God's law. As we have seen already, even Paul the Pharisee had placed great confidence in his heritage and merit before God (Phil. 3:4–6). But as God chose in Israel in the Old Testament, so he chooses today—by his "mercy" (Rom. 9:14–16) and **grace**. In other words, it is God's plan that is being worked out in the nation of Israel. He is the one who is ordaining, working out, and ensuring the completion of his plan (see his sovereignty at work in Rom. 8:28–30 on an individual basis).

While there was an election of the nation of Israel as a whole (Amos 3:2), there has constantly been at work a separation, another election, within the nation, by which believers were being separated from unbelievers. In the Old Testament, it did not "depend on man's desire or effort [whether good or bad], but on God's mercy" (Rom. 9:16). In the New Testament, God is continuing his acts of separation/preservation by grace. **And if by grace, then it is no longer by works.**

Paul never lets up on his preaching of the grace of God. Of the 119 mentions of grace in Acts to Revelation, 86 of them occur in Paul's epistles, with 21 of them in Romans. Perhaps nothing arrested Paul as much as the idea that his salvation was by grace (Eph. 2:8)—totally a gift from God. This was so contrary to everything he had learned and practiced up to that point in his life, and yet he found that it was consistent with how God had always acted, even in the "age of law," the Old Testament. To trace Paul's mention of grace in salvation in Romans is to easily understand his mention of it in Romans 11:5–6:

- Romans 1:5: Paul, a Jew, has received grace from God personally.
- Romans 4:16: The promise comes by faith, so that it may be by grace and may be guaranteed to all Abraham's offspring (Jew and Gentile alike).
- Romans 5:2: Those who have received salvation stand in grace.
- Romans 5:15,17: It was God's grace that overcame the sin of Adam and provided redemption for the human race through Christ.
- Romans 5:20: No human sin is so grievous that it has not been overcome by God's grace.
- Romans 5:21: God's grace is the controlling element in salvation history. Grace, not sin, is reigning and will ultimately reign.

It is Paul's emphasis on **grace** that reminds us that salvation is of God. Human beings, being dead in sin, can do nothing to initiate and produce their own salvation. If a **remnant** is going to be preserved in Israel, it is going to be by God's **grace**—*because he has a divine and appointed purpose for Israel to play in the salvation history of the whole world.* It is this realization that Paul wants his readers to understand. Neither in Abraham's day, nor Isaac's, nor Jacob's, nor Elijah's, nor Paul's, nor in ours, was there any reason for God to choose to continue saving some in Israel—except for his **grace**.

Remember from whence we have come since Genesis 12:1–3 when God's promises first were given to Abraham. Following the Flood, and the Tower of Babel, seventy "nations" (people groups) had populated the earth. God, because of mercy and **grace**, wants to take salvation to them all. He chose one man, Abram, and began building a "seventy-first" nation, one that would serve as the light of salvation to the rest who were in darkness (the Gentiles). Though the new nation (Israel) had failed by Paul's time to fulfill God's missionary mandate for them, God's promises to them stood and stand today. In calling out a new people, a spiritual people (the church), made up of both Jews and Gentiles, God continues in the modern day his missionary task of reaching the world with the salvation message.

But, by his **grace**, his promises to Israel stand, and because of his love for the nation and its fathers (see below in Romans 11:28), he preserves a **remnant** of believers by which the nation is kept "alive" until the day when "all Israel will be saved" (Rom. 11:26). This, in a nutshell, is the story Paul is telling to the church in Rome (and to us). Understanding this, it is almost superfluous to say that **if by grace, then it is no longer by works.** Salvation is God's idea and he is working it out according to his plan, which is always by grace.

11:7–10. Paul now raises (for his readers) a very legitimate question: **What then?** That is, "Where do we go from here, Paul? God has elected Israel as a nation, but only elected some of Israel to believe. Why has God done this—and what does the future hold?" Paul's basic answer, which he goes on to explicate in the rest of the chapter, deals with one of the most profound parts of Scripture: the hardening of the nation Israel. Only the **elect**, Paul says, obtained what they were seeking—right standing before God, which they obtained by faith. The rest, pursuing the goal on the basis of works and self-righteousness, did not obtain it and were **hardened** in their sinful ways. This hardening occurred in the Old Testament (and continues today) and was ultimately manifested in both the ten northern and the two southern tribes of Israel being carried into captivity.

The truth is that God gives spiritual wisdom and understanding (Prov. 2:1–8). In fact, spiritual things, apart from the enlightenment of God, are foolishness to humans (1 Cor. 2:1–16). But the truth is also that God hardens against spiritual understanding to keep people from acquiring it, a point that Paul proves by quoting once again the two greatest of Israel's prophets, Moses and Isaiah (Moses calls himself a prophet in Deut. 18:15). Paul puts together a verse based on Deuteronomy 29:4 and Isaiah 29:10 to demonstrate God's active hardening of Israel.

Deuteronomy 29:4 occurs in the context of the renewal of the covenant for the new generation of Israelites following the forty years of wandering in the desert. Moses reminds them that they had seen God's miracles in Egypt (actually only those who had been under twenty years of age at the Kadesh-barnea incident), "But to this day the LORD has not given you a mind that understands or eyes that see or ears that hear." The generation to whom Moses was speaking was, for the most part, natural Israel. They were coming off of forty years of discipline in the wilderness, and Moses was introducing them to God's covenant before they crossed into the promised land. At that time, their minds, eyes, and ears were closed to the truths and the glory of God. They had no personal experience with him. There had been no "Aha!" moments in their spiritual journey. And if there were to be, it would be because God gave them eyes to see and ears to hear, either individually or through his servants the prophets (cf. 1 Sam. 9:9; 2 Kgs. 17:13).

Isaiah 29:10 is the other verse Paul references. This passage is in a time of Israel's abject sinfulness, a time when her leaders staggered from wine and reeled from beer. Prophets and priests lived in such states of alcoholic intoxication that they staggered "when seeing visions" and stumbled "when rendering decisions" (Isa. 28:7). As a result, God through Isaiah says that he will make them "drunk, but not from wine, stagger, but not from beer" (Isa. 29:9). He will bring over them a "deep sleep" (Paul's **spirit of stupor**) by sealing their eyes and covering their heads (Isa. 29:10). God, as a form of discipline, simply made it impossible for Israel, save the elect, to understand spiritual truth. If Israel was not going to fulfill God's missionary mandate—to deliver the light of salvation to the Gentiles—then she would be prevented from receiving the light herself.

The comparison could be made to a person who collects all the newest and fanciest tools in his workshop, but never builds anything, versus the carpenter who owns a few basic, well-worn tools with which he has constructed shelters and furniture for many. Israel's workshop was beyond compare when it came to available resources (Rom. 9:4–5). The problem was that they had not used their tools for God's purposes, and God took their tools away.

The most profound connection between God's hardening of Israel and God's explaining of the hardening of Israel is found in Jesus' use of Isaiah 6:9–10. God tells Isaiah to go to Israel to pronounce God's hardening upon them: a calloused heart, and ears and eyes that are closed. When Isaiah asks how long the "curse" will last, God says it will be until the land is utterly forsaken, the people are scattered far away, and there is nothing but a "stump in the land" (Isa. 6:11–13). But that stump will be a "holy seed," implying that it will one day sprout anew (cf. the same imagery in Isa. 11:1,10; 53:2; cf. Paul's reference to the holy root in Rom. 11:16).

But for the moment, Jesus said, "this people's heart has become calloused; they hardly hear with their ears, and they have closed their eyes" (Matt. 13:15). His statement was in response to the disciples asking why he spoke so frequently in parables. The answer is that parables conceal the truth in their structure. Only the spiritually hungry— those who "call out for insight and cry aloud for understanding (Prov. 2:3)—and the spiritually seasoned and mature—those who have developed expertise in "understanding proverbs and parables, the sayings and riddles of the wise" (Prov. 1:6)—can receive the truths of the kingdom of God.

The religious leaders of Jesus' day were neither spiritually hungry nor spiritually seasoned and mature. As a result they did not understand Jesus's parable of the sower and the seeds. They did not understand at all the concept of the heart being like the earth into which seeds of spiritual truth are planted. They did not understand that the cares of the world, worldly temptations, and even Satan himself could—*at any time and on any day*—snatch the seed from their hearts. They thought that because they were the sons of Abraham they had all the spiritual discernment they needed. The religious leaders dramatically illustrated the spiritual axiom that "deceived people do not know they're deceived." How could they? It is only when God grants the removal of spiritual blindness that understanding can come.

Amazingly, Jesus said something about the parable of the sower that he said about no other story or parable that he told. He said that the parable of the sower and the seeds is the key to understanding all the other parables about the kingdom of God. Mark is the only gospel writer who records this statement of Jesus, and because this parable is usually studied in Matthew's fuller version, Mark's record is usually overlooked. But in Mark 4:13, Jesus said, "Don't you understand this parable? How then will you understand any parable?" It is also instructive to note that Jesus did not begin this parable with the familiar introductory words, "The kingdom of heaven is like . . ." (cf. Matt. 13:24,31,33,44,45,47,52).

Rather, this parable appears, based on its lack of the introductory formula and Jesus' own words as to its importance, to be a key to the others. And that key appears to have to do with the way spiritual truth is received and held onto (something that the disciples would need in order to understand the other parables)—and the reason Israel could not receive the spiritual truth Jesus was giving them. Truth is received in direct correlation to the condition of the heart-ground it falls upon. Truth is maintained in direct correlation to the defensive methods (against trials, temptations, and the Tempter) employed to insure its taking root and bearing fruit.

There are different levels of fruitfulness—"a hundred, sixty or thirty times what was sown" (Matt. 13:23)—based on the condition of the heart-ground and the diligence in bringing the seed to fruition. As Luke's account records, "the seed on good soil stands for those with a noble and good heart, who hear the word, retain it, and by persevering produce a crop" (Luke 8:15). But if a person is like Israel, blinded to spiritual truth to begin with, then the seed might just as well have been sown on the sidewalk.

It is obvious from Isaiah 6:10, and from Jesus' use of the Isaiah passage, that it was not God's intent for Israel to "see with their eyes, hear with their ears, [and] understand with their hearts" (Isa. 6:10). Jesus spoke in parables to maintain their blindness. "Otherwise they might see with their eyes, hear with their ears, understand with their hearts and turn, and I would heal them" (Matt. 13:15). While Isaiah was speaking eternal truth to Israel's leaders, here is how it sounded in their ears: "Do and do, do and do, rule on rule, rule on rule; a little here, a little there." As a result, Isaiah said, "They will go and fall backward, be injured and snared and captured" (Isa. 28:13).

Being "snared" turns our attention to the next verse Paul quotes from the Old Testament, Psalm 69:22–23. In this psalm, David is pictured as under threat of attack from vicious enemies. He asks that their "table" (the covenant made at a fellowship meal?) become a snare and a trap, and that their eyes fail (cf. Ps. 6:7) and their backs (bodies) suffer in retribution. Paul takes David's description of the fate of his enemies and applies it to what God has done to Israel, who "are enemies on your account" (Rom. 11:28). Because of Israel's opposition to the gospel, Paul says in verse 28, they have become the enemies of God (just as all are before becoming reconciled to God; cf. Rom. 5:10). Their strategies have worked against them, just as David prayed his enemies' strategies would work against them. Israel thought they saw it all; now they see nothing.

Israel thought they could do it all; now they can do nothing. Israel thought they could hear it all; now they can hear nothing. To have ears that hear and eyes that see is a prerequisite of entering the kingdom. Otherwise, the response will be like that of the deaf and blind: "What kingdom?"

Having explained the "how" of Israel's blindness, Paul now moves to explain the "why" in greater detail than he has. We already know that the "why" is because of disobedience (cf. Isa. 5:1–2 as the basis for the judgment of Isa. 6:9–10). But from a missiological perspective, the "why" is because the gospel was not getting to the Gentiles. Israel was God's chosen vessel in which he deposited the promise of his blessings for all the world, but Israel had failed to dispense those blessings obediently. Now, they were to be set aside temporarily so that God might call the Gentiles to himself through a new agency, the church. Paul does not go into detail here about the union of Jew and Gentile in the church (cf. Eph. 2:11–3:13), but rather focuses on the setting aside of Israel so that the Gentiles may be reached (by the church) with the gospel.

B God Has Delivered the Gospel to the Gentiles (11:11–22)

> **SUPPORTING IDEA:** *God is making Israel envious by delivering the gospel to the Gentiles.*

In this section of chapter 11, Paul reveals how the hardening of Israel has resulted in blessings for the Gentiles—blessings accompanied by the responsibility for humility. To keep the Gentiles from falling into the same sin as Israel, Paul's description of blessing is followed by a warning against pride.

11:11–16. Having demonstrated that Israel **stumbled** (cf. 9:33–11:9), the apostle now must answer the question, To what degree? Did they **fall beyond recovery?** Again comes Paul's typical, emphatic answer: *me genoito* (**Not at all!**). Whether Israel has fallen permanently from the grace of God is answered quickly when Paul reveals that **salvation has come to the Gentiles to make Israel envious.** Paul had already hinted at this in Romans 10:19 (quoting Moses in Deut. 32:21), but here the details become clearer.

"Provoke to jealousy" is *parazeloo*, which derives from *zeloo*, to be jealous. In modern culture the concept of jealousy has a primarily negative moral sense. We think of a jilted lover going to all extremes to win back the object of his or her affections, primarily because of an emotional dysfunction with roots in possessiveness or insecurity. Nothing could be further from the truth in this case. God is in no sense "jealous" in a romantic sense, or operating out of possessiveness or insecurity or control that so characterizes the soap-opera portrayals of jealousy so familiar to our culture.

The primary difference between God's "jealousy" for Israel and the modern version of jealousy lies in the beneficiary. In modern terms, the jealous person wants someone back for his or her own benefit. In God's case, he wants Israel back for Israel's benefit. God is self-sufficient and has no need, especially one that could be met by his creation. Israel (and all the human race) has needs that can only be met in God, and thus he wants Israel to return to him. Thus the NIV rendering of *zeloo* by "envy" rather than "jealousy" (in Rom. 10:19; 11:11,14; but see 1 Cor. 10:22). But even envy can at times border on covetousness, so it has its own limitations.

Other English words used in the NIV to translate *zeloo* expand the semantic range of this term. Paul encourages the Corinthian believers to "eagerly desire" the most profitable spiritual gifts (1 Cor. 12:31; 14:1), to be "eager" to prophesy (1 Cor. 14:39). The Judaizers were "zealous" to win over new converts in the Galatian region (Gal. 4:17). This zeal is good if it is properly directed (Gal. 4:18). God's intentions toward Israel in winning converts among the Gentiles was certainly properly directed. He is doing so in order to make Israel "eagerly desire," or be "zealous," to return to him. Echoing the truth of Romans 8:28, Paul points out how even the **transgression** of Israel (their failure to accept God's Messiah and his gospel) is going to result in **greater riches** in the long run. **The world (the Gentiles)** will receive spiritual **riches**, but even Israel will be blessed with **life from the dead.**

There is a general parallelism between verses 12 and 15. In verse 12, **their transgression** refers to Israel's sin, **their loss** refers to Israel's loss of favor with God, and **their fullness** refers to the reversal of **their loss**—a time in the future when Israel will experience God's blessing again. In verse 15, **their rejection** is a combination of **their transgression** and **their loss** in verse 12, and **their acceptance** is the same as **their fullness** in verse 12. **Life from the dead** must surely refer to the seeming resurrection of a nation that appears to have died.

Could Paul have in mind any less than Ezekiel's magnificent vision of the valley of dry bones (Ezek. 37:1–14), where God asked the prophet, "Son of man, can these bones live?" While directed immediately at the nation in exile in Babylon, Ezekiel's vision included a second mountaintop of prophetic import—the return of Israel to her homeland in the last days: "O my people, I am going to open your graves and bring you up from them; I will bring you back to the land of Israel. Then you, my people, will know that I am the LORD, when I open your graves and bring you up from them. I will put my Spirit in you and you will live, and I will settle you in your own land" (Ezek. 37:12–14).

And if not the words of Ezekiel, were not the words of the Lord Jesus himself in Paul's mind as he wrote, recalling the story of the prodigal son? The father's words to the son—"For this son of mine was dead and is alive again; he was lost and is found.' So they began to celebrate" (Luke 15:24)— describe exactly the condition of the nation of Israel when it "comes to its senses" (see Luke 15:17) and realizes that true **riches** are to be found in the father's house, not in the world.

The final reason Paul offers for Israel not stumbling **beyond recovery** is based on the **firstfruits** image from Numbers 15:17–21. The consecration of **part of the dough** made all of the dough **holy** before the Lord. Therefore, if the firstfruits of the nation of the Israel were **holy** before the Lord, **then the whole batch is holy** (meaning "set apart for special service" to the Lord). Israel would never "not" be set aside for the Lord. Likewise, if a **root is holy, so are the branches**. Just as the branches of any tree will be the same as the root, so latter-day Israel will be the same (have the same purpose and place before God) as the **root**.

The commentaries vary in their conjecture concerning the identity of the **firstfruits** and the **root**. While identity is not Paul's main point here (rather the principle of solidarity), it seems most reasonable to trace the nation's purpose, place, and purity before God to the patriarchs—those who believed God's promises and walked in faithfulness prior to enslavement and the apostasy during the divided monarchy (see 11:28 for further support for this view). The point is that the nation had a **holy** (set apart) beginning and will therefore have a **holy** (set apart) end.

11:17–22. In this section overall (Rom. 11:11–22), Paul is talking directly to the Gentiles (v. 13): first, to let them know that they have not replaced Israel in God's plan (vv. 13–16), and now to warn them that lest they **consider . . . the kindness and sternness of God**, they also could be **cut off** as Israel was.

Paul's famous image of the cultivated and **wild olive** trees portrays beautifully what God has done for the Gentiles. Here is how the two types of olive trees compare (Israel is pictured as an olive tree before God in Jer. 11:16):

Israel	Gentiles
the cultivated olive tree	the wild olive tree
pruned and cultivated to bear much fruit	from lack of care in the wild, had never produced fruit
while the root was good, the branches were failing to be fruitful	the root was weak, but had branches which were strong

Israel	Gentiles
the fruitless branches are trimmed, keeping the root, and branches from the wild olive are grafted in	fruitless branches are cut off and grafted into the healthy root so that they may begin to bear fruit for the first time

Normally, the process for turning a wild olive tree into a fruit-bearing tree was to graft a branch from a cultivated tree into the trunk of a wild tree. Here, Paul describes a reverse process, calling his image "contrary to nature" (Rom. 11:24), by saying that God has preserved the holy root, pruned off the worthless **branches**, and **grafted** them in so that they could **share in the nourishing sap from the olive root.** While this is a graphic portrayal of what God has done for the Gentiles—allowing them to share in Israel's covenant blessings—Paul's primary point is a warning: **Do not be arrogant, but be afraid. For if God did not spare the natural** [cultivated] **branches, he will not spare you** [the wild branches] **either.**

Nothing has changed here, Paul is saying. Israel is still God's chosen (elect) nation, the steward of the riches of God. Israel is still, albeit in different form, the fountainhead for the riches of salvation the Gentiles enjoy. The Gentiles have not become the chosen people. In short, he says to the Gentiles, **You do not support the root** [Israel], **but the root supports you.**

C. S. Lewis's Aslan comes to mind with Paul's final words. The great beast who could tend the tiniest wound could also shake Narnia with his roar. **Kindness** and **sternness** are what the Gentiles must know about the God who has grafted them. Just as his **sternness** was exercised toward Israel, so it will replace his **kindness** toward the Gentiles if they become **arrogant** and do not continue to **stand by faith.**

Ⓒ God Will Deliver the Gospel to Israel Again (11:23–32)

> **SUPPORTING IDEA:** *When the Gentiles' salvation is complete, Israel will once again turn and embrace the gospel of grace.*

But what of Israel's future? Paul, still addressing the Gentiles, explains the mystery of Israel's hardening and how it will result in future blessings for the nation, and provides even further insight into God's overall plan for his human creation.

11:23–24. Paul, having begun with a horticultural metaphor, now leaves the realm of known practice and creates a "what if" based on his prior illustration. Paul's emphasis to the Gentiles had been to remain faithful, and he reminds them that if (when) Israel regains faith, **they will be grafted** into their own original root once again! **After all,** he says, God has already done

one thing **contrary to nature**—grafting wild branches into a cultivated root. How much less difficult could it be for him to graft **the natural branches back into their olive tree!**

11:25–27. But when might that happen? How long will Israel remain "cut off" from the root through which their salvation and blessings had flowed since their beginning? The short answer is, **Until the full number of the Gentiles has come in.** The longer answer, that Paul wants his Gentile readers (**brothers**) to understand, is that Israel's **hardening** is not complete, it is only **in part.** It is not permanent, it is only temporary—**until** the elect among the Gentiles are saved. Paul does not want the Gentile believers in Rome to become **conceited** or arrogant in their new-found position of blessing. Israel is waiting in the wings to enter back into **covenant** fellowship with God, as the prophets had declared.

As he has done before in Romans, Paul draws on several Old Testament prophetic passages to put together a description of future events, in this case, Isaiah 59:20–21; 27:9 and Jeremiah 31:33–34. God prophesied to Israel in the Old Testament that her **sins** would one day be removed, and here Paul confirms that they will be—when the **deliverer [comes] from Zion to turn godlessness away from Jacob.** At that time (apparently at the return of Christ), **all Israel will be saved.**

All Israel is not best understood numerically any more than "the Gentiles" should be taken to mean every individual Gentile. The implication is not that at the *parousia* of Christ all Jews alive at that time will be saved. The best understanding is that offered by F. F. Bruce: "'All Israel' is a recurring expression in Jewish literature, where it need not mean 'every Jew without a single exception,' but 'Israel as a whole'" (Bruce, p. 209). Paul's point here is that in the future, when the elect of the Gentiles have been saved, the **hardening** currently afflicting Israel will be removed and **all Israel** will resume its position as the elect people of God before him. At that point, salvation of individuals will occur as it did for Paul and always has—on the basis of personal faith in Israel's Savior and Messiah, Jesus Christ.

11:28–32. Paul concludes this eschatological survey of the future of Israel, and Gentiles as they relate to Israel, by revealing what is behind the plan of God for both: **God has bound all men over to disobedience so that he may have mercy on them all.** This universalist-sounding summary is not what the cynic might propose, that "after all this" God is going to have **mercy** on, and save, everyone. Rather, Paul is saying that both categories of humanity, Jews and Gentiles, will one day find themselves in the favor of God solely on the basis of his **mercy.** While it might have been said before Israel's hardening that it was only the Gentiles who were shown **mercy,** now Israel has **become disobedient in order that they too may now receive mercy.**

This statement takes us back to the end of Genesis 11 when God looked out across the earth and found a human family disobedient to him. A flood did not keep the newly reproduced race from rallying together in the plains of Shinar and attempting to make a name for themselves apart from God. If they were going to be saved, it would simply be because of God's **mercy**. God first saved Abraham, then sent his descendants to tell the others that God would forgive them if they would turn to him. Abraham's descendants failed in their mission, so God has set them aside temporarily. He exercised mercy on the rest of the human race apart from the Jews, but will ultimately exercise mercy toward the Jews as well in order that all the human race, Jew and Gentile, may see and receive the mercy of God.

At the moment, Israel is the enemy of the **gospel**, but **as far as election is concerned, they are loved on account of the patriarchs**. God's promises made to Abraham and his descendants still stand today since **God's gifts and his call are irrevocable**. While there is only one people of God, the spiritually faithful from both Jews and Gentiles, the nation of Israel still stands as the God-preserved testimony to all the earth of his faithfulness to his promises. One day, when the glory of the Lord covers the earth, it will be because the mercy of God is being praised by both Jew and Gentile alike. The Jews received mercy in the calling of Abraham because of the Gentiles' disobedience, and the Gentiles received mercy because of the Jews' disobedience.

𝔻 Praise to the God of the Gospel (11:33–36)

SUPPORTING IDEA: *Praise is the natural response to God's merciful plans for the salvation of the human race.*

Paul could have moved immediately from mercy in 11:32 to mercy in 12:1, but he was apparently overcome by the reality and profundity of the mercy of God. Perhaps afresh as he wrote the letter to the Romans, it dawned on him that he himself was a recipient of the mercy of God. He had previously been one of the hardened in Israel, one of the disobedient, and then for reasons known only to God he was chosen to receive mercy. Having come full circle in Israel's salvation scenario—part of the elect nation that was set aside for disobedience, only finally to receive mercy—he is well qualified to praise the wisdom, counsel, and glory of God.

11:33–34. In language reminiscent of a psalmist, Paul begins in his own words to praise the wisdom and counsel of God. He concludes these two verses with a quote from Isaiah 40:13. Martin Luther pointed out that Paul's doxology does not bring closure to what was a mystery before we began reading the chapter: "There is still something which is hidden and too deep for us to understand" (Luther, p. 163). Though we have read all of Romans 9–11, we do not know all that God knows.

We do not fully understand election. We do not fully understand hardening. We do not fully understand God closing the eyes and ears of people who need his truth, people whom he wants to receive it. We do not fully understand his timetable. We do not fully understand (though we try because we want to) the eternal destinies of those who live and die in the period of Israel's hardening. We do not fully understand what makes those who live at a time when Israel's disobedience is removed more "deserving" of mercy (to speak in human terms) than those who did not receive mercy. And least of all, we do not understand why those who write about Romans, and teach others about Romans, have received mercy, knowing ourselves as we do. Paul was right. **The riches of the wisdom and knowledge of God** are too deep for us.

A person can go down only so far into the ocean before the capacities of the human body are tested to the breaking point. We were made to operate at only a certain depth in water; beyond that, the pressure is too much to bear. So it is with the **depth** of God's **wisdom and knowledge**. We cannot bear what he can bear, nor can we follow his **paths**. But there is praise and glory in our distance from him. We know that we are saved, and by that fact we know that what Paul is writing is true. Paul's praise and worship of God is prompted by what he does not know as well as by what he does.

11:35–36. Paul then turns to Job 41:11 as the basis for praising the self-sufficient glory of God. Job, who thought he knew a thing or two about the ways and works of God, had spent an extended session doing remedial work when God finally came to him to quiz him. In Job 41:1–9, God asks Job whether he is sufficient to tame leviathan, the legendary monster of the deep. With an obvious "No" hanging in the air, God asks Job, "No one is fierce enough to rouse him. Who then is able to stand against me?" (Job 41:10). In fact, God continues, since I own everything under heaven, who can confront me with any kind of claim at all? (Job 41:11).

This last quote from Paul, plus his own words reminding us that everything begins and ends in God, is enough to silence those who are not satisfied not knowing all that God knows. In truth, no one can make a claim on God for anything since no one except God owns anything. As one contemporary preacher said, "We are change in God's pocket for him to spend as he pleases." While that may wrinkle the brow of the nobility-of-man set, it is nonetheless true. God owns everything and everyone—Jews, Gentiles, the world they live in, and the means and ends of their salvation. Paul's words here are a just, though gentler, reminder of his question in Romans 9:20, "But who are you, O man?"

Being self-sufficient, God is not required to answer man. His glory begins in himself and ends in himself and encompasses all of his purposes and actions. To the degree humans are included in an awareness of the glorifying purposes of God, they should offer him praise. To the degree humans are excluded from an awareness of the purposes of God, they should likewise offer him praise. In the first degree we praise him for what we understand, in the second for what we do not understand. After all, how much motivation would there be in worshiping a God whose purposes were totally exhausted by the finiteness of our intellect?

> **MAIN IDEA REVIEW:** *The gospel, the power of God unto salvation for the Jew first and then for the Gentile, will be dramatically vindicated by events in Israel's future.*

III. CONCLUSION

Eyes to See, Ears to Hear

Here is an experiment that may help illustrate a central theme of Romans 11—and help apply it. Paul says that Israel is under a partial hardening from God—a "spirit of stupor," to be exact. The result of that hardening is that "all Israel" (Paul's words in v. 26 concerning "all Israel's" salvation apply equally to her hardening; the issue is not numerical inclusiveness, but solidarity as a people) cannot see or hear the truth of God "to this very day" (v. 8).

With that in mind, talk with a Jewish friend about this and see what sort of reaction you get. Ask the person if he feels stupefied. Observe him carefully. Does he look stupefied? How so? If you have any sort of conversation with the person at all, it could easily lead to feelings of resentment on the Jewish person's part (and understandably so, humanly speaking). After all, how would you feel if someone approached you and said you were afflicted by a spirit of stupor and were blind and deaf to spiritual truth? Your Jewish friend neither looks nor feels stupefied, and yet Paul says, in a general way, that they are.

Given Paul's clear statements, there are still some things that are true about Israel's hardening that we do not know. We do not know the day it began, and we do not know the day it will end. In fact, we do not know if it is a binary event (either on or off), or a gradual event. There is a (slowly) growing number of Jewish people in the world today who have accepted Christ as their Messiah and Savior—does that mean there is a "thaw" in God's hardening? When Israel was reestablished as a nation in 1948, was that politically-motivated Zionist movement in any way a sign that Jews wanted to return to the land, and perhaps even the God, of their fathers? The truth of the matter is that the hardening of Israel—the spirit of stupor that has overcome them—is a mystery.

But before we pat ourselves on the back for having 20/20 spiritual vision regarding Israel's blindness, perhaps we should ask ourselves the same question we were going to ask our Jewish friend: Is it possible that we are more blind than we thought—even as believers? How would we know? What reference point does a blind person have? How do deceived people know they are deceived? When Jesus spoke the parable about the sower and the seeds to the disciples, the implication was that it is a battle to receive and retain spiritual truth. The harvest (fruitfulness) in our lives—thirty-, sixty-, or one hundred-fold increase—is probably evidence of how we are doing in the battle.

The unnerving part about the parables Jesus told the disciples is that even they did not understand all of them. After the one about the wheat and tares, when the disciples were alone with Jesus, they asked him to explain it. They did not get it! This in itself is probably a good sign. They were hungry and wanted to know more, which God always honors (Prov. 2:1–10).

Let us give the disciples a break—they were young in the faith, and kingdom truth was new to them. Remember, they had been eating a diet of the Roman civil kingdom with a side order of the Pharisaical legal kingdom all their lives. The truths of the kingdom of heaven (where you die to live, give to get, be last to become first—pretty radical stuff) were totally new to them. But at least they were asking. At least they were hungry. At least they wanted to go deeper into this new kingdom of heaven that Jesus was describing in his parables.

You will note in the Gospels that it is not the Pharisees—those with a spirit of stupor—who are asking the tell-me-more-about-the-kingdom questions, which brings us to the scary part. When we hear "the message about the kingdom" (Matt. 13:19)—and that does not just mean the gospel; it might be kingdom truth about finances, marriage, personal morality, relationships, or any such subject—how do we react? It was those with a spirit of stupor who did not ask for more; it was those babes in the kingdom nursery who did just what real babies do—they kept bugging Jesus to explain it in detail.

Since harvests are variable (thirty-, sixty-, hundred-fold), and since it appears that hardening is gradual, perhaps we should ask how thawed out we really are from the spiritual stupor we were in before the merciful warmth of the grace of God allowed us to begin to see. In the spiritual life, there are not just two categories—seeing and not seeing. That is only the beginning. After that, there is seeing more and more and more.

As we pray for God's mercy to fall upon Israel, that their eyes and ears may be opened to the gospel, let us also pray for our own eyes and ears. Let us not assume that we are not blind because we can see our physical reflection in the mirror. Let us assume that there is much more about the kingdom that even we have not seen—and then ask Jesus to explain it to us.

PRINCIPLES

- God keeps his promises.
- God is willing to harden those who are disobedient to his revelation.
- God is willing to create conditions that motivate the wayward to desire him.
- Jewish believers today are part of the remnant in Israel.
- Gentile believers are part of a witness to attract Jews to God and his blessings.
- All who believe do so by God's mercy.

APPLICATIONS

- What fears in my life can be relieved by trusting in God's promises?
- In what areas of my life have I become casual about obedience to God?
- Have I failed to thank God for a situation that he used to renew my love for him?
- How do I see Jewish people today? Do I see them as part of the plan of God?
- What is there about my life that would attract a Jewish person to Christ?
- Have I thanked God for what I understand of the mercy that led to my salvation, and praised him for what I do not yet understand?

IV. LIFE APPLICATION

The Up and Down of Israel's Existence

If the nation of Israel had a corporal existence—a singular body with a mind and personality that could communicate to the world—one of the first things we might hear her say is, "I need a rest!" No other nation in history has had the kind of trying, up and down existence that Israel has. Four thousand years old, driven from her homeland and scattered around the world, nearly extinguished as a race in World War II Germany, Israel has been limping back home and regathering her strength since 1948. In the half-century since then, she has become a central player on the world's political stage, and is rapidly gaining status in the global economy as a leader in commercial technology ventures. But fifty years of catching her breath is only typical for

Israel. She has had these brief respites from turmoil all of her life. Will we hear Israel cry, "Oh no, not again!" in the near future?

Students of biblical prophecy, especially those of a dispensational and premillennial persuasion, would answer "Yes"—that Israel has yet many troubles ahead of her at the hands of anti-Israeli forces in the world. Other Bible students would be less quick to agree that grisly prophetic pictures are yet to be painted—that Israel's future as a nation has less to do with God's plan for her than for the contentious place she occupies in the volatile Middle East. But regardless of one's eschatological persuasion concerning Israel, there is another "up and down" part of Israel's existence which, if history is the judge, should give the nation great comfort concerning her future.

The "up and down" assurance to Israel is found in Jeremiah 31:37. God, speaking through the prophet Jeremiah, essentially told the nation to look up, and look down, and take great comfort in what they could *not* see: "'Only if the heavens above can be measured and the foundations of the earth below be searched out will I reject all the descendants of Israel because of all they have done,' declares the Lord." Compared to what we know today, the ancient Israelites enjoyed little scientific expertise. The Egyptians and Mesopotamians had gained scientific acumen, especially concerning the heavens, but Israel had not. Israelis were naturalists—they were great observers of nature, and drew lessons for life from what they observed—but not scientists. One has to wonder then, what Jeremiah 31:37 meant to them when it was written. Based on the remarkable knowledge that we have today, we can safely say that God will never "reject all the descendants of Israel."

Consider the "upside" of God's promise—measuring the heavens. We now know that our earth, and the sun around which it orbits, are tiny parts of the Milky Way galaxy. If we wanted to travel from one edge of our galaxy to another, it would take 100,000 years—*if* we were traveling at the speed of light, which is 186,000 miles *per second*. The Milky Way galaxy contains about 200 billion stars, one of which is our sun, which is located about 30,000 light years (a light year is 5.88 trillion miles) from the center of the galaxy (our earth is about 93,000,000 miles from the sun). In addition to our Milky Way galaxy, there are about 200 billion galaxies in the universe, some of which are several billion light years (remember, a light year is 5.88 trillion miles) away. A galaxy (actually, a quasar, the supposed nucleus of a galaxy) was discovered in 1991 which is 12 billion *light years* from earth (12 billion x 5.88 trillion = the distance in miles we are talking about).

Our point here is that "only if the heavens above can be measured" will God reject the descendants of Israel. If the numbers concerning the size and number of the galaxies are not daunting enough to consider ever accomplishing such a measuring job, there is more bad news.

Not only is the universe (the heavens above) huge; it is apparently expanding (making the measuring job increasingly difficult!). In 1929, the American astronomer Edwin P. Hubble discovered evidence indicating that all galaxies are moving away from us—and the farther away a galaxy is, the faster it is moving. The best guess scientists have regarding the rate of expansion is that it is between five and ten percent every billion years.

If that is the "upside" of the promise, how about the "downside"—our ability to search out the foundations of the earth? The distance from earth's surface to its center is 3,960 miles. Going straight down, the first 30 miles constitutes the crust. The next 1,800 miles is the mantle, made mostly of rock, and the final 2,160 miles to the center is the core, which is mostly fluid except for a solid center. The interior of the earth is believed to be about 12,000 degrees Fahrenheit. How much of the earth's foundations have we searched out? Relatively speaking, almost none. At most, we have drilled mines and wells a few miles into the earth's outer crust—a mere pinprick compared to what remains.

Israel should take heart about their future, don't you think? How much progress have we made in measuring the heavens and searching out the foundations of the earth? Think it will be a while before this is accomplished? At least the earth is limited in size—we could search it all out one day. But the ever-expanding universe? It will never happen. Therefore, if we let God's words in Jeremiah 31:37 have meaning, God will never reject the descendants of Israel. Their existence may have been filled with ups and downs of a spiritual and geo-political nature, but there is an upside and a downside to their existence that says they will always have a place in God's sight.

If God's promises to Israel are that permanent, should you not also take heart concerning your future? You may have had ups and downs in your life, but God has given you "his very great and precious promises" (2 Pet. 1:4) to give you hope for your future. The existence and longevity of Israel as a nation is a sign to every believer to trust in the Lord. (Scientific data adapted from Richard P. Brennan, *Dictionary of Scientific Literacy,* New York: John Wiley & Sons, Inc., 1992, and *Encarta 98 Desk Encyclopedia,* Microsoft Corporation, 1996–1997.)

V. PRAYER

Heavenly Father, I thank and praise you for your plan of salvation that encompasses all the peoples of the earth. I thank you for your faithfulness to Israel, as I know you will likewise be faithful to me. Help me to see your elect nation with new eyes, and to hear their needs with new ears. Help me to be a small part of what creates a hunger in them, and in others, for you. Amen.

VI. DEEPER DISCOVERIES

A. Grace (11:5–6)

Twenty-one times in the letter to the Romans Paul mentions grace (*charis* occurs twenty-four times, twice translated as "thanks" [6:17; 7:25] and once as "gift" [4:4]). If there is a championing theme in Paul's preaching, it is the grace of God. But what is grace? In Romans 11:5–6, Paul casts grace in stark contrast with works as the foundation for God's choice in election. God chooses not on the basis of works, but on the basis of grace: "So too, at the present time there is a remnant chosen by grace." Choosing on the basis of works is what we are all too familiar with; for the most part, it is how people choose in every realm of life. We choose "what works."

Vine's Complete Expository Dictionary of Old and New Testament Words says that grace (*charis*), in an objective sense, is "that which bestows or occasions pleasure, delight, or causes favorable regard." Subjectively, on the part of the bestower, *charis* is "the friendly disposition from which the kindly act proceeds, graciousness, loving-kindness, goodwill generally, etc. . . . In this respect there is stress on its freeness and universality, its spontaneous character, as in the case of God's redemptive mercy, and the pleasure or joy He designs for the recipient; thus it is set in contrast with debt . . . with works . . . and with law."

On the part of the receiver, grace is "a sense of the favor bestowed, a feeling of gratitude." "Favor" is an English word closely associated with "grace." Anyone who bestows grace shows favor. Anyone who receives grace is the object of favor. And anyone who stands in grace stands in favor.

Grace is most often described by theologians as "unmerited favor," since the grace originates on the initiative of the bestower, not the recipient. Grace is the expression and result of self-generated pleasure and delight. Therefore, when God chooses the elect on the basis of grace and not works, he does it for his own good pleasure. The source of grace is internal to the bestower; it is motivated by nothing externally.

B. Olive Trees and Grafting (11:17–24)

Paul's beautiful use of the picture of grafting is one of the most remarkable images in Scripture. Like Jesus' use of pruning as an image in John 15, however, illustrations that served as metaphors in biblical days are foreign to those not familiar with agrarian cultures. The teacher of the Bible who does background research into these agricultural examples will benefit his or her students greatly.

For instance, learning about the differences between the wild olive tree (vv. 17,24; *agrielaios*) and the cultivated olive tree (v. 24; *kallielaios*) can be instructive. Primarily, the differences can be seen as the results of care and cultivation. The wild olive tree is more like a large shrub, a few feet in height, and produces an inferior quality of oil. The cultivated olive tree, however, can reach heights of thirty feet and produce a fine quality of oil for hundreds of years. The cultivated olive tree, planted from a seedling, bears no fruit for its first ten years. Only then, having matured sufficiently, does it begin to provide a harvest for its owner. And when the harvest is taken in October and November, it is done by thrashing the trees with large sticks, or violently shaking the trees, knocking the olives to the ground, after which they are crushed to release their oil.

It is normal to transform a wild olive tree into a fruit-bearing tree by grafting a branch from a cultivated tree into the trunk of a wild tree. Paul interestingly reverses the order, saying that God has grafted a wild branch (the Gentiles) into the trunk of a cultivated tree (Israel). Rather than accuse Paul of horticultural ignorance (he admits his illustration is "contrary to nature," v. 24), is he possibly depending on awareness of olive trees in the Mediterranean culture to heighten his point?

The Gentiles were like wild shrubs—uncared for, fruitless, springing up randomly across the earth. The Jews, however, had been cultivated and cared for by God, given order and direction from the master gardener. The root of Israel was what held value. For hundreds of years it had been established and prepared; it only made sense for him to picture the Gentiles as being grafted into that historic, cultivated root of spiritual life so that they might bring forth the fruit thereof (fruit only harvested through violence and "suffering").

Care must always be given in expanding metaphors beyond the simple point addressed by the biblical writer. But where pictures abound in God's created order, there are often helpful spiritual parallels and insights to be discovered.

C. Doxology (11:33–36)

Paul's words in verses 33–36 form one of the clearest examples of doxology in Scripture. *Doxologia* is from *doxa* (praise, honor, glory) and *logos* (word, utterance). Therefore, a doxology is a word in praise of, or ascribing honor and glory to, another.

The basic form of the doxology was the "Blessed be" or "Praise be to" formula seen in both the Old Testament and New Testament (Gen. 24:27; Exod. 18:10; 1 Chr. 16:36; Luke 1:68; 2 Cor. 1:3; Eph. 1:3; 1 Pet. 1:3). In congregational settings, doxologies were voiced by the audience at the end of prayers and hymns (many hold that the doxologies following the five books of the psalms were added by editors; Pss. 41:13; 72:18–19; 89:52; 106:48; 150:1–6), and this seems to be the place at which Paul inserts his. His three-chapter treatise on Israel is such a unified section thematically that it can support its own doxology. Paul then concludes the letter as a whole with a separate doxology (Rom. 16:25–27).

Several forms of doxologies have become well-used in contemporary Christendom, though their roots are well established in the history of the church. The most popular doxology is that composed by Anglican Bishop Thomas Ken (1637–1711), which begins, "Praise God from whom all blessings flow." This doxology was originally a stanza composed by Ken to be added to the end of several hymns used by the church in praise of Christ or at times in the church calendar.

Liturgical worshipers are also familiar with the *Gloria Patri,* the "Lesser Doxology" (found in use at the end of psalms as early as the fourth century):

> "Glory be to the Father, and to the Son, and to the Holy Ghost; As it was in the beginning, is now, and ever shall be, world without end. Amen" and the *Gloria in Excelsis,* the "Greater Doxology" (also in use as early as the fourth century): "Glory be to God on high, and on earth peace, good will toward men. We praise thee, we bless thee, we worship thee, we glorify thee, we give thanks to thee for thy great glory, O Lord God, heavenly King, God the Father Almighty.
>
> "O Lord, the only-begotten Son, Jesus Christ; O Lord God, Lamb of God, Son of the Father, that takest away the sins of the world, have mercy upon us. Thou that takest away the sins of the world, receive our prayer. Thou that sittest at the right hand of God the Father, have mercy upon us.
>
> "For thou only art holy; thou only art the Lord; thou only, O Christ, with the Holy Ghost, art most high in the glory of God the Father. Amen."

D. Eschatology and Israel

There are sharp differences in the Christian church over the purpose, presence, and prophetic place of Israel in God's redemptive plan. The Bible teacher who expounds Romans 9–11, but especially chapter 11, must be schooled in these differences based on his or her audience and the purpose and goal of the teaching.

The theological school of thought known as dispensationalism has done more to popularize a singular perspective on Israel's place in God's plan than any other tradition. It is safe to say that there is the dispensational view on Israel, and then there is everything else. While there has been some moderation among dispensational scholars and teachers in recent years, the fundamental framework that sets dispensationalism apart is still in place. And the most distinguishable part of that framework has to do with the nation of Israel.

In short, dispensationalists have long taught (as popularized by the *Scofield Bible* and works such as the systematic theology of L. S. Chafer, and taught by such institutions as Dallas Theological Seminary, Moody Bible Institute, Talbot Theological Seminary, and Grace Theological Seminary) that God has two distinct plans running on parallel tracks: one plan for the nation of Israel and one plan for the church. Israel's plan is an earthly plan, centered around the messianic kingdom which will be established on earth, while the church's plan is a heavenly plan, focused on citizenship in heaven.

Dispensationalists do not believe that the church has replaced Israel in God's plan, that all the promises and prophecies made to Israel still stand today and will be fulfilled as originally given. Nondispensationalists believe (in general) that the church is spiritual Israel, and that Israel's mission in God's plan has been replaced by his mission through the church.

While the dispensational view on Israel has continuity and cohesiveness on its side (notwithstanding the aforementioned "moderating" approaches offered in recent years), it is accused of hermeneutical literalness not warranted by Scripture. Nondispensationalists are accused of spiritualizing the portions of Scripture dealing with Israel and ignoring the modern developments in the nation which would seem to indicate a literal fulfillment of prophecies regarding the nation. It appears that the moderating approach taken by some is bridging the gap between strict dispensationalists and their two redemptive programs, and nondispensationalists who nonetheless acknowledge an obvious future for Israel based on Romans 11.

VII. TEACHING OUTLINE

A. INTRODUCTION

1. Lead Story: The Bible in a Word
2. Context: With Romans 11, Paul is concluding a three-chapter exposition on the salvation history of Israel. He is doing this in the larger scope of the letter to the Romans in order to prove that the God of the gospel is a God who keeps his promises. Israel was, and still is, God's elect nation. Because the church in Rome (and churches today) are made up of Gentile and Jewish believers, the relationship of Gentiles to Jews, and both groups to God, must be clearly understood in order to separate appearances from reality regarding the promises of God in salvation.
3. Transition: Though it may appear that Israel has been permanently removed from the favor of God, they have not. They have been set aside partially and temporarily in order that what God commissioned them to do from the beginning—take the gospel of salvation to the Gentiles—may be accomplished. After that task is accomplished, Paul reveals that once again Israel's status as the elect nation of God

will be manifested. God is saving Gentiles without Israel's help in order to woo Israel back to himself.

B. COMMENTARY

1. God Has Always Preserved the Elect in Israel (11:1–10)
   a. God has not rejected Israel (11:1–2a)
   b. A remnant was preserved in the Old Testament (11:2b–4)
   c. A remnant is being preserved in the New Testament (11:5–6)
   d. God's hardening of the non-elect in Israel (11:7–10)
2. God Has Delivered the Gospel to the Gentiles (11:11–22)
   a. The results of Israel's hardening (11:11–16)
   b. A warning to the Gentiles (11:17–22)
3. God Will Deliver the Gospel to Israel Again (11:23–32)
   a. Israel's potential future blessing (11:23–24)
   b. The mystery of Israel's hardening (11:25–27)
   c. God's ultimate purpose for Israel and the Gentiles (11:28–32)
4. Praise to the God of the Gospel (11:33–36)
   a. The wisdom and counsel of God (11:33–34)
   b. The self-sufficient glory of God (11:35–36)

C. CONCLUSION: THE UP AND DOWN OF ISRAEL'S EXISTENCE

VIII. ISSUES FOR DISCUSSION

1. Is it possible that within the church at large, a true, believing "remnant" exists just as there is a remnant of believers in Israel today? How does Jesus' parable of the wheat and tares (Matt. 13:24–30) speak to the issue of the confessing remnant versus the professing remainder?
2. How can Christians stimulate one another to increase the fruitfulness of their lives, i.e., to avoid being blinded to spiritual realities by sin? What should you do if a professing Christian appears insensitive to spiritual truth? How is spiritual blindness or hardness removed?
3. Should Gentile Christians have any sense of gratitude toward the Jewish race for the role Israel has played in the inclusion of Gentiles? What role should Gentile believers in the body of Christ take in stimulating Israel's desire to seek a true relationship with God?
4. If God saves all by his mercy, what role should mercy play in the life of the Christian? How do we decide whether justice (i.e., getting what an offender deserves) or mercy (i.e., not getting what is deserved) is appropriate in a given situation?

Romans 12:1–21

The Gospel Expects Sacrifice

Quote

"*The* problem with living sacrifices is that they keep

crawling off the altar!"

(U n k o w n)

Romans 12:1–21

I N   A   N U T S H E L L

At the end of Romans 11, Paul completes his exposition of the gospel of Jesus Christ. It was certainly the most thorough and systematic presentation of Christian truth up to that time in the church, and most would agree since that time as well. Romans 1–11 forms the basic outline, or framework, on which a Christian understanding of sin, salvation, sanctification, and sovereignty have been based for nearly two thousand years. But now Paul turns his attention to the implications of the truth he has just presented. Romans 12 is where Paul says, "In light of what God has done, here is how we should live." The primary theme is sacrifice—its expression and evidence in the life of the Christian and the church. Ministry to one another through spiritual gifts and love for one another form the two major emphases of Paul in this chapter.

The Gospel
Expects Sacrifice

I. INTRODUCTION

Practical Theology

*M*ost theological seminaries have a department in which courses on pastoral duties are taught—things such as preaching, counseling, hospital visitation, evangelistic methods, polity (church structure and organization), staff management, conflict resolution, leadership skills, church growth, and related topics. If one looks at that list of courses and wonders if that is how the contemporary church views pastors—more as CEOs than spiritual shepherds of the flock—the answer is basically "Yes." Heavy regimens of theology, Bible, and biblical languages notwithstanding, today's pastor has his hands full with the day-to-day running of the local church. And given that the majority of churches in America are under a few hundred people in size, the pastor is usually shouldering most of the "practical" side of church life alone—with the assistance of volunteers and a life-saving secretary/assistant.

Is it any wonder that, for many years, the departments in seminaries that taught the "pastoral" courses were called the "Practical Theology" departments? While some still retain that title, most of these departments have changed to other names: Department of Ministry, Pastoral Theology Department, etc. Perhaps an unstated reason for the gradual change is the implication inherent in the title "Practical Theology" that all other areas of theology are "impractical." In fact, the chairman of the Practical Theology department at one leading evangelical seminary was well known for his annual joke made to incoming, first-year students, that his department taught practical theology as opposed to the impractical theology the students could expect to learn in the other curriculum areas.

His comments, while made in jest, reflect a problem among Bible readers that is well illustrated by Romans 12—the division in Paul's writing between doctrinal theology and "practical matters." Nothing could be further from the truth than to draw a line of demarcation between Romans 1–11 and Romans 12–16, labeling the latter "practical" and implying the opposite for the former.

It is easy to fall into the "doctrinal/practical" dichotomy with Paul's letters, since several of them contain an obvious separation between the two different emphases (cf. Gal. 5:1; Eph. 4:1; Col. 3:1; 1 Thess. 4:1). The problem is not in recognizing Paul's different emphases; it is the erroneous conclusion that is often drawn from his transitions from one emphasis to another—the conclusion that doctrine is in a separate category from practical Christian living. Romans 12:1 is perhaps Paul's clearest indication that the two are vitally linked.

Where did this false dichotomy originate? Several factors can be cited. First, the post-Enlightenment age, with its emphasis on reason and academics, has contributed to the intellectualizing of pastoral training. The average seminary student has as role models scholars with one or two doctorate degrees who place a high value (and rightly so) on theologizing in the academic setting. The seminary, rather than being part of a church, is separate from the church. We learn theology in the seminary, and we do preaching, counseling, and other practical tasks in the church. No one means for this dichotomy to exist, and certainly no one promotes it intentionally. It just happens.

Secondly, wittingly or unwittingly, the church acts as a mirror to corporate structural and operational models that develop in the business world. Therefore, the pastor becomes a CEO of the church with a board of directors (elders and/or deacons) who serve as the "management" team. The goal for the church (just as in the business world) is to be "profitable," to grow by adding new "customers." Therefore, since there is an unspoken assumption that new "customers" are not going to be attracted by boring theology and doctrine, these areas become separated from emphases on what will make the church grow, not only numerically but maturationally. There is nothing wrong with multifaceted church growth, and no one intends to separate doctrine from the process. Again, it just happens.

Finally, perhaps as a result of the first two factors, very few pastors preach and teach doctrine in a creative, vibrant fashion that demonstrates its relevance to everyday Christian living. Many churches establish Bible training centers or institutes for their members—miniseminaries, if you will—to meet the need of teaching doctrine, once again promoting the idea that theology (the classroom) is separate from Christian living (the pulpit).

The root concept behind the idea of a seminary is a "seed plot." The word semen, or seed, is obvious in "seminary," and in its earliest English uses a seminary was a seed plot used for raising small seedlings prior to being transplanted to a permanent location. It gradually was applied to instructional settings, and eventually even to settings in which priests, and later Protestant ministers, were trained. The concept is a good one if the ultimate, permanent product is a pastor who, like the apostle Paul, correctly integrates theology with Christian living. Unfortunately, seminaries in the modern era have perhaps produced more specialists than balanced generalists—theologians who cannot pastor or pastors who cannot theologize.

Paul's opening phrase in Romans 12:1—"Therefore, I urge you, brothers, in view of God's mercy"—contains two clues that his exhortations are based on the doctrine he has just presented. "Therefore" is obvious, referring to what has come before. "Mercy" is less so, unless one has just read Romans 11:32, where mercy is God's action toward all the elect. God's mercy, Paul says, has consequences, implications, results, and applications—meaning theology and practice are vitally linked. The idea that theology is separate from practice will be clearly dispelled from Romans 12:1 to the end of the letter.

The theology that Paul has presented in Romans 1–11 is what informs the actions of Romans 12–16. If we are not making practical decisions in the church on the basis of Pauline doctrine, then how do we know that our actions are correct? And if we try to carry out the exhortations of Romans 12–16 without the power of the Holy Spirit presented in Romans 8, how long will our efforts last? If we try to love our brother or sister, much less our enemy, without realizing the universality of sin—that we ourselves deserve condemnation—how will there be any grace in our lives? If we try to spread the gospel without understanding God's love in sovereign election, what confidence will we have in the outcome? If we do not know that the basis for peace with God is justification by faith, how will we ever be free from the condemnation that we have not done enough in the church or in our relationships to please God?

No, doctrine is not separate from practical Christianity. Rather, it is the force behind it. It would not take a very astute observer to look at the weakness in Christian practices around the world and be able to trace that weakness to a lack of comprehension of Christian doctrine and theology.

II. COMMENTARY

The Gospel Expects Sacrifice

> **MAIN IDEA:** *The believer's response to God's mercy is personal sacrifice that will strengthen life in the church as well as personal relationships.*

A The Exhortation to Personal Sacrifice (12:1–2)

> **SUPPORTING IDEA:** *Sacrificing oneself to God is accomplished by applying a renewed mind to the pursuit and achieving of the will of God.*

12:1. This verse is one of the most important in all the Bible, and contains more key theological terms and truths for its size than perhaps any other verse of Scripture. Having completed his explanation of sin, salvation, sanctification, and sovereignty, Paul now does to the Roman believers, in a manner of speaking, what the Holy Spirit does in our lives—he urges the Rome believers to act on the truth they have received. **I urge you** is the translation of *parakaleo* (to urge, call, exhort, encourage), from which is derived the noun *parakletos,* or *paraclete.* This is the term Jesus used to refer to the promised Holy Spirit who would come to the disciples after his ascension into heaven (John 14:16,26; 15:26; 16:7).

Paraclete is translated by "Helper" in the NASB and NKJV, "Comforter" in the KJV, and "Counselor" in the NIV. As is widely understood, the paraclete's ministry is pictured from the formation of the word *para* (along, beside, together) and *kaleo* (to call). Therefore, the paraclete is one called alongside to do that which the verb, *parakaleo,* suggests—exhort, urge, comfort, counsel.

It is striking how closely Paul fulfills the ministry of the Holy Spirit predicted by Jesus: "But the Holy Spirit . . . will teach you all things and will remind you of everything I have said to you" (John 14:26). Paul has certainly taught the Roman Christians "all things," and is now about to remind them of the consequences and application of what he has taught them. Paul is going to urge them to act on the truth they have received, letting that truth be the foundation of their Christian practice.

The key action verb in Paul's urging is **to offer.** But before getting to that key action step, Paul justifies his exhortation. He does not simply command them **to offer** themselves; he appeals to their reason (*logikos*). **In view of God's mercy,** Paul says, it is only reasonable that you offer yourselves **to God.** Prior to this verse in Romans, Paul has mentioned the **mercy** of God ten times (Rom. 9:15 [twice], 16,18 [twice], 23; 11:30,31 [twice], 32), and mentions it two more times following this verse (12:8 [the mercy of God manifested by human instruments]; 15:9). His conclusion to chapter 11 summarizes all that he has taught on the sovereignty of God in salvation by saying that "God has bound all men over to disobedience so that he may have mercy on them all" (Rom. 11:32).

The only thing that saves a human race lost in sin is the **mercy** of God. Mercy is *oiktirmos* (compassion, pity; besides this verse, cf. 2 Cor. 1:3; Phil. 2:1; Col. 3:12; Heb. 10:28), that compassion-based response of God to the plight of humans that causes him to forego what they deserve, punishment for sin, and give them what they do not deserve, forgiveness.

In view of God's mercy, Paul urges his readers (and us) **to offer [their] bodies as living sacrifices, holy and pleasing to God.** What would be a reasonable (*logikos*) response to the cancellation of judgment? Offering oneself in gratitude for the grace that has been shown would not be unreasonable. F. F. Bruce quotes Thomas Erskine, who said that "'in the New Testament religion is grace, and ethics is gratitude' (*Letters,* 1877, p. 16). It is not by accident that in Greek one and the same noun (*charis*) does duty for both 'grace' and 'gratitude'" (Bruce, p. 213).

The reason that offering oneself to God is both reasonable and **spiritual** is based partly on the meaning of *logikos* and partly on Paul's context. *Logikos* derives from *logos*, the Greek term for word or reason. But Paul is also drawing a contrast here between the physical sacrifices of the Old Testament and the spiritual sacrifice of the New Testament. The **spiritual act of worship** which Paul is encouraging is one that springs from the inner man, the realm of the mind (see v. 2). It is therefore a reasonable as well as **spiritual** form of **worship.**

Worship has always been accompanied by sacrifice, but the form of sacrifice has changed under the new covenant:

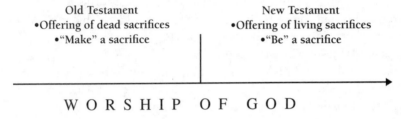

Old Testament	New Testament
•Offering of dead sacrifices	•Offering of living sacrifices
•"Make" a sacrifice	•"Be" a sacrifice

W O R S H I P   O F   G O D

In the Old Testament, there were sacrifices for sin as well as sacrifices of gratitude and praise. Christ has obviously fulfilled the sacrifice for sin once for all (Heb. 9:26; 10:10,12,14), and there is nothing that the believer can add to that sacrifice. But **living sacrifices** of gratitude and praise are the appropriate (reasonable, spiritual) sacrifices to be made by those who live only by the mercy of God. These sacrifices are as much the **act of worship** of the believer today as the sacrifices of dead animals were the **act of worship** of Old Testament Israelites. *Latreia* is the word Paul used for the worship practices of Israel in Romans 9:4, so he obviously has the same concept in mind for New Testament believers. The root of worship is *latreuo,* to serve. God was served in the Old Testament by sacrifices of property owned by the believer, but he is served in the New Testament by the sacrifice of the believer himself or herself. Paul does not tell believers to "make" a sacrifice, but to "be" a sacrifice.

It was the great missionary to Africa, David Livingstone, who put "making a sacrifice" in perspective: "I never made a sacrifice. We ought not to talk of 'sacrifice' when we remember the great sacrifice which he made who left his Father's throne on high to give himself up for us" (Ward, p. 180). The sacrifice we are to offer is our **bodies,** which recalls Paul's earlier words in Romans 6:13: "Do not offer the parts of your body to sin . . . but rather offer yourselves to God . . . as instruments of righteousness." **God's mercy** resulted in our being bought out of the slave market of sin and adopted into the household of righteousness. Therefore, our **bodies** are to become **living sacrifices** as we **worship** the one who redeemed us by his **mercy**.

It takes many times of hearing this truth for the contemporary believer to get it right. God is not asking the believer to dedicate his gifts, abilities, money, time, ideas, creativity, or any such thing. He is asking the believer to sacrifice himself or herself. Oswald Chambers says, "We have the idea that we can dedicate our gifts to God. However, you cannot dedicate what is not yours. There is actually only one thing you can dedicate to God, and that is your right to yourself. If you will give God your right to yourself, He will make a holy experiment out of you—and His experiments always succeed. The one true mark of a saint of God is the inner creativity that flows from being totally surrendered to Jesus Christ" (*My Utmost*, June 13).

On a continual, daily basis, our attitude should be that of Theodore of Heraclea, a Christian martyr from Pontus who died around A.D. 306: "I know not your gods. Jesus Christ, the only Son of God, is my God. Beat, tear or burn me, and if my words offend you, cut out my tongue; every part of my body is ready when God calls for it as a sacrifice" (Ward, p. 26). God, through the apostle Paul, is calling for the body of every believer to be offered daily as a sacrifice in worship—and if necessary, in death.

12:2a. The person who has truly sacrificed himself or herself to God will be distinguished by one overriding characteristic that informs the rest of life. That characteristic is the unwillingness to be conformed to **the pattern of this world**. Or, as J. B. Phillips put it in his widely-known translation of this verse, "Don't let the world . . . squeeze you into its mold." Paul gives the offensive key to this defensive posture—but first a closer look at that which the believer is committed to avoiding.

The NIV rendering of *aion* by **world** is not quite as telling as its primary translation, "age." The NIV's **pattern** is not in the Greek text. It is an expansion of the verb *suschematizo*, to conform to. Literally, the verse says: "Do not be conformed to this age." "Age" carries with it a sense of the beliefs, the philosophies, the methodologies, and the strategies of the fallen world in which we live. It is not just the world and its people in their fallen state. It is the worldviews and practices that derive from the fallen state that define the age in which humans live at any time in history.

Paul elsewhere calls this age "evil" (Gal. 1:4), and says that "the god of this age has blinded the minds of unbelievers" to the gospel (2 Cor. 4:4). This age has wise men, scholars, and philosophers who believe that their answers to life are to be preferred over God's (1 Cor. 1:20), but whose wisdom will lead them to nothing (1 Cor. 2:6). Paul warns believers against being deceived into measuring true wisdom by "the standards of this age," and suggests instead that believers become "fools" with regard to this age so that they might become truly wise (1 Cor. 3:18). This age (world) is a dangerous place: "We know . . . that the whole world is under the control of the evil one" (1 John 5:19).

If we do not allow ourselves to be conformed (present passive imperative of *suschematizo*), then we will not be one with (*sun*) the schemes (*schema*) of the age in which we live. While the same word for schemes is not used in the Greek text (*schema*), the same sense is implied by Paul's words in 2 Corinthians 2:11 and Ephesians 6:11 where he makes reference to Satan's schemes and strategies against believers. If Satan is the god of this world (and he is), and if the whole world lies in his power (and it does), then the believer must resist the pressure to conform morally, intellectually, and emotionally—and ultimately behaviorally—to Satan's schemes for life. We are not to act like the "wise" of this age—those who follow their own satanically-inspired will and practices rather than God's.

And what offensive measure keeps the believer from being conformed to this present evil age? The consistent and deliberate **renewing** of the mind. To make new (Paul here uses the noun, renewal, *anakainosis*, instead of the verb *anakainoo*, to make new) is a combination of "new" (*kainos*) and "again" (*ana*). Paul uses the verb form in 2 Corinthians 4:16 where he says "we are being renewed day by day," and in Colossians 3:10 where he says that the new self "is being renewed in knowledge in the image of its Creator."

Both of these uses of the verb shed light on his use of the noun here, especially the Colossians reference where he highlights a renewal of knowledge "in" (*kata*, according to) the image of God. In other words, believers are coming out of Satan's domain where lies and depravity are the language and currency, and depraved minds (Rom. 1:28) are the norm. Therefore, our minds must be renewed in knowledge according to the image of God, not the age in which Satan rules.

The ongoing, repetitive nature of the renewal is drawn from the present passive imperative of *metamorphoo*, to change form. It is from this Greek word that our "metamorphosis" derives—"a transformation; a marked change in appearance, character, condition, or function" (*American Heritage Dictionary*). The English definition describes perfectly the "metamorphosis" which took place before the disciples' eyes as Jesus was transfigured (*metamorphoo*) before them: "His face shone like the sun, and his clothes became as white as the light" (Matt. 17:2), "whiter than anyone in the world could bleach them" (Mark 9:3).

These dramatic images are a picture of how different the believer is to become as, day after day, he or she is being transformed by the renewing of the mind. Instead of being *conformed* to the present evil age, believers are to be *transformed* into the image of God insofar as knowledge and behavior are concerned. Paul has already stated that it is God's ultimate goal for believers "to be conformed to the likeness of [God's] Son" (Rom. 8:29). But in this verse, the "conformation" is of a different sort than the "conformation" to the world that we are warned against in our present verse. We are warned against being shaped into (*suschematizo*) the patterns and schemes of the world system in which we live.

On the other hand, Paul says that we are being "made like" Christ. Here the word conformed is *summorphos,* made up of *sum* (with) and *morphe* (shape or form). The former word for conformed has to do with exterior structures and designs, things which are changeable, not permanent. The latter word, suggesting how we are being conformed to Christ, has to do with being made like something else in essence or in form, something that is durable and not just an exterior structure. W. E. Vine clarifies, saying "*Suschematizo* could not be used of inward transformation" (Vine, p. 122).

12:2b. But how exactly is the renewing to take place? What is to "fuel" the metamorphosis that takes place in the believer's life? Transformation ("conformation" to the image of Christ) happens when the renewed mind begins **to test and approve what God's will is—his good, pleasing and perfect will.** It is the will of God—his standards, his desires, his motives, his values, his practices—which gradually pull the monarch butterfly of the believer out of the world's cocoon into which he or she has been squeezed. It is a knowledge and practice of the will of God that leads to spiritual growth and maturity in the Christian's life.

Ultimately, the will of God is all that matters, as Martin Luther King, Jr., so eloquently said, "Like anybody else, I would like to live a long life. Longevity has its place. But I'm not concerned about that now. I just want to do God's will" (Ward, p. 282).

Test and approve in the NIV is actually one word, *dokimazo,* which means to test and (by implication or extension) to approve. Both words can be subsumed under the idea of "prove," as rendered by the NASB—"that you may prove what the will of God is." The idea here is that the renewed mind can discover and put into action—thereby proving or demonstrating— the will of God. His will is **good, pleasing and perfect,** and in doing his will, the believer demonstrates sacrificial living.

That is, when a person chooses to sacrifice the preferences of the flesh (the normal human disposition), and chooses to do the will of God instead, the life of sacrifice is seen. It is as the seventh-century Spanish archbishop and scholar Isidore of Seville said: "The whole science of the saints consists in finding out and following the will of God" (Ward, p. 45). And as one whose safety was threatened on many occasions said, "The centre of God's will is our only safety" (Betsie ten Boom, sister of Corrie ten Boom, in Ward, p. 239).

This concludes Paul's introductory exhortation following eleven chapters of doctrinal foundation. It would not be off the mark to say that all of Romans 1–11 could be summarized under the rubric of "the mercy of God." Starting with the initial chapters when the utter sinfulness of humans is revealed, it quickly becomes obvious that mercy is all that can save the human race. By the time we get to the end of chapter 11, Paul declares that God's grand purpose is to have mercy on all (the elect) without exception. Therefore, when Paul says in Romans 12:1, "in view of God's mercy," he is saying, "in view of Romans 1–11"; "in view of your sin, God's salvation, your sanctification, and God's sovereignty, it really is a spiritually reasonable thing for you to sacrifice yourself for him." That is Paul's conclusion to Romans 1–11 and his introduction to Romans 12–16.

If the first eleven chapters of Romans demonstrate God's mercy, the next four chapters are how believers respond to God's mercy by demonstrating sacrificial living. In the rest of chapter 12, sacrifice is expressed and evidenced in the body of Christ and in personal relationships. In chapter 13, sacrifice is seen as believers submit to civil authorities and to the dual commands to love God and neighbor. And finally, in chapters 14 and 15, sacrifice is seen as believers give up their personal preferences in the church so as not to cause a weaker Christian to stumble and sin.

To return to the point made in the introduction to this chapter, the contents of the next four chapters contain much practical advice for Christian living. But to disconnect these chapters from Romans 1–11 is to disconnect them from their power source, for the motivation to sacrifice in the Christian life is the mercy of God.

ⓑ The Expression of Sacrifice in the Church (12:3–8)

> **SUPPORTING IDEA:** *A sacrificial believer will discover his or her place in the body of Christ and seek to build it into a unified body.*

Becoming a living sacrifice calls to mind Paul's earlier words in Romans 6 about being a slave to righteousness (Rom. 6:15–23). When one is a slave to God (Rom. 6:22), the assignment from the Master becomes one way to prove and carry out God's good, pleasing, and perfect will. Using himself as an example of one who has sacrificed himself to God, and who has received a grace-assignment from God, Paul now exhorts the believers in Rome to carry out the assignment in the body of Christ that God has given them.

12:3. The **grace** (assignment for ministry) given to the apostle Paul is clear in Scripture. He was called to be an apostle, to reveal long-hidden mysteries to the church, and to preach the gospel to the Gentiles, starting and nurturing churches in the process. That definitive statement is pieced together from the apostle's life more so than lifted from a text in the Bible.

What was the grace given to Paul? Here are the key verses that reveal the grace that was given to him:

- Romans 1:5: Grace and apostleship to call Gentiles to faith.
- Romans 15:15: Grace given to be a minister of Christ to the Gentiles.
- 1 Corinthians 15:10: The grace of apostleship was at work in him.
- Galatians 2:9: The grace given to him was evident to church leaders.
- Ephesians 3:7: Grace to be a servant of the gospel.
- Ephesians 4:7: Grace that was apportioned to him by Christ.

Interestingly, it is by the **grace given to [him]** that he writes authoritatively to the church in Rome concerning the **grace** given to them. He is speaking as an apostle in almost the same terms as his statement in verse 1. There he said, "I urge you," and here he says, **I say to every one of you.** Paul has his apostle's hat on firmly as he exhorts the church concerning life as a living sacrifice. No one knows better than Paul how irrelevant the question of "status" is in terms of the grace of God. Grace comes by way of mercy, not by merit or by heritage.

Had there been a problem with "status" in the church at Rome? Very possibly, "Yes," especially in light of what Paul says to the church in chapters 14–15. But here he says, **Do not think of yourself more highly than you ought, but rather . . . with sober judgment.** Perhaps the Jews regarded themselves as special because of their heritage. Perhaps the Gentiles regarded themselves as preferred because of Israel's status of being hardened by God. But Paul reiterates to them: a renewed mind sees everything through mercy-colored glasses. Living sacrifices have no status, especially sacrifices who have sinned and fallen short of the glory of God.

What living sacrifices do have is a **measure of faith God has given.** This corresponds to the **grace** that Paul himself received from God. Paul said in Ephesians 4:7 that "to each one of us grace has been given as Christ apportioned it." Peter said that, "Each one should use whatever gift [of grace] he has received to serve" (1 Pet. 4:10). God's gifts of grace—the **measure of faith** God has given each believer—levels the playing field. No one is better than another, so no one should think more highly of himself than he ought. **Sober judgment** renews the realization that living sacrifices owe all to God, and the grace they have received is simply God's assignment for them in the body of Christ.

As Paul saw himself as the chief of sinners who had mercifully received grace from God, he wants the believers in Rome to view themselves the same way. Only then will the church discover the will of God for the body of Christ as God intends it to be.

12:4–5. About two years before writing to the church in Rome, Paul had penned his first letter to the church in Corinth (1 Corinthians, about

A.D. 55). In that letter, written to a church with many internal problems, rivalries, factions, and sinful practices, he takes two chapters (1 Cor. 12, 14) to cover what he covers here in five verses: the church as a body with many parts, and spiritual gifts (1 Cor. 13 is paralleled by Rom. 12:9–21). It may be a testimony to the maturity of the church in Rome (at least in some areas compared to the Corinthian church) that Paul does not give extended space in his letter to "body life" vis-à-vis the gifts of the Holy Spirit. But what he does say is instructive for the church in any age.

Working backward, Paul says in these two verses that the church is **one body**. But it can only function as a body if members view themselves soberly in light of their grace assignments (v. 3), each believer doing his or her part. And this kind of perspective comes only from a mind renewed daily, committed to the perfect will of God (v. 2). Finally, the only people renewing their minds daily are those who have offered themselves as living sacrifices to God in light of the mercy of God. Is healthy body life in the church related to the mercy of God? It is when you follow the connections Paul makes between doctrine and practice.

Finding the link between the mercy of God and healthy body life may be like discovering the link between black holes in space and fast food, or the link between cornflakes and Einstein's Theory of Relativity—links exposed by best-selling British author James Burke in his enormously popular television series *Connections*. Watching his presentations is like turning over a tapestry of history and knowledge and discovering the maze of knots and threads on the back side which go to make up the cohesive picture on the front. Until the connections are exposed, one would hardly think that topic "A" had anything to do with topic "Z." Christianity is not primarily a human, historical, or social event. It is primarily a theological event. Therefore, to view it only in human dimensions—such as trying to effect body life in the church solely on the basis of group dynamics and organizational skills, omitting the theological dimension—is to view it incorrectly, and to invite less than satisfactory results.

Paul's point here is that when every person in the church views himself or herself with "sober judgment" (v. 3), each will accomplish the part of the church's task that he or she has been gifted (graced) to accomplish. All Christians **do not . . . have the same function** in the **body** of **Christ**, and it is only **in Christ** that diversity finds expression in unity. Connecting Paul's first reference in Romans to believers being "in Christ" (Rom. 6:11) with this reference provides another link between the theological and practical: "Therefore, there is now no condemnation for those who are in Christ Jesus (Rom. 8:1). . . . so in Christ we who are many form one body, and each member belongs to all the others" (Rom. 12:5).

It is the theological truth of death, burial, and resurrection *with* Christ (Rom. 6:4–5) that spiritually and positionally places believers *in* Christ free from condemnation. And if no believer in the body of Christ is condemned by God, no believer should be condemned by another. Thus believers are diverse in their grace assignments and giftedness, but unified in their freedom from condemnation in Christ Jesus.

12:6–8. The good, pleasing, and perfect will of God for the church is unity based on the contributions of its diverse members. Here Paul presents a sampling of the different ways members of the body of Christ are gifted for service and ministry in the church. He returns to the point made in verse 3 where Paul mentioned "the grace given me." Here he expands that dynamic to **the grace given us.** Just as Paul was gifted as an apostle, so every member is gifted in some way to serve and build up the body of Christ. Gifts (*charisma*, sing., *charismata*, pl.) originate in grace (*charis*), which means they are freely bestowed according to the good pleasure of the giver, the Holy Spirit (1 Cor. 12:11). Grace-gifts are manifestations of the presence and activity of the Holy Spirit—he not only gives the gifts "just as he determines" (1 Cor. 12:11) but he also empowers their use "for the common good" (1 Cor. 12:7).

To the detriment of the church, "discussions" over spiritual gifts have resulted in Corinthian-like carnality in the church. How ironic that the very instruments given to manifest and encourage the unity of the body of Christ should so divide it! In Romans, Paul's point is not to correct abuses of the gifts but to teach on their primary purpose—to meet needs in the body of Christ and to build up the body in preparation for the accomplishment of its God-given mission.

Paul's statement that **we have different gifts, according to the grace given us** is amplified in 1 Corinthians: "God has arranged the parts in the body, every one of them, just as he wanted them to be" (1 Cor. 12:18). And what are the parts? It appears from the New Testament that Paul's penchant for list-making is not for the purpose of exhaustiveness as much as for illustration. For example, his lists for the qualifications of church elders are not the same in 1 Timothy 3 and Titus 1. And he only gives qualifications for deacons to Timothy, not to Titus. Does this mean that the elders in Ephesus where Timothy was had different qualifications than those on the island of Crete where Titus was? And did the church on Crete not need deacons because Paul did not mention them?

Not at all. This question falls into the same category as the "exception" concerning divorce as taught by Jesus. Matthew records Jesus' words concerning an exception to the "no divorce" statute (Matt. 19:9) whereas Mark (10:1–12) and Luke (16:18) do not. Does this mean that a different standard concerning divorce existed for Matthew's Jewish readers than for Luke's Gentile readers or Mark's Roman readers? A final example is the list of the fruit of the Holy Spirit (Gal. 5:22–23). Does the Holy Spirit manifest himself in only the nine ways mentioned in Galatians?

Lists of spiritual gifts should be afforded the same fluidity of interpretation and allowance for human dynamics in the process of the inspiration of Scripture that is required to accommodate the alleged "inconsistencies" in the above examples. The gifts of the Spirit are mentioned in four places in Scripture. A comparison of the gifts mentioned in each passage will illustrate the point that, even by combining all four lists, the intent of Scripture is not to arrive at an airtight list. Rather, the lists indicate some of the ways the Holy Spirit manifests the grace of God in the church:

Romans 12:6–8	1 Corinthians 12:8–11; 28–31	Ephesians 4:11	1 Peter 4:10–11
Prophecy	Prophecy	Prophecy	
Service			Service
Teaching	Teaching	Pastor-Teacher (same as teacher?)	Speaker (same as teacher?)
Encouraging			
Giving			
Leadership	Administration (same as leadership?)		
Showing mercy	Helping others (same as mercy?)		
	Wisdom		
	Knowledge		
	Faith		
	Healing		
	Miraculous powers		
	Distinguishing between spirits		
	Tongues		
	Interpreting tongues		
	Apostle	Apostle	
		Evangelists	

From these four lists, it is obvious that there is not one single list of the gifts of the Spirit—or at least one that we have in our possession. But since three of the lists are from Paul, and given that his general topic was the same in all three instances of his discussions of gifts (the unity and building up of the body of Christ), it would seem that if a codified list were to have been given, he would have done so.

The implication of a fluid approach to the matter of spiritual gifts is to reflect on Jesus' words in John 3:8: "The wind blows wherever it pleases. You hear its sound, but you cannot tell where it comes from or where it is going." While Jesus' specific application in that context was to the new birth through the Spirit, the insight into the ministry of the Spirit is helpful regarding spiritual gifts. We know that everyone has been gifted by God, but we probably should not be dogmatic in asserting whether with one or more than one *charisma*. Nor should we be dogmatic about whether any or all gifts are permanent as a rule, or whether or not gifts may be given to believers according to the need of the moment. Many believers give testimony of having been aware of an unusual anointing by the Holy Spirit to meet a need in the church on a temporary basis. Was that an anointing or a gifting?

We probably should not yield to our Occidental tendencies to isolate Oriental matters into categories. The Hebrew culture was much more serendipitous than ours. "Going with the flow" was the norm. We should incorporate into our understanding the clear teaching that the Holy Spirit has gifted us and expects us to use our gifts for the building up of the body of Christ—and then be prepared to be surprised by the Spirit if and when he dispenses grace "as he determines" (1 Cor. 12:11).

The gifts Paul mentions in Romans are presented in such a way as to make them self-explanatory. It is as if Paul is answering questions from those new to the idea of spiritual gifts: "Paul, what should I do if I am a prophet?" *Prophesy!—but only by faith.* "What if my gift is serving?" *Then serve!* "What about teaching?" *Teach!* "Encouraging?" *Encourage someone!* "Giving to others?" *Give generously!* "Leading?" *Start leading!* "Showing mercy?" *Stop frowning—people who need mercy also need good cheer!* In other words, the implication seems to be that we are not to wait around for instructions or for a mystical move of the Spirit in order to minister to the body of Christ. We are to do that which is obvious to us and which we feel compelled and capable of doing.

That last phrase—"which we feel . . . capable of doing"—will raise the question of the confusion of natural talents with spiritual gifts. Teachers on this topic often insist on drawing a firm line of demarcation between the two, suggesting that a person's natural gifts (in the area of church life and social dimensions) should not be considered when assessing spiritual gifts. This is not a biblical distinction; Paul never addresses the issue. He himself was an up-and-coming leader in Judaism on the basis of natural talent, displaying apostolic propensities as he traveled from city to city tearing down the church. Then he met Christ, was born again, and graced by the Holy Spirit as an apostle, after which he continued going from city to city only then to build up the church, not tear it down.

Paul was compelled to lead both before and after his conversion. Following his example, we should not be so quick to put a new believer on hold in ministry until it becomes clear what his or her spiritual gifts are. Who is to say that the Holy Spirit would not sanctify a carnal or profane ability and use it in the church? Plenty of mundane and profane objects in the Old Testament (knives, pots, pans, building materials, people) were sanctified (set apart and declared holy) for use by the Lord. Natural talents could fall into that same category. (See this chapter's "Deeper Discoveries" for notes on the gifts mentioned by Paul in Romans.)

The bottom line of Paul's move from sacrifice to a healthy body of Christ is, "Do what God has gifted you to do. Sacrifice your own likes, dislikes, preferences, and partisan positions for the sake of the one who had mercy on you."

The Evidence of Sacrifice in Relationships (12:9–21)

SUPPORTING IDEA: *A sacrificial believer will overcome evil with love in all personal relationships, especially those in which he or she is persecuted.*

If the sacrificed life is expressed when believers use their five senses and their bodies to build up the body of Christ based on their giftedness, then it is evidenced in the nitty-gritty of day-to-day relationships that happen in the midst of the expression of gifts. Love of others—love especially of enemies—is a key test of the reality of a living sacrifice. The final section of Romans 12, as mentioned previously, parallels 1 Corinthians 13 on the subject of love within the context of the body of Christ. While the two sections are totally different in style, their message is similar—love is the highest value.

In 1 Corinthians it is a higher value than spiritual gifts (which were being used carnally), and in Romans it is a higher value than retaliating against those who persecute you (which gives insight into the condition of the church in Rome, or the condition of Jewish and Gentile relations *within* the church in Rome).

12:9. The final thirteen verses of this chapter defy outlining. At best, it is possible to identify the hilltops that poke above the plain of Paul's thought on the topic of love. If a single theme is to be identified, it would have to be "love in the face of evil," as that is Paul's first word—**hate what is evil; cling to what is good**—and his last—"Do not be overcome by evil, but overcome evil with good" (v. 21). Almost every other evidence of love he mentions will fit under this theme. The question is, Whence the evil, or persecution, that was tempting the Rome believers to retaliate instead of love?

Most certainly, it could have been from Rome. Within a decade of Paul's writing this letter, he himself would die under Rome's sword. The wickedly infamous Nero was Emperor at the time of Paul's writing, and while the worst of his atrocities against Christians did not occur until nearer the end of his reign, there was steadily growing pressure against Christians. Jews had already suffered in Rome, having been expelled from the city several years before the writing of this letter by the emperor Claudius, who ruled prior to Nero (Acts 18:2).

But Paul's words could possibly have been directed in reference to strife within the Roman church itself. Jewish and Gentile conflicts were not new in the early church, and it is quite possible that animosities had developed to the extent that words like "vengeance," "conceit," and "enemy" were not out of place among the fellowship in Rome. Given that Paul addresses both categories (the civil situation in chap. 13 and the internal, church situation in chaps. 14–15), it is likely that both were fueling his thoughts on love in this section.

The **love** of which Paul speaks is, of course, *agape*, the selfless, unconditional expression of grace and compassion exemplified by the love of God for sinners (John 3:16; Rom. 5:5,8). Just as nothing can separate the believer from the benefits of God's *agape* (Rom. 8:35,39), so nothing should be able to come between a believer and his or her love for sinners (Rom. 13:10; 14:15). By dissecting **sincere**, it is easy to see what Paul means. *Anupokritos* is simply the negative (negative prefix "*a*" plus "n") of *hupokrites*, from which derives our "hypocrite." Therefore, **sincere** is not hypocritical. "Hypocrite" was used in the Greek world of the actor who wore masks to portray the emotion of his character—sincere Christians wear no masks. What you see is (should be) what you get, and Paul says that others should see **love**. It would be hypocritical to hate what is good and cling to what is evil; therefore, **hate what is evil; cling to what is good.**

12:10. Was Paul thinking of David's Song of Ascents in Psalm 133 when he exhorted the Rome believers to **be devoted to one another in brotherly love**?:

How good and pleasant it is
when brothers live together in unity!
It is like precious oil poured on the head,
running down on the beard,
running down on Aaron's beard,
down upon the collar of his robes.
It is as if the dew of Hermon
were falling on Mount Zion.
For there the LORD bestows his blessing,
even life forevermore (Psalm 133:1–3).

Or was he thinking of how eleven of the sons of Jacob turned on their brother Joseph out of jealousy and anger and consigned him to Midianite slavery? Could he even have been thinking back seven years earlier when he and Barnabas "had such a sharp disagreement" that they could not continue ministering together (Acts 15:36–41)? Only those who are living sacrifices to God could possibly carry out the exhortation to **honor one another above yourselves.** "Looking out for number one" may be a modern mantra, but it was written in the Garden of Eden. Considering others better than yourselves (Phil. 2:3) is just as offensive to the ancient carnal mind as it is to the modern one. Only a renewed mind can tell that it is the "good, pleasing and perfect will" (Rom. 12:2) of God.

Paul's special commendation of the believers in Thessalonica for how they loved "the brothers throughout Macedonia" is worthy of note (1 Thess. 4:9–10), especially since Paul seems to indicate that they learned to do so from God (as opposed to a human instrument such as Paul or another apostle).

12:11. Here Paul touches a theme mentioned to the Corinthian church after a long exposition concerning the future resurrection of the body, the putting on of immortality for eternity. Though that is not the subject here, maintaining zeal in service is, especially in the face of persecution or partisanship. He told the Corinthians, "Therefore, my dear brothers, stand firm. Let nothing move you. Always give yourselves fully to the work of the Lord, because you know that your labor in the Lord is not in vain" (1 Cor. 15:58).

12:12. While Paul refers to life in the church in verse 10 (referring to "brotherly love"), here is the first hint of persecution—**Be . . . patient in affliction.** Paul, no stranger to affliction for the sake of the gospel, stated a principle in Acts 14:22 which summarizes what he is beginning to share with the believers in Rome: "We must go through many hardships to enter the kingdom of God." Only the believer who has made a decision to be a living sacrifice can maintain zeal and patience in affliction. Joy **in hope** was a theme in Romans 5:2, as was prayer in Romans 8:26–27. Once again we see Paul going back to the doctrinal part of his letter and making application for the present situation. The knowledge that the Holy Spirit is able to intercede through us in times of trouble can be a lifeline to the other side of the quagmire.

12:13. Another evidence of a living sacrifice is a person who gives generously. Does sharing **with God's people who are in need,** and the exhortation to **practice hospitality,** refer just to materially poor believers in Rome, or to those who have been made poor or destitute through persecution and affliction? Here is a good example of a practice that has been mentioned as a grace-gift in some believers' lives—giving (v. 8) to meet the needs of others—being presented as a responsibility of the church at large. Certainly some believers have been gifted and resourced by God so as to be able to give more than others, but all believers have a responsibility to **practice hospitality** and meet the needs of **God's people.**

12:14. Now comes the hard evidence that believers in the church were being persecuted, and with it the need for evidence that these believers were responding as living sacrifices. Paul paraphrases Jesus' words to "love your enemies and pray for those who persecute you," and "bless those who curse you" (Matt. 5:44; Luke 6:27–28). Jesus himself was the chief example of blessing the enemy when he prayed for those who were torturing and crucifying him: "Father, forgive them, for they do not know what they are doing" (Luke 23:34).

To be expected from the Son of God, you might say, but what about the mere mortal Stephen, who opened his mouth in a blessing upon those who were stoning the life out of him as he spoke: "Lord, do not hold this sin against them" (Acts 7:60)? Peter told his readers to repay evil with blessings, "because to this you were called so that you may inherit a blessing" (1 Pet. 3:9). He invokes the covenant promises of Psalm 34:12–16 to show that God is ready to reward with "life and . . . good days" (1 Pet. 3:10) whoever turns from evil and does good.

12:15. Identity with others in their joys and sorrows is evidence of love flowing from one who is a living sacrifice. These are admonitions that Paul had made in his lengthy writing on body dynamics in 1 Corinthians 12 (cf. v. 26). He also touches the subject in 2 Corinthians 1:3–4 and Galatians 6:2.

12:16. This verse provides evidence of possible internal conflicts within the church in Rome—class and racial distinctions that caused some to look down on others in contempt. There were no doubt slaves in the church, as well as people of means (cf. Paul's personal greetings to members of the church in Rom. 16). Also, there was the possibility that Jews in the church were maintaining a position of superiority over the Gentile believers (see Rom. 2:17–24).

Paul's teaching in places such as 1 Corinthians 12:13; Galatians 3:28; and Ephesians 2:15–16 confirm the principles underlying all of Romans 12: all have been leveled by sin, and any who have been redeemed have been so by God's mercy. Therefore, anyone who would look upon another believer with contempt or conceit because of status or position in life has not grasped the enormous implications of having been redeemed solely by grace.

12:17–21. Finally, Paul concludes the chapter with the most lengthy, and perhaps the most difficult to manifest, evidence of being a living sacrifice: loving when wronged. The clear command is, **Do not repay anyone evil for evil**—whether a fellow believer or an unbeliever outside the church. There are at least two reasons for not taking **revenge** into one's own hand. First, it puts an individual, a part of the creation, in the place of judge over another part of creation. God has made it abundantly clear in Scripture, as Paul attests with his quote of Deuteronomy 32:35, that it is his prerogative and responsibility to avenge sin—and that he will do it: "For God will bring every act to judgment, everything which is hidden, whether it is good or evil" (Eccl. 12:14, NASB).

The second reason not to seek revenge is that it could bring disrepute and harm to the cause of the gospel. When Paul told Timothy to lead the church in Ephesus in prayers for "kings and all those in authority," it was so that those same subjects of prayer would not bring trouble to the church; so that believers could live "peaceful and quiet lives in all godliness and holiness" (1 Tim. 2:2). Since "God . . . wants all men to be saved and to come to a knowledge of the truth" (1 Tim. 2:3–4), any disruption of a quiet and peaceful society would hinder the spread of the gospel.

To that same end, Paul tells the Roman believers, **If it is possible, as far as it depends on you, live at peace with everyone**. That would include peace with believers and nonbelievers, those in the church and outside the church. Since it takes two to fight, if the believers do not seek **revenge**, there will be no long-lasting disruption of peace. Doing **what is right in the eyes of everybody** includes not only "the eyes of the Lord but also . . . the eyes of men" (2 Cor. 8:21; cf. also 1 Thess. 5:15).

What should they do when persecuted? In essence, the same thing that Paul has already said in verse 14: "Be a blessing." The lengthy quotation from Proverbs 25:21–22 may represent an Egyptian ritual in which hot coals carried in a basin on the head would cause the guilty to repent. If that is the basis of the Proverbs quote, then the application would be that love—food and drink—will bring about shame and thus repentance in the enemy. But the admonition can be carried out simply as a gesture of kindness, as Elisha requested in the case of the Aramean army which, though trapped and primed for destruction, was given a feast and then sent home (2 Kgs. 6:21–23; cf. 2 Chr. 28:15). Even the law code in Israel commanded that an Israelite return to an enemy an ox or donkey that had wandered off, or give assistance to an enemy's beast of burden (Exod. 23:4–5).

The point of this last section is to do toward others what God has done toward us: forgive as we have been forgiven (Eph. 4:32). God loved us when we were enemies (Rom. 5:10; Col. 1:21). Though Israel is an enemy of the gospel still (Rom. 11:28), God loves her. And we are to love those who are our enemies. We are not to be **overcome** by evil but to **overcome evil with good**.

MAIN IDEA REVIEW: *The believer's response to God's mercy is personal sacrifice that will strengthen life in the church as well as personal relationships.*

III. CONCLUSION

Nickeled and Dimed to Death

Paul starts off this chapter talking about sacrifice, which invariably brings to mind grand images of martyrdom. Even though he is not talking about physical sacrifice—indeed, just the opposite—the fleshly nature of man cannot help but pridefully contemplate what it would be like to leave this life in the proverbial blaze of glory for Christ. What would it be like to have been included in *Foxe's Book of Martyrs?* Fred Craddock, in an address to a group of ministers, brings us back to real life by connecting Paul's initial topic, sacrifice, to the reality of his closing section on love: for most Christians, true sacrifice will be measured in a thousand small acts of love, not in the martyr's fire.

> "To give my life for Christ appears glorious. To pour myself out for others . . . to pay the ultimate price of martyrdom—I will do it. I'm ready, Lord, to go out in a blaze of glory. We think giving our all to the Lord is like taking a $1,000 bill and laying it on the table— "Here's my life, Lord. I'm giving it all." But the reality for most of us is that he sends us to the bank and has us cash in the $1,000 for quarters. We go through life putting out 25 cents here and 50 cents there. Listen to the neighbor kid's troubles instead of saying, 'Get lost.' Go to a committee meeting. Give a cup of water to a shaky old man in a nursing home. Usually giving our life to Christ is not glorious. It is done in all those little acts of love, 25 cents at a time. It would be easy to go out in a flash of glory; it is harder to live the Christian life little by little over the long haul." (Larson, p. 200)

Though there is a great difference between a one-time sacrifice of physical martyrdom and daily small acts of love, the sacrifice Paul is talking about is synonymous with love for others—whether fellow believers or non-Christians. That is because Paul's sacrifice requires dying spiritually to self, not dying physically. A living sacrifice is a person who, in view of the mercy of God, lives his or her life with a renewed mind and a ready gift of mercy for others. A sure sign of whether one understands and appreciates the love and mercy God has shown in salvation is whether that person expresses love and mercy to others.

PRINCIPLES

- The proper response to God's mercy is sacrificing myself in order to pursue his will.

- Becoming more like Christ and less like the world is a process of renewing the mind.
- Every Christian has been gifted by God for service in the church.
- Love for friends and enemies is the evidence of a living sacrifice.
- Because God has overcome the evil in us by love, we are to overcome the evil in others by love.
- Vengeance and judgment are God's responsibility, not ours.

APPLICATIONS

- What evidence can be found in my life of an unwillingness to be a living sacrifice?
- What disciplines do I pursue daily that will renew my mind in accordance with God's will?
- To what acquaintance, friend or enemy, do I need to show more love?
- By what specific action this week can I demonstrate love to one who is my enemy?
- What actions could any of my "enemies" cite to show that I have tried to take revenge against them?

IV. LIFE APPLICATION

The Cost of a Living Sacrifice

The roster of names is long of Christian martyrs in the history of the church, men and women who followed the example of the apostle Paul, living a life following a "Romans 12" pattern. For all Christians, a commitment to offer oneself as a living sacrifice to God will almost always lead to persecution of some sort. But for Christian martyrs, that persecution comes full circle back to the point of sacrifice for the cause of Christ. William Tyndale of England was one such martyr.

Tyndale, upon whose English translation of the Bible the KJV was based, was born near the end of the fifteenth century and lived until 1536. From an early age, he was consumed with a love for the Scriptures—his mind was "singularly addicted" to them, in the words of John Foxe, a contemporary of Tyndale's in England (and author of *Foxe's Book of Martyrs,* the source of quotes to follow). But it was not head knowledge; his life reflected what he read in Scripture: "His manners and conversation being correspondent to the same [the Scriptures], were such, that all they that knew him, reputed him to be a man of most virtuous disposition, and of life unspotted."

"Life unspotted" sounds like a man "above reproach" (1 Tim. 3:2), a man who had offered his body as a living sacrifice to God. Tyndale, unlike most people of his day, had the kind of education (Magdalen Hall at Oxford University, and Cambridge University) that allowed him to read the Scriptures in the original biblical languages. As there were no English translations available, Tyndale would instruct the learned and the unlearned in his clear understanding of what the Scriptures said from the Reformers' perspective. This, naturally, attracted the attention of those in the Catholic leadership who were beginning to seek out and persecute the Protestant factions in the country. There were no moral charges to bring against Tyndale. His life as a living sacrifice left him unapproachable. The only charge to bring against him was his teaching of the truth of God, and ultimately his translation of that truth into the English language of his countrymen.

When speaking with a learned Catholic scholar on one occasion, Tyndale's refutation of the man's teaching caused the scholar to blurt out, "We were better to be without God's laws than the Pope's." Tyndale's zeal, not allowing for such heresy, manifested itself in his response (which won him no favor with the established church): "I defy the Pope, and all his laws." He went on to say that if God spared his life, he would in time cause a boy that drives the plow in England to know more of the Scripture than did the learned divine. Ultimately, Tyndale's life and sacrificial adherence to the truth of God cost him his life.

In 1536 William Tyndale was tied to a stake, strangled by a hangman, and then burned in the fire by decree of the emperor—but not before crying out from the stake, "Lord! Open the king of England's eyes!" Even to the end he lived as a sacrifice before God. In the year and a half he was imprisoned before his death, he led the prison keeper, the keeper's daughter, and others of his household to a knowledge of Christ. Tyndale was a man after Paul's own heart (Acts 16:25–34), and the heart of God.

Even while losing all of his translation manuscripts in a shipwreck and having to start from the beginning, while being pursued by secret agents, while enduring the police raiding his printer, while being betrayed to authorities by his friends—Tyndale remained faithful as a living sacrifice. Let all who would offer their bodies as living sacrifices to God learn from Tyndale. With sacrifice comes persecution, the requirement to love one's enemies, and possibly the call from God to lay down one's life for the gospel—the ultimate sacrifice.

V. PRAYER

Heavenly Father, thank you for your mercy! Please deepen in my own heart an understanding of what you have done for me in Christ. In light of your mercy, I offer myself to you as a living sacrifice, fully committed to be used to accomplish your perfect will through my life. May my understanding of what it means to receive mercy from you be reflected in my ministry in the body of Christ and in my relationship with others. Amen.

VI. DEEPER DISCOVERIES

A. Living Sacrifice (12:1)

The idea of a "living" sacrifice was a new thought in religious observance in the Graeco-Roman world as well as in Israel and surrounding Semitic peoples. Animals were the sacrifice of choice in most religious observances, killed in place of the human supplicant. Crops (fruits, vegetables, and grains) were used in some instances. Human sacrifice was known among Canaanites, but in those cases the human (children usually) was offered in the same vein as an animal, only with a higher worth because of its humanity and its relation to the offerer.

Paul's use of "living sacrifice" does not imply a sacrifice for sin, but a sacrifice for service. Other instances in the New Testament expand this concept:

- Ephesians 5:2: While referring to Christ's sacrifice for our sins, the idea that he "gave himself up . . . as a . . . sacrifice" is helpful. The Christian, as a living sacrifice, gives himself or herself up to God, while remaining alive to serve.
- Philippians 2:7: Paul saw the Philippians' service in the gospel as a sacrifice, accompanying which he was prepared to have his life poured out as a drink offering (see Exod. 29:38–41 for background).
- Hebrews 8:3; 1 Peter 2:5,9: The function of priests was to offer sacrifices, and Peter speaks of believers as a "royal (holy) priesthood." Therefore every believer is spiritually in a position to offer himself or herself as a living sacrifice to God.

While Paul calls on believers to submit their bodies and their entire person as a living sacrifice, every act of obedience to and worship of God can be seen as part of the offering of the body. For instance, Peter says that believers are to offer "spiritual sacrifices acceptable to God" (1 Pet. 2:5); we are to offer "a sacrifice of praise" (Heb. 13:15); and we are "to do good and to share with others, for with such sacrifices God is pleased" (Heb. 13:16). Just as the components of the human body go together to comprise "the body," so a multitude of daily sacrifices in worship and work comprise the "body" that is a living sacrifice to God.

B. Spiritual Gifts (12:6–8)

As outlined in the commentary above, spiritual gifts are mentioned in four of the New Testament epistles. Here are the gifts mentioned by Paul in Romans 12:6–8 and a brief description of each:

1. *Prophecy* (cf. 1 Cor. 12:10, 28–29; 14:1–40; Eph. 4:11). The ability to receive and proclaim a message for God. Prophecy has two dimensions: foretelling and forthtelling. The former occurs when a prophet speaks about a future event. When the contemporary believer thinks of "prophecy," foretelling is usually what comes to mind vis-à-vis the prophets in the Old Testament. In the New Testament, however, forthtelling is more common, when one who prophesies "speaks to men for their strengthening, encouragement and comfort" (1 Cor. 14:3). This may occur in settings of preaching, teaching, exhortation, or other settings. Many Spirit-centered Christians include revelations through dreams, visions, or the audible or inaudible voice of God within the prophetic dimension. These revelations are not normative for the church, nor are they to be received or dispensed on a par with canonical prophecy (the Scriptures). Congregational prophecy, that discussed by Paul in 1 Corinthians 14, should be verified by church leaders, given in love, edify the church, and be consistent with Scripture.

2. *Service* (cf. 1 Pet. 4:11). The person given this grace is burdened for ministering to and serving people. The Greek word for "service" is the same as the word translated by "ministry" and "deacon," but care must be maintained to separate a grace-gift from an office. Not everyone who has the gift of service will be a deacon; not all deacons will necessarily have the gift of service.

3. *Teaching* (cf. 1 Cor. 12:28–29; Eph. 4:11). A person with this gift is able to cause others to learn. Teaching in the New Testament context probably initially referred to the explaining of the Old Testament Scriptures to demonstrate the fulfillment of kingdom and messianic promises in Jesus Christ. Today, however, with the completion of the canon of Scripture, the gift of teaching would encompass communicating all of Scripture—research, organization, and presentation—and related subjects in a manner that causes others to understand and apply what is taught.

4. *Encouraging (or exhortation).* A person with this gift ministers in the mold of the *paraclete*, the Holy Spirit. An encourager comes alongside another with words of counsel, encouragement, and motivation so that people are encouraged to take actions and develop attitudes consistent with their Christian calling.

5. *Giving.* When this gift is present, a person lives a life of material liberality, regardless of the amount of resources possessed. There is a freedom to be a channel of blessing from God to others by consistently using material resources to meet needs. The focus in this gift is not on resources possessed that can be given, but on the giver being free

from possession by resources so that he or she is free to be a channel of God's riches.

6. *Leadership.* God gives grace to some members of the body of Christ to help determine priorities, set goals, establish directions, and achieve results. The model for all Spirit-led leaders in Scripture is that of the "servant-leader" or "shepherd-leader." A person with this spiritual gift would therefore lead as a servant and/or shepherd, without manipulation, coercion, or harshness. People are usually eager to follow a person with this gift because such leadership helps them accomplish things that are important to them.

7. *Showing mercy.* This word for mercy is different from "mercy" in verse 1 (more literally translated "compassions"), but is from the same root as the mercy shown by God to all in Romans 11:31–32. The person gifted with mercy acts like God—showing great compassion for the sufferings and needs of people without judgment. People with this gift, like God, can often identify (judge) the cause of a person's condition, but their focus is not on judgment; it is on healing and ministry to the person's needs.

C. Love (12:9)

Four words for love occur in the Greek language in the classical period (prior to the New Testament, which was written in *koine* or common Greek). Only two of the four occur in the New Testament, with a third appearing in a modified form. The four words are:

1. *Eros* denoted the love between man and woman that embraces longing, craving and desire; a physical or sensual love. Eros was the Greek god of love, the son of Aphrodite, goddess of love and beauty. This word does not occur in the New Testament.

2. *Stergo* meant to love, i.e., to feel affection, especially the affection manifested between parents and children. It was also used of the love of people for a ruler, a guardian god for the people, or a dog for his master. It does not appear in the New Testament except for the negative compound *astorgos* in Romans 1:31 (heartless) and 2 Timothy 3:3 (without love) and *philostorgos* in Romans 12:10 (devoted).

3. *Phileo* is the most general word used for love or affection. It mainly represents the attraction of people to one another both inside and outside the family where concern, care, hospitality, and connections of faith are important (cf. *philadelphia*, love for a friend or brother, in 2 Pet. 1:7). Used in compounds, it can also show the love of inanimate objects, e.g., *philosophia*, the love of knowledge (Col. 2:8).

4. *Agape* (noun) and *agapao* (verb) are the words for love that take on special significance in the New Testament period. Used alongside *eros*

and *phileo* in the classical period, *agape* had an unremarkable presence in the Greek language, but it was the word used to translate the primary Hebrew word for love (*aheb*) in the Septuagint, the Greek version of the Old Testament. In the New Testament, it is the word used distinctively to describe God's love for man, and man's love for man in imitation of God's love. *Agape* is the word used in Romans 12:9 to describe the love believers must have for each other and for their enemies (but note also *philadelphia* and *philostorgoi* in 12:10). (Information summarized from Brown, *New International Dictionary of New Testament Theology*, 2:538–551.)

D. Taking Revenge (12:19)

The principle of proportional retaliation, permitted by the *lex talionis* (Latin for "law of retaliation") is repudiated in the New Testament. Exodus 21:23–25, Leviticus 24:19–21, and Deuteronomy 19:21 spelled out the "life for life, eye for eye, tooth for tooth, hand for hand, foot for foot, burn for burn, wound for wound, bruise for bruise" retaliation that was allowed under Mosaic Law in Israel (Lev. 19:18; Prov. 20:22; 24:29). But even in these cases, retaliation was judicial, not personal, and the individual was given no right to exact personal retribution beyond the legal limits. Jesus, in the Sermon on the Mount, repudiates the *lex talionis*, citing "eye for eye, and tooth for tooth" (Matt. 5:38) as opposed to the way of the kingdom. The Christian standard is now to meet violence with love (Rom. 12:17–21; 1 Cor. 13:4–7; 1 Thess. 5:15).

The question for Christian interpreters and ethicists has been whether the New Testament's prohibition on revenge excludes self-defense in the case of personal attack. When Jesus says, "Do not resist an evil person" and "turn to [the evil person who has slapped you] the other [cheek] also" (Matt. 5:38–39), is that to be applied to the thief who enters a home and physically assaults the Christian occupants? Self-defense can be seen as instant, on-the-spot retaliation, and therefore forbidden. Or it can be seen as an attempt to limit the spread of evil by protecting life and liberty, those "unalienable rights" granted to man by his Creator. The questions of pacifism in time of war and of the Christian's obligation to submit to the decisions of civil authorities (Rom. 13:1–7) are also part of the discussion of appropriate limits on revenge and retaliation. (For further information, see "Self-Defense" in Henry, *Dictionary of Christian Ethics*.)

VII. TEACHING OUTLINE

A. INTRODUCTION

1. Lead Story: Practical Theology

2. Context: Through the first eleven chapters of Romans, Paul lays out the most systematic and thorough presentation of the gospel written up to that time, and perhaps in all of church history. Man's sin, salvation, sanctification, and the sovereignty of God over all the human race, Jews and Gentiles alike, are thoroughly explained. As he does in other of his letters, Paul now turns to the implications of what he has written for the believers in the church at Rome. If God's mercy in salvation has been presented in chapters 1–11, then the response of those receiving God's mercy begins in chapter 12.

3. Transition: How should those receiving the mercy of God respond? That is Paul's opening exhortation in this chapter: "In view of God's mercy . . . offer your bodies as living sacrifices." For the remainder of this letter (chaps. 12–15; chap. 16 consists primarily of his greetings to friends in Rome), Paul demonstrates what it means to live as a "living sacrifice"—in the church through personal ministry, in relation to other individuals, in relation to civil authorities, and as one willing to balance personal freedom with spiritual responsibility. The gospel is the power of God not only to save, but to empower the recipient of God's mercy to live sacrificially by displaying God's mercy to others.

B. COMMENTARY

1. The Exhortation to Personal Sacrifice (12:1–2)
    a. Offering the body of the believer (12:1)
    b. Renewing the mind of the believer (12:2a)
    c. Discovering the will of God (12:2b)
2. The Expression of Sacrifice in the Church (12:3–8)
    a. The renewed mind's view of self (12:3)
    b. The renewed mind's view of others (12:4–5)
    c. The will of God for the church (12:6–8)
3. The Evidence of Sacrifice in Relationships (12:9–21)
    a. Sincere love (12:9)
    b. Devotion to others (12:10)
    c. Zeal in service (12:11)
    d. Perseverance in trials (12:12)
    e. Generosity in giving (12:13)
    f. Blessing in persecution (12:14)
    g. Identity with others (12:15)
    h. Humility in community (12:16)
    i. Love when wronged (12:17–21)

C. CONCLUSION: THE COST OF A LIVING SACRIFICE

VIII. ISSUES FOR DISCUSSION

1. How does the New Testament change the focus of worship from its Old Testament roots? Where does Paul's reference to "spiritual act of worship" fit into the church's understanding of how worship should be accomplished today?

2. How many believers in the average church minister with a confident understanding of the grace given to them by God? How can we replace "recruiting" people to "work" in the church with helping people understand the grace for ministry given them by God?

3. Where do Christians in North America have the greatest need— learning to love those within the church or those outside the church? What are some subtle forms of revenge-seeking that Christians practice against those who have "harmed" them? How does the church's practice of love influence how the world thinks about the God of love?

Romans 13:1–14

The Gospel Requires Understanding the Times

"[T]here were] sons of Issachar, men who understood the times, with knowledge of what Israel should do."

1 Chronicles 12:32, NASB

Romans 13:1–14

I N A N U T S H E L L

Paul continues his explanation of what it means to be a living sacrifice to God in view of his mercy toward all people. In chapter 13 he turns to the tension of living as a believer under the rule of pagan authorities and in light of the eschatological end of history. Should Christians rebel against pagan rulers? Should they live as they please in light of the approaching end of the age? Paul provides answers for the church in Rome, and for all churches today that exist under the same tensions and conditions.

The Gospel Requires
Understanding the Times

I. INTRODUCTION

No One Said Submission Was Easy

*W*hen Paul urged the believers in Rome to offer their bodies as living sacrifices to God (Rom. 12:1), he was not using idle language to paint a picture of devotion. In using the language of death—"sacrifice"—he was acknowledging an ever-present reality in the Roman Empire: emperors were free to take the life of anyone at any time. Israel had already witnessed the ruthlessness of Herod the Great. In an attempt to destroy the newborn king of Israel (Jesus), he decreed the murder of all male children two years old and younger in Bethlehem and its vicinity (Matt. 2:16–18). Three decades later, Herod's son, Herod Antipas, celebrated his birthday by having John the Baptist beheaded (Mark 6:14–29). What had appeared to be an empathetic strain in Antipas's rule (Mark 6:20) vanished capriciously when he found himself captive to a promise made to a young woman.

Without question, the value of life in the Roman Empire changed like the weather. Peaceful conditions on one day could give rise to the black clouds of persecution and death on the next. To people who could be sacrificed for their faith—or for any other reason—on the altar of an emperor's whim, the exhortation to be a "living sacrifice" found understanding ears. At the risk of putting it too casually, Paul might have been saying, "Live as though you have died for your faith. You might be dead soon anyway." Had Paul spoken those words, he would have been remembered as a prophet as well as an apostle, since the murderous rampages of Nero were only a few short years into the future.

Emperors under which the church in Rome lived began with the infamous Caligula (reigned from A.D. 37–41). His reign began just a few years after the resurrection of Christ and founding of the church, and though there were undoubtedly already some Christians resident in Rome (Acts 2:10), there is little evidence of his persecution of believers. The Christian "sect" would have appeared to Roman officials as little more than a disruptive branch of Judaism. While the Roman Empire as a whole was tolerant of Judaism, Caligula on one occasion commanded Petronius, governor of Syria, to place a statue of Caligula in the Temple at Jerusalem for purposes of adoration. The Jews in Jerusalem were so strident in their opposition that Caligula withdrew the command, fearing an uprising. Just because Caligula was tolerant of Christians and Jews, however, does not mean he was an emperor to be loved.

Caligula and Tiberius Gemellus were first appointed joint emperors, the Senate and people later choosing Caligula as sole ruler. One of his first acts was to have Gemellus murdered. Following a calm initial six months in office, Caligula suffered a severe illness after which he appeared to go insane. He murdered most of his relatives, had people tortured and killed while he ate, named his favorite horse as a counselor, declared himself a god, and had temples and sacrifices dedicated to himself. Not surprisingly, he was assassinated in A.D. 41 by the officers of his guard.

Following Caligula was Claudius I, uncle of Caligula, who reigned from A.D. 41–54. He delegated most of his responsibilities to his wife Messalina, whom he had murdered in A.D. 48. He then married his niece, Agrippina the Younger, who was responsible for poisoning Claudius. Though Claudius treated the Jews in Rome with indulgence, he banished them all from Rome midway through his reign because of disturbances related to "Chrestus"— probably a reference to Jewish unrest over the preaching of the gospel of Christ in Rome (Acts 18:2).

After Claudius's death in A.D. 54, Nero assumed the throne and reigned until A.D. 68. Nero was emperor when Paul wrote Romans (A.D. 57)—the "governing authority" to whom Paul made specific reference in Romans (Rom. 13:1). His reign was no more salutary than those of his predecessors—and ultimately was much worse as far as believers in Christ were concerned. Nero became emperor at age 15, and at age 22 he had his mother murdered, followed three years later by the divorce (and later murder) of his wife. It is thought by many historians that the great fire that swept Rome in A.D. 64 was instigated by Nero, who blamed it on the Christians. He had Christians tortured and burned publicly, ultimately taking the lives of both the apostles Peter and Paul. Nero committed suicide under pressure against his policies in A.D. 68.

Leaping forward more than two centuries, we come to a brighter moment in the church's history—at least as far as physical safety was concerned. The emperor Diocletian, in the late third century, had divided the empire into western and eastern portions, each with its own emperor. Constantine secured a hold on the eastern portion of the empire, and brought to an end a fearful reign of terror upon Christians perpetrated by the emperor Galerius (d. A.D. 311).

In A.D. 312, Constantine had seen a cross of light in the sky bearing the inscription, "In this sign conquer." Later, Christ appeared to Constantine in a dream bearing the same sign (a cross in the shape of the "chi" and "rho," the first two letters of the Gr. *christos*), instructing him to mark his soldiers' shields with the sign, which he did. He was victorious in his next battle, which helped him secure his hold on the empire. Wishing to thank Christ for his victory, in A.D. 313 Constantine and Licinius, the emperor in the west, issued the Edict of Milan granting religious freedom in the empire. He restored property and granted money to the Christian church, and took an active role in church matters, calling councils such as the now-famous one at Nicea in A.D. 325.

Wresting power from Licinius in A.D. 324, Constantine became emperor of the entire Roman Empire, as a result of which the church moved from being persecuted to enjoying great privilege and power. This was not a totally good transition, however, as it caused the church of Jesus Christ to adapt itself to the formal and structured paradigms of imperial governance. Discussions about the relationship between church and state have continued apace ever since.

This lengthy introduction to Romans 13 sets the stage for the very difficult words the apostle Paul writes to the church at Rome (and to the modern church as well): submit yourself to the governing authorities because they have been established by God. Given the tumultuous and dangerous practices of the Roman rulers the church had seen in the Holy Land and in Rome in the first half of the first century, this was no small order Paul was giving. How is it possible that murderous rulers are in place by God's will? And why would God want us to submit to them? And what if a "Christian" ruler like Constantine comes along? Is the church supposed to become the spiritual arm of the state?

At any time in history, these are important questions. For a church that had lived under Caligula, Claudius, and Nero, they were especially relevant. But there was something else Paul needed to tell the church that would make his instructions more understandable: we are in a holding pattern—these governing authorities are not permanent. We are destined to inherit something far more permanent and better than this. In light of that, submit to the authorities, love one another, and walk in the light. That is the message of Romans 13 to the church at Rome—and for the church today.

II. COMMENTARY

The Gospel Requires Understanding the Times

MAIN IDEA: *In light of the end of the age, believers should honor their civil rulers, fulfill the law of love, and walk in the light of salvation in Christ.*

A Understanding Leads to Submission to Civil Authority (13:1–7)

SUPPORTING IDEA: *In light of the end of the age, believers should honor their civil rulers since they are appointed by God.*

Because sin is a reality in human culture, Paul knew that it would be to the advantage of Christians to be sheltered by the civil authorities from the effects of sin in society—especially in light of the likelihood of the escalation of sin as the present age draws to a close. Therefore, what seems contradictory at first—for believers in Christ to submit themselves to pagan "lords"—is really for the believers' own good.

13:1. When it came to presenting oneself as a living sacrifice to God, Paul "urged" the Christians to do so (Rom. 12:1). But when it came to submitting oneself to the governing authorities of the land, urging was replaced by commanding: **Everyone must submit himself** (*hupotasso;* present passive imperative) **to the governing authorities.** Why the imperative, the command? Because, in principle (though not always in specifics), to submit to the civil authority is to submit to God. The statement in this command which unlocks its meaning, and which gives Christians ground to accept it and apply it, is this: **There is no authority except that which God has established.** This is a statement of the overarching sovereignty and rule of God in the affairs of this world. If God has appointed every civil ruler, every governing authority, then why should any Christian fear submitting to that which God has appointed?

Daniel said that God "sets up kings and deposes them" when he praised God in prayer for revealing to him the meaning of King Nebuchadnezzar's dream (Dan. 2:21). When Daniel conveyed the dream and its meaning to the king, he said plainly, "The God of heaven has given you [Nebuchadnezzar] dominion and power and might and glory . . . he has made you ruler" (Dan. 2:37–38). Daniel continued illustrating Paul's point: "After you [Nebuchadnezzar], another kingdom will rise. . . . Next, a third kingdom . . . will rule. . . . Finally, there will be a fourth kingdom" (Dan. 2:39–40). Then, "the God of heaven will set up a kingdom that will never be destroyed" (Dan. 2:44).

Daniel's point is conclusive: from Nebuchadnezzar's kingdom to God's final kingdom, God is in control, setting up and taking down kings to accomplish his perfect will. Later, Nebuchadnezzar recounted another dream he had in which he was told by "holy ones" (angels) that "the Most High is sovereign over the kingdoms of men and gives them to anyone he wishes and sets over them the lowliest of men" (Dan. 4:17). Unfortunately, Nebuchadnezzar was to become a living illustration of his own dream as he was driven from his throne for seven years (Dan. 4:24–27).

What Paul wanted the believers in Rome to understand was that, in the Roman Empire (or any other), "No one from the east or the west or from the desert can exalt a man. But it is God who judges: He brings one down, he exalts another" (Ps. 75:6–7). And even after he is in office, "The king's heart is in the hand of the LORD; he directs it like a watercourse wherever he pleases" (Prov. 21:1). Therefore, Caligula, Claudius, and Nero (those Roman emperors spanning the lifetime of the Roman church up until Paul's writing) had ascended to power with God's permission—actually, by his direction **(have been established by God)**—as have the rulers of today.

As an aside, it should be noted in the name of thoroughness that Paul does not contradict himself between what he says here and in 1 Corinthians 6:1–8. In the latter passage, where Paul commands believers not to air their dirty laundry in front of civil magistrates, he is not encouraging them to bypass the duly constituted legal process for redress of grievance. Rather, he is asking the Corinthian believers, "Why do you have any grievance at all?" This is not a matter of being unwilling to obey the governing authorities. It is a matter of the shameful condition the church was in when they could not find among themselves enough wisdom to settle differences without having to ask for the help of unspiritual, civil judges.

To admit that, with God's help, in the body of Christ we cannot solve our differences, is to admit defeat. It would be better to suffer the wrong than to admit to the world the inability to solve the dispute (1 Cor. 6:7–8). A private defeat with a believer's name shamed is better than a public defeat with God's name shamed.

13:2. Rebelling against what God has instituted will bring the judgment of God, more than likely through the rulers themselves. While we are painfully (shamefully) aware of the fist we raise against God in some areas of life, it is sometimes hard to see it here. If an earthquake destroys our town, or a disease ravages our body, or a deranged person violates our personal or property rights, we can rest in the sovereignty of God more easily than we can when a twenty-something police officer pulls us over for rolling through a stop sign. We looked both ways, we slowed almost completely to a stop, we have a (reasonably) good driving record, we were under the influence of nothing—and yet we still got a ticket.

Paul says that to rebel against that ticket is to rebel **against what God has instituted**. If we rebel against it loudly enough, or aggressively enough, or persistently enough, we may be punished with an additional fine for disorderly conduct, interfering with a police officer's duty, or touching (assaulting) a police officer.

The fact that "governing authorities" are *human* authorities—sinners just like us—is perhaps what makes it so difficult. Earthquakes and natural disasters have no will. Diseases and congenital deformities have no will. Deranged assailants have a will, but one that is obviously deserving of pity. But when an otherwise competent individual, set apart from us by nothing but a gold badge, asserts his or her authority over us, it is hard to see God in that blue suit. But God says he is there, and to resist him is to invite his blue-suited judgment.

The example of a policeman and a traffic ticket is almost trivial in today's world of moral, ethical, religious—and ultimately legal—quagmires. But it does illustrate Paul's point. Far more difficult to deal with is the question of limits. How far is the Christian expected to go in obeying civil authorities—

especially when those authorities demand that which goes against the will of God?

The question of civil disobedience is not an easy one, nor a new one (see "Deeper Discoveries"). When the apostles Peter and John were told by Jewish leaders "not to speak or teach at all in the name of Jesus . . . Peter and John replied, 'Judge for yourselves whether it is right in God's sight to obey you rather than God . . . . We must obey God rather than men'" (Acts 4:18–19; 5:29). There obviously comes a time when governing authorities are to be "resisted" (the question of "How?" is another worthy discussion) through disobedience to their injunctions. The key to discerning when that time has come is found in Paul's words, **what God has instituted**. When rulers put themselves in the place of God by legislating moral or spiritual positions (all acts have moral and spiritual roots) which are contrary to the revealed positions of God, resistance is warranted.

Generally speaking, the church historically has differentiated between governing authorities forcing versus allowing a moral or spiritual condition contrary to the laws of God. If the position is commanded (such as Herod's killing of male children two years old and younger, or Hitler's decree that Jews and other minorities were to be eliminated, or the prohibition against religious activities on public property), then the injunction is to be resisted in all possible ways. If the position is allowed but not commanded (such as modern laws allowing abortion), then resistance is to be voiced by the church in an attempt to have immoral standards changed; to restore God's standards to society.

Concerning Paul's words here, F. F. Bruce says, "It is plain from the immediate context, as from the general context of the apostolic writings, that the state can rightly command obedience only within the limits of the purposes for which it has been divinely instituted—in particular, the state not only may but must be resisted when it demands the allegiance due to God alone" (Bruce, pp. 223–224). He proceeds to cite the words of Sir T. M. Taylor (*The Heritage of the Reformation*, 1961), who says, "The obedience which the Christian man owes to the State is never absolute but, at the most, partial and contingent. It follows that the Christian lives always in a tension between two competing claims; that in certain circumstances disobedience to the command of the State may be not only a right but also a duty. This has been classical doctrine ever since the apostles declared that they ought to obey God rather than men" (cited by Bruce, p. 224). The moral and spiritual standards that God **has instituted** are to be upheld whenever the positions of **the authority** come in conflict with them.

It must be stated here that this is not actually Paul's point in these verses. In fact, in his epistles, he does not directly address the topic of the Christian's response to the *ungodly* acts of the civil governing authorities. His point is much more related to the example of the policeman given above—those times when the Christian is called upon to submit to governing authorities when their standards do not violate the standards of God.

When Paul was brought by the Jews before Gallio, the proconsul of Achaia, he was accused of advocating a religion not allowed by the Romans. Gallio wisely and properly did not interfere, saying the Jews were upset not about Roman legal matters but about matters pertaining to their own religion. "Settle the matter yourselves. I will not be a judge of such things," he told the Jews (see Acts 18:12–15).

On another occasion, Paul did not fare as well, almost bringing **judgment on [himself]** when he called Ananias the high priest a "whitewashed wall," after Ananias had him struck. But when Paul "discovered" that Ananias was the high priest, he "apologized," citing Exodus 22:28: "Do not blaspheme God or curse the ruler of your people" (see Acts 23:1–5).

Paul's emphasis here is a civil version of his words in Romans 12:18: "If it is possible, as far as it depends on you, live at peace with everyone." Live within the system and do not rebel against the rulers on nonessential matters—the gospel will be spread more effectively when you do.

13:3–5. Paul next explains the "why?" behind his statement in verse 2 that to rebel against authorities is to invite judgment upon oneself. In an "ideal" world, governing authorities are **God's servant[s] to do you good . . . to bring punishment on the wrongdoer.** The world is not a governmental theocracy in which God is king. Since Israel abandoned the direct theocratic rule God desired for them, and asked God for a king like "all the nations around us" (1 Sam. 8:5,20), even his chosen people have been governed by human rulers. There is no direct, geopolitical theocratic rule in place today; all people on earth are ruled by some sort of human authority. In Israel's case, this was to be a good thing (witness the moral and civil law codes given to Israel to protect their best interests) and should be a good thing for all nations.

Most governing authorities implement law codes that are basically moral, designed to protect citizens and **to bring punishment on the wrongdoer.** Inherent in God's assignment of responsibility for authorities is not only the provision of **good** but the use of force **(the sword)** to restrain evil. There is no conflict here between Paul's words in Romans 12:19–20 about not taking vengeance, and his words about the use of **the sword** to restrain evil. The former is personal, the latter is constitutional. In the former, hatred (vengeance) is at work; in the latter, justice is at work.

This is the fundamental principle espoused in Samuel Rutherford's time-honored work, *Lex Rex: or The Law and the Prince* (1644). In his book, Rutherford said that the law, not the human authority, is king, and the law is to be based on God's law. Therefore, when the human authority uses **the sword,** he is doing so not on a personal basis but as a servant of the king-law. King Lemuel's (Solomon?) mother illustrated this principle in her maxims to her son: "It is not for kings . . . to drink wine . . . lest they drink and forget *what the law decrees, and deprive all the oppressed of their rights* (Prov. 31:4–5; emphasis added). The king's job is to apply righteous standards to the people (Prov. 31:8–9), to be a servant of the law.

Again, in an ideal setting (all rulers are not moral or lawful), no one should live in fear of a governing authority. God has put them in place to provide for order and safety until the king of all kings comes to establish his righteous rule over all the earth. God commends right living through the intermediary of **rulers**. The idea is that if you are living in peace, you are living right. If you are living in trouble, you are not living right. **Rulers** are God's arm of correction for people on earth.

As it does for many topics, Proverbs presents a multitude of images concerning kings that support the ideas and ideals Paul is presenting in these verses. While the king of Israel was the immediate reference point for these verses, "kingship" in general is a valid application given the nature of the Book of Proverbs:

- Prov. 8:15: Kings (should) reign by wisdom and make laws that are just.
- Prov. 14:28: A large (read "prosperous") population brings glory to the king.
- Prov. 14:35: Shameful servants incur a king's wrath.
- Prov. 16:10: Kings should not speak unjustly.
- Prov. 16:12: Kings should be righteous and detest wrongdoing.
- Prov. 16:13: Honest subjects are honored by kings.
- Prov. 16:15: A happy king means life for subjects.
- Prov. 20:2: Angering a king is a sentence of death.
- Prov. 20:26: Kings are supposed to filter the evil out of the kingdom.
- Prov. 21:1: A king is God's instrument.
- Prov. 24:21: Subjects should fear God and (his representative) the king.
- Prov. 29:4: A king's justice brings stability to a country.

Paul's last word in his explanation concerns motivation. While avoiding **punishment** is always a legitimate motivation for submitting to an authority, there is a higher motivation for the Christian's submission to **the authorities**—the motivation of a clear **conscience**. One of the verses cited above—Proverbs 24:21—illuminates Paul's words: "Fear the LORD and the king, my son, and do not join with the rebellious." For one to say that he or she fears God while acting with impudence toward governing authorities presents a contradiction which cannot stand in the face of **conscience**.

That is, in order to keep a clear **conscience**, the Christian must submit to governing authorities (Rom 13:1). Christians must pay their taxes, obey the speed limit, buy fishing and hunting licenses, wear their seat belts, and do a myriad of other things they would rather not do—and do them all in both the letter and spirit of the law. A **conscience** is not an infallible guide, as Paul said—"My conscience is clear, but that does not make me innocent" (1 Cor. 4:4)—but it is a place to start.

13:6–7. Shades of Levitical legislation are apparent in Paul's next words. Just as the Levites in Israel were to be supported by the twelve tribes, so governing authorities are to be supported by taxes on the people. Added impetus is given to Paul's words by his change of terms from verse 4. There, God's "servant" is twice designated by *diakonos,* the word which is also used to describe those who minister and serve in the church (e.g., Rom. 16:1; 1 Tim. 4:6). But in verse 6, Paul uses a different word for servant, *leitourgos,* a word used for someone who serves in behalf of another. The former word speaks of the activity, the latter the activity as representing another (see *leitourgos* used of Christ [Heb. 8:2], angels [Heb. 1:7], Paul [Rom. 15:16], and Epaphroditus [Phil. 2:25]).

In the Old Testament, the Levites were God's intermediaries, his priests, to represent his will (minister to) the nation. As such, they received no inheritance of land in the Promised Land (the Lord himself was their inheritance; Num. 18:20), and they received tithes from the whole nation for their support "in return for the work they do while serving at the Tent of Meeting" (Num. 18:21; see also Num. 18:22–24; 26:62; Deut. 10:9; 12:12; 14:27).

While civil ruling authorities in no way take the place of or succeed the role of the Levites in Israel, the principle of support is not dissimilar. Just as you should not "muzzle an ox while it is treading out the grain" (Deut. 25:4; 1 Cor. 9:9; 1 Tim. 5:18), so "the worker deserves his wages" (Luke 10:7; 1 Tim. 5:18). Because governing authorities are God's authorities, they are to be supported since they give **full time to governing,** just as the Levites did (and just as do those elders "who direct the affairs of the church . . . especially those whose work is preaching and teaching"; 1 Tim. 5:17).

With regard to the government, the Christian is to be "debtless"—he or she is not to be found owing **taxes . . . revenue . . . respect . . .** [or] **honor** to any governing authority. Jesus Christ himself validated Paul's position in his famous "give to Caesar what is Caesar's" statement (Matt. 22:15–22). Paul does allow for one debt to remain outstanding, however, but not to public officials. He mentions that debt in the next part of chapter 13 before getting to the real reason for living in obedience to the ruling authorities—the approaching end of the age (13:11–14).

Ⓑ Understanding Leads to Love for One Another (13:8–10)

SUPPORTING IDEA: *In light of the end of the age, believers should fulfill their obligation to love one another.*

Living at peace with society and at peace with one's **fellowman**—both in light of the approaching end of the age—are the two practical dimensions of life as a living sacrifice. Having commanded submission to ruling authorities, he now turns to another commandment—the law of love for one another.

13:8. Paul's words in this section are not as much an exhortation to life within the body of Christ (he touched this in Rom. 12:9–13) as they are a balance to what he has just commanded the church in 13:1–7. Paul's overall emphasis in this chapter is to live submissively as living sacrifices in light of the coming end of the age—"The trip is almost over; this is no time to rock the boat." Living respectfully toward the king and loving one's **fellowman** are the two dimensions of every person's public life. If there is a key word in verses 1–7 it is "submit" (vv. 1,5), which contains within it the range of words such as "honor," "respect," and "obey." When it comes to one's **fellowman**, Paul draws upon a range of words found in the Decalogue, the Ten Commandments given by God to Israel through Moses. He summarizes all those words in the operative word **love**.

Love (and its attendant synonyms) is the one sanctioned unpaid **debt**. Indeed, it is a debt that cannot be paid; it is a **continuing debt**. While it appears that Paul's words are church-related, his use of **fellowman** seems to broaden the intent of his instruction. In light of the previous verses dealing with society and governance at large, it would seem his focus is still on the wider scope of Christian responsibility. It is not Christian to love fellow church members while hating a pagan neighbor.

No, Paul is saying something larger to the believers in Rome: "The way to open doors for the gospel in Rome is to avoid entanglements. We are on a kingdom mission of spreading the gospel, not morally rehabilitating the Roman Empire or its citizens. Obey the emperor and love your neighbors. If you do this you will live at peace and have greater opportunity to focus on the mission of the church in light of the coming end of the age."

There is a certain paradox in Paul's words: in order to get out of debt to **the law** we have to go into debt to **love**—we fulfill **the law** when we love. The difference is a liberating one. Instead of focusing on what we could never do (perfectly meet the demands of the law), we are freed to focus on what we can always do (love one another).

13:9. When Christ reduced the Ten Commandments (themselves a summary of the whole moral law) to two, he simplified the process of obeying

God for the Pharisees. The Jewish leaders were more interested in the details and particularities of "how" to obey God than in actually obeying God, and reducing the details of the moral law to two simple statements removed their excuses: love God and love your neighbor (Matt. 22:34–40). Paul does the same thing here (not that the Roman believers had been offering excuses that we know of, but just to remind them of how the law had been subsumed under love).

Apparently in random order, Paul mentions four of the six commandments dealing with relations with one's neighbor (in the Ten Commandments, commandments one through four focus on God; five through ten on one's neighbor; see Exod. 20:1–17). His words, **whatever other commandment there may be** does not mean he cannot remember the others. He is saying that all commandments and laws and regulations governing one's relationship with others are essentially commands to **love your neighbor as yourself.** This summary command was initially taken by Christ (Matt. 22:39; see also Mark 12:31; Jas. 2:8; Gal. 5:14) from Leviticus 19:18 and coupled with the *Shema,* the great statement of Judaism that the Lord is one and to be loved with all the heart, soul, and strength (Deut. 6:5).

Loving one's neighbor as oneself does not imply a self-focused infatuation with self. Rather, it is a simple way of saying, "Take care of your neighbor with the same natural motivation that you take care of yourself." It is the same sense that Paul used when telling the Ephesian men to "love their wives as their own bodies" because "he who loves his wife loves himself. After all, no one ever hated his own body, but he feeds and cares for it" (Eph. 5:28–29).

And who is this neighbor that we are to feed and care for, that we are to **love** (love here is *agapao,* not *phileo;* the command is to sacrifice oneself, not be merely friendly or affectionate)? It is the person who has a need that I can meet, according to Christ's story in Luke 10:25–27. There, the neighbor was the man who had the resources, not the man in need. But a person who is a neighbor is a person who also has neighbors, so Paul's admonition to **love your neighbor** is the same as Christ's admonition to be a neighbor who loves.

13:10. In his final word on **love,** what did Paul have in mind by mentioning **harm?** Were there incidents of the Christians in Rome acting unkindly toward their Roman neighbors, or toward anyone? Were there reports of unkind relations between members of the church in Rome? Or was Paul simply going back to the source of "love your neighbor" and drawing on the context—which was rich in examples: do not steal, lie, deceive, defraud, rob, hold back wages, curse the deaf or cause the blind to stumble, be unjust, show partiality, slander, endanger, hate, seek revenge, bear a grudge—"but love your neighbor as yourself" (Lev. 19:11–18)?

The most specific indication that we have as to the motivation for his words is found in the next verse. We are to love our neighbors because the darkness is receding and the light of a new (eschatological) day is dawning.

⬤ Understanding Leads to Pleasing the Lord (13:11–14)

SUPPORTING IDEA: *In light of the end of the age, believers should put off the deeds of darkness and walk in the light of salvation in Christ.*

In this chapter, Paul has hung the keys to understanding by the back door. He now reveals, in these last four verses, the eschatological reality that confronts all believers: a new age is dawning. Rather than spending our time gratifying the desires of the flesh, we should be clothing ourselves with the righteousness that is about to envelop the entire world.

13:11. When Paul says **do this**, to what is he referring? While we have presented two distinct categories of responsibilities outlined by Paul—submit to the civil rulers and love one's neighbor—the singular **this** could be taken not to refer to both; perhaps only the latter, the responsibility to love one's neighbor. But in a way, the "debt" to love one's neighbor is an extension of the responsibility (debt) to submit to civil authorities, to whom no debt was to remain outstanding. Therefore, there is a "singular" sense about the whole chapter: the responsibility to live submissively and in love with those over you and those beside you in light of the end of the present age.

It is **understanding the present time**, much as the men of Issachar were gifted with doing (1 Chr. 12:32), that is the key to Paul's words. The **present time** is the age of salvation that has come in the person of Jesus Christ. One of Paul's key themes in all his writing is the line drawn between "this age" and the "age to come" (which was inaugurated with Christ; see 1 Cor. 1:20; 2:6,8; 3:18; 2 Cor. 4:4; Gal. 1:4,14; Eph. 1:21; 1 Tim. 6:19; Titus 2:12; see also Matt. 12:32; Heb. 6:5). **Salvation** for Paul and his readers was much more tangible than it is to the contemporary church. **Salvation** was the equivalent of being rescued from darkness and transferred into the kingdom of God (Col. 1:13). Certainly this was positional, but it was also a rescue that was going to take place in the future—"he [Christ] will appear a second time . . . to bring salvation to those who are waiting for him" (Heb. 9:28). And that **salvation** draws **nearer** with each passing day—**it is nearer now than when we first believed**.

The image of waking from slumber to welcome the dawning of the glory of God is probably derived from Isaiah 60:2: "Arise, shine, for your light has come, and the glory of the LORD rises upon you. See, darkness covers the earth and thick darkness is over the peoples, but the LORD rises upon you and his glory appears over you." That eschatological glimpse into the future by Isaiah is now being refined by Paul as he tells the Romans that the glory of God (the second advent of Christ) is growing nearer day by day. But what are the implications of the fast-approaching day of **salvation?**

13:12–13. These two verses are paralleled thematically in Paul's writing in 1 Thessalonians 5:4–11 and Ephesians 5:1–20. The need to come out of the **darkness** and into the **light** behaviorally is what every believer must do in light of the imminent Day of the Lord. Positionally, the believer has been justified and declared holy by God, as Paul has clearly shown. But when Christ returns, when salvation is at hand, he will not come for his own in the realm of darkness on this earth. He will come looking for his own in the light.

"We do not belong to the night or to the darkness," Paul told the Thessalonians (1 Thess. 5:5). Therefore, do not be like those of the night, those who are asleep morally, who participate in **orgies and drunkenness . . . debauchery . . . dissension and jealousy,** and who practice "sexual immorality . . . impurity . . . greed . . . obscenity . . . foolish talk [and] coarse jesting" (Eph. 5:3–4). Why? Because all of those things will be made visible on the day of our salvation. Better to come out of the darkness now and be found pure and holy when the light of the glory of God shines on all people at the end of this age. Light and darkness are incompatible in the spiritual realm just as they are in the physical realm. They cannot be in the same place.

To come out of darkness means to **put on the armor of light.** Because of the contextual parallels between the 1 Thessalonians and Ephesians passages, the **armor of light** is without question the "armor of God" found in Ephesians 6:11–18 (see a shorter version of the armor in 1 Thess. 5:8).

What did Paul mean by **the night is nearly over; the day is almost here?** Was his reference to time literal or metaphorical—or both? Without question, it was, at the very least, metaphorical. To Paul had been revealed things that the prophets of old had not seen or understood, and he was in a position to know that the light destined to shine on the Gentiles was now shining (Isa. 42:6; 49:6; Luke 2:32; Acts 13:47; 26:23). Even Matthew realized that "the people living in darkness have seen a great light; on those living in the land of the shadow of death a light has dawned" (Matt. 4:16, quoting Isa. 9:2). Matthew was, of course, writing after the death and resurrection of Christ, which all recognized as being the watershed event between the testaments— that display of power and light which separated the ages.

But how soon would the **day,** the age to come, appear? The *NIV Study Bible* represents the position that Paul had no timetable in mind: "These texts do not mean that the early Christians believed that Jesus would return within a few years (and thus were mistaken). Rather, they regarded the death and resurrection of Christ as the crucial events of history that began the last days. Since the next great event in God's redemptive plan is the second coming of

Jesus Christ, 'the night,' no matter how long chronologically it may last, is 'nearly over'" (Barker, note on Rom. 13:12).

But is there evidence to the contrary in the New Testament? And must we conclude that, if the early church did anticipate a prompt return of Christ (in their lifetime), they were mistaken—any more than the prophets were mistaken about their lack of understanding? The New Testament writers could certainly be excused if they thought that Christ would return soon. Given their limited knowledge of the world (i.e., what it would take to fulfill the Great Commission; cf. Matt. 24:14), and their failure to anticipate the sluggishness (carnality? disobedience?) of the church to enter fully into the task of completing its mission after their demise, one can read an expectation of a soon-return of Christ into their words.

In fact, in light of the plain meaning of the many words they wrote to others, a strong case can be made for their anticipation that Christ might return while they were still alive (see "Deeper Discoveries" for further study).

The doctrine of imminence—the any-moment return of Christ—is an eschatological doctrine, not a chronological one. Regardless of when Christ returns on the calendar, the church is warned by Paul to be found in the light, not in the darkness. And the way to do that is the message of his last verse.

13:14. When considering the meaning of **clothe yourselves with . . . Christ,** one cannot but think of the story of Joseph and his brothers (Gen. 37:2–24)—especially in light of Paul's words concerning the envy of Israel over the fruit of the gospel (Rom. 10:19; 11:11,14). To put something on, or to clothe oneself, is to display it outwardly. When the patriarch Jacob gave his favorite son, Joseph, a beautiful coat to wear, Joseph put it on and thereby displayed the glory of his father Jacob—and his love for Joseph. The anticipated response of Joseph's eleven brothers was jealousy: "When [Joseph's] brothers saw that their father loved [Joseph] more than any of them, they hated [Joseph] and could not speak a kind word to him" (Gen. 37:4). The brothers realized that Joseph had received the love and favor of their father more than they had—perhaps in no small measure because of the bad report Jacob had received about their activities (Gen. 37:2).

A bad report about the descendants of the sons of Jacob has once again reached the Father's ears, and he has clothed another (the church) with the glory of his love so that the sons of Jacob may one day turn back to him to receive their own cloak of righteousness. The church—those faithful, spiritual descendants of Abraham—are clothing themselves **with the Lord Jesus Christ,** and displaying the glory of God to the world.

And because Paul is talking about spiritual cloth, how do we tell who is clothed with the Lord Jesus and who is not? Those clothed in Christ are the ones who **do not think about how to gratify the desires of the sinful nature.**

They are the ones moving out of the darkness and putting on the armor of light (v. 12). They are the ones baptized into Christ and clothing themselves with him (Gal. 3:27). They are the ones who are putting on a new self, a self created to be like God in true righteousness and holiness (Eph. 4:24) in the image of their Creator (Col. 3:10).

Many of Paul's words in 1 Corinthians 7 (esp. v. 17) would apply in his message to the Roman believers: "This is not a time to be starting new things. The Son of Righteousness is about to dawn over the whole earth. Wherever you were when God called you, sit tight. Do not make trouble with the law and do not fail to keep the law—the law of love. Our highest priority is to witness to the glorious love of God that has been made known to us in Christ Jesus. If you can endure these limitations for the sake of the gospel, you will be rewarded with the salvation Christ is preparing, at this moment, for you."

MAIN IDEA REVIEW: *In light of the end of the age, believers should honor their civil rulers, fulfill the law of love, and walk in the light of salvation in Christ.*

III. CONCLUSION

Disobedient Unto Death

The aged bishop, Polycarp, disciple of the apostle John and bishop of Smyrna, honored the Roman authorities under whom he lived—until they asked for more honor than he gave to his Lord and Savior Jesus Christ. The following is a paraphrased version of the Christian historian Eusebius's (*History of the Church*, IV, 15) account of Polycarp's final hours:

"Are you Polycarp?" the Roman proconsul asked.

"Yes."

"Swear to Rome, and I will set you free. Execrate Christ!"

"For eighty-six years," replied Polycarp, "I have been his servant, and he has never done me wrong. How can I blaspheme my king who saved me?"

"I have wild beasts," said the proconsul. "I shall throw you to them if you don't change your attitude."

"Call them," replied the saint. "We cannot change our attitude if it means a change from better to worse."

"If you make light of the beasts," retorted the governor, "I'll have you destroyed by fire, unless you change your attitude."

Polycarp answered: "The fire you threaten burns for a time and is soon extinguished. There is a fire you know nothing about—the fire of the judgment to come and of eternal punishment, the fire reserved for the ungodly. But why do you hesitate? Do what you want."

The proconsul was amazed, and sent the crier to stand in the middle of the arena and announce three times: "Polycarp has confessed that he is a Christian." The crowd roared in unison that Polycarp must be burned alive.

When the wood was laid around his feet, Polycarp prayed:

> O Father of thy beloved and blessed Son, Jesus Christ, through whom we have come to know thee, the God of angels and powers and all creation, and of the whole family of the righteous who live in thy presence; I bless thee for counting me worthy of this day and hour, that in the number of the martyrs I may partake of Christ's cup, to the resurrection of eternal life of both soul and body in the imperishability that is the gift of the Holy Spirit.

Upon his "Amen," the pyre was lighted and Polycarp gave up his life in submission to the governing authority—after submitting himself to his chief Governing Authority.

It has happened countless times in history—believers living in submission to their civil rulers with honor and respect, until those rulers ask them to give up their faith in Christ. Because so many years separate the modern Western church from martyrs like Polycarp, it is easy to read about them and marvel at their faith. But the faith of modern Christians is beginning to be tested around the world as it has not been since the days of the Roman Empire. Not so much in America (yet), but in many other parts of the world believers are being persecuted simply for being Christians. Many have lost property, family, limbs, and yes, even their lives.

When Peter and John said, "We must obey God rather than men" (Acts 5:29), they meant it, and proved it—Peter by being crucified and John by being exiled for his faith. The modern Western church has to ask itself whether it is prepared to give up all, if asked to, for the sake of allegiance to Christ. The Lord is not above testing his people (Exod. 16:4). The first test may seem small: Will you obey the rulers I have established over you (when you break the speed limit)? The second test may be large: Will you obey the rulers I have established over you (when they ask you to deny me)? If we answer the first test affirmatively, we pass; if the second, we fail.

PRINCIPLES

- Where no clear biblical command or principle is violated, believers are to obey their governing authorities.
- All governing authorities have been established by God.
- Authorities exist to reward good and restrain evil in society.
- All of God's Old Testament commands concerning relationships are summed up in the command to love one's fellowman.

- The present evil age is almost over; the final act of history, the return of Christ, could happen at any time.
- Christians are to live righteously, walking in the light of Christ, in light of his return.

APPLICATIONS

- Is there any area of civil life in which I have exercised a cavalier or disobedient spirit?
- Do I treat my governing authorities with the same respect I treat God, who appointed them?
- When was the last time I thanked God for the safety I enjoy daily, or thanked those authorities who provide it for me at the risk of their own lives?
- Do I try to rationalize my failure to love on the basis of "technicalities" instead of simply obeying the law of love?
- Have I made any plans for the future that are more important to me than the return of Jesus Christ?
- If Christ appeared today, is there any lifestyle, thought, or activity that I would be ashamed to have brought into his light?

IV. LIFE APPLICATION

The Cost of Discipleship

No modern Christian, and few in all of history, have so lived out the dual emphases of Paul in Romans 13 as did the German Lutheran Dietrich Bonhoeffer. His interaction with the Nazi government in Germany in World War II, and his costly decision to remain committed to his fellow believers, and non-believing fellow German citizens as well, are a model for living out Paul's admonitions.

Bonhoeffer lived from 1906 to 1945, when he was hanged by the Nazi regime for treasonous activity—specifically, he was imprisoned on charges of smuggling fourteen Jews out of Germany to safety in Switzerland. But that act, in obvious violation of Nazi policy, was the end result of years of trying to live under a totalitarian regime and maintain his Christian convictions at the same time. It gradually became impossible, which caused him to repudiate his government's policies and live in violation of them as a citizen of the kingdom of God.

Bonhoeffer was a privileged German from a well-to-do family. He received a doctorate in theology from the University of Berlin at the age of 21, and did postgraduate work in New York City at Union Seminary. He was the chaplain and a lecturer at the University of Berlin when Hitler came to power in 1933. He became part of the *Kirchenkampf* (church-struggle) as Protestant and Catholic leaders tried to discern a role for the church in an increasingly anti-Christian state. The "Confessing Church" arose, consisting of about one-third of Protestant German pastors who were committed to repudiating Hitler's advances. After pastoring from 1933–1935, he became head of the Confessing Church seminary which the Nazis closed in 1937. He was forbidden to speak publicly or publish his writings. He was at a moral and spiritual crossroads.

Offered the opportunity to leave Germany and go to America where he could speak out freely against Hitler, he chose to remain in Germany with the increasingly persecuted church and other Germans who were resisting Nazism. He actually joined the anti-Nazi resistance as a double agent in the German military intelligence, working directly against the success of his own "governing authorities." At one point, under the guise of using his international ecumenical connections for the Nazis, he transmitted to the British news about the group of Germans who were plotting to assassinate Hitler.

Bonhoeffer had moved deeper in his sacrificial commitment to help the people of his homeland, though it meant working in channels committed to the death of his own civil ruler. His priorities had come into full focus, and became clear for all who knew him well—and for others—to see.

Bonhoeffer was imprisoned from 1943 to 1945 (hanged in 1945), during which time he wrote prodigiously. In his *Letters and Papers from Prison,* he expressed the costly grace which he believed every Christian should be willing to enter into: "It is infinitely easier to suffer in obedience to a human command than to accept suffering as free, responsible men. It is infinitely easier to suffer with others than to suffer alone. It is infinitely easier to suffer as public heroes than to suffer apart and in ignominy. It is infinitely easier to suffer physical death than to endure spiritual suffering. Christ suffered as a free man alone, apart and in ignominy, in body and in spirit, and since that day many Christians have suffered with him."

When outward religion in Germany failed to stand up against unrighteousness, Bonhoeffer saw it as unbiblical. When many suffered under unrighteous leaders, he saw it as a call to put love into action. Bonhoeffer's pattern in all of this was Christ. Jesus Christ was "there only for others," and being there for others is what genuinely points to the reality of God. Bonhoeffer did not seek out conflict with his government, but he ran headlong into it in pursuit of God's kingdom. At that point, loving his fellowman became more important than saving himself. While the cost of discipleship for Dietrich Bonhoeffer ended up being his very life, it was no more a price than his Savior had paid for him.

V. PRAYER

Heavenly Father, forgive me for my failure to appreciate and honor those authorities which you have set over me for my good and my protection. I recognize that your hand, and your plan, have placed them where they are. And forgive me for justifying my lack of love. Help me, in light of the any-moment return of your Son, to live honorably in my community, and lovingly with my fellowman, in order that the spread of the gospel will not be hindered. Amen.

VI. DEEPER DISCOVERIES

A. Civil Obedience/Disobedience (13:2)

As stated in the commentary, the question of civil obedience (and disobedience) is neither an easy, nor a new, one. Once the focus of God's work on earth moved outside of the context of Israel's theocracy (where a perfectly just God was both civil and spiritual ruler), things changed. The church is not a geopolitical entity. It has no earthly king, no constitution, no homeland, and no armies by which to propagate or defend its views. The church is a scattered body, a guest, so to speak, in the nations of earth that do have all those things. Thus the obvious tension: What does the church do when the rulers of the lands in which it is a guest-resident either allow or command practices and policies which are contrary to Christian doctrine (God's will)?

In the words of philosopher-theologian Francis Schaeffer, "What is the final relationship to the state on the part of anyone whose base is the existence of God?" And, "Has God set up an authority in the state that is autonomous from Himself?" (Schaeffer, *Manifesto,* pp. 89–90). Schaeffer's work is the primary resource for this discussion). Schaeffer goes on to point out that when Jesus said to "Give to Caesar what is Caesar's, and to God what is God's" (Matt. 22:21), he did not mean it this way,

GOD and CAESAR

but this way,

GOD

and

CAESAR.

Schaeffer continues:

"The civil government, as all of life, stands under the Law of God. In this fallen world God has given us certain offices to protect us from the chaos which is the natural result of that fallenness. But when *any office* commands that which is contrary to the Word of God, those who hold that office abrogate their authority and they are not to be obeyed. And that includes the state." Paul's words in Romans 13:1–5, and Peter's parallel in 1 Peter 2:13–17, do not suggest that God has given the state absolute power, but power to act justly and morally. "God has ordained the state as a *delegated* authority; it is not autonomous. The state is to be an agent of justice, to restrain evil by punishing the wrongdoer, and to protect the good in society. When it does the reverse, it *has no proper authority.* It is then a usurped authority and as such it becomes lawless and is tyranny."

Schaeffer goes on to cite numerous times in the history of the church when its leaders and members have resisted the tyranny of civil authority. Those who died in Roman arenas for their faith were persecuted not for their religion but because they would not obey the state. Schaeffer cites Francis Legge, who in *Forerunners and Rivals of Christianity from 330 B.C. to A.D. 330* (University Books, 1964), writes, "The officials of the Roman Empire in times of persecution sought to force the Christians to sacrifice, not to any heathen gods, but to the Genius of the Emperor and the Fortune of the City of Rome; and at all times the Christians' refusal was looked upon *not as a religious but as a political offense*" (emphasis added).

Beyond the martyrs of the church's first century stand others who resisted the civil and religious tyranny of governing authorities: England's William Tyndale (1490–1536) and John Bunyan (1628–1688); Dutch Protestants in sixteenth-century Holland; the Vasa family in sixteenth-century Denmark who broke away and established Sweden as a Lutheran country; Protestants in sixteenth-century Denmark who overthrew the Danish dynasty and set up a new government; Luther in Germany who was protected from the emperor by the Duke of Saxony; Protestants in sixteenth-century Bern, Switzerland, whose military presence secured the right to preach the gospel; John Calvin's resistance to the House of Savoy in Geneva, Switzerland; John Knox of Scotland, whose pamphlet *Admonition to England* set off a firestorm for his assertion that common people (not just rulers, as Luther and Calvin had said) had the right and duty to disobedience and rebellion if state officials ruled contrary to the Bible. To do otherwise, for Knox, was rebellion against God. Knox wrote that "kings then have not an absolute power in their regiment to do what pleases them; but their power is limited by God's word." A ruler is "Lieutenant to One whose eyes watch upon him" (historical survey summarized from Schaeffer, *Manifesto*, p. 98).

It was on the heels of Knox's fiery formulations that Samuel Rutherford (1600–1661) wrote his *Lex Rex: or The Law and the Prince* (1644) mentioned in the commentary. Rutherford's attack on the divine right of kings—the king or state ruled as God's regent making his (its) word law—formed the bedrock of all post-seventeenth-century dissent against political tyranny in Europe, and eventually in America as well. Rutherford argued that all men, kings included, are under the Law of God, not above it. The state is to be administered according to God's Law, and acts of the state which contradict God's law are tyranny—i.e., ruling without the sanction of God.

Schaeffer cites two of Rutherford's fundamental premises: first, since tyranny is satanic, not to resist it is to resist God. And second, because rulers are granted power conditionally by God, if rulers do not meet those conditions (just rule according to God's laws), then the people have the right (the duty) to withdraw their sanction. The civil ruler is a "fiduciary figure," according to Rutherford, holding authority in trust for the people. Violation of the trust is grounds for resistance.

Citizens, therefore, have a moral obligation to resist unjust and tyrannical government. While the office that God has established is to be honored, the man or woman in that office is disqualified from ruling when policies violate God's standards. Schaeffer points out that Rutherford was careful to warn that it is not single breaches of trust that call for resistance. Rather, it is when the governing structure of the country is being destroyed through unjust and ungodly acts over time that the ruler is to be relieved of his or her privilege to rule.

In the modern day, there are many forms of "resistance." Prayer (resistance in the spiritual realm), letter writing, face-to-face meetings, elected office, legislation, peaceful demonstration, civil disobedience, resistance by force, and overthrow. Certainly, Scripture calls on every peaceful means of resistance and change to be employed first. But in the end, when peaceful resistance to tyranny has failed, disobedience to authorities, according to Peter and John (Acts 4:19; 5:29) and Knox and Rutherford, is justified. Schaeffer's words are a sobering wake-up call: "*If there is no final place for civil disobedience, then the government has been made autonomous, and as such, it has been put in the place of the Living God*" (Schaeffer, p. 130, emphasis his).

B. Church and State (13:3–5)

In addition to the question of civil disobedience, the relationship between church and state is another outgrowth of Paul's words in Romans 13:1–5. In essence, should the two be totally separate, as modern proponents of separation doctrines hold? A review of the evolution of the relationship provides background.

Following three centuries of persecution by the Romans, the church emerged protected and legalized in the Roman Empire under Constantine through the Edict of Milan in A.D. 313. In some ways, the state was "Christian" since Constantine had embraced Christianity, but it was clear that, though the church was supported, it still existed by permission of the state. The Eastern Orthodox Church's entanglement with the state remains to this day as a result of Constantine's merging of the two. The Western church in

Rome fared little better, the Vatican finally becoming its own state in 1929, making it the world's smallest country (population around 750).

In the fifth century, Augustine of Hippo penned *De Civitate Dei* (*The City of God;* written 413–426), in which he divided humanity into two groups: the city of God (the church) and the city of man (the state). Both were ordained by God, the state to be concerned with civil matters and the church with spiritual affairs. Augustine's view laid the foundation for the basic view held by "Christianized" Western nations until the Middle Ages in Europe when the secular and spiritual roles of the church were merged, culminating in the divine right of kings in which the head of the state is also head of the church. In post-Reformation Geneva, Switzerland, Calvin attempted to establish Augustine's two distinct arms of society again, a model which Puritan fathers brought to American shores when England refused to separate the two institutions.

As religious pluralism and post-Enlightenment secularism made their way into the American culture, duly-elected officials not sharing biblical convictions made their way into the state house. The conflicts between church and state—no prayer in school, abortion on demand, spiritual authority of parents over their children, etc.—are the outgrowth of two centuries of a widening gap between church and state.

It is the widening gap between Augustine's (Scripture's) two arms of society that have raised the issues of civil disobedience. What does the church do when the state's biblical heritage is lost in the gradual devolution of standards to the lowest common denominator? (See Henry, *Dictionary of Christian Ethics*, pp. 101–103.)

C. The End of the Night (13:12)

Just six years before Paul wrote to the Roman believers, he wrote a letter to the believers in Thessalonica that offers some insight into Romans 13:12: "The night is nearly over; the day is almost here." Paul knew that the church was living in tumultuous times in the Roman Empire. He also knew that Christ had told his disciples that when certain disruptive events started to happen they were to "lift up [their] heads, because [their] redemption is drawing near" (Luke 21:28). What Paul understood about the details of Christ's words, we do not know. But we do know that he foresaw a time when a "man of lawlessness" would be revealed who would exalt himself over God and proclaim himself to be God (2 Thess. 2:1–12). Paul knew that the "secret power of lawlessness" was "already at work" (v. 7) but was being held back by a restrainer, ready to be "revealed" (v. 8).

Was the man of lawlessness in Paul's mind when he told the Romans that "the night is nearly over"? Did Paul see the Roman Empire as the force that would attempt to snuff out the light of the church? Did he think that in just a short time, the confrontation between lawlessness and righteousness—"the Lord Jesus will overthrow [him] with the breath of his mouth" (2 Thess. 2:8)—was on the verge of taking place? If so, why did he not go into the same detail with the Roman believers as he had with the Thessalonians? What had he learned in six years about the eschatological conclusion of the age?

It is interesting that Paul spoke most boldly about eschatological realities in his two earliest epistles (following Galatians), 1 and 2 Thessalonians (A.D. 51–52). As he prepared to go to Rome himself, and wrote to the believers there, he became less specific and more practical: submit to the authorities and love those around you. Was Paul preparing the church for a conflagration, the dawning of a new day in God's timetable, that he thought would happen in his lifetime? (See the next "Deeper Discoveries" for further notes on this topic.)

D. The Time of Christ's Return (13:11–12)

Scholars have debated whether Paul thought that the culmination of the present age would occur in his lifetime with the second advent of Christ. Arguments of "inclusive" language (using first-person language to refer to the church regardless of chronology) notwithstanding, the following verses give some indication that Paul and the other New Testament writers never anticipated a two-thousand-plus year hiatus between the first and second advents—that they might have considered that the Great Commission would have been fulfilled in their lifetime:

- 1 Corinthians 7:29–31: "The time is short" serves as an explanation for his advice in verses 17–28 concerning marriage, etc. Because the time is short, do not expend great efforts in changing the present or planning for the future.
- 1 Corinthians 10:11: "Us, on whom the fulfillment of the ages has come." Paul seemed to think the fulfillment *had come.* Certainly, the fulfillment was Christ. But Christ's temporary departure while the Holy Spirit empowered the church to announce the fulfillment to the rest of the world does not seem to imply a lengthy period of time.
- Philippians 4:5: "The Lord is near."
- 1 Thessalonians 4:13–18: "We who are still alive, who are left till the coming of the Lord." Paul seems to put himself in the camp of those who will be alive at the coming of the Lord.
- 2 Thessalonians 2:1: "Concerning the coming of our Lord . . . and our being gathered to him." Again, first person language.
- 2 Thessalonians 3:6–15: Paul's admonition against idleness. In light of his teaching on the coming of the Lord, was there a

temptation among the Thessalonians to cease their daily responsibilities?

- Hebrews 10:25: "Let us not give up meeting together . . . as you see the Day approaching." Had some even stopped meeting together for encouragement and edification as the church in anticipation of the return of Christ?
- James 5:7–9: "Be patient . . . until the Lord's coming . . . because the Lord's coming is near."
- 1 Peter 4:7: "The end of all things is near."
- 1 John 2:18,28: "This is the last hour . . . continue in him, so that when he appears." John appears to be writing to people whom he thought would see the appearance of the Lord.

Other verses give indication that Paul may have included himself among those who would be buried before the return of the Lord (1 Cor. 6:14; 2 Cor. 4:14). A key verse linking Paul's mission to the return of Christ is Matthew 24:14 where Christ said that the end would come when the gospel of the kingdom had been preached in the whole world. Understanding this, one can understand Paul's urgency to enlist the Roman church's support in his mission to reach Spain and the regions beyond.

Eschatologically, the apostles were correct in thinking that world evangelization could be accomplished "quickly" and the Lord would return. Practically, it is hard to imagine that it could have happened by the end of the first century, given what we now know about world population distributions at that time. The value in discovering the apostles' viewpoint on the timetable of the Lord's return is this: *if they were urgent and expectant, we should be urgent and expectant as well.* Had the church been completely obedient from the first century onwards, world evangelization could probably have been completed long before the present time. It is at that point that the discussion has to find its resting place in the way God's sovereignty overshadows and accounts for the will (or lack of will) in human beings.

VII. TEACHING OUTLINE

A. INTRODUCTION

1. Lead Story: No One Said Submission Was Easy
2. Context: In the last chapter of Romans (chap. 12), Paul urged the Christians in Rome to present themselves as living sacrifices to God. Everything he instructs them in from that point on is a sacrificial act of one sort of the other—the picture presented is that the Christian life is a sacrificed life. In the church or with fellow believers, we are called to sacrifice our desires for what God has called us to do to

build his church. Paul continues that theme in chapter 13, but now with reference to the community and our fellowman.

3. Transition: Because Paul's heart is set on getting the gospel to the Gentiles, he wants the church at Rome to do nothing that would hinder that process—whether aiding him on his way to Spain or in their own evangelistic efforts in Rome. Therefore, he instructs them to honor the Roman rulers and their laws and to obey God's laws that are summarized in the command to love one's neighbor. In obeying these directives, the church at Rome will live in peace and provide no reason for hindering the spread of the gospel, the power of God unto salvation.

B. COMMENTARY

1. Understanding Leads to Submission to Civil Authority (13:1–7)
   a. Recognition of God's authorities (13:1)
   b. Results of rebelling against God's authorities (13:2)
   c. Role of God's authorities (13:3–5)
   d. Responsibility toward God's authorities (13:6–7)
2. Understanding Leads to Love for One Another (13:8–10)
   a. One legitimate debt (13:8)
   b. One summary command (13:9)
   c. One way to fulfill the law (13:10)
3. Understanding Leads to Pleasing the Lord (13:11–14)
   a. Understanding the present time (13:11)
   b. Living in the present time (13:12–13)
   c. Pleasing the Lord in the present time (13:14)

C. CONCLUSION: THE COST OF DISCIPLESHIP

VIII. ISSUES FOR DISCUSSION

1. What are the key arenas of public life in which today's church has manifested disagreement with the national government? How have they done so? What have been the results? How much of the church has voiced its objection? Why is not the number of objectors larger? What would be the impact on our government if 100 percent of the church spoke out?

2. How much love is there in the church of Jesus Christ with regard to fellow Christians? With regard to non-Christians? What are the hardest ways to show love within the church? To those outside the church? What relationship is there between love and evangelism (see John 13:35)? Is there any correlation between the number of non-

Christians eager to become disciples of Jesus and the amount of true love in the church?

3. How often does the average Christian think about the return of Christ—that it could be today? Why does this most important doctrine carry so little relevance to believers? Given what many Christians have invested of their time, talent, and treasure in this life, what evidence is there that their hopes are fixed on the salvation Christ will bring at his appearing? If Christians invested less in this world and more in "the next," what impact would that have on fulfilling the Great Commission?

Romans 14:1–15:13

The Gospel Unifies the Body of Christ

Quote

"A Christian is a most free lord of all, subject to none.

A Christian is a most dutiful servant of all, subject to all."

Martin Luther

Romans 14:1–15:13

 IN A NUTSHELL

*P*aul continues his exposition on living sacrificially by dealing with an apparent problem in the church at Rome: conflicts between the Jewish and Gentile believers over preferences regarding food and the observance of holy days. He knows that the church cannot be unified behind him in the spread of the gospel if they are not one with one another in daily Christian living. He emphasizes that unity requires liberality, unity is an evidence of love, and unity exemplifies the life of the Lord Jesus Christ.

The Gospel Unifies the Body of Christ

I. INTRODUCTION

Focus On Who, Not What

$\mathcal{T}$he great Methodist churchman and missionary E. Stanley Jones (1884–1973) gives an example of why every pastor would do well to spend some time on the mission field: Talk about *what* you believe and you have disunity. Talk about *who* you believe and you have unity (cited in Larson, p. 170).

Like most truisms, Stanley's words are not 100 percent reliable—but they are close. Generally speaking, when Christians get their focus off the center of their faith, Jesus Christ, and get it onto peripheral matters, disunity sets in. On the mission field, where the greatest priority is telling people about Jesus, it is much easier to stay focused than it is in congregations where evangelism and discipleship have lost their priority. Once institutionalism sets in, the church finds lots of things to disagree about.

Such was the case with the church in Rome—to a degree. At first blush, we might think that the church at Rome had not had time to become institutionalized. But assuming the church started around A.D. 35 (there were Jewish and Gentile visitors from Rome at Pentecost when the postresurrection giving of the Holy Spirit occurred and three thousand were converted; see Acts 2:10–11,41), it had been in existence at least twenty years by the time Paul wrote this letter. Think how many churches there are in your community that have been in existence less than twenty years and have had "unity" problems. It does not take long to get the focus off of "who" and on to "what."

To be fair to the church at Rome, however, their problems with disunity do not appear to have been severe. And their differences were admittedly over serious and complicated theological matters—as opposed to the somewhat trivial matters over which modern churches disagree. A story is told of two churches located only blocks from each other in a small community. They felt it would be wiser for them to merge into one larger, stronger congregation, and plans to do so were set in motion. But it never happened. Why? They could not agree on the wording of the Lord's Prayer. One group preferred "forgive us our trespasses," while the other wanted "forgive us our debts." A newspaper article reporting the failed merger noted that the one group went back to its "trespasses" while the other returned to its "debts" (cited in Hughes, *Stories*, p. 418).

At least the Roman church (as far as we know) had not gone as far down the disunity road as the Corinthian church had. At Corinth, internal factions, based on loyalty to individuals, were dividing the church (1 Cor. 1:11–17; 3:4–21). This was totally unacceptable to Paul, and he told them so. He was far more gentle with the Roman Christians based on the topic of their concern, as he himself had been through serious "unity" discussions on the same topic (cf. Acts 15 and Gal. 2). At least the Roman church was still just "the church (singular) at Rome." But we cannot help wondering what Paul would say if he surveyed the current landscape of Christendom—or what he must think about it from his perspective in heaven. There are some differences so large as to make it appear that two or more different religions exist—all under the name "Christian."

Consider the Protestant, the Roman Catholic, and the Orthodox branches of Christianity. The differences there are so large as to make members of each branch suspicious of the spiritual integrity of the others. But even from those major trunks have sprung branches complex enough to strain a genealogist's patience. And then, visit any community and you will discover congregations *of the same affiliation* which, if pressed, would admit to reasons for not joining in fellowship with those with which they profess to agree!

Are the differences that divide the body of Christ justifiable? Theoretically, no. There is only one Lord, one faith, one baptism, and one God and Father of all who is over all (Eph. 4:5). If we were somehow able to get the apostle Paul, Martin Luther, John Calvin, John Wesley, Billy Graham, the Pope, and the various Orthodox patriarchs together two thousand years after the inauguration of Christianity, and asked them to survey the current state of the unity of the church, what would they say? Would the differences that divided the church along its historical path still seem as relevant—especially in the face of an unfulfilled Great Commission resulting in thousands dying daily and entering a Christless eternity? Which of the issues that seemed so important at the time—everything from disagreements over staffing for evangelism (Acts 15:36–41) to the authority of earthly leaders (the Reformation) would remain in the "essentials" column?

For the Roman believers, unity as an outgrowth of liberty and love was Paul's goal. The things that they were disagreeing over were nonessentials, things in which loving liberty needed to be extended. But Paul's message was not an academic one—it was a practical one that the church today needs to hear and practice: unity is at the heart of evangelization. Unity among Christians is how the world knows that Jesus is our Lord (John 13:35), and unity among Christians provides the stable, ongoing base needed for extended evangelistic efforts to be successful.

Because Paul hoped to visit the church at Rome as soon as possible after writing this letter, he wanted to find in place a unified and loving fellowship of house churches that would unite with him in extending the gospel to Spain and the regions beyond. Though the geography has changed in two millennia, the task Paul was pursuing remains unfulfilled. Do we have a lesson in liberality and love to learn? It would appear that we do. May the church today become unified in the essentials, extend liberty in the nonessentials, and love one another in all things—that the gospel of the kingdom may go forth in power and purity to those yet to hear.

II. COMMENTARY

The Gospel Unifies the Body of Christ

MAIN IDEA: *Unity in the body of Christ encompasses liberty, evidences love, and follows the example of the Lord Jesus Christ.*

A Unity Encompasses Liberty (14:1–12)

SUPPORTING IDEA: *Unity is more important than agreement on nonessential matters in the Christian life.*

One wag said that if you tie two alley cats together by the tails and hang them over a clothesline, you will see an example of being united without being unified! The Christians in Rome were united by their faith in Christ, but Paul detected a lack of unity between the Jewish and Gentile believers. By identifying the fundamental issue—differences over religious standards and ordinances—he was able to prioritize those matters in the larger scheme of kingdom values.

14:1–4. In these first four verses, Paul identifies the fundamental problem that the believers in Rome were having, and he gives a one-sentence corrective. The problem was that the Christians in Rome were **passing judgment on** [each other over] **disputable matters.** The **disputable matters** were primarily two: food (v. 2) and the observance of sacred days on the calendar (v. 5). In a nutshell, Paul's answer to the problem is to stop judging one another—**Who are you to judge someone else's servant?** Paul pictures Christians as the servants of God, and accountable to him alone. To one's own **master he stands or falls,** not to one's fellow servants. The rest of this lengthy section of the letter deals with the rationale behind his instruction to stop judging one another.

Does this problem exist in the modern church? How often do believers find themselves guilty of passing judgment on one another over matters which are in the "gray zone"—that area to which the Bible does not address clear guidelines, especially on cultural matters that were not even part of the biblical world? More often than not, modern believers are forced to look for principles from which guidelines can be extrapolated. And when believers arrive at different practices, it causes them to judge one another.

Just think of the areas which have been "hot buttons" in the twentieth-century church: the consumption of alcoholic beverages, the ownership of luxury goods, forms of recreation such as movies and dancing, tithing, Christian schools versus public education—and the list goes on. Clearly, the practice of judging one another over **disputable matters** is not a modern sin—the believers in Rome were guilty as evidenced by Paul's directives. But their plight is at least a bit more understandable. The early church was on the cusp of a whole new way of doing "religion"—the transition from the old covenant to the new covenant was not an easy one for Jewish believers.

And, Paul's words to them were their first guidelines, following on the heels of the letter from the Jerusalem Council seven years earlier (A.D. 50), and his letter to the Galatian churches (perhaps as early as A.D. 48/49) and the church in Corinth (A.D. 55) where the same issues were addressed. It is to the modern church's shame that we have been living under the new covenant for nearly two thousand years, and have full access to Paul's guidance on **disputable matters**, and yet still judge one another.

The reason that food and sacred days were a problem derives from the integration of old covenant Jewish standards with new covenant church practice. Jewish life in the Old Testament was governed by "the law"—all the way from the fourth commandment which required the appropriate keeping of the Sabbath to scores of ordinances about eating. The kinds of foods, how they could be produced and prepared, and even the source of the foods were all governed. The purpose of this, of course, was national identity (along with purity-based health concerns). God's people, the Jews, were to be separate and distinct from all the peoples on the earth, thereby attracting legitimate attention to themselves and their God.

But the laws proved to be too burdensome for people with sinful and weak constitutions. The laws were good—it was the people who were not. So when God sent his Son to fulfill the law righteously for humankind—thereby doing away with the laws as a source of righteousness—the question immediately arose, What do we do with the laws and regulations that we used to follow in a quest for righteousness now that righteousness, is based on faith instead of works?

In comparison to the relatively mild forms of disagreement over this question in our day, the early church, only a score of years removed from the event that caused the debate (Jesus' death and resurrection for the redemption of law-breaking humans, putting an end to law-based redemption), argued vociferously over this subject. Paul even dressed down Peter and Barnabas in front of the church in Syrian Antioch because of their hypocrisy

(Gal. 2:11–21). They knew that it was not necessary for Gentiles to adopt Old Testament practices in order to be accepted by God, and yet were being influenced by Jewish believers from Jerusalem precisely in that direction. As a result, Gentile believers in Antioch were being alienated.

Paul took this issue very seriously—"I [Paul] opposed him [Peter] to his face, because he was clearly in the wrong" (Gal. 2:11). This problem was a microcosm of the issue Paul later addressed in 1 Corinthians 8, 10 and here in Romans 14, where it centered around food. Eventually as the church grew following the ascension of Christ, church leaders wrestled with these issues at the famous Jerusalem Council (Acts 15). There, they heard Paul and Barnabas, fresh off their first missionary journey (Acts 13–14), recount how God had opened the door of acceptance to the Gentiles on the basis of faith alone.

Under the leadership of James (the very James who had sent Judaizers to Antioch to influence Peter and Barnabas; Gal. 2:12), the council of church leaders in Jerusalem drew up a letter to send to "the Gentile believers in Antioch, Syria and Cilicia" (Acts 15:23) advising—*not legislating*—certain things that would be helpful in building unity between Jewish and Gentile believers. James's goal was to "not make it difficult for the Gentiles who are turning to God" (Acts 15:19) by asking them to adopt Jewish standards or practice regarding old covenant life. Rather, the council, in their letter, asked Gentile Christians to "abstain from food sacrificed to idols, from blood, from the meat of strangled animals and from sexual immorality. *You will do well to avoid these things*" (Acts 15:29; emphasis added).

It is important to note that the recommendations are in the form of advice, not prohibitions. The first three all had to do with Jewish prohibitions concerning the consumption of meat—prohibitions unknown by Gentiles. The last, sexual immorality, is not to be taken as "advice" in the sense that it can be practiced or not practiced. Rather, the point is that Gentiles had almost no standards regarding sexual practices, especially those associated with pagan religious festivals which some may have wanted to introduce into Christianity. Gentiles were advised by the Jerusalem Council to stop offending Jewish believers in all these areas as a way to build unity in the church.

It is hard for the modern believer to identify with the "wild West" mentality of the early church, fresh out of Gentile paganism. While we know from years of meditation on Scripture that even a lustful look at a person is to be avoided (Matt. 5:28), in the early days of the church there were much more flagrant forms of immorality that needed to be addressed and eliminated. While we may find it surprising that Gentiles were "advised" by the council to cease their sexual immorality, this was a gentle way to begin implementing standards into a fairly chaotic environment. Within a short time, issues such as sexual immorality in the church became grounds for being barred from fellowship (1 Cor. 5).

So, when Paul heard that the Jewish and Gentile believers in Rome were at odds over the issue of food regulations and the keeping of sacred days, he was not surprised. He set about to instruct them as he had done several years earlier with the Corinthians. But in this case, consistent with his style and purpose in Romans, he goes into greater detail with a more lengthy explanation.

As to questions over food, it appears that some believers were avoiding meat altogether for religious reasons. These were most likely Jewish believers (but could have been Gentile believers influenced by their Jewish brethren) who held one or more fears: the kind of meat they were purchasing in the market was forbidden in the Old Testament; the meat had possibly been part of a sacrifice to a pagan deity before ending up for sale in the market; the meat had not been drained of blood properly—all of which would have violated their strict Jewish sensibilities. As a result of not being able to control the source and method of preparation of marketplace meat, these believers were eating **only vegetables.**

Paul gives his hand away as to where he stands on the issue by calling these believers those **whose faith is weak**—but he does not do so in a derogatory manner. In fact, he defends their right to hold to their convictions in order to keep their consciences clear before God. But his use of the adjective **weak** is an indication that their view is not his since he identifies himself with the "strong" (Rom. 15:1).

The only person Paul chastises is the person who would **look down on** or **condemn** one who holds to a different view than one's own. Do you eat everything in the market? Fine, but do not **look down** on those who pick and choose. Do you pick and choose? Fine, but do not **condemn** those who shop and eat with their eyes closed. Paul's main point in this entire section is that there is a kingdom of God, not a cuisine of God, that is the priority. And in God's kingdom, there is only one thing on the menu: unity—manifested by "righteousness, peace and joy" (Rom. 14:17).

Paul says to think of God's kingdom like a house—God is the **master**, we are the **servant[s].** The goal of the house is peace and harmony among all who live there. The **master** sets the standards, and as long as each **servant** is at peace with the **master**, peace will be maintained among the servants. If one of the **servant[s]** usurps the role of **master** and implements standards for the other **servant[s]**, discord erupts. And that is precisely what was about to happen in Rome.

14:5–8. In the first four verses, Paul disallowed judging one another. In these verses, he turns to the positive and says that **each [man] should be fully convinced in his own mind** when it comes to disputable matters. "Disputable matters" must be emphasized here. Paul is not saying that one may commit any act or indulge in any behavior as long as he or she is **convinced in his [or her] own mind.** Rather, the point is that, among those spiritual behaviors that people do for **the Lord**, giving **thanks** and glory to him in the process, all are acceptable to God—and therefore should be acceptable to each other.

For instance, in the period of the Babylonian captivity, Daniel and his friends were convinced that they would honor God more by not eating the meats offered them in the courts of the Babylonians (Dan. 1:8–16), meats perhaps sacrificed to their pagan deities. Others of the Hebrew youth undoubtedly did not share their conviction (though Daniel 1:16 may indicate that they were invited by the Babylonian guards to develop the conviction anyway!). Daniel's and his friends' choices illustrate what Paul is saying here: we must choose on the basis of our convictions before God, and as we do so, we should be free from criticism from others in the body of believers.

A few years after writing on these matters to the church in Rome, Paul took a more strident approach with the believers in Colossae (Col. 2:16–23). There, however, believers were being influenced by false teachers of an unknown origin. Apparently, strict rules of worship and religious conduct were being foisted upon the church, and Paul says clearly, "Do not let anyone judge you . . . [for] these are a shadow of the things that were to come; the reality, however, is found in Christ" (Col. 2:16–17).

There are clues to suggest that the problem in Colossae was different from the problem in Rome. The criticizers had false humility, unspiritual minds, idle notions, the appearance of wisdom, sensual indulgences, and were basing their judgments on human commands and teachings (see Paul's warnings to Timothy about the same problem in 1 Tim. 4:3–5). This was not the case in Rome. There, the Jewish and Gentile believers were going about different ways of giving genuine **thanks to God**, but without agreement or understanding on the right way.

Paul's words to the Roman believers echo his words to the Corinthians: "So whether you eat or drink or whatever you do, do it all for the glory of God" (1 Cor. 10:31). Here he says **whether we live or die**, we belong to the Lord, but the implication is the same. The person **who eats meat** and **he who abstains** from meat **does so to the Lord and gives thanks to God** (cf. 1 Tim. 4:4–5). We should not be about the business in the spiritual life of making up our own rules, i.e., living to ourselves alone. Our life is to be lived **to the Lord**, and if our convictions about how to live to him include something that another person does not include, Pauls says it is fine.

Some consider one or more days in the week **sacred**, others consider **every day alike**, i.e., every day sacred. While the Sabbath day comes immediately to mind, there were any number of other days in the religious calendar that Jewish believers could have been observing. And Paul is saying that he does not object to that, nor should anyone else.

14:9–12. In this final section of Paul's opening words, he reminds his readers that **we will all stand before God's judgment seat**. There is only one judge of all people; for that reason, people can afford to live liberally (generously) with one another. Unity in the body of Christ is bigger than anyone's personal perspective, and should therefore encompass generous amounts of liberality toward one another. The truly confident Christian is the one who, like Paul, can live caring "very little if I am judged by . . . any human court" because "the Lord . . . will bring to light what is hidden in darkness and will expose the motives of men's hearts" (1 Cor. 4:3,5).

Paul's justification for saying that we should mind our own business, and not that of others, is the death and resurrection of Christ. There is no one over whom Christ is not Lord, as demonstrated by his death and resurrection. Because Christ was raised by the power of God (2 Cor. 13:4), God has made him Lord of **both the dead and the living.** John Stott says, "It is wonderful that the apostle lifts the very mundane question of our mutual relationships in the Christian community to the high theological level of the death, resurrection and consequent universal lordship of Jesus" (Stott, p. 362).

If Christ is going to judge every person one day, Paul asks the obvious questions: **Why do you judge your brother?** (probably referring to those "weak" in faith, the Jewish believers, who believed that Christians should not eat the meat from the marketplace), and **Why do you look down on your brother?** (probably referring to the "strong" in faith, those who believed it was acceptable to eat all things with thanksgiving).

Interestingly, Paul once again appeals to the Old Testament for support. Gentile believers would not intuitively stand to be corrected by a passage from the Hebrew Scriptures as much as the Jewish believers—an indication that the Jewish believers were the ones doing most of the "judging"? Regardless, Paul quotes Isaiah 45:23 (here and in Phil. 2:10–11) in a context speaking of the future submission of Gentiles (everyone else in addition to Israel) to God. Paul obviously interprets this to refer to Christ, even mentioning the *bema,* **God's judgment seat,** referred to as "the judgment seat of Christ" in 2 Corinthians 5:10 (see also 1 Cor. 3:10–15).

Whenever a human being puts himself in a position of judge of another, he or she usurps the position of the true judge of all, Jesus Christ. Because **each of us will give an account of himself to God,** no Christian should judge another or be intimated by the judgments of another—Paul's next point in this part of the epistle.

B Unity Evidences Love (14:13–23)

> **SUPPORTING IDEA:** *Unity reveals the only thing that can bring together people who differ: love.*

In this section Paul raises the discussion of food and sacred days to a higher level. He is not interested in debating the fine points of the law; rather, he is interested in focusing on the highest value in the kingdom of God: love (1 Cor. 13:13).

14:13–18. In this section of the epistle Paul reveals where he stands personally on the issue of "disputable matters." At the other end of the table from those weak in faith—those whose conscience will not allow them to eat meat from the pagan marketplace or miss the observance of sacred days—are the strong in faith, the group with which Paul specifically identifies himself in Romans 15:1. Here, without using the word *strong*, he says that he is **fully convinced that no food is unclean in itself**—adhering to his own advice to be "fully convinced in his own mind" (14:5).

But then he introduces into the discussion that which makes the Christian perspective in human relationships so radical: even if you believe you are right, if your actions cause a spiritually weaker (less mature) brother or sister to stumble in his or her own faith, you are to stop what you are doing.

Paul is now moving in a more focused direction than he was earlier in this chapter. He began by suggesting that eating or not eating were equally valid choices; and they are, depending on where we are in our understanding. But here he is making it clear that, as an apostle—**one who is in the Lord Jesus**—he believes it is less mature to be bound to regulations based in the law. In other words, it is totally acceptable from God's point of view to eat meat from the marketplace in Rome (cf. 1 Cor. 10:23–11:1). But there is something more important in the **kingdom of God** than being right. The most important thing is to act **in love**. And when a Christian insists on his or her rights to the detriment of a fellow Christian, that person is **no longer acting in love**.

Jesus went to extreme efforts to try to convince the Jews that things in the **kingdom of God** are different than in human kingdoms. Whereas we are focused on external issues—who one is, how one dresses or acts, what one eats or drinks—God is concerned with the heart: "What goes into a man's mouth does not make him 'unclean,' but what comes out of his mouth, that is what makes him 'unclean'" (Matt. 15:11; cf. Matt. 15:10–11,16–20; Mark 7:14–23). And if what comes out of our mouth is, "I have the right to eat whatever I want!" then we have defiled ourselves since those are not the words of a person acting **in love**—the highest **kingdom** value.

Paul has here returned to the concept of being a living sacrifice before God (Rom. 12:1). A person who has sacrificed all of his or her rights and prerogatives on the altar of service to God discovers that God's "good, pleasing and perfect will" is to "honor one another above yourselves" (Rom. 12:2,10). And in the matter of the rights of a mature Christian is found a perfect example of what he means. If a mature Christian in the church at Rome brought meat purchased in the marketplace into a communal meal at which are present those brothers or sisters who felt the eating of that meat was wrong—then the more mature Christian is at fault. Why? Because the weaker brother or sister would be encouraged to participate in something which for them was sin.

Fast forward to today. Perhaps a church home group celebrates the Lord's Supper together, and the leader decides to use real wine instead of a nonalcoholic grape juice. If there are those in the group who have strong feelings about the use of alcoholic beverages, so much so that they would be in a position of compromising their convictions, then the wine should be excluded (v. 21). Or if some members of a group of Christians chooses a movie for the group to see together, and some in the group are reluctant to attend because of the nature of the movie's content, they should choose a movie that does not offend any in the group.

This is radical!—from the world's point of view. The world would say to the weaker brother or sister, "Get a life! Grow up! Stop whining!" But Paul says to the stronger brother or sister, **Make up your mind not to put any stumbling block or obstacle in your brother's way.** In other words, he takes the focus of responsibility off what the weaker believer *cannot* do in good conscience and puts it on what the stronger believer *can* do in good conscience. The stronger believer's conscience is like an umbrella that is large enough to cover the weaker believer's conscience. Therefore, the stronger believer has the responsibility to "cover" the situation instead of asking the weaker believer to cover more than his or her umbrella of conscience can handle.

What is it that one might stumble into? Sin, as Paul will explain in the next section (v. 23). Just look at some of the "dark" words Paul uses in describing this situation: **stumbling block, obstacle, distressed, destroy, evil.** Just looking at those terms, one might suspect Paul was talking about a conflict between darkness and light or good and evil. That is exactly how serious Paul wants to make this issue. He wants no division to enter the church in Rome, no opportunity for the devil to get a foothold (Eph. 4:27) and perpetrate his schemes among people who all thought they were "right" (2 Cor. 2:11; Eph. 6:11).

Paul almost seems to have Christ's words in mind when he says that **the kingdom of God is not a matter of eating and drinking, but of righteousness, peace and joy in the Holy Spirit.** This is, of course, the opposite of what life was like under the old covenant. Though **righteousness, peace and joy** were to be had, there was quite a bit of emphasis given to **eating and drinking.** The **Holy Spirit** was active in the Old Testament, but not as an indwelling reality in the life of the believer. Under the new covenant, it was the opposite. **Righteousness, peace and joy** derive not from what one eats or drinks but from who one is filled with—the **Holy Spirit** (Eph. 5:18).

Therefore, if a brother or sister does not understand that truth from the point of view of all things being acceptable, then the stronger brother or sister must apply it from the perspective of having **joy** in life even if some of his or her preferences and desires are given up. The reason that this is the wisest course for the stronger believer is twofold: it is **pleasing to God** and will cause the stronger believer to be **approved by men.**

A missionary who had served in Laos told of an interesting situation that illustrates what Paul is saying here. Years ago, before national boundaries were set, the kings of Laos and Vietnam reached an agreement on taxation in the border areas where it was hard to tell "who was who." But values saved the day. For example, the Laotians ate short-grained rice, built their houses on stilts, and decorated them with Indian-style serpents. The Vietnamese, on the other hand, ate long-grain rice, built their houses on the ground, and decorated them with Chinese-style dragons. As for taxation, the location of a person's house was not what determined the nationality. Instead, each person was taxed by the country (kingdom) whose values they exhibited in their way of life. It should be the same with believers in Christ.

Regardless of how circuitous the boundaries between believers and unbelievers are (the church is *in* the world but not *of* the world), it should be obvious where the Christians are by the values they exhibit. Unlike kingdoms of this world, or other religions of this world, Christians should not be known for what they eat or drink, or how they decorate their houses or churches, but for their **love, righteousness, peace and joy in the Holy Spirit.**

14:19–23. Paul is moving toward a conclusion in light of what he has just stated. And the conclusion is that the building up of the church—**peace and . . . mutual edification**—is the goal. *Oikodome*—the act of building up, edification, strengthening; a building—is an oft-employed theme of the apostle in his letters. If anything, it can be said that the apostle Paul loved the church, the body of Christ. After all, it was the church that was the great mystery revealed to him, a mystery hidden from the Old Testament saints. It was the church that he set out to destroy as a zealous Pharisee. And it was the church to which he had given the rest of his life after being confronted by its Head on the road to Damascus.

Paul's desire was to build the church larger and more glorious day by day by spreading the gospel of the kingdom further and further into regions where it had not been taken—and risking his life in the process (2 Cor. 6:3–10; 11:16–29). It was Paul who felt responsibility and concern for the churches (the "church," the body of Christ) which he had planted all over the Mediterranean region (2 Cor. 11:28).

The church was God's building that Paul was helping to build (1 Cor. 3:9; Eph. 2:21). Spiritual gifts were to be employed for the edification of the church (1 Cor. 14:5,12,26; Eph. 4:12). Paul's authority as an apostle was for the building up of the church (2 Cor. 10:8; 13:10). Love was the key ingredient in the recipe for building up the church (Eph. 4:16). Everything he did was to strengthen the church (2 Cor. 12:19). With that kind of heartbeat for the church, it is no wonder that Paul wanted the believers in Rome to **make every effort to do what leads to peace and to mutual edification.** The apostle was concerned about the possibility of division and spiritual impurity in Christ's body, "like a mother caring for her little children" (1 Thess. 2:7). The very idea that **the work of God** could be destroyed **for the sake of food** was unthinkable to him.

It is worth noting that Paul makes no attempt to convince the Roman believers (the "weaker" brothers) of the integrity of his own position (that all foods are acceptable to eat). He mentions it only as part of his discussion. His chief priority is clearly the spiritual integrity of the church: it is wrong to do anything **that causes someone else to stumble.** In fact, he says, **whatever you believe about these things keep between yourself and God.** What a refreshing perspective from the most doctrinally conscious pillar of the early church! Paul clearly knew where to draw the line between essentials and nonessentials in theology.

Paul's fear for believers is that they would end up with a defiled conscience. He does not mention the conscience in his letter to the Romans, but it dominates his discussion on the same topic undertaken with the Corinthian believers (1 Cor. 8:7,10,12; 10:25,27,29). Both the weaker Christian and the stronger Christian are in danger of condemning themselves by violating their conscience. The stronger Christian, by insisting on acting according to **what he approves** thereby causing a weaker Christian to stumble, **condemn[s] himself.** The weaker Christian, by giving in to the influence of the stronger Christian and participating in something that he or she believes is sin, **is condemned . . . because [the act] is not from faith.**

Everything, Paul concludes, **that does not come from faith is sin**—both for the weaker and the stronger Christian. Paul seemed to believe that individual believers had the authority, in disputable matters, to go before the Lord in faith and "be fully convinced in his own mind" (v. 5) about what he or she believes—and then hold that position!

The ability to agree to disagree is a marvelous gift in human relations, but one thing is necessary for the gift to spring to fruition—a focus on a higher purpose. In marriage, spouses can agree to disagree for the sake of the higher purpose of remaining true to their vows and leaving a godly legacy for their children. In business, partners can agree to disagree while pursuing profitability and growth. In the church, what is the higher calling that allows members to agree to disagree? For Paul, it was the task of world evangelization and obedience to the Great Commission of Christ. Regarding food sacrificed to idols, Paul is saying that is not a critical factor in spreading the gospel; we can agree to disagree. Sacred days? Not a critical factor, so we can hold different views in tension while we continue on our mission.

In the modern church, when congregations lose sight of the mission and become inwardly focused on who is right about what points of doctrine or practice, they do not agree to disagree—they just disagree. It takes lifting the eyes above the horizon of disputable matters and focusing afresh on the person of Christ and his commission to take the gospel into all the world that allows the church to hold disputable matters lightly. When the church lives sacrificially, Christians are willing to give up personal rights in order to speed the gospel to those waiting to hear. It is that unity which Paul longs to see in Rome.

The famed creator of the "Peanuts" cartoon strip once had the easygoing Charlie Brown sprawled out watching television when Lucy storms in, demanding he change the channel. When Charlie Brown asks meekly what gives her the right to make him change the channel, she responds, "These five fingers!" shoving her clenched fist in front of his nose. After changing the channel, Charlie Brown is seen walking out of the room, holding up his open hand and saying to his fingers, "Why can't you guys get organized like that?" (cited by Swindoll, p. 599). There is power in unity, but only in unity characterized by righteousness, peace, joy, love, clear consciences, and focus on the mission. When the "fingers" judge and criticize each other over matters that are nonessential to the "hand's" mission in life, disorganization and disunity results.

In Paul's final exhortation on this matter to the church in Rome, he demonstrates how maintaining unity in the church requires the heart of a servant—the same heart that Jesus Christ demonstrated by uniting Jews and Gentiles together in one body.

C Unity Exemplifies the Lord (15:1–13)

SUPPORTING IDEA: *Unity follows the example of the Lord Jesus Christ, who united Jews and Gentiles into the body of Christ.*

By imitating the example of the Lord Jesus Christ, the church will do three things: bear with the weak, glorify God, and accept one another.

15:1–4. The English novelist Jane Austen might have had this passage of Scripture in mind when she wrote, "Incline us, oh God, to think humbly of ourselves, to be severe only in the examination of our own conduct, to consider our fellow-creatures with kindness, and to judge of all they say and do with that charity which we would desire from them ourselves" (Ward, p. 161). Her words certainly reflect the emphasis of the apostle Paul throughout his entire discussion of "disputable matters."

First, he summarizes the responsibility of the **strong**—those whose convictions allow them greater latitude when it comes to debatable issues. The strong are to **bear with** the weaknesses of their fellow believers—not just tolerate, or condescend to, but participate by showing understanding for the conviction they hold. A good illustration of bearing with (*bastazo*) is Paul's use of it in Galatians 6:2: "Carry each other's burdens." Carrying another person's weakness in the spiritual sense is the same as carrying their burden in the physical sense—we help them get where they are going with what they have in their hand or heart. Instead of criticizing them, we encourage them in their desire to glorify and thank God for his provision and blessing (Rom. 14:6). Instead of tearing them down with theological explanations for why they are wrong, we **build [them] up** in the Lord.

By definition, we cannot **please ourselves** while we are tending to the needs of another. If the strong Christian, one like Paul (**We who are strong**), turns from his own needs to the needs of another, the end result is the building up of that one who is weak in faith.

The example we are to follow in all things, and especially in serving one another, is **Christ.** He did not come to serve himself but to serve those who were in need (Mark 10:45). Though he was rich, he became poor that through his poverty we might become rich (2 Cor. 8:9). He willingly divested himself of his rights and prerogatives as God and took upon himself the very nature of a servant (Phil. 2:5-8). Paul followed the example of **Christ** (1 Cor. 11:1) as he sought not his own good, "but the good of many, so that they may be saved" (1 Cor. 10:33).

To demonstrate to his readers that there is something larger in life than one's own personal concerns, Paul uses a quotation from Psalm 69. In that psalm of David, the king of Israel suffers at the hand of the enemies of God because of some sin (Ps. 69:5). But the king refuses to separate himself from the temple or from God, preferring rather to identify with God in suffering than to identify with those who are persecuting him. The early church, as they did with many royal psalms, saw foreshadowings of **Christ** in the words of the psalmists, and this psalm is no exception (no psalm except Ps. 22 is quoted in the New Testament more than this one).

The entire verse from which Paul quotes (Ps. 69:9), reads, "For zeal for your house consumes me, and the insults of those who insult you fall on me." In John 2:17, the disciples of Jesus apply the first part of Psalm 69:9 to the occasion of Christ's cleansing of the temple in Jerusalem. And Paul applies the second part of verse 9 to Christ here, showing how Christ was more concerned to do the will of God as a servant than he was to seek his own comfort ("Not my will, but yours be done," Luke 22:42). In the same way, Paul says Christians are not to **please** themselves but those whom it is their responsibility to serve.

In citing Psalm 69:9 and applying it to Christ, Paul is making a transition to the last part of this major section on maintaining unity in the church. He is about to cite four major passages from the Old Testament to support his point that Christ sought to bring people together by uniting Jews and Gentiles together in one body—exactly what Paul is desirous of seeing happen in the church in Rome. To tie Psalm 69:9 together with the upcoming four passages, he says that **everything that was written in the past was written to** teach us, so that through endurance and the encouragement of the Scriptures we might have hope.

This statement, along with its parallel written to the Corinthians (1 Cor. 10:6,11), establishes a sound hermeneutical footing for the new covenant believer's use of the Old Testament Scriptures. Here, Paul says they were **written to teach us.** In the Corinthian parallel, he says they were written "as warnings for us." Obviously, they were written for both those reasons, and more. It is a shame that the modern Christian knows so little of the Old Testament. We forget (many contemporary Christians have never realized) that the church was founded on the Old Testament, and functioned for many years that way prior to the canonization of the apostles' writings. Paul did not set out to write the "other half" of the Bible. The purpose of his epistles to the churches was to reveal the mystery which was contained in the Old Testament—the revelation that God was making one new man out of both Jews and Gentiles (Eph. 2:15). To do that, he is continually quoting the Old Testament and explaining its meaning and relevance in light of the ministry and death and resurrection of Christ.

The old witticism, "If the King James Bible was good enough for Paul, it's good enough for me!" has an embarrassing element of truth to it in terms of the perceptions of many Christians. It was not Paul's intent to teach new theology, but to reveal and explain the theology that had been unseen and unheard by the blind eyes and deaf ears of Israel for centuries.

In both verse 4 here, and in 1 Corinthians 10:11, Paul gives an eschatological reason for our need to understand the Old Testament Scriptures. Here, it is so **that through endurance and the encouragement of the Scriptures we might have hope** for the future. In the Corinthians passage, Paul says the Old Testament contains warnings for us "on whom the fulfillment of the ages has come." In both passages, his point is this: there are bigger things happening in God's plan for the ages than our relatively small concerns of the moment. Eating and drinking (Romans) and yielding to temptation to sin (Corinthians) are flashing billboards designed to take our eyes off the road to heaven. When we get distracted by insignificant matters, and stop serving the larger purposes of God by maintaining the unity of the body of Christ, we have left the will of God.

15:5–6. The "endurance" and "encouragement" that comes from reading the Old Testament, identifying the ministry example of Christ, and serving one another gives the church a **spirit of unity.** When that **spirit of unity** is at work in the church, the church speaks with **one heart and mouth** to give glory to God. Here we see allusions to Paul's "body" metaphor so prevalent in 1 Corinthians 12 (mentioned seventeen times in that chapter alone) and Ephesians 3–5 (eight occurrences). Paul believed that the church should act as one body, following the lead of Christ the head.

The last verse of Mark, describing how "the disciples went out and preached everywhere, and the Lord worked with them" (Mark 16:20), is a graphic illustration of how Paul must have envisioned the church continuing to work together to accomplish the fulfillment of Christ's Great Commission. To the extent that, two millennia later, we have not fulfilled Christ's last command, to that same extent we probably have failed to glorify God with **one heart and mouth** in accomplishing his will.

15:7–13. This final section of verses begins with a summary statement followed by four illustrations from the Old Testament and concludes with a benediction. The summary statement Paul gives (vv. 7–9) is perhaps one of the most theologically dense statements in all of Paul's writing. Condensed in one statement is a summary of Romans 9–11, pointing out that God in **Christ** came as a **servant** to **confirm the promises** made to the **patriarchs** which resulted in **mercy** being extended to the **Gentiles.** Had not **Christ** taken on the form of a **servant** and gone first to the "lost sheep of Israel" (Matt. 10:6; 15:24; Rom. 1:16) in confirmation of the **promises** made to the **patriarchs,** the unfolding of the mercy of God to the Gentiles would not have occurred as we know it.

It was Christ's willingness to be led as a "lamb to the slaughter" (Isa. 53:7) that brought closure to the Old Testament messianic prophecies and paved the way for both Jews and Gentiles to be bound over to disobedience so that God might have mercy on them all (Rom. 11:32). Given the content of the Old Testament passages with which Paul is about to support his argument, all of which emphasize the inclusion of the **Gentiles,** it could be suggested that the primary problem in the Roman church was the Jews being exclusionary regarding Gentile believers. Paul may be saying to the Jews in the Roman church, "Be like Christ who, as a servant, completed the purposes of God for his life so that mercy might be extended to the Gentiles. You need to do the same thing toward the Gentiles in the church. Do not worry if they eat meat from the marketplace. Realize they have been brought into the same spiritual union with God that you have through the servanthood of Christ."

While Paul had been speaking to the "strong" in verses 1–6, he seems to broaden his appeal to the whole church beginning in verse 7 (**Accept one another, then**), suggesting an "if the shoe fits, wear it" approach. In verses 9–12 the shoe would likely fit best on the feet of Jewish believers who were not willing to act like **Christ** in serving their Gentile brethren.

Paul cites four Old Testament passages illustrating that it was always God's intent for the Gentiles to be brought into the fold of God's love and mercy. This became possible when Christ came as the Jewish Messiah (came as **a servant of the Jews**) and died for the sins not only of Israel but of the whole world (1 John 2:2). Thus Christ's servanthood provided the means whereby both Jews and Gentiles were unified in one body—Paul's goal for the church in Rome:

1. *2 Samuel 22:50:* This song of praise by David is also included in the Psalms as Psalm 18, and is typical of the Old Testament perspective on "gospelizing" the nations of the world (the Gentiles). As a result of God's favor to Israel (in this case, his deliverance of David from them militarily; 2 Sam. 22:48–49), Israel would praise God among the Gentiles, and they would hear of his power and might.

2. *Deuteronomy 32:43:* In the Song of Moses, Israel's first national leader issues an invitation in the last verse of his song: "Rejoice, O nations [Gentiles], with his people." The rest of the verse, not quoted by Paul, issues a warning to the Gentiles as well: "[God] will take vengeance on his enemies." The Gentiles will meet God at the fellowship table or the bar of justice, and they are invited to come willingly in peace before being forced to come submissively in subjection.

3. *Psalm 117:1:* These verses call on the nations to praise the God of Israel for "his love toward us" and "the faithfulness of the LORD."

4. *Isaiah 11:10:* This messianic passage follows verse 1 of Isaiah 11 which predicts a branch rising from the "stump of Jesse" (Jesse being the father of King David) which would **rule over the nations; the Gentiles will hope in him.** That branch was obviously Jesus Christ.

Paul uses all of these verses to demonstrate that the Gentiles were not an afterthought in God's plan, but were destined to inherit salvation through the instrumentality of Israel and her Messiah (see other references to the Gentiles in Pss. 47:1; 67:3–5; 96:7; 98:4; 100:1). In light of God's plan from the beginning to bring Jews and Gentiles together to share in his blessings (Gen. 12:3), disunity and contention among believers in a given assembly is unacceptable. By not living together in unity, they become an affront to God's purpose and plan for sending his Son as the Jewish Messiah.

Paul's final benediction to them is a gentle one. What he is asking them to do is not easy—certainly not something to be accomplished in the power of human ability. **Joy and peace** are supernatural manifestations of the **Holy Spirit** (Gal. 5:22), and any **hope** they have of learning to love those of a different racial and ethnic background than themselves can only come through him. **Hope** for the present—"Can I truly accept my brother or sister in Christ?"—and **hope** for the future—"Are my efforts going to be consummated in God's final deliverance from all of life's stresses and troubles?"—will only **overflow** in the believer as the believer overflows with the **Spirit**.

MAIN IDEA REVIEW: *Unity in the body of Christ encompasses liberty, evidences love, and follows the example of the Lord Jesus Christ.*

III. CONCLUSION

How Many Angels?

A disturbing poster made the rounds in Christian bookstores a number of years ago. In the foreground of the poster were two wizened old saints who were down on their hands and knees, seemingly in a discussion, or more likely an argument, about something on the floor between them. Their appearance cast a negative spell on the scene—dark clothes, wrinkled and unhappy faces, tense bodies, argumentative expressions and gestures. This part of the poster was clear at first glance, and the viewer was immediately drawn closer to discover the object of their apparent disagreement.

Upon closer inspection, one discovered that stuck upright in the floor between them was an ordinary sewing pin. On the head of the pin the artist had drawn an innumerable host of tiny angels—and suddenly the men's preoccupation was evident. They represented the church of the ages engaged in a fruitless and endless debate over the unanswerable question, "How many angels can fit on the head of a pin?"

This question is thought to have originated in the Middle Ages when great energy and speculation was expended on defining such matters as the size and constitution of angelic beings. Since then, the question has served to represent those occasions when the church loses its focus and becomes overly involved in "disputable matters" to the detriment of the church itself.

That in itself made an interesting poster—but not a compelling one. Almost unnoticed by the viewer until close enough to see the object of the men's debate was an additional background image. The foreground of the poster gave way in an upper corner to a horrifying sight—an image of a cliff. Leading up to the precipice of an abyss was a long line of naked human beings with abject terror and fear written on their faces. The line was obviously inching closer and closer to the cliff, up the sides of which were licking red-hot flames of fire. At various stages of descent into the flames were human figures as they fell off the edge of the cliff into the flames.

Upon taking in this image, the import of the poster was fully realized. The church, represented by the two crusty old theologs, was arguing over a totally irrelevant and unanswerable issue, while humanity, stripped bare of all hope and righteousness, was falling steadily into the pit of hell. The message is a powerful one: How often do we get sidetracked into debating "disputable matters" with one another at the expense of a world that is waiting upon us to deliver the good news of the gospel, the power of God unto salvation, to them?

This was Paul's message to the church in Rome. Some may believe a million angels can fit on the head of a pin, while others believe a million pins can fit on the head of an angel. Fine either way. We are to love one another, manifesting the unity that Jesus Christ bought for us by coming as a servant to redeem us from sin. Those who are inching closer and closer to a Christ-less eternity will thank us, one day, for staying focused on the "nondisputable matters" of the faith.

PRINCIPLES

- There is no place for judging fellow believers on disputable matters of faith.
- Every Christian is a servant of God and answerable to him alone.
- When our lifestyle choices cause another to stumble, we should put our neighbor's good above our own.
- Unity, a kingdom value, is more important than any individual's preferences.
- Choices not from faith (firm conviction of appropriateness) are sin.
- We are to serve one another for the sake of unity, following Christ's example.

APPLICATIONS

- Have I been guilty of judging, i.e., forcing my views on another?
- Have I made a fellow believer answerable to me instead of God?
- Is there any lifestyle behavior of mine that is causing another Christian problems? Am I willing to stop that behavior for the sake of unity if necessary?
- Can I trace any failings of unity in the body of Christ to my preferences?
- Have I violated my own conscience by participating in activities or choices that I did not believe were appropriate for me as a Christian?
- What opportunity to model unifying, Christlike service has God placed before me?

IV. LIFE APPLICATION

Strong's for the Weak

In modern days, few Christians find themselves at odds with other Christians over meat sacrificed to idols. Nor do we argue with one another over the observance of sacred days, except perhaps for the Sabbath. But that does not mean that our propensity to judge has matured; it only means that the occasions for our judging have changed with the times. The great preacher

Donald Grey Barnhouse told of a story from his own experience that provides a twentieth-century version of the first-century problem in Rome.

At a ministers' luncheon Barnhouse was attending, the conversation turned to the clergy of a different denomination—and not in a particularly positive fashion. It seems that the group Barnhouse was with felt the other group of ministers did not accomplish much in their churches. At that point, Barnhouse spoke up and relayed his knowledge of a particular minister in the other group. Seminary trained and ordained, this minister never went to prayer meetings and often would fail to attend church for several weeks at a time. On top of that, he seemed to have little concern for people, spending all of his time in the library—when he was not engaging in habits that many found to be undisciplined and not Christian.

As the luncheon progressed, the conversation turned to Bible study resources. Barnhouse asked the group which concordance they felt was the best to use, and all readily agreed that *Strong's Concordance,* with its links to Hebrew and Greek definitions, was superior to others. ("*Strong's* for the strong" was a saying that developed about James Strong's concordance. In this case, however, it was "*Strong's* for the weak;" the weak in faith.).

Barnhouse agreed with them, then shocked the group by revealing that the "unproductive" minister he had spoken of earlier was none other than James Strong, the compiler of *Strong's Concordance.* Those who before had thought that Barnhouse was being overly critical of a fellow minister suddenly saw Barnhouse's point. They realized he had revealed their own lack of appreciation for a brother in Christ whose Christian ministry and lifestyle was not like their own, but greatly productive nonetheless (Boice, 4:1727–28).

Many tales are told about the greatest preacher of the nineteenth century, England's Charles Haddon Spurgeon. He ruffled the feathers of not a few Christians in his day by his lifestyle choices—particularly his penchant for fine cigars. Compared to today, there was relatively little public awareness of the ill effects of tobacco on the human body, but smoking was shunned nonetheless by many Christians—but not Spurgeon. On one occasion, a young man approached Spurgeon and asked what he should do about a box of cigars he had been given. "Give them to me," Spurgeon replied, "and I will smoke them to the glory of God."

On another occasion, America's greatest preacher, Dwight Moody, visited London and in conversation with Spurgeon, asked the British preacher when he was going to give up smoking those awful cigars. "When you get rid of this," Spurgeon replied, poking a finger into Moody's considerable midsection, "I shall get rid of these," referring to his cigars. Moody somehow failed to see his weight problem as being as severe as Spurgeon's smoking problem.

In the case of Barnhouse's ministerial friends, who was the strong and who was the weak? Is the strong the one who attends prayer meetings and visits hospitals (and criticizes those who do not), or the one who violates convention and obediently pursues the calling of God regardless of whether conventional wisdom approves? Comparing this situation with Jesus and the Pharisees, who was who?

In all cases, what was more important? Most important was that the body of Christ not be divided in spirit or in fact by the judgmental attitudes of its members. Jesus' words in Matthew 7:3–5 warn against the judgments that can come from either a weak or a strong brother. We may have weak faith on one issue and strong faith on another. In either case, we are prone to judge the one who thinks or acts differently than we do. May God help the church to be judgment-free and unified so that those outside the church, who are under a legitimate judgment for sin, may see the church as a sanctuary—a place where they find forgiveness from the true Judge and judgment from no one else.

V. PRAYER

Heavenly Father, thank you for accepting and loving me in spite of my weaknesses. Where I am weak, help me to live by convictions born of faith. Where I am strong, help me to accept others' weaknesses. In all things, may I contribute my love to the unity of the body of Christ so that those outside the body will know that I am a disciple of Christ. Amen.

VI. DEEPER DISCOVERIES

A. The Jerusalem Council

The council of church leaders held in Jerusalem (Acts 15) has been referred to throughout church history as the Jerusalem Council (it is not referred to by that label in the text of Acts). It is also thought by some to be the purpose of Paul and Barnabas's visit to Jerusalem as described in Galatians 2:1–10 (though some would place the Galatians entry as making reference to an earlier famine relief visit of Paul and Barnabas as described in Acts 11:30).

The Jerusalem Council was pivotal in the development of the earlier church in terms of doctrine and practically in terms of uniting the Jewish and Gentile portions of the church. The early church was predominantly Jewish, having been birthed through a Jewish Messiah and Jewish disciples in the capital of the Jewish nation on a prominent Jewish feast day. It was not until the conversion of the apostle Paul, and Christ's commission to him to take the gospel to the Gentiles, that large numbers of Gentile converts began entering the fold. Two millennia later, the situation is exactly the reverse. The church is predominantly Gentile with only a modicum of Jewish believers.

The situation for a nonreligious Gentile becoming a Christian was totally different than for a Jew to become a Christian. In the former case, no change in religion was necessary; the convert went from irreligious to religious. Jews, however, were *changing* religions—going from one set of religious practices and understanding to another. It is quite easy to understand the tendency on the part of Jewish believers to bring with them into Christianity some, or many, of the tenets of the Jewish faith—and in many cases, as Paul explains in Romans, this was not a problem. The fact that, in some cases, it had become a problem is the reason that the Jerusalem Council was convened.

A key verse that reveals this is Acts 15:1: "Some men came down from Judea [Jerusalem] to Antioch and were teaching the brothers: 'Unless you are circumcised, according to the custom taught by Moses, you cannot be saved'" (see also Acts 15:5). This statement puts a Jewish condition—circumcision—on salvation. It takes circumcision—something that Paul himself indicated was a nonessential (see Acts 16:1–5 where Paul circumcised Timothy not as a matter of salvation but as a cultural courtesy for purposes of evangelism)—and makes it an essential.

At the council in Jerusalem, Peter, Paul, and Barnabas gave testimony that it was wrong to put "on the necks of the disciples a yoke that neither we nor our fathers have been able to bear" (Acts 15:10). And thankfully, the council agreed that they "should not make it difficult for the Gentiles who are turning to God" (Acts 15:19). At this first major church council, a stake was driven in the ground which ensured that salvation would remain by faith alone.

B. The Sabbath (14:5)

In Romans 14:5, Paul cites the keeping of sacred days as being among the "disputable matters" under consideration in the church in Rome. Sabbath day observance was perhaps the most visible sacred day on the Hebrew calendar, given its occurrence every seventh day. The Sabbath is mentioned forty-nine times in the four gospels; its proper observance was a constant standard of spirituality for the Jews. While there were many other sacred days on the Jewish calendar (the feasts of Passover, Unleavened Bread, Firstfruits, Pentecost, Tabernacles, Hanukkah, and Purim, as well as the Day of Atonement), the Sabbath has remained a topic of debate among believers since the first century.

Why do many Christians believe that the Sabbath should be observed? Two reasons are given: first, because the Sabbath was instituted by God at creation before the laws of sacred days were given to Moses (the "Sabbath" is not mentioned by name; rather a "seventh day" is mentioned on which God "rested" [Heb. *shabat;* Gen. 2:2–3]), and second, because the Sabbath is mentioned as the fourth of the Ten Commandments, thereby giving it permanence along with the rest of the moral code in the Decalogue.

Should Christians observe a Sabbath rest on a weekly basis? It is most likely that the early church continued to observe the Sabbath (Saturday) simply out of custom, but gradually transitioned to the first day of the week (our

Sunday) since it was the "Lord's Day" (Rev. 1:10; see also 1 Cor. 16:1–2; Acts 2:1), the day of the resurrection. In time, the church, especially the Gentile portion that had no customary or religious ties to a Sabbath, began meeting exclusively on the first day of the week (Sunday) instead of the last day of the week (Saturday, the Jewish Sabbath).

The question of Sabbath observance was problematic among the early churches. Besides the church in Rome, Paul chastised the churches in Galatia for observing not only the Sabbath but also "months and seasons and years" (Gal. 4:10). Also, some false teachers in Colossae were accusing believers of not keeping religious festivals, celebrations, and the "Sabbath day" (Col. 2:16). Nowhere does Paul give any indication that the Sabbath should be observed by the church. If anything, he seems to warn against the dangers of mixing old covenant observances with new covenant realities. Why live in the "shadows" when the "reality" has come (Col. 2:17)?

But in Romans Paul does allow that the observance of a sacred day should not be criticized, though he apparently puts that conviction, along with the conviction about not eating certain foods, into the category of "weak" faith. In any event, he says, "each one should be fully convinced in his own mind" (Rom. 14:5).

C. Legalism

Legalism, also called Pharisaism, enters any discussion of "disputable matters" like the ones Paul addresses in Romans 15. Legalism is the belief that one gains favor and ultimate acceptance by God through the performing of works prescribed by God's laws. The Pharisees held as their highest value the reverencing and keeping of the law and the traditions of their own elders. Because the name "Pharisee" derived from the Hebrew *parush,* meaning "separated," it was characteristic of the Pharisees to separate themselves from any who did not keep God's laws.

A problem arose when Jews who had been influenced by Pharisees (as all first-century Jews in Judea had been) became Christians and discovered that their acceptance with God was no longer based on the keeping of the law. Paul was no doubt the radical exception to the Jews who would have had a difficult time releasing themselves from the Pharisaism under which they had lived most of their lives. Legalism's subtle encroachment into the salvific realm comes when, as believers, we cross the fine line that separates "I desire to do this to honor God" and move into "I must do this to gain merit before God."

Paul says to the believers in Rome, "Eat what you want to eat and observe the days you want to observe"—with this caveat: "No one will be declared righteous in [God's] sight by observing the law" (Rom. 3:20). Believers in the twentieth century as well as the first must stay on the proper side of the line that divides liberty and legalism.

D. Vegetarianism (14:2)

The vegetarianism mentioned by Paul in Romans 14:2 is not the same as the vegetarianism practiced by many Christians today. The abstaining from meat that Paul refers to was based on grounds of religious purity—the desire not to eat meat which had been part of sacrifices to pagan idols and may not have been prepared in accordance with Jewish *kosher* practices.

But there is a biblically-based vegetarianism that is gaining acceptance in the contemporary church. It is based not on Romans 14:2 but on the diet God apparently prescribed in Genesis 1:29 immediately after humans were created—a diet of fruits and vegetables (see also Gen. 2:16). Even the animals were created to be vegetarian (Gen. 1:30), and humanity apparently remained vegetarian by precept after the fall into sin (Gen. 3:18). It was not until after the Flood that God gave Noah and his family (and apparently the human family) permission to eat meat (Gen. 9:2–4). Many Christians today see God's permission to eat meat as being a concession much like divorce—an exception to a divine ideal. Many are moving beyond vegetarianism to a total exclusion of meat products such as milk, eggs, cheese, and the like (referred to as a "vegan" lifestyle).

The positive side of vegetarianism is that there may be health benefits; the negative side is that what is a nonessential part of the Christian life could be made an essential part by those who practice it. Just as some Jewish believers in Rome no doubt looked down on their Gentile brethren for eating meat, Christians today who are vegetarians must guard against judging their meat-eating brethren.

E. The Kingdom of God (14:17)

One of the most noticeable differences between the gospels and the epistles is the difference in the number of times the kingdom of God is referred to (primarily the difference is between the synoptics and the epistles; "kingdom" as a subject occurs 117 times in Matthew, Mark, and Luke, and only four times in John). Paul mentions the kingdom of God only fifteen times in his epistles (Rom. 14:17; 1 Cor. 4:20; 6:9,10; 15:24,50, Gal. 5:21; Eph. 5:5; Col. 1:12,13; 4:11; 1 Thess. 2:12; 2 Thess. 1:5; 2 Tim. 4:1,18), and only once in Romans. Does this mean that the emphasis on the kingdom of God changed between Jesus and Paul? That the kingdom was not a topic of preaching and teaching in the postresurrection ministry of the apostles? A survey of Acts would prove otherwise.

For forty days after his resurrection, Jesus spoke to the apostles "about the kingdom of God" (Acts 1:3,6). Philip the evangelist preached the same "good news of the kingdom" (Acts 8:12) that Jesus did. Entering into the present fullness and future consummation of the kingdom was a topic of encouragement from Paul to those he instructed (Acts 14:22). Paul argued "persuasively" with Jews in synagogue settings about the kingdom of God (Acts 19:8). Paul preached (proclaimed; *kerusso*) the kingdom of God in his ministry (Acts 20:25). In the last months of his life, "from morning till evening he (Paul) explained and declared to them the kingdom of God" while confined to house arrest in Rome (Acts 28:23), doing so "boldly" (Acts 28:31).

The kingdom of God received no token attention from the apostle Paul in his ministry, nor should it in the preaching and teaching ministry of the modern church. The incursion of the kingdom of God into Satan's domain of darkness is what has made possible the setting free of the captives (Luke 4:18–19). Our salvation is nothing less than a "rescue" out of Satan's kingdom into God's (Col. 1:13). Sadly, this truth, and the implications of it, are missing from much contemporary ministry of the word of God—but they were not missing from Paul's.

VII. TEACHING OUTLINE

A. INTRODUCTION

1. Lead Story: Focus On Who, Not What
2. Context: Since the beginning of chapter 12, Paul has been detailing the consequences of being justified by faith, of living life under the mercy of God. Paul called it being a living sacrifice—giving up one's life for others (being as merciful toward others) in response to what God has done for us. His initial exhortations were general—use your spiritual gifts, love those who persecute you, submit to the authorities, and love your neighbor. But his final set of exhortations seems to be in response to a problem in the church in Rome—believers judging one another over matters of preference and belief that were not germane to the faith.
3. Transition: Many things in the Christian life are essential, but many are not. Two of the nonessentials—sacred observances of certain days and convictions about the sanctity of foods—had become matters of dispute among Christians in Rome (as they had in the church in Corinth). Paul has a message for those on both sides of any such issue: do not judge your brother or sister for their convictions. In this chapter we discover Paul's rationale for his strong exhortation to the church on disputable matters.

B. COMMENTARY

1. Unity Encompasses Liberty (14:1–12)
   a. Do not judge another's convictions (14:1–4)
   b. Be firm in your own convictions (14:5–8)
   c. God is the only judge of all (14:9–12)

2. Unity Evidences Love (14:13–23)
   a. Kingdom values are the priority (14:13–18)
   b. Peace and edification are the goals (14:19–23)
3. Unity Exemplifies the Lord (15:1–13)
   a. Learn from Christ and bear with the weak (15:1–4)
   b. Follow Christ and glorify God (15:5–6)
   c. Imitate Christ and accept one another (15:7–13)

C. CONCLUSION: *STRONG'S* FOR THE WEAK

VIII. ISSUES FOR DISCUSSION

1. What are five of the top "disputable matters" in the modern North American church today? Why are they disputable? What evidence is there that some groups of Christians have made them "nondisputable?" What results occur when nonessential matters are made essential?

2. Cite some contemporary examples of how a stronger believer's actions can put a stumbling block in the path of a weaker believer. What actions should a weaker believer take in regard to such a problem? What should the stronger believer's response be? How often are you aware of this dialogue having taken place among Christians you know? What does the frequency (often? rarely?) indicate either way?

3. Which portion of the Bible are you most familiar with—the Old or New Testament? What conclusions can you draw from the relative neglect of the Old Testament in contemporary preaching and daily reading? What is your response to the frequency with which Paul uses the Old Testament in his letter to the Romans? How do you think a deeper knowledge of the Old Testament could increase your understanding and appreciation of the New?

Romans 15:14–16:27

The Gospel: The Heart of the Apostle Paul

"*R*emember, you are God's sword, His instrument—I trust a chosen vessel unto Him to bear His name. In great measure, according to the purity and perfection of the instrument, will be the success. It is not great talent God blesses so much as likeness to Jesus. A holy minister is an awful weapon in the hand of God."

Robert Murray McCheyne

Romans

15:14—16:27

IN A NUTSHELL

*H*aving completed the two major parts of his letter to the Romans—an exposition of the gospel and its application to daily life—Paul now concludes his magnum opus. In his final words Paul reveals his heart to the church in Rome, and to us. He is a builder, a servant, a shepherd, and an apostle of the church, a person whose entire life is being spent in the spread of the gospel

The Gospel: The Heart of
the Apostle Paul

I. INTRODUCTION

The Mark of a Leader

*T*he famous radio journalist Paul Harvey, in one of his "Rest of the Story" segments, told the story of a physician whose character bore a striking resemblance to that of the author of Romans (as told by Paul Aurandt, *More of Paul Harvey's The Rest of the Story*; this account summarized from Swindoll, p. 515):

Like most physicians of great experience, Dr. Evan O'Neil Kane had become preoccupied with a particular facet of medicine. His strong feelings concerned the use of general anesthesia in major surgery. He believed that most major operations could and should be performed under local anesthetic, for, in his opinion, the hazards of a general anesthesia outweighed the risks of the surgery itself. For example, patients with heart trouble or anesthesia allergies ran the risk of severe complications when placed under general anesthesia for surgery. Kane's medical mission was to prove to his colleagues once for all the viability of local anesthesia. It would take a great deal of convincing.

To prove the viability of major surgery using only a local anesthetic, Kane would have to find a patient brave enough to go through what he hoped all patients would one day experience—major surgery without the dangers of general anesthesia. In his thirty-seven years as a surgeon, Kane had performed nearly four thousand appendectomies. This freed him from worrying about the complications of the surgery and focusing on the local anesthesia aspect. Having found a volunteer, he proceeded.

The patient was prepped in all the normal ways, but in the operating room was given only a local anesthetic. As he had thousands of times before, Kane entered the abdomen, slicing tissues and clamping blood vessels as he went. Locating the appendix, the surgeon nimbly clipped it away from its surrounding tissue, folded the stump back in place, and sewed up the patient's wound—all with the patient being wide awake and experiencing only minor discomfort. After a restful recovery of two days—faster than most general anesthesia cases—the patient was released from the hospital to recuperate at home.

Kane had achieved his goal—to demonstrate that successful general surgery could be accomplished without the risks of general anesthesia. Since Dr. Kane's experiment in 1921, his breakthrough technique has changed the face of surgery—but not only for scientific reasons. For Dr. Kane's name was added to a short list of pioneers in the medical field who, so utterly convinced of the validity of their theories, chose to use them first on themselves. Kane's first volunteer appendectomy patient was none other than himself. To prove his theory regarding local anesthesia, Dr. Evan Kane had removed his own appendix.

It has long been said that great leaders ask their followers to go nowhere they have not first been themselves. Where severe physical pain was a possibility, a doctor chose to test his theory on himself before asking anyone else to run the risk. And where losing one's entire life was at stake (Luke 14:26–27), the apostle Paul chose to demonstrate personally what he wanted the church in Rome—and the believers in all the churches he started—to do. Paul's life is at the heart of this last section of the letter to the Rome believers, and the gospel was at the heart of Paul's life. Not in so many words—Paul would never set out to boast about himself. Rather, in concluding his letter, four aspects of his life are visible to the reader who looks closely beneath the surface of his words: Paul was a builder of the church, a servant of the church, a shepherd of the church, and an apostle of the church.

All four aspects of Paul's life as revealed in this final section of Romans represent priorities that he would want every Christian to possess. Build the church by mediating the pure gospel of Christ. Serve the church by going to any lengths to demonstrate the love of God on which the gospel is based. Shepherd the church by developing genuine and time-tested relationships with its members. And have the vision of an apostle of the church, wanting constantly to see the gospel taken wherever it has not been preached and received. But these were not mere academic initiatives dreamed up by Paul from some behind-the-lines bunker safe from the shelling of the enemy. No, these were the things that Paul himself had done, and was in the process of doing, as he wrote to the Roman believers. This was Paul's life—and what he considered the normal Christian life.

Paul did use himself as an example for other Christians to follow, but almost always his exhortation was tied to his following the example of Christ (1 Cor. 4:16; 11:1; Phil. 3:17; 4:9; 1 Thess. 1:6; 2 Thess. 3:9). Paul does not intentionally set himself up as an example in these verses of Romans, but the example is there all the same. In wrapping up his words to the Roman Christians, the values and priorities of his life surface and become a model of genuine Christianity, a person committed to the gospel—the power of God unto salvation.

II. COMMENTARY

The Gospel: The Heart of the Apostle Paul

> **MAIN IDEA:** *A passion for the gospel is revealed in Paul's roles as a builder, servant, shepherd, and apostle of the church.*

Paul, Builder of the Church (15:14–22)

> **SUPPORTING IDEA:** *As a builder of the church, Paul was responding in obedience to his commission from God to preach the gospel to the Gentiles.*

If the modern believer envied the apostle Paul in anything, it might be for the clarity of his life's calling. He was to proclaim the gospel to the Gentiles—mediating the gospel as a "priest," promoting the gospel as that of Jesus Christ, and pioneering the gospel where it had not been preached by any other.

15:14–16. We get another brief glimpse of the condition of life in the church in Rome by Paul's introductory words to this section of his epistle. His words are complementary—not flattering—and indicate the esteem with which he held the believers in Rome in spite of the Jewish-Gentile tensions that might have existed. As a point of contrast, one could note Paul's uncomplimentary words to the Corinthians who were "worldly . . . infants" (1 Cor. 3:1), or the writer to the Hebrews' words to his audience: "You are slow to learn. In fact, though by this time you ought to be teachers, you need someone to teach you the elementary truths of God's words all over again. You need milk, not solid food! Anyone who lives on milk, [is] still an infant" (Heb. 5:11–13).

Paul's three points of commendation speak well of the Roman church's progress in sanctification.

First, they were **full of goodness.** Paul indicates elsewhere that **goodness** is a fruit of walking in the Spirit (Gal. 5:22) and walking in the light (Eph. 5:9), and reflects the moral desire and intent of the faithful believer (2 Thess. 1:11). The Roman Christians were good men and women (brought to light even more by the immoral/amoral nature of their hometown—a place where Caligula ruled a few years earlier).

Second, they were **complete in knowledge.** It would not seem that Paul refers here to the **knowledge** imparted through his letter; rather, it seems to be a reference to the quality of instruction they had received since their founding. Why then, it would be legitimate to ask, does Paul write his most lengthy and systematic epistle to saints already **complete in knowledge** (cf. 2 Pet. 1:12–15)? His answer will come in the next verse.

Finally, they are **competent to instruct one another**. *Noutheteo* can carry a stronger meaning than simply instruction. It comes from two words, *nous* (mind, comprehension) and *tithemi* (to put, place, lay), conveying the idea of putting something into someone's mind or understanding. In addition to **instruct**, it could mean counsel, warn, or admonish, as most other modern translations render it. Jay Adams popularized the concept of "nouthetic counseling" in his volume *Competent to Counsel*, drawing on Paul's words in this verse. The Roman believers were able, on the basis of their moral ground in the Spirit and their knowledge, to be a self-correcting entity—to admonish and counsel one another toward continued godliness and kingdom fruitfulness.

Again, why has Paul **written** to them? Buried in the midst of his collection of clauses in verses 15–16 is the essence of his reminder, more easily understood as summarized by Eugene Peterson in *The Message*: "I'm simply underlining how very much I need your help in carrying out this highly focused assignment God gave me, this priestly and gospel work of serving the spiritual needs of the non-Jewish outsiders so they can be presented as an acceptable offering to God, made whole and holy by God's Holy Spirit" (Peterson, pp. 336–337). Paul probably notes his boldness in writing to them because he was not their spiritual father, the founder of the church in Rome. But what he is should make up for his lack of prior relationship with them: **a minister of Christ Jesus to the Gentiles**.

He has mentioned the **grace** given to him twice already in the letter (1:5; 12:3), meaning that it is his assignment from God. The subtle reality is that to disavow the grace given to Paul is to disavow the will of God (and the same with the grace given to any other believer). What is unique about Paul's description here is the Levitical terminology he uses—**priestly duty** and **offering acceptable to God**. Offerings of various sorts are mentioned 264 times in Leviticus (NIV text), being that which the Israelites would bring, and the priests would offer, to God. Offerings were by their very nature sacrificial, something owned or possessed by the offerer.

In a metaphorical way, Paul saw his mission to win the non-Jewish population of the world to Christ as his offering to God. He wanted to bring the Gentiles to God as one who would go and "possess" the nations for Christ; he offered them as a "priest," dedicating them and setting them apart (sanctifying them) through the ministry of the **Holy Spirit** to be God's own possession. Paul has written his most lengthy letter to the church in Rome to remind them of this, his calling from God.

But in this case, his calling has also become their calling. He has not revealed to them yet his intention to go to Spain (see vv. 24,28), but their place on his westward route makes them exactly what he needs: a partner in the power of the gospel. Herein lies the key to understanding the depth to which Paul has gone in systematizing the gospel for the believers in Rome. If he had set his sights on, say, the far east, beyond Asia Minor, then perhaps we would have a letter to the church in (Syrian) Antioch in our hands instead of one to the church in Rome. But Paul's focus is on his calling from God, and he has done his best to explain that calling to the Roman believers so they might join with him in fulfilling it—as he wants to join with them in fulfilling their individual callings from God (Rom. 1:11–12).

15:17–19. In spite of the pride and presumption which might easily have arisen out of a calling such as Paul's, he repeatedly sought to decrease himself and increase the preeminence of Christ (John 3:30). Perhaps his most well-known defense against boasting is what he wrote to the Corinthian believers: "Yet when I preach the gospel, I cannot boast, for I am compelled to preach. Woe to me if I do not preach the gospel!" (1 Cor. 9:16; see also 2 Cor. 10:17; 11:30; 12:5,9; Gal. 6:14).

For one who was a bondservant (*doulos*) of Christ (Rom. 1:1), Paul could take no credit at all for his ministry. And it was important for the believers in Rome to understand this since their future support of Paul's ministry would depend on it. As believers in Christ, they likewise were Christ's bondservants (Rom. 6:16–20), and should be prepared to offer themselves to him to accomplish his will. Just as Paul could say, "Woe is me if I don't preach the gospel," so every believer should say, "Woe is me if I don't faithfully carry out my Lord's desires for my life!" And Paul's goal for the Roman church was to develop a partnership with them which would see the gospel taken to Spain and beyond.

Two things stand out in Paul's exaltation of Christ: first, it is Christ's mission that he is on, not his. Paul was called into service by Christ and told that he would take the name of Christ far away to the Gentiles and their kings (Acts 9:15; 22:21). Second, it was Christ who was **leading the Gentiles to obey God.** The mission was Christ's and the fruit was Christ's. Left to his own desires, Paul would have continued acting murderously toward those who embraced Christ. Now, he marvels at what Christ has **accomplished through** [**him**]. If the church in Rome gets in step with what Christ is doing in the world, then they will also be in step with what Paul is doing, since Paul is doing nothing more than obeying Christ.

Even in the **signs and miracles** that he worked, Paul pointed to the **power of the Spirit.** Whether healing a crippled man in Lystra (Acts 14:8–10), casting a demon out of a slave girl in Philippi (Acts 16:16–18), or restoring life to a dead man in Ephesus (Acts 20:9–12), Paul worked in the **power of the Spirit** alone. Had he been working in his own power, would he not have, by natural human instinct, prevented the severe beating that he and Silas received after casting the demon out of the slave girl in Philippi (Acts 16:19–23)? Not only was their beating a fulfillment of Christ's word to Paul about suffering for his name (Acts 9:16), but it was an avenue to the salvation of the Philippian jailer and his family (Acts 16:25–34). It was clear that Paul, like Jesus himself, operated with kingdom power and initiative, not his own.

Paul uses the Hebrew figure of speech called merism, where the totality is indicated by citing its two opposite extremes (see Ps. 139:8–10), to indicate the arena in which he has preached the **gospel of Christ** in the **power of the Spirit**. Illyricum, though unmentioned in Acts, is on the northern border of Macedonia into which Paul traveled on his way into Greece (Acts 20:1–6). This was the western extent of his travels. While his mission trips began geographically in Antioch (Acts 13:1–3), Jerusalem was both the easternmost point of his preaching missions (unless one counts his years in Arabia; Gal. 1:17) and the spiritual center of the Great Commission (Acts 1:8; see also Isa. 2:3b and Mic. 4:2b for Old Testament references to Jerusalem as the starting point for "the word of the LORD"). Therefore, **from Jerusalem all the way around to Illyricum** describes Paul's "circuit," to use the language of the Methodist circuit riders on the American wilderness.

Fully proclaimed does not mean that he preached **the gospel** to every living being between **Jerusalem** and **Illyricum**. Rather it means that he covered all of that area, planting churches through which the gospel would continue to spread. In our day of fast and comfortable travel, it is difficult to imagine the personal price Paul paid in his efforts to obey Christ's calling in his life.

15:20–22. As a builder of the church, Paul acted as a priest of Christ, a promoter of Christ's gospel, and finally, as a pioneer for Christ. Paul was hesitant to preach where someone had already preached before him, of **building on someone else's foundation**. This was not a prideful issue for Paul, rather one of strategy—he wanted to continue to expand the boundaries of the kingdom.

The brilliant scholar-pastor Harold John Ockenga learned a lesson in this regard while on a thirty-day preaching tour with Donald Gray Barnhouse. Each night they were in a different church, and they alternated each night who would preach first. Ockenga preached a different sermon each night, while Barnhouse preached the same identical message night after night. Having sat through Barnhouse's sermon the first few nights, Ockenga decided to memorize it while listening to Barnhouse throughout the rest of the tour. Arriving at the last church on their tour, it being Ockenga's night to preach first, he rose and preached Barnhouse's sermon which he had by that time memorized completely. When his turn came, Barnhouse rose and preached another sermon, never missing a beat.

After the service, Ockenga, pleased with the trick he had played on his friend, said to Barnhouse, "The congregation seemed to have enjoyed 'your' sermon this evening." To which Barnhouse replied, "Yes, but not nearly as much as when I preached it here three months ago!" (Swindoll, p. 462).

It is unlikely that Paul's **ambition to preach the gospel where Christ was not known** arose from a fear of duplicating another's sermon. Rather, it arose because of his commission from Christ as an apostle. Paul states in Ephesians 2:20 that the church is built on the foundation of the apostles and prophets, and to the Corinthian believers he stated that his strategy was to lay a foundation upon which others would build (1 Cor. 3:10). Paul was a man of singular focus (as evidenced by his conflict with Barnabas over Mark; Acts 15:36–41), and he had no desire to become entangled with other foundation-laying apostles.

He would have agreed with John Bunyan, the author of *Pilgrim's Progress*, who said, "Let every tub stand upon its own bottom" (Ward, p. 113). The civilized world, the Roman Empire, in which his ministry of spreading the gospel had been successful, lay before him to the west. He knew no one had taken the gospel there yet, and that is where he intended to go. Once a "region" such as that of Jerusalem to Illyricum had received the gospel, it was time to go to **those who were not told . . . and those who have not heard.** This quotation from Isaiah 52:15 is yet another effort by Paul to document the fulfillment of the ministry prophesied in the Old Testament and now being revealed and fulfilled in the New—the taking of the gospel to the non-Jewish world. It was his effort to complete his ministry as far west as Macedonia that had **hindered** him from making it to Rome before now.

𝔹 Paul, Servant of the Church (15:23–33)

> **SUPPORTING IDEA:** *As a servant of the church, Paul risked his life to meet the needs of fellow believers in distress.*

Paul was in the vicinity of Corinth as he wrote Romans—how easy it would have been for him to deliver his letter to Rome himself and continue on to Spain. Had Paul been concerned only about himself and his personal desires, he would likely have done that. Instead, his servant's heart reveals a parallel set of priorities that would delay his arrival in Rome: the need to visit the predominantly Jewish church in Jerusalem—to deliver funds for the poor and to strengthen ties with the leaders.

15:23–24. If anything may be said of the apostle Paul, it was that he took the long view. While at the same time that he modeled the immediacy found in the words of the Puritan Richard Baxter—"I preached as never sure to preach again, and as a dying man to dying men" (Ward, p. 110)—he also practiced the wisdom of Solomon—"We should make plans—counting on God to direct us"; Prov. 16:9, TLB). Here we find Paul making plans to complete a **plan** he had been working on for **years**—to visit the church in Rome. And in the restatement of his **plan** we find a snapshot of his long-term goal and desire for the church in Rome—that they might assist him on his journey to **Spain**. Paul was not "using" the believers in Rome to help him accomplish a self-serving goal. Rather, he was involving them in the priority of the church—reaching all nations with the gospel.

Unknown to Paul, he would eventually realize his plan to get to Rome, but in a way that he had not anticipated. But for a man who lived as a servant, any plans he made were subject to God's direction.

15:25–29. Paul was about to turn his back on Rome and head in the opposite direction—to Jerusalem, **in the service of the saints there.** He had a financial gift from the saints in **Macedonia and Achaia** to be distributed for **the poor among the saints in Jerusalem.** In addition to delivering the gift, he hoped by his presence in Jerusalem to strengthen his ties, as the apostle to the Gentiles, with the Jewish branch of the church still headquartered in Jerusalem.

But this was no mean decision on his part. John Stott has calculated what Paul's servant heart was about to cost him in terms of personal travel (Stott, p. 384). Assuming he traveled by sea, the first leg of his journey from Corinth to Jerusalem would be around eight hundred miles. The second, from Jerusalem to Rome, would be fifteen hundred miles. And the third, from Rome to Spain, would be seven hundred miles, making a total of three thousand miles by ship. However, had he gone straight from Corinth to Spain, the trip would have been approximately fifteen hundred miles.

So, for the good of the saints in Jerusalem and the unity of the church, he doubled the length of his journey. In our modern age of jet travel, this does not seem like such a sacrifice. But all one need do is read the accounts of Paul's ultimate journey to Rome when he is shipwrecked on the island of Malta (Acts 27:13–28:11), not to mention three previous shipwrecks, once spending a day and a night in the open sea (2 Cor. 11:25), to realize the cost of his decision. Such is the nature of a servant.

Norman Cousins, in his volume on Dr. Albert Schweitzer, *Albert Schweitzer's Mission*, wrote of the days he spent with the renowned physician in his small hospital at Lambarene in French Equatorial Africa: "The biggest impression I had in leaving Lambarene was of the enormous reach of a single human being. Yet such a life was not without punishment of fatigue. Albert Schweitzer was supposed to be severe in his demands on the people who worked with him. Yet any demands he made on others were as nothing compared to the demands he made on himself. . . . History is willing to overlook almost anything—errors, paradoxes, personal weaknesses or faults—if only a man will give enough of himself to others" (cited by Swindoll, pp. 512–513).

The illustration applies, not because history is replete with the shortcomings of the apostle Paul, but because of the example he set for others as a servant. The next time we are asked by God to serve another saint or the church at large in a way that taxes our strength, we might only remember the apostle to the Gentiles who gave himself for others.

Paul does not tell us here, or in parallel passages concerning the offering for the church in Jerusalem (1 Cor. 16:1–4; 2 Cor. 8:1–9:15), what occasioned their need. It could have been a famine like the one predicted by the prophet Agabus which occurred during the reign of Claudius (around A.D. 44–46). Or it might have been due to the ongoing persecution of the church in which Paul had participated shortly after the ascension of Christ (cf. the martyrdom of Stephen, Acts 8:1–3).

Some have even speculated that the communal lifestyle of the church, consuming its capital base to meet daily needs in the burgeoning early days of its existence (Acts 2:42–47), had finally taken a toll on the long-term economic viability of its members. For Paul, what is more important than the cause of the need in Jerusalem is the reason why the churches in **Macedonia and Achaia** (as well as Galatia; cf. 1 Cor. 16:1) were obligated to respond sacrificially. The churches in the Gentile portion of the world owed a debt to the Jewish portion of the church—still located in Jerusalem.

Think of it with Paul's "big picture" perspective. If one looks at a map of the Mediterranean world in the first century, Jerusalem represents the Jewish portion of the church, and Asia Minor and Macedonia the Gentile portion of the church. Obviously, there were Jews living in Asia Minor and Macedonia, and undoubtedly some Gentiles were mixed in with the church in Jerusalem. But the two "halves" of the church can be located in these regions. To grasp how Paul feels about the debt owed by the Gentile churches to their brethren in Jerusalem, take a ruler and draw straight lines on your map radiating out from Jerusalem to all the cities that Paul, Silas, Barnabas, Timothy, and others had visited in proclaiming the gospel.

The gospel came from Jerusalem (Rom. 15:19), from the nation of Israel, and was received by the non-Jewish parts of the world. Paul has made this clear already in Romans. Israel's was the adoption, the glory, the covenants, the law, the temple worship, the promises, the patriarchs, and from within Israel "is traced the human ancestry of Christ, who is God over all" (Rom. 9:4–5). Israel is the cultivated olive tree into which have been grafted the branches of the Gentiles' wild olive trees (Rom. 11:17–21). Paul could not have said it more clearly than when he told the Gentile believers in Rome, "You do not support the root, but the root supports you" (Rom. 11:18).

Therefore, Paul's bold wording should come as no surprise: **For if the Gentiles have shared in the Jews' spiritual blessings, they owe it to the Jews to share with them their material blessings.** And while he does not mention it here, we know that the words of Jesus on giving (which we know only from Paul) are informing Paul's desire for the churches in **Macedonia and Achaia** to receive a blessing by giving one: "It is more blessed to give than to receive"

(Acts 20:35). While it is good that the Gentile churches **were pleased** to give, the fact is that they owed it to the Jews. Paul made it clear to the church in Corinth that he was not "commanding" them to give, but giving them an opportunity to respond to the grace of God in Christ who became poor so that, through his poverty, we might become rich (2 Cor. 8:8–9).

The cynic would see this as a form of manipulation, and indeed many modern fundraisers have used a spin on Paul's words to pressure people to give. But in reality, Paul's words are the truth—there is no manipulating at all! Christ became poor, we became rich. Our love will best be revealed when we follow his example by taking of what we have and giving it (becoming poor) to those who are poor (making them rich). This is simply the reality of the kingdom of God.

The **blessing** (*eulogia*) **of Christ** which Paul would bring with him to Rome is the same blessing that is twice translated "gift" in 2 Corinthians 9:5. Paul would bring with him the overflow from **Christ** of the gift-blessings that the churches in **Macedonia and Achaia** were giving to **Jerusalem**. Paul speaks of the gifts to the Jerusalem church as **fruit**—the natural result of life lived for God. As Paul transfers the fruit to the church in **Jerusalem**, he will be nourished by it and will become a **blessing** to the church in Rome when he sees them.

Paul next asks for prayer for two things: physical protection from unbelievers in Judea and productive relations with the church in Jerusalem, so that he can eventually arrive safely in Rome. Even the apostle to the Gentiles knows that his plans, be they ever so carefully conceived, will succeed only by the blessing and oversight of God.

15:30–33. Paul had apparently made no effort to ask the Roman believers to participate in the collection he made for the saints in Jerusalem. Logistically, the distance separating Corinth, where Paul was writing his letter, and Rome, would have made it impractical to wait upon a return gift before leaving for Jerusalem. Nevertheless, Paul invites the participation of the Roman church in his mission of mercy to Jerusalem. In fact, he appeals to them on the basis of two imperatives: the will of God (the meaning of **by our Lord Jesus Christ**, or by the authority Paul has as an apostle of **our Lord Jesus Christ**), and the **love of the Spirit** requires it. That is, if they are servants of Christ and are manifesting the fruit of the Spirit, which includes **love**, they will join with him in his **struggle**.

The **struggle** Paul refers to needs amplification. The noun supplied by the NIV is actually a verb, *sunagonizomai*. Comprised of *sun* (with), and *agonizomai* (to compete, fight, labor earnestly, strive), *sunagonizomai* means to "strive with, contend with, join with in the fight" ("with" not meaning "against," but as a partner). It does not appear that Paul is inviting the Roman believers to join with him in a fight in the realm of prayer, but in the larger mission—their part of which will be in prayer. That is, Paul wants them to be partners with him ("be my allies in the fight," NEB) in the struggle he is about to engage in by going to Jerusalem. And their part of that struggle will be in the realm of prayer to God for Paul.

Paul requests prayer for two specifics: first, that he **may be rescued from the unbelievers in Judea,** and second, that his **service in Jerusalem may be acceptable to the saints there.** The **unbelievers** are obviously the Jewish leadership who will have viewed Paul as a traitor for the last twenty years. If he shows his face in Jerusalem, the chances are good that he will be accused by the Jewish leaders of being a troublemaker—blaspheming their religion and stirring up divisions among the populace. And that is exactly what they do, trying to use whatever trumped-up charges they can to prove to the Roman authorities that Paul deserves to be incarcerated.

The second request for prayer is that Paul's **service**—meaning the gift he is bringing to the Jerusalem church from the churches in Macedonia and Achaia—would be **acceptable to the saints there.** This request for prayer is an admission by Paul of the tension that probably remains concerning his ministry to the Gentiles. Ever since the Jerusalem Council (Acts 15), the question of how to integrate Jews and Gentiles into one body, the church, had been a delicate one. Nearly fifteen hundred years of Jewish culture were being held up to scrutiny by the doctrine of justification by faith alone that Paul preached—and it had not been a trouble-free transition, as evidenced by Paul's own words on the subject to the Roman church (Rom. 14:1–15:13).

Dr. Luke does a good job in Acts of covering the events that transpire in Jerusalem, and a chronology of the high points will reveal how God chose to answer the prayers that Paul had requested:

Acts 20:1–3a	Paul in Greece (either Corinth or Cenchrea) where he penned the letter to Rome.
Acts 20:3b–38	Paul, in the company of representatives from the churches, departed Greece, making several stops along the way, the last of which was the emotional meeting at Miletus with the elders and others from the church in Ephesus. In his words to the Ephesian elders, note the numerous prophetic references Paul made about his future, lending further insight into his request for prayer from the Roman believers (Acts 20:22–25,32). The fact that he was traveling with a group of representatives from the churches who could easily have taken the monetary gift to Jerusalem, indicates that more than delivery of money was involved for Paul. He personally had to go, as the founder of the Gentile churches, to demonstrate to the leaders and members of the Jerusalem church that there was solidarity in the body of Christ; that the Gentile churches, and he as their founder, wanted to honor and serve the "mother church," the Jewish church in Jerusalem.

Acts 21:1–16	The group left Miletus and sailed to Tyre, where they remained with the believers for a week. They, in the Spirit, urged Paul not to go to Jerusalem. The same thing happened at their next stop, Caesarea. The prophet Agabus, who had correctly predicted the A.D. 42–44 famine (Acts 11:27–28), dramatically warned Paul that he would be handed over to the Gentiles in Jerusalem. Paul declared his willingness to die for Christ in Jerusalem, for which they departed.
Acts 21:17–26	Paul's entourage arrived in Jerusalem, where they met with James and the leaders of the Jerusalem church. Their report of God's work among the Gentiles was received gladly. To demonstrate further solidarity with Jewish believers in Jerusalem, Paul was asked by the elders to go up to the temple and participate in a purification ritual.
Acts 21:27–22:29	A week later, some Jews from Asia stirred up the crowds in Jerusalem against Paul. Roman soldiers intervened and prevented his being murdered, but placed him under arrest. Paul spoke to the Jewish crowd and delivered the testimony of his conversion, which they rejected. He was taken into custody by the Roman guards.
Acts 22:30–23:11	The next day, Paul was brought by the Roman commander before the Jewish Sanhedrin for examination. Again, Paul's testimony was rejected by the Jewish rulers who caused such an uproar that Paul was again taken into custody for his own protection. In jail, Christ appeared to Paul and comforted him, telling him he would give his testimony in Rome! Paul's desire to visit the church in Rome would be granted, but in a very different way than Paul expected.
Acts 23:12–26:32	Paul was transferred to Caesarea for his safety and to be examined by the Roman governor, Felix. Paul remained in prison in Caesarea for two years. Paul appealed to the new governor, Festus, for a trial before Caesar in Rome rather than a trial before the Jews in Jerusalem. Festus ordered Paul to be taken to Rome. Before leaving, Paul gave his testimony to King Agrippa (Herod Agrippa II), beginning the fulfillment of Acts 9:15.
Acts 27:1–28:16	Paul, under guard, set sail for Rome. After shipwreck and wintering on the island of Malta, they arrived in Rome around A.D. 59, where Paul was placed under house arrest. He finally met with members of the church in Rome (Acts 28:15).
Acts 28:17–31	Paul immediately gathered the leaders of the Jews in Rome to explain his presence there. For two years, under house arrest, Paul met with Jews and any who would come, "Boldly and without hindrance [preaching] the kingdom of God and [teaching] about the Lord Jesus Christ" (Acts 28:31). Tradition, and some other biblical references (cf. Phil. 2:24; Phlm. 22), suggest an anticipated or actual release from imprisonment in Rome, during which time Paul could have ventured as far as Spain. There is no evidence that he actually ever made it. Paul was ultimately martyred by the Roman emperor Nero around A.D. 68 after a second imprisonment (2 Tim 4:6–8).

The prayers of the Roman church were answered. The gift from the Gentile churches, and Paul's submissive posture toward the Jerusalem church leadership, were both apparently received gladly by the church. Likewise, he was protected from harm by the **unbelievers in Judea**, though just barely—he came within a moment of being flogged by the Roman authorities (Acts 22:25–29), which would have been his sixth such punishment, the first five coming from the Jews themselves (2 Cor. 11:24).

John Bunyan's definition of prayer, which he wrote while in prison, seems to fit perfectly with the prayerful striving-together of the Roman church for Paul: "Prayer is a sincere, sensible, affectionate pouring out of the heart or soul to God, through Christ, in the strength and assistance of the Holy Spirit, for such things as God has promised, or according to the Word of God, for the good of the church, with submission in faith to the will of God" (Hughes, *Stories,* p. 326).

Did Paul ultimately arrive in Rome **with joy?** Knowing Paul, though it was in chains and on the heels of almost losing his life at sea, we would have to say an unqualified "Yes." Paul asked the Roman believers to pray that he might arrive in Rome **by God's will . . . with joy.** Paul's associates had ample opportunity to learn from Paul that the will of God is always a cause for **joy.** For instance, when his friends in Caesarea tried to convince him not to go up to Jerusalem for fear that he would die, Paul replied to them, "Why are you weeping and breaking my heart? I am ready not only to be bound, but also to die in Jerusalem for the name of the Lord Jesus." His friends then adopted the Pauline perspective on life: "The Lord's will be done" (Acts 21:13–14).

Paul wrote his epistle on joy, Philippians (joy mentioned sixteen times), while under house arrest in Rome (cf. Phil. 1:13–14; he was not in the Mamertine dungeon from which he wrote 2 Timothy during his second arrest under Nero), so we can only conclude that he indeed arrived in Rome full of joy (he left Corinth on his way to Jerusalem "full of joy" over the Roman believers; Rom. 16:19). Paul's constant source of joy was the presence of Christ his Master and obedience to his will—perhaps the chief characteristics of a true servant.

Paul's concluding benediction, **The God of peace be with you all. Amen,** along with the nature of the content of chapter 16, has led some commentators to suggest that the letter to the Romans originally ended here. See "Deeper Discoveries" for a fuller discussion of that possibility.

🅒 Paul, Shepherd of the Church (16:1–24)

SUPPORTING IDEA: *As a shepherd of the church, Paul nurtured relationships with many who were his colaborers in the gospel*

Not only was Paul a builder of the church and a servant of the church he was a shepherd of the church. A remarkable, intense, and loyal relationship to many of the believers in Rome is evidenced in the final chapter of Paul's letter.

16:1–2. Before Paul begins his greetings to his friends in the church in Rome, he commends to them a fellow believer, **Phoebe, a servant of the church in Cenchrea.** It is widely agreed that **Phoebe** was likely the carrier of Paul's letter to Rome. Her designation as a **servant** (here not *doulos,* bondservant, but *diakonos,* servant, minister, or deacon) probably implies a position of responsibility in the church at Cenchrea, perhaps that of deaconess. Paul's request that she be given **any help she may need** is doubtless a response to the **great help** she had been to many. Paul's reference to Phoebe as a **great help** is probably more than just physical assistance. **Help** here is *prostatis,* used only here in the New Testament. It often referred to a patroness or benefactress (Stott, p. 393), meaning that Phoebe was possibly a woman of means who had helped to support the Cenchrean church and possibly Paul himself.

16:3–16. Next, Paul enters into a lengthy list of greetings to acquaintances in Rome. Immediately coming to mind is the image of Christ as the Good Shepherd of his sheep, whose "sheep hear his voice, and he calls his own sheep by name and leads them out" (John 10:3, NASB). As "a" shepherd of the church in Rome (in an apostolic sense, not an immediate, pastoral sense), Paul obviously knows many of the sheep there by name. Yet another side of the apostle Paul is seen in his conveyance of personal greetings and expressions of well-being to so many by name.

At the dawn of the twenty-first century, when life is supposedly more impersonal than ever, a person with the apostle Paul's preoccupations could be excused for overlooking personal greetings. He *could* be, but *should not* be—neither he, nor any modern-day shepherd either. Theology does not exist in a vacuum. It may be the queen of the sciences, but in truth it exists as the servant of people who want to know God. To exclude personal references to individuals at the end of a theological letter would suggest a one-dimensional approach of which, thankfully, the apostle Paul was not guilty.

Most technical commentaries do an adequate job of exploring the identities of those named in Paul's greetings (especially helpful are the comments of the classicist F. F. Bruce as he ferrets out identity clues based on Roman names found in the list; see Bruce, pp. 257–262). A concordance will aid the student of Romans in linking many names in Paul's list to other occurrences of those individuals in the New Testament. What is often lacking is a survey—a big picture—of the names and what such a survey might indicate about the nature of the church in Rome. Therefore, the following breakdown will add a different perspective (some of the following was gathered from the commentary by Stott, pp. 395–396):

From a short list of twenty-eight individuals, several characteristics of the church in Rome may be noted:

Individuals: 28	Twenty-six are mentioned by name, plus two other individuals not mentioned by name (Rufus's mother, v. 13; Nereus's sister, v. 15).
Groups: 5	The church in **Priscilla's** and **Aquila's** house (v. 5); the household of **Aristobulus** (v. 10); the household of **Narcissus** (v. 11); the brothers associated with Asyncritus, Phlegon, Hermes, Patrobas, and **Hermas** (v. 14); the saints with **Philologus, Julia, Nereus,** and **Olympas** (v. 15).
Men: 17	Seventeen are greeted (excluding the male heads of households named, but not necessarily greeted as members of the church: **Aristobulus** and **Narcissus**): **Aquila** (v. 3), **Epenetus** (v. 5), **Andronicus** (v. 7), **Ampliatus** (v. 8), **Urbanus** (v. 9), **Stachys** (v. 9), **Apelles** (v. 10), **Herodion** (v. 11), **Rufus** (v. 13), **Asyncritus** (v. 14), **Phlegon** (v. 14), **Hermes** (v. 14), **Patrobas** (v. 14), **Hermas** (v. 14), **Philologus** (v. 15), **Nereus** (v. 15), **Olympas** (v. 15).
Women: 9	Nine are mentioned: **Priscilla** (v. 3), **Mary** (v. 6), **Junias** (v. 7), **Tryphena** and **Tryphosa** (twin sisters?, v. 12), **Persis** (v. 12), Rufus's **mother** (v. 13), **Julia** (v. 15), Nereus's **sister** (v. 15).
Couples: 2	**Priscilla** and **Aquila** (v. 3); **Andronicus** and **Junias** (v. 7; see the commentaries on why Junias is most likely a female name).
Households: 2	**Aristobulus** (v. 10); **Narcissus** (v. 11).
Slaves: 5	From Roman inscriptions, the following names were often those of slaves: **Ampliatus** (v. 8), **Urbanus** (v. 9), **Hermes** (v. 14), **Philologus** and **Julia** (v. 15).
Persons of distinction: 2	**Aristobulus** (v. 10) was possibly the grandson of Herod the Great and friend of the Emperor Claudius. **Narcissus** (v. 11) was likely a well-known freedman who exercised great influence on Claudius. It is not certain that these famous individuals had become Christians (they were possibly dead at the time of Paul's writing), but that their families (households) were represented by members of the church. **Rufus** (v. 13) was possibly the son of Simon the Cyrene, who carried Jesus' cross to Golgotha (Mark 15:21).
Fellow Jews: 3	**Andronicus** and **Junias** (v. 7); **Herodion** (v. 11). (There could have been others not designated as such.)
Apostles: 2	The married couple **Andronicus** and **Junias** (v. 7). Possibly apostles for having seen the risen Christ (1 Cor. 15:7); possibly among the Grecian Jews of Acts 6:1 based on their names; were Jewish believers (Paul's kinsmen and cell-mates, 2 Cor. 11:23) (cf. Bruce, p. 258).
Paul's descriptives:	Those who worked hard: four women (**Mary,** v. 6; **Tryphena, Tryphosa,** and **Persis,** v. 12). Fellow workers: **Priscilla** and **Aquila** (v. 3); **Andronicus** and **Junias** (v. 7; not mentioned as fellow workers, but obviously were based on Paul's description); **Urbanus** (v. 9). Dear friends or beloved: **Epenetus** (v. 5); **Ampliatus** (v. 8); **Stachys** (v. 9); **Persis** (v. 12).

Individuals: 28	Twenty-six are mentioned by name, plus two other individuals not mentioned by name (Rufus's mother, v. 13; Nereus's sister, v. 15).
Receiving special note:	Deserved the gratitude of all the churches: **Priscilla** and **Aquila** (v. 3). First convert to Christ in Asia: **Epenetus** (v. 5). Been in prison with Paul: **Andronicus** and **Junias** (v. 7). Outstanding among the apostles: **Andronicus** and **Junias** (v. 7). Tested and approved: **Apelles** (v. 10). Been like a mother to Paul: **Mother** of Rufus (v. 13; the wife of Simon of Cyrene who carried the cross for Jesus? cf. Mark 15:21).

1. It was extremely diversified. There were males, females, slaves, freedmen, Jews, Gentiles, well-to-do, and well thought of.

2. Women are mentioned prominently. A third of those mentioned are women; all the ones described as working hard (*kopiao*) are women; one of the women is called an apostle.

3. House churches are mentioned at least once (v. 5), probably three times (if adding vv. 14–15), and possibly five times if including the references to households in verses 10–11.

4. Based on Paul's words concerning the "weak" and "strong" members of the church (Rom. 14:1–15:13), it seems unlikely that the house churches were segregated into Jewish, Gentile, or other homogeneous groups. The likely heterogeneity of the groups is probably what caused the tensions that Paul addressed.

5. The language Paul uses (honest, positive, affirming) suggests a level of intimacy reflecting what he has heard about the maturity of the Roman church.

Two final words from Paul in verse 16 add additional insights into the state, or the need, of the church at Rome. First, for the fourth time in his letters, Paul urges the believers to **greet one another with a holy kiss** (cf. 1 Cor. 16:20; 2 Cor. 13:12; 1 Thess. 5:26; see also 1 Pet. 5:14). Was this exhortation (command; aorist middle imperative of *aspazomai*) because they were lacking affection for one another or because they were being encouraged to continue it? Either way, it is a good word for the church today. J. B. Phillips gives the verse a formal British twist—"Give one another a hearty handshake all round for my sake"—while Eugene Peterson (*The Message*) calls for "holy embraces all around!" Whether rubbing noses in Eskimo land or elbows in the jungle, affectionate greetings are appropriate and encouraged in the church.

Second, **all the churches of Christ send greetings** to the church in Rome. These greetings most likely came from the members of Paul's entourage who were about to leave with him on the journey to Jerusalem (Acts 20:4). They would represent churches in Macedonia and Achaia as well as Asia Minor (Galatia). How often do churches today send words of greeting and encouragement to other churches? Paul worked hard at doing whatever might increase the unity of the body of Christ.

16:17–20. Part of the job of the shepherd is to protect the sheep from "ferocious wolves" (Matt. 7:15) and thieves who come to "steal and kill and destroy" (John 10:10). In the realm of truth, physical barriers such as hedges, gates, and corrals do not deter the enemy, those who prey upon the minds of the sheep. Paul has two weapons at his disposal in his role as apostolic shepherd: declaring the truth and warning against intruders. He has taught the Roman church the truth in his letter, and now he warns them against those who would seek to lead them astray.

In Paul's words can be found the kernels of the Genesis story of the fall—not so much to claim that Paul is mirroring that story, but enough to suggest its presence as a constant paradigm in Paul's thinking:

1. Adam and Eve were taught the truth; the Roman believers are reminded of the **teaching [they] have learned.**

2. Adam and Eve should have kept away from the one who came to tempt them; the Roman believers are warned **to watch out for** and **keep away from** those who would lead them astray.

3. The one who deceived Adam and Eve was not serving God, but himself; the Roman believers are warned that their tempters **are not serving our Lord Christ, but their own appetites.**

4. Adam and Eve were deceived by smooth talk; the Roman believers are warned to beware of **smooth talk and flattery.**

5. Just as God pronounced the ultimate doom of the one who deceived Adam and Eve (Gen. 3:15), so Paul repeats that promise to the Roman believers: **the God of peace will soon crush Satan under your feet.**

In the midst of his warnings, Paul reaffirms his **joy,** first mentioned in Romans 1:8, over their faith and **obedience.** But he does not want them to be **naive** about their faith. His **wise** (*sophos*) **about what is good** and **innocent** (*akeraios*) **about what is evil** parallels Jesus' words to his disciples when he sent them out to proclaim the kingdom of God (Matt. 10:16): "Therefore be as shrewd (*phronimos*) as snakes and as innocent (*akeraios*) as doves." From a different direction, it is similar to what he told the church in Corinth: "In regard to evil be infants, but in your thinking be adults" (1 Cor. 14:20). The life of faith must be received with the innocence and purity of faith of a child (Mark 10:15) but lived in the maturity and reality of an adult who knows there is a war going on.

The harshness of Paul's words—**will soon crush**—is cast in stark contrast to the backdrop of his earlier declaration—**I am full of joy.** Both are true in the Christian life—joy in the midst of war. The joy comes from knowing that the war has been and will be won. Our part (the Roman church's part) is to be alert and vigilant until the final armistice. It is the **grace** of God that empowers us to understand, and stand in, the conflict.

16:21–24. In addition to greeting his personal friends in Rome, Paul now sends personal greetings from his friends who are with him in Corinth. Three of those sending greetings to the church in Rome were among those listed in Acts 20:4 as part of Paul's travelling partners on the way to Jerusalem:

Acts 20:4	Romans 16:21–24
Timothy	Timothy (Acts 16:1–3; like a son to Paul [Phil. 2:22])
	Lucius (possibly Lucius of Cyrene [Acts 13:1]? Some have suggested Luke the physician, but Luke was a Gentile and Lucius is Paul's kinsman, or a Jew)
	Jason (the Jason of Acts 17:6–9? But he is not listed as a Thessalonian delegate in Acts 20:4)
Sopater	Sosipater (probably the same as Sopater in Acts 20:4; Bruce, p. 265)
	Tertius (Paul's scribe, or amanuensis, who penned the letter as Paul dictated. For Paul's other end-of-letter notes see Gal. 6:11 and 2 Thess 3:17)
Gaius (Acts 19:29; 1 Cor. 1:14; 3 John 1?)	Gaius ("hospitality" may refer to Acts 18:7 making him Gaius Titius Justus)
	Erastus (a public official in Corinth who was a Christian. He has been identified in archaeological ruins in Corinth. Possibly the same Erastus as in Acts 19:22 and 2 Tim. 4:20)
Aristarchus (Acts 19:29)	
Secundus (from Thessalonica; no other mention)	
Tychicus (an oft-mentioned fellow traveler and representative of Paul; cf. Eph. 6:21; Col. 4:7; 2 Tim. 4:12; Titus 3:12)	
Trophimus (mentioned again after arriving in Jerusalem with Paul [Acts 21:29; implication is that he was a Gentile] and toward the end of Paul's life [2 Tim. 4:20])	

It is easy to read the New Testament and gloss over the many names of individuals who contributed to the spread of the gospel and the building of the church in the first century. The temptation now is the same as it was then, to think that history will not record or remember what we do for Christ in our corner of the kingdom. That is correct—"history" will know little and care less of what the average believer does in his or her life of faith. The faithful first-century men and women who, in the midst of the same fears, testings, limitations, and insecurities that we face, continued to build the church, did so not in hopes of finding their names on the pages of history. They did it because they were faithful, and because their names were already written on far more important pages than those of history (Rev. 21:27).

May the church today honor the memory of the few whose names we know, and the millions whose names we will not know until "the roll is called up yonder." May we honor their memory by being as faithful in our day as they were in theirs.

D Paul, Apostle of the Church (16:25–27)

SUPPORTING IDEA: *As an apostle of the church, Paul focused on bringing glory to God through proclaiming the gospel of Jesus Christ.*

16:25–27. When it comes time for Paul to conclude this greatest of all epistles, he summarizes much of what he said in the first five verses of the letter. The focus is on the gospel of Christ, given through the revelation of an Old Testament mystery, as the power of God unto salvation so that all—Jews and Gentiles (the nations)—might be saved. But in the doxology, his train of thought runs in a series of ascriptions to God's glory that are bracketed by the subject (**him**) and verb (**be glory**) of his statement. Breaking down Paul's lengthy doxology will help us understand it.

Here is the essence of what he is saying: **Now to him** (v. 25) . . . **to the only wise God be glory forever through Jesus Christ! Amen** (v. 27). God's wisdom is the focus. What has God done that is so **wise** that makes him deserving of **glory**? Between his opening and closing words, Paul specifies why God deserves **glory**: because he **is able to establish you** (save you). Paul then lays out the wisdom of God: in the gospel Paul preaches, a long-hidden mystery has been revealed so that all the people of the earth might reclaim the obedience to God lost in the garden by Adam and Eve:

- The means: **My gospel and the proclamation of Jesus Christ.**
- The mystery: **according to the revelation of the mystery hidden for long ages past, but now revealed and made known through the prophetic writings by the command of the eternal God.**
- The mandate: **That all nations might believe and obey him.**

For that, Paul says, God deserves glory—and he does. That God, out of his own loving initiative, designed a plan by which disobedient men and women might once again obey him and regain their heritage as children of God, is worthy of glory.

MAIN IDEA REVIEW: *A passion for the gospel is revealed in Paul's roles as a builder, servant, shepherd, and apostle of the church.*

III. CONCLUSION

A Reason to Praise

Charles Colson, former White House counsel to president Richard Nixon and founder of Prison Fellowship ministry, tells a remarkable story of a doxology in an unusual place and for an unusual reason. It seems that a young man named Fred, a convicted thief and heroin addict, had been led to Christ in prison by the family of one of his robbery victims. They visited him and showed the love of Christ so consistently to him that he was won to the Lord. The impact of his conversion on his conscience was so dramatic that, at a parole hearing, Fred confessed to other robberies for which he had not been caught or convicted. As a Christian, he felt that it was his obligation to be completely honest about his sins.

Because Fred's original conviction was overturned based on a legality, he was released from prison. He joined a church, got involved in an ex-prisoners' fellowship group, and continued to grow in Christ. At his retrial for the crimes he was originally accused of, he again confessed, this time to the trial judge, to the additional wrongs he had committed. He told the judge he was willing to accept whatever punishment was appropriate. An awkward silence ensued while the judge considered what to do with Fred and his previously-known and newly-confessed crimes. When the judge announced the sentence, it reflected a wisdom that gave Fred back his life: ten years for each robbery— suspended (no jail time)—and restitution to his victims for their losses with 50 percent interest.

For a moment no one in the courtroom moved. Then Fred's pastor jumped to his feet and shouted, "Let's sing it!" and proceeded to lead the entire packed courtroom in the singing of the doxology. The *Seattle Times* newspaper captured the scene: "Everyone stood up, little old ladies in spring dresses, ex-cons, girls in jeans, men in business suits, a biker with his motorcycle jacket and helmet, prison guards—and they began to sing: 'Praise God from whom all blessings flow . . . .'" Officials later said that it was the first time a Seattle Superior Court case had ever closed with the Doxology (cited by Hughes, pp. 313–315).

Fred and his friends had a great reason to burst forth with praise to God—the reasonable response to a wise judge. After writing the longest and most detailed letter in the New Testament, Paul is awed at the wisdom of God. It was the wisdom of God that confronted him on a road to Damascus, where he was going to persecute the people of God. It was the wisdom of God that revealed the gospel, long concealed in the Old Testament. It was the wisdom of God that commissioned him to preach the gospel to the Gentiles so that all the nations might come to faith in Christ. By the wisdom of God, Paul had become a builder, servant, shepherd, and apostle of the church of Jesus Christ. Are we surprised that Paul burst forth in his own doxology to the wisdom of God?

The reader of Romans has surely learned by now that Paul was a man passionate about the gospel and its God. What should surprise us is not that Paul had a doxology in his heart and on his lips, but that we do not more often! We may not have been called as apostles, but we have been called as "gospelizers"—those who have experienced the power of the gospel and who enjoy the privilege of telling others as we build, serve, and shepherd the church of Jesus Christ. When was the last time you shouted, "Let's sing it!" to the glory of God?

PRINCIPLES

- Believers must be continually reminded of Christian truth.
- True Christian service is accomplished by Christ in us.
- Plans are wise, but must be submitted to the larger plan of God.
- Spiritual debts should be paid just as material debts are paid.
- The best-laid plans must be undergirded by prayer.
- People are the true fruit of the gospel.
- The gospel evidences the wisdom of God to his glory.

APPLICATIONS

- Do I study my Bible daily for the purposes of confirming what I believe?
- Do I ever take credit for what Christ does through me?
- Are there any plans I have made that I am not willing for God to change?
- To whom do I owe a spiritual debt that I have not repaid with thanksgiving?
- Do I remember to pray about what I have planned?
- Is my ministry in the gospel adorned by close relationships in the Lord?
- How awed am I by what God has done in and through the gospel?

IV. LIFE APPLICATION

Go Thou and Do Likewise

A conclusion to the last chapter of any Bible book is by default a conclusion to the whole book as well. William Tyndale (1494?–1536), the English martyr whose translation of the New Testament into English unlocked the riches of Scripture for the masses, concluded his own prologue to the Book of Romans in a way that becomes a fitting application at the end of the book:

"Now go to, reader, and according to the order of Paul's writing, even so do thou. First behold thyself diligently in the law of God, and see there thy just damnation. Secondarily turn thine eyes to Christ, and see there the exceeding mercy of thy most kind and loving Father. Thirdly remember that Christ made not this atonement that thou shouldest anger God again: neither cleansed he thee, that thou shouldest return (as a swine) unto thine old puddle again: but that thou shouldest be a new creature and live a new life after the will of God and not of the flesh. And be diligent lest through thine own negligence and unthankfulness thou lose this favour and mercy again" (cited in Bruce, pp. 269–270).

Paul's letter to the Romans is an orderly progression through the Christian experience: sin (chaps. 1–3), salvation (chaps. 4–5), sanctification (chaps. 6–8), God's sovereignty over all (chaps. 9–11), sacrifice, submission, and service (chaps. 12–15), and being sent (chap. 16). In the last half of chapter 15 and all of chapter 16, Paul summarizes his letter by revealing his heart—committed to building, serving, and shepherding the church of Jesus Christ. Paul never stopped being an apostle, a sent one. He lived his life for one thing, to obey the one who called and sent him to the nations of the world bearing the gospel—the power of God unto salvation.

Thankfully, his plan to make the Roman church his partner in the power of the gospel—to spread the good news of Jesus and his kingdom to Spain—occasioned the writing and sending of this letter. While we do not know whether he made it to Spain, we know the most important thing was accomplished—the writing of his letter to the believers in Rome. For in the writing of this letter, Paul ultimately equipped hundreds of thousands of churches and millions of believers to go not only to Spain but to "the regions beyond" as well.

It is not enough to read the letter to the Romans and come to grips with sin, to be saved, to make progress in sanctification, to understand God's sovereignty, and to live sacrificially, submissively, and as a servant. If we have not agreed to be sent by God to those who do not yet embrace the Lord Jesus Christ, then we have not embraced all of Romans. God may send us across the street to a neighbor, or across the ocean to another nation. But we must be willing to go. Our salvation, sanctification, and service are all means to the ultimate end of the Christian life—"That all nations might believe and obey him" (Rom. 16:26).

V. PRAYER

Heavenly Father, thank you for the faithfulness of the apostle Paul. Thank you for leading him to write the letter to the believers in Rome. May the fruit of my study of Romans be that I, like Paul, recognize my ultimate obligation to be willing to be a "sent one" so that all the nations may believe and obey you. Amen.

VI. DEEPER DISCOVERIES

A. Reminders (15:15)

Used only here in the New Testament, Paul employs an intense verb to explain to the Roman church why he has written to them "quite boldly on some points." *Epanamimneskw* is a verb that means to remind again. The preposition *epi* (over, upon) is added to the verb *anamimneskw* (to remind) to produce, in a literal sense, "over-remind." It is as if he is saying that he cannot tell them enough times of his calling by God ("the grace God gave me") to be a minister of Christ Jesus to the Gentiles (Rom. 15:16). Paul considered this to be a fundamental concept that the Roman church had to understand in order to understand him, what he was writing to them, and his future plans to visit them and venture on to Spain.

Though *epanamimneskw* is employed only here, the idea of reminding believers of the fundamentals of the faith can be found throughout the New Testament:

- 1 Corinthians 15:1–12: Paul reminds the church in Corinth of the gospel which they have believed.
- Philippians 3:1: Paul takes up matters which he had either discussed personally with the Philippian church or in an earlier letter.
- 2 Thessalonians 2:15: Paul reminds the believers in Thessalonica to stand firm in the teachings they have received, either orally or by letter.
- 2 Timothy 1:13; 3:14: Timothy is exhorted to keep as a pattern what Paul has taught him.
- Hebrews 2:1: The writer admonishes his readers to pay more careful attention to what they have heard lest they "drift away."

- 2 Peter 1:12–15; 3:1—Peter cites the value of perpetual reminders even to people who are established in the truth. He says both his letters are to stimulate his readers to "wholesome thinking."

The great creeds of the church developed not only as a means for systematizing the faith, but for systematizing and preserving it in a way that is easy to memorize and pass from one generation to another. However, even creeds can fall into rote use, and so the Spirit-led teaching and preaching of the Word of God (the proclamation of kingdom truth) continues to be the best way for reminding the church of what it believes. Just as the New Testament epistles served as reminders when originally written, they should do so in our day as well.

B. Paul as Priest (15:16)

One of the richest verses for exposition in this section of Romans is 15:16, where Paul refers to his apostolic ministry as a priestly duty and the Gentiles as an offering to God. Five key terms will repay expanded study in providing background for Paul's meaning here (summarized from Stott, p. 379):

1. *leitourgos*. "Minister" can mean a public servant (Rom. 13:6), but both the noun and its cognate verb, *leitougeo*, are used in the New Testament to refer to the Jewish priesthood and also to Christ as our high priest (Heb. 8:2).

2. *heirourgeo*. "Priestly duty" refers to the service of the priests (*hiereus*) in the temple and suggests the entire background of the priestly ministry as detailed in Leviticus. Hebrews 4:14–10:39 provides background on the Aaronic priesthood and Christ's role as high priest.

3. *prosphora*. "Offering" or "sacrificial offering" is used in the New Testament nine times, all in the context of offerings as sacrifice to God.

4. *euprosdektos*. "Acceptable to God" refers to sacrifices that please the one to whom they are offered.

5. *hagiazo*. "Sanctified" refers to setting something aside for holy use. As the Jews were set aside as God's holy people in the Old Testament, now the Gentiles are being offered as holy to the Lord as well.

Besides the Levitical background of Paul's words in verse 16, there is also an eschatological reference to his actions of bringing Gentiles as an offering to God. Given Paul's intimate knowledge and use of Isaiah throughout his writings, he could have been thinking here of Isaiah 66:19–20: "I will set a sign among them [the sign of the Son of Man? cf. Matt. 24:30 with Isa. 5:26; 11:10–12], and I will send some of those who survive [God's judgment] to the nations—to Tarshish [possibly Spain], to the Libyans and Lydians . . . to Tubal and Greece, and to the distant islands that have not heard of my fame or seen my glory. They will proclaim my glory among the nations. And they will bring all your brothers, from all the nations, to my holy mountain in *Jerusalem as an offering to the LORD . . .* as the Israelites bring their grain offerings" (emphasis added; cf. also Zech. 8:23). Did Paul see his proclaiming of the gospel of Jesus Christ as part of the fulfillment of Isaiah's prophecy about the Son of Man becoming a banner to the nations?

This verse in Paul's letter is a good example of how a deep knowledge of the Old Testament enlightens understanding of the New Testament. If the above considerations concerning Paul's use of Isaiah 66:19–20 are correct (in addition to all his other many uses of the Old Testament), one can only imagine his response of awe as his apostolic role was revealed to him by the Lord in the period following his conversion.

C. Deacon/Deaconess (16:1)

The question of women in leadership and service roles in the church is a matter of continual debate. The reference in Romans 16:1 regarding Phoebe's ministry adds support to the idea that women were possibly appointed or elected to the deaconess position in the early church.

"Deacon" comes from the common word *diakonos,* meaning servant, minister, or attendant. It is used in a variety of ways in the New Testament to describe numerous aspects of service or ministry. By the time Paul writes Philippians (A.D. 61), he mentions deacons along with elders as leaders in the church (Phil. 1:1). When he writes a few years later to Timothy, he gives a full range of qualifications for deacons (1 Tim. 3:8–13).

The growth of the role and office of deacon appears to have its roots in the infant days of the church. Because the twelve apostles were about to be distracted from their primary tasks of prayer and the ministry of the word to "wait on tables" (*diakoneo,* the verb form of "deacon;" Acts 6:2), seven men were selected to handle the food distribution. They were not called deacons, but their tasks were those of "serving" (*diakoneo*) the body of believers. A good case could be made for "the Twelve" (Acts 6:2) and "the Seven" (Acts 21:8) being the prototypes for the future elder and deacon offices in the church.

But the fact still remains that the seven original "ministers," or deacons, were men (Acts 6:3). Two indications in the New Testament allow that women may have been included in the office as it developed (there is no such evidence for women filling the office of elder).

First, Phoebe is called by Paul a *diakonon tes ekklesias*—a servant or minister or deacon—of the church in Cenchrea (Rom. 16:1). Did Paul mean she was simply a woman with a servant's heart and hands, aiding the church in sacrificial ways, or that she held the office of *diakonos,* deacon?

Second, when Paul is outlining the qualifications for deacons in 1 Timothy 3, he includes a reference to the *gunaikas* (feminine accusative plural of *gune,* wife or woman; 1 Tim. 3:11). Is he referring to the wives of the deacons (deacons are called "men" in 1 Tim. 3:8,10,12) or to women who are deacons? As evidence of the debate, the NIV takes the former view ("their wives"), while the NASB calls them "women," but not "deaconesses."

At the very least, Phoebe, along with the four women who are cited by Paul as working "very hard" in the church in Rome (Rom. 16:6,12), give ample evidence to the strong contribution of women in the early church. Whether Phoebe, and others like her, served in official or unofficial capacities cannot be determined from the evidence at hand.

D. The End of Romans (15:33)

Some measure of discussion has taken place among scholars regarding the end of Romans, for several reasons. The presence of a benediction and "Amen" in 15:33 (the third in this chapter, see 15:5,13) could signal the end of the letter (though see 1:25; 9:5; 11:36 preceding it, and 16:27 following). Shorter versions of the letter have been preserved in ancient manuscripts, some ending with 14:23 and others with 15:33. The absence of chapter 16 in some manuscripts is the easiest to understand. If Paul's epistles were copied and circulated for the benefit of other churches, it is understandable that his personal greetings to friends in Rome (chap. 16) might have been omitted.

More serious objections have been raised about the legitimacy of chapter 16. Primarily, is it reasonable to believe that Paul would have so many friends in a church he had never visited? If not the church in Rome, to whom might these greetings have been addressed, and how did they get tacked on to the end of Romans if they were not written for the believers in Rome? F. F. Bruce summarizes arguments for and against the legitimacy of chapter 16 being an original part of the letter to the Rome church (Bruce, pp. 253–255):

For the idea that Romans 16 was originally intended for the church in Ephesus:

1. Paul could not have known more than twenty-five individuals and five households (house churches?) in a city he had never visited. However, he had spent between two and three years in Ephesus and would easily have known that many people.

2. Priscilla and Aquila (16:3) appear at last sighting to have been in Ephesus (Acts 18:26; 1 Cor. 16:9), though they may originally have been from Rome (Acts 18:1–2).

3. Epenetus (16:5), Paul's first convert to Christ in Asia, would more likely be found in Ephesus, not Rome.

4. Verses 17–20 are out of character with the rest of Paul's letter, while they fit well with Paul's words to the Ephesian elders in Acts 20:28–31. Paul seems in this passage to adopt a stronger attitude of authority, unusual for him in a church he did not found, but to be

expected in his relationship with the churches he did found, such as the one in Ephesus.

For the idea that Romans 16 was an original part of the letter, meant for the church in Rome:

1. Paul's greetings are to be expected more in a church with which Paul was *not* familiar than one with which he was *very* familiar. He undoubtedly, in two to three years, would have known everyone in the Ephesus church. To have singled out particular individuals for greetings and commendations would have been insulting, hurtful, or at the least confusing, to the rest of the body. On the other hand, only those whom Paul knew in Rome would have expected a greeting, which are the ones he does greet.

   Additionally, if the end of Claudius's reign in A.D. 54 ended his edict of Jewish expulsion (Acts 18:2), then perhaps many Jews who had left Rome (e.g., Priscilla and Aquila) and whom Paul met during the expulsion returned to Rome where Paul greets them one to three years later (recall that Romans was written in A.D. 57).

2. More of the names mentioned in chapter 16 have been attested archaeologically in Rome than in Ephesus.

3. Paul's greetings *from* all the churches in Asia (16:16), and the presence of Trophimus, an Ephesian (Acts 21:29), in the party Paul assembled just prior to leaving Corinth for Jerusalem (Acts 20:4), make it unlikely that the group with Paul representing the Asian churches would be sending greetings to Ephesus (Trophimus would be greeting his own church); Rome makes much more sense.

4. Paul's strong admonition makes more sense in a brief, postscript fashion, after demonstrating restraint and a spirit of gentleness with a church of which he was not the founder. His apostolic role, emphasized in the letter, would legitimize his strong words. Though they are not paralleled in the rest of the letter, they can easily be seen as the exception to the rule.

The idea that Phoebe was bound for Ephesus (due east from Corinth when Rome was due west) with a letter of greeting to the church there, before turning west for Rome—or that a separate letter to the church in Ephesus has for some reason been attached to the end of Romans—is "highly improbable" in the words of Bruce. Since "possession is nine points of the law," he says, "it is natural to suppose that [chapter 16] was equally addressed to [the Roman Christians]."

VII. TEACHING OUTLINE

A. INTRODUCTION

1. Lead Story: The Mark of a Leader

2. Context: Paul is concluding his letter to the church in Rome. He has demonstrated the reality of sin, the means of salvation, the promise of sanctification, and the sovereignty of God. He has also urged the believers in Rome to live lives of sacrifice, submission, and service as a demonstration of the power of the gospel. In the final chapter-and-a-half of his letter, Paul pulls back the curtain on his own heart and reveals some of the internal realities that account for the single-mindedness of his life.

3. Transition: Has anything happened in your life that is so radical that it consumes you from that moment on? Ask Paul that question and he will say it was his encounter with Christ and the calling he received from him. To build the church throughout the world (the Gentile, non-Jewish world beyond Israel) was his calling and hence his passion. In this final section of Romans we meet Paul, the builder, servant, shepherd, and apostle of the church of Jesus Christ.

B. COMMENTARY

1. Paul, Builder of the Church (Rom. 15:14–22)
   a. Priest of Christ (15:14–16)
   b. Promoter of Christ's gospel (15:17–19)
   c. Pioneer for Christ (15:20–22)
2. Paul, Servant of the Church (15:23–33)
   a. Plan to serve the church in Rome (15:23–24)
   b. Priority of serving the church in Jerusalem (15:25–29)
   c. Prayer for safety and effectiveness in service (15:30–33)
3. Paul, Shepherd of the Church (16:1–24)
   a. Phoebe, messenger of Paul (16:1–2)
   b. Personal greetings to friends in Rome (16:3–16)
   c. Protection from enemies of the gospel (16:17–20)
   d. Personal greetings from friends in Corinth (16:21–23)
4. Paul, Apostle of the Church (16:25–27)
   a. Praise for the proclamation of the gospel (16:25a)
   b. Praise for the revelation of the mystery (16:25b–26)
   c. Praise for the God of the gospel (16:27)

C. CONCLUSION: GO THOU AND DO LIKEWISE

VIII. ISSUES FOR DISCUSSION

1. What methods do you use in your personal life to remind yourself of the truths of Christianity? How easy is it to "float along" as a Christian without having to bring the truths of the faith to bear upon your life? What connection is there between being actively involved in ministry and the need to have "at hand" the truths of the faith?

2. To whom are you indebted spiritually? Besides salvation, in what ways can people be indebted to others spiritually? What have you done to acknowledge your "indebtedness" to the persons who somehow invested spiritually in you?

3. How many "dear friends" do you have in the Lord? What binds people together as Christians? What constitutes "working hard" in the Lord in our modern era? Is fellowship a goal we seek or a by-product in which we share? How do we know when we are having true fellowship in the Lord?

4. Paul wrote a doxology to God based on his personal spiritual experience with God. Following Paul's outline (Rom. 16:25–27), write your own doxology based on your personal observations of God and his work in your life.

Glossary

Abraham—The father of the Hebrew race, from whom the Jews are descended. The spiritual father of those who are granted a righteous standing before God on the basis of faith alone

Abba—Aramaic word for father, but in the intimate sense of "daddy," or "papa"

Achaia—A Roman province of which Corinth was the capital. The phrase "Macedonia and Achaia" is used in Scripture as a reference to Greece.

Adam—The father of the human race, through whose sin all the rest of the human race was born in a condition of sin deserving of God's judgment

apostle—From Greek *apostolos;* a sent one. Generally refers to the eleven original disciples, plus Matthias chosen to replace Judas; "the Twelve" (Acts 6:2). Paul and others were designated apostles as well; those sent with the gospel

atonement—Old Testament root meaning was "to cover" (*kaphar*), referring to the lid of the ark of the covenant where the blood of the sacrifice was poured. Atonement results from a sacrifice that satisfies the righteousness of God.

Baal—Name of a pagan deity, the most significant in the Canaanite pantheon during the days of the monarchy in Israel. Elijah, by the power of God, defeated 450 prophets of Baal on Mt. Carmel (1 Kgs. 18:16–40).

baptism—A Christian initiatory rite identifying a believer with the death and resurrection of Christ.

Benjamin—One of twelve tribes of Israel, named for Jacob's youngest son. Adjacent to Jerusalem, Benjamin allied with Judah to form the Southern Kingdom of Israel during the divided monarchy. Paul was from the tribe of Benjamin.

calling—God's foreknowledge and election expressed in the human realm; God's drawing the elect to himself

circumcision—The cutting off of the male foreskin. Practiced today for cultural and health reasons, it was originally a sign of the covenant between God and Abraham and his descendants (Gen. 17:11).

covenants—The promises made to Abraham and his descendants ensuring a particular place of favor for the Jewish people in the outworking of God's universal plan of redemption. Often referred to as "the promises"

depravity—The moral condition of being spiritually dead toward God. It suggests a total inability of humans, in and of themselves, to do that which would commend them to God.

diatribe—A Greek literary device used by Paul for proving a point through hypothetical questions and objections which allow points of truth to be conveyed through the answers.

elect—Those whom God foreknew and chose to belong to himself for eternity

Esau—The firstborn of twin sons of Isaac and Rebekah. Should have received his father's blessing but was tricked out of it by his younger brother Jacob

faith—From Greek *pistis*. Trust in the word and actions of God; that human decision, itself a gift from God (Eph. 2:8), which, when directed toward Christ, prompts forgiveness of sin and declaration of righteousness by God

forbearance—Patience, tolerance, or restraint at a time when judgment is warranted and would be justified

foreknowledge—More than just "knowledge before the fact," but knowledge that is effectual and causative, producing the results that are foreknown

Gentiles—Non-Jewish peoples of the world; all the world's peoples except the Jews

Glossary

glorification—The ultimate and eternal state of transformation of the believer from mortality to immortality when sin is done away with forever

glory—From Hebrew *kabod*, weight. Value was originally measured by physical weight; then someone's word "carried weight." The glory (weight) of God implies his trustworthiness and infinite value.

gospel—From Greek *euangelion;* originally the report of victory in a military conflict, later glad tidings or good news. Used in the New Testament to refer to the good news of the presence of God's kingdom ("the gospel of the kingdom") and deliverance from the domain of Satan based on the death and resurrection of Christ (1 Cor. 15:1–5)

grace—From Greek *charis;* unmerited action of love and compassion originating from within and by the will of the giver. In Scripture, salvation is a gift of grace; the extension of forgiveness and love to those not deserving it

hope—That bright anticipation of the future that arises out of a character that has been flooded with the love of God

Isaac—The second son of Abraham, but the first through Sarah. Isaac was the son of promise, through whom God's promises to Abraham would be fulfilled.

Israel—The name given by God to Jacob and which became the national name of his descendants (Gen. 32:28).

Jacob—The second born of twin sons of Isaac and Rebekah. By trickery, and with Rebekah's help, Jacob received Isaac's blessing instead of his older brother Esau.

Jews—Physically, those descended from Jacob (Israel) and his sons. Spiritually, those who share in the faith of Abraham as a basis for right standing with God

judgment—Evaluation based on standards. God's judgments, based on his standards, are righteous; human judgments, based on self-defined standards, are unrighteous. God will ultimately judge every human action according to his righteous standards.

justification—God's legal act of freeing a person from the condemnation and penalty of sin and reckoning the same person as completely righteous. Justification is a legal, positional act, not necessarily resulting in perfectly righteous behavior.

kingdom of God—That domain where God's rule is acknowledged and submitted to, where his values are those embraced and practiced; in this age, a spiritual domain, in the age to come a geopolitical as well as spiritual one

Last Adam—A description of Jesus Christ used by Paul to contrast the life won back by Christ through obedience with the loss of life resulting from the first Adam's sin (1 Cor. 15:45)

law—The Ten Commandments and hundreds of subsequent standards given to Israel through Moses. Also used in Scripture to refer to human laws or other standards by which people attempt to prove or gain righteousness

Law and the Prophets—Specifically, the first five books of the Old Testament written by Moses and the seventeen books of the prophets (written by four major, twelve minor prophets). Generally, came to be used as a reference to the Old Testament as a whole (Luke 16:6)

Macedonia—A Roman province, but part of the kingdom of Greece, lying north of Achaia. The first entrance of the gospel into Europe was in Macedonia. The phrase "Macedonia and Achaia" is used in Scripture as a reference to Greece.

olive tree—Used by Paul to compare Israel with the Gentiles. Israel was a cultivated olive tree, the Gentiles a wild olive tree whose branches were grafted into Israel so as to receive her life and bear fruit to God

peace—The absence of the wrath or displeasure of God directed at human sinfulness

perversion—Immoral sexual activity that not only violates God's revealed standards but the standards of natural laws

Pharaoh—Title of Egyptian rulers. The Pharaoh of the Exodus served as an example of God's hardening the heart of an unrepentant sinner.

predestination—The securing of the ultimate destiny of the elect

reconciliation—The bringing together of enemies at the cessation of hostility. Man, the enemy of God, has been reconciled to God on the basis of the death of God's Son.

redemption. A slave-market term referring to the release from bondage by the payment of a price. Christ's death was the price paid for the redemption of sinners from slavery to sin.

resurrection—In Scripture, refers to the raising of the physical body from death to life

righteousness—From Greek *dikaosyne*. An attribute of God which makes him right and just in his actions; a positional attribute of Christians who are declared "right" before the law of God on the basis of faith in Christ

Root of Jesse—A dual reference to the descendants of Jesse of the tribe of Judah. The first reference was to Jesse's son David, anointed king over Israel, the second to Jesse's descendant Jesus Christ, Israel's greater king and Messiah (Isa. 11:10)

Rome—Capital of the Roman Empire; home to a large contingent of Christian believers; site of Paul's next-to-last and last imprisonments and his martyrdom

saint—From Greek *hagios*; holy, holy one. Holiness implies set-apartness; therefore a saint is one set apart by and for the Lord.

salvation—Rescue or deliverance from peril; God's act of rescuing sinners from spiritual and eternal death through the forgiveness of sin and the gift of eternal life

servant—From Greek *doulos*; one who willingly indentures himself to the service of another

sin—From Greek *hamartia*; missing the mark. Implies the human condition, both constitutionally and behaviorally, to fail to live up to God's standards of righteousness

Son of God—A messianic title (Ps. 2:7) which Jesus received for himself (Matt. 26:63–64; Mark 14:61–62; John 5:18)

spiritual gift—A measure of grace apportioned to each believer equipping him or her for service in the body of Christ

stumbling stone—A prophetic reference to the Messiah (Isa. 8:14; 28:16) which Paul applies to his preaching of the gospel about Christ (Rom. 9:32–33)

wrath of God—The manifest anger and displeasure of God toward sin and those who commit it

Bibliography

Barker, Kenneth. *The NIV Study Bible,* New International Version. Grand Rapids: Zondervan Bible Publishers, 1985.

Barrett, C. K. *The Epistle to the Romans* (2nd. ed.). Black's New Testament Commentary. London: A & C Black, Limited, 1991.

Boice, James Montgomery. *Romans-Galatians.* The Expositor's Bible Commentary. Grand Rapids: Zondervan Publishing House, 1976.

Boice, James Montgomery. *Romans, An Expositional Commentary.* 4 vols. Grand Rapids: Baker Book House, 1991, 1992, 1993, 1995.

Bray, Gerald, ed. *Romans.* Ancient Christian Commentary on Scripture. Downers Grove, Ill.: InterVarsity Press, 1998.

Brown, Colin. *The New International Dictionary of New Testament Theology.* Grand Rapids: Zondervan Publishing House, 1976.

Bruce, F. F. *The Letter of Paul to the Romans, An Introduction and Commentary.* The Tyndale New Testament Commentaries. Grand Rapids: William B. Eerdmans Publishing Company, and Leicester, England: InterVarsity Press, 1985.

Chambers, Oswald. *My Utmost for His Highest.* An Updated Edition in Today's Language. Edited by James Reimann. ©Oswald Chambers Publications Association, Ltd., 1992. Original edition copyright © 1935 by Dodd, Mead & Company, Inc. United States publication rights held by Discovery House Publishers which is affiliated with Radio Bible Class, Grand Rapids, Michigan.

Cranfield, C. E. B. *Romans, A Shorter Commentary.* Grand Rapids: William B. Eerdmans Publishing Company, 1985.

Douglas, J. D., gen. ed. *The New International Dictionary of the Christian Church.* Grand Rapids: Zondervan Publishing House, 1974.

Elwell, Walter A., ed. *Evangelical Dictionary of Biblical Theology.* Grand Rapids: Baker Book House, 1996.

Erickson, Millard J. *Christian Theology.* 3 vols. Grand Rapids: Baker Book House, 1985.

Geisler, Norman L. *Baker Encyclopedia of Christian Apologetics.* Grand Rapids: Baker Book House, 1999.

Godet, Frederic Louis. *Commentary on Romans,* 1879. Reprint. Grand Rapids: Kregel, 1977.

Grudem, Wayne. *Systematic Theology, An Introduction to Biblical Doctrine.* Leicester: InterVarsity Press, and Grand Rapids: Zondervan Publishing House, 1994.

Harrison, Everett F. *Romans-Galatians.* The Expositor's Bible Commentary. Grand Rapids: Zondervan Publishing House, 1976

Henry, Carl F. H., ed. *Baker's Dictionary of Christian Ethics.* Canon Press, 1973.

Hughes, R. Kent. *Romans, Righteousness from Heaven.* Wheaton: Crossway Books, 1991.

Larson, Craig Brian, ed. *Illustrations for Preaching & Teaching.* From *Leadership Journal.* Grand Rapids: Baker Books, 1993.

Lewis, C. S., ed. *George MacDonald, 365 Readings.* New York: Collier Books, Macmillan Publishing Company, 1947, 1974.

Luther, Martin. *Commentary on Romans.* Trans. by J. Theodore Mueller. Grand Rapids: Zondervan Publishing House, 1954. Reprint edition by Kregel Publications, 1976.

———. *A Heritage of Great Evangelical Teaching.* Nashville: Thomas Nelson Publishers, 1996.

MacArthur, John F., Jr. *Romans 1–8, Romans 9–16.* The MacArthur New Testament Commentary. Chicago: Moody Press, 1991, 1994.

Bibliography

Moo, Douglas J. *The Epistle to the Romans*. Grand Rapids: William B. Eerdmans Publishing Company, 1996.

Morris, Leon. *The Epistle to the Romans*. Eerdmans and InterVarsity Press, 1988.

Mounce, Robert. *Romans*. The New American Commentary. Nashville: Broadman & Holman Publishers, 1995.

Murray, John. *The Epistle to the Romans*. The New International Commentary on the New Testament. Grand Rapids: Wm. B. Eerdmans Publishing Co., 1959, 1965.

Robertson, A. T. *Word Pictures in the New Testament*. 6 vols. Nashville: Broadman Press, 1931.

Rowell, Edward K., ed. *Quotes and Idea Starters for Preaching and Teaching*. Grand Rapids: Christianity Today, Inc., and Baker Books, 1996.

Schaeffer, Francis A. *A Christian Manifesto*, rev. ed. Wheaton, Ill.: Crossway Books, 1982.

Schaeffer, Francis A. *The Finished Work of Christ, The Truth of Romans 1–8*. Wheaton, Ill.: Crossway Books, 1998.

Sjogren, Bob. *Unveiled at Last*. Seattle: YWAM Publishing, 1992.

Spicq, Ceslas. *Theological Lexicon of the New Testament*. 3 vols. Translated and edited by James D. Ernest. Peabody, MA: Hendrickson Publishers, 1995.

Stott, John. *Romans, God's Good News for the World*. Downers Grove, Ill.: InterVarsity Press, 1994.

Schreiner, Thomas R. *Romans*. Baker Exegetical Commentary on the New Testament. Grand Rapids: Baker Book House, 1998.

Swindoll, Charles R. *The Tale of the Tardy Oxcart and 1,501 Other Stories*. Nashville: Word Publishers, 1998.

Vine, W. E., Merrill F. Unger, William White, Jr. *Vine's Complete Expository Dictionary of Old and New Testament Words*. Nashville: Thomas Nelson Publishers, 1996.

Ward, Hannah, and Jennifer Wild. *The Doubleday Christian Quotation Collection*. New York: Doubleday, 1997.

Wiersbe, Warren. *Be Right*. Colorado Springs, Colo.: Chariot Victor Publishing, 1977.

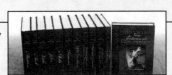